15.95

Indexed in Essay &
General Literature

D0583886

ATE DUE

NEW WORLD ENCOUNTERS

In memory of Michel de Certeau

New World Encounters

Edited by Stephen Greenblatt

A Representations Book

University of California Press
BERKELEY   LOS ANGELES   LONDON

Twelve of the essays in this volume were originally published in various issues of *Representations* as follows:

Inga Clendinnen, "'Fierce and Unnatural Cruelty': Cortés and the Conquest of Mexico": 33 (Winter 1991): 65–100.

Rolena Adorno, "The Negotiation of Fear in Cabeza de Vaca's *Naufragios*": 33 (Winter 1991): 163–99.

Anthony Pagden, "*Ius et Factum*: Text and Experience in the Writings of Bartolomé de Las Casas": 33 (Winter 1991): 147–62.

Sabine MacCormack, "Demons, Imagination, and the Incas": 33 (Winter 1991): 121–46.

Frank Lestringant, "The Philosopher's Breviary: Jean de Léry in the Enlightenment": 33 (Winter 1991): 200–211.

David Damrosch, "The Aesthetics of Conquest: Aztec Poetry Before and After Cortés": 33 (Winter 1991): 101–20.

Louis Montrose, "The Work of Gender in the Discourse of Discovery": 33 (Winter 1991): 1–41.

Mary C. Fuller, "Ralegh's Fugitive Gold: Reference and Deferral in *The Discoverie of Guiana*": 33 (Winter 1991): 42–64.

David Quint, "Voices of Resistance: The Epic Curse and Camões's Adamastor": 27 (Summer 1989): 111–41.

Jeffrey Knapp, "Elizabethan Tobacco": 21 (Winter 1988): 27–66.

Luce Giard, "Epilogue: Michel de Certeau's Heterology and the New World": 33 (Winter 1991): 212–21.

Michel de Certeau, "Travel Narratives of the French to Brazil: Sixteenth to Eighteenth Centuries": 33 (Winter 1991): 221–26.

An earlier version of Sara Castro-Klarén's essay "Dancing and the Sacred in the Andes: From the Taqui-Oncoy to Rasu Ñiti" appeared in *Dispositio* 14 (1989): 169–85.

University of California Press
Berkeley and Los Angeles, California

University of California Press, Ltd.
London, England

Library of Congress Cataloging-in-Publication data
appears at the end of the book.

Printed in the United States of America
9 8 7 6 5 4 3 2

The paper used in this publication meets the minimum requirements of American National Standard for Information Sciences—Permanence of Paper for Printed Library Materials, ANSI Z39.48-1984. ⊗

Contents

Stephen Greenblatt, Introduction: New World Encounters   vii

Margarita Zamora
Christopher Columbus's "Letter to the Sovereigns":
Announcing the Discovery   1

Inga Clendinnen
"Fierce and Unnatural Cruelty":
Cortés and the Conquest of Mexico   12

Rolena Adorno
The Negotiation of Fear in Cabeza de Vaca's *Naufragios*   48

Anthony Pagden
Ius et Factum: Text and Experience
in the Writings of Bartolomé de Las Casas   85

Sabine MacCormack
Demons, Imagination, and the Incas   101

Frank Lestringant
The Philosopher's Breviary: Jean de Léry in the Enlightenment   127

David Damrosch
The Aesthetics of Conquest: Aztec Poetry
Before and After Cortés   139

Sara Castro-Klarén
Dancing and the Sacred in the Andes:
From the Taqui-Oncoy to Rasu-Ñiti   159

Louis Montrose
The Work of Gender in the Discourse of Discovery   177

Mary C. Fuller
Ralegh's Fugitive Gold: Reference and Deferral in
The Discoverie of Guiana   218

David Quint
Voices of Resistance: The Epic Curse and Camões's Adamastor   241

Jeffrey Knapp
Elizabethan Tobacco   272

Luce Giard
Epilogue: Michel de Certeau's Heterology and the New World   313

Michel de Certeau
Travel Narratives of the French to Brazil:
Sixteenth to Eighteenth Centuries   323

Contributors   329

Index   333

STEPHEN GREENBLATT

Introduction: New World Encounters

AT THE CLOSE OF Samuel Eliot Morison's monumental study, *The European Discovery of America: The Southern Voyages, 1492–1616,* the great historian salutes the ships—*Santa María, Niña, Golden Hind,* and so forth—that carried Europeans across the face of the earth in what he views as a secular epiphany. This century of voyages was also, Morison observes, an epiphany in the religious sense:

The main conception and aim of Columbus, to carry the Word of God and knowledge of His Son to the far corners of the globe, became a fact: Christ had been made manifest to a new race of Gentiles. By 1615 the Christian Mass was being celebrated in hundreds of churches from the St. Lawrence through the Antilles to the River Plate, and along the west coast from Valdivia to Lower California. To the people of this New World, pagans expecting short and brutish lives, void of hope for any future, had come the Christian vision of a merciful God and a glorious Heaven. And from the decks of ships traversing the two great oceans and exploring the distant verges of the earth, prayers arose like clouds of incense to the Holy Trinity and to Mary, Queen of the Sea.[1]

Morison's words, published in 1974 near the end of his long and distinguished career, can conveniently stand as the articulation of a traditional position—let us call it "the vision of the victors"—against which all of the essays in this volume, however diverse their interests and conclusions, are written.[2] It is not that these essays are explicitly concerned to refute this position; rather, they seem to inhabit a different century, one that has seen all of the assumptions behind Morison's eloquent sentences decisively challenged.

For the contributors to this volume, the European voyages of the sixteenth century did not constitute an epiphany—though not because these essays simply dismiss the Europeans' religious motives. Such a dismissal was characteristic of an earlier critique of colonialist apologetics, a critique exemplified by a famous passage in *Gulliver's Travels*:

A Crew of Pyrates are driven by a Storm they know not whither; at length a Boy discovers Land from the Top-mast; they go on Shore to Rob and Plunder; they see an harmless People, are entertained with Kindness, they give the country a new Name, they take formal Possession of it for their King, they set up a rotten Plank or a Stone for a Memorial, they murder two or three Dozen of the Natives, bringing away a Couple more by Force for a Sample, return home, and get their Pardon. Here commences a new Dominion acquired with a Title by *Divine Right*. Ships are sent with the first Opportunity; the Natives driven out or destroyed, their Princes tortured to discover their Gold; a free Licence given to all Acts of Inhumanity and Lust; the Earth reeking with the Blood of its Inhabitants: and this execrable Crew of Butchers employed in so pious an Expedition, is a *modern Colony* sent to convert and civilize an idolatrous and barbarous People.[3]

There is, in my view, much to be said for Swift's vision, but it is no more that of the contributors to this volume than is Morison's. If there are in these essays few pious sailors hymning the Virgin from the decks of their stout ships, there are equally few cheerily cynical pirates. Even Sir Walter Ralegh, who was rumored in his own time to be an atheist, figures in these pages not as a man who stands coolly outside the ideological codes of his time but as someone who was engaged in a complex and often desperate negotiation with values he could neither securely manipulate nor comfortably embrace. Other Europeans whose texts are analyzed here—Pedro de Cieza de León, Bartolomé de Las Casas, Jean de Léry—are deeply engaged with the fate of Christianity in the New World, but their religious vision and its practical consequences bear little resemblance to that celebrated by Morison.

One way in which these essays differ sharply from the positions exemplified by Morison and Swift is that they are centrally concerned with what Nathan Wachtel called "the vision of the vanquished."[4] They share with other recent scholarship in Europe and the Americas a sense of alternative histories, competing accounts, and muffled voices. They attempt in a variety of ways to register the powerful presence of otherness—not an abstract, quasi-allegorical figure of the Other, whether brute or victim, but a diverse range of cultures and representations and individuals with whom the Europeans were forced to interact. Reading these essays, we come to realize that between Morison's celebrants and Swift's predators the very possibility, let alone the necessity, of such interaction had been lost. The American natives had in either case been rendered virtually transparent—either as Hobbesian pagans in a state of nature, condemned to lives that are solitary, nasty, brutish, and short, or as mute, naive, miserable victims, condemned only to deception and enslavement. The essays in this volume, by contrast, give to the encounter between Europeans and American peoples a remarkable specificity and historical contingency. The Indians have lost the transparency of allegory, gaining instead the density of historical subjects struggling to come to terms with figures from a perplexingly different culture. For their part, the Europeans are also not to be understood as allegorical representatives of monolithic traditions, but as figures who are improvising sinuous paths through fiercely competing claims.

This mutual density does not necessarily signal successful communication between the historical subjects. On the contrary, as Inga Clendinnen shows in her brooding and powerful essay, the cultural understandings specific to Indian as well as Spanish warfare make communication virtually impossible. But the point is that even failed communication is two-way. The Spanish and the Mexicans had a common desire, the desire to make a meaningful story out of the disorienting, almost incomprehensibly violent events in which they were plunged.

The radical incompatibility of these compelling stories plays a crucial role, Clendinnen argues, in the outcome of their struggle—and it plays a crucial role as well in the story that she has to tell. For, as she acknowledges, the historian is by no means exempt from the compulsion to fashion a coherent and satisfying narrative out of the tangled traces of the past. This acknowledgment leads her to skepticism about her own sources, particularly the fragmentary early accounts of the initial clash between the small band of conquistadors and the Aztec empire. She proposes that we resist the Spanish presumption that their civilization gave them greater access to the mind of the other, and hence a strategically crucial advantage, a claim that has dominated accounts from those of Hernan Cortés to W. H. Prescott in the nineteenth century and to Tzvetan Todorov in our own. For Clendinnen, Cortés is not a model of intercultural understanding, strategic or otherwise, nor is he the embodiment of rational calculation. His gift, in her view, lay in his ability "to coax, bully, and bribe his men, dream-led, dream-fed, into making his own gambler's throw; to participate in his own desperate personal destiny." Her essay is a somber warning against confusing this fantastic exercise of the will—a violent imposition, in effect, of narrative on reality—with actual knowledge of another culture.

But if the historian herself is committed to imposing narrative on reality, how can she avoid replicating the very process she is attempting to analyze? There is no simple solution to this problem, I think, but one can glimpse in Clendinnen's essay repeated attempts to unsettle the very condition of a coherent and satisfying narrative of these events. Hence her account turns upon a central, structural incoherence, an untranslatability (as much for the Spaniards as for the Mexicans) that had and, she suggests, continues to have terrible consequences. What looks like communication is noncommunication; what looks like relationship is the absence of relationship; what looks like strategic understanding and cultural manipulation is the bloody clash of incompatible and mutually uncomprehending worlds. And the deepest incompatibility is the incompatibility of story making: Spanish stories trace "an intricate sequence of action" in order to produce "the familiar, powerful cumulative explanation through the narrative form"; Indian stories are founded on a different principle, one based on a conception of time "as multidimensional and eternally recurrent." The absolute non-coincidence of these modes did not cause the violent encounter of the Spanish invaders—"men without a city," as Clendinnen characterizes them—and the inhabitants of Mexico: blood would have been shed had both peoples understood each other perfectly. But the noncoincidence made it impossible to contain the killing within either culture's established ways of managing violence, impossible to bring the war to a close until the men without a city had utterly destroyed the city they had meant to conquer.

We can perhaps usefully apply to the situation Clendinnen analyzes a concept that Fernand Braudel terms "the structure of the conjuncture." As adapted by Marshall Sahlins, the concept refers to the historical intersection of radically divergent cultural categories.[5] Each side in an encounter between peoples who do not understand each other tries to make sense of the other's actions, and the particular meeting of these interpretations—the way they happen to fit together or to clash in a given historical situation—has profound consequences. In the conjuncture of Europeans and New World peoples not only were the respective cultural understandings vastly different, but the historical situations on each side, though superficially identical (ships arrive, objects are traded, blows are struck), were in fact equally far apart. For a historical situation is never simply that of the moment: it is the expression of long-term trajectories, material necessities, social structures, enduring, largely unconscious patterns of will and constraint, not necessarily identical with the culture's own understanding of itself or others.

Thus in the momentous encounters after 1492 four distinct elements repeatedly converge: the operative cultural understanding of the Europeans, the historical situation in which this understanding is deployed, the operative cultural understanding of the natives, and the historical situation in which this understanding is deployed. The convergence has its own structuring force, quite apart from what any of the participants may be thinking. The crucial point, for our purposes, is that the asymmetries, the virtually inevitable misunderstandings and confusions, were as consequential as any carefully crafted strategy—and not only in the production of violence. Hence, as Rolena Adorno's essay shows, Cabeza de Vaca stumbled into a situation where his actions, which initially threatened the security of the Indians among whom he found himself, subsequently became an essential instrument for their spiritual coherence. It is not clear how much Cabeza de Vaca himself understood his role in the strange and complex ritualized pillages he had triggered. He is a figure, in Adorno's account, at the center of a structural conjuncture that manipulates him at least as much as he manipulates it.

Does this mean that Cabeza de Vaca's understanding of his situation is irrelevant to his fate? Not at all. To survive and to make his way back to his countrymen, he had somehow to "negotiate away" the terrible fear with which he and his companions were understandably afflicted, and he had at the same time to negotiate away the fear that his presence aroused in the various groups of Indians he encountered. But, in the event, this negotiation of fear required the fortuitous conjunction of fundamentally divergent expectations, understandings, and practices. The acts of healing by which the Spanish ingratiated themselves to the Indians came to be strangely bound up with "ritual patterns of intertribal exchange and/or warfare." The two cultures produced, in effect, a discourse that neither could have fully understood—and it is as a result of this fusion, Adorno shows, that Cabeza de Vaca's extraordinary expedition narrated in the text known as the *Naufragios* came to "symbolize the benevolent and paradigmatic encounter of two worlds."

Faced with the challenge of radical difference, both Europeans and natives often behaved as if groping their way blindly through dense fog. The problem posed for action and understanding alike, in the wake of the European landfall in the Americas, is the need, as Anthony Pagden puts it, "to create a text where none had existed before" and "to make the text, once created, authoritative." Hence from the moment of landfall Columbus attempts to translate the practices of the alien world he observes into the practices of his own. This attempt to reduce the distance between the self and the other by "direct substitution" is one of the enduring principles of the early European response to unfamiliar lands and peoples, but it is set against the opposite response, the recognition of baffling and confounding otherness in the newly discovered lands and peoples. As Pagden demonstrates in a subtle analysis, the pivotal figure of Bartolomé de Las Casas conjoined the two responses, for Las Casas appeals both to a principle of identity (the Indians are "men like us") and a principle of eyewitness (only those who have seen for themselves can speak with authority). Pagden lines up these two principles with a tension in Las Casas between *ius* and *factum*, law and fact, canonical text and direct experience of the external world. Why should Las Casas's long personal experience of the New World not serve as a reliable basis for an authoritative text, a sure guide to the interpretation of the law as it applies to the peoples of America? The problem is that to European readers the experiences of the New World sounded like "the fables and lying tales of *Amadis of Gaul*"; the only way to confer a convincing reality upon them, Pagden suggests, would have been through a convincing "I"—an "I" that Las Casas the writer, whose passionate intelligence was not matched by his rhetorical skills, could never become.

Las Casas also has a critical role in Sabine MacCormack's essay, "Demons, Imagination, and the Incas." Starting with the Aristotelian conception, followed by Aquinas, that "the soul never thinks without a phantasm," MacCormack explores the ways in which Europeans tried to understand Inca religion. In classifying and categorizing what they were attempting to destroy, the Spanish tended, MacCormack notes, to detach Andean religious beliefs and ritual practices from the mythic and historical narratives that gave them meaning. The consequence was that the Spanish could not hope to comprehend Andean religion. Yet they feared its obvious power in the daily lives of the people, and they took seriously the many visionary manifestations of the Inca gods. Since the Aristotelian tradition held that sense perceptions, in themselves, could not be in error, European observers concluded that the Incas' beliefs in false gods must originate in an imagination that was led astray by demons. Hence, insofar as they recognized the cultural power of Andean religion, the Spanish could only attribute that power to the founding intervention of the devil.

MacCormack argues that Las Casas made an important conceptual break with this explanatory tradition by demoting direct demonic intervention from primary cause to merely one of several causes of religious difference. But only when the indigenous culture no longer represented a significant threat, only when Andean religion no longer had teeth—and hence, to recall Durkheim's view, was scarcely a religion—could it be freed from the theory that its origin lay in satanic intervention in the imagination. For the Spanish observers in the first generations after the conquest, the power of Indian culture was inextricably intertwined with the agency of Satan. The Andean imagination was freed from the imputation of the demonic only by stripping it of its power—the power, for example, to induce widows to immure themselves in the graves of their dead husbands. At the far end of the intellectual development initiated by Las Casas is Spinoza, for whom the imagination is not the unreliable faculty that mediates between infallible sense perception and right reason, but rather the faculty that in itself lies outside the possibility of error. "For," Spinoza writes, "if the mind while it imagines nonexistent things as present to it at the same time knows that those things do not exist, it attributes this power of imagining to a virtue of its nature, not to a vice." But, of course, this view, if applied to Andean (or any other) religious imagination, would imply that its visions are empty, mere spectacles of "nonexistent things."

In "The Philosopher's Breviary," Frank Lestringant makes a somewhat comparable point about the French Enlightenment. The account of the Tupi Indians in Jean de Léry's extraordinary *Histoire du Brésil*—the text Lévi-Strauss has called "the breviary of the ethnologist"—is bound up with the Huguenot Léry's conviction that the "savages" among whom he lived for several months were under a divine curse and were predestined to eternal damnation. The philosophy of the Enlightenment, full of confidence in the triumph of Reason over gloomy superstition, took up the wonderfully evocative Huguenot discourse of the New World in order to produce the idealized figure of the Noble Savage. But in doing so the Enlightenment philosophers drastically reduced Léry's vision, for in stripping it of its "fanaticism"—its conviction that the natives were devil-worshipers doomed to the fires of hell—they also stripped it of its ethnographic intelligence and its emotional force. "Once the omnipresent curse springing from original sin is left out of Léry," Lestringant asks, "what remains of the poignancy of condemned children? His remarks become insipid when deprived of their theological dimension." The Enlightenment rationalized the uncanniness of Léry's cannibals, so profoundly appealing and so morally disturbing, and transformed them into nature's noblemen. In place of Léry's stunned vision of what Michel de Certeau calls "insurmountable alterity," the philosophers projected onto the Brazilian natives the phantasms and desires of the European imagination, in the process reducing their religion to mere trickery and imposture.

What would it mean neither to demonize an American culture nor to transform it into an idealized exotic reverie? Several answers are at least implied in these essays, particularly David Damrosch's "The Aesthetics of Conquest" and Sara Castro-Klarén's "Dancing and the Sacred in the Andes." As Damrosch notes, many contemporary Mesoamericanists see Aztec culture as sharply split between the terrifying violence of its military and religious practices and the haunting delicacy of its melancholy poetry. He proposes not that we abandon both views— they are too bound up in our sense of the world simply to discard—but rather that we place them in relation to each other in an act of cultural interpretation. Damrosch thus suggests that we view Aztec aestheticism not as a redemptive alternative to Aztec imperial policy but as "deeply implicated" in it. The poems are in this sense "impure": for all of their exquisite otherworldliness, they are actions in the world. They are impure in another sense as well: their blend of Christian and Aztec references cannot be neatly rearranged to reveal a pre- and post-Conquest religion and aesthetic. For Damrosch, this impurity—which renders us unable to know whether a given poem is responding to events of 1460 or 1560, or perhaps to both—is not so much a liability of these texts as a source of their compelling power.

Damrosch posits a pre-imperial mode of poetry that was changed by the Aztec militarization of culture into a celebration of the beauty and terror of warfare: "Warfare is seen as an artistic act, and the warrior becomes a poet." The old images that evoked the fragility of life and the moral urgency of friendship are repeated, but now to cast an aura of beauty around imperial expansion and the suppression of revolts. After the Spanish conquest, this cycle of repetition and difference continues: "Within their own lifetimes, the Aztec poets were compelled to sing their poems in the light of the overturning of the world in which they were first composed." Their poems paradoxically insist on the continuity of their culture even in registering its destruction, and we are in consequence compelled to read many of them in a kind of double or triple sense. "The same images and verses that aided and even heightened the brutality of the imperial regime were turned to new purposes some years later: to strengthen the resolve of a conquered people to resist their total destruction."

The ruses and transcodings that enable continuity in the midst of disaster and oblivion are the subject of Sara Castro-Klarén's essay, "Dancing and the Sacred in the Andes." But the survival that principally interests her is located not in the sixteenth century, at the time that the "extirpators of idolatries" were doing their relentless work, but in the twentieth. In the cult and ritual dance known as the "Taqui-Oncoy"—a millenarian vision of the end of Spanish domination and the return of the Andean gods—Castro-Klarén finds the hermeneutic key to a resonant short story by a contemporary Peruvian writer, José María Arguedas. Her essay serves as an important reminder that this volume is not about peoples and cultures that "have vanished without a trace," but about encounters, strategies, contradictions, and struggles that continue into the present.

If one of the key principles of this collection is that the native cultures were, in Damrosch's phrase, "impure"—that is, neither transparent nor timeless, but opaque, complex, and constantly changing—an equally important corollary is that the discourse of the colonizers was similarly impure. Their texts are over-determined, crisscrossed by tiny fracture lines, characterized by unresolvable contradictions. These contradictions have famously plagued interpretation of Columbus's first letter, for which we now have an alternate version, translated into English for the first time by Margarita Zamora. This version, as Zamora observes, differs significantly from the celebrated letter that circulated in Europe in the wake of Columbus's first voyage, and its startling resurfacing after so many centuries subjects that letter to what Louis Montrose, in his illuminating analysis of Sir Walter Ralegh's *Discoverie of Guiana*, calls "epistemological and ideological destabilization."

The newly discovered version makes far more visible the peculiar yoking in Columbus's rhetoric, and perhaps in his consciousness, of piety and greed—the longing to recover for Christianity the holy places of Jerusalem and the equally intense longing to get the natives' gold in exchange for trash. This conjunction of apparently contradictory impulses is no accident; it is built into the structure of much of the period's colonialist discourse. Hence Ralegh's text, Montrose shows, attempts to mount a moral argument based on a cynical design, indeed boasts of a cynical use of moral pretense even as it insists on its ethical uprightness. In consequence, the *Discoverie* constructs for its author and reader alike a set of mutually contradictory positions—roughly akin to the pious evangelists and the ruthless pirates with which we began this introduction—whose incompatibility threatens fatally to undermine the manifest rhetorical intention of the work.

In "Ralegh's Fugitive Gold," Mary Fuller points out a comparable contradiction between the triumphalism of Ralegh's account of his expedition and the expedition's failure to bring back any substantial material proof of Ralegh's claims. Therefore, Fuller observes, Ralegh's *Discoverie* is forced perpetually to defer the completion of the quest, to point just beyond the horizon to the place where the gold of El Dorado forever awaits and eludes the seeker.

Ralegh's discourse, as Fuller and Montrose both observe, was not meant—any more than was Columbus's letter—to be an intriguing puzzle, a delicious game of vanishing points, dissolving promises, and ethical contradictions. It was meant to testify, to persuade, to provoke action. But how, given its internal rifts, could the *Discoverie* successfully intervene in the world? How could it persuade its readers—and, above all, its royal reader—of anything? Faced with this dilemma, Montrose argues, Ralegh employs gendered language. In an attempt to stabilize the categories and shore up the distinctions on which he wishes to base his claim for the moral superiority of English imperialism, Ralegh writes of Guiana as a woman. This use of the figure of the woman is a time-honored expedient in such shaky rhetorical structures, but the problem for Ralegh is that he is in the service of a powerful female monarch toward whose authority he feels a deep and unresolvable conflict. Therefore, Montrose argues, while the "gendering" of Guiana ostensibly serves the imperial designs of Elizabeth I, it actually "stages a covert resistance to the queen's power." This resistance serves in turn further to destabilize Ralegh's errant text: a rhetorical strategy aimed at composing the conflicting elements of a troubled discourse into harmonious accord only intensifies the dissonance. For Ralegh there is no safe haven, no home port.

Textual dissonance is the subject as well of David Quint's "Voices of Resistance." Quint shows that the curses of the vanquished, so powerfully represented in Gaspar Perez de Villagrá's *Historia de la Nueva Mexico* and in Alonso de Ercilla's *Araucana*, are an epic *topos* that can be traced back to the *Odyssey* and the *Aeneid*. But what function does this *topos*, that seems to pull sharply against the triumphalism of epic, serve? In Quint's analysis, it appears to serve a double or split function: on the one hand, "it makes a good story"; on the other hand, it "calls the idea of ending"—and hence, perhaps, of making a good story—"into question." The epic curse raises the specter of people who will never be assimilated to the imperialists' new world order, never reconciled to their own subjugation. Like most curses, it is uttered from a position of powerlessness, but also in the expectation that powerlessness will not endure forever. It registers a tenacious refusal to submit to the narrative of the victors.

And yet, Quint points out, the epic curse is precisely one of the hallmarks of this narrative. As such, its presence can be viewed as a kind of sublime trophy of conquest, a sign of the containment of the rebellious spirit of the savage, the point at which barbarous speech submits to civilized writing. It may signal not a crack in the imperial ideology but the need for unceasing vigilance and the endless renewing of disciplinary will. In a subtle analysis of the Adamastor episode in Camões's *Lusíadas*, Quint shows that the half-stifled voices of resistance can be made to serve the celebration of the victors, and at the same time he argues that the unsettling power of the *topos* asserts itself even when it appears to be most repressed.

In an "Afterword," Quint associates the epic curse with a still more virulent curse that at least some Europeans felt had originated in America: syphilis. To this we may add another American specter that came to haunt Europe: tobacco. Jeffrey Knapp's "Elizabethan Tobacco" points out, however, that for many Englishmen tobacco was one of the highest blessings of the New World. Compared with the gold bullion that the Spanish treasure fleet regularly carried home from the Caribbean, tobacco seems, of course, like the most negligible trifle, but the apologists for the English colony in Virginia—a territory notably deficient in gold mines—persuaded themselves or tried to persuade others that tobacco was an even greater treasure. Tobacco's proponents praised the weed not only for its fabled medicinal powers—its ability to open the pores, clear the lungs, and warm the brain—but also for its exemplary spiritual qualities: its link to the imagination, its superiority to filthy lucre, its emblematic transformation of matter into spirit. Let the Spanish have the gold their slaves claw from the bowels of the earth, let the papists have the wafer-god they profess to swallow in the Mass; the stout Protestant Englishmen, happier by far, have "divine tobacco."

Were such arguments ever made seriously? Not quite. Yet, as Knapp shows, they were the hyperbolic articulation of a set of assumptions, ambitions, and compensatory dreams that characterize much of the discourse of colonialism, the religious ideology, and the poetry of early modern England. Even James I's angry denunciation of tobacco was not enough to turn his nation away from its obsession with turning smoke into profit and profit into smoke.

As this brief review should make apparent, the essays collected here represent a wide range of interests and approaches. But, with the exception of Margarita Zamora's translation of Columbus's letter and Sara Castro-Klarén's "Dancing and the Sacred," all have appeared in the journal *Representations*, most of them in a single issue dedicated to the memory of Michel de Certeau, and this common ground is not a neutral fact. Context does not constitute a unified or prescriptive program, but it does, as I have already hinted, imply certain shared critical principles that bring together the very different enterprises of history, ethnography, and literary criticism.

What are these principles? First, an assumption of textual opacity. All the essays start from the conviction that discourse neither can nor should be rendered transparent. We are allowed access to the European encounter with the New World chiefly through what de Certeau calls the colonists' "scriptural economy." Writing is itself freighted with meaning, particularly in texts about peoples whose identity the texts repeatedly characterized as bound up with their supposed lack of even the most rudimentary writing. The scholar's goal must not be to strip away or look behind European texts in order to discover the naked truth. The problem is not that there is no truth or that we are forever doomed to ignorance—though considerable ignorance is certainly inescapable in these matters—but that the discourses of colonialism actually do much of the crucially important work of colonialism. Consequently, if we treat the texts as clear or even as distorting windows, we inevitably miss much of what we most need to understand.

Second, a recognition of textual complexity. The early European accounts of the encounter are not monolithic or single-minded. The essays in this volume are concerned with the half-hidden stress points in the official structures, the tensions, ideological negotiations, and rifts that are often plastered over in later accounts, all but disappearing from view. Many of the texts discussed here create complex intertwinings of potentially competing discourses, systems that are perilously close to explosion or collapse. It was, de Certeau argued, Montaigne's genius in "Of Cannibals" to bring matters to a crisis: the rival discourses "destroy one another as soon as they touch: a shattering of mirrors, the defection of images, one after the other."[6]

Third, a search for textual otherness. The voices of the other do not reach us in pure or uncontaminated form—as if such a condition were ever possible! Indeed the whole European project of writing about the New World rests upon the absence of the object—landscape, people, voice, culture—that has fascinated, repelled, or ravished the writer. "The scriptural operation which produces, preserves, and cultivates imperishable 'truths,'" de Certeau writes, "is connected to a rumor of words that vanish no sooner than they are uttered, and which are therefore lost forever."[7] Yet, despite this loss, the "rumor of words" must somehow be attended to. The difficulty of this task is the subject of many of these essays, as is the peril of a failure to attend.

Fourth and finally, a questioning of textual authority. Once they are written, texts do not simply appear in the world (or routinely survive in archives): they are marked, placed, licensed, authorized. "Writing," de Certeau observes, "designates an *operation organized about a center*."[8] But in the case of the New World, the center very often does not hold. Textual authority is fraught with particular difficulties, not only because of perennial tensions in overburdened command structures, but because of the immense distance from Europe of the newly discovered lands and, consequently, the immense problem of verification, a problem exacerbated by the strangeness of the stories that had to be told. At the moment that Europeans embarked on one of the greatest enterprises of appetite, acquisition, and control in the history of the world, their own discourses became haunted by all that they could not control. They had embarked, without quite realizing it, on "a subtle, permanent, practice of distances."[9]

Notes

1. Samuel Eliot Morison, *The European Discovery of America: The Southern Voyages, 1492–1616* (New York, 1974), 737.
2. Among the many articulations of this traditional position, one might cite Leonardo Olschki's characterization of Spanish imperialism as "a human activity which transformed within a short lapse of time a rudimentary stone-age society into a lively colonial organization"; "What Columbus Saw on Landing in the West Indies," *Proceedings of the American Philosophical Society* 84 (1941): 635.
3. Jonathan Swift, *Gulliver's Travels*, ed. Ricardo Quintana (New York, 1958), 241.
4. Nathan Wachtel, *The Vision of the Vanquished: the Spanish Conquest of Peru through Indian Eyes, 1530–1570*, trans. Ben and Sian Reynolds (1971; New York, 1977).
5. See Marshall Sahlins, *Islands of History* (Chicago, 1985), esp. 125.

6. Michel de Certeau, "Montaigne's 'Of Cannibals': The Savage 'I,'" in *Heterologies: Discourse on the Other* (Minneapolis, 1986), 71.
7. Michel de Certeau, *The Writing of History*, trans. Tom Conley (New York, 1988), 212.
8. Ibid., 217.
9. de Certeau, *Heterologies*, 68.

MARGARITA ZAMORA

Christopher Columbus's "Letter to the Sovereigns": Announcing the Discovery

As the *Diario* of the first voyage tells it, on 14 February in the midst of a life-threatening storm, Christopher Columbus wrote to Ferdinand and Isabela announcing the Discovery. He sealed the letter inside a barrel, along with a note asking whoever might find the letter to deliver it to the sovereigns unopened and promising a substantial reward if the instructions were followed. He then tossed it overboard to the fate of wind and waves.[1] On 4 March Columbus wrote to the king of Portugal and, again, to the Spanish sovereigns. Both letters were apparently posted overland, since on this day according to the *Diario* he was anchored near the mouth of the Tagus River by the Portuguese town of Cascais. Two other almost identical letters announcing the Discovery, and bearing the date of 15 February (undoubtedly false), have been attributed to Columbus.[2] They were addressed to Luis de Santángel and Rafael [*sic*] Sánchez,[3] officials of the Crown of Aragón who had been instrumental in facilitating the enterprise of discovery.

Until very recently only one of the four versions of the announcement was known to have survived—the "twin" letters addressed to Santángel and Sánchez, which were published in various editions and in three different languages throughout Europe within a few months of Columbus's triumphant return from "the Indies." The letters of 4 March, to João II of Portugal and to Isabela and Ferdinand, seemed to have fared no better than the one entrusted to the storm on 14 February; this last one apparently never made it to shore, probably falling victim to official suppression, however, rather than to the elements.[4] Not so the letters dated 15 February, which, on the contrary, were so vigorously and widely circulated that it is not difficult to see in their promotion a concerted propaganda campaign. The publicizing of this version of the announcement was so successful in fact that for almost five centuries it has served as the original, indeed only, representation of Europe's first encounter with the New World. Until 1989, that is, when Antonio Rumeu de Armas published a transcription of an authenticated sixteenth-century copy of Columbus's *Libro Copiador*.[5] The "copy book," the original of which consisted of Columbus's personal copies of documents he must have deemed especially worthy of preservation, contains various texts previously

1

thought lost and opens with the long-missing 4 March "Letter to the Sovereigns" announcing the Discovery, translated into English here for the first time.[6]

The publication of this text is probably the single most significant scholarly event of the quincentennial, making available for the first time since the nineteenth century a new Columbian source on the Discovery. Of more transcendental importance than the find itself, however, is the fact that the appearance of the "Letter to the Sovereigns" has in effect set up a dialogue on the Discovery from within its own sources, so that we no longer have only one Columbian version of it but two. Whether both can be considered authentically Columbus's has been a subject of considerable debate.[7] The (probably unanswerable) question of authorship, however, seems to be less important than the fact that each version identifies the narrator as Columbus, thereby assuming the authority and privilege of eyewitness testimony by the protagonist of the events.

Even a cursory comparison of the two announcements suggests, however, that the image of the Discovery heralded by the Santángel-Sánchez version is not identical to the one contained in the royal missive, but a sanitized rendition of it.[8] Not only did the Santángel-Sánchez letter undergo stylistic revision for the sake of economy and ease of reading, but the royal text was also purged on its way to becoming the public announcement of the Discovery. Whereas the descriptions of the land and peoples for which the Santángel-Sánchez version is famous are not significantly different in the 4 March "Letter to the Sovereigns," the interpretation that the latter assigns to the larger significance of the enterprise does differ, as does its much more candid, albeit discreet, discussion of some of the problems the expedition experienced. On comparison the targets of suppression begin to suggest a pattern corresponding to one or more of the following general categories:

· information that could serve competitors, such as the elaborate discussion on the advantages of the caravel over the larger *nao* for voyages of discovery;
· comments that could put the expedition in a bad light or suggest discord among the various parties involved—for example, the grounding of the *Santa María*, the insubordination of Martín Alonso Pinzón (captain of the *Pinta*), or the ridicule to which Columbus was subjected in Spain before the first voyage;
· petitions that the Crown grant privileges and favors to Columbus in recompense for his services;
· plans that link the enterprise of discovery to a projected reconquest of the Holy Land, rendering the liberation of Jerusalem its ultimate goal.

The most readily perceptible effect of these suppressions is to expose in the Santángel-Sánchez version a bureaucratic blandness or flatness, a somewhat antiseptic aftertaste of the sanitation. The image of the Discovery conveyed by the royal missive is less guarded, more human, and consequently more vibrant than its public counterpart. It unabashedly speaks of Columbus's personal concerns, even self-interest, the lingering bitterness of his earlier humiliation, his pride in the success of the endeavor, his rather arrogant demands for compensation, and so on. In contrast to the heroic but one-dimensional figure portrayed in the public version, the "Letter to the Sovereigns" reveals an undoubtedly less mythical yet more accessible Columbus. Moreover, it represents the Discovery unequivocally as a joint commercial venture between an individual who was driven by personal worldly and spiritual ambitions and the state that was contractually bound to compensate him for the initiative and would benefit from his efforts. This is not the image of the Discovery or the portrait of Columbus we are accustomed to, but in both we should be able to recognize our legacy.

Letter to the Sovereigns of 4 March 1493 Announcing the Discovery

†

Most Christian and lofty and powerful sovereigns:

That eternal God who has given Your Highnesses so many victories now gave you the greatest one that to this day He has ever given any prince.[9] I come from the Indies with the armada Your Highnesses gave me, to which [place] I traveled in thirty-three days after departing from your kingdoms; after fourteen of the thirty-three there were light winds in which I covered very little ground. I found innumerable people and very many islands, of which I took possession in Your Highnesses' name, by royal crier and with Your Highnesses' royal banner unfurled, and it was not contradicted.[10] To the first [island] I gave the name of San Salvador, in memory of His Supreme Majesty [Jesus Christ], to the second Santa María de la Concepción, to the third Fernandina, to the fourth Isabela, to the fifth Juana, and to the others almost a new name.[11] After I arrived at Juana I followed its coast to the west and found it to be so large that I thought it was probably not an island, but rather a mainland, and most likely the province of Cathay; but I could not verify this because everywhere I arrived the people fled and I could not speak with them. And because I was unable to find a notable settlement, I thought that by hugging the coast I could not fail to find some town or great city, such as those who have gone to that province overland tell it.[12] And after following this land for a long while, I found that I was veering away from the west and it was leading me to the north and I found the wind came from that direction, with which I tried to contend until it passed and a different one arrived, because it was already winter and I had no other intention but to avoid the south wind,[13] and so I turned back. In the meantime I already understood something of the speech and signs of certain Indians I had taken on the island of San Salvador, and I understood [from them] that this was still an island. And thus I came to a very good harbor, from which I sent two men inland, three days' journey, with one of the Indians I brought, who had become friendly with me, so that they could see and determine if there were any cities or large settlements, and which land it was, and what there was in it. They found many settlements and innumerable people, but no government of any importance. And so they returned, and I departed and took certain Indians at the said harbor so that I could also hear or learn from them about said lands. And thus I followed the sea coast of this island toward the east one hundred and seven leagues to where it ended. And before leaving it, I saw another island to the east, eighteen leagues out from this one, which I later named Española. And then I went to it and followed its coast on the north side, just as in the case of Juana, due east for one hundred and eighty-eight very long leagues. And I continued to enter very many harbors, in each of which I placed a very large cross in the most appropriate spot, as I had done in all the other [harbors] of the other islands, and in many places I found promontories sufficient [for this purpose]. So I went on in this fashion until the sixteenth of January, when I determined to return to Your Highnesses, as much because I had already found most of what I sought as because I had only one caravel left, because the *nao*[14] that I brought I had left in Your Highnesses' village of La Navidad, with the men who were using it for fortification. There was another caravel, but one from Palos whom I had put in charge of her, expecting good service, made off with her, with the intention of taking much[15] [*damaged*] . . . of [from?] an island about which an Indian had given news, that with him I [*damaged*] . . . after doing whatever. [*damaged*] . . . and it is the sweetest [thing] to navigate and with the least danger for ships[16] of all sorts. For discovering, however, small caravels are better suited, because going close to land or rivers, in order to discover much, [vessels] must require but little depth and be capable of being assisted with oars. Neither is there ever stormy weather, since in every place I have been I see the grass and trees growing into the sea.

Besides the above-mentioned islands, I have found many others in the Indies, of which I have not been able to tell in this letter. They, like these others, are so extremely fertile, that even if I were able to express it, it would not be a marvel were it to be disbelieved. The breezes [are] most temperate, the trees and fruits and grasses are extremely beautiful and very different from ours; the rivers and harbors are so abundant and of such extreme excellence when compared to those of Christian lands that it is a marvel. All these islands are densely populated with the best people under the sun; they have neither ill-will nor treachery. All of them, women and men alike, go about naked as their mothers bore them, although some of the women wear a small piece of cotton or a patch of grass with which they cover themselves. They have neither iron nor weapons, except for canes on the end of which they place a thin sharp stick. Everything they make is done with stones [stone tools]. And I have not learned that any of them have any private property, because while I was spending a few days with this king in the village of La Navidad, I saw that all of the people, and the women in particular, would bring him *agís*, which is the food they eat, and he would order them to be distributed; a very singular sustenance.[17]

Nowhere in these islands have I known the inhabitants to have a religion, or idolatry, or much diversity of language among them, but rather they all understand one another. I learned that they know that all powers reside in heaven. And, generally, in whatever lands I traveled, they believed and believe that I, together with these ships and people, came from heaven, and they greeted me with such veneration. And today, this very day, they are of the same mind, nor have they strayed from it, despite all the contact they [the Spaniards at La Navidad] may have had with them. And then, upon arriving at whatever settlement, the men, women, and children go from house to house calling out, "Come, come and see the people from heaven!"[18] Everything they have or had they gave for whatever one gave them in exchange, even taking a piece of glass or broken crockery or some such thing, for gold or some other thing of whatever value. One sailor got more than two and a half *castellanos* [in gold] for the ends of leather latchets. There are ten thousand like occurrences to tell.

The islands are all very flat and low-lying, except for Juana and Española. These two are very high lands, and there are mountain chains and very high peaks, much higher than those of the island of Tenerife. The mountains are of a thousand different shapes and all [are] most beautiful, and fertile and walkable and full of trees; it seems they touch the sky. And both the one and the other of the said islands are very large, such that, as I have said, I traveled in a straight line . . . [*damaged for the next three lines, not enough context to translate*][19] . . . is much larger than England and Scotland together; this other one [*stained*] is certainly larger than the whole of Española such that, as I said above, I traveled in a straight line, from west to east, one hundred and eighty-eight large leagues that comprise that side [of the island].[20] Juana has many rivers, and great mountains, and very large valleys and meadows and fields, and it is all full of trees and huge palms of a thousand varieties, such as to make one marvel. La Spañola[21] has the advantage in every respect; the trees are not so tall or of the same kind, but rather very fruitful and broad; and [they are] delectable lands for all things, and for sowing and planting and raising livestock, of which I have not seen any kind on any of these islands. This island has marvelously temperate breezes, and marvelous meadows and fields incomparable to those of Castile; and the same can be said of the rivers of great and good waters, most of which are gold-bearing. There are so many and such good sea harbors that it has to be seen to be believed. I have not tarried in these islands or the others for many reasons, as I said above, but especially because it was winter when I sailed these coasts, which did not allow me to go south because I was on their north side and the [winds] were almost always easterly, which were contrary to continuing my navigation. Then I did not understand those people nor they me, except for what common sense dictated, although they were saddened and I much more so, because I wanted to have good information concerning everything. And what I did to remedy this was the Indians I had with me, for they learned our language and we theirs, and the next voyage will tell. So, there was no reason for me to tarry at any harbor wasting time when the opportunity came to set sail. Moreover, as I have said, these vessels I brought with me were too large and heavy for such a purpose, especially the *nao* I brought over, about which I was quite troubled before leaving Castile. I would much have preferred taking small caravels, but since this was the first voyage and the people I brought were afraid of running into high seas and uncertain about the voyage, and there was and has been so much opposition, and anybody dared to contradict this route and ascribe to it a thousand dangers without being able to give me any reasons, they caused me to act against my own judgment and do everything that those who were to go with me wanted, in order to get the voyage finally under way and find the land. But Our Lord, who is the light and strength of all those who seek to do good and makes them victorious in deeds that seem impossible, wished to ordain that I should find and was to find gold and mines and spicery and innumerable peoples . . . [*the next four lines are damaged, not enough context to translate*] I left in it [Española], in possession of the village of La Navidad, the people I brought on the *nao* and some from the caravels, stocked with provisions to last over a year, [with] much artillery and quite without danger from anyone, but rather with much friendship from the king of that place, who prided himself in calling me and having me for a brother; who [also] appeared to accept everything as the greatest boon in the world, as I said. And the others [feel] just as the king does, so that the people I left there suffice to subjugate the entire island without danger. This island is in a place, as I have said, signaled by the hand of Our Lord, where I hope His Majesty will give Your Highnesses as much gold as you need, spicery of a certain pepper [to fill] as many ships as Your Highnesses may order to be loaded, and as much mastic as you may order to load, which today can be found only on the island of Chios, in Greece, and the government[22] sells it as they see fit, and I believe they get more than 45,000 ducats for it each year. And as much lignum aloe as you may order to be loaded, and as much cotton as you may order to be loaded, and so many slaves that they are innumerable; and they will come from the idolaters. And I believe there are rhubarb and cinnamon. All this I found on this hasty trip, but I have faith in God that upon my return the people I left there will have found a thousand other things of importance, because that is the charge I left them with. And I left them a boat and its equipment and [the tools] to make boats and *fustas*,[23] and masters in all the nautical arts. And above all I consider all the above-mentioned islands as belonging to Your Highnesses and you may command them as you do the kingdoms of Castile, and even more completely, especially this one of Española.

I conclude here: that through the divine grace of Him who is the origin of all good and virtuous things, who favors and gives victory to all those who walk in His path, in seven years from today I will be able to pay Your Highnesses for five thousand cavalry and fifty thousand foot soldiers for the war and conquest of Jerusalem, for which purpose this enterprise was undertaken. And in another five years another five thousand cavalry and fifty thousand foot soldiers, which will total ten thousand cavalry and one hundred thousand foot soldiers; and all of this with very little investment now on Your Highnesses' part in this beginning of the taking of the Indies and all that they contain, as I will tell Your Highnesses in person later. And I have reason for this [claim] and do not speak uncertainly, and one should not delay in it, as was the case with the execution of this enter-prise, may God forgive whoever has been the cause of it.

Most powerful sovereigns: all of Christendom should hold great celebrations, and especially God's Church, for the finding of such a multitude of such friendly peoples, which with very little effort will be converted to our Holy Faith, and so many lands filled with so many goods very necessary to us in which all Christians will have comfort and profits, all of which was unknown nor did anyone speak of it except in fables. Great rejoicing and celebrations in the churches [*damaged*] . . . Your Highnesses should order that [many] praises should be given to the Holy Trinity [*damaged*] your kingdoms and domains, because of the great love [the Holy Trinity?] has shown you, more than to any other prince.

Now, most serene sovereigns, remember that I left my woman and children behind and came from my homeland to serve you, in which [service] I spent what I had. And I spent seven years of my time and put up with a thousand indignities and disgrace and I suffered much hardship. I did not wish to deal with other princes who solicited me, although Your Highnesses' giving of your protection to this voyage has owed more to my importuning [you] than to anything else. And not only has no favor been shown to me, but moreover nothing of what was prom-ised me has been fulfilled. I do not ask favors of Your Highnesses in order to amass treasure, for I have no purpose other than to serve God and Your High-nesses and to bring this business of the Indies to perfection, as time will be my witness. And therefore I beseech you that honor be bestowed upon me according to [the quality of] my service.

The Church of God should also work for this: providing prelates and devout and wise religious; and because the matter is so great and of such a character, there is reason for the Holy Father to provide prelates who are very free of greed for temporal possessions and very true to the service of God and of Your High-nesses. And therefore I beseech you to ask the Church, in the letter you write regarding this victory, for a cardinalate for my son, and that it be granted him although he may not yet be of sufficient age, for there is little difference in his age and that of the son of the Medicis of Florence, to whom a cardinal's hat was granted without his having served or having had a purpose so honorable to Christianity, and that you give me the letter pertaining to this matter so that I [myself] may solicit it.

Furthermore, most serene sovereigns, because the sin of ungratefulness was the first one to be punished, I realize that since I am not guilty of it I must at all times try to gain from Your Highnesses the following [favor], because, without a doubt, were it not for Villacorta,[24] who every time it was necessary persuaded and worked on [the enterprise's] behalf, because I was already sick of it and everyone who had been and was involved in the matter was tired, [the enterprise would not have succeeded]. Therefore, I beseech Your Highnesses that you do me the favor of making him paymaster of the Indies, for I vouch that he will do it well.

Wherefore Your Highnesses should know that the first island of the Indies, closest to Spain, is populated entirely by women, without a single man, and their comportment is not feminine, but rather they use weapons and other masculine practices. They carry bows and arrows and take their adornments from the copper mines, which metal they have in very large quantity. They call this island Matenino, the second Caribo, [*blank*] leagues out from this one. Here are found those people which all those of the other islands of the Indies fear; they eat human flesh, are great bowmen, have many canoes almost as big as oar-powered *fustas* in which they travel all over the islands of the Indies, and they are so feared that they have no equal. They go about naked like the others, except that they wear their hair very full, like women. I think the great cowardice . . . [*damaged*] peoples of the other islands, for which there is no remedy, makes them say that these of Caribe are brave, but I think the same of them as of the rest. And when Your Highnesses give the order for me to send slaves, I hope to bring or send [you] these for the most part; these are the ones who have intercourse with the women of Matenino, who if they bear a female child they keep her with them, and if it is a male child, they raise him until he can feed himself and then they send him to Cardo. Between the islands of Cardo and Española there is another island they call Borinque,[25] all of it is a short distance from the other region of the island of Juana that they call Cuba. In the westernmost part [of Cuba], in one of the two provinces I did not cover, which is called Faba, everyone is born with a tail. Beyond this island of Juana, still within sight, there is another that these Indians assured me was larger than Juana, which they call Jamaica, where all the people are bald. On this one there is gold in immeasurable quantities; and now I have Indians with me who have been on these [islands] as well as the others and they know the language and customs. Nothing further, except that may the Holy Trinity guard and make Your Highnesses' royal estate prosper in Its service. Written in the Sea of Spain,[26] on the fourth day of March in the year fourteen ninety-three. At sea.

Notes

1. Columbus strapped another barrel with similar contents to the ship's stern; (Consuelo Varela, *Textos y documentos completos* (Madrid, 1984), 127. Ferdinand Columbus, in his account of the first voyage, quotes his father's description of this first letter announcing the Discovery:

> Escribí en un pergamino, con la brevedad que el tiempo exigía, cómo yo dejaba descubiertas aquellas tierras que les había prometido; en cuántos días y por qué camino lo había logrado; la bondad del país y la condición de sus habitantes, y cómo quedaban los vasallos de Vuestras Altezas en posesión de todo lo que se había descubierto. Cuya escritura, cerrada y sellada, dirigí a Vuestras Altezas con el porte, es a saber, promesa de mil ducados a aquél que la presentara sin abrir. A fin de que si hombres extranjeros la encontrasen, no se valiesen del aviso que dentro había, con la avidez del porte. Muy luego hice que me llevaran un gran barril, y habiendo envuelto la escritura en una tela encerada, y metido ésta en torta u hogaza de cera, la puse en el barril. Y bien sujeto con sus aros, lo eché al mar, creyendo todos que sería alguna devoción. Y porque pensé que podría suceder que no llegase a salvamento, y los navíos aun caminaban para acercarse a Castilla, hice otro atado semejante al primero, y lo puse en lo alto de la popa para que, si se hundía el navío, quedase el barril sobre las olas a merced de la tormenta. (*Vida del Almirante don Cristóbal Colón*, ed. Ramón Iglesias [Mexico City, 1947], 123).
>
> ["Therefore I wrote on a parchment, as briefly as the state of things required, how I had discovered those lands as I had promised to do; the length of the voyage and the route thither; the goodness of the country and the customs of its inhabitants; and how I had left Your Highnesses vassals in possession of all I had discovered. This writing, folded and sealed, I addressed to Your Highnesses with a written promise of a thousand ducats to whoever should deliver it sealed to you; this I did so that if it should fall into the hands of foreigners, they would be restrained by the reward from divulging the information it contained to others. I straightaway had a great wooden barrel brought to me, and having wrapped the writing in a waxed cloth and put it in a cake or loaf of wax, I dropped it into the barrel, which I made secure with hoops and cast into the sea; and all thought this was an act of devotion. I still feared the barrel might not reach safety, but as the ships meanwhile were drawing closer to Castile, I placed a similar cask at the head of the stern, so that if the ship sank it might float on the waves at the mercy of the storm.] (*The Life of the Admiral Christopher Columbus by His Son Ferdinand*, trans. Benjamin Keen [Westport, Conn., 1978], 92).

2. In the entry for this day the *Diario* places the fleet in midstorm somewhere off the Azores and still over a week away from the European mainland. It does not mention that Columbus wrote any such letter on this day.
3. The correct name was Gabriel Sánchez, treasurer of the Crown of Aragon.
4. The only traces of the 14 February text are the references found in the *Diario* and in the subsequent histories of the Discovery derived from it: Ferdinand Columbus's biography of his father, *Vida del Almirante don Cristóbal Colón* (1571 [in Italian]), and Bar-

tolomé de Las Casas's *Historia de las Indias* (composed 1527–ca. 1560; pub. 1875; repr. Mexico City, 1951). The letters of 4 March also seemed to have disappeared without a trace. Their previous existence was betrayed only in passing references to the Portuguese king in the *Diario*, and to the Spanish sovereigns in a postscript to the published letters to Santángel and Sánchez as well as in correspondence from the Crown to Columbus acknowledging receipt of what most scholars believe was the letter in question.

5. Antonio Rumeu de Armas, ed., *El Libro Copiador de Cristóbal Colón*, 2 vols. (Madrid, 1989).

6. Notably absent from the collection is the famous version of 15 February. As of August 1991 only two U.S. libraries held copies of the *Libro Copiador*, perhaps because of its steep price tag of approximately one thousand dollars. As a result, regrettably, the letter of 4 March has yet to be discussed in the scholarly literature here in the United States.

7. Most recently in the works of Demetrio Ramos, *La primera noticia de América* (Valladolid, 1986), and Rumeu de Armas, ed., *El Libro Copiador*, vol. 1.

8. For a more detailed comparison of the two versions see Margarita Zamora, *Reading Columbus* (Berkeley, forthcoming).

9. A small cross appears heading the text in the original manuscript. My translation is based on Rumeu de Armas's transcription in *El Libro Copiador*. I have attempted to follow the Spanish as literally as possible, in order to recreate in the English version the awkwardness or clumsiness that characterizes much of Columbus's written Spanish. Where literal translation verged on incomprehensibility, I have added a word or phrase in brackets for clarification. Rumeu de Armas modernized the punctuation in his transcription; therefore I have done the same in the English translation.

10. "Y no fue contradicho" has the sense of "without resistance or opposition." In this context it implies that there was no verbal or physical opposition to the taking of possession by Columbus.

11. Rumeu de Armas's transcription reads "y a las otras, casi nombre nuevo." An almost identical passage in the letter to Santángel says "e así a cada una nombre nuevo"; Varela, *Textos y documentos completos*, 140. Until I can verify it in the facsimile, I have translated Rumeu's transcription literally, but as such it makes little sense. My best guess is that there was either a copying error in the original or a transcription error by Rumeu. It probably should read "e así nombre nuevo," that is, "and [to the others] likewise a new name."

12. This is probably an allusion to the accounts of Marco Polo and the papal embassies to the Far East of the thirteenth and fourteenth centuries by John Plano Carpini, William of Rubruck, John of Monte Corvino, and Oderic of Pordenone. Columbus certainly would have known Pordenone's account, as distilled in John Mandeville's *Travels* (1470), a book Columbus knew well.

13. I believe there is another error here: "porque ya era el ynbierno encarnado, y no tenía el propósito salvo de huir al austro" should probably read "y[o] no tenía," that is, "I had no other purpose but to avoid a south wind."

14. Columbus sailed with two caravels (*Niña* and *Pinta*) and a larger *nao*, the *Santa María*, which grounded on the night of 24–25 December.

15. This passage appears to be an allusion to Martín Alonso Pinzón, who throughout the voyage had a tendency to disregard Columbus's orders and strike out on his own.

16. The Spanish reads "naos y navíos," both of which were larger vessels than the caravels Columbus preferred.

17. The "king" in question here must be Guacanagarí, who befriended Columbus and came to his aid when the *Santa María* ran into a reef on Christmas Eve, 1492. La Navidad fort was erected, at least partially with lumber from the *Santa María*, to house the Spaniards who remained on the island. *Agí* is a hot red pepper. It was one of the very first Taino words to be introduced to Europeans.
18. *Cielo* has the connotations of both sky and heaven. I have preferred to translate it as heaven because the context in which it appears suggests that the term was used with intention of implying to the reader that the Indians saw the Europeans as beings of divine origins.
19. Throughout the transcription Rumeu de Armas has noted various places as damaged and has included the mutilated passages. In most cases, I have translated the fragments, but some (like this one) do not provide sufficient context for translation.
20. The original reads "que en ella hay en aquella quadra." None of the Spanish connotations of "quadra" that I found made sense in this context. In Italian the word means "quadrant," which also seemed anomalous here. I have based my translation of "quadra" on *quartum*, which is used in an almost identical passage in the Latin version of the letter of 15 February addressed to Sánchez. See R. M. Major, ed. and trans., *Four Voyages to the New World: Letters and Selected Documents* (Gloucester, Mass., 1978), 11.
21. Variant spelling of "Española."
22. The term used here is *señorío* (seigneury), literally meaning feudal lordship.
23. *Fusta*, a small vessel of Moorish or Turkish origin. See James J. Pontillo, "Nautical Terms in Sixteenth-Century American Spanish" (Ph.D. diss., State University of New York at Buffalo, 1975).
24. Pedro de Villacorta, a member of the crew of the first voyage and a favorite with Columbus.
25. Later named by Columbus San Juan de Puerto Rico.
26. The *Diario* puts Columbus in the Atlantic just off the coast of Portugal, near Lisbon and the mouth of the Tagus River, on 4 March 1493.

"Fierce and Unnatural Cruelty": Cortés and the Conquest of Mexico

I

THE CONQUEST OF MEXICO matters to us because it poses a painful question: How was it that a motley bunch of Spanish adventurers, never numbering much more than four hundred or so, was able to defeat an Amerindian military power on its home ground in the space of two years? What was it about Spaniards, or about Indians, that made so awesomely implausible a victory possible? The question has not lost its potency through time, and as the consequences of the victory continue to unfold has gained in poignancy.

Answers to that question came easily to the men of the sixteenth century. The conquest mattered to Spaniards and to other Europeans because it provided their first great paradigm for European encounters with an organized native state;[1] a paradigm that quickly took on the potency and the accommodating flexibility of myth. In the early 1540s, a mere twenty years after the fall of Mexico-Tenochtitlan before the forces led by Hernando Cortés, Juan Ginés Sepúlveda, chaplain and chronicler to the Spanish emperor Charles V, wrote a work that has been described as "the most virulent and uncompromising argument for the inferiority of the American Indian ever written." Sepúlveda had his spokesman recite "the history of Mexico, contrasting a noble, valiant Cortés with a timorous, cowardly Moctezoma, whose people by their iniquitous desertion of their natural leader demonstrated their indifference to the good of the commonwealth."[2] By 1585 the Franciscan Fray Bernardino de Sahagún had revised an earlier account of the Conquest, written very much from the native point of view and out of the recollections of native Mexicans, to produce a version in which the role of Cortés was elevated, Spanish actions justified, and the whole conquest presented as providential.[3]

The Mexican Conquest as model for European-native relations was reanimated for the English-speaking world through the marvelously dramatic *History of the Conquest of Mexico* written by W. H. Prescott in the early 1840s, a bestseller in those glorious days when History still taught lessons.[4] The lesson that great history taught was that Europeans will triumph over natives, however formidable the apparent odds, because of cultural superiority, manifesting itself visibly in equipment but residing much more powerfully in mental and moral qualities.

Prescott presented Spanish victory as flowing directly out of the contrast and the relationship between the two leaders: the Mexican ruler Moctezoma, despotic, effete, and rendered fatally indecisive by the "withering taint" of an irrational religion, and his infinitely resourceful adversary Cortés. Prescott found in the person of the Spanish commander the model of European man: ruthless, pragmatic, single-minded, and (the unfortunate excesses of Spanish Catholicism aside) superbly rational in his manipulative intelligence, strategic flexibility, and capacity to decide a course of action and to persist in it.[5]

The general contours of the Prescottian fable are still clearly discernible in the most recent and certainly the most intellectually sophisticated account of the Conquest, Tzvetan Todorov's *The Conquest of America: The Question of the Other*. Confronted by the European challenge, Todorov's Mexicans are "other" in ways that doom them. Dominated by a cyclical understanding of time, omen-haunted, they are incapable of improvization in face of the unprecedented Spanish challenge. Although "masters in the art of ritual discourse," they cannot produce "appropriate and effective messages"; Moctezoma, for example, pathetically sends gold "to convince his visitors to leave the country." Todorov is undecided as to Moctezoma's own view of the Spaniards, acknowledging the mistiness of the sources; he nonetheless presents the "paralyzing belief that the Spaniards were gods" as a fatal error. "The Indians' mistake did not last long . . . just long enough for the battle to be definitely lost and America subject to Europe," which would seem to be quite long enough.[6]

By contrast Todorov's Cortés moves freely and effectively, "not only constantly practicing the art of adaptation and improvisation, but also being aware of it and claiming it as the very principle of his conduct." A "specialist in human communication," he ensures his control over the Mexican empire (in a conquest Todorov characterizes as "easy") through "his mastery of signs." Note that this is not an idiosyncratic individual talent, but a European cultural capacity grounded in "literacy," where writing is considered "not as a tool, but as an index of the evolution of mental structures": it is that evolution which liberates the intelligence, strategic flexibility, and semiotic sophistication through which Cortés and his men triumph.

In what follows I want to review the grounds for these kinds of claims about the nature of the contrast between European and Indian modes of thinking during the Conquest encounter, and to suggest a rather different account of what was going on between the two peoples. First, an overview of the major events. Analysts and participants alike agree that the Conquest falls into two phases. The first began with the Spanish landfall in April of 1519, and Cortés's assumption of independent command in defiance of the governor of Cuba, patron of Cortés and of the expedition; the Spaniards' march inland, in the company of coastal Indians recently conquered by the Mexicans, marked first by bloody battles and then by alliance with the independent province of Tlaxcala; their uncontested entry into the Mexican imperial city of Tenochtitlan-Tlatelolco, a magnificent lake-borne city of 200,000 or more inhabitants linked to the land by three great causeways; the Spaniards' seizing of the Mexican ruler Moctezoma, and their uneasy rule through him for six months; the arrival on the coast of another and much larger Spanish force from Cuba under the command of Panfilo Narváez charged with the arrest of Cortés, its defeat and incorporation into Cortés's own force; a native "uprising" in Tenochtitlan, triggered in Cortés's absence by the Spaniards' massacre of unarmed warriors dancing in a temple festival; the expulsion of the Spanish forces, with great losses, at the end of June 1520 on the so-called "Noche Triste," and Moctezoma's death, probably at Spanish hands, immediately before that expulsion. End of the first phase. The second phase is much briefer in the telling, although about the same span in the living: a little over a year. The Spaniards retreated to friendly Tlaxcala to recover health and morale. They then renewed the attack, reducing the lesser lakeside cities, recruiting allies, not all of them voluntary, and placing Tenochtitlan under siege in May of 1521. The city fell to the combined forces of Cortés and an assortment of Indian "allies" in mid August 1521. End of the second phase.

Analysts of the conquest have concentrated on the first phase, drawn by the promising whiff of exoticism in Moctezoma's responses—allowing the Spaniards into his city, his docility in captivity—and by the sense that final outcomes were somehow immanent in that response, despite Moctezoma's removal from the stage in the midst of a Spanish rout a good year before the fall of the city, and despite the Spaniards' miserable situation in the darkest days before that fall, trapped out on the causeways, bereft of shelter and support, with the unreduced Mexicans before and their "allies" potential wolves behind. This dispiriting consensus as to Spanish invincibility and Indian vulnerability springs from the too eager acceptance of key documents, primarily Spanish but also Indian, as directly and adequately descriptive of actuality, rather than as the mythic constructs they largely are. Both the letters of Cortés and the main Indian account of the defeat of their city owe as much to the ordering impulse of imagination as to the devoted inscription of events as they occurred. Conscious manipulation, while it might well be present, is not the most interesting issue here, but rather the subtle, powerful, insidious human desire to craft a dramatically satisfying and coherent story out of fragmentary and ambiguous experience, or (the historian's temptation) out of the fragmentary and ambiguous "evidence" we happen to have to work with.

Against the consensus I place Paul Veyne's bracingly simple test: "Historical criticism has only one function: to answer the question asked of it by the historian: 'I believe that this document teaches me this: may I trust it to do that?'"[7] The document may tell us most readily about story-making proclivities, and so take us into the cultural world of the story maker. It may also tell us about actions, so holding the promise of establishing the patterns of conduct and from them inferring the conventional assumptions of the people whose interactions we are seeking to understand. It may tell us about sequences of actions that shed light on impulses and motivations less than acknowledged by the writer, or (when he is recording the actions of others) perhaps not even known to him. The following pages will yield examples of all of these. The challenge is to be at once responsive to the possibilities and yet respectful of the limitations of the material we happen to have.

The story-making predilection is powerfully present in the major Spanish sources. The messy series of events that began with the landfall on the eastern coast has been shaped into an unforgettable success story largely out of the narratives of Cortés and Bernal Díaz, who were part of the action; the superb irresistible forward movement that so captivated Prescott, a selection and sequence imposed by men practiced in the European narrative tradition and writing, for all their artfully concealed knowledge of outcomes, when outcomes were known. The foot soldier Díaz, completing his "True History" of the Conquest in old age, can make our palms sweat with his account of yet another Indian attack, but at eighty-four he knew he was bequeathing to his grandchildren a "true and remarkable story" about the triumph of the brave.[8] The commander Cortés, writing his reports to the Spanish king in the thick of the events, had repudiated the authority of his patron and superior the governor of Cuba, and so was formally in rebellion against the royal authority. He was therefore desperate to establish his credentials. His letters are splendid fictions, marked by politic elisions, omissions, inventions, and a transparent desire to impress Charles of Spain with his own indispensability. One of the multiple delights in their reading is to watch the creation of something of a Horatio figure, an exemplary soldier and simplehearted loyalist unreflectively obedient to his king and the letter of the law: all attributes implicitly denied by the beautiful control and calculation of the literary construction itself.[9]

The elegance of Cortés's literary craft is nicely indicated by his handling of a daunting problem of presentation. In his "Second Letter," written in late October 1520 on the eve of the second thrust against Tenochtitlan, he had somehow to inform the king of the Spaniards' first astonishment at the splendor of the imperial city, the early coups, the period of perilous authority, the inflow of gold, the accumulation of magnificent riches—and the spectacular debacle of the expulsion, with the flounderings in the water, the panic, the loss of gold, horses, artillery, reputation, and altogether too many Spanish lives. Cortés's solution was a most devoted commitment to a strict narrative unfolding of events, so the city is wondered at; Moctezoma speaks, frowns; the marketplace throbs and hums; laden canoes glide through the canals; and so on to the dark denouement. And throughout he continues the construction of his persona as leader: endlessly flexible, yet unthinkingly loyal; endlessly resourceful, yet fastidious in legal niceties; magnificently daring in strategy and performance, yet imbued with a fine caution in calculating costs.

J. H. Elliott and Anthony Pagden have traced the filaments of Cortés's web of fictions back to particular strands of Spanish political culture, and to his particular and acute predicament within it, explaining the theme of "legitimate inheritors returning" by demonstrating its functional necessity in Cortés's legalistic strategy, which in turn pivoted on Moctezoma's voluntary cession of his empire and his authority to Charles of Spain—a splendidly implausible notion, save that so many have believed it. Given the necessity to demonstrate his own indispensability, it is unsurprising that along the way Cortés should claim "the art of adaptation and improvisation" as "the very principle of his conduct," and that we, like his royal audience, should be impressed by his command of men and events: dominating and duping Moctezoma; neutralizing Spanish disaffection by appeals to duty, law, and faith; managing Indians with kind words, stern justice, and displays of the superiority of Spanish arms and the priority of the Spanish god.

The "returning god-ruler" theory was powerfully reinforced by Sahagún's *Florentine Codex*, an encyclopedic account of native life before contact compiled from the recollections of surviving native informants. Book 12 deals with the Conquest. It introduces a Moctezoma paralyzed by terror, first by omens and then by the conviction that Cortés was the god Quetzalcoatl, Precious-Feather Serpent, returned.[10] We are given vivid descriptions of Moctezoma's vacillations, tremulous decisions, collapses of will, as he awaits the Spaniards' coming, and then of his supine acquiescence in their depredations, while his lords abandon him in disgust. Sahagún's was a very late-dawning story, making its first appearance thirty and more years after the Conquest, and by the Veyne test it conspicuously fails. In the closed politics of traditional Tenochtitlan, where age and rank gave status, few men would have had access to Moctezoma's person, much less his thoughts, and Sahagún's informants, young and inconsequential men in 1520, would not have been among those few. In the first phase they can report on certain events (the entry of the Spaniards into the city, the massacre of the warrior dancers) that were public knowledge, and to which they were perhaps witness, although their reporting, it is worth remembering, will be framed in accordance with Mexican notions of significance. They speak with authority and precision on the fighting, especially of the second phase, in which some at least seem to have been involved. But the dramatic description of the disintegration of Moctezoma, compatible as it is with "official" Spanish accounts, bears the hallmarks of a post-Conquest scapegoating of a leader who had indeed admitted the Spaniards to his city in life, and so was made to bear the weight of the unforeseeable consequences in death. What the informants offer for most of the first phase is unabashed mythic history, a telling of what "ought" to have happened (along with a little of what did) in a satisfying mix of collapsed time, elided episodes, and dramatized encounters as they came to be understood in the bitter years after the Conquest. With the fine economy of myth Moctezoma is represented as being made the Spaniards' prisoner at their initial meeting, thenceforth to be their helpless toy, leading them to his treasures, "each holding him, each grasping him," as they looted and pillaged at will.[11] In the Dominican Diego Durán's account, completed sixty years after the Conquest, and built in part from painted native chronicles unknown to us, in part from conquistador recollections, this process of distillation to essential "truth" is carried even further, with Moctezoma pictured in a native account as being carried by his lords from his first meeting with Cortés already a prisoner, his feet shackled.[12] It is likely that Durán made a literal interpretation of a symbolic representation: in retrospective native understanding Moctezoma was indeed captive to the Spaniards, a shackled icon, from the first moments.

Throughout the first phase of the Conquest we confidently "read" Cortés's intentions, assuming his perspective and so assuming his effectiveness. The Spanish commander briskly promises his king "to take [Moctezoma] alive in chains or make him subject to Your Majesty's Royal Crown." He continues: "With that purpose I set out from the town of Cempoalla, which I renamed Sevilla, on the sixteenth of August with fifteen horsemen and three hundred foot soldiers, as well equipped for war as the conditions permitted me to make them."[13] There we have it: warlike intentions clear, native cities renamed as possessions in a new polity, an army on the move. Inured to the duplicitous language of diplomacy, we take Cortés's persistent swearing of friendship and the innocence of his intentions to Moctezoma's emissaries as transparent deceptions, and blame Moctezoma for not so recognizing them or, recognizing them, for failing to act.[14] But Cortés declared he came as an ambassador, and as an ambassador he appears to have been received. Even had Moctezoma somehow divined the Spaniards' hostile intent, to attack without formal warning was not an option for a ruler of his magnificence.[15] We read Moctezoma's conduct confidently, but here our confidence (like Cortés's) derives from ignorance. Cortés interpreted Moctezoma's first "gifts" as gestures of submission or naive attempts at bribery. But Moctezoma, like other Amerindian leaders, communicated at least as much by the splendor and status of his emissaries, their gestures and above all their gifts, as by the nuances of their most conventionalized speech. None of those nonverbal messages could Cortés read, nor is it clear that his chief Nahuatl interpreter, Doña Marina, a woman and a slave, would or could inform him of the protocols in which they were framed: these were the high and public affairs of men. Moctezoma's gifts were statements of dominance, superb gestures of wealth and liberality made the more glorious by the arrogant humility of their giving: statements to which the Spaniards lacked both the wit and the means to reply. (To the next flourish of gifts, carried by more than a hundred porters and including the famous "cartwheels" of gold and silver, Cortés's riposte was a cup of Florentine glass and three holland shirts.)[16] The verbal exchanges for all of the first phase were not much less scrambled. And despite those reassuring inverted commas of direct reportage, all of those so-fluent speeches passed through a daisy chain of interpreters, with each step an abduction into a different meaning system, a struggle for some approximation of unfamiliar concepts. We cannot know at what point the shift from the Indian notion of "he who pays tribute," usually under duress so carrying no sense of obligation, to the Spanish one of "vassal," with its connotations of loyalty, was made, but we know the shift to be momentous. The identifiable confusions, which must be only a fraction of the whole, unsurprisingly ran both ways. For example, Cortés, intent on conveying innocent curiosity, honesty, and flattery, repeatedly informed the Mexican ambassadors that he wished to come to Tenochtitlan "to look upon Moctezoma's face." That determination addressed to a man whose mana was such that none could look upon his face save selected blood kin must have seemed marvelously mysterious, and very possibly sinister.

So the examples of miscommunication multiply. In this tangle of missed cues and mistaken messages, "control of communications" seems to have evaded both sides equally. There is also another casualty. Our most earnest interrogations of the surviving documents cannot make them satisfy our curiosity as to the meaning of Moctezoma's conduct. Historians are the camp followers of the imperialists: as always in this European-and-native kind of history, part of our problem is the disruption of "normal" practice effected by the breach through which we have entered. For Cortés, the acute deference shown Moctezoma's person established him as the supreme authority of city and empire, and he shaped his strategy accordingly. In fact we know neither the nature and extent of Moctezoma's authority within and beyond Tenochtitlan, nor even (given the exuberant discrepancies between the Cortés and Díaz accounts) the actual degree of coercion and physical control imposed on him during his captivity. From the fugitive glimpses we have of the attitudes of some of the other valley rulers, and of his own advisers, we can infer something of the complicated politics of the metropolis and the surrounding city-states, but we see too little to be able to decode the range of Moctezoma's normal authority, much less its particular fluctuations under the stress of foreign intrusion. Against this uncertain ground we cannot hope to catch the flickering indicators of possible individual idiosyncrasy. We may guess, as we watch the pragmatic responses of other Indian groups to the Spanish presence, that as *tlatoani* or "Great Speaker" of the dominant power in Mexico Moctezoma bore a special responsibility for classifying and countering the newcomers. From the time of his captivity we think we glimpse the disaffection of lesser and allied lords, and infer that disaffection sprang from his docility. We see him deposed while he still lived, and denigrated in death: as Cortés probed into Tenochtitlan in his campaign to reduce the city, the defenders would ironically pretend to open a way for him, "saying, 'Come in, come in and enjoy yourselves!' or, at other times, 'Do you think there is now another Moctezoma to do what you wish?'"[17] But I think we must resign ourselves to a heroic act of renunciation, acknowledging that much of Moctezoma's conduct must remain enigmatic. We cannot know how he categorized the newcomers, or what he intended by his apparently determined and certainly unpopular cooperation with his captors: whether to save his empire, his city, his position, or merely his own skin.[18] It might be possible, with patience and time, to clear some of the drifting veils of myth and mistake that envelop the encounters of the first phase, or at least to chart our areas of ignorance more narrowly.[19] But the conventional story of returning gods and unmanned autocrats, of an exotic world paralyzed by its encounter with Europe, for all its coherence and its just-so inevitabilities, is in view of the evidence like Eliza's progression across the ice floes: a matter of momentary sinking balances linked by desperate forward leaps.

Of Cortés we know much more. He was unremarkable as a combat leader: personally brave, an indispensable quality in one who would lead Spaniards, he lacked the panache of his captain Alvarado and the solidity and coolness of Sandoval. He preferred talk to force with Spaniards or Indians, a preference no doubt designed to preserve numbers, but also indicative of a personal style. He knew whom to pay in flattery, whom in gold, and the men he bought usually stayed bought. He knew how to stage a theatrical event for maximum effect, as in the plays concocted to terrify Moctezoma's envoys—a stallion, snorting and plunging as he scented a mare in estrus; a cannon fired to blast a tree. When he did use force he had a flair for doing so theatrically, amplifying the effect: cutting off the hands of fifty or more Tlaxcalan emissaries freely admitted into the Spanish camp, then mutilated as "spies"; a mass killing at Cholula; the shackling of Moctezoma while "rebellious" chiefs were burned before his palace in Tenochtitlan. He was careful to count every Spanish life, yet capable of conceiving heroic strategies—to lay siege to a lake-girt city requiring the prefabrication of thirteen brigantines on the far side of the mountains, eight thousand carriers to transport the pieces, their reassembly in Texcoco, the digging of a canal and the deepening of the lake for their successful launching. And he was capable not only of the grand design but of the construction and maintenance of the precarious alliances, intimidations, and promised rewards necessary to implement it. In that extraordinary capacity to sustain a complex vision through the constant scanning and assessment of unstable factors, as in his passion and talent for control of self and others, Cortés was incomparable. (That concern for control might explain his inadequacies in combat: in the radically uncontrolled environment of battle, he had a tendency to lose his head.)

He was also distinguished by a peculiar recklessness in his faith. We know the Spaniards took trouble to maintain the signs of their faith even in the wilderness of Mexico; that bells marked the days with the obligatory prayers as they did in the villages of Spain; that the small supplies of wine and wafers for the Mass were cherished; that through the long nights in times of battle men stood patiently, waiting for the priests to hear their confessions, while the unofficial healer "Juan Catalan" moved softly about, signing the cross and muttering his prayers over stiffening wounds. We know their faith identified the idols and the dismembered bodies they found in the temples as the pitiless work of a familiar Devil. We know they drew comfort in the worst circumstances of individual and group disaster from the ample space for misfortune in Christian cosmology: while God sits securely in His heaven, all manner of things can be wrong with His world. Those miserable men held for sacrifice in Texcoco after the Spanish expulsion who left their forlorn messages scratched on a white wall ("Here the unhappy Juan Yuste was held prisoner") would through their misery be elevated to martyrdom.[20]

Even against that ground Cortés's faith was notably ardent, especially in his aggressive reaction to public manifestations of the enemy religion. In Cempoalla, with the natives cowed, he destroyed the existing idols, whitewashed the existing shrine, washed the existing attendants and cut their hair, dressed them in white, and taught these hastily refurbished priests to offer flowers and candles before an image of the Virgin. There is an intriguing elision of signs here. While the pagan attendants might have been clad suitably clerically, in long black robes like soutanes, with some hooded "like Dominicans," they also had waist-long hair clotted with human blood, and stank of decaying human flesh. Nonetheless he assessed them as "priests," and therefore fit to be entrusted with the Virgin's shrine.[21] Then having preached the doctrine "as well as any priest today," in Díaz's loyal opinion (filtered though it was through the halting tongues of two interpreters), he left daily supervision of the priests to an old crippled soldier assigned as hermit to the new shrine and Cortés moved on.[22]

The Cempoallan assault was less than politic, being achieved at the sword's point against the town on whose goodwill the little coastal fort of Vera Cruz would be most dependent. Cortés was not to be so reckless again, being restrained from too aggressive action by his chaplain and his captains, but throughout he appears to have been powerfully moved by a concern for the defense of the "honor" of the Christian god. It is worth remembering that for the entire process of the Conquest Cortés had no notion of the Spanish king's response to any of his actions. Only in September of 1523, more than two years after the fall of Tenochtitlan, and four and a half years after the Spanish landfall, did he finally learn that he had been appointed captain general of New Spain. It is difficult to imagine the effect of that prolonged visceral uncertainty, and (especially for a man of Cortés's temperament) of his crucial dependence on the machinations of men far away in Spain, quite beyond his control. Throughout the desperate vicissitudes of the campaign, as in the heroic isolation of his equivocal leadership, God was perhaps his least equivocal ally. That alliance required at best the removal of pagan idols and their replacement by Mary and the Cross, and at the least the Spaniards' public worship of their Christian images, the public statement of the principles of the Christian faith, and the public denunciation of human sacrifice, these statements and denunciations preferably being made in the Indians' most sacred places. Cortés's inability to let well alone in matters religious appears to have effected the final alienation of the Mexican priests, and their demand for the Spaniards' death or expulsion from their uneasy perch in Tenochtitlan.[23] Cortés's claim of his early, total, and unresisted transformation of Mexican religious life through the destruction of their major idols was almost certainly a lie. (He had to suppress any mention of Alvarado's massacre of the warrior dancers in the main temple precinct as the precipitating factor in the Mexican "revolt" as too damaging to his story, for the Mexican celebrants would have been dancing under the serene gaze of the Virgin.) But the lie, like his accommodation to the cannibalism of his Tlaxcalan allies, was a strategic necessity impatiently borne. With victory all obligations would be discharged, and God's honor vindicated.[24] That high sense of duty to his divine Lord and his courage in its pursuit must have impressed and comforted his men even as they strove to restrain him.

None of this undoubted flair makes Cortés the model of calculation, rationality, and control he is so often taken to be. There can be some doubt as to the efficacy of his acts of terror. It is true that after the "mutilated spies" episode the Tlaxcalans sued for peace and alliance, but as I will argue, routine acts of war in the European style were probably at least as destructive of Indian confidence of their ability to predict Spanish behavior as the most deliberate shock tactics.[25] The Spaniards' attack on the people of Cholula, the so-called "Cholula massacre," is a muddier affair. Cortés certainly knew the therapeutic effects of a good massacre on fighting men who have lived too long with fear, their sense of invincibility already badly dented by the Tlaxcalan clashes, and with the legendary warriors of Tenochtitlan, grown huge in imagination, still in prospect. As other leaders have discovered in other times, confidence returns when the invisible enemy is revealed as a screaming, bleeding, fleeing mass of humanity. But here Cortés was probably the unwitting agent of Tlaxcalan interests. Throughout the first phase honors in mutual manipulation between Spaniard and Indian would seem to be about even. The Cempoallan chief Cortés hoaxed into seizing Moctezoma's tax gatherers remained notably more afraid of Moctezoma in his far palace than of the hairy Spaniards at his elbow. Tricked into defiance of Moctezoma, he immediately tricked Cortés into leading four hundred Spaniards on a hot and futile march of fifteen miles in pursuit of phantom Mexican warriors in his own pursuit of a private feud, a deception that has been rather less remarked on.[26] There are other indications that hint at extensive native manipulations, guile being admired among Indians as much as it was among Spaniards, and Spanish dependence on Indian informants and translators was total. But they are indications only, given the relative opacity and ignorance of the Spanish sources as to what the Indians were up to. Here I am not concerned to demonstrate the natives to have been as great deceivers as the Spaniards, but simply to suggest we have no serious grounds for claiming they were not.

Cortés's political situation was paradoxically made easier by his status as rebel.

That saved him from the agonizing assessment of different courses of action: once gone from Cuba, in defiance of the governor, he could not turn back, save to certain dishonor and probable death. So we have the gambler's advance, with no secured lines back to the coast, no supplies, no reinforcements, the ships deliberately disabled on the beach to release the sailors for soldiering service and to persuade the faint-hearted against retreat. Beyond the beach lay Cuba, and an implacable enemy. The relentless march on Mexico impresses, until one asks just what Cortés intended once he had got there. We have the drive to the city, the seizing of Moctezoma—and then the agonizing wait by this unlikely Micawber for something to turn up, as the Spaniards, uncertainly tolerated guests, sat in the city, clutching the diminishing resource of Moctezoma's prestige as their only weapon. That "something" proved to be the Spanish punitive expedition, a couple of providential ships carrying gunpowder and a few reinforcements, and so a perilous way out of the impasse. Possibly Cortés had in mind a giant confidence trick: a slow process of securing and fortifying posts along the road to Vera Cruz and, then, with enough gold amassed, sending to the authorities in Hispaniola (bypassing Velázquez and Cuba) for ships, horses, and arms, which is the strategy he in fact followed after the retreat from Tenochtitlan.[27] It is nonetheless difficult (save in Cortés's magisterial telling of it) to read the performance as rational.[28]

It is always tempting to credit people of the past with unnaturally clear and purposeful policies: like Clifford Geertz's peasant, we see the bullet holes in the fence and proceed to draw the bull's-eyes around them. The temptation is maximized with a Cortés, a man of singular energy and decision, intent on projecting a self-image of formidable control of self and circumstance. Yet that control had its abrupt limits. His tense self-mastery, sustained in face of damaging action by others, could collapse into tears or sullen rage when any part of his own controlling analysis was exposed as flawed, as with his fury against Moctezoma for his "refusal" to quell the uprising in the city after Alvarado's attack on the unarmed dancers.[29] He had banked all on Moctezoma being the absolute ruler he had taken him to be. He had seized him, threatened him, shackled him to establish his personal domination over him. But whatever its normal grounds and span, Moctezoma's capacity to command, which was his capacity to command deference, had begun to bleed away from his first encounter with Spaniards and their unmannerliness, as they gazed and gabbled at the sacred leader.[30] It bled faster as they seized his person. Durán's account of Moctezoma pictured in native chronicles as emerging shackled from his first meeting with Cortés is "objectively" wrong, but from the Indian perspective right: the Great Speaker in the power of outsiders, casually and brutally handled, was the Great Speaker no longer.[31] Forced to attempt to calm his inflamed people, Moctezoma knew he could effect nothing; that his desacralization had been accomplished, first and unwittingly by

Cortés, then, presumably, by a ritual action concealed from us; and that a new Great Speaker had been chosen while the old still lived: a step unprecedented to my knowledge in Mexican history.

Cortés could not acknowledge Moctezoma's impotence. Retrospectively he was insistent that his policy had been sound and had been brought down only through the accident of the Mexican ruler's final unreliability. Certainly his persistence in its defense after its collapse in debacle points to a high personal investment: intelligence is no bar to self-deception. Nonetheless there must have been some relief at the explosive end to a deeply uncanny situation, where experience had offered no guide to action in a looking-glass world of yielding kings and arrogant underlings; of riddling speech, unreadable glances, opaque silences. The sudden collapse of the waiting game liberated him back into the world of decisions, calculated violence, the energetic practicalities of war—the heady fiction of a world malleable before individual will.

His essential genius lay in the depth of his conviction, and in his capacity to bring others to share it: to coax, bully, and bribe his men, dream-led, dream-fed, into making his own gambler's throw; to participate in his own desperate personal destiny. Bernal Díaz recorded one of Cortés's speeches at a singularly low point on the first march to the city. With numbers already dangerously depleted, the remaining men wounded, cold, frightened, the natives ferocious, Cortés is reported as promising his men not wealth, not salvation, but deathless historical fame.[32] Again and again we see Cortés dare to cheat his followers in the distribution of loot and of "good-looking Indian women," but he never discounted the glory of their endeavors. Not the least factor in Cortés's hold over his men was his notary's gift for locating their situation and aspirations in reassuringly sonorous and legalistic terms: terms necessary to please the lawyers at home, who would finally judge their leader's case, but also essential for their own construction of an acceptable narrative out of problematical actions and equivocal experience. But he also lured them to acknowledge their most extreme fantasies; then he persuaded them, by his own enactment of them, that the fantasies were realizable.[33]

So Cortés, his men regrouped, his strategies evolved, stood ready for the second phase of the attack. What he was to experience in the struggle to come was to challenge his view of himself and his capacities, of the Mexican Indian, and of his special relationship with his God.

II

Analysts, save for military historians, have overwhelmingly concentrated on the first phase of the Conquest, assuming the consummation of Spanish victory to be merely a matter of applying a technological superiority: horsemen against pedestrian warriors, steel swords against wooden clubs, muskets and crossbows against bows and arrows and lances, cannon against ferocious courage. I would argue that it is only for the second phase that we have sufficiently solid evidence to allow a close analysis of how Spaniards and Indians made sense of each other, and so to track down issues that must remain will-o'-the-wisps for the first phase. I would also argue that the final conquest was a very close-run thing: a view in which the combatants on both sides, as it happens, would agree. After the Spanish ejection from Tenochtitlan the Mexicans remained heavily favored in things material, most particularly manpower, which more than redressed any imbalance in equipment. Spanish technology had its problems: the miseries of slithering or cold-cramped or foundering horses, wet powder, the brutal weight of the cannon, and always the desperate question of supply. Smallpox, introduced into Mexico by one of Narváez's men, had swept through the native population, but its ravages had presumably affected Spanish "allies" equally with the Mexicans.[34] The sides were approximately matched in knowledge: if Cortés was to profit from his familiarity with the fortifications and functioning of the lake city, the Mexicans at last knew the Spaniards as enemies, and were under the direction of a ruler liberated from the ambiguities that appear to have bedeviled them earlier.

We tend to have a *Lord of the Flies* view of battle: that in deadly combat the veils of "culture" are ripped away, and natural man confronts himself. But if combat is not quite as cultural as cricket, its brutalities are nonetheless rule-bound. Like cricket, it requires a sustained act of cooperation, with each side constructing the conditions in which both will operate, and so, where the struggle is between strangers, obliging a mutual "transmission of culture" of the shotgun variety. And because of its high intensities it promises to expose how one's own and other ways of acting and meaning are understood and responded to in crisis conditions, and what lessons about the other and about oneself can be learned in that intimate, involuntary, and most consequential communication.

The sources for the second phase are sufficiently solid. Given it is cultural assumptions we are after, equivocation in recollection and recording matter little. Cortés edits a debacle on the Tacuba causeway, where more than fifty Spaniards were taken alive through his own impetuosity, into a triumph of leadership in crisis; Díaz marvels at Spanish bravery under the tireless onslaughts of savages; both are agreed as to the vocabulary through which they understand, assess, and record battle behavior. Sahagún's informants, able to report only bitter hearsay and received myth on the obscure political struggles of the first phase, move to confident detail in their accounts of the struggle for the city, in which at least some of them appear to have fought, naming precise locations and particular warrior feats; revealing through both the structure and the descriptions of the accounts their principles of battle. Those glimpses can be matched against admittedly fragmentary chronicles to yield the general contours of Indian battle behavior.

Here the usual caveats of overidealization apply. If all social rules are fictions, made "real" through being contested, denied, evaded, and recast as well as obeyed, "rules of war," war being what it is, are honored most earnestly in the breach. But in the warrior societies of Central Mexico, where the battlefield held a central place in the imagination, with its protocols rehearsed and trained for in the ordinary routines of life, the gap between principle and practice was narrow. War, at least war as fought among the dominant peoples of Mexico, and at least ideally, was a sacred contest, the outcome unknown but preordained, revealing which city, which local deity, would rightfully dominate another.[35] Something like equal terms were therefore required: to prevail by mere numbers or by some piece of treachery would vitiate the significance of the contest. So important was this notion of fair testing that food and weapons were sent to the selected target city as part of the challenge, there being no virtue in defeating a weakened enemy.[36]

The warriors typically met outside the city of the defenders. Should the attacking side prevail, the defenders abandoned the field and fled, and the victors swept unresisted into the city to fire the temple where the local deity had its place. That action marked victory in occurrence and record; the formal sign for conquest in the painted histories was a burning temple. Free pillage continued until the increasingly frantic pleas of the spokesmen for the defeated were heard, and terms of tribute set. Then the victors withdrew to their home city with their booty and their captives, including not only the warriors taken in the formal battle but "civilians" seized during the period of plunder. Their most significant captive was the image of the tutelary deity of the defeated city, to be held in the "god captive house" in Tenochtitlan. Defeat was bitter because it was a statement and judgment of inferiority of the defeated warriors, who had broken and run; a judgment the victorious warriors were only too ready to reinforce by savage mockery, and which was institutionalized by the imposition of tribute.[37]

The duration of the decision remained problematic. Defeated towns paid their tribute as a regular decision against further hostilities, but remained independent, and usually notably disaffected, despite the conquering city's conviction of the legitimacy of their supremacy. Many towns in the valley, whether allied or defeated or intimidated by the Mexicans, paid their token tribute, fought alongside the Mexicans in Mexican campaigns, and shared in the spoils, but they remained mindful of their humiliation and unreconciled to their subordination. Beyond the valley the benefits of empire were commonly smaller, the costs greater, and disaffection chronic. The monolithic "Aztec empire" is a European hallucination: in this atomistic polity, the units were held together by the tension of mutual repulsion. (Therefore the ease with which Cortés could recruit "allies," too often taken as a tribute to his silver tongue, and therefore the deep confusion attending his constant use of that meaning-drenched word *vassal* to describe the relationship of subject towns first to Tenochtitlan, and later to the Spanish crown.)

If war was a sacred duel between peoples, and so between the "tribal" gods of those peoples, battle was ideally a sacred duel between matched warriors: a contest in which the taking of a fitting captive for presentation to one's own deity was a precise measure of one's own valor, and one's own fate. One prepared for this individual combat by song, paint, and adornment with the sacred war regalia. (To go "always prepared for battle" in the Spanish style was unintelligible: a man carrying arms was only potentially a warrior.) The great warrior, scarred, painted, plumed, wearing the record of his victories in his regalia, erupting from concealment or looming suddenly through the rising dust, then screaming his war cry, could make lesser men flee by the pure terror of his presence: warriors were practiced in projecting ferocity. His rightful, destined opponent was he who could master panic to stand and fight. There were maneuverings to "surprise" the enemy, and a fascination with ambush, but only as a device to confront more dramatically; to strike from hiding was unthinkable. At the outset of battle Indian arrows and darts flew thickly, but to weaken and draw blood, not to pierce fatally.[38] The obsidian-studded war club signaled warrior combat aims: the subduing of prestigious individual captives in single combat for presentation before the home deity.

In the desperation of the last stages of the battle for Tenochtitlan, the Mexican inhibition against battleground killing was somewhat reduced: Indian "allies" died, and Spaniards who could not be quickly subdued were killed, most often, as the Mexicans were careful to specify, and for reasons that will become clear, by having the backs of their heads beaten in. But the priority on the capture of significant antagonists remained. In other regards the Mexicans responded with flexibility to the challenges of siege warfare. They "read" Spanish tactics reasonably accurately: a Spanish assault on the freshwater aqueduct at Chapultepec was foreseen, and furiously, if fruitlessly, resisted. The brigantines, irresistible for their first appearance of the lake, were later lured into a carefully conceived ambush in which two were trapped. The horses' vulnerability to uneven ground, to attack from below, their panic under hails of missiles, were all exploited effectively. The Mexicans borrowed Spanish weapons: Spanish swords lashed to poles or Spanish lances to disable the horses; even Spanish crossbows, after captive crossbowmen had been forced to show them how the machines worked.[39] It was their invention and tenacity that forced Cortés to the desperate remedy of leveling structures along the causeways and into the city to provide the Spaniards with the secure ground they needed to be effective. And they were alert to the possibilities of psychological warfare, capitalizing on the Spaniards' peculiar dread of death by sacrifice and of the cannibalizing of the corpse.[40] On much they could be innovative. But on the most basic measure of man's worth, the taking alive of prestigious captives, they could not compromise.

That passion for captives meant that the moment when the opponent's nerve broke was helplessly compelling, an enemy in flight an irresistible lure. This pursuit reflex was sometimes exploited by native opponents as a slightly shabby trick. It provided Cortés with a standard tactic for a quick and sure crop of kills. Incurious as to the reason, he nonetheless noted and exploited Mexican unteachability: "Sometimes, as we were thus withdrawing and they pursued us so eagerly, the horsemen would pretend to be fleeing, and then suddenly would turn on them; we always took a dozen or so of the boldest. By these means and by the ambushes which we set for them, they were always much hurt; and certainly it was a remarkable sight for even when they well knew the harm they would receive from us as we withdrew, they still pursued us until we had left the city."[41] That commitment bore heavily on outcomes. Had Indians been as uninhibited as Spaniards in their killing, the small Spanish group, with no secured source of replenishment, would soon have been whittled away. In battle after battle the Spaniards report the deaths of many Indians, with their own men suffering not fatalities but wounds, and fast-healing wounds at that: those flint and obsidian blades sliced clean. It preserved the life of Cortés: time and again the Spanish leader struggled in Indian hands, the prize in a disorderly tug of war, with men dying on each side in the furious struggle for possession, and each time the Spaniards prevailing. Were Cortés in our hands, we would knife him. Mexican warriors could not kill the enemy leader so casually: were he to die, it would be in the temple of Huitzilopochtli, and before his shrine.[42]

If the measurable consequences of that insistence were obvious and damaging, there were others less obvious, but perhaps more significant. We have already noted the Spanish predilection for ambush as part of a wider preference for killing at least risk. Spaniards valued their crossbows and muskets for their capacity to pick off selected enemies well behind the line of engagement: as snipers, as we would say. The psychological demoralization attending those sudden, trivializing deaths of great men painted for war, but not yet engaged in combat, must have been formidable. (Were the victim actively engaged in battle, the matter was different. Then he died nobly; although pierced by a bolt or a ball from a distance, his blood flowed forth to feed the earth as a warrior's should.) But more than Indian deaths and demoralization were effected through these transactions. To inflict such deaths—at a distance, without putting one's own life in play—developed a Mexican reading of the character of the Spanish warrior.[43]

Consider this episode, told by a one-time conquistador. Two Indian champions, stepping out from the mass of warriors, offered their formal challenge before a Spanish force. Cortés responded by ordering two horsemen to charge, their lances poised. One of the warriors, against all odds, contrived to sever a horse's hooves, and then, as it crashed to the ground, slashed its neck. Cortés, seeing the risk to the unhorsed rider, had a cannon fired so that "all the Indians in the front ranks were killed and the others scattered." The two Spaniards recovered themselves and scuttled back to safety under the covering fire of muskets, crossbows, and the cannon.[44]

For Cortés the individual challenge had been a histrionic preliminary flourish: he then proceeded to the serious work of using firepower to kill warriors, and to control more territory, which was what he took war to be about. Throughout, Spaniards measured success in terms of body counts, territory controlled, and evidence of decay in the morale of the "enemy," which included all warriors, actively engaged in battle or not, and all "civilians" too. Cortés casually informed the king of his dawn raids into sleeping villages and the slaughter of the inhabitants, men, women, and children, as they stumbled into the streets: these were necessary and conventional steps in the progressive control of terrain, and the progressive demoralization of opposition. To an Indian warrior, Cortés's riposte to the Indian champions' challenge was shameful, with only the horses, putting themselves within reach of the opponents' weapons, emerging with any credit. Cortés's descents on villages are reported in tones of breathless incredulity.[45]

There is in the *Florentine Codex* an exquisitely painful, detailed description of the Spaniards' attack on the unarmed warrior dancers at the temple festival, the slaughter that triggered the Mexican "uprising" of May 1520. The first victim was a drummer: his hands were severed, then his neck. The account continues: "Of some they slashed open their backs: then their entrails gushed out. Of some they cut their heads to pieces. . . . Some they struck on the shoulder; they split openings. They broke openings in their bodies."[46] And so it goes on. How ought we interpret this? It was not, I think, recorded as a horror story, or only as a horror story. The account is sufficiently careful as to precise detail and sequence to suggest its construction close after the event, in an attempt to identify the pattern, and so to discover the sense, in the Spaniards' cuttings and slashings. (This was the first view the Mexicans had of Spanish swords at work.) The Mexicans had very precise rules about violent assaults on the body, as the range of their sacrificial rituals makes clear, but the notion of a "preemptive massacre" of warriors was not in their vocabulary.

Such baffling actions, much more than any deliberately riddling policy, worked to keep Indians off balance. To return to an early celebrated moment of mystification by Cortés, the display of the cannon to impress the Mexican envoys on the coast with the killing power of Spanish weapons: the men who carried the tale back reported the thunderous sound, the smoke, the fire, the foul smell— and that the shot had "dissolved" a mountain, and "pulverised" a tree.[47] It is highly doubtful that the native watchers took the intended point of the display, that this was a weapon of war for use against human flesh. It was not a conceivable weapon for warriors. So it must have appeared (as it is in fact reported) as a gratuitous assault upon nature: a scrambled lesson indeed. Mexican warriors learned, with experience, not to leap and shout and display when faced with cannon fire and crossbows, but to weave and duck, as the shield canoes learned to zigzag to avoid the cannon shot from the brigantines, so that with time the carnage was less.[48] But they also learned contempt for men who were prepared to kill indiscriminately, combatants and noncombatants alike, and at a secure distance, without putting their own lives in play.

What of Spanish horses, that other key element in Cortés's mystification program? We have early evidence of swift and effective warrior response to these exotics, and of a fine experimental attitude to verifying their nature. A small group of Tlaxcalan warriors having their first sight of horses and horsemen managed to kill two horses and to wound three others before the Spaniards got the upper hand.[49] In the next engagement a squad of Indians made a concerted and clearly deliberate attack on a horse, allowing the rider, although badly wounded, to escape, while they killed his mount and carted the body from the field. Bernal Díaz later recorded that the carcass was cut into pieces and distributed through the towns of Tlaxcala, presumably to demonstrate the horse's carnal nature. (They reserved the horseshoes, as he sourly recalled, to offer to their idols, along with "the Flemish hat, and the two letters we had sent them offering peace.")[50]

The distribution of the pieces of the horse's flesh possibly held further implications. Indians were in no doubt that horses were animals. But that did not reduce them, as it did for Spaniards, to brute beasts, unwitting, unthinking servants of the lords of creation. Indians had a different understanding of how animals signified. It was no vague aesthetic inclination that led the greatest warrior orders to mimic the eagle and the jaguar in their dress and conduct: those were creatures of power, exemplary of the purest warrior spirit. The eagle, slowly turning close to the sun; then the scream, the stoop, the strike; the jaguar, announcing its presence with the coughing rumble of thunder, erupting from the dappled darkness to make its kill: these provided unmatchable models for human emulation. That horses should appear ready to kill men was unremarkable. The ferocity and courage of these creatures, who raced into the close zone of combat, facing the clubs and swords; who plunged and screamed, whose eyes rolled, whose saliva flew (for the Mexicans saliva signified anger) marked them as agents in the battle action, as had the charge of the two horses against their Indian challengers. In the Mexican lexicon of battle, the horses excelled their masters. They were not equal in value as offerings—captured Spanish swords lashed to long poles were typically used against horses to disembowel or hamstring them, but not against their riders, judged too valuable to damage so deeply—but their valor was recognized. When the besieged Mexicans won a major victory over Cortés's men on the Tacuba causeway, they displayed the heads of the sacrificed

Spaniards on the skull rack in the usual way, and below them they skewered the heads of the four horses taken in the same melee.[51]

There is one small moment in which we see these contrary understandings held in counterpoise. During a skirmish in the city some Spanish horsemen emerging from an unsprung ambush collided, a Spaniard falling from his mare. Panicky, the riderless horse "rushed straight at the enemy, who shot at and wounded her with arrows; whereupon, seeing how badly she was being treated, she returned to us," Cortés reported, but "so badly wounded that she died that night." He continued: "Although we were much grieved by her loss, for our lives were dependent on the horses, we were pleased she had not perished at the hands of the enemy, for their joy at having captured her would have exceeded the grief caused by the death of their companions."[52]

For Cortés the mare was an animal, responding as an animal: disoriented, then fleeing from pain. Her fate had symbolic importance only through her association with the Spaniards. For the Indians the mare breaking out from the knot of Spaniards, rushing directly and alone toward enemy warriors—white-eyed, ferocity incarnate—was accorded the warrior's reception of a flight of arrows. Her reversal, her flight back to her friends probably signaled a small Indian victory, as her capture and death among enemies would have signaled to the Spaniards, at a more remote level, a small Spanish defeat. That doomed mare wheeling and turning in the desperate margin between different armies and different systems of understanding provides a sufficiently poignant metaphor for the themes I have been pursuing.

Spanish "difference" found its clearest expression in their final strategy for the reduction of the imperial city. Cortés had hoped to intimidate the Mexicans sufficiently by his steady reduction of the towns around the lake, by his histrionic acts of violence, and by the exemplary cruelty with which resistance was punished, to bring them to treat.[53] Example-at-a-distance in that mosaic of rival cities could have no relevance for the Mexicans—if all others quailed, they would not—so the Spaniards resorted, as Díaz put it, to "a new kind of warfare." Siege was the quintessential European strategy: an economical design to exert maximum pressure on whole populations without active engagement, delivering control over people and place at least cost. If Cortés's own precarious position led him to increase that pressure by military sorties, his crucial weapon was want.

For the Mexicans, siege was the antithesis of war. They knew of encircling cities to persuade unwilling warriors to come out, and of destroying them too, when insult required it. They had sought to burn the Spaniards out of their quarters in Tenochtitlan, to force them to fight after their massacre of the warrior dancers.[54] But the deliberate and systematic weakening of opposition before engagement, and the deliberate implication of noncombatants in the contest, had no part in their experience.

As the siege continued the signs of Mexican contempt multiplied. Mexican warriors continued to seek face-to-face combat with these most unsatisfactory opponents, who skulked and refused battle, who clung together in tight bands behind their cannon, who fled without shame. When elite warriors, swept in by canoe, at last had the chance to engage the Spaniards closely, the Spaniards "turned their backs, they fled," with the Mexicans in pursuit. They abandoned a cannon in one of their pell-mell flights, positioned with unconscious irony on the gladiatorial stone on which the greatest enemy warriors had given their final display of fighting prowess; the Mexicans worried and dragged it along to the canal and dropped it into the water.[55] Indian warriors were careful, when they had to kill rather than capture Spaniards in battle, to deny them an honorable warrior's death, dispatching them by beating in the back of their heads, the death reserved for criminals in Tenochtitlan.[56] And the Spaniards captured after the debacle on the Tacuba causeway were stripped of all their battle equipment, their armor, their clothing: only then, when they were naked, and reduced to "slaves," did the Mexicans kill them.[57]

What does it matter, in the long run, that Mexican warriors admired Spanish horses and despised Spanish warriors? To discover how it bore on events we need to look briefly at Indian notions of "fate" and time. We can compare the structure of the Indian and Spanish accounts of the final battles, to discover the explanatory strategies implied in that structuring. The Spanish versions present the struggles along the causeways, the narrow victories, the coups, the strokes of luck, the acts of daring on each side. Through the tracing of an intricate sequence of action we follow the movement of the advantage, first one way, then the other. God is at the Spaniards' shoulders, but only to lend power to their strong arms, or to tip an already tilting balance. Through selection and sequence of significant events we have the familiar, powerful, cumulative explanation through the narrative form.

The Indian accounts look superficially similar. There are episodes, and they are offered serially: descriptions of group or individual feats, of contemptible Spanish actions. But these are discrete events, moments to be memorialized, with time no more than the thread on which they are strung: there is no cumulative effect, no significance in sequence. Nor is there any implication that the human actions described bore on outcomes. The fact that defeat was suffered declares it to have been inevitable.

The Mexicans, like Mesoamericans generally, conceptualized time as multidimensional and eternally recurrent, and men attempted to comprehend its complex movement through the use of intermeshing time counts, which completed their complex permutations over fifty-two years, a *Xiumolpilli* or "Bundle of Years." (Note how that word *bundle* denies any significance to mere adjacency.) Under such a system, each "day" was not the outcome of the days preceding it: it had its own character, indicated by its complex name derived from the time counts, and was unique within its Bundle of Years. It also was more closely connected with the similarly named days that had occurred in every preceding Bundle of Years than with those clustered about it in its own bundle. Thus the particular contingent event was to be understood as unfolding in a dynamic process modeled by some past situation. But just as those anomalous events presumably noted before the Spanish advent could be categorized as "omens" and their portent identified only retrospectively, the identification of the recurrent in the apparently contingent was very much an after-the-event diagnosis, not an anterior paralyzing certitude. The essential character of the controlling time manifested itself in subtle ways, largely masked from human eyes. Events remained problematical in their experiencing, with innovation and desperate effort neither precluded nor inhibited. In human experience outcomes remained contingent until manifested.[58]

Nonetheless, some few events were accorded special status, being recognized as signs of the foretold. At a place called Otumba the Spaniards, limping away from Tenochtitlan after the expulsion of the Noche Triste, were confronted by a sea of Mexican warriors: a sea that evaporated when Cortés and his horsemen drove through to strike down the battle leader, and to seize his fallen banner. The "battle of Otumba" mattered, being the best chance from our perspective for the Mexicans to finish off the Spaniards at their most vulnerable. The Spanish accounts identify the striking down of the commander as decisive, but while the fall of a leader was ominous (and an attack on a leader not actively engaged in combat disreputable) it was the taking of the banner that signified. Our initial temptation is to elide this with the familiar emotional attachment of a body of fighting men to its colors: to recall the desperate struggles over shreds of silk at Waterloo; the dour passion of a Roman legion in pursuit of its lost Eagle and honor.[59] There might have been some of this in the Indian case. But the taking of a banner was to Indians less a blow to collective pride than a statement: a sign that the battle was to go, indeed had gone, against them.

Cortés reported his determined attack on "the great cue," the pyramid of Huitzilopochtli, during the first struggle in Tenochtitlan, claiming that after three hours of struggle he cleared the temple of Indians and put it to the torch. He also noted that the capture of the pyramid "so much damaged their confidence that they began to weaken greatly on all sides": the sign noted.[60] Had the capture been as decisive as Cortés claims, we could expect more than "weakening," but just how complete it was remains problematical: in Díaz's account the Spaniards, having fired the shrine, were then tumbled back down the steps. The event clearly mattered to the Indians, Díaz remarking how often he had seen that particular battle pictured in later Indian accounts. He thought this was because the Indians took the Spanish assault as a very heroic thing, as they were represented as "much wounded and running with blood with many dead in the pictures they made of the setting afire of the temple, with the many warriors guarding it."[61] My thought is that what the representations sought to make clear was that despite the firing of the shrine the Spaniards had not achieved the uncontested mastery which would indeed have constituted and marked "victory." The vigor of the attack must have made even more urgent the putting of the temple to rights after the Spaniards' expulsion—that period when we, with our notions of strategy, wait in vain for the Mexicans to pursue the weakened Spaniards and finish them off, while they prepared instead for the set-piece battle at Otumba, "read" the message of the taking of the banner, and yielded the day.

Deep into the second phase of the conquest, Spanish banner carriers remained special targets, being subjected to such ferocious attack that "a new one was needed every day."[62] But the Mexicans had come to pay less heed to signs, because they had discovered that Spaniards ignored them. In the course of the causeway victory a major Spanish banner had actually been taken: "The warriors from Tlatelolco captured it in the place known today as San Martín." But while the warrior who had seized the banner was carefully memorialized, "They were scornful of their prize and considered it of little importance." Sahagún's informants flatly record that the Spaniards "just kept on fighting."[63] Ignoring signs of defeat, the Spaniards were equally careless of signs of victory. When a Spanish contingent penetrated the marketplace of Tlatelolco, where the Mexicans had taken their last refuge, they managed to fight their way to the top of the main pyramid, to set the shrines on fire and plant their banners before they were forced to withdraw. ("The common people began to wail, expecting the looting to begin," but the warriors, seasoned in Spanish ways, had no such expectation. They knew the fighting would go on: these enemies were as blind to signs as they were deaf to decency.) Next day from his own encampment Cortés was puzzled to see the fires still burning unquenched, the banners still in place. The Mexicans would respect the signs and leave them to stand, even if the barbarians did not, even if the signs had lost efficacy, even if the rules of war were in abeyance.

John Keegan has characterized battle as "essentially a moral conflict [requiring] a mutual and sustained act of will between two contending parties, and, if it is to result in a decision, the moral collapse of one of them."[64] Paradoxically, that mutuality is most essential at the point of disengagement. To "surrender," to acquiesce in defeat and concede victory, is a complex business, at once a redefinition of self and one's range of effective action, and a redefinition of one's relationship with the erstwhile enemy. Those redefinitions have somehow to be acknowledged by the opponent. Where the indicators that mark defeat and so allow "moral collapse" to occur are not acknowledged, neither victory nor defeat is possible, and we approach a sinister zone in which there can be no resolution save death.[65]

That, I think, came to be the case in Mexico. "Signs" are equivocal things, especially when they point not to a temporary submission of uncertain duration, but to the end of a people's imperial domination. The precarious edifice of "empire" had not survived the introduction of the wild card of the Spaniards—

men without a city, and so outside the central plays of power and punishment. Its collapse had been proclaimed by Quauhtemoc, "He Who Falls Like an Eagle," who had replaced the dead Cuitlahuac as Great Speaker, when he offered a general "remission" of tribute for a year in return for aid against the Spaniards: tribute is a product of the power to exact it. In the final battles the Mexicans were fighting for the integrity of their city, as so many others had fought before. They knew the settled hatred of the Tlaxcalans and the envy of other peoples. Perhaps even against indigenous enemies they might have fought on, in face of the signs of defeat. Against the Spaniards, cowardly opportunists impossible to trust, who disdained the signs of victory and defeat, they lacked any alternative.[66] The Mexicans continued to resist.

The chronicles record the stories of heroic deeds: of warriors scattering the Spaniards before them, of the great victory over Cortés's troop, with terrified Spaniards reeling "like drunken men," and fifty-three taken for sacrifice.[67] Spanish accounts tell us that the victory that had given so many captives to the Mexican war god was taken at the time to indicate the likelihood of a final Mexican victory, hopefully prophesied by the priests as coming within eight days. (The Indian records do not waste time on false inferences, misunderstood omens.) Cortés's allies, respectful of signs, accordingly removed themselves for the duration. But the days passed, the decisive victory did not come, and the macabre dance continued.[68]

And all the while, as individual warriors found their individual glory, the city was dying: starving, thirsting, choking on its own dead. This slow strangling is referred to as if quite separate from the battle, as in the Mexican mind it presumably was. Another brief glory occurred, when Eagle and Ocelot warriors, men from the two highest military orders, were silently poled in disguised canoes to where they could leap among looting native allies, spreading lethal panic among them. But still the remorseless pressure went on: "They indeed wound all around us, they were wrapped around us, no one could go anywhere. . . . Indeed many died in the press."[69]

The Mexicans made their endgame play. Here the augury component, always present in combat, is manifest. Quauhtemoc and his leading advisers selected a great warrior, clad him in the array of Quetzal Owl, the combat regalia of the great Ahuitzotl, who had ruled before the despised Moctezoma, and armed him with the flint-tipped darts of Huitzilopochtli; thus he became, as they said, "one of the number of the Mexicans' rulers." He was sent forth to cast his darts against the enemy: should the darts twice strike their mark, the Mexicans would prevail. Magnificent in his spreading quetzal plumes, with his four attendants, Quetzal Owl entered the battle. For a time they could follow his movements among the enemy: reclaiming stolen gold and quetzal plumes, taking three captives, or so they thought. Then he dropped from a terrace, and out of sight. The Spaniards record nothing of this exemplary combat.

After that ambiguous sign another day passed with no action: the Spaniards, disreputable to the end, "only lay still; they lay looking at the common folk."[70] On the next evening a great "bloodstone," a blazing coal of light, flared through the heavens, to whirl around the devastated city, then to vanish in the middle of the lake. No Spaniard saw the comet of fire that marked the end of imperial Tenochtitlan. Perhaps no Indian saw it either. But they knew great events must be attended by signs, and that there must have been a sign. In the morning Quauhtemoc, having taken counsel with his lords, abandoned the city. He was captured in the course of his escape, to be brought before Cortés. Only then did his people leave their ruined city.[71]

So the Mexicans submitted to their fate, when that fate was manifest. A certain arrangement of things had been declared terminated: the period of Mexican domination and the primacy of Tenochtitlan was over.

A particular section of the Anales de Tlatelolco is often cited to demonstrate the completeness of the obliteration of a way of life and a way of thought. It runs:

> Broken spears lie in the roads;
> we have torn our hair in our grief.
> The houses are roofless now, and their walls
> are red with blood.
>
> Worms are swarming in the streets and plazas,
> and the walls are splattered with gore.
> The water has turned red, as if it were dyed,
> and when we drink it,
> it has the taste of brine.
>
> We have pounded our hands in despair
> against the adobe walls,
> for our inheritance, our city, is lost and dead.
> The shields of our warriors were its defense,
> but they could not save it.[72]

And so it continues. But what is notable here (apart from the poetic power) is that the "lament" was a traditional form, maintaining itself after the defeat, and so locating that defeat and rendering it intelligible by assaying it in the traditional mode. If the Mexican vision of empire was finished, the people, and their sense of distinctiveness as a people, were not. The great idols in the temples had been smuggled out of the city by their traditional custodians before its fall, and sent toward Tula, a retracing of their earlier migration route. A cyclical view of time has its comforts. And if the "Quetzalcoatl returned" story as presented in the *Florentine Codex* is a post-Conquest imposition, as is likely, and if indeed it does move away from traditional native ways of accounting for human action in the world, with Moctezoma's conduct described not merely to memorialize his shame but in order to explain the outcome of defeat, as I believe it does—then its fabrication points to a concern for the construction of a viable and satisfying public history for the conquered, an emollient myth, generated in part from within the European epistemological system to encompass the catastrophe of Mexican defeat.

III

Now, at last, for the consequences.

There is something appealing to our sense of irony in the notion that the Spaniards' heroic deeds, as they saw them, were judged shameful by the Mexican warriors. But attitudes of losers have little historical resonance. Attitudes of victors do. Here I want to pursue an impression. Anyone who has worked on the history of Mexico—I suspect the case is the same for much of Latin America, but I cannot speak for that—is painfully impressed by the apparent incorrigibility of the division between the aboriginal inhabitants and the incomers, despite the domestic proximity of their lives, and by the chronic durability, whatever the form of government, whatever its public rhetoric, of systemic social injustice grounded in that division. In Mexico I am persuaded the terms of the relationship between the incoming and the indigenous peoples were set very early. A line of reforming sixteenth-century missionaries and upright judges were baffled as much as outraged by what they saw as the wantonness of Spanish maltreatment of Indians: cruelties indulged in the face of self-interest. Spaniards had been notoriously brutal in the Caribbean islands, where the indigenes were at too simple a level of social organization to survive Spanish endeavors to exploit them. Yet in their first encounters with the peoples of Mexico the Spaniards had declared themselves profoundly impressed. Cortés's co-venture with the Tlaxcalans seems to have involved genuine cooperation, a reasonably developed notion of mutuality, and (not to be sentimental) some affection between individuals.[73]

Then something happened, a crucial break of sympathy. It is always difficult to argue that things could have been other than they turn out to be, especially in the political maelstrom of post-Conquest Mexico.[74] But despite the continuing deftness of his political maneuverings in the aftermath of the Conquest, I have a sense of Cortés relinquishing both his control over the shaping of Spanish-Indian relations and his naturally conservationist policies—a conservationism based in pragmatism rather than humanity, but effective for all that—earlier and more easily than his previous conduct would have us expect. His removal to Honduras in October 1524 was an extraordinary abdication of the official authority he had sought so long and had worn only for a year, and marked the end of his effective role in "New Spain." We tend to like our heroes, whether villains or saints or Machiavels, to be all of a piece: unchanging, untinctured emblems of whatever qualities we assign them, impervious to experience. But there are indicators in his writings as in his actions that Cortés was changed by his experience in Mexico, and that the change had to do with the obstinate, and to Spanish eyes profoundly "irrational," refusal or incapacity of the Mexicans to submit.

Cortés was sensitive to the physical beauty and social complexity of the great city of Tenochtitlan. It was the dream of the city that had fired his ambition, and provided the focus for all his actions. We must remember that Tenochtitlan was a marvel, eclipsing all other cities in Mesoamerica (and Europe) in size, elegance, order, and magnificence of spectacle. Cortés had contrived the complex, difficult strategy of the blockade, and pursued the mammoth task of implementing it, in order to preserve the city by demonstrating the futility of resistance. Then he watched the slow struggle back and forth along the causeways, as the defenders, careless of their own lives, took back by night what had been so painfully won by day. He moved his men onto the causeways, into physical misery and constant danger, and then was forced to undertake the systematic destruction of the structures along the causeways to secure the yards won, a perilous prolongation of a task already long enough.

So, with patience, access to the city was gained, and the noose of famine tightened. From that point victory was in Spanish (and our) terms inevitable. Yet still the resistance continued, taking advantage of every corner and rooftop. So the work of demolition went on. At last, from the top of a great pyramid Cortés could see that the Spaniards had won seven-eighths of what had once been the city, with the remaining people crammed into a corner where the houses were built out over the water. Starvation was so extreme that even roots and bark had been gnawed, with the survivors tottering shadows, but shadows who still resisted.[75]

Cortés's frustration in being forced to destroy the city he had so much wanted to capture intact is manifest, as is his bewilderment at the tenacity of so futile a resistance: "As we had entered the city from our camp two or three days in succession, besides the three or four previous attacks, and had always been victorious, killing with crossbow, harquebus and field gun an infinite number of the enemy, we each day expected them to sue for peace, which we desired as much as our own salvation; but nothing we could do could induce them to it." After another largely unresisted thrust into the city, "We could not but be saddened by their determination to die."[76]

He had no stomach to attack again. Instead he made a final resort to terror. Not to the terror of mass killings: that weapon had long lost its efficacy. He constructed a war-engine, an intimidatory piece of European technology that had the advantage of not requiring gunpowder: the marvelous catapult. It was a matter of some labor over three or four days, of lime and stone and wood, then the great cords, and the stones big as demijohns. It was aimed, as a native account bleakly recorded, to "stone the common folk." It failed to work, the stone dribbling feebly from the sling, so still the labor of forcing surrender remained.[77]

Four days patient waiting, four days further into starvation, and the Spaniards entered the city again. Again they encountered ghostly figures, of women and gaunt children, and saw the warriors still stationed on the rooftops, but silent now, and unarmed, close-wrapped in their cloaks. And still the fruitless pretense at negotiation, the dumb, obdurate resistance.

Cortés attacked, killing "more than twelve thousand," as he estimated. Another meeting with some of the lords, and again they refused any terms save a swift death. Cortés exhausted his famous eloquence: "I said many things to persuade them to surrender but all to no avail, although we showed them more signs of peace than have ever been shown to a vanquished people for we, by the grace of our Lord, were now the victors."[78] He released a captured noble, charging him to urge surrender: the only response was a sudden, desperate attack, and more Indians dead. He had a platform set up in the market square of Tlatelolco, ready for the ceremony of submission, with food prepared for the feast that should mark such a moment: still he clung to the European fiction of two rulers meeting in shared understanding for the transference of an empire. There was no response.

Two days more, and Cortés unleashed the allies. There followed a massacre, of men who no longer had arrows, javelins, or stones; of women and children stumbling and falling on the bodies of their own dead. Cortés thought forty thousand might have died or been taken on that day. The next day he had three heavy guns taken into the city. As he explained to his distant king, the enemy, being now "so massed together that they had no room to turn around, might crush us as we attacked, without actually fighting. I wished, therefore, to do them some harm with the guns, and so induce them to come out to meet us."[79] He had also posted the brigantines to penetrate between the houses to the interior lake where the last of the Mexican canoes were clustered. With the firing of the guns the final action began. The city was now a stinking desolation of heaped and rotting bodies, of starving men, women, and children crawling among them or struggling in the water. Quauhtemoc was taken in his canoe, and at last brought before Cortés, to make his request for death, and the survivors began to file out, these once immaculate people "so thin, sallow, dirty and stinking that it was pitiful to see them."[80]

Cortés had invoked one pragmatic reason for holding his hand in the taking of Tenochtitlan: if the Spaniards attempted to storm the city the Mexicans would throw all their riches into the water, or would be plundered by the allies, so some of the profit would be lost. His perturbation went, I think, very much deeper. His earlier battle narratives exemplify those splendid Caesarian simplicities identified by John Keegan: disjunctive movement, uniformity of behavior, simplified characterization, and simplified motivation.[81] That style of high control, of magisterial grasp, falters when he must justify his own defeat on the causeway, which cost so many Spanish lives. It then recovers itself briefly, to fracture, finally and permanently, for the last stages of his account of the battle for Tenochtitlan. The soldierly narrative loses its fine onward drive as he deploys more and more detail to demonstrate the purposefulness of his own action, and frets more and more over native mood and intentions.[82]

Cortés's strategy in the world had been to treat all men, Indians and Spaniards alike, as manipulable. That sturdy denial of the problem of otherness, usually so profitable, had here been proved bankrupt. He had also been forced into parodying his earlier and once successful strategies. His use of European equipment to terrify had produced the elaborate threat of the catapult, then its farcical failure. "Standard" battle procedures—terror-raiding of villages, exemplary massacres—took on an unfamiliar aspect when the end those means were designed to effect proved phantasmal, when killing did not lead to panic and pleas for terms, but a silent pressing on to death. Even the matter of firing a cannon must have taken on a new significance: to use cannon to clear a contended street or causeway or to disperse massed warriors was one thing: to use cannon to break up a huddled mass of exhausted human misery was very much another. It is possible that as he ran through his degraded routine of stratagems in those last days Cortés was brought to glimpse something of the Indian view of the nature and quality of the Spanish warrior.

His privilege as victor was to survey the surreal devastation of the city that had been the glittering prize and magnificent justification for his insubordination, and for the desperate struggles and sufferings over two long years, now reduced by perverse, obdurate resistance to befouled rubble, its once magnificent lords, its whole splendid hierarchy, to undifferentiated human wreckage. That resistance had been at once "irrational," yet chillingly deliberate.

He had seen, too, the phobic cruelty of the "allies," most especially the Tlaxcalans. He had known that cruelty before, and had used and profited from it. But on that last day of killing they had killed and killed amid a wailing of women and children so terrible "that there was not one man amongst us whose heart did not bleed at the sound."[83]

Those luxurious killings are at odds with what I have claimed to be the protocols of Indian combat. Tlaxcalan warrior-to-warrior performance had been conventional enough: we glimpse them exchanging insults and dueling with Mexican warriors; quarreling over the place of danger while escorting the brigantines over the mountains. It is possible that they came to judge the inadequacies of Spanish battle performance with the leniency of increased knowledge, or (more plausibly) that they thought Spanish delicts none of their concern. During the conquest process they performed as co-venturers with the Spaniards, associates in no way subordinate and, given their greater investment, probably defining themselves as the senior partners in the association.[84] It is in their attitude to Tenochtitlan and its inhabitants that their behavior appears anomalous. Cortés recalled that when he took the decision to raze the buildings of the city, a dauntingly laborious project, the Tlaxcalans were jubilant. All non-Mexicans would have longed to plunder Tenochtitlan, had they dared, and all had scores to settle against Mexican arrogance. No victor would have left the city intact, built as it was as the testament of the Mexican right to rule. Nonetheless the Tlaxcalan taste for destruction was extravagant. Only the Tlaxcalans were relentless in their hatred of the Mexicans: other cities waited and watched through the long struggle for the causeways, "reading the signs" in the ebb and flow of what we would call the fortunes of battle, moving, deft as dancers, in and out of alliance. Only the Tlaxcalans sought neither loot nor captives as they surged into Tenochtitlan, but to kill. Where is the exemption of nonwarriors, the passion for personal captures, for the limited aims of tribute exaction, in those killings? Is this a liberation into ecstatic violence after a painfully protracted and frustrating struggle?

Licensed massacres are unhappily unremarkable, but there are more particular explanations. The Tlaxcalans had signaled their peculiar hatred of the Mexicans early: on the Spaniards' first departure for the Mexican city the Tlaxcalans, warning of chronic Mexican treachery, offered chillingly explicit advice: "In fighting the Mexicans, they said, we should kill all we could, leaving no one alive: neither the young, lest they should bear arms again, nor the old, lest they give counsel."[85] Their long-term exclusion from the play of Mexican alliance politics, coupled with the massive power of the Mexicans, liberated them as underdogs from "normal" constraints. While other formidable Nahua-speaking cities and provinces were recruited into the empire, the Tlaxcalans were kept out. I have come to see their exclusion, their role as outsiders, not as an unfortunate quirk but a structural requirement, a necessary corollary, of the kind of empire it was. Asked whether he could defeat the Tlaxcalans if he so chose, Moctezoma was said to have replied that he could, but preferred to have an enemy against whom to test his warriors and to secure high-quality victims. I believe him.[86] How else, with campaigns increasingly fought far afield, to make real the rhetoric, the high glamor, the authenticity of risk of warriordom? The overriding metaphor of Mexican life was contest, and the political fantasy of destined dominance required a plausible antagonist/victim. That essential role had devolved onto the Tlaxcalans. They made absolutely no obeisance to the Mexican view of themselves, and they were proximate enemies, penned like gamecocks in a coop—until the Spaniards came. Those wandering men without a city could not be pursued, subdued, or incorporated: they could only be destroyed, and that Cortés's conservationist talents and the Mexican cultural predilection for capturing significant enemies alive combined to preclude. The house of cards structure of the wider empire had been rendered unstable by their mere presence. Then they challenged the mutuality of interest bonding the valley city states, so opening Tenochtitlan to assault, and the Tlaxcalans took their chance to destroy people and city together.[87]

Writing later of that day of killing, and what he saw his Indian "friends" do there, Cortés was brought to make one of his very rare general statements: "No race, however savage, has ever practiced such fierce and unnatural cruelty as the natives of these parts."[88] "Unnatural" cruelty. Against nature. A heavily freighted term in early sixteenth-century Spain. He had described Moctezoma as a "barbarian lord" in his earlier letter, but he had done so in the course of an elaborate description of the Mexican city and its complex workings that demonstrated the Mexican ruler was a "barbarian" of a most rare and civilized kind. I think his view was changed by the experience of the siege. There he saw "fierce and unnatural cruelty," an unnatural indifference to suffering, an unnatural indifference to death: a terrifying, terminal demonstration of "otherness," and of its practical and cognitive unmanageability. Todorov has called Cortés a master in human communication. Here the master had found his limits.[89]

In the aftermath of the fall of the city the Spaniards expressed their own cruelties. There was a phobic edge in some of the things done, especially against those men most obviously the custodians of the indigenous culture. There was a special death for priests like the Keeper of the Black House in Tenochtitlan, and other wise men who came from Texcoco of their own free will, bearing their painted books. They were torn apart by dogs.[90]

I do not suggest that any special explanation is required for Spanish or any other conquerors' brutalities. All I would claim at the end is that in the long and terrible conversation of war, despite the apparent mutual intelligibility of move and counter-move, as in the trap and ambush game built around the brigantines, that final nontranslatability of the vocabulary of battle and its modes of termination divided Spaniard from Indian in new and decisive ways. If for Indian warriors the lesson that their opponents were barbarians was learned early, for Spaniards, and for Cortés, that lesson was learned most deeply only in the final stages, where the Mexicans revealed themselves as unamenable to "natural" reason, and so unamenable to the routines of management of one's fellow men. Once that sense of unassuageable otherness has been established, the outlook is bleak indeed.

Notes

An earlier version of this paper, "Cortés, Signs and the Conquest of Mexico," has been published in Anthony Grafton, ed., *Culture and Communication in Early Modern Europe* (Philadelphia, 1990). It was first presented before the Shelby Cullom Davis Center for Historical Research, Princeton University.

1. Anthony Padgen notes several editions of Hernando Cortés's letters to his emperor in five languages between 1522 and 1525; *The Fall of Natural Man* (Cambridge, 1982), 58.
2. Ibid., 117, referring to Juan Ginés de Sepúlveda's "Democrates secundus sive de justis causis belli apud Indos."

3. S. L. Cline, "Revisionist Conquest History: Sahagún's Revised Book XII," in J. Jorge Klor de Alva, H. B. Nicholson, and Eloise Quiñones Keber, eds., *The Work of Bernardino de Sahagún, Pioneer Ethnographer of Sixteenth-Century Aztec Mexico* (Albany, N.Y., 1988). The claim as to the providential, indeed miraculous character of the Spanish achievement was not novel, having been made earlier by Fray Toribio de Motolinía in his *History of the Indians of New Spain* (1541), trans. Elizabeth Andros Foster (New York, 1950). It infuses Franciscan attitudes as described by John Leddy Phelan, *The Millennial Kingdom of the Franciscans in the New World*, 2nd ed. (Berkeley, 1970).

4. W. H. Prescott, *History of the Conquest of Mexico and the History of the Conquest of Peru* (New York, n.d.).

5. For Prescott see the fine study by David Levin, *History as Romantic Art* (Harbinger, N.Y., 1963); and more succinctly in his "History as Romantic Art: Structure, Characterization, and Style in *The Conquest of Mexico*," *Hispanic American Historical Review* 39, no. 1 (February 1959): 20–45.

6. Tzvetan Todorov, *The Conquest of America: The Question of the Other*, trans. Richard Howard (New York, 1984), part 2, passim but esp. 63–67, 80–81, 86–89. For Todorov's rather metaphysical notion of the defeat enclosed within the Spanish victory, see p. 97.

7. Veyne continues: "Other than the techniques of handling and checking documents, there is no more a method of history than one of ethnography or of the art of travelling," which might just possibly be true if the notion of "checking" is sufficiently expanded; Paul Veyne, *Writing History: Essay on Epistemology* (Middletown, Conn., 1984), 12.

8. Bernal Díaz del Castillo, *Historia verdadera de la Conquista de la Nueva España*, introduction and notes by Joaquín Ramirez Cabañas (Mexico City, 1966), 40, 45. For information on Spanish and native Conquest-related materials, see Robert Wauchope, ed., *Handbook of Middle American Indians*, (Austin, Tex., 1964–76), vols. 12–15, *Guide to Ethnohistorical Sources*, ed. Howard F. Cline.

9. *Hernán Cortés: Letters from Mexico*, trans. and ed. Anthony Pagden, with an introduction by J. H. Elliott (New Haven, 1986), "Second Letter," 88. See also J. H. Elliott, "The Mental World of Hernán Cortés," *Transactions of the Royal Historical Society*, 5th ser., 17 (1967): 41–58.

10. Fray Bernardino de Sahagún, *Florentine Codex: General History of the Things of New Spain*, trans. Charles E. Dibble and Arthur J. O. Anderson (Salt Lake City, Utah, 1950–82); hereafter cited as *Florentine Codex*, with book, chapter, and page. Quetzalcoatl-Topiltzin, ruler of the mythic "Tollan," or Tula, the previous great imperial power in the valley, before he withdrew to the east in some shadowy former time, was ambiguously associated with Quetzalcoatl-Ehecatl, the Wind God. For the confusions clustering around the stories to do with the self-exiled Quetzalcoatl-Topiltzin, legendary ruler of Tollan, see H. B. Nicholson, "Topiltzin Quetzalcoatl of Tollan: A Problem in Mesoamerican Ethnohistory" (Ph.D. diss., Harvard University, 1957).

11. *Florentine Codex*, 12.16.17–18, 45, 48–49.

12. "This I saw in a painting that belonged to an ancient chieftain from the province of Texcoco. Moctezoma was depicted in irons, wrapped in a mantle and carried on the shoulders of his chieftains"; Fray Diego Durán, *Historia de las indias de Nueva España y islas de Tierra Firma*, ed. José F. Ramirez, 2 vols. plus atlas (Mexico City, 1967), chap. 74, pp. 541–42.

13. Cortés, "Second Letter," 50.

14. Cortés's own confusion deepens our confidence in our reading, as he aggressively seeks to collect what he called "vassals" along the way, with no demur from Moctezoma. For example, the lord "Pánuco" sent gifts, and freely offered to supply certain Spaniards in his region whom he took to be members of Cortés's party with food; "Second Letter," 54. See also the reception offered by "Sienchimalen," ibid. These were almost certainly not gestures of political subordination but the normal courtesies—the provision of supplies, and if necessary fuel and shelter—extended to official travelers within the more effectively subdued Mexican territories. Where Cortés made the condition of "vassal" more explicit by requesting not food or carriers but gold, the request was denied.

15. The lodging of the Spaniards in a royal palace is not especially remarkable, visiting rulers and ranking ambassadors being routinely luxuriously housed and feted, in the not unfamiliar determination to impress potentially troublesome visitors while keeping an eye on them; Durán, *Historia*, chap. 43; *Florentine Codex*, 12.15.41. Despite the intense traditional hostility between Tlaxcala and the Mexicans, a Mexican embassy numbering more than two hundred people sought out Cortés during his first stay in Tlaxcala, its members being permitted to come and go without hindrance; "Second Letter," 69. The phrasing of the *Florentine Codex* on the Spanish assault on the warrior dancers affords a dizzying perspective on Spanish-Mexican relations, the Spaniards being described as "friends" to that point, and then as having "risen up against us [the Mexicans]" to become "enemies"; 12.29.81.

16. Díaz, *Historia*, chap. 39.

17. Cortés, "Third Letter," 188.

18. Unsurprisingly few commentators are prepared to be so austere. For an attractive display of indulgence, see R. C. Padden, *The Hummingbird and the Hawk* (Columbus, Ohio), 1967.

19. Possible, but difficult: e.g., for art historians' divisions on the meanings of a pleasantly substantial and certainly pre-contact artifact, the "Hamburg Box," a superb lidded greenstone box carved on both inner and outer surfaces, compare Esther Pasztory, *Aztec Art* (New York, 1983), 255–56; and her "El arte Mexica y la Conquista Española," *Estudios de cultura Nahuatl* 17 (1983): 101–24; with H. B. Nicholson and Eloise Quiñones Keber, *The Art of Ancient Mexico: Treasures of Tenochtitlan* (Washington, D.C., 1983), 64–66.

20. Cortés, "Third Letter," 184.

21. Díaz, *Historia*, chap. 52. For a discussion see Richard C. Trexler, "Aztec Priests for Christian Altars: The Theory and Practice of Reverence in New Spain," in Paola Zambelli, ed., *Scienze credenze occulte livelli di cultura* (Florence, 1982), 175–96.

22. Díaz, *Historia*, chaps. 51, 52.   23. Ibid., chap. 107.

24. In the ordinances he proclaimed in Tlaxcala in December 1520, preparatory to the great campaign against the lake cities, Cortés emphasized the necessary disciplines of war (no private booty, no gambling of weapons, no breakaway attacks, no insults or brawling in the ranks). But he prefaced it with the declaration that justified all: that the Spaniards' principal motive was to destroy idolatry and to bring the natives to the knowledge of God and of the Holy Catholic Faith. Without that primary justification, the war to come would be unjust, and everything taken in it liable to restitution; "Ordenanzas militares dadas por Hernando Cortés in Tlaxcallan," in Mario Hernandez Sánchez Barba, ed., *Hernán Cortés: Cartas y documentos* (Mexico City, 1963), 336–41.

25. Cortés, "Second Letter," 60–62.

26. Díaz, *Historia*, chaps. 46, 47, 51.   27. Ibid., chap. 95.

28. As John Elliott puts it: "It would be hard to think of a crazier strategy"; J. H. Elliott, *New York Review of Books*, 19 July 1984.

29. Díaz, *Historia*, chap. 126.

30. Sahagún's informants emphasize physical contact far beyond Spanish reports, "recalling" Moctezoma as being prodded and pawed by any and all of the newcomers, with the disgrace of the unabashed glance marked equally keenly: "They caressed Moctezoma with their hands"; they "looked at him; they each looked at him thoroughly. They were continually active on their feet; they continually dismounted in order to look at him"; *Florentine Codex*, 12.16.43–46; Díaz, *Historia*, chap. 88.

31. See note 30 above.

32. "Recorded" is putting it rather too high: here we have to take the "captain's speech" for the literary convention it is. But it is, at best, close to what Cortés claims he said: at worst, the gist of what Díaz thought a man like Cortés ought to have said on such an occasion; Díaz, *Historia*, chap. 61, e.g., "Now and from henceforth, through God, the history books will make much more of this than of anything done in the past. . . . The most famous Roman captain has not achieved such great things as we have." Cf. "Second Letter," 63.

33. For a contrary view of the whole conquest phenomenon as very much more pragmatic and routinized, see James Lockhart, *The Men of Cajamarca* (Austin, Tex., 1972). On the importance of the model of the Mexican Conquest for later conquerors: "[The Conquest of] Mexico had no major impact on Peru merely by virtue of some years' precedence. . . . Pizarro was certainly not thinking of Cortés and Moctezoma when he seized Atahualpa; he had been capturing *caciques* [chiefs] in Tierra Firme long before Mexico was heard of"; James Lockhart and Stuart B. Schwartz, *Early Latin America* (Cambridge, 1983), 84.

34. Skin afflictions were commonly understood as coming from Tezcatlipoca, the Mexican interventionist deity, but we do not know if the Mexicans identified smallpox pustules with more familiar lesions. As always, they noted the month of the epidemic's coming and of its diminishing (a span of sixty day signs), but smallpox does not appear in the *Florentine Codex* list of Spanish-related events (12.27–29.81–83).

35. Wars of conquest waged against distant "barbarians" were a rather different matter. For an exhaustive description from a steadfastly pragmatic perspective, see Ross Hassig, *Aztec Warfare: Imperial Expansion and Political Control* (Norman, Okla., 1988). Dr. Hassig is persuaded that "in fact, Aztec [warrior] practices were shaped by political realities and practical necessities" (10). The question is to discover what the Aztec/Mexican understood those "realities and practical necessities" to be.

36. Durán, *Historia*, chap. 34.

37. Cf. the deliberate humiliation of the Tlatelolcan warriors, discovered hiding in the rushes after the Mexican victory, and ordered to quack. "Even today," Durán noted, decades after the debacle, "the Tlatelolca are called 'quackers' and imitators of water fowl. They are much offended by this name and when they fight the name is always recalled"; *Historia*, chap. 34, p. 264.

38. Contrast the fate of Spaniards when faced with the arrows projected from the short powerful bows of the Chichimeca, the Indians of the northern steppes whose territory lay athwart the road to the silver mines; Philip Wayne Powell, *Soldiers, Indians and Silver* (Tempe, Ariz., 1975).

39. Díaz, *Historia*, chap. 153; Durán, *Historia*, chap. 77.

40. Indian cannibalism is a vexed question. In very brief, insult displays pivoted on the

threat of eating and being eaten. While the eating of the flesh of a warrior's sacrificed captive was hedged by ritual, more casual references suggest its debasing function, and it is possible that battlefield behavior was more relaxed. For ritual cannibalism, see *Florentine Codex*, 2.25.49–54; and Inga Clendinnen, "The Cost of Courage in Aztec Society," *Past and Present* 107 (May 1985): 44–89, esp. 56–60 and 69; for the debasing function, see Durán, *Historia*, chap. 9.

41. Cortés, "Third Letter," 230.
42. E.g., the attack on Cortés in the Xochimilco battle, and the desperate rescue, Cortés sustaining a "bad wound in the head"; Díaz, *Historia*, chap. 145.
43. Spaniards valued muskets equally with crossbows, a musketeer being allocated the same share of the spoils as a crossbowman, yet oddly muskets are mentioned infrequently in Indian accounts, perhaps because the ball could not be followed in flight, while crossbow bolts whirred and sang as they came; *Florentine Codex*, 12.22.62. For a succinct and accessible account of sixteenth-century cannon, in their enormous variety, see Pagden, *Cortés*, 507–8. Most of the small guns used in America could fire a ball of twenty pounds over some four hundred meters (ibid., n. 59). For a more extended account, see Alberto Mario Salas, *Las armas de la Conquista* (Buenos Aires, 1950).
44. Durán, *Historia*, chap. 72, pp. 529–30.
45. E.g., on the Spanish retreat from Tenochtitlan they "quickly slew the people of Calacoaya . . . [they] did not provoke them; without notice were they slain. [The Spaniards] vented their wrath upon them, they took their pleasure with them"; *Florentine Codex*, 12:25:73.
46. *Florentine Codex*, 2.20.55. It appears from the funerary rites accorded the fragmented corpses of the warrior dancers that the Mexicans somehow decided that the victims had found death in a mode appropriate to warriors.
47. Ibid., 12.7.19.   48. Ibid., 12.30.86.
49. Cortés, "Second Letter," 58.
50. Díaz, *Historia*, chap. 63.
51. Note also the offering of the entire skins of five horses, "sewn up and as well tanned as anywhere in the world," in Texcoco. These captives had been taken in a situation where they were riderless at the time of engagement. Cortés, "Third Letter," 184.
52. Ibid., 252.   53. Ibid., 192.
54. Díaz recalls them yelling, whistling, and calling the Spaniards "rogues and cowards who did not dare to meet them through a day's battle, and retreated before them"; *Historia*, chap. 126.
55. *Florentine Codex*, 12.31.89. For an account of those exemplary battles, see Clendinnen, "Cost of Courage."
56. E.g., *Florentine Codex*, 12.35.87.
57. Ibid., 12.33.96; 12.34.99 (*tlacotli*, a secular slave performing lowly tasks, not *tlaaltilli*, those selected captives ritually purified to be especially acceptable to the gods).
58. Rather too much has been made of the Mexican concern for "day signs," the determining authority of the auguries associated with one's day of birth over the individual's *tonalli*, or destiny. It is true that in some passages of the *Florentine Codex*—the only source with the kind of "spread" to make this sort of concept mapping viable—the individual is presented as quite mastered by his or her "fate." That clarity blurs on broader acquaintance, emerging as part of the characteristic stylistic movement of much of the codex between firm statements of the ideal and the tempering qualifications necessary to catch the messiness of actuality. Day signs had about as much deter-

mining power as horoscopes hold today for the moderate believer. They mattered, but more as intimations or as post-hoc diagnoses (and even then, one suspects, most readily invoked by others, not the individuals concerned) than as iron determinants of fate. Cf. Todorov: "To know someone's birthday is to know his fate"; *Conquest of America*, 64.

59. John Keegan, *The Face of Battle* (New York, 1977), 184–86.
60. Cortés, "Second Letter," 134–35.
61. Díaz, *Historia*, chap. 126.   62. Ibid., chap. 151.
63. Miguel Leon-Portilla, *The Broken Spears* (Boston, 1962), 107. The captor was the *Tlapanecatl* Hecatzin—see *Florentine Codex*, 12.35.103, n. 2. For an earlier exploit of the Otomí warrior, see *Florentine Codex*, 101.
64. Keegan, *Face of Battle*, 296.
65. As in the interspecies mayhem described by Konrad Z. Lorenz, where signs of submission are not "understood" in the battle between the turkey and the peacock; *King Solomon's Ring* (London, 1961), 194–95.
66. Cortés was desperate to treat with Quauhtemoc in the last days of the siege, but Díaz reports that the ruler would not show himself, despite all reassurances, because he feared he would be killed by guns or crossbows, Cortés having behaved too dishonorably to be trusted; *Historia*, chap. 155.
67. *Florentine Codex*, 12.35.104.
68. Díaz, *Historia*, chap. 153; Cortés, "Third Letter," 242. Cortés for his part deletes any reference to the withdrawal of his Indian "vassals," the admission of such a withdrawal casting altogether too much light on the nature of their commitment to the Spanish cause.
69. *Florentine Codex*, 12.38.117.   70. Ibid., 12.38.118.   71. Ibid., 12.40.123.
72. I offer Miguel Leon-Portilla's translation as the version most likely to be familiar; *Broken Spears*, 137–38. Cf. Leon-Portilla, *Pre-Columbian Literatures of Mexico* (Norman, Okla., 1969), 150–51; and Gordon Brotherston and Ed Dorn, *Image of the New World* (London, 1979), 34–35. For other songs in traditional form to do with the Conquest, see John Bierhorst, *Cantares Mexicanos* (Stanford, Calif., 1985), esp. no. 13, pp. 151–53; no. 60, p. 279 (obscurely); no. 66, pp. 319–23; no. 68, for its early stanzas, pp. 327–41; no. 91, pp. 419–25.
73. For example, Cortés approvingly noted the courage of the chief Chichimecatecle, who "having always gone with his warriors in the vanguard," took it as an affront when put to the rear in the transport for the brigantines: "When he finally agreed to this, he asked that no Spaniards should remain accompanying him, for he is a most valiant man and wished to keep all the glory for himself"; "Third Letter," 185.
74. For the multiple demands on Cortés in this period see J. H. Elliott, "The Spanish Conquest and the Settlement of America," in Leslie Bethell, ed., *The Cambridge History of Latin America*, vol. 1 (Cambridge, 1984), 149–206.
75. Cortés, "Third Letter," 256.   76. Ibid., 232–33.
77. Ibid., 257; Díaz, *Historia*, chap. 155; *Florentine Codex*, 12.38.113.
78. Cortés, "Third Letter," 258.   79. Ibid., 262.
80. Díaz, *Historia*, chap. 156.
81. Keegan, *Face of Battle*, 65–66. This is not to claim any direct classical influence; see Pagden, *Cortés*, xlvii; and Elliott, "Mental World of Cortés," for Cortés's slight acquaintance with classical authors. Caesar's *Commentaries* had been published in Spanish by 1498, and it is possible that Cortés had read them, although perhaps unlikely.
82. For the control: "While the alguacil-mayor was at Matalcingo, the people of [Tenoch-

titlan] decided to attack Alvarado's camp by night, and struck shortly before dawn. When the sentries on foot and on horseback heard them they shouted, 'to arms!' Those who were in that place flung themselves upon the enemy, who leapt into the water as soon as they saw the horsemen. . . . Fearing our men might be defeated I ordered my own company to arm themselves and march into the city to weaken the offensive against Alvarado"—and so on; Cortés, "Third Letter," 247. For the dislocation:

> When we came within sight of the enemy we did not attack but marched through the city thinking that at any moment they would come out to meet us [to surrender]. And to induce it I galloped up to a very strong barricade which they had set up and called out to certain chieftains who were behind and whom I knew, that as they saw how lost they were and knew that if I so desired within an hour not one of them would remain alive why did not Guatimucin [Quauhtemoc], their lord, come and speak with me. . . . I then used other arguments which moved them to tears, and weeping they replied they well knew their error and their fate, and would go and speak to their lord. . . . They went, and returned after a while and told me their lord had not come because it was late, but that he would come on the following day at noon to the marketplace; and so we returned to our camp. . . . On the following day we went to the city and I warned my men to be on the alert lest the enemy betray us and we be taken unawares.

And so to more worried guesses and second guesses; ibid., 259–60.

83. Ibid., 261.
84. The Tlaxcalans refused to participate in any expedition (like the sortie against Narváez) not in their direct interest; they withdrew at will, taking their loot with them; they required payment for aid given the Spaniards after the expulsion from Tenochtitlan, having considered the utility of killing them; Díaz, *Historia*, chap. 98. Their self-representation as faithful friends and willing servants to the Spaniards, as pictured in the Lienzo de Tlaxcala, came a generation or more after the Conquest as part of a campaign for privileges.
85. Ibid., chap. 79.
86. Andrés de Tápia, "Relación hecha por el señor Andrés de Tápia sobre la Conquista de México," in Joaquin García Icazbalceta, ed., *Colección de documentos para la historia de México*, 2 vols. (Mexico City, 1858–66), 2:343–438.
87. It was possibly in the decimation of native leaders who had learned how to deal with each other that the smallpox epidemic had its most immediate political effect.
88. Cortés, "Third Letter," 262.
89. Those limits were to be drawn more narrowly through the shaking experience of the Honduran expedition. The Cortés who early in the Mexican campaign could dismiss "omens" in the confidence that "God is more powerful than Nature" learned in Honduras how helpless men are when Nature, not men, opposes them, and where God seems far away. There he discovered that God is bound by no contract, and that he, like all men, must wait upon His will. The "Fifth Letter" reads like a mournful antiphon to the sanguine assurance of Cortés's early Conquest accounts.
90. *Anales de Tlatelolco: Unos anales historicos de la Nación Mexicana*, prepared by Heinrich Berlin (Mexico City, 1948), 371–89, 74–76.

ROLENA ADORNO

The Negotiation of Fear
in Cabeza de Vaca's *Naufragios*

Introduction

WHEN THE GENTLEMAN OF ELVAS begins his account of the expedition of Hernando de Soto to Florida, he tells how a certain *hidalgo* (nobleman) arrived at court after the concession to de Soto had been granted.[1] This gentleman, "Cabeza de Vaca by name," had survived the disastrous Pánfilo de Narváez expedition of 1527 to conquer "Florida," the territory along the Gulf of Mexico coast that reached all the way from the Florida peninsula to the province of Pánuco (near present-day Tampico) in Mexico. Cabeza de Vaca now returned to Spain after years of hardship in the wilderness to seek the favor of the emperor. According to the Gentleman of Elvas, Cabeza de Vaca brought with him a written *relación* (relation), which said in some places, "Here I have seen this; and the rest which I saw I leave to confer of with His Majesty" (136). Whether this relation was one that narrated the fate of the expedition from its departure through the survivors' arrival at the Texas coast, or the famous one of the complete journey that was published in 1542 and 1555 and came to be known as the *Naufragios* (Shipwrecks), is not clear.[2]

In any case, the Gentleman from Elvas says that the relation described the poverty of the country visited by Cabeza de Vaca and the hardships undergone by him. At the same time, however, Cabeza de Vaca gave those at court to understand that the country he had visited was the richest in the world. In fact, declares our Portuguese gentleman, Cabeza de Vaca's report to the emperor was so compelling that all the men of breeding who had sold their lands and signed up for the de Soto expedition could not be accommodated on the voyage and so "remained behind in Sanlúcar for want of shipping" (138).

There is a noticeable gap in Cabeza de Vaca's account between the impoverishment of the land about which he wrote and the visions of wealth that he conjured up for the emperor. In an analogous fashion, there is a gap between what one may read in the famous *Naufragios* and what is generally said about it, starting from sixteenth-century interpreters right through our own present day. A modest relation and its author have been the subject of countless recreations that have found their way into the historiography of the Indies through the eigh-

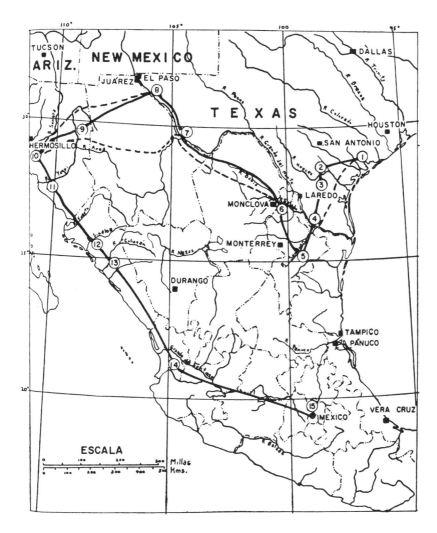

FIGURE 1. Alex D. Krieger's interpretation of the Cabeza de Vaca route. Broken lines indicate alternate route. From Krieger, "The Travels of Alvar Núñez Cabeza de Vaca in Texas and Mexico, 1534–1536," in *Homenaje a Pablo Martínez del Río* (Mexico City, 1961). Courtesy Instituto nacional de antropología e historia, Mexico City.

teenth century, and poetic and novelistic versions of his experience continue to be produced and published in our own.[3] I would like to place my own consideration of the Cabeza de Vaca story in that interpretative gap, working through the evidence he presents and trying to pick up its most faithful resonances.

To do this, I shall offer a *razonamiento* or reasoning that follows the course of the narration itself, which in the story's unfolding reproduces an emerging process of cultural adaptation and, consequently, physical survival. This process becomes visible less through the interpretation that the author provides of his experience than through the information that he so often "lets drop."[4] Such information constitutes part of the experience being recorded but tends to lack direct bearing on the author's interpretation of it. Occasionally, this data contradicts the larger interpretation or at least casts its major themes in a different light. Coordinating my reading with the best interpretations of the Cabeza de Vaca route (fig. 1), I want to elucidate the process of adaptation and survival in his interaction first solely with native Amerindian groups and subsequently with native groups already familiar with European colonizers. Both of these encounters take place in the portion of the journey that begins off the east coast of Texas and ends in northwestern Mexico.[5] I reserve for another occasion questions of later textual interpretations and the influence of texts, both of which are brought into the foreground in the history of the history of Cabeza de Vaca's adventures.

Two key and somewhat contrastive sources will suffice for the present purpose: Alvar Núñez Cabeza de Vaca himself and Gonzalo Fernández de Oviedo y Valdés. Oviedo wrote his version of the journey on the basis of the so-called joint report prepared in Mexico by the three Spanish survivors and sent to the *audiencia* (high court) of Santo Domingo, which had jurisdiction over Florida.[6]

Cabeza de Vaca's journey of survival began during the fall and winter of 1527, spent in Cuba, when losses due to a hurricane and desertions were followed by a disastrous inland expedition into northwestern Florida, an attempt to leave Florida by sea on five makeshift barges, and Narváez's abandonment of command after passing the mouth of the Mississippi. Cabeza de Vaca and an undetermined number of men landed on an island in Galveston Bay on 6 November 1528.[7] From that date till September or October of 1534 the ultimately four survivors, Cabeza de Vaca, Andrés Dorantes de Carranza, his African-born slave Estevanico, and Alonso Castillo Maldonado, lived among groups of shoreline Indians of Texas.[8] This time and location are the starting point of the following discussion.

When they left for Pánuco in 1529, Dorantes, Estevanico, and Castillo were enslaved by the Mariames at a distance of some sixty leagues from Malhado (fig. 1, point 1). Cabeza de Vaca was united with them in 1533, and in 1534 they managed to escape together (point 2). According to Alex D. Krieger (461, 472), there ensued a two-year odyssey whose last twenty-one or twenty-two months, from September 1534 to July 1536, constitute the entirety of the overland journey (points 2 to 15). However, the travelers were continuously on the move only during the last thirteen months of that time, that is from May or June 1535, when they left south-central Texas, to 22–24 July 1536, when they arrived in Mexico-Tenochtitlán (points 3 to 15). This period of slightly less than two years occupies about half the bulk (chapters 20 to 36) of Cabeza de Vaca's published narrative account.

Contrary to the romantic image that tales of captivity and escape tend to foster, none of their time was spent in aimless wandering. They learned important lessons on survival in the years they lived among nomadic and semisedentary groups, and these lessons were put to use in their swift overland trek (May–December 1535) from the Avavares people of south Texas to the mouth of the Río Yaqui on the Sonoran (west) coast of Mexico, where they made their first sightings of other Europeans (points 3 to 11). Furthermore, they always traveled accompanied by natives who led them from one group to another over established trails that were used by nomadic groups for annual migrations in search of food and by sedentary groups for communication and commerce. Although the native role has been underplayed in most period interpretations of the journey and even those of the twentieth century, information in Cabeza de Vaca's account itself allows us to reexamine the more common interpretations under the powerful light of the survivors' own testimony.

The ethnic groups with which Cabeza de Vaca came into contact, during what I consider to be the crucial part of his journey, inhabited the most poorly known region of Indian North America. This area is today constituted by southern Texas, northeastern Coahuila, and the greater parts of Nuevo León and Tamaulipas.[9] The extinct groups were small, apparently autonomous Indian groups who lived by hunting and gathering. The hypothesis of widespread linguistic and cultural uniformity among them has now been seriously challenged.[10] The Indians that Cabeza de Vaca encountered in southern Texas at the lower sections of the Guadalupe and Nueces Rivers would not be the object of European observation for the next one hundred fifty years. Among the groups he named, only the Mariames can be identified clearly in the eighteenth-century sources.[11] The only portion of the journey for which there are contemporary accounts consists of the north-northwesterly corridor of Mexico, from the Río Yaqui to Compostela.[12]

The common interpretation of Cabeza de Vaca's experience, suggested by his testimony but made explicit in Oviedo's version, is that the healing practices and miraculous cures performed by the Spaniards were responsible for their successful deliverance. This assessment has been emphasized in the subsequent accounts over the succeeding centuries by Francisco López de Gómara, Antonio de Herrera y Tordesillas, Fray Antonio Tello, Fray Matías de la Mota Padilla, and Antonio Ardoino, among others.[13] In them, the role that the curing played in the safe return of the "pilgrims," as Oviedo and later writers called them, becomes more and more pronounced. Jacques Lafaye has reviewed the history of the miracle cure interpretations,[14] and scholarly interest continues to be drawn to the importance of the healing episodes.[15]

The curing practices, however, constitute only one aspect of a complex web of negotiations between the shipwreck survivors and the native peoples they encountered. Thus I would like to place the healings in relation to another set of practices that the Europeans observed and adapted from native tradition. These were ritual patterns of intertribal exchange and/or warfare to which the Spaniards appended their healing practices (themselves an adaptation of native custom) and that made possible their transport and passage across native trade routes from one ethnic group to another. I will show that they learned about these practices among the coastal and inland groups of the Gulf of Mexico shoreline when the survivors of the five makeshift barges were thrown up along the shores of the island in Galveston Bay that the Spanish dubbed "Isla de Malhado," the "Isle of Ill Fate."

The subject of fear in the original Cabeza de Vaca and Oviedo accounts suggested a way to examine European/Amerindian interaction, and so it shall be the theme of this inquiry. Fear of the other was a weapon employed by both sides, the native American and the European. Both groups created, managed, and manipulated it, depending on who had the upper hand. The "negotiation of fear" can thus be read in three ways. The first concerns what Cabeza de Vaca says about how he and his companions controlled their own fear and terror of the aboriginal peoples. The second involves the manner in which they subsequently inspired fear in the native groups they encountered. A third and the most significant deals with the way in which Cabeza de Vaca and his party, at last returned to lands occupied by Spaniards (Nueva Galicia), negotiated away the natives' fears of Spanish settlers and slave hunters and secured the natives' peaceful resettlement. In following the trajectory of this old *relación*, we may discover the elements that have made it symbolize the benevolent and paradigmatic encounter of two worlds, long after the social type represented by its author—the Spanish *hidalgo* of noble lineage who wanted the king's license for a territory to conquer—has ceased to be revered.

Christian Suffering and the Practice
of Terror by the Natives

The discourse of miracles and the discourse of terror are both present in the early accounts. Oviedo's narrative brings to our attention the specter of terror and fear that Cabeza de Vaca himself expresses explicitly but less emphatically. Oviedo compared the trials and hardships of Spanish captivity in America to enslavement under the Muslims, declaring that the members of Cabeza de Vaca's party were subjected to "greater cruelties than even a Moorish slave master could impose," and that natives came from many regions to enslave the luckless Spaniards because "they had heard what good slaves Christians made" (599). The image of the Moorish slave master would have had chilling resonances for the Spanish reader, and more chilling still were the techniques of terror, described by Cabeza de Vaca and Oviedo, to which the Spaniards under captivity were subjected.

According to Oviedo, this torment was borne by the three Castilian *hidalgos* with the fortitude supplied them by their noble birth and breeding and their religious faith. The echoes of Job in his statement are clear and, in a comparison that neither Oviedo nor others chose to repeat, Cabeza de Vaca described his own sufferings by recalling the greater torments of Jesus Christ (102). To endure hardship and cruelty in the best tradition of the Christian *hidalgo* was to achieve the nobility of Christian suffering and martyrdom. Cabeza de Vaca had placed himself far from the scene of pathetic victimization by terror, within a biblical tradition of spiritual grace and a literary one of chivalric dignity and courage. Nevertheless, until the point in the narration at which Dorantes, Estevanico, Castillo, and Cabeza de Vaca were reunited and fled together in 1534, the life Cabeza de Vaca and Oviedo described was one of nightmarish terror.

At the same time, the shipwreck survivors' apprenticeship in fear among the coastal and inland groups of the Gulf of Mexico shoreline taught them important tactics of survival. To begin with, the Spaniards were pressed into service as medicine men on the island of Malhado during that first winter of 1528 (56). Because so many deaths had occurred since the Spaniards' arrival, and since the deaths of many of the Spaniards themselves apparently convinced the Karankawas that the Spaniards were not responsible, the logical alternative was to enlist their help in curing. According to Cabeza de Vaca, shamans were regarded most highly in Karankawa society; they were allowed to have several wives, and when they died, they were cremated, their bones being crushed to powder and drunk a year later by their family members.[16] In his general description of Karankawa healing, Cabeza de Vaca tells how, after being cured, the patient not only gave the healer all he had but also obtained more goods from his relatives in order to reward more generously the shaman (53–56; *DII*, 14:277).

Cabeza de Vaca makes it clear that he and his companions joined in the healing practices only under duress; they were denied food until they agreed to participate. As a result, they were given food in abundance. On taking up healing, Cabeza de Vaca reports that their patients told the others that they were cured, and "for this reason, they gave us good treatment, and refrained from eating in order to give food to us, and they gave us hides and other things" (57; *DII*, 14:278).[17] Since starvation was a threat in the area at this time of year, becoming shamans was an effective way to fend off starvation and assure the friendly attitude of the natives in spite of the devastating population losses they suffered.[18]

Cabeza de Vaca was taught a second lesson in survival during the year he and one Lope de Oviedo spent on Malhado, due to the fact that neither had been able-bodied enough to continue to head for Pánuco in 1529. There he learned patterns of intertribal exchange that would prove to be crucial in his subsequent experiences. He understood the practices of various groups as pertaining to a related set of patterns or principles. The specificity with which he described native groups gives important early testimony on Karankawa, Avavares-Caddo, Coahuiltecan, Jumano, Suma, Opata, Seri, Nabame, and other cultures.

Below is his description of local custom on Malhado (58; *DII*, 14:278), to which I am assigning, based on evidence accumulated throughout his account, a paradigmatic value:

There are two distinct languages spoken on the island; those of one language are called Capoques, those of the other, Han. They have the custom, when they know each other and meet from time to time, before they speak, to weep for half an hour. After they have wept, the one who receives the visit rises and gives to the other all he has. The other takes it, and in a little while goes away with everything. Even sometimes, after having given and obtained all, they part without having uttered a word. There are other very queer customs, but having told the principal ones and the most striking, I must now proceed to relate what further happened to us. (Bandelier, 60)

This "principal and most striking" custom, as Cabeza de Vaca called it, was to be repeated and varied countless times in the course of his subsequent overland journey. It is important to note two things: first, this form of exchange was an independent custom of the Karankawa, unrelated to their healing practices. Second, in the healing practices, the shaman was always handsomely rewarded. In my view, the two practices, described as early as Malhado, will be articulated together in such a way that they make an interlocking whole. The "miracle cure" episodes and healing rituals thus become part of larger intertribal negotiations and ritual exchange, acquiring meaning within those more complex patterns. Our challenge is to see these practices not as the Spaniards reported them but as the natives understood them.

Finally, the third aspect of that early apprenticeship occurred when Cabeza de Vaca was able to flee to the mainland to the Charrucos after about a year on Malhado (59). Once thus freed, he took up his existence as a trader, for a period of some four years.[19] Because of constant hostilities and continuous wars, the native groups could not traverse the country or engage in barter. Thus Cabeza de Vaca carried sea items inland and brought to the coastal Karankawas the hides and red ochre with which they colored their faces and hair, as well as flint for arrow points and tassels made of deer hair (60; *DII*, 14:278). He reports that he traveled inland as far as he cared to go, and along the coast some forty or fifty leagues (60).[20] Considering the goods that he acquired, it is clear that Cabeza de Vaca was not wandering aimlessly but following established routes to acquire the commodities desired by his trading clients.

He insists that he had liberty to go where he wanted, without any kind of obligation or the danger of being enslaved; wherever he went, he was treated well and given food and provisions out of respect for his trade. He was well known and well received by those who knew him and sought out by those who did not, "because of my fame" (60–61; *DII*, 14:278–79)—and, we might add, because of his skill: he had learned to negotiate between tribes which were at war with each other. His life was spared and vouched safe for the goods he was able to convey. How is his survival to be explained?

Cabeza de Vaca's travels and trade were possible only as long as the warfare was not total. Did he understand this because of traditions of warfare in Christian-Muslim Spain before the Catholic kings, or because he learned it in America? The answer may lie in both directions; in the immediate context, he elsewhere remarks that native women were often designated to communicate between groups at war with one another (93). The principle is clear: the outsider to the native male war community could perform a neutral, mediating function.

At the same time, Cabeza de Vaca would have been familiar with pre-1492 warfare against the Muslim kingdom of Granada from his grandfather, who participated in the conquest and colonization of the Canary Islands as well as the war that definitively defeated the Muslims of Granada early in 1492. The spirit of the Crusades returned with the Catholic kings,[21] but prior to that time warfare was limited, not total, with the Crown of Castile obtaining great economic benefit from the taxes paid by Granada. Over the period 1350–1460, only twenty-five years had been spent at war; sporadic and presumably independent warfare undertaken by nobles broke the peace that was the common objective of all.[22] Numerous types of intermediaries mediated between both sides of the frontier, with special judges and investigators assigned to restore and keep the peace. These officials (*alfaqueques*), assigned the task of locating and exchanging captives, were immune to frontier hostilities and traveled freely in the fulfillment of their obligations.[23] Given the native American practices observed by Cabeza de Vaca and his companions, and the precedents established in his native Andalusia, we may surmise that the three white men and one black man became keys or catalysts to intertribal exchange even as they pursued their goal of return to the Spanish settlements.

Cabeza de Vaca and Dorantes independently survived another apprenticeship: the negotiation of fear. This emerges clearly in Cabeza de Vaca's account when he tells how he returned from his inland trading area year after year to Malhado to try to persuade Lope de Oviedo to accompany him and escape. He was finally successful in 1533, yet when the Karankawas of Galveston Bay had accompanied them to Matagorda Bay,[24] they met the fearsome Quevenes (61–63; *DII*, 14:279). Cabeza de Vaca's brief unpublished *relación* ends here, but in the *Naufragios* he goes on to narrate that, as a result of the Quevenes' boastful reports of the torture and killings of other Spaniards whom they named (61–63; also Oviedo, 592), and their taunts, beatings, and death threats against him and Lope de Oviedo, the latter went back to Malhado in spite of all of Cabeza de Vaca's pleadings, while Cabeza de Vaca remained alone with the Quevenes.[25] Lope de Oviedo was never heard from again.

Lope de Oviedo, who had not had contact with groups other than the Karankawas of Malhado, was intimidated by the Quevenes to retreat once again to the island, but Cabeza de Vaca was not. Apart from personal courage, his superior experience of some four plus years of negotiating with various native groups had taught him how to cope under harrowing circumstances and how to negotiate between groups at war with one another. In any case, at Matagorda Bay Cabeza de Vaca was in a familiar situation of negotiating with people who were the enemies of those from and with whom he had come.

Dorantes's testimony regarding another Karankawa group, with whom he and others had spent a year and a half, paints a similar picture.[26] The chronicler Oviedo reports how the natives treated the white men poorly "in word and deed" (599–600). Native boys pulled at the Spaniards' beards as a pastime; surprising them, they would pull their hair "and take from it the greatest pleasure in the world." At other times, they would claw the Spaniards' bodies until the blood ran, for the natives grew such nails that they used them as their principal weapons and ordinary knives. If the Spaniards responded by throwing stones, the natives thought it was a game and a new source of amusement. Not being able to endure it any longer, Dorantes escaped to the Mariames. Clearly, Cabeza de Vaca's and Dorantes's initiation as targets of terrorist tactics and taunting prepared them to survive and to turn the tables when the opportunity arose.

The escape of the Cabeza de Vaca party to the Mariames marks the beginning of their journey homeward (point 1). The Mariames were a treacherous group, from the Europeans' perspective, for some of them, as Cabeza de Vaca and Lope de Oviedo had learned, had killed Esquivel, a member of the Narváez expedition, because of a dream and tortured two others before they fled (Cabeza de Vaca, 68–69). The Mariames are the best described of all the native groups encountered by Cabeza de Vaca and his fellow travelers.[27] Dorantes had spent some four years with the Mariames, and Cabeza de Vaca some eighteen months (in 1533–34); both learned to speak their language.[28] Dorantes reported (in Oviedo) that the Mariames, like the Karankawas with whom he had lived, also engaged in taunting and threats. While digging roots, Dorantes could not see a single native come upon him without fear of Esquivel's fate, i.e., being killed because of a native dream omen, and he did not feel safe until the person was past him. Many times, says Oviedo, the Mariames showed themselves very fierce to "poor Dorantes," and often they came running at him, placing arrows in his chest or sending arrows whistling past his ears (600). And afterward they would laugh and say, "Were you afraid?"

In September or October of 1534, the four survivors managed to reunite and slip away from the Mariames at the end of the prickly pear harvest (point 2). Fleeing the Mariames "in great fear [*con harto temor*] lest the Indians follow us" (Bandelier, 81), they were welcomed by the Avavares (point 3), the Spaniards' fame as healers having preceded them. Since the Christians had performed no cures among the Mariames, the question arises as to how their fame as healers could have been known to the Avavares. Cabeza de Vaca reveals that the curing he had done among the Susolas during the time he was living with the Mariames is now remembered by other Susolas who meet him with the Avavares at the prickly pear grounds (82). The little party finds the Avavares to be "very docile and with some news about Christians, although very little, because they did not know that the others had treated them badly" (Oviedo, 602; my translation). Cabeza de Vaca interprets the experience in recounting it as follows:

The community directly brought us a great many prickly pears, having heard of us before, of our cures, and of the wonders our Lord worked by us, which, although there had been no others, were adequate to open ways to us through a country poor like this, to afford us people where oftentimes there were none, and to lead us through immediate dangers, not permitting us to be killed, sustaining us under great want, and putting into those nations the heart of kindness, as we shall relate hereafter. (77–78; Hodge, 73–74)

It is this "putting into those nations the heart of kindness" that I wish to examine next.

"Moving the Hearts of the People to Treat Us Well"

With the clarity of vision that hindsight provides, Cabeza de Vaca draws a definitive line at this place in the narration into a "before" and "after."[29] Once freed from their Mariames masters, the group reunited seems to step neatly and unequivocally into a world of friendly natives. Suddenly the tables of fear are turned: the natives now express enormous fear of the Spaniards, and Cabeza de Vaca and Oviedo feature this reaction in their narrations. Here is the negotiation of fear in a second sense, and the exceptions to the rule merely serve to support the argument. Oviedo and subsequent narrators interpret this fear as inspired by reverence, not terror. They offer a simple equation: where the Christians had formerly feared the irrational violence of the natives, the natives now appropriately recognized and feared the Christians' spiritual and cultural superiority. However, the evidence that Cabeza de Vaca presents requires a more complex explanation. Although accounts of healings and even resuscitations of the dead were frequent in missionary writings of the period for native North America, Cabeza de Vaca provides details as to how they were carried out.[30]

In Cabeza de Vaca's narrative, the full-scale healing practices begin with the Avavares, to whom the party fled upon leaving the Mariames.[31] Oviedo's narration lacks any account of healing among the Avavares (602), but Cabeza de Vaca's *Naufragios* elaborates them in detail (78). Accommodated on the day of their arrival in the dwellings of two shamans, the party is called upon the first night to cure certain native maladies of the head. There are two things to note here: the "healings" commenced with Castillo's curing of natives' headaches, at their request; this type of complaint would be of possibly psychosomatic origin and thus malleable to shamanic ritual.[32] As a result, the natives bring food—prickly pears and venison—in such quantity that Cabeza de Vaca does not know where to store it (78). He, Dorantes, and Estevanico go to the settlement, accompanied by "nuestros indios" whom he identifies as the Cutalchuches, and Cabeza de Vaca tells how he then cured a man who was to all appearances dead. More specifically, he says that the natives said that the man recovered. "This caused great wonder and fear, and throughout the land the people talked of nothing else" (83; Hodge, 78).

During the eight months that the Spaniards spent with the Avavares, people came from all over to be cured, most complaining of maladies of the head and alimentary tract.[33] Cabeza de Vaca explained that he and his companions were taken to be "children of the sun" (*hijos del sol*), and that during this time, all four members of their party became healers (83–84).[34] So effective were the cures—according to the reports of the natives—and so confident were the natives in them, that as soon as the Spaniards were among them the natives "thought that they would not die" (Cabeza de Vaca, 84).

Here the expectations of the group are a critical element. For Claude Lévi-Strauss, the shamanic complex, consisting of the three inseparable elements of shaman, sick person, and the public, is organized around the poles of the intimate experience of the shaman and of group consensus (173). In Cabeza de Vaca's narration, and in others of the area in this period, the role of social consensus is obvious. He and his fellows no doubt did cure some psychosomatic maladies, yet this point is subordinate to a more fundamental one: it is not that they became great shamans because they performed cures but rather that they performed cures because they were perceived to be great shamans.[35]

Citing a case close to the present subject, Lévi-Strauss provides an explanation of the phenomenon of the innocent bystander becoming a shaman and balancing attitudes of credulity and skepticism. The source is the account by M. C. Stevenson, an ethnographer who worked among the Zuni of New Mexico, of the case of an innocent boy accused of shamanism. Entering into a confession of magical powers as his best defense against the accusation of possessing them, the young boy persuaded his accusers of his magic and thereby satisfied them, corroborating their system of belief. Thus, the one whose actions had at first threatened the security of the group "became the guardian of its spiritual coherence."[36] The principle was the same in Cabeza de Vaca's case, and it was repeated with dozens of groups. Moreover, the number of cures cited by other sixteenth- and seventeenth-century travelers through the area supports the notion that the cures served to compensate for the unclear threat implicit or explicit in the white man's presence.

Miracle Cures and Mala Cosa

There is a native context for interpreting these events among the Avavares, although Oviedo, Herrera, and the others do not report it. Their suppression of the following tale is not surprising, given its remarkable account of bodily dismemberment and restoration. Cabeza de Vaca tells how the Avavares, as well as "those whom we left behind," which we can assume meant and included at least the Mariames, reported the existence of a man who, some fifteen or sixteen years earlier, that is in 1519 or 1520, had terrorized the people. This stranger had come into their homes, seized victims, and cut them open. This terrifying visitor was called, descriptively, "Mala Cosa" (Evil Thing; Cabeza de Vaca, 84).

Mala Cosa was described as bearded and short. Whenever he came upon the natives, their hair stood on end and they began to tremble. Carrying a torch, he would enter a house, select a man, and perform two surgical operations: with a large flint knife, he would cut open the side of whomever he chose, pull out the entrails, and cut out a piece therefrom to throw into the fire. Then he would lacerate one of the victim's arms in three places and sever the arm at the elbow. Next he would "pass his hand over the separated parts and the arm came together again, healing instantly" (Cabeza de Vaca, 84).[37] He had sometimes appeared during native ceremonies, occasionally dressed as a woman, other times as a man. He could send a hut flying through the air and ride it to the ground (85). Many times, the natives said, they gave him food to eat, but he never consumed it. Asking him whence he came, he pointed to the earth and said that his home was there below. Given the difficulties of communication, this account of Mala Cosa probably represents a fair summary of the information that Cabeza de Vaca received from the Avavares and others such as the Mariames.

Several features of this account stand as important guides to these people's assessment of the Spaniards' presence and activity. Mala Cosa was bearded, although they never were able to see his features clearly; thus he obviously resembled the Europeans. Being unlike the natives, he clearly came from some other place, just as the Europeans did. Though a terrorist and torturer, he was also a healer. This band of four strangers, so far as we know, did not harm, but did heal. Apparently the natives did make an association between the Spaniards and Mala Cosa. We need only recall Cabeza de Vaca's accounts of 1) the offering of highly prized flint stones to him for the resuscitation of an apparent dead man (83); 2) the offer (to them by all the natives) of much food; and 3) finally, and most importantly, the constant registering of great fear of the strangers.

According to Krieger's and the Campbells' readings of the Cabeza de Vaca account, the myth of bodily dismemberment that Cabeza de Vaca mentions would be associated with the Avavares-Caddoan peoples on both sides of the lower Nueces River in Texas.[38] Regrettably, the only primary documents on this area are those recording Cabeza de Vaca's experience.[39] Thus, there is a problem in pursuing the myth of bodily dismemberment he describes in the gap between his 1534–35 experience and the subsequent sources on these peoples that appear a century and a half later.[40] To date, I have found no similar accounts from reports by these sources.[41] Nevertheless, there are some analogies from the central valley of Mexico, if not from the northern Mexican area of the Coahuiltecas.

In materials collected as part of his research on Mexica (Aztec) language and culture, Fray Bernardino de Sahagún's account of "magicians and mountebanks" is pertinent. He tells of one called "the destroyer" (*el destrozador*) who would perform in the patios of the elite a daring stunt of cutting off hands, feet, and other parts and placing them at various locations. Then he would cover all with a red mantle, and the parts would grow back together as if they had not been cut asunder. At this point, he would reveal the restored body.[42] Ángel María Garibay K. describes this as a "curious case of magicianship in old Anahuac," a form of amusement that depended on visual suggestion. Sahagún, suggests Garibay, must have considered this phenomenon an enchantment, due to diabolical arts.[43] One malevolent character in Sahagún's catalog was a being who, out of malice and hatred, bewitched people and devoured the calves of their legs or their hearts. The victim would call on his attacker to be cured, and then give him the goods he wanted; Garibay notes that the verb for "to cure," *patia*, meant "to heal" in the medical sense as well as "to undo a magical spell."[44]

According to Cabeza de Vaca the natives, in order to attest the existence of Mala Cosa, brought people who bore scars in the very places where they said he had lacerated them (100). Cabeza de Vaca goes on to tell how the Christians responded that the man was evil and that, if the natives were to believe in the Christians' god and become Christians, they would not have to fear Mala Cosa, nor would he dare come to do those things to them. They should be assured that as long as the Christians were in their territory, Mala Cosa would not dare to set foot there. It is the natives' response to this speech that is of interest to us: "With this they were very pleased and lost a great part of the fear that they had" (85; my translation). Fear of what or whom? Of Mala Cosa, as Cabeza de Vaca seems to imply? I think, rather, that the fear they lost was of the Christians, due to the assurances that they gave that they *were not like* Mala Cosa as well as by their promise to protect the natives from him.

Mysterious nocturnal visitors doing bodily harm to native peoples and leaving evidence of their attacks is a motif not uncommon in other reports of European/ Amerindian contact. As in Cabeza de Vaca's narration about Mala Cosa, such bedevilments provided an occasion for the Christians to preach of their god and to offer their religion's protection of the natives from further harm. A pertinent incident is recorded by El Inca Garcilaso de la Vega in his history of the de Soto expedition to Florida. An Indian guide of the expedition, not yet baptized, was attacked at night and pummeled in his room by an intruder whose presence could be verified only by the victim's beaten and broken body. Identified as the devil, the intruder's flight was attributed to the demon's fear of Christians. The report of the attack became the motive for the preaching of Christianity and, in this case, the baptism of the faithful Marcos.[45]

The Spaniards slipped away from the Avavares, heading still in a general south-southwestward direction toward Pánuco (point 3 and southward). They passed on to the Maliacones and accompanied them in seed collecting. They next came to the Arbadaos, who were starving. Interestingly, they performed no cures in these circumstances and were subjected to labor so burdensome that here Cabeza de Vaca remarks that his own suffering made him recall the torments of Jesus Christ. Leaving the Arbadaos, they came to the Cuchendados, the first group they had seen to occupy more than one settlement at a time. Here the Spaniards were met by great fear. They performed cures, and the Cuchendados gave them food in abundance, depriving themselves in order to do so (Cabeza de Vaca, 89–90).

After his narration of the visit to the Cuchendados, Cabeza de Vaca pauses to describe all the groups encountered up until that time (summer 1535). In part, this parenthesis in his narration is a conclusion, for here ends that portion of his experience during which he and his companions had come to know well the native groups they encountered.[46] Among his general observations, two stand out: first, these are all warrior peoples who were so astute in protecting themselves from their enemies that one might think they "had been raised in Italy and in continuous wars" (91). When Cabeza de Vaca describes them as the most alert and ready warriors of all the peoples he has seen in the world (93), he is comparing them with the adversaries he had encountered during his military service in the Italian campaigns.[47] Second, he observes that all these peoples were expert at perceiving fear in others and at knowing how to manipulate it:

Whosoever would find them must be cautious and show no fear, or desire to have anything that is theirs. . . . If they discover any timidity or covetousness, they are a race that well discerns the opportunity for vengeance, and gather strength from the weakness of their adversaries. (94; Hodge, 86)

The survival of Cabeza de Vaca's party had depended on showing no fear, and now they had—thanks to their curing rituals and the news thereof that spread far and wide—opportunities of their own to instill fear. They were mediators between the groups that led them and those that received them, serving in the same slot in the paradigm occupied by the native women who were designated to serve as emissaries between warring groups and who had often ended the fighting and negotiated the peace (Cabeza de Vaca, 91, 93, 99, 111; Oviedo, 606). Others whose identity placed them outside the limits of the respective war communities could serve in similar roles. However, the Europeans and Estevanico were not merely mediators but mediators embued with magical powers. They were the magical elements in the drama that unfolded, and this becomes clear in the next episode, which occurs after their crossing the Río Grande.

Guided by some women who served them from the previous settlement of

Cuchendados, they crossed the river at a settlement of some one hundred huts (point 4; 98–99; Oviedo, 604). Here the people came out to greet them and received them with so much shouting and slapping of thighs that it caused a great fright. So great was the fear and agitation that these people suffered, says Cabeza de Vaca, that to arrive first to touch the Christians they crowded and almost crushed them. Without letting our feet touch the ground, he said, they took us to their homes. They crowded around the Spaniards so tightly that, once in the houses they had prepared for them, they forbade them to make any further ceremony or feast that night (99–100; Oviedo, 604).

Clearly, this reception reveals that this Cuchendado group considered the visitors to have magical powers: the natives rushed forward fearfully to touch and to make contact with these divine or magical beings. By lifting them up and carrying them, they meant to ensure that their magical powers would not enter the ground or contaminate it.[48] This potency perceived by the natives is confirmed in what follows.

The people greeted them with sacred ceremonial gourds filled with stones that they used only in dancing or in healing (99; Oviedo, 604). Cabeza de Vaca explains that no one apart from the indicated persons was allowed to use these objects, and "they say that those gourds have special powers [*virtud*] and that they come from the sky" (99; my translation). Two observations are pertinent here. The offering and receipt of the gourds confirms the association made by the natives between the special powers of the gourds and those of the Spaniards. Secondly, the natives did not have the gourds in their own region nor did they know their origin (*ni saben dónde las haya*); they came upon them floating in the rivers (99). Not knowing the ultimate origin of the gourds, they said they came from the sky. Here we have a first and important indication that "coming from the sky" is a way of expressing "origin unknown," although available translations make it apparent how often that cue has been missed.[49] We shall return to this problem of "sky origins" later.

After the natives passed the night of the Spaniards' arrival in celebration, the next day they brought all the people from that settlement "so that we could touch and bless them as we had done to the others with whom we had been" (100; my translation). Afterward these natives gave many arrows to the women from the other (Cuchendado) village who had come with the Cabeza de Vaca party. The key to this remarkable event, in which the new settlement brought forth their sacred gourds and gave itself over to the most extraordinary expressions of awe, is that the Cuchendado women who brought the strangers had sent scouts ahead to let the new village know of the impending arrival of the Spaniards and of their deeds of blessing and curing. This pattern of interaction will be continued throughout the rest of the journey, and the breakdown of the system will be seen by Cabeza de Vaca as a cause for much concern.

Pillages, Ritual and Real

At this juncture (points 4 to 5 on the map), a new custom came into use: according to Cabeza de Vaca, the natives who accompanied the Christians took bows and arrows, shoes and beads, if they had any, from those who came for curing, and placed these things before the Christians so that they would perform cures (100). Once blessed by the Spanish party, the natives went away saying they were healthy. Oviedo reports that the accompanying natives pillaged those who came forward for healing; they took what they had and even went through their houses robbing them of their possessions, "and it seemed that the victimized hosts took pleasure in their plight" (604; my translation).

Cabeza de Vaca is careful to express his chagrin at this wholesale sacking and tries to assure his readers how much he and his companions had opposed it, since it was wrong to do so much ill to "those who had received us so well" (101). At the same time, he recalls a greater apprehension, namely that the pillaging might have provoked conflict between the visiting and host groups. Yet, he explains, his own band of four was powerless to change it, or even to dare to punish those who did it. So they decided to suffer it until such time as they had the authority to change it. He explains that the victims consoled the Christians, saying that their properties were thus put to good use and that, ahead, they would be compensated by others who were rich in possessions.

It is clear that the pattern the Spanish party developed among the Coahuiltecas crossing the Río Grande into Nuevo León had been in the making since their escape from the Mariames and the healings done since Malhado. The following of native roads, the accompaniment by native groups, the advance messengers who foretold their arrival and arrived at an understanding with the new village as to the reception demanded of them, made possible the remarkable journey whose wonders Cabeza de Vaca often would repeat. At this point, however, the Spaniards decided to abandon their southward course and instead head west to the Mar del Sur (Pacific Ocean) (point 5). Yet instead of traveling westward, they were forced to head northwest in order to skirt the range of the Sierra Madre Oriental.[50]

One of the next episodes recorded by Cabeza de Vaca and repeated by Oviedo is revealing for what it tells about the motivations and manipulations of the marauding bands, in Cabeza de Vaca's account, and the desire to suppress it, substituting a purely religious interpretation, in Oviedo's. Arriving at sunset at a village of twenty huts, the Spanish party was received by the village's inhabitants with great weeping and sadness (104; Oviedo, 605). This episode in Cabeza de Vaca's narrative is crucial, for it reveals the source of these people's fear: "They received us weeping and with great sadness because they knew that wherever we went, all the people were sacked and robbed by those who accompanied us, and when they saw us alone, they lost their fear, and gave us some prickly pears and *not another single thing*" (104; translation and emphasis mine). Without their marauding army, the Christians were not feared and did not fare well.

An insight into the creation of subsequent interpretations is presented to us by Oviedo. He narrates the Spanish arrival at this village and also describes the weeping natives. However, he ignores or suppresses the information Cabeza de Vaca provides, explaining that the natives wept not out of fear of being sacked but rather out of spiritual devotion: "And they found the Indians weeping in devotion, and they received them, as it has been stated, as in other places, and they gave them food to eat from their own stores" (Oviedo, 605; my translation).

Returning to Cabeza de Vaca's account, we discover that the natives' generosity always depended on external motivation. The next day the marauders arrived, taking the people unprepared and off guard. The newcomers took all that they found, giving their victims no time to hide anything. Because of this, the inhabitants wept greatly and the robbers, to console them, told them that the Christians were "hijos del sol" (children of the sun) and that they had the power to cure the sick and to kill them, and they told "other lies even greater than these, as they know how to tell them when they feel it suits them" (104; my translation). And they told them to show the Spaniards much respect and to be careful not to anger them in any way, to give them all they had, and to try to take them to wherever there were many people. When they arrived, they should rob and sack the inhabitants, because such was the custom (104–5). Cabeza de Vaca reveals here that the fear of the strangers by the natives who did not know them was created by force and skillfully manipulated by those groups who did. This is clearly a fear produced by intimidation; it is not the fear inspired by reverence as taken up by Oviedo and reiterated by successive interpreters.[51]

Cabeza de Vaca goes on to tell how the marauders left, after having indicated to the current hosts the manner in which the Christians were to be treated and having robbed everything they had. The newly enlightened natives now began to treat the Christians "with the same fear and respect as had the others" (105). Their "conversion" consisted in learning how they might exploit the Spaniards' presence. Accompanying the Christians on three days' travel, they took them to well-populated areas and sent out messengers who proclaimed all the things that the others had taught them about the Christians and much more, "because all these people are greatly enamored of making up things and are very deceptive, especially where their personal interest is involved" (105, my translation). The Spaniards added the gourds to their repertoire, which Cabeza de Vaca said gave them greater authority (105). The natives who accompanied the Europeans robbed the new settlements, and since these were many and the pillagers few, they had to leave more than half their spoils (106).

Cabeza de Vaca's and Oviedo's accounts of the above episode offer differing interpretations of the actions and beliefs of the natives. Oviedo, at second hand, fails to see the armies of native marauders and interprets the new group's cowering anticipation and dread as spiritual sentiment or presentiment. Cabeza de Vaca sees the armies sweeping before him, their leaders telling their victims that they too can share in future spoils. Cabeza de Vaca's refusal to dismiss as extravagant and deceitful the native groups' claims about him and his fellows is the Europeans' own participation in the deceit (105).

The Europeans added gourds to their own repertoire to grant themselves the greater authority that Cabeza de Vaca admits had been exaggerated by the natives (105). In some respects, Oviedo's solution and the subsequent interpretations are the only possible ones. Cabeza de Vaca inadvertently reveals how the nonshaman, "with a mixture of cunning and good faith, progressively constructs the impersonation which is thrust upon him," as Lévi-Strauss observes (168). Cabeza de Vaca recognized the deception perpetrated by the natives (and enhanced by him and his companions) as a way of achieving a greater good: the making of peace among all the warring groups. Later, in the lands of Nueva Galicia once conquered by the Spaniards, this greater good will take the form of the peaceful resettlement of groups driven from their lands by Spanish slave hunters.

After following the skirts of the mountains for some fifty leagues, the Spanish party came to a village of forty huts; they encountered a mountain whose rocks contained iron and crossed a "very beautiful river" (point 6; 106; Oviedo, 606).[52] Continuing to head north-northwest, and being told of great copper deposits, Cabeza de Vaca sums up this part of their travels by saying that they passed through territories of so many types of people and diversity of languages that memory was inadequate to recount them all, and that the travelers always sacked the hosts; thus those who lost like those who gained were very content. He adds, "The number of our companions became so large that we could no longer control them" (Bandelier, 116).[53]

This was an area of great abundance of food, such as rabbits and deer, birds, quail, and other game (109; Oviedo, 606). Cabeza de Vaca observes that "everything that those people found and hunted and killed they placed before us, without them daring to take any single thing, even though they might be dying of hunger," and, "Everyone with the share he had been given came to us so that we could breathe on it and bless it; without it they would not dare to eat of it; and many times we brought with us three or four thousand persons" (109, my translation). Oviedo repeats how, without the Christians' blessing it first, the Indians would take no food: "And the Christians took what they wanted and blessed the rest; and with this practice they went over the entire road until arriving at the land of Christians" (606).

Naturally, the implication is that that act of breathing on, and blessing, the share of food that each was given was a sign of the reverence for the Christians and the power that they represented. More likely, however, given the sacking and robbing and the huge numbers of people, is the notion that this act was part of the negotiation between the marauding and the victim/host group, rather than between the Christians and either. Here, the role of the lord who accompanied them (*el principal de la gente que con nosotros venía*), mentioned briefly in a single remark, is likely to be the key figure in the negotiations: "Of each we took a little, and the remainder we gave to the principal personage of the people coming with us, directing him to divide it among the rest" (109; Hodge, 98).

It is probable that this lord was the one giving the commands, that it was he who organized the ritual blessing by the Christians as the way to exercise his own control. In this light, the blessing by the Christians was the sign of truce, signaling that food could be partaken without its possession being disputed. Given the enormous numbers of people, it was a way of organizing and systematizing the distribution of food, controlled by the natives' lords. The problem of checking this interpretation against other period sources and modern ethnographic studies is that there are no other European testimonies for this crucial portion of the itinerary, between present-day Coahuila and eastern Chihuahua in northern Mexico (points 6 to 7).

Cabeza de Vaca next describes a change in the rules of sacking, thus again suggesting the magical powers they had been assigned by the lords and crowds leading them forward. The victims no longer came forth with goods but rather awaited the newcomers in their huts, offering the Christians whatever they had, and their houses with them (110). He explains how he and his companions again turned everything over to the "chief personages who accompanied us, that they should divide them" (110; Hodge, 99), and how those thus robbed always joined the expedition, when there grew greatly the number of people who had to "make up their losses." He goes on to explain how, again, the new hosts were instructed not to hide anything but to surrender everything they had, because they could not keep the knowledge of it from the Christians. Furthermore, the Christians could make them die, because the sun had given the Christians the power to kill. So great, explains Cabeza de Vaca, were the fears the people suffered from this threat that, during the first days they were with the Spaniards, they were constantly trembling, without daring to speak or raise their eyes (110).

These fears were further extended by an epidemic that affected more than three hundred people and that occurred, coincidentally, after the Spaniards' anger and threats about not being led in the direction they wished to go.[54] The natives were so fearful, thinking that the Spaniards had caused these deaths out of their anger, that they dared neither to look the Christians in the face nor to raise their eyes from the ground (Oviedo, 607). For more than two weeks, none talked with any other nor did any child laugh or cry. One who did weep was carried away and scratched from head to toe in punishment (Cabeza de Vaca, 113; Oviedo, 607–8). Cabeza de Vaca remarks: "These terrors they imparted to all those who had lately come to know us, that they might give us whatever they had; for they [the marauders] knew we kept nothing and would relinquish all to them" (113; Hodge 101). In spite of Cabeza de Vaca's commentary, the generosity of the Spanish party was not the major attribute perceived. The magical or divine nature attributed to them by the natives was the source of the fear noted.

However, this magical power did not mean that the Spaniards were the principal parties in the negotiations between the marauding groups and their victims, but rather the catalysts to the exchange: they helped produce the desired pillaging and could be counted upon not to covet its rewards. In other words, the role the Spanish party played was not unlike that of the sacred gourds whose use they had taken up; the four strange men lent authority to the native groups just as the gourds had lent authority to the Spaniards (105). The Spanish party's presence legitimized the pillages and explained the deaths of the natives. Under these circumstances, the white and black strangers were feared as agents of destruction and death, and their apparent "generosity" in keeping nothing for themselves was irrelevant to the events that attended them. From the native point of view, the assignment of divine powers to the strangers and the attribution of deaths and cures to them would have been important factors within their field of interpretation. By emphasizing the sole action of the robbery and redistribution of goods, however, Cabeza de Vaca narrows the scope of the events he interprets. As a result, his discussion (not to mention those of Oviedo and subsequent historians) of native actions and reactions is much more restricted than the information he imparts about them.

As the Cabeza de Vaca party traversed Coahuila and came upon the first agricultural peoples they had met since leaving Florida on their barges, Cabeza de Vaca tells how another new custom came into use among these so-called "people of the cows" (point 7).[55] Instead of coming out to the roads to receive the Spaniards, as previous groups had done, the people they encountered now stayed in their houses, and had other houses made for the Spaniards. All were calm and had their faces turned to the wall, heads lowered and eyes covered, with all their possessions arranged in the middle of the floor (114–15; Oviedo, 606), "and they had nothing they did not bestow" (Hodge, 103).

Cabeza de Vaca tells how he and his party brought peace to all: "Through all these lands, those who had wars with each other later became friends in order to come to see us and bring us all they had, and in this manner we left the entire land in peace" (120, my translation). They also told them about Christianity, as best they could. Oviedo, not surprisingly, details this discussion, saying that the natives commended themselves to the all-powerful god and believed that the Christians had come from heaven, and they were much pleased when they were told some things about it (610). Oviedo's claims are extravagant in comparison to Cabeza de Vaca's account. There, the only indication of native reaction is his declaration that henceforth, when the sun rose, the natives raised their hands to the sky with great shouting and afterward ran them over their bodies; and they did the same when the sun set (120). Cabeza de Vaca himself seemed content with this description, and added that, if the mutual understanding of language had permitted, they would have left them all Christians. He ended the chapter by declaring: "They are a people of good condition and substance, capable in any pursuit" (120; Hodge, 108).

People from the Sky

Oviedo's interpretation of what *gente del cielo* meant begins a long line of interpretations and translations to the effect that the phrase meant "people from heaven." Such a practice was not without antecedents; the reports of many first encounters, starting with those of Christopher Columbus in the Antilles, insisted that the natives understood that the European strangers came "from heaven." The interpreters of Columbus's text, from Las Casas to Don Hernando Colón and Hernán Pérez de Oliva, all claimed that the natives meant that the Spaniards "came down from heaven." Only the ethnographic text of Fray Ramón Pané, and the treatise on it by Hernán Pérez de Oliva, offer more reasonable interpretations.[56] These serve to support the explicit findings in Cabeza de Vaca's text.[57]

At this point in the narration, Cabeza de Vaca introduces a notion that has become the subject of erroneous interpretations. After telling of the Spaniards' arrival in the land of *frijoles* and *calabazas* and the "people of the cows" (point 7), Cabeza de Vaca tells how native groups came from far and wide to be touched and blessed by the Spaniards, and how native women in their retinue who gave birth came forward, asking that their newborn infants be touched and blessed. Here Cabeza de Vaca makes a declaration, the final phrase of which was omitted in the 1555 and all later editions:[58] "Among all these peoples, it was held for very certain that we came from the sky, because about all the things that they do not understand or have information regarding their origins, they say that such phenomena come from the sky" (1542, fol. 55v, my translation).[59] Only the Bandelier translation, which is based on the 1542 edition,[60] carries the phrase.

This casts a different light on the natives' apprehension of the Europeans and Estevanico. Certainly "coming from the sky" continues to have a magical connotation, because both the ritual gourds and the never-before-seen black and white men are associated by them with extraordinary powers. Nevertheless, the sense of the premonition or intuition of Christianity through the interpretation of the concept as "heavenly" or divine in the Christian sense must be set aside. Cabeza de Vaca makes no such claim and is careful to give as precise a meaning as possible to the notion of sky origins.

A subsequent reference to "people from the sky" comes at the Río Yaqui (point 11), where Cabeza de Vaca and his companions saw their first evidence of Europeans. At this river, where they arrived around Christmas 1535,[61] they found a native with ornaments of iron that he had obtained from white men like themselves; Castillo saw a little buckle from a sword belt with a horseshoe nail on a native's neckpiece. Taking it from the Indian, they asked what it was, and he replied that it had come from the sky. They questioned him further, and he said that some men with beards like the Christians, who had come from the sky,[62] had arrived at that river, and had horses and lances and swords and had killed two of the natives with their lances (122).[63] Again, the question of "origin unknown" is handled by the natives by attribution to the sky. However, the Spaniards' brutal murders by lancing of two natives leaves no doubt as to the negative value assigned to these visitors. Of magical and extraordinary powers they were, but hardly were they seen as heavenly visitors long awaited. Rather, they were the agents of death and destruction. Nevertheless, the interpretation of these remarks as evidence of heavenly or divine intervention was taken up readily by subsequent European interpreters of the Cabeza de Vaca account.

Nuño de Guzmán's Conquest of Nueva Galicia

From this point on in the narration, from the Río Yaqui to Compostela (points 11 to 14), Cabeza de Vaca's narrative is concerned with the effects of the conquest of Nueva Galicia, which had been undertaken by Nuño Beltrán de Guzmán in 1530–31, when he was president of the first Audiencia de México (the supreme judicial court of New Spain).[64] Cabeza de Vaca's account of the trip south from the Yaqui is a description of depopulated lands and sick and thin people (123). Interestingly, accounts of healing, in both the Cabeza de Vaca and Oviedo accounts, are all but absent. Nuño de Guzmán's destruction of these lands and peoples is depicted from the native point of view in the Lienzo de Tlaxcala (figs. 2 and 3), from the destruction of Michoacan northward to the area of Chiametla, the area immediately south of Culiacán,[65] the latter area being where Cabeza de Vaca and his companions spent two and a half months resettling the native population (point 13).

The work described by Cabeza de Vaca in the last few chapters of his *relación* is precisely that of pacifying or resettling abandoned lands. Among eighteenth- to twentieth-century commentaries on the work, this section of the narrative has been given far less emphasis than in the original. The real challenge was to come not from hostile natives but from the Spaniards' hostile countrymen, after they had crossed the Río Yaqui in Sonora and continued to head south. "We always found more signs of Christians," said Cabeza de Vaca, and although he does not make explicit reference to the slave-hunting activities of Nuño de Guzmán's men, he acknowledges them on recounting how his party promised the natives they found that they would neither murder nor enslave them, nor carry them away from their lands nor do them any other harm (123).

This is a third and final moment in the negotiation of fear: Cabeza de Vaca

FIGURE 2. Nuño de Guzmán's conquest of Michoacán as portrayed in the sixteenth-century Lienzo de Tlascala. From Alfredo Chavero, *Antigüedades mexicanas* (Mexico City, 1892). Courtesy William L. Clements Library, Ann Arbor, Mich.

FIGURE 3. Nuño de Guzmán's conquest of Chiametla, with the help of Tlascalan allies, in the Lienzo de Tlascala. From ibid.

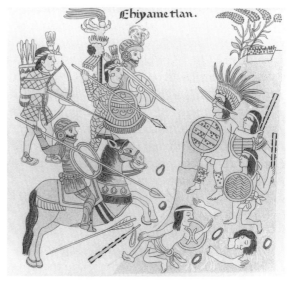

and his party are asked to negotiate away the terrible fears of the natives who have been terrorized by the slave-hunting Christians. Cabeza de Vaca does not mince words:

The sight was one of infinite pain to us . . . the people thin and weak. . . . We bore a share in the famine along the whole way . . . and they related how the Christians at other times had come through the land, destroying and burning the towns, carrying away half the men and all the women and boys. . . . They would not, nor could they till the earth, but preferred to die rather than live in dread of such cruel usage as they had received. (Hodge, 110)

His advocacy of humane treatment for these peoples makes him a Lascasian by experience rather than reading. In fact, his own return to Spain coincides with Fray Bartolomé de Las Casas's "peaceful conversion" experiments in Vera Paz in Guatemala (1537–50).[66] To attract the natives to Christianity and obedience to his Imperial Majesty, kind treatment is the "only way," according to Cabeza de Vaca: "This is the road most sure, and no other" (124, my translation).

With these remarks, Cabeza de Vaca anticipates Las Casas's first major work, *The Only Way to Attract the People to the True Religion*.[67] Cabeza de Vaca's account echoes the type of peaceful conversion attempted by Fray Pedro de Córdoba on the Pearl Coast, Fray Jacobo de Testera in Yucatán, and Las Casas in Vera Paz.[68] Although Las Casas was a layman when he undertook his 1521 peaceful conversion experiment in Cumaná (present-day Venezuela), Cabeza de Vaca represents, de facto, the only lay attempt to do the same completely without armed assistance. The radical character of Cabeza de Vaca's effort, and the success claimed by him and borne out by others, make his account an ideal conquest history. Before considering why this remarkable portion of the Cabeza de Vaca experience was downplayed in subsequent interpretations, it will be necessary to follow again the unfolding story.

Crossing the Sinaloa River, Cabeza de Vaca's party met Diego de Alcaraz, whose men's acts of cruelty had driven away their native suppliers of food and labor (point 12). When Cabeza de Vaca fulfilled Alcaraz's request of bringing hidden stores of food out of the hills and six hundred native men came along, the Alcaraz party expected to be able to enslave the natives who had succored them. The "trial by fire" occurred when Cabeza de Vaca negotiated away Alcaraz's demands by giving him precious goods, including five "emeralds" that Cabeza de Vaca had received from some natives earlier. Cabeza de Vaca's most salient claim to leadership and heroic service to his king occurs here, on persuading his compatriots to desist from their nefarious plan.[69]

As in the case of the shamanic rituals, Cabeza de Vaca's authority to direct the natives was drawn from the people themselves. His party spent two and one half months at Culiacán (point 13) at the request of Captain Melchior Díaz, and here Cabeza de Vaca succeeded in resettling the area, which the accounts of Guzmán's *entradas* (incursions) had shown to be one of the most well-populated and well-developed areas in the Indies. Cabeza de Vaca's fear that he would not be able to accomplish this feat hinged on the fact that his group no longer had with them "any native of our own, nor any of those who accompanied us according to custom, intelligent in these affairs" (132; Hodge, 117). However, there were two captives of the same group, who had been with the Alcaraz party when Cabeza de Vaca and his men encountered them.[70] Thus, these two natives had seen the huge number of natives that accompanied them, and they were familiar with the "great authority and command we carried and exercised throughout those parts, the wonders we had worked, the sick we had cured, and the many things besides we had done" (132; Hodge, 117). So they sent the two captives out with a "gourd of those we were accustomed to bear in our hands, which had been our principal insignia and evidence of rank" (133; Hodge, 117). In seven days, they brought back three lords of those people who had rebelled (133; Oviedo, 613, agrees with this account).

Melchior Díaz recited to them the *Requerimiento*, the declaration by which the natives were given the option to accept Spanish dominion or war, slavery, and death: if they chose to be Christian, they would be their friends; if not, they would be treated very badly and would be taken as slaves to other lands (133–34; Oviedo, 613). The reading of the *Requerimiento* had been legally imposed in 1526 as a requisite feature of Spanish conquests, and it presumably would have been applied in the conquest of Florida, had the Narváez expedition enjoyed a more felicitous fate.[71] To its reading at Culiacán in 1536, Cabeza de Vaca reports, the natives replied through their interpreter that they would serve God and become Christians (134).

Cabeza de Vaca tells how they then instructed the Indians, who represented those from the Río Petatán (Sinaloa) and the sierras, to resettle and place a cross at the entrances to their homes. When Christians came, they were to go out and receive them with crosses in their hands, rather than bows or arms, and give them to eat of what they had. If they did this, the Christians would not harm them, but would be their friends (134). They agreed. According to Cabeza de Vaca, Melchior Díaz gave them blankets and treated them very well, so that all returned to their homes, including the two captives who had served as intermediaries. All this was noted down by a notary and before many witnesses (135).

With the news of the returning natives, more came down to visit the Spaniards, bringing them beads and feathers. They commanded the natives to build churches, and Cabeza de Vaca notes that "until that time, none had been raised" (135). That is, no realization of the evangelizing mission had occurred in the five years since the arrival of the Guzmán expeditions. The other important event was the "covenant with God made by the Captain" Melchior Díaz neither to invade nor to consent to invasions, nor to enslave any peoples; and he would do this until the king, the governor, or the viceroy determined what ought to be done (135).[72]

Now Cabeza de Vaca presents two reports as to how the natives went about resettling the depopulated areas. One comes from natives arriving at San Miguel on 1 April 1536, when the Cabeza de Vaca party arrived; the other report came two weeks later, when Alcaraz returned with his party to say that the "Indians had come down and peopled the plain":

The towns were inhabited which had been tenantless and deserted, the residents, coming out to receive them with crosses in their hands, had taken them to their houses, giving of what they had, and the Christians had slept among them over night. They were surprised at a thing so novel; but, as the natives said they had been assured of safety, it was ordered that they should not be harmed, and the Christians took friendly leave of them. (Hodge, 119–20)

At this point, Cabeza de Vaca's narrative comes to its plenitude as a treatise on Christian colonization:

God in His infinite mercy is pleased that in the days of your Majesty, under your might and dominion, these nations should come to be thoroughly and voluntarily subject to the Lord, who has created and redeemed us. We regard this as certain, that your Majesty is he who is destined to do so much, not difficult to accomplish; for in the two thousand leagues we journeyed on land, and in boats on water, and in that we travelled unceasingly for ten months after coming out of captivity, we found neither sacrifices nor idolatry. (Hodge, 120; see also Oviedo, 614)

The skills of the Cabeza de Vaca party to negotiate between groups and work with native strategies of contact and movement had prepared them well for the challenge later to be placed upon them by the Spanish colonizers of Nueva Galicia: "Throughout all these countries the people who were at war immediately became friends, that they might come to meet us, and bring what they possessed. In this way, we left all the land at peace" (Hodge, 97, 107). Hostility and war were replaced by negotiation and exchange through the "magical" powers of these three Spaniards and one black man from Azamor.

Melchior Díaz's recitation of the *Requerimiento*, the devastation seen in the hundred leagues' journey from Culiacán to Compostela, and Nuño de Guzmán's reception of the Cabeza de Vaca party, fit into the theme of the miracle of pacification as part of the ideology of empire.[73] From Compostela to Mexico-Tenochtitlán, now Spanish, not Amerindian, natives lined the roadways to greet these extraordinary survivors, who were received as well by Hernando Cortés and the Viceroy Antonio de Mendoza. Cabeza de Vaca and his party had not only survived hardship; they had survived their own fears and learned to manipulate those of others. At the same time, they came to protect those others from the source of the greatest fear of all.

The Miracle of Pacification
and the Ideology of Empire

The accounts of Oviedo, and over half a century later Antonio de Herrera, agree on two crucial aspects found in Cabeza de Vaca's account: the curing episodes and the final miracles of the pacification of the native peoples. The episodes of healing spread over chapters 15 through 31 of the thirty-eight-chapter Cabeza de Vaca account. The culmination toward which these events, called "miraglos" by Oviedo, moved was the complete pacification of the land and its inhabitants as narrated in Cabeza de Vaca's chapters 35 and 36.

I insist upon pacification of the land and the people and not the religious conversion of their souls as the effective denouement of the tale because Cabeza de Vaca himself underscored the fact that conversion did not take place (125); he tells how they tried to make the natives understand that the deity Aguar was really the Christian god.[74] Yet these are only penultimate gestures, for the finalization of all these efforts is the "pacification" of the territory, that is, the resettlement of groups in their own native areas after having been frightened or driven off by the Spanish slaving parties. In Cabeza de Vaca's narrative as in Oviedo's, the most dramatic confrontation was that which took place between countrymen, between Cabeza de Vaca's group and the Spanish slave hunters.

Cabeza de Vaca described the contestants in this moral struggle and defended his own position by placing on the lips of the natives the arguments by which he refuted the demands of his enemies. This speech is in itself a pamphlet on the virtues of peaceful conquest. The slavers had their interpreter tell the natives that the Cabeza de Vaca group had been lost a long time and were men of little luck and valor and that they, the slave traffickers, were the true lords whom the natives should serve and obey. According to Cabeza de Vaca, the natives replied that the "Christians" (the Spanish slaving party) lied: the Cabeza de Vaca group came from where the sun rose, the others came from where it set; Cabeza de Vaca and his fellows cured the sick, while the others killed those who were well; Cabeza de Vaca and his companions were naked and barefoot, while the others came dressed and carried lances and rode horses; Cabeza de Vaca and all had no greed but rather gave back everything they were given and took nothing for themselves; the others had no other goal than to rob all that they could, and never gave anything to anyone (132). By the light of their natural reason, Cabeza de Vaca implies, these people recognized good and evil, and followed the saintly example of the Cabeza de Vaca group in promising to accept the Christian gospel. Furthermore, they were persuaded by those whom they so much admired to return to the care and cultivation of their native lands.

That this was the culmination of their experience, in Cabeza de Vaca's view, is easily argued from the fact that immediately after commenting on the natives' successful resettlement, the author directs himself in the next sentence to his king. As noted earlier, he implores Charles to see to their full Christianization, a goal Cabeza de Vaca saw as possible and in fact "not difficult to achieve" (137). Cabeza de Vaca thus insists upon his triumph over his personal enemies and his service to god and king, by bringing the natives peacefully to submission and resettlement without the force of arms. That this was seen as the truly admirable achievement of Cabeza de Vaca and his noble companions is made explicit in the interpretations of Oviedo.

Oviedo painted the conflict in full color, and, in case his readers did not understand the point, he added an aside:

Does it seem to you, Christian reader, that this conduct and exercise of the four pilgrims is lenient in contrast to that of the Spaniards who were in that land? or that there is cause to reflect upon the fact that some went about attacking and enslaving people, as has been said, and that others went about curing the sick and performing miracles? (612, my translation)

He told how the four survivors were asked to give an account of their experiences to be sent to the emperor, and he described the topic as "the manner in which they came and brought those peoples who followed them in peace and with good will" (612). To my mind, Oviedo's reading confirms the fact that the object sought and achieved was the resettlement of the native peoples of Culiacán and Chiametla (now Nueva Galicia). His reading thus bears out the final, unequivocal mes-

FIGURE 4. Nuño de Guzmán's torture and execution of the Caltzontzin of Michoacán. From the Théodore de Bry Latin edition (Frankfurt, 1598) of Bartolomé de Las Casas's *Brief Account of the Destruction of the Indies*. Courtesy John Carter Brown Library, Brown University.

sage Cabeza de Vaca communicated and that represented a most pressing issue of his time.

Aside from the evidence provided by the accounts themselves, legislative history also reveals the importance of the resettlement issue. The story of Cabeza de Vaca's successful resettlement of native peoples in the areas devastated by Nuño de Guzmán's conquests represented a triumph not *of* the law but *over* the law. With or without the Second Audiencia de México's total abolition of slavery,[75] the reports provided by Cabeza de Vaca represented the triumph of conquest as understood by López de Gómara, as he commented on the failure of the Narváez expedition: "Whoever fails to populate the lands does not make a good conquest; without conquering the land, the people will not be converted. Thus, the maxim of the conqueror must be to people the land."[76]

Throughout the decade of Cabeza de Vaca's first edition, Nuño de Guzmán had attempted to defend his conquests and his administrative record against criminal charges. Accounts of his reign of terror appeared in 1552 in Las Casas's *Brevísima relación de la destrucción de las Indias* and Gómara's *Historia general de las Indias*. Both emphasized Guzmán's torture and execution of the Caltzontzin of Michoacán, the most wealthy and powerful lord of Mexico after Moctezuma (fig. 4).[77] Guzmán's cruelty is well documented by the testimony of eyewitness sources in the *Proceso* against Guzmán.[78] In contrast, Cabeza de Vaca provided what was, to date, the most successful and the most peaceful of conquests. It was the prototype of expeditions that were to be called, according to Philip II's 1573 laws, not "conquests" but rather "acts of pacification."

Epilogue

In spite of the neat narrative resolution of an exemplary conquest conduct reported by Cabeza de Vaca and celebrated by subsequent interpreters, there are several questions left open. One is the issue of the actual source of fear. At both extremes of the narration of cures, that is at their initiation on Malhado and among those carried out in northwestern Mexico, death and epidemics accompanied the Spaniards. From the natives' perspective, since the strangers did not die, they had power over death and evidently the power to extend it over others. The natives' fear of the Spaniards and Estevanico was the fear of the death that these strangers all too often brought by their very presence, in the dozens of encounters that occurred among communities that had never known the parties of slave hunters.

A second problem concerns the native interpretation of the Europeans as being the divine "children of the sun" (not the "people from Heaven"). Although it is impossible to resolve here what it meant to the various groups who, according to Cabeza de Vaca, used it to identify the Spaniards, it is clear that Cabeza de Vaca expressed ambivalence about this as a belief. Among the Avavares, he said, the strangers were thought to be "hijos del sol." Yet subsequently he described how the natives instructed other groups to spread this account of the Spaniards in order to inspire aboriginal generosity toward them. Did he see this declaration not as the belief of some native groups but as a ruse perpetrated by others? Or was his description concerned with his assessment of native societies and with his views on how they should be colonized? We recall that he later proclaimed that he had witnessed no idolatry, as he presented a case for the peaceful subjugation and conversion of these cultures. In Cabeza de Vaca's view, were these native groups the deceivers or the deceived regarding belief in solar divinity?

Third, there is the problem of religious conversion to Christianity itself, the very heart of the colonialism debate. Cabeza de Vaca rejected all wishful thinking about the natives' conversion. With regard to his own experiences, he had no illusions about religious conversion being possible, due to the great gap in communication caused by mutual ignorance of languages. Yet Oviedo and the others who had not had Cabeza de Vaca's direct experience fell into the trap of assigning attitudes of religious devotion to the natives. The irony of their doing so was that it meant that they accepted the testimony and the interpretations offered by the natives, or rather those attributed to the natives by Cabeza de Vaca and his companions. What Cabeza de Vaca's account reveals perhaps more clearly than most colonial writings is the fact that conquest histories could not do *with* the natives (that is, convert them easily to Christianity) and yet could not do *without* them (that is, do without some type of experience with Christians interpreted to have some tinge of the supernatural). In the end, those who would promote the interests of Christian empire were required to accept the interpretations of those (the natives) whom they considered inadequate to judge it and perhaps unworthy to share it.

Finally, Jacques Lafaye's essay on the prevalent interpretations of the Cabeza de Vaca account reminds us of the degree to which Cabeza de Vaca's resettlement of native territories subsequently was ignored or suppressed. Eighteenth-century accounts, such as those of Fray Matías de la Mota Padilla, Antonio Ardoino, and especially Fray Pablo de Beaumont, paid little or no attention to Cabeza de Vaca's account of the resettlement activities. A familiar generalization is borne out once again: the further away we move from foundational acts (even those of colonialism), the more irrelevant that founding becomes. What takes their place instead is apology, that is the apology for what went before and a rigidity of interpretation in which authors from the foundational period itself would have found it difficult to recognize themselves. All traces of shamanic ritual had been replaced by missionary faith healing, and the negotiation of fear had been substituted by the triumph of the faith.

It is not necessary, however, to go to eighteenth-century interpretations of Cabeza de Vaca's account to contemplate the distance between that which was reported and that which was understood. We need only to return to Cabeza de Vaca's visit to court in 1537 and contemplate the distance between what he said, about the poverty of "Florida," and what the other noble gentlemen around him understood, that it was the richest country in the world. One can only imagine what reports Cabeza de Vaca whispered into the emperor's ear, or in those of his kinsmen Baltasar de Gallegos and Cristóbal de Espindola, who decided to go with de Soto. Yet one thing seems sure: whatever he said about his own experiences, it seems likely to have been misunderstood.

Notes

I would like to thank Sabine MacCormack for her helpful commentary, and the John Simon Guggenheim Memorial Foundation and the University of Michigan for their support of research contributing to this paper.

1. Gentleman of Elvas, *The Narrative of the Expedition of Hernando de Soto*, trans. Buckingham Smith, ed. Theodore H. Lewis, in *Spanish Explorers in the Southern United States, 1528–1543*, ed. Frederick W. Hodge and Theodore H. Lewis (1907; reprint ed., New York, 1959), 132–272; further references in the text.

2. The full title of Cabeza de Vaca's published relation is *La relación que dio Alvar Núñez Cabeza de Vaca de lo acaescido en las Indias en la armada donde yua por governador Pánfilo de Narváez desde el año de veynte y siete. . . .* The title *Naufragios* came into use after it had appeared in the heading of the 1555 edition's table of contents: "Tabla de los capítulos contenidos en la presente relación y naufragios del governador Alvar Núñez Cabeza de Vaca" (Madrid, 1555), fol. 55r. The edition used here is *Relación de los naufragios y comentarios de Alvar Núñez Cabeza de Vaca*, vol. 1, ed. Manuel Serrano y Sanz (Madrid, 1906); references cited in the text. Cabeza de Vaca repeats this account in the brief *relación* he wrote of the journey that extended from the original 1527 departure of the Narváez expedition to the arrival at the bay of Espíritu Santo, off the Texas coast. This unpublished and undated *relación*, found in the Archivo general de Indias of Seville, is reproduced in the *Colección de documentos inéditos relativos al descubrimiento, conquista, y colonización de las posesiones españolas en América y Oceanía*, 55 vols. (Madrid, 1864–84; hereafter *DII*), 14:269–79; see p. 278.

3. See, for example, Walter Brooks Drayton Henderson, *The New Argonautica: An Heroic Poem in Eight Cantos of the Voyage Among the Stars of the Immortal Spirits of Sir Walter Raleigh, Sir Francis Drake, Ponce de León, and Nuñez da Vaca* (New York, 1927); John Upton Terrell, *Journey into Darkness* (New York, 1962); Helen Rand Parish, *Estebanico* (New York, 1976); Daniel Panger, *Black Ulysses* (Athens, Ohio, 1982).

4. My thanks to Sabine MacCormack for specific suggestions in conceptualizing this paper.

5. Donald Chipman, "In Search of Cabeza de Vaca's Route Across Texas: An Historiographical Survey," *Southwestern Historical Quarterly* 91, no. 2 (October 1987): 142–43, persuasively argues that the most recent and reliable interpretations of the Cabeza de Vaca route across Texas and Mexico are those proposed by Alex D. Krieger, "Un nuevo estudio de la ruta seguida por Cabeza de Vaca a través de Norte América" (Ph.D. diss., Mexico City, 1955); Krieger, "The Travels of Alvar Núñez Cabeza de Vaca in Texas

and Mexico," in *Homenaje a Pablo Martínez del Río en el vigésimoquinto aniversario de la primera edición de "Los orígenes americanos"* (Mexico City, 1961; references cited in the text), 459–74; and T. N. and T. J. Campbell, *Historic Indian Groups of the Choke Canyon Reservoir and Surrounding Area, Southern Texas* (San Antonio, Tex., 1981). Other historical scholars of the area such as Robert S. Weddle, *Spanish Sea: The Gulf of Mexico in North American Discovery, 1500–1685* (College Station, Tex., 1985), 203, 206; and W. W. Newcomb, Jr., "Karankawa," in *Handbook of North American Indians*, vol. 10, *Southwest*, ed. Alfonso Ortiz (Washington, D.C., 1983), 366, agree that the proposals of Krieger and the Campbells best coordinate the original sources with the topography, ethnology, and plant and animal life of the regions concerned. Krieger's map (463) is reproduced here.

6. Gonzalo Fernández de Oviedo was in Santo Domingo at the time. His account appeared in his *Historia general y natural de las Indias*, ed. José Amador de los Ríos (Madrid, 1851–55; hereafter Oviedo, with further references in the text), book 35, chaps. 1–7. Oviedo evidently wrote his own account before he saw Cabeza de Vaca's published version of 1542, from which he subsequently added information to his own book 35, chap. 7 (1853), 3:614–18. See Henry R. Wagner, *Alvar Núñez Cabeza de Vaca: Relación* (Berkeley, 1924), 7.

7. Chipman, "Cabeza de Vaca's Route," 127–28.

8. One additional survivor of the Narváez expedition, Juan Ortiz, was found inland from Charlotte Harbor or Tampa Bay in present-day Florida by Hernando de Soto in 1539 or 1540. Ortiz had lived among the natives for twelve years; upon joining the de Soto expedition, he served as an interpreter until his death in 1542. See Gentleman of Elvas, *Narrative of de Soto*, 149–52, 158, 224; El Inca Garcilaso de la Vega, *The Florida of the Inca*, trans. John Grier Varner and Jeannette Johnson Varner (Austin, Tex., 1962), 59, 63–75, 78–84.

9. T. N. Campbell, "Coahuiltecans and Their Neighbors," in *Handbook of North American Indians*, 10:ix, 343–44.

10. The lack of systematic investigation of unpublished archival documentation in Europe and America and limited archaeological investigations are among the reasons for this gap in information; ibid., 344.

11. Campbell and Campbell, *Historic Indian Groups*, 1; Campbell, "Coahuiltecans," 353.

12. These are the accounts of the Nuño de Guzmán expeditions of 1530–31, that of Diego de Guzmán (1533), Fray Marcos de Niza (1538), the reports of the Viceroy Antonio de Mendoza in the 1530s, the Coronado expedition of 1540, and that of Antonio de Espejo in 1582.

13. See Francisco López de Gómara, *Historia general de las Indias y vida de Hernán Cortés*, 2 vols. (1552; Caracas, 1979), 1:68–69; Antonio de Herrera y Tordesillas, *Historia general de los hechos de los castellanos en las islas y tierra firme del mar océano*, 17 vols. (1601–15; Madrid, 1953), vol. 12, decade 6; Fray Antonio Tello, *Crónica miscelánea de la Sancta Provincia de Xalisco*, 3 vols. (early 17th c.; Guadalajara, 1968), 1:247, 253; Fray Matías Angel de la Mota Padilla, *Historia del reino de Nueva Galicia en la America Septentrional* (1742; Guadalajara, 1973), 80–81; Antonio Ardoino, *Examen apologético de la histórica narración de los naufragios, peregrinaciones, i milagros de Alvar Núñez Cabeza de Baca en las tierras de la Florida i del Nuevo México* (1736), 13–14.

14. Jacques Lafaye, "Los 'milagros' de Alvar Núñez Cabeza de Vaca, 1527–1536," in *Mesías, cruzadas, utopías: El judeo-cristianismo en las sociedades ibéricas*, trans. Juan José Utrilla (Mexico City, 1984), 65–84.

15. Enrique Pupo-Walker, "Pesquisas para una nueva lectura de los *Naufragios* de Alvar

Núñez Cabeza de Vaca," *Revista iberoamericana* 140 (July–September 1987): 517–39; Pupo-Walker, "Los *Naufragios* de Alvar Núñez Cabeza de Vaca: Notas sobre la relevancia antropológica del texto," *Revista de Indias* 47, no. 181 (1987): 755–76; Maureen Ahern, "The Semiosis of Miracles in *La relación* of Alvar Núñez Cabeza de Vaca, 1542," Paper presented at the 12th International Congress of the Latin American Studies Association, 18–20 April 1985, Albuquerque, N.M.; Ahern, "Signs of Power: The Cross and the Gourd in the *Relaciones* by Alvar Núñez Cabeza de Vaca and Fray Marcos de Niza," Paper presented at the Symposium on Colonial Literature and Historiography, Kentucky Modern Language Conference, 22 April 1985, Lexington; Ahern, "*Cruz y calabaza*: The Appropriation of Ritual Signs in the *Relaciones* of Alvar Núñez Cabeza de Vaca and Fray Marcos de Niza," in *Early Images of the New World: Transfer and Creation*, ed. Robert E. Lewis and Jerry M. Williams (forthcoming).

16. W. W. Newcomb, Jr., *The Indians of Texas: From Prehistoric to Modern Times* (Austin, Tex., 1961), 75, describes this practice according to the principle of "contagious magic" whereby the recipients are expected to receive the special powers of the donors.

17. My translation. I have also consulted translations of Cabeza de Vaca by Frederick W. Hodge, *The Narrative of Alvar Núñez Cabeza de Vaca*, in *Spanish Explorers*, 12–136 (hereafter Hodge, with references in the text); and Fanny Bandelier, *The Narrative of Alvar Núñez Cabeza de Vaca* (1905; reprint ed., Barre, Mass., 1972; hereafter Bandelier, with references in text).

18. The success with which Cabeza de Vaca and his fellows adapted themselves to the circumstances is underscored by the fact that, on another part of the island during that first winter, five Spaniards engaged in cannibalism in order to sustain themselves: "Five Christians, of a mess [quartered] on the coast, came to such extremity that they ate their dead; the body of the last one only was found unconsumed"; Cabeza de Vaca, *Relación*, 52; Hodge, *Narrative*, 49.

19. Oviedo, *Historia general*, 592, seems confused on this score, saying Cabeza de Vaca suffered slave labor for five years, while telling also that he became a trader. Cabeza de Vaca's own account is clear: he had complete freedom of movement and action during that time.

20. According to Krieger, "Travels of Cabeza de Vaca," 464, the distance of a league in Cabeza de Vaca's account was about three miles. Thus, Cabeza de Vaca's trading journeys carried him over some 120 to 150 miles of territory.

21. Angus MacKay, *La España de la edad media desde la frontera hasta el imperio, 1000–1500*, trans. Angus MacKay and Salustiano Moreta (Madrid, 1985), 222.

22. Ibid., 214.   23. Ibid., 215.

24. Newcomb, "Karankawa," 360.

25. The chronicler Oviedo reports the same events: the Quevenes gave the names of the murdered Spaniards, told of the sufferings and mistreatment of the other survivors, made death threats against their two interlocuters, and shot warning arrows into the two men's chests; *Historia general*, 592. (A printer's or other error makes Dorantes, not Cabeza de Vaca, the protagonist in these particular events in Oviedo's account (593). The subsequent passage confirms the error, because the subject of the sentence is described as meeting Dorantes and Castillo.)

26. Weddle, *Spanish Sea*, 198, identifies the natives by whom the Spaniards were terrorized as Karankawas.

27. Krieger, "Travels of Cabeza de Vaca," 466; Campbell and Campbell, *Historic Indian Groups*, 13.

28. Campbell and Campbell, *Historic Indian Groups*, 13, 14.

29. The title of this section comes from Bandelier's translation; *Narrative*, 83.
30. Luis Weckmann, *La herencia medieval de México*, 2 vols. (Mexico City, 1984), 1:320–38, cites some dozen period texts on the performance of miraculous cures, carried out by religious and even lay persons, as part of missionary activity in northern New Spain.
31. This group is referred to in the 1542 edition both as Avavares and the variant Chavavares; Campbell and Campbell, *Historic Indian Groups*, 24. As to their location, placing them on either side of the lower Nueces River in Texas accommodates the recorded facts. Cabeza de Vaca makes it clear that the Avavares spoke a different language than the Mariames, but since the Avavares could speak the language of the Mariames, it was possible for the Spaniards to communicate with the Avavares on their first encounter; ibid, 25.
32. Claude Lévi-Strauss, *Structural Anthropology*, trans. Claire Jacobson and Brooke Grundfest Schoepf (Garden City, N.Y., 1967), 174–75; further references in the text.
33. Campbell and Campbell, *Historic Indian Groups*, 26.
34. "The sons of the sun" seems to suggest the concept of the sun as a deity (ibid., 27) and the Spanish party as divine. In subsequent interpretations and translations, the probable indigenous notions of divinity (*hijos del sol*) are integrated with another reported description of the black and white strangers as being "people from Heaven." We shall discover later that this conflation is more convenient than correct, and that "gente bajada del cielo" (people come down from the sky) has more to do with native notions of geography than cosmology.
35. Lévi-Strauss, *Structural Anthropology*, 174.
36. Ibid., 167–68; previously cited by Pupo-Walker, "Notas," 764.
37. Campbell and Campbell, *Historic Indian Groups*, 27.
38. Krieger, "Travels of Cabeza de Vaca," 466, locates this area to the north and south of the Nueces River, and Campbell and Campbell, *Historic Indian Groups*, 10, 24–25, place it between the lower Guadalupe and lower Nueces Rivers, inland between Lake Corpus Christi and Copano Bay.
39. Campbell and Campbell, *Historic Indian Groups*, 24.
40. Campbell, "Coahuiltecans," 353.
41. This area of Texas and northeastern Mexico was next visited by the expedition of Alonso de León in the mid seventeenth century. León's account, the *Historia de Nuevo León con noticias sobre Coahuila, Tejas, Nuevo México* (1649; Mexico City, 1909), plus Cabeza de Vaca's, reveal enormous cultural diversity over this poorly known area. However, León did not get as far north as the Avavares; he describes instead the natives in Nuevo León from "Monterrey and Cadereyta northeastward to Cerralvo"; Campbell, "Coahuiltecans," 344, 350. Harbert Davenport and Joseph Wells, "The First Europeans in Texas, 1528–1536," *Southwestern Historical Quarterly* 22, no. 3 (January 1919): 217–22, considered it possible that an official inquiry of 1777 into the character and occupancy of the lands of today's southwest Hidalgo County and Cameron County in Texas could have encountered some of Cabeza de Vaca's Avavares group, then known as Pauragues. Although I have not been able to consult these *testimonios*, it seems unlikely that they contain information on native customs.
42. Fray Bernardino de Sahagún, *Historia general de las cosas de Nueva España*, trans. and ed. Angel María Garibay K. (Mexico City, 1979), 906.
43. Angel María Garibay K., "Paralipómenos de Sahagún," *Tlalocan* 2, no. 3 (1946): 244.
44. Angel María Garibay K., "Paralipómenos de Sahagún," *Tlalocan* 2, no. 2 (1946): 168, 173.
45. El Inca Garcilaso, *Florida of the Inca*, 196–97.

46. Until the early summer of 1535, when Cabeza de Vaca's group began a period of swift travel, Cabeza de Vaca had been among the shoreline and inland groups of the Gulf Coast of southern Texas from Galveston Bay to Corpus Christi Bay. He had spent a year with the Karankawas on and near Malhado, some four years trading between Karankawa groups, and a year with the Mariames, the easternmost Coahuila group.

47. Morris Bishop, *The Odyssey of Cabeza de Vaca* (New York, 1933), 9–10.

48. I am grateful to Sabine MacCormack for the suggestion about the importance and meaning of this gesture regarding the magical or divine being; see "Children of the Sun and Reason of State: Myths, Ceremonies, and Conflicts in Inca Peru," 1992 Lecture Series, Working paper no. 6 (College Park, Md., 1990), 6.

49. The original text states: "Dicen que aquellas calabazas tienen virtud y que vienen del cielo, porque por aquella tierra no las ay, ni saben donde las aya, sino que las traen los ríos quando vienen de auenida" (99). Hodge translates: "They say there is virtue in them, and because they do not grow in that country, they come from heaven; nor do they know where they are to be found, only that the rivers bring them in their floods"; *Narrative*, 90. Bandelier translates: "They claim that those gourds have healing virtues, and that they come from Heaven, not being found in that country; nor do they know where they come from, except that the rivers carry them down when they rise and overflow the land"; *Narrative*, 107.

50. Krieger, "Travels of Cabeza de Vaca," 467.

51. In contrast to Cabeza de Vaca's lengthy explanation, Oviedo simply says that the marauders came and sacked and "told the others the way they were to behave with the Christians"; *Historia general*, 606; my translation.

52. Krieger, "Travels of Cabeza de Vaca," 468, has identified the place as the Sierra de la Gloria, southeast of Monclova in Coahuila and the Río Nadadores or one of its tributaries. The party continues to travel among little-known Coahuilteca groups.

53. This portion of their journey lies between the area of Monclova in Coahuila and the junction of the Río Conchos and the Río Grande in eastern Chihuahua, ibid., 468.

54. In Cabeza de Vaca's account, it is he whose show of anger produced a contrite native response; in Oviedo's work, Dorantes is the protagonist of this episode.

55. Krieger, "Travels of Cabeza de Vaca," 469.

56. See Fray Ramón Pané, *Relación acerca de las antigüedades de los indios*, ed. José Juan Arrom (Mexico City, 1974); and Hernán Pérez de Oliva, *Historia de la inuención de las Indias* (Bogotá, 1965).

57. Fray Ramón Pané learned about the Tainos on Columbus's second voyage, and the latter commissioned him to write about what he had learned about their beliefs from living with them. The notion that the sky should be the place where the Spaniards came from is quite logical. In this case, the sky had no supernatural connotation but a geographical one; the Tainos located the sites of the before-life and the afterlife on their own landmass. Clearly, being from the sky did not mean being from the place of the origin of creation or of the afterlife. In Pané's text, the identification of the bearded strangers is not based on their being "from heaven" but rather their being the source of destruction. In his *Historia*, Pérez de Oliva lay bare the cross-purposes of ethnographic data collection and interpretation when he failed to integrate the information he had about Taino beliefs into his own poetically true account of the discovery of the Indies, while at the same time accepting it in the separate chapter ("Narración novena") in which he summed up Pané's findings.

58. Wagner states that the 1555 Valladolid edition was the basis for the modern ones of Vedia, Serrano y Sanz, and others; *Cabeza de Vaca*, 6.

59. The key phrase in the 1542 edition of Cabeza de Vaca (fol. 55v) is: "Porque todas las cosas que ellos no alcanzan ni tienen noticia de donde vienen dizen que vienen del cielo"; cf. *Relacíon*, 119.
60. John Francis Bannon, "Introduction," in Bandelier, *Narrative*, xiii. However, Mrs. Bandelier has it both ways, proclaiming heavenly origins and offering the more prosaic explanation simultaneously: "And all those people believed that we came from Heaven. What they do not understand or is new to them they are wont to say that it comes from above" (129). Hodge translates the phrase as "All held full faith in our coming from heaven"; *Narrative*, 107.
61. Krieger, "Travels of Cabeza de Vaca," 472.
62. Bandelier, *Narrative*, 132, and Hodge, *Narrative*, 109, translate the origin of both the metal ornament and the murdering Spaniards as being "from heaven."
63. According to Krieger, "Travels of Cabeza de Vaca," 472, this was the "exploring expedition of Diego de Guzmán in 1533, which came from Culiacán to the Río Yaqui and then turned back." Guzmán had reached the lower Pima area and covered the whole Cahita range; Carl O. Sauer, "The Road to Cíbola," *Ibero-Americana* 3 (1932): 11–12.
64. Appointed governor of Nueva Galicia in 1530, Nuño Beltrán de Guzmán occupied that post when he received Cabeza de Vaca and his companions in Compostela in May 1536. He was removed from his post in January 1537, being arrested by Diego Pérez de la Torre, judge of *residencia* of Nueva Galicia. Guzmán was kept in the public prison of Mexico City from then until 30 June 1538, when he returned to Spain and spent the rest of his life, still listed as a *contino* (member of the royal bodyguard), but with the royal court as his prison. He died in Valladolid on 26 October 1558; J. Benedict Warren, *The Conquest of Michoacán: The Spanish Domination of the Tarascan Kingdom in Western Mexico, 1521–1530* (Norman, Okla., 1985), 242.
65. José López-Portillo y Weber, *La conquista de la Nueva Galicia* (Mexico City, 1935), 38.
66. On Las Casas's peaceful conversion experiment in Vera Paz, see Lewis Hanke, *The Spanish Struggle for Justice in the Conquest of America* (1949; reprint ed., Boston, 1965); and Henry Raup Wagner, with Helen Rand Parish, *The Life and Writings of Bartolomé de Las Casas* (Albuquerque, N.M., 1967).
67. The work probably was written in Mexico in 1539, according to Wagner and Parish, ibid., 265.
68. Ibid., 87.
69. Regrettably, Oviedo's account reveals that the reprieve was only temporary; *Historia general*, 613. Once the Cabeza de Vaca party left and had been led over a torturous inland route on which they would have no further contact with the natives of this area, the *caudillo* Alcaraz and his men went off into the hills to capture more slaves.
70. Diego de Alcaraz's recollections of that meeting are also recorded. He had seen a large troop of advancing Indians and sounded the alarm to prepare arms. On going forward to capture them, he stopped in his course upon seeing, amidst this huge throng, "three men of strange figure"; Sauer, "Road to Cíbola," 20.
71. See Lewis U. Hanke, "The *Requerimiento* and Its Interpreters," *Revista de Historia de América* 1, no. 1 (1938): 25–34; and Hanke, "The Development of Regulations for Conquistadores," in *Contribuciones para el estudio de la historia de América* (Buenos Aires, 1941), 71–87.
72. Melchior Díaz, who was in 1535 *alcalde principal* and captain of the province of Culiacán, was involved in later explorations to the north. In 1539, he and Juan de Saldívar were ordered by Coronado to head north and verify Fray Marcos de Niza's reports; they went some two hundred leagues, to Chichilticalli, "where the wilderness

begins," according to Pedro Castañeda y Nájera; Hodge, *Narrative*, 296, and returned, not finding anything important. Castañeda lists Díaz as a companion of Coronado and one of the captains who went to Cíbola: "Melchior Díaz, a captain who had been mayor of Culiacán, who, although he was not a gentleman, merited the position he held"; George Parker Winship's translation of the Castañeda report, reprinted in Hodge and Lewis, *Spanish Explorers*, 292–93. As to the suspension of conquest activities he promised, I have found no evidence to date.

73. About this event and on his own behalf in an undated *memorial*, Nuño de Guzmán declared that he had always helped wayfarers with the provisions to save their lives, aiding them as Christians, be they the survivors of Cortés's disastrous expedition to California, Franciscan monks, or, after them, the survivors of Pánfilo de Narváez's expedition to Florida; *Memoria de los servicios que había hecho Nuño de Guzmán, desde que fue nombrado Gobernador de Pánuco en 1525*, ed. Manuel Carrera Stampa (Mexico City, 1955), 85.

74. Bartolomé de Las Casas (*Obras escogidas de Fray Bartolomé de las Casas*, ed. Juan Pérez de Tudela Bueso, 5 vols. [Madrid, 1958], 3:428–29), however, would later take Cabeza de Vaca's account of the native deity Aguar and cite it verbatim in his *Apologética historia sumaria*. He found Cabeza de Vaca's interpretation useful in supporting his fundamental argument that the natives of the New World did have knowledge of the Judeo-Christian god and that they had forgotten it or remembered it imperfectly. Cabeza de Vaca's assertion that he had found no idolatry or sacrifices throughout the vast area over which he had traveled made his outlook in general one that Las Casas could applaud.

75. J. M. Ots Capdequí, *El Estado español en las Indias* (1941; reprint ed., Mexico City, 1975), 25.

76. López de Gómara, *Historia general*, 1:67.

77. Bartolomé de Las Casas, *Brevísima relación de la destrucción de las Indias*, in *Obras escogidas*, 5:154–55; Gómara, *Historia general*, 1:302–3.

78. Guzmán, *Memoria*, 93–193.

ANTHONY PAGDEN

Ius et Factum:
Text and Experience in the Writings of Bartolomé de Las Casas

I

GONZALO FERNÁNDEZ DE OVIEDO, author of one of the earliest histories of America, the *Historia general y natural de las Indias*, tells this story of Columbus:

The Admiral Don Christopher Columbus, first discoverer of these parts, as a Catholic captain and a good Governor, after he had heard about the mines at Cibao, and saw that the Indians gathered gold in the waters of the streams and rivers, without having to dig for it, with the ceremony and the piety that has been mentioned, refused to allow the Christians to collect gold without first confessing and communicating. The Indians, he said, spent the twenty days beforehand without touching their wives (nor any other woman) and fasting; and they said that if they touched a woman they would find no gold. Therefore, he said, if those bestial Indians observed such rituals, there was even more reason for the Christians to cease from sin and to confess their errors, and that, being in a state of Grace with God Our Saviour, He would give them more freely the temporal and spiritual goods they sought.[1]

The Arawak of Hispaniola knew that material in transition between the natural and the artificial is dangerous. They knew that what lies in water is neither above nor below the ground. They knew, too, that such material is always close to the numinous. As one of Columbus's companions, Ramon Pané, had observed, the Arawak exercised similar ritual caution when "making idols," for wood and clay were possessed, in their transitional state, by the same instability.[2] Columbus, as a "Christian Captain," knew nothing about the perils adhering to transitional substances. He was trying to make sense of a seemingly senseless pattern of behavior at what was probably the first significant moment of contact between European normative expectations and the practices of an Amerindian culture. And he was highly sensitive to the numinousness of gold, which, he seems to have believed, "can even drive souls into Paradise."[3]

What is striking about Oviedo's account, however, is not Columbus's attitudes toward gold, nor his failure to understand what the Arawak were doing, nor even the assumption that any ritual preparation that involved sexual abstinence *must* be a sacred one; it is the unmediated laying of Christian practices, whose objective is to acquire grace, over non-Christian practices, whose purpose—as Columbus perceived it—was to acquire gold "without having to dig for it."[4] Since for the Christian fundamentalist sexual abstention is perceived as a good no matter what the intention, it might be argued, as Oviedo seems to imply, that the ready availability of gold *was* a sign of divine favor. The Indians had understood this through natural reason; Columbus knew it through revelation. But Columbus was also doing something else, something that others, who shared none of his messianic veneration for precious metals, would replicate in different ways. He was translating varieties of experience from an alien world into the—in this case sacramental—practices of his own. But he was doing this not by analogue or metaphor but in terms of what Ernst Cassirer called "the pure category of relation."[5] European and Amerindian sacred rites are not said to be similar, as many later commentators would say they were, one either a diabolic inversion or a residual memory of the other. Instead, one is perceived as a substitution for the other. The stark incommensurability of the two is dissolved in the supposed common recognition of the danger of sex and of the cosmic worth of gold. Here the bestial Indian and the Christian are made to share a common ritual terrain. In the process the "otherness" of their world, although not eliminated (they still remain "bestial," a mark by which Columbus's men can measure their own "errors") has been made accountable.

All of Columbus's acts, and the language in which he described them, were similarly intended to shrink the distance between Europe and America, between himself and the geographical and cultural "other." His initial calculations, by reducing the real length of the degree, shrunk the globe by two-thirds. And all his life he insisted that what he had discovered was not a new world but a new route to the old, familiar, world of Asia. "His constant endeavour," as Acton later observed of him, "was *not* to be mistaken for the man who had discovered the new world."[6]

Columbus's strategies were, in many ways, unprecedented and unrepeatable. But the process of reducing distance by direct substitution was an enduring feature of most early European efforts to steady the initially vertiginous experience of being in a "new" world. Columbus's attempt to register Arawak practices by Christian analogues is matched by attempts to name, and to map, the new continent. Since categories of the "new" imply comparison with a known and familiar "old," they have the immediate and intended effect of denying complete novelty. If what its autochthonous inhabitants called "Anahuac" could be rendered as "New Spain," what survived was less its newness than its proximity to Old Spain: even within Iberia itself there was, after all, both an Old and a New Castile.

But Columbus's act of ritual appropriation could never accommodate the range of alternatives that America presented. Even Amerigo Vespucci, for whom America was, at first, the repository for a variety of classical exotica—the Earthly Paradise, the ceaselessly fertile, persistently ageless, Amazons and Hyperboreans, the cannibals and the giants—soon came finally to realize that when one got up close enough, "nothing shows any conformity with the things of this part [of the world]."[7]

For the migrant, unlike the traveler, such incommensurability was inescapable. Here is another, in this case imaginary, moment of encounter between a European and the experience of "being in" America. In a dialogue written in 1555, the Franciscan Pedro de Quiroga imagined a conversation between two of his fellow religious, "Barchilon," a long-time resident of Cuzco, and "Justino," a neophyte who has just arrived, ignorant and enthusiastic, from Spain. Barchilon's advice to Justino is to forget everything he thought he knew at home. Open your eyes, he says, and you will see that "everything is the reverse of what it is in Castile." What appear to be correspondences are often, in fact, inversions. Indeed, it is the apparent similarities between Europe and America, between Indian and Christian devotional customs, which for Columbus had seemed to offer the possibility of immediate and direct translation, that Barchilon now points to as evidence of their incommensurability. Certainly, Justino admits, "This land weakens the judgment, disturbs the spirit, harms and corrupts good customs, engenders unfamiliar conditions, and creates in men effects contrary to those which they previously had." But even such powerful forces as these can, surely, be countered by prayer and a meticulous attention to duty. No, replies Barchilon, "Have nothing to do with the things of this land until you understand them, because they are different matters, and another language."[8] Here the neophyte has to learn to speak again. Literally nothing that "he imagines in Castile" will be of any service to him.

For Barchilon it is incommensurability that is, ultimately, the *only* certainty. So, too, was it for Jean de Léry, the Huguenot author of the *Histoire d'un voyage fait en la terre du Brésil*, one of the most painstaking attempts to represent America as it appeared to a single individual. "If you wish to represent to yourself a savage," he wrote of the Tupinamba of Brazil, "imagine in your understanding (*entendement*) a nude man, well-formed and with well-proportioned limbs, all of whose hair has been scraped off him," and so on. Léry is here inviting his reader to perform a traditional Aristotelian act of *phantasia*. And, like Aristotle, he makes no clear distinction between mental images and the reception of sensory perception.[9] The final picture will, as he says, be not unlike that of some tangible object in the natural world, "similar to the figure of the fruit they call *Ananas*"—and to make the point his illustrator has added to the line drawing in the text an over-large pineapple. Léry's account of the Tupinamba is one of the most sensitive we have. He even includes an imaginary conversation with his "savages," and provides his readers with an elementary Tupi vocabulary. But in the end, even Léry seems to have recognized that representation, the creation of mental images through language, could never be an adequate means of making the "other" fully intelligible. "Their gesture and countenances," he at last felt compelled to admit, "are so very different from ours that I confess my difficulty in representing them in words, or even in pictures. So that, to enjoy the real pleasure of them, you will have to go and visit them in their own country."[10] But of course, few of us—and fewer still of Léry's readers—are ever in a position to "visit them in their own country." *Phantasia* is all we have. And since *phantasia*, as Léry also knew, seeks to translate initial sensory perceptions into mental images via language, it is a process that inevitably lays great stress upon the presence of the translator. Hence the repetition in so many of these narratives of first-person "utterance markings"—to use Michel de Certeau's term—"I saw," "I heard," "I was there." "My intention," as Léry claimed of his *Histoire*, "has been to set down only what I did, saw, heard and observed."[11] "Only the appeal to the senses," as de Certeau has said of Montaigne's use of such phrases, "and a link to the body . . . seem capable of bringing closer and guaranteeing, in a single but indisputable fashion, the real that is lost in language."[12]

The claims of Barchilon and Léry, however, can only be fully understood in the context of a theory of knowledge that relied very largely upon exegesis and hermeneutics. In the terms of this theory the representation of the external world depended upon the interpretation of a determined body of texts: the Bible, the Church Fathers, and a regularly contested corpus of ancient writers.[13] All attempts at representation had to be presented within the "structure of norms" provided by this canon.[14] The objects of description might, of course, appear, as they sometimes did to Barchilon, to fall so far outside this structure as to seem to be merely an inversion of it. America, as one traveler mockingly noted, was a place where rivers ran uphill and women urinated standing up.[15] But nothing could be made intelligible in terms of some alternative structure. The world of the Amerindians, and of all those other "others" whose behavior seemed initially unaccountable, could not be explained, as later ethnographers were to demand, "in their terms" since, for these early writers, "their terms" could never be detached from "ours."[16] And our terms were always those determined by the authoritative canon.

The tensions that the very different responses to the presence of the "new" of America revealed derived, at one level, from the problem of how to create a text where none had existed before. This led to the creation of new genres or, at least, to new versions of old genres. First-person narratives, such as that of Bernal Díaz de Castillo, declaring to be "True Histories"; overextended letters, part descriptive and part evaluative, such as Hernán Cortés's *Letters of Relation*; even attempts, such as Oviedo's *Historia general*, to impose a loose Plinian structure upon the natural and human history of America—all these belong to recognizable European genres—chronicle, natural history, legal deposition—but they are all also sufficiently unlike those genres for Carlos Fuentes to be able, without undue hyperbole, to claim them as the first "novels" to be written about America.[17] At another, and far more complex, level, however, the question, in a culture whose scientific procedures were so bound by the appeal to *auctoritates*, was how to make the text, once created, authoritative. The answer was an appeal not to other texts (for there were none), nor to internal coherence, the logic of argument, the structure of analogy, and so on, but to the authorial voice. It is the "I" who has seen what no other being has seen who alone is capable of giving credibility to the text. If the reader chooses to believe what he or she reads, it is because he or she is willing to privilege that writer's claims to authority over all others and not, in this case, because it might seem to the reader to be inherently plausible or internally consistent. Indeed, as the Jesuit historian José de Acosta pointed out, it was only the authorial voice, the inherent credibility of the "I" who has "been there," that distinguished between reading about America and reading the romances of chivalry.[18] The same, of course, holds true for the texts within the authoritative canon itself. We—the members, that is, of this particular discursive culture—believe what Aristotle, Aquinas, or St. Jerome have to say not, at least in the first instance, because of any particular properties of their texts themselves but because the texts are the works of Aristotle, Aquinas, and St. Jerome.[19]

II

I want now to look more closely at the writings of the author who perhaps best illustrates the problems inherent in the construction of an authoritative representation of America, and of the corresponding tensions between the appeal to authorial experience and the demands of the canon: Bartolomé de Las Casas. Las Casas wrote a large number of quasilegal tracts in defense of the rights of the Amerindian peoples. But he is, perhaps, best known today for his descriptive works—the *History of the Indies* (*Historia de las Indias*), composed between 1527 and 1559; the *Apologetic History of the Indies* (*Apologética historia sumaria*), written sometime after 1551; and the only one to appear during his own lifetime, the *Short Account of the Destruction of the Indies* (*Brevísima relación de la destrucción de las Indias*), published in 1552. In these, as in his more formal texts, Las Casas reiterated two related claims: that the Indians were "men like us,"[20] and that only those who had "been there" could possibly have any significant understanding of America and its inhabitants. Las Casas insisted, in all his writings, on the primacy of firsthand experience. But his arguments for the property and political rights of the Indians, and for their unassailably human status, are couched in the language of the neo-Thomism in which he had been educated, a language that was, like most theological discourse, heavily text-dependent.[21] His ultimate objective, furthermore, was to demonstrate that his own reading of the canon, as it applied to America, its inhabitants, and to the legitimacy of the conquests, was the only true one.

Since his project was to establish the unique status of his voice, most of his writings are, implicitly or explicitly, autobiographical. No historian of America is so tirelessly self-referential. And it is as an account of a personal experience, the most significant of his entire life, that he provides what is, in effect, a representation of the necessary relation between the cognitive status of text and experience. Although he was to become the most outspoken defender of Indian rights, Las Casas spent much of his early life as a priest and a colonist in Cuba. He was, on his own account, better, more gentle perhaps, than other colonists, but he was also, like them, the master (*encomendero*) of Indians whose labor he, like they, unquestioningly exploited. Las Casas's transformation into the "Apostle to the Indians" was the outcome of a now famous conversion, which he describes in the *History of the Indies* in terms intended to convey a discreet, but inescapable, analogy with the conversion of St. Paul. Las Casas's moment of illumination, however—conceived precisely as the bestowal of a power to understand through experience—was not the consequence of an encounter with a divine revelation of the kind that had struck Paul from his horse on the way to Damascus, nor did it come to him as the result of his observation of the misery of the Indians, although, as he says, he had seen much of that. It was the consequence of an encounter with a text, Ecclesiasticus 34.21–22, which he "began to consider" in preparation for his Easter sermon. "The bread of the needy is their life," he read. "He that defraudeth him thereof is a man of blood. He that taketh away his neighbour's living slayeth him, and he that defraudeth the labourer of his hire is a bloodletter." For Las Casas it was this text that led directly back to, and gave meaning to, the sufferings of the Indians of which he had been a hitherto unreflective witness. It was God's word that, in characteristically Augustinian terms, had restored through grace the eye's capacity to see.[22] But it was, he tells us, yet further texts, "every book" he had read, "in either Latin or the vernacular which in forty-four years were infinite," which verified precisely what it was that the moment of illumination had revealed to him.[23] Here the text made sense of what he had seen, but what his blinded eyes had never allowed him to "witness" for years, and what he had thus experienced led back around the hermeneutical circle to yet more texts.

The project to which Las Casas subsequently dedicated the remainder of his long life—the establishment of the Indians' claims to full humanity, and hence full legal equality with the Spaniards—depended precisely upon the reconciliation of the competing claims to authority of text and experience that his "conversion" had allowed him to achieve. Only an interpretation of the canonical texts, primarily of course those texts that the "cruel and implacable enemies of the Indians" had used against them, could secure the human status of the Indians before a community for whom exegesis was the only access to knowledge. His own knowledge of the canon was, he insisted, equal to that of any professional jurist or theologian, and to prove it he loaded his writings with more citations than any contemporary jurist or theologian would have thought necessary. As the great Dominican natural-law theorist Domingo de Soto said wearily of one of his depositions, and could have said of all, "It was as copious and diffuse as have been the years of this affair."[24] Such learning was the result of an intense and prolonged intellectual labor. "For forty-eight years," he told his colleagues in Chiapas and Guatemala, with pardonable exaggeration, "I have worked to inquire and to study and to set down clearly the law [on these matters]. And I think that, unless I deceive myself, I have delved so deep into the waters of these matters that I have reached their source."[25] But it was also the case that the primacy of his *interpretation* of "the Law" depended not upon the range of his knowledge but upon the depth of his direct, unmediated contact with what he called "the fact." As in the court of law, before which he so frequently imagined himself, it was the facts of the case that provided the basis for an authoritative reading of the text. For, he wrote, "it is, the jurists say, from the true account [*relación*] of the fact, that the Law is born."[26] In order, however, to ensure the authority of *his* account over that of all possible others, his experience of the facts had to be presented as uniquely privileged. "God has given no man," he claimed, "neither living nor dead (and that only through His goodness and through no worth of my own) so much experience [*noticias*] and understanding [*sciencia*] of the facts and the Law natural, divine and human, as I have of the things of these Indians."[27] "Facts and the Law," "hecho y Derecho," "ius et factum"[28]—the coupling, which occurs again and again in all his writings, determined the crucial relationship between the canonical text and a direct experience of the external world as the only certain instrument of interpretation.

If this was true for any act of interpretation, it was particularly so for the interpretation of anything to do with America. For everything about America, in the words of the opening sentence of the *Short Account*, was "so extraordinary that the whole story remains quite incredible to anyone who has not experienced it at first hand."[29] And only Las Casas had fully understood what that involved. "I can," he wrote in 1535, "swear before God that, until I went to this royal court, even in the time when the Catholic King Don Ferdinand was still alive, no one knew what thing the Indies were, nor of their greatness, their opulence, their prosperity," nor, he added, "of the destruction which had been wrought in them."[30] It had been, he said in the prologue to the *History of the Indies*—a long, somewhat disjointed essay on the identity and purpose of the historian's task—his objective "to give clarity and certainty for readers of ancient things, to the principles which have been discovered about the machine of this world."[31]

In order to achieve this end, he had become a recorder, an historian in the proper, ancient sense of the Greek term *historein*, "which," he said, quoting Isidore of Seville, "means 'see' or 'know'; for no one among the ancients dared place himself in any position other than among those where he had been present, and had seen with his own eyes that which he had determined to describe."[32] Only a history of this kind could provide the data necessary for the correct interpretation of the authoritative canon, as it applied to America. And only the "'I' witness," to borrow Clifford Geertz's pun, could be relied upon to compose such a history.

Throughout all of Las Casas's writings there is the same insistence on the primacy of *his* eye, and consequently of the uniqueness of *his* text. Seeing constitutes a form of possession, analogous to that by which (and this was a claim Las Casas never denied) the Castilian crown "possessed" the New World.[33] Columbus had taken possession of the Indies when he had first "set eyes upon them."[34] The claim to prior possession through sight also assured the uniqueness and authority of the text composed by the seer. "I am," Las Casas told Charles V's minister the seigneur de Chievres, "the oldest of those who went over to the Indies, and in the many years that I have been there and in which I have seen with my eyes, I have not read [other] histories which could be lies, but instead I have experienced."[35] "Only I," he told the Council of the Indies, who have been "an eyewitness for all the years since they [the Americas] were discovered," who had "wandered through these Indies since very nearly the year 1500";[36] "Only I can be trusted to know what I write."[37] By contrast Fernández de Oviedo—"this utterly empty trifler"[38]—the only other contemporary to attempt a task in any way comparable to Las Casas's, and the only other indisputable eyewitness, had been made literally blind by his crimes, and had, thus, "fabricated his history—or better, his trifles—from stories" and had turned for his evidence not to what lay before him but to "histories that are nothing but sheer fables and shameless nonsense."[39] All such men, wrote Las Casas in a remarkable, if also characteristically obscure, passage,

who have written not what they *saw*, but what they did not hear so well . . . and wrote with great detriment to the truth, [have been] occupied only in dry sterility and with the fruitlessness of the surface, without penetrating into the reason of men. . . . Because they failed to till the field of this dangerous material [*peligrosa materia*] with the rake of Christian discretion and prudence, they sowed an arid seed, wild and unfruitful of any human or worldly sentiment, and as a result a mortal discord has greatly grown, produced, burst forth, in many, in very many, scandalous and erroneous sciences, and perverse consciences, so that, as a consequence, the very Catholic faith and Christian customs, and the greater part of the human race has suffered irreparable harm.[40]

The agricultural metaphor holds together the notions of experience, ocular testimony—that "dangerous material"—and the skillful manipulation of hermeneutic knowledge—"Christian discretion and prudence." From the cultivation of the one by the other comes the true science that has eluded all previous commentators. Experience, as Las Casas's own "conversion" had shown, was not an alternative to hermeneutics; it alone made true prudential interpretation possible.

The true witness, the historian is, then, the only reliable guide to those "ancient things" that constitute our knowledge of "the machine of this world." The historian, however, provided more than the accurate grounding for the interpretation of an old text in a new context. From Diodorus Siculus, whom he declared to be "more like a holy theologian than a damned pagan philosopher," Las Casas had learned that, "through such a presentation of events," the historian may also provide his readers with "a most excellent kind of experience," for just as providence had "brought together the orderly arrangement of the visible stars and the natures of men into one common relationship," so history, "in recording the common affairs of the inhabited world as though they were those of a single state have made of their treatises a single reckoning of past events and a common clearing-house of knowledge concerning them."[41]

But the process of transmuting personal experience into a text that would itself then provide "a most excellent kind of experience" was not unproblematical. Historians, Las Casas knew, were not, for the most part, recording angels. They wrote with a purpose. Most had done so for the glory of their patrons, or because they "have felt within them a great number of polished and limpid words, the sweetness and beauty of gentle speech" or, like the "Greek chroniclers," who were "very partial to their own worth and particular honor," because they had written "not what they had seen and experienced, but that which formed the subject matter of their [personal] opinion."[42] Las Casas's own motives, however, like those of Josephus, the historian of another race—the Jews—that had been destroyed by a rapacious imperial power, and to whom his own theoretical remarks are heavily indebted, were "to bear witness to great and noteworthy deeds for the benefit of man," deeds that the official record would prefer to have silently forgotten or presented as something other than what they were. *He* had been compelled to utter only by the enormity of what he has seen, by "so much harm, so many calamities, so much destruction, so many kingdoms devastated." The result of this strict adherence to the immediate fact had been a text that was, inescapably, "uncured." The very "poverty of vocabulary, humanity of the style, and lack of eloquence" of the *History of the Indies* will therefore, he claimed, "be the good witnesses" both to its accuracy and of its author's sincerity.[43] Such a claim, known in the formal language of sixteenth-century rhetoric as *captatio benevolentiae*, was a familiar one.[44] But in Las Casas's case it was intended to do more than appeal to native simplicity, or to ward off potential criticism from his remarkably unwieldy prose. It was a declaration of faith in the essential innocence of *his* eye.

For in order to secure the authority of the "I," he had to return to the language of description not merely its directness—its lack of formal rhetorical elegance—but also its transparency. There was, Las Casas claimed, a sense in which those who stood most to gain by misdescribing the Spanish enterprise in America had created for themselves a new and wholly mendacious vocabulary. The *conquistadores*, he bitterly recorded, frequently compared their activities to those of the Christian heroes of the Reconquest of Spain from the Arabs. New arrivals in the Americas often had masses said on landing for the soul of that legendary hero of the Reconquest, El Cid.[45] By such acts of self-representation, these men were explicitly and self-consciously acting out in another place what had come to be thought of as the defining event of the Spanish past. And because the Indians, unlike the Arabs, were not "worthy enemies,"[46] their "conquerors" had been compelled to redescribe their military capabilities and their political and technological expertise. America, Las Casas insisted, had not been "conquered." It had been overrun, invaded. "This term 'conquest,'" he wrote in a memorandum of 1542, "is tyrannical, Mahommedan, abusive, improper, and infernal." A conquest, he argued, can be conducted only against "Moors from Africa, Turks, and heretics who seize our lands, persecute Christians, and work for the destruction of our faith."[47] One can only speak to the woefully underinformed about "conquering" peoples so gentle that they would flee rather than fight, whose wars were "no more deadly than our jousting, or than many European children's games,"[48] and whose arms—even those of the Inca—were "a joke."[49] "Conquest" belonged with those other terms by which the *conquistadores* had transformed their shabby deeds into events from the romances of chivalry and the Spanish border-ballads—with "victories," which designated only massacres;[50] "uprisings," which described the Indians' terrified attempts to escape their persecutors; "rebellion," which characterized legitimate resistance to "the forces of plague and carnage";[51] "pacification," which meant "killing God's rational creatures with the cruelty worthy of the Turk."[52] For Las Casas the ballads and the romances of chivalry, where his fellow countrymen had found a lexicon with which to fashion for themselves a comforting image of their "pestiferous deeds," served as a model only because they offered a compelling image of a world gone mad. "All that I have seen," he wrote to his fellow Dominicans in 1563, "and your reverences have heard, will seem perhaps like the fables and lying tales of *Amadis of Gaul*, for all that has been done in these [Indies] is by natural, divine, and human law, null, inane, and invalid, and as if it had been done by the Devil."[53]

Las Casas's claims for the transparency of his own vocabulary, as with the crucial coupling of "Law and fact," are heavily indebted to forensic rhetoric. The "true" historian, like the witness under examination, can appeal to precisely those features of the text that, in any other circumstances, would have reduced its value in the readers' eyes, as evidence that the translation from lived experience into language has been direct.

Similar analogies with recognized legal practices not only determined Las Casas's methodological claims; they also informed the formal structures of much of his narratives. The rapid transition within single chapters from recorded action and recorded speech to lengthy quotations from authoritative texts; the use, in the *History of the Indies*, of different temporal registers for the events of his own life, for those of Columbus's voyages, for the discovery and conquest of the Canary Islands, and for the subsequent conquests in America, all have identifiable legal analogues. So, too, does the frequent and circumscribed use of secondary evidence. Las Casas, of course, had not been present at all the events he describes. He had witnessed the conquest of Cuba, had spent some time in Venezuela and parts of Mexico. But he had never set foot in the areas of the largest, most devastating conquests, central Mexico and Peru. When dealing with these areas he substitutes another's eyes for his own. "I was told," "I heard it from one who was there," "He told me so," and similar "utterance markings" are employed to retain, as far as possible, the illusion of the immediate personal contact with "the real." Sometimes, too, he incorporates entire documents into the texts. The Franciscan Marco de Niza's account of the killing of the Inca Atahualpa, for instance, reproduced in the *Short Account*, is a deposition, a sworn testimony, countersigned by the bishop of Mexico, and written by one who had had "first-hand experience of these people" and was thus able to bear "true witness."[54] Much of the text of the *History of the Indies* and of the *Short Account*, despite the former's claim to be organized according to the traditional causal divisions of Aristotelian logic, reads less like a "history" than a series of overlapping depositions.

Las Casas was not, of course, an ethnographer in any strong sense of the term. He observed, and he collected such data as came his way. But he had never intended to "get himself into a culture."[55] His project had always been to establish the Amerindians as peoples who could be made fully familiar to the European gaze. If not yet entirely civil, he argued, they were nonetheless no more "barbarous" than some of the remote cultural ancestors—the Greeks, Egyptians, and Romans—of the modern Europeans had been. To prove this point the *Apologetic History* provided the reader with a series of detailed analogies between the practices of those cultures and the practices of the Indians. For Las Casas the new did not indicate, as it did for Léry, a stark unfamiliarity.[56] It indicated a precise cultural relationship in which distances in space could be expressed as distances in time. America was new in the sense of being initially unaccountable; it was new, too, in the sense that its peoples were still culturally unformed, just as, centuries before, the Greeks, Egyptians, and the Romans had been. Given time, and now the instruction the Christian missionaries could provide, Indian cultures would come to resemble in all important respects European ones. However difficult the act of imagination required to find the analogies between the ancient Mediterranean and modern American worlds might be, those analogies made the seemingly incommensurable commensurable. The "other" was, after all, like "us," albeit a now remote, barely imaginable "us." In Diodorus Siculus's striking phrase, Las Casas had, indeed, succeeded "in recording the common affairs of the inhabited world as though they were those of a single state" and had thus made his "treatises a single reckoning of past events and a common clearing-house of knowledge concerning them."[57]

Columbus in Hispaniola, Barchilon in Peru, and Léry in Brazil had all attempted to counter incommensurability by the ultimate appeal to unmediated experience. Las Casas's turn to authorial experience, by contrast, seemed to offer a means of mediating between an authority-dependent hermeneutic culture and the presence of the "facts." But it also placed upon the author just that weight of asseveration that direct appeals to the senses were intended to avoid. Las Casas was not, by formal training or institutional affiliation, even a member of a recognized interpretative cadre. He may, as he claimed, have had a profound knowledge of both theology and the law, but he was neither a professional theologian nor a jurist, something of which his enemies frequently reminded him. He had, therefore, to mediate between the extreme solipsism of his claims to authority and the equally extreme limitations imposed by the interpretative community to which he belonged. Las Casas's story of his conversion was intended to hint at the presence of a semidivine source for his experience. God, he implied on more than one occasion, had sent him to America to act as a witness, the sole witness who, if any would listen to him, could prevent God's anger from ultimately destroying Spain, "as divine punishment for the sins against the honour of God and the true faith."[58] But since he could make no more claim to prophetic status than he could to apostolic status, he could only hint and suggest. In the end, his ability to interpret the authoritative canon relied solely upon his own, purely human, vision.[59] It was, indeed, central to his claim for the rationality and humanity of the Indians that *all* men, even the hated *conquistadores*, would be able to see, and hence of course read, as he did if only they were not so "anaesthetized to human suffering by their own greed and ambition."[60] And since his claims to what he *had* seen, and his interpretations, were often singularly bizarre, he was open to the charge that, as one of his most polemical critics, Bernardo de Vargas Machuca, put it, "if one proposition can be shown to be false in part, it may be presumed that the rest is false too."[61] The authority of the "I" may save "true history" from confusion with romance. But it cannot silence criticism of the author himself. As Clifford Geertz has noted of the modern ethnographer's not dissimilar dilemma, "To be a convincing 'I' witness one must . . . first become a convincing 'I,'" and Las Casas was never a wholly convincing "I."[62] His polemical objectives were always too stridently in evidence. As Acosta was the first to realize, only a history that replaced the single voice by an analysis of several voices could escape precisely those criticisms that Las Casas himself had leveled against those infamous "Greek chroniclers."[63] But, then, neither the *Apologetic History* nor the *History of the Indies*, despite their titles, despite Las Casas's extended defense of his own historical practice, are truly "histories." They conform, in part, to Diodorus Siculus's prescriptions—or, at least, to one of them—but they do not describe processes over time. (This is particularly so of the *Apologetic History*, which has no temporal frame at all, other than the analogies between modern Indian and past classical cultures, and those have no narrative structure.) Both works led, as Las Casas's own conversion had done, round the hermeneutic circle from the text to the experience and back again, in an attempt to find a place for America within the authoritative canon, to use the "Fact" to interpret the "Law" and the "Law" to situate the "fact." In this respect, at least, Las Casas's writings constitute a dead end in the history of the historiography of the Americas. The future, from Acosta to Francisca Clavigero to William Robertson and the Abbé Raynal, belonged with a "philosophical history" of the kind that Acosta had attempted to write, a history that, by offering causative explanations for "the customs and deeds of these peoples,"[64] would be able to break out of that particular hermeneutical circle altogether.

Notes

1. Gonzalo Fernández de Oviedo y Valdes, *Historia general y natural de las Indias*, ed. José Amador de los Rios, 4 vols. (Madrid, 1851–55), 1:136.
2. Pané's account of the customs of the Arawak has not survived, but sections of it are quoted by the Milanese humanist Peter Martyr, *De orbe novo decades* (Alcala de Henares, 1516), [cviii]r.
3. Christopher Columbus, *Textos y documentos completos: Relaciones de viajes, cartas, y memoriales*, ed. Consuelo Varela (Madrid, 1982), 302.
4. Much of what Columbus has to say about gold seems to have been conditioned by the language of alchemy; see Alan Milhou, *Colón y su mentalidad mesiánica en el ambiente franciscanista español* (Valladolid, 1983), 131.
5. "Language takes up the pure category of relation hesitantly, as it were, and learns to apprehend it only deviously, through other categories, particularly those of substance and attribute"; Ernst Cassirer, *The Philosophy of Symbolic Forms*, trans. Ralph Manheim, 3 vols. (New Haven, 1953–57), 1:312.
6. Lord Acton, *Lectures on Modern History* (London, 1960), 71.
7. Angelo Maria Bandini, *Vita e lettere di Amerigo Vespucci* (Florence, 1745), 68; and see Antonello Gerbi, *La natura delle Indie nuove* (Milan, 1975), 45–58.
8. Pedro de Quiroga, *Libro intitulado coloquios de la verdad*, ed. Julian Zarco Cuevas (Seville, 1922), 44–52.
9. The classic source is Aristotle *De anima* 3.3. See Malcolm Schofield, "Aristotle on the Imagination," in Jonathan Barnes, Malcolm Schofield, and Richard Sorabji, eds., *Articles on Aristotle*, vol. 4, *Psychology and Aesthetics* (London, 1979).
10. Jean de Léry, *Histoire d'un voyage fait en la terre du Brésil, autrement dit Amérique*, 2nd ed. (n.p., 1588), 105–6; and quoted in J. H. Elliott, *The Old World and the New* (Cambridge, 1970), 22; and see Steven Mullaney, "Strange Things, Gross Terms, Curious Customs: The Rehearsal of Cultures in the Late Renaissance," in Stephen Greenblatt, ed., *Representing the English Renaissance* (Berkeley, 1988), 69.
11. Léry, *Histoire*, 2.
12. Michel de Certeau, "Montaigne's 'Of Cannibals': The Savage 'I,'" in *Heterologies: Discourse on the Other*, trans. Brian Massumi (Manchester, 1986), 68, 72.
13. The obvious difference in status between the Bible and all other texts served, when required, to discredit the authority of those other texts, particularly when they were written by pagan authors. Las Casas could, thus, defer to the authority of Aristotle on the necessary conditions for civility but, when it came to describing the condition of the Amerindian soul, dismiss him as "a pagan burning in Hell." On the distinction between biblical exegesis that relies upon "a theology which claims Yahweh as the agent of a history of deliverance" and what he calls "philosophical hermeneutics," see Paul Ricoeur, *Du texte à l'action*, vol. 2 of *Essais d'herméneutique* (Paris, 1986), 122–23.
14. The phrase is Stanley Fish's: "Meaning comes already calculated, not because of norms

embedded in the language but because language is always perceived, from the very first, within a structure of norms." That structure, however, is not, he claims, "abstract and independent" but determined by an "assumed background of practices, purposes [and] goods"; *Is There a Text in This Class?: The Authority of Interpretive Communities* (Cambridge, Mass., 1980), 318.

15. Fray Francisco de Ajofrín, *Diario del viaje que . . . hizo a la América septentrional en el siglo XVIII*, ed. Vicente Castañeda y Alcover, 2 vols. (Madrid, 1958–59), 1:84.

16. See Anthony Pagden, *The Fall of Natural Man: The American Indian and the Origins of Comparative Ethnology* (Cambridge, 1987), 200.

17. Few of the early writers, however, make any direct reference to the problem of genre. What Bartolomé de Las Casas, in traditional Aristotelian manner, describes as the "formal, material, and efficient causes" of his *History* refer only to the author's intention; *Historia de las Indias*, ed. Augustín Millares Carlo, 3 vols. (Mexico City, 1951), 1: 19–22. The first to claim to have created a new genre is the Jesuit historian José de Acosta in 1590. See Pagden, *Fall of Natural Man*, 149–51.

18. Bartolomé de Las Casas, *Historia natural y moral de las Indias* (Seville, 1590), 11. The phrase "true history" was one also used, by their authors, to describe a number of the romances of chivalry.

19. This is Michel Foucault's point: "It [the author's name] has other than indicative functions: more than an indication or a gesture, a finger pointed at someone, it is the equivalent of a description"; "What Is an Author?" in Josué V. Harari, ed., *Textual Strategies: Perspectives in Poststructuralist Criticism* (Ithaca, N.Y., 1979), 146. This is not, of course, to deny that the reasons for which a given text came to form part of the canon in the first place *did* have something to do with its inherent properties.

20. For this part of Las Casas's project, see Pagden, *Fall of Natural Man*, 119–45.

21. Las Casas was also perhaps the only one of Columbus's contemporaries to support his view, as late as the 1550s, that America was a part of Asia. See Bartolomé de Las Casas, *Apologética historia sumaria*, ed. M. Serrano y Sanz (Madrid, 1909), 53–55.

22. Cf. Charles Taylor: "We might say that where for Plato the eye already has the capacity to see, for Augustine it has *lost* this capacity. This must be restored by Grace. And what Grace does is to open the inward man to God, which makes us able to see that the eye's vaunted power is really God's"; *Sources of the Self: The Making of the Modern Identity* (Cambridge, Mass., 1989), 139. Las Casas was always "God's eye," "God's witness," in America.

23. Las Casas, *Historia*, 1:92–93.

24. *Aqui see contiene una disputa o controversía*, in *Obras escogidas de Fray Bartolomé de Las Casas*, ed. Juan Perez de Tudela Bueso, Biblioteca de Autores Españoles, vol. 110 (hereafter *Obras escogidas*; Madrid, 1958), 308.

25. Bartolomé de Las Casas, "Carta a los Dominicos de Chiapa y Guatemala" [1563]; in *Obras escogidas*, 470.

26. Las Casas, *Historia*, 1:19.

27. Ibid., 471. See Bartolomé de Las Casas, *Treinta proposiciones muy iurídicas*; in *Obras escogidas*, 257.

28. See, e.g., his attack on the Scottish theologian John Major as one who, in American matters at least, "knew neither the law nor the facts"; Bartolomé de Las Casas, *Argumentum apologiae adversus Genesium Sepulvedam theologum cordubensem* (1550), 228v; transcribed in Fray Bartolomé de las Casas, *Obras completas*, vol. 9, ed. Angel Losada (Madrid, 1988). There is also an excellent English translation by Stafford Poole, *In Defense of the Indians* (De Kalb, Ill., 1974).

29. Bartolomé de Las Casas, *Brevísima relación de la destrucción de las Indias*, ed. André Saint-Lu (Madrid, 1987), 69. This, and all subsequent translations, come from a new English version by Nigel Griffin, with an introduction by Anthony Pagden, published in 1991 by Allen Lane and Penguin Books.

30. Bartolomé de Las Casas, "Carta a un personaje de la corte," 15 October 1535; in *Obras escogidas*, 63.

31. Las Casas, *Historia*, 1:20

32. Ibid., 1:6. Las Casas's reference to Isidore is, as with most of his references, incorrect. It should read *Etymologiarum*, book 1, sec. 41.

33. Las Casas denied that the crown had property rights in America (*dominium rerum*), but he never challenged its claim to sovereignty (*dominium jurisdictionis*). In the political language in which Las Casas wrote, both constituted a form of possession.

34. According to Las Casas, Columbus had promised 10,000 *maravedís* to the first man to sight land. This he took himself because although "a sailor called Rodrigo de Tirana first saw land," it was Columbus who "had first seen the light, which meant that it was he who had first sighted land"; *Historia*, 1:199. It is significant that it is at this point in his narrative that Las Casas ceases to refer to Columbus by name and shifts to his title, "The Admiral"; *Historia*, 1:200.

35. Ibid., 3:342.

36. Bartolomé de Las Casas, "Carta al Consejo de Indias," 15 October 1535; in *Obras escogidas*, 59.

37. Las Casas, *Historia*, 1:22.

38. "Vanissimus hic nugator"; Las Casas, *Argumentum apologiae*, 240r. Las Casas regarded Oviedo, who had been an overseer (*veedor*) on Hispaniola, a defender of the slave trade and an *encomendero*, as his, and the Indians', archenemy.

39. Las Casas, *Argumentum apologiae*, 243v. There is a strong linguistic similarity between this passage and the description in the *History* (1:3) of the "Greek chroniclers."

40. Las Casas, *Historia*, 1:13.

41. Diodorus Siculus *History* 1.3–5.

42. Las Casas, *Historia*, 1:3.

43. Ibid., 1:12. Las Casas's writings are strewn with observations on style—his own and others. Columbus's prose, for instance, is similarly praised for its directness. He had, he said, copied out a passage "so that it may be seen how simply the Admiral lived and wrote, and also how, in those times, there was not the elevated, illustrious and magnificent mode of writing which is now used in the world, and that the words which are now used to puff up the titles used in letters were lacking" (2:316).

44. Some two hundred years later, Francisco Javier Clavigero, similarly engaged in writing a "true"—and apologetic—history of the Indians, would make exactly the same claims for very much the same ends. See Anthony Pagden, *Spanish Imperialism and the Political Imagination* (New Haven, 1990), 100.

45. See Stuart B. Schwartz, "New-World Nobility: Social Aspirations and Mobility in the Conquest and Colonization of Spanish America," in Miriam Usher Chrisma and Otto Grendler, eds., *Social Groups and Religious Ideas in the Sixteenth Century* (Kalamazoo, Mich., 1978).

46. On this notion see Stephen Greenblatt, "Murdering Peasants: Status, Genre, and the Representation of Rebellion," in *Representing the English Renaissance*, 10–11.

47. Bartolomé de Las Casas, "Memorial de los remedios"; in *Obras escogidas*, 121.

48. Las Casas, *Brevísima relación*, 81.

49. Ibid., 159.   50. Ibid., 125.   51. Ibid., 169.

52. Las Casas, *Argumentum apologiae*, 241v.

53. Las Casas, "Carta a los Dominicos," 472.

54. Las Casas, *Brevisima relación*, 160–3.

55. Clifford Geertz, *Works and Lives: The Anthropologist as Author* (Stanford, Calif., 1988), 17.

56. On which grounds, as he pointed out, "Asia or Africa might well be described as a new world"; Léry, *Histoire d'un voyage*, ciiv.

57. See p. 155 above.

58. Las Casas, *Brevisima relación*, 174.

59. This did not, however, prevent him from making prophetic utterances; see Alain Milhou, "Las Casas à l'âge d'or du prophétisme apocalyptique et du messianissme," in *Autour de Las Casas: Actes du colloque du cinquième centenaire* (Paris, 1984), 77–106.

60. Las Casas, *Brevisima relación*, 69.

61. Bernardo de Vargas Machuca, *Apologías y discursos de las conquistas occidentales . . . en controversía del tratado Destrucción de las Indias escrito por Don Fray Bartolomé de Las Casas*, in *Colección de documentos inéditos para la historia de España*, vol. 71 (Madrid, 1879), 219. The proposition he is referring to is the population figures that Las Casas gives for pre-Conquest Hispaniola.

62. Geertz, *Works and Lives*, 79.

63. Las Casas, *Historia natural*, 10.

64. Ibid., 11.

Demons, Imagination,
and the Incas

In the later sixteenth century, a Spanish poet, perhaps John of the Cross, imagined encountering, around Christmastime, the pregnant Virgin Mary on the road he was walking:

> Del Verbo divino
> La Virgen preñada
> Viene de camino
> Si le dais posada.[1]

These verses were recited in Carmelite communities every Christmas by way of calling the monks and nuns to celebrate the festival as a present reality. Indeed, sometimes the Virgin was actually visible. Between 1505 and 1513, a shepherd from León, one Alvar Simon, had seen an apparition of the Virgen del Camino, the Virgin of the Road, for whom therefore, a few years later, a shrine was built on that road where she had been seen.[2] Stories abounded in late medieval and Renaissance Spain of such occurrences, impingements by supernatural beings into the doings of everyday. The Virgin and the saints were represented as permanently present in earthly life through their statues, but at times they were perceived to be concretely and truly present in their own persons (fig. 1). In a different sense, Christ was present in the consecrated eucharistic host. This sacramental presence was made concrete in both sacred legend and daily experience. Legend had it that when speaking the words of consecration, Pope Gregory had seen Christ the man of sorrows standing on the altar (fig. 2).[3] In the more tangible reality of ordinary life, the pope's vision was shared by many medieval and Renaissance Christians who sought to experience the savior's human nature in terms of a personal and tender intimacy.[4] At the same time, such visions raised a set of thorny cognitive problems that Thomas Aquinas and other theologians reflected on repeatedly.

What exactly did the visionary see when instead of or with the host there seemed to be on the altar the figure of Christ? Aquinas addressed this question by differentiating the substance of an object, what it actually was, from that object's accidents, its external appearance. The substance of the consecrated host, he explained, remained unchanged, for Christ could not be more truly present in a vision than he already was in the eucharistic bread and wine. Instead, the

101

FIGURE 1. The twofold presence of the Virgin Mary as depicted by Pedro Berruguete (d. before 1504); she appears to a community of Dominican friars, while the triptych on the altar displays her seated statue with the Christ child on her lap. Prado, Madrid.

vision was brought about because of "a miraculous mutation in the accidents [of the host], for instance in its contours and color . . . so that Jesus is seen."[5] This mutation in the appearance of the host was external to the visionary's eyes; it was, as it were, an objective reality. Alternatively, the visionary's eyes could be miraculously transformed by divine intervention so that they beheld a vision.[6]

The reasoning that underlay these distinctions between an object's substance or true nature from its accidents such as color, shape, and texture was derived by Aquinas from Aristotle's writings on the soul. So was the idea that a mutation could occur in a person's sense perceptions. Aristotle distinguished reasoning, the activity of the intellect, from the activity of the five senses whereby a person takes cognizance of external reality. The findings of the senses were mediated to the intellect by imagination. Whatever reasoning might be formulated by the intellect had to be preceded by and anchored in mental images that were created on the basis of sense perceptions by the imagination. As Aristotle, followed later by Aquinas, concisely expressed it, "The soul never thinks without a phantasm,"[7] that is, a mental image formed by the imagination.

Sense perceptions observed an object's accidents, while intellect reflected on

FIGURE 2. The Mass of St. Gregory by Diego de la Cruz; late 15th c. The pope with his clerics kneels before the apparition of Jesus on the altar. Blood from the side of Jesus flows into the chalice containing the consecrated eucharistic wine. The background of the picture is filled with faces and objects evocative of the Passion. At right, donor and her patron saint. Collection Torello, Barcelona.

its substance. Sense perceptions, according to Aristotle and his Christian followers, were never in error; a person was never mistaken in seeing that a given object was white. Intellect, by contrast, was frequently mistaken with regard to the inferences it derived from this fact as to the true nature of the object.[8] This was the case because the imagination was prone to lead intellect astray by composing a distorted or erroneous synthesis of data supplied by the five senses.[9] The genesis of such error was inherent in the process whereby imagination produced a synthesis from different, potentially divergent, or conflicting sense impressions. A different kind of error in the imagination resulted from the fact that the soul dwelt in a material body, for the condition of the body, its health or disease, satiety or hunger, affected imagination's functioning.[10] Intoxication, a disorderly style of life, passion, and disease were likely to bring about misleading and erroneous phantasms. Such phantasms could also be lodged in the imagination by the demonic spirits with whom late antique and medieval Christians populated the sublunary world.[11] But on the other hand, God himself in his omnipotence was capable of conditioning body and imagination to produce divine and truthful visions.

A distinction therefore had to be drawn between visions sent by God and illusions resulting from excess and disease, or from sorcery and the intervention of demonic spirits in human affairs. Aquinas suggested that divine visions were recognizable by virtue of communicating a theological truth, while visions induced by a sorcerer or by demons deluded the visionary with misleading appearances, images that had no true substance.[12] This distinction, however useful in theoretical terms, entailed a variety of cognitive difficulties, some of which were explored by late medieval painters.

The holy hermit Anthony, for example, was tempted, in a picture by Joachim Patinir that was acquired by Philip II of Spain, by three lovely young ladies (fig. 3). Anthony has slipped and is about to fall at the very moment when the ladies approach him. One of the three is thus shown in the act of arresting his fall, while another innocently holds out an apple to him. Things are not as they appear, however, for behind the three ladies an ugly old hag emits a piercing scream, while the train of one young lady's gown terminates in a tiny devilish dragon. The saint turns away in anguish, as though knowing yet not knowing what confronts him. Hieronymus Bosch depicted the temptations of St. Anthony several times. In one of these paintings, Anthony sits sheltered by a hollow tree, his faithful companion pig at his side (fig. 4). Plants flower at his feet and in front of him flows a small tranquil brook. Yet all is not well, for the entire landscape is littered with aberrations of nature both great and small. Behind the saint, a figure half dragon and half human carries a pitcher of water; out of the brook, a creature yells at Anthony while reaching up toward him with a clawlike hand; and in the distance, deformed humans play at war. Evidently, the sense perceptions could

FIGURE 3. Joachim Patinir (d. 1524), *Temptation of St. Anthony*. Prado, Madrid.

FIGURE 4. Hieronymus Bosch (d. 1516), *Temptation of St. Anthony*. Prado, Madrid.

not be trusted to collect from the environment usable data out of which imagination might present to the intellect phantasms fit for thought. Anthony is thus resting his chin on folded hands, resolved to endure the demonic visitation, but his face speaks of wordless dismay.

Such problems notwithstanding, Aquinas's account of eucharistic visions along with the Aristotelian writings on which he drew described part of the framework within which Christians understood cognition, the order of nature, and sacred power. In late medieval and Renaissance Spain, his ideas were thus widely utilized for apologetic purposes. In the early fifteenth century, Don Lope de Barrientos, bishop of Segovia and confessor to King Juan II of Castile, wrote about dreaming and divination by way of defending Christianity against Judaizers and other dissenters from orthodox doctrine. The issue was that dream visions and divinatory apprehensions could be called into service to validate spiritual truths not authorized in official Christian teaching. In the footsteps of Aristotle and Aquinas, Barrientos explained that dreams resulted from sense perceptions that remained latent in the imagination during sleep. The quality of dreams, like that of waking visions, was conditioned by an individual's character and physical condition. Virtuous recollected individuals "of subtle imagination," such as Joseph the patriarch and the prophet Daniel, were regarded as likely to see truthful, even prophetic dreams. By contrast, the imagination of a dissolute person would receive vaporous, unclear dream images and would mistake these for divine revelation. Such a person was easily deceived by "mistaking the image for the thing itself," or was captivated by demonic illusions.[13]

The dangers that Barrientos and some contemporaries considered to confront Christian society from alternative belief systems, or simply from beliefs not controlled by the Church, loomed larger than ever in the early sixteenth century, when Spanish politicians and churchmen, having first expelled from the peninsula those Jews who would not convert to Christianity, also set themselves against Protestant reform. At issue were not merely the finer points of theology but the entire order of society.[14] This was why the priest Pedro Ciruelo, author of a bestselling treatise on witchcraft published in 1530, highlighted the authority of scripture but only as interpreted by the Catholic clergy and other officially recognized experts. In Ciruelo's mind, the distribution of natural and divine power in the universe was mirrored and made effective in society by designated experts. Ordained priests were authorized to administer words imbued with divine power, while physicians after prolonged study administered the natural power inherent in certain plants and minerals. There existed no such thing as knowledge "infused by God without the need of a teacher's instruction or the study of books."[15] Practices described by Ciruelo as "idolatrous superstition" threatened, not only true religion and scientifically accurate knowledge, but also the proper ordering of society. For where in the realm of theory truth confronted falsity, in society the ranks of true experts, priests, physicians, and theologians administering words and things of power confronted clandestine groups of false experts administering words and things that had no power.

Nonetheless, demonic power was seen as real, not imaginary. Its most profound impact on human affairs was to be looked for not so much in open displays of control over situations or individuals but in its far more subtle workings in the imagination. However vaguely Ciruelo conceptualized the exact process whereby a demonic impulse lodged itself in the imagination, he did specify that the devil in human or animal shape, or as one of the dead, was capable of appearing before a devotee's waking eyes or in dreams, so as to inspire actions subverting true religion and legitimately constituted society.[16]

This was how, in the early sixteenth century, the Flemish painter Juan de Flandes, who had spent some of his life in Spain, depicted the temptation of Christ. The devil, dressed in the habit of a Franciscan friar, appears before Jesus in the wilderness (fig. 5). Piously holding a rosary in one hand and a stone in the other, the Evil One suggests that Jesus, who has been fasting for forty days, should manifest his divinity by turning the stone into bread. Jesus, however, recognizes the substance of the devil behind the accidents of the Franciscan friar's habit and wearily lifts his hand by way of making a gesture of negation.

Seeing that human beings could not be expected to act with Christ's exem-

FIGURE 5. Juan de Flandes (d. 1519), *Temptation of Jesus in the Wilderness*. Alisa Mellon Bruce Fund, National Gallery of Art, Washington, D.C.

plary fortitude, society was ordered by diverse landmarks—rituals both secular and sacred, groups of publicly designated experts, learned and religious traditions—that guided the individual imagination toward an acceptance of divine and a rejection of demonic power. But such landmarks notwithstanding, there existed many potential rifts between demonic and divine power defined as polar opposites. Demonic power was recognizable in rituals not practiced by the Catholic Church, in authority not defined by canonical texts, and in experts lacking Catholic approval. However, the mode of describing and analyzing things divine and things demonic was one and the same. Because demons acted in the same human and natural universe as God, it followed that they obeyed the same psychological and physical laws. There was thus no need to devise a distinct vocabulary of otherness or difference with which to describe religious phenomena and experiences beyond or to one side of the Catholic Church in Spain, where the long familiar religions of Islam and especially Judaism were primary targets of Christian hostility. Indeed, all sides in this conflict found themselves riveted in the spell of the same vocabulary, so that for Jews "idolatrous superstition" was Christianity.[17]

Demons, Imagination, and the Incas   107

These tensions in the perception of good and evil and of right and wrong that pervaded Spanish politics and culture during the fifteenth and sixteenth centuries were replicated in the Americas. In Peru, as earlier in Mexico, Spaniards continued defining religious difference and otherness by using a terminology that had been crystalized during centuries of use. Inca temples were described as *mezquita*, "mosque"; one of the great Andean pilgrimages was found to be comparable to the Muslim pilgrimage to Mecca; and the devil was thought to talk to Andeans just as at home in Spain he talked to individuals who stood outside the social order sanctioned by the Church (fig. 6).[18]

However, to look only at such continuities is misleading, for a deep chasm unmodified by long coexistence gaped between Andean realities and the European norms that were deployed to describe them. In religious terms, Catholic Spaniards confronted the utterly alien religious world of Andeans, and in political terms Spaniards were the conquerors, ministers of their victorious God. The very first encounters between the two sides made this clear. In 1532, the Inca Atawallpa, ruler of an empire comprising contemporary Ecuador, Peru, Bolivia, and northern Chile, was taken prisoner by the Spaniards. This act of aggression, which took place in the central square of Cajamarca in northern Peru, was followed by the systematic ransacking of Inca temple treasures, allegedly for Atawallpa's ransom.

FIGURE 6. The demon Pachacamac talks to Indians in Peru. Illustration to Agustín de Zárate's *Historia del descubrimiento y conquista del Perú* (Antwerp, 1555).

Three Spanish eyewitnesses described how Hernando Pizarro, with a band of followers, made a violent entry into one of the greatest of Peruvian sanctuaries, the pyramid of the god Pachacamac near Lima. Pachacamac was consulted for oracles, and people came to him in pilgrimage from far and wide. The sanctuary predated the Inca conquest of the region, but the Incas incorporated it into the imperial network of holy places by erecting next to Pachacamac's pyramid another taller one to their own imperial deity, the divine Sun.[19] The treasure-seeking Spaniards who arrived there in January 1533 were received by the local nobility and the attendants of the deity Pachacamac. Some of the temple's precious objects were reluctantly handed over, but the priests were unwilling to admit the intruders into the sanctuary, because "no one was permitted to see the god." Indeed, pilgrims felt honored to be allowed merely to touch the walls of the great pyramid, and the privileged few who were admitted into the proximity of the god fasted for twenty days before ascending the pyramid's first step and for an entire year before reaching its peak.[20] The priests who met the Spanish newcomers thus offered to convey a message to Pachacamac but would not admit them to the temple. However, Hernando Pizarro and his men overrode all objections and insisted on being accompanied into the divine presence. Passing many doors during the winding ascent of the pyramid, they finally reached its peak, where a small open space gave access to a cavern made of branches, its posterns decorated with leaves of gold and silver. A door bejeweled with coral, turquoise, and crystal and flanked by two guardians closed off this holy spot. Upon the Spaniards demanding that the door be opened, a tiny dark room was revealed, in the center of which stood a wooden pole, its top carved into the figure of a man. All around, the ground was covered with small offerings of gold and silver, which had accumulated there over many years. This was the seat of Pachacamac, "the maker of the world," a two-faced deity who on the one hand created and sustained human beings, made the crops grow, and cured disease, but on the other hand brought disease and caused earthquakes and the overflowing of the sea. So it was that, in the words of one of the god's worshippers, "all things in the world lie in his hands."[21]

But the Spaniards had no ears for such reasoning. The jeweled door of Pachacamac's dwelling had led them to expect on the other side some elaborately worked treasure chamber. Finding instead an unadorned holy place of ancient simplicity they expressed a profound contempt. "Seeing how vile and despicable the idol was," related a member of the expeditionary force,

we went outside to ask why they paid such reverence to something so worthless. And they were astounded at our boldness and, defending the honor of their god said that he was Pachacamac, who healed their infirmities. As we understood it, in the cavern the devil appeared to those priests and spoke with them, and they entered with the petitions and offerings of those who came in pilgrimage, and indeed, the entire kingdom of Atawallpa went there. Seeing the vileness that was there and the blindness in which all those people lived, we brought together the leaders of the town and opening their eyes in the presence of all, that cavern into which very few people had ever entered was opened and broken down. And when they saw our resolve and grasped what we said of how they had been deceived, they themselves gave a show of being glad. Thus, with great solemnity, we erected a tall cross on that dwelling place which the devil had held so much as his own.[22]

Whether this show of being glad was sincere or not, the Spaniards had stumbled upon a point of tension in Andean and Inca religion. Oracular shrines both great and small abounded in the Andes; their principal role was to legitimate political power by establishing and then articulating consensus. In the course of doing this, the oracular deities also predicted the future. Such predictions were taken very seriously, if only because they were capable of generating either support or dissent at times of political uncertainty. Making prophecies could be a perilous undertaking, for the cost of being wrong was high. Some years before the Spanish invasion, Atawallpa had consulted Catequil, a regionally respected oracular deity in Guamachuco, so as to assess his chances of success in the war against his brother Guascar. Since Catequil was known to be a partisan of Guascar, Atawallpa may have hoped to win the region of Guamachuco peacefully by gaining the support of one of its principal deities. However, Catequil responded negatively. When thus the victorious Atawallpa gained control of Guamachuco, he exacted spectacular vengeance on the oracle and its priests. Catequil's image was overthrown and its head thrown into a river. His treasures were confiscated and the entire cult site was devastated in a fire that burned for over a month.[23]

Pachacamac also was found to have been wrong, and that on more than one occasion. The Spaniards witnessed the resulting showdown between Atawallpa and Pachacamac's priests in 1532, some sixty days after they had captured the Inca. On that occasion, Atawallpa ordered the representatives of Pachacamac who were in Cajamarca to surrender the god's treasures to the Spaniards for his ransom, because "this Pachacamac of yours is not God." The Inca's reason for challenging Pachacamac's deity was that the cure Pachacamac had recommended to his father Guayna Capac during the latter's last illness failed to work and Guayna Capac had died. Next, during the war between Guascar and Atawallpa, Pachacamac predicted that Guascar would win, which he did not, and finally, the god had erroneously predicted that Atawallpa would defeat the Spaniards. Francisco Pizarro used the Inca's disenchantment to inform him that "Pachacamac was the devil who was talking to them in that place, and was deceiving them. [And he said] that God was in heaven, and other things of our holy faith."[24] Yet, as seen by Atawallpa and the priests of Pachacamac, the problem was not so simple. Bearing in mind what had happened to Catequil, Pachacamac's priests may well have intended to support Atawallpa by predicting his victory over the invaders, although earlier the much more cogent policy obviously was to ally the oracle to the Inca Guascar in Cuzco, rather than to Atawallpa in distant Quito. Thus, where Andeans found themselves with the task of stage managing a delicately tuned but not infallible network of sacred power that had developed over centuries, Spaniards viewed that network as the fruit of demonic delusion.

In 1535, Pedro de Cieza de León, the most intelligent and observant of all historians of the Andes, reached South America. He traveled in Peru for twelve years. The land he saw was very different from the land that had greeted the first conquerors in 1532. The river Apurimac had to be crossed with the help of a rope, because the Inca suspension bridge had been destroyed, and the formerly renowned oracle of Apurimac, the "Lord who Speaks," was a memory only. The great Inca palace and temple of Tumebamba where Guayna Capac had held court were deserted, and the local curaca had become a Christian. The temple of Vilcas, built by the Incas to mark the geographical center of their empire, was likewise in ruins—"It was what it is no longer," as Cieza phrased it. The curaca of Xauxa had been baptized and called himself Don Cristóbal; he showed Cieza round the local Inca temple of the Sun and the temple of the regional prophetic deity Guaribilca, who also was the divine ancestor of the people of Xauxa. The sacred images had been destroyed by the friar Valverde in 1533, so that the oracle fell silent; the buildings were in ruins and overgrown with shrub.[25]

Yet in many places the old religious customs endured unchanged. Of one such incident Cieza wrote:

I still remember, when I was in the province of Cartagena some twelve or thirteen years ago, while the licenciado Juan de Vadillo was its governor and resident judge, how a boy escaped from a village called Pirina and fled to where Vadillo was staying, because they wanted to bury him alive with the lord of the village, who had died at that time.[26]

To bury the living seemed to Cieza an "accursed custom," which was explicable only if one bore in mind the extraordinary power of demonic illusion in the lives of "these gentiles."[27] There were thus concrete reasons why one should wish to convince the Indians of the Christian "path of truth."

However, on his long travels through the former Inca empire and adjacent regions, Cieza was confronted again and again with the disquieting reality that God continued to permit the demons to hold dominion over Andean souls. Pedro Ciruelo had distinguished on the one hand between the public idolatry and superstition of the gentiles of classical antiquity and the clandestine superstition of his own day, and on the other between the vain words and actions of enchanters and sorcerers and Christian rituals of power. Cieza did the same.[28] Public idolatry had come to an end with the fall of the Inca empire, but clandestine idolatry persisted, especially in rituals of divination. Ciruelo's devil, who thanks to his great age and fine memory was an "excellent historian," and who easily deceived the simple with probable but incomplete prophecies, was thus the exact counterpart of Cieza's devil, who "because of his subtlety and astuteness and because of his great age and the experience he has in everything speaks to the simple and they listen to him."[29]

Cieza recorded a variety of Andean funerary observances that documented, he thought, not only a belief in the afterlife and in the existence of the soul, but also the immense power of demonic delusion in the Andes. "When the will of God was pleased to give the devil power," he wrote,

it allowed him to adopt the appearance of lords already dead, and to show himself in their very own guise and stature exactly as they were in the world, with some semblance of servants and adornment. Thus [the devil] led them to suppose that [their lord] lived happily and peacably in another realm, just as they had seen him here. Therefore the Indians, considering those false appearances to be true, give more care to preparing their tombs and burials than to any other matter.[30]

Similarly in Guanuco, as in so many other places, Cieza heard that women stayed by the side of their deceased husbands; the very thought of their fate appalled him.

When the lords of these villages died, [the people] did not place them into their graves alone, but had them be escorted by the most beautiful live women. . . . Thus, when [the lords] are dead and their souls outside the body, these women whom they bury [alive] await the dread hour of death, which it is so fearful to endure, in order to join the deceased, having been placed into those great caverns which are their graves. And [the women] consider it to be a great felicity and blessing to go with their husband or lord and believe that soon they will attend to serving him as they have been accustomed to do in this world.

"This custom," Cieza continued,

arises from what I have said on earlier occasions, which is that they see, according to what they say, on their farms and in the sown fields appearances of the devil who looks like the lords who have already died and they are accompanied by their wives and have the objects that were placed in the tomb with them.[31]

The capacity of the devil to create illusions, pictures in the imagination that had no true substance, affected even Christians[32]—and Andeans, Cieza thought, were doubly vulnerable because they lacked the guidance of revealed religion. Nonetheless, there was an Andean reality in the idea of the dead walking about the fields and appearing, even talking, to the living. In Cuzco the *mallquis*, embalmed bodies of deceased Incas, stood at the hub of an elaborate ceremonial order. They participated in the affairs of the living and invited and toasted each other in the main square (fig. 7).[33] Elsewhere, the dead were remembered for generations as being present in the tomb.

These tombs were often located in the very fields where the dead were observed walking about,[34] and sometimes the spot was chosen by the deceased while still alive.[35] Just as the living Incas shared their capital city with dead ancestors, so throughout the Andes the countryside was inhabited by the living and the dead jointly. When Cieza described these countryside burials, he thought of individual tombs of lords whose funerary possessions attracted the attention of

FIGURE 7. An Inca ruler pours a libation of maize beer into a sacrificial receptacle for the deceased Inca and his consort, whose bodies are watching the transaction. In the burial tower in the background may be seen the bones of a dead person of long ago. Drawing from the *Nueva crónica* of 1615 by the Andean lord Guaman Poma de Ayala (fol. 287).

treasure-hunting Spaniards. But much more was at issue. The full pattern of coexistence between the living and the dead was revealed during ecclesiastical inquiries of the seventeenth century, which showed that all the members of entire lineages, not merely isolated individuals, were buried, generation after generation, in the open country, in the fields and wastelands belonging to each individual's lineage.[36]

Andeans perceived the land differently than Spaniards. It was not merely that the majestic heights of the Andes and the far-flung plains of the lowlands sustained the presence of the living as much as that of the dead. It was also that these heights and plains, and the springs and lakes that demarcated them, were so many pointers to humankind's remote origin from and identity with that august environment. Cieza glimpsed something of this Andean perception of the land. On his way to La Paz, traveling on the Inca royal road of Collasuyo, he passed through Urcos, in the valley of Cuzco, where he was told a myth of origins. "In times past," he wrote, the people of Urcos

greatly venerated a temple which they called Auzancata. Near it, they say, their ancestors saw an idol or demon whose appearance and dress was like their own, and with whom they held converse, offering sacrifices according to their custom. And these Indians tell that in times past they were convinced that souls which left the body went to a great lake . . . which was their place of origin, and from there the souls entered the bodies of those who were being born. Later, when the Incas ruled over them, they became more polished and intelligent and adored the Sun, although they did not forget to revere their ancient temple.[37]

The lake whence the people of Urcos first came was also the place to which their souls returned at death and whence again they set forth for a new life. Throughout the Andes, people thought their ancestors had sprung from the land itself, from mountain or rock, lake or spring. A place of origin, often described as *pacarina* (from *pacari*, "dawn"),[38] was a fixed point, always present, immovable. To be buried in the open country thus meant in some general sense to return to one's origin. However, since tombs were located on land belonging to one's lineage, this return could also be conceptualized as specific and concrete. Places of origin, like the dead, were recipients of cults for the increase of crops, animals, and humans. Ritual action spelt out the connection between a lineage's origin and its living and dead members, which myth for the most part left open.

The relationships Andeans perceived between life and death, and between humankind and the natural environment, were thus profoundly different from Spanish and Christian equivalents. The land surrounding one told the story of one's first ancestors as much as it told one's own story and the story of those yet to come. It was right that the familiar dead were seen walking through the fields they had once cultivated, thus sharing them with both the living and with the original ancestors who had raised the first crops in the very same fields. Death was thus the great leveler not because, as in Christian thought, it reduced all human beings to equality in relation to each other and before God. Rather, death was a leveler because by means of it humans were reintegrated into a network of parents and offspring that embraced the entire natural order.

Cieza looked at this order of things with a certain puzzlement, because he thought Andean religious ideas, diverse, contradictory, and demonically inspired as they appeared to him, were out of step with Andean political and economic achievements, which he greatly admired. However, the Incas had imposed a certain regularity, dignity, and predictability on this vast diversity of belief and practice. A parallel change had taken place in the development of Andean political forms. Cieza produced a penetrating analysis of the functioning of stateless societies beyond the frontiers of the Inca empire,[39] where, as he understood it, religious observance centered around the dead of a given social group and accordingly varied from one region to the next. In Inca lands, by contrast, religion had become unitary and more rational in that regional cults of the dead had in part been superseded by the Inca solar cult.

But that rationality had its limitations in Spanish eyes. In 1552, the year after Cieza returned to Spain, the Augustinian Order founded a convent in the Inca palace of Guamachuco; eight years later, the friars wrote an account of their work there. Cieza had commented in passing both on the Inca state cult and on the regional cults of Guamachuco;[40] it was these latter that most occupied the attention of the Augustinian friars. Local myths told of Catequil, offspring of the creator Ataguju's son Guamansuri and a woman belonging to an earlier generation of human beings. On another mountain, Catequil, who was also conceptualized as lightning, was worshiped along with his mother and a brother. He was represented in human form as Apu, "the Lord," Catequil and gave oracles, one of which had been the mistaken prediction that Atawallpa would be defeated by Guascar.[41] At the foot of the mountain was a village where lived the priests and attendants of this holy place.

The Augustinian friars destroyed the image of Catequil, taking care that not one fragment of it could be retrieved for future worship. But the deity resurrected manyfold, in that the Indians thinking of him as they walked and worked in their fields saw his many sons being revealed to them in certain rocks and stones, which they therefore set aside as focal points of cult where converse could be had with the holy presences. For in Guamachuco, as everywhere in the Andes, the plains and mountains, the sky and the waters were both the theater and the *dramatis personae* of divine action.

But the friars viewed this as so many manifestations of demonic activity. It was the devil who appeared to Andeans in dreams as an eagle or in waking visions as a serpent—as that serpent who figured so prominently in Inca thought as a figure for lightning or a sign of prosperity and first origins. And when the friars had destroyed the statue of Catequil, it was the devil who spoke from the stones that the people of Guamachuco came to regard as Catequil's sons. Finally, the devil could lead those he desired for his service to mountain retreats so as to deceive them the more easily in a remote solitude; and if such gentle and gradual deception failed, the devil entered a person violently, depriving him of his senses.[42] In short, the friars brought with them a variegated vocabulary for interpreting the religious experiences of Andeans. Yet, their interpretation could hardly have been more distant from Andean self-perception.

For the holy places of Guamachuco, and the *guacas*, divine presences that resided in them, represented the history and the concerns of the community. The principal deity of the local people was their originator Catequil, while the creator Ataguju, like other Andean creator gods, was a more distant presence. These Andean creator gods gave expression to a first beginning that was logically satisfying and necessary but remote both historically and in terms of daily cult and daily concerns. Closer at hand was "the common guardian of the entire village . . . the eye of the village,"[43] conceptualized as a great stone standing in or next to each village of the region. The friars were reminded by these standing stones of the guardian angels of the nations, of whom they had read in the church fathers:

As the theologians write, there is an angel who guards every republic and nation, but . . . the devil imitates what he sees and contrives to transform himself into an angel of light. Although here, he transformed himself into rock.[44]

The Incas left the established beliefs of Guamachuco intact, but their presence brought about a restructuring of the divine world just as it did of the social and political world. Institutionally, the Inca cults, especially that of the divine Sun, were distinct from the regional ones, for they were supported from separate revenues and maintained by a separate staff of experts. But conceptually the different cults, whether local or Inca in origin, were continuous with each other. It had thus been the Inca Guayna Capac who had responded to a local need by instituting a cult dealing with irrigation, and the same Inca had chosen a local *guaca* to accompany him on his campaigns. The people of Guamachuco in their turn served the state temple of the Sun, but they also included the Sun along with their other holy presences when making sacrifice at times of sickness, and they offered coca to the Sun as a remedy for fatigue during journeys.[45] The cult of the divine Sun thus did not merely consist of observing the great imperial festivals that were organized from Cuzco; rather, it comprised much more humble daily observances that were adhered to long after the Inca empire had fallen.

Another Spaniard who scrutinized Andean religion in the mid sixteenth century was the lawyer Polo de Ondegardo. Some of his extant writings resemble the work of the friars of Guamachuco in that they also display the mind of the extirpator endeavoring to classify and categorize Andean religious beliefs and practices in the light of Christian norms. As a result, religious practice and ritual are often separated from the beliefs that provided their conceptual content, and the mythic and historical narratives that allowed ritual and belief to fuse into a coherent unity are ignored altogether. Polo's subject matter thus was not a religious system with its own inner coherence and rationale; rather, it was the superstitions of the Andes. Reminiscences of erudite descriptions of European witchcraft hover in the background. Hence Polo suggested that in the Andes, as in Europe, witches flew through the air, spoke to the devil, and learned of matters that it would not be possible to know by natural means.[46] Such activities were far removed from the divinatory deities whom Andeans actually consulted and the utterances of Andean priests whose bodies the gods had chosen as their dwelling place.

Yet Spaniards recognized, even feared, the power that crystalized in Andean expressions of worship and concepts of deity and sought to understand these phenomena by applying to them the cognitive vocabulary of imagination and illusion. Polo de Ondegardo was convinced of the erroneous, illusory quality of Andean religious concepts and the practices that arose from them. Andeans believed in the immortality of the soul, as Christians did, Polo conceded, but at the same time this belief resulted in the pernicious custom of burying the living with the dead: "From the great good of believing in the immortality of souls, the devil brought upon them a very great evil by causing the death of so many people."[47] Religious error came about, in the first instance, thanks to demonic illusion. However, once launched, it persisted and ramified quite independently of further demonic intervention. Polo could thus write of all Andean burial customs, vain as he thought them to be, as having been devised "in accordance with their imagination." The same applied to other aspects of religion. The foundation myth of the Incas, in which were anchored many of their religious institutions and their claim to empire, thus was a product of the untutored Andean imagination, seeing that the true account of human origins after Noah's flood had been forgotten.[48] Like the Incas, so all other Andeans told stories about their different origins, "each one according to his imagination."[49] It was the same with all other aspects of religious thought and observance. Referring to his account of the network of shrines surrounding Inca Cuzco, Polo thus wrote:

There were in this city, and within a radius of a league and a half of it, some four hundred sites where sacrifices were offered, and much property was expended on them for different purposes from which the Indians imagine they derive benefit.[50]

The very greatness and holiness of Cuzco was the outcome of "imaginations and opinions" that the Incas fostered about this city among their subjects. It was thanks to these imaginations and opinions that year by year the Inca subjects brought their sacrifices and tribute to the center of empire, and enhanced the splendor and glory of the city by their labor.

Like other Spaniards, Polo was caught in the grip of two conflicting impressions of Amerindian civilizations. On the one hand, he could not withhold his admiration for Andean administrative, cultural, and economic achievements and thought that Andean and Inca institutions should be preserved within colonial government. On the other hand, the "false" religion of Andean people was a product of demonic illusion and had to be extirpated, however much it might be inseparable from all other aspects of Andean life.

This conflict and its resolution in the New World at large is the central theme of the *Apologética historia* that the Dominican friar and missionary Bartolomé de Las Casas completed in 1559, after many years of research and writing.[51] Like everyone else who thought about American religions, Las Casas was deeply preoccupied with the role of imagination in religious perception. But he addressed the question in a new way by describing American religions in their social, cultural, and historical context, and by examining the impact of demons and the devil on imagination, not only in America but also in the ancient Mediterranean and his own contemporary Europe.

As many sixteenth-century Europeans were agreed, the stars were moved in their courses by angelic intelligences, invisible spiritual energies. The demons also were invisible spiritual energies, but they, the angels who had fallen with Lucifer, were evil, a continuously active negative force in the universe. According to Las Casas, the Incas had understood something about this force, for in one of their myths they related that before he made the world, the Creator

Viracocha had a son called Taguapica Viracocha, who contradicted his father in every-thing. Whereas the father made men good, this son made them evil, both in body and soul. . . . The father made springs and the son dried them up . . . so that finally, the father became wroth and threw his son into the sea to die an evil death, but he never did die. This fiction or imagination appears to signify the fall of the first evil angel, who was created a son of God, but his pride made him evil and always contrary to God his creator. He was thrown into the sea, according to the words of the *Apocalypse*, chapter 20: "The devil was cast down into the deep."[52]

Like the two-faced Pachacamac of whom Hernando Pizarro had been told, Vira-cocha the Creator was also Viracocha the destroyer. But to Las Casas, the myth made a different point. Just as the Bible and the early Christian apologists in Europe told of the vigor and destructiveness of demonic power, so did this myth in the Andes.

It was thus by invoking demons that the magicians of Pharaoh had trans-formed their rods into serpents; for the demons, Las Casas explained, substi-tuted the rods with putrid matter from which the serpents were engendered.[53] Incited by magical rituals, the demons moved air, clouds, and lightning, thereby unleashing tempests.[54] At other times, demons appeared in the guise of the dead and spoke with their voices,[55] just as Cieza, whose *Crónica* Las Casas had read, thought had been observed in the Andes. Thus it was that the many exegetes of the *Book of Kings* could not agree whether the witch of Endor had brought up the spirit of the prophet Samuel himself to speak to Saul, or whether it was a demon who spoke in the guise of Samuel.[56] Certainly at Delphi a demon in the guise of a long-dead king named Apollo had possessed the Pythia to deliver oracles. For when the Pythia

ascended the sacred seat, the devil entered into her from the secret lower parts and she became filled and enraged with an infernal fury, unloosened her hair and foamed at the mouth so that a hundred men could not hold or hinder her. In this state of rage, she threw herself on the ground and thus recumbent the petition for an oracle was put before her. She responded what the demon commanded her to say, without feeling anything or knowing what she said. . . . This was the divine and holy rage that the gentiles thought came from heaven.[57]

But the rage did not come from heaven. Rather, the demon who had seized the body of the priestess deranged her senses so that her imagination could not convey true images to her intellect, and she raved of the phantasms the demon put before her. The demons were able to do such things because, as Aquinas had so carefully explained regarding the eucharist and eucharistic visions, the acci-dents of an object, its external appearance, were separable from its substance.

Similarly, Cieza's demons walking in the fields in the guise of dead Andean lords displayed the accidents of those lords and the substance of demons.

Throughout the ancient Mediterranean, demons had spoken ambiguously in the guise of the dead or from hollow statues and had possessed themselves of human beings. At the advent of the cross they took flight, and hence, not surprisingly, were to be found in large numbers in the Americas. Las Casas heard from an eyewitness how the Dominican Pedro de Córdoba exorcized one such demon from a young Indian priest in Paria. Before coming out this demon claimed that he would take the souls of his devotees to certain "pleasant and delightful places," but the friar forced the demon to confess that the destination of those souls was hell. The fraud that the serpent had perpetrated on Adam and Eve in paradise was no different.[58]

The ubiquity of demonic illusion in Europe both ancient and modern and in the New World disqualified it as a means of evaluating the Indian imagination as somehow more prone to error or more childlike than the imagination of Europeans. For vulnerability to demonic illusion and hence to the idolatrous worship that the demons fostered was the common human lot. By way of explaining this state of affairs, Las Casas appealed, in the footsteps of Augustine, to "the secret judgments of God, which are many, but never unjust."[59]

In this way, Las Casas removed from the discussion of Amerindian religions those grounds for negative value judgments that had been implicit in earlier accounts. The task at hand was not to contrast the true Christian religion with the false religions of classical antiquity and the Americas. Rather, it was to understand the origin and nature of human perceptions of God. Las Casas approached this task from two different angles. On the one hand, he argued that the perception of God originated in each individual. On the other hand, this perception was conditioned by the culture and the political ordering of the individual's society. Religion could thus not be understood in isolation from its historical and social context. With this vision of the totality of any given society, the contradiction that Polo de Ondegardo and to a lesser extent Cieza de León perceived in Andean religion and statecraft was suspended.

Therefore, given that the demons did influence an individual's perception,[60] it was possible to inquire after the other factors that, as Aristotle had found, conditioned the five senses, imagination, and hence intellect. The Indians, Las Casas argued, were as chaste and temperate "as the holy fathers in the desert,"[61] while the climate of the New World produced in its inhabitants a natural equanimity and gentleness of temperament,[62] a harmonious working of the faculties of the soul. The Indians were thus not victims of those vaporous images that blur the imaginations of intemperate persons who are ruled by their passions. Instead, Indian customs had allowed those Aristotelian "seeds of virtues" with which every human being was endowed to grow into actual virtues, practiced in daily life,[63] so that the Indians had reached a knowledge of God by natural reason.

The customs and habits of the individual were writ large in society and in a society's historical evolution. Las Casas thus analyzed Amerindian societies according to the criteria of Aristotle's *Politics* so as to show that the growth of cultural and political sophistication went hand in hand with increasingly refined theological ideas. The religion of the Inca empire was one of several examples that Las Casas elaborated. Viracocha, the creator god whom the Incas had super-imposed on lesser regional deities approximated closely to the God who had revealed himself in Scripture. And the divine Sun of the Incas had been appro-priately revered not as God but as "the principal creation of God." The divine Sun thus made clear to the Incas "what God commands." Las Casas wrote:

Here, they did not wander far from the truth, because as we read in the *Divine Names* of St. Dionysius, apart from men and angels no creature shows forth the attributes and excel-lencies of God as clearly as does the Sun. . . . Therefore they served and honored him and offered him sacrifice.[64]

But the sun in the *Divine Names* of Dionysius the Areopagite was a long way from the divine Sun of the Incas and its cult image that was displayed in Cuzco's Coricancha, "the enclosure of gold." For this golden image represented the Sun as a young boy, and inside it were preserved the hearts of deceased Inca rulers.[65] Elsewhere, also, Las Casas recast Andean religious ideas in conformity with his comparative framework. But he achieved one thing: the *Apologética historia* laid the groundwork required to consider American religions as, *inter alia*, cultural phenomena capable of being studied independently of Christian theological con-viction.[66] Las Casas did this by insisting on the conditioning of the imagination by a person's moral habits and social and cultural environment. Demonic violence and destruction were not discounted, but neither were they the indispensable means of explaining religious difference.

Few of his contemporaries, and almost no one in subsequent generations, took much notice of this breakthrough. Instead, historians and missionaries continued elaborating the theory that the personal and cultural deficiencies of Andeans, and of all other people living in that "less noble part of the world,"[67] had facilitated the grip of the demons on their imagination. In addition, sixteenth-century ethnographic investigation yielded in the seventeenth century to repetition of stereotypes.

Yet, Las Casas did point to a way of the imagination being free of the demons that had a future. We catch a glimpse of the direction of this change in Francisco Zurbarán's painting of the temptation of St. Jerome, which was commissioned by the Jeronymite monks of Guadalupe in Extremadura. Like Anthony the hermit as depicted by Patinir, Jerome is tempted by women (fig. 8). But there is nothing sinister or demonic in the exquisitely poised lady musicians whose melody has taken the saint's attention away from his book. It is the choice between two dif-ferent goods that confronts the aged ascetic, who must reject the melody of feminine beauty so as to remain faithful to his earlier choice of learned chastity. The experience of temptation as here depicted by Zurbarán has nothing to do with demons. Rather, temptation is a state of mind.

Elsewhere in Europe, likewise, the demons were losing their explanatory usefulness. This is particularly clear in the writings of Zurbarán's contemporary, the philosopher Baruch Spinoza. Spinoza lived all his life in the Netherlands, but his parents were Portuguese.[68] Spinoza himself was interested in Spanish literature; indeed, apart from a number of Greek and Latin classics, the only literary works he owned were by Cervantes, Góngora, Quevedo, and Gracián.[69] As a philosopher, also, he addressed issues that had been important in Spain, although he did this by redefining both the issues in themselves and the terms that had been used to formulate them. To begin with, he discounted the demons as nonexistent because no clear and unequivocal ideas could be formed about them.[70] In addition, he considered the inscrutable but never unjust judgments of God that permitted demonic activity to be an appeal to human ignorance, not to divine justice.[71] And finally, he did not regard the prophets of the Hebrew Bible as the rational and philosophically inclined individuals that medieval Aristotelians had

FIGURE 8. Francisco Zurbarán, *Temptation of St. Jerome*, ca. 1635. Sacristy of the monastery of Guadalupe, Spain.

Demons, Imagination, and the Incas   121

made of them. The prophet Daniel, for instance, far from being endowed with a lucid imagination attuned to receive prophetic revelation, could not understand the revelation he received, and was moreover terrified of the divine utterance.[72] In any case, Spinoza did not construe imagination as the Aristotelian faculty of the soul that conceived of those true or false phantasms without which no thought is possible. Instead, to imagine was to think speculatively and independently of any external physical reality:

In order to begin to indicate what error is, I should like you to note that the imaginations of the mind, considered in themselves, contain no error, or that the mind does not err from the fact that it imagines, but only in so far as it is considered to lack an idea that excludes the existence of those things that it imagines to be present to it. For if the mind while it imagines nonexistent things as present to it, at the same time knows that those things do not exist, it attributes this power of imagining to a virtue of its nature, not to a vice—especially if this faculty of imagining depended only on its own nature, i.e., if the mind's faculty of imagining were free.[73]

Freedom, according to Spinoza, was a product of virtue, and the practice of virtue, as Las Casas had already pointed out, was independent of cultural tradition. An adherent of Spinoza's philosophy would therefore not argue that Indians were more prone to vain imaginings than other people. But Spinoza did not think about Indians, and his arguments remained unknown to the men who framed and implemented policies in vice-regal Peru. In addition, European ideas about the Americas were changing. In the experience of Spanish colonial administrators during the late seventeenth and early eighteenth centuries, Indians were rarely opponents in warfare who for this reason alone had in one way or another to be taken seriously. Nor were they perceived to be the heirs of the great culture that Cieza and his contemporaries had admired, or the targets of evangelizing rhetoric passionate with contempt and ferocity. Rather, Indians in their new enlightenment guise of noble savages figured in quiet and sometimes profound inquiry into man's origin and true nature. But those noble savages had nothing in common with the Incas recently dead, or the living Andeans who so deeply preoccupied those Spaniards whose voices we have heard. In this way, while the European imagination came to be free of demons, there was also a price to be paid for that freedom. For the possibility of forming unequivocal ideas such as Spinoza might acknowledge ousted from European minds that unencumbered curiosity and capacity for engagement with which Cieza and some of his contemporaries had looked at the New World and its people.

Notes

1. John Frederick Nims, *The Poems of St. John of the Cross* (Chicago, 1979), 95, translates the verses quoted: "The wayfaring virgin, / Word in her womb / comes walking your way—/ haven't you room?" See also his note, p. 149.
2. William A. Christian, Jr., *Apparitions in Late Medieval and Renaissance Spain* (Princeton, N.J., 1981), 150.
3. Joseph de Borchgrave d'Altena, "La Messe de Saint Grégoire," *Bulletin des Musées royaux des beaux arts*, May–June 1959, 3–34; Andrée de Bosque, *Quentin Metsys* (Brussels, 1975), 132ff. See Clemente Sanchez de Vercial, *Libro de los Exemplos por A.B.C.*, ed. John Esten Keller (Madrid, 1961), 337ff., for the legend of a monk who sees the Christ child on the altar.
4. See Carolyn Walker Bynum, *Holy Feast and Holy Fast: The Religious Significance of Food to Medieval Women* (Berkeley, 1987).
5. Aquinas *Summa theologica* 3.76.8 resp.; "contours" translates the Latin *figura*. Aquinas was here thinking not of the legendary vision of Pope Gregory but of appearances of the child Jesus or of his human flesh in the host during his own time.
6. Ibid.
7. Aristotle *De anima* 3.431a16; Aquinas *Summa theologica* 1.84.7.
8. Aristotle *De anima* 3.428b21.
9. Aristotle *De anima* 3.431a17ff.; I am using the term "synthesis" to paraphrase Aristotle's *mesotes* or "mean." See also E. P. Mahoney, "Sense, Intellect, and Imagination in Albert, Thomas, and Siger," in Norman Kretzmann et al., eds., *Cambridge History of Later Medieval Philosophy* (Cambridge, 1982), 609.
10. Aquinas *Summa theologica* 1.84.7 resp.
11. The importance of demons in Christian thinking can be gauged from the argumentative ferocity with which Augustine addressed problems generated by them in his *City of God*; see in particular books 8–11.
12. Aquinas *Summa theologica* 3.76.8 resp.
13. Lope de Barrientos, *Tratado del dormir*, in Fray Luis G. A. Getino, *Vida y obras de Fray Lope de Barrientos*, in *Anales Salmantinos*, vol. 1 (Salamanca, 1927), 52ff., 56.
14. Among the tasks of the Inquisition was that of assisting in the maintenance of this order. See, most recently, Stephen Haliczer, *Inquisition and Society in the Kingdom of Valencia* (Berkeley, 1990).
15. Pedro Ciruelo, *Reprobación de las supersticiones y hechicerías* (1538; reprint ed., Valencia, 1978), part 3, chap. 1.
16. Ibid., part 1, chap. 3; part 2, chap. 1; part 2, chap. 6.
17. Yosepf ha-Kohen, *'Emeq ha-Bakra*, trans. Pilar Leon Tello (Madrid, 1964), 127ff.
18. See Sabine MacCormack, "The Fall of the Incas: A Historiographical Dilemma," *History of European Ideas* 6, no. 4 (1985): 422–23.
19. Pedro de Cieza de León, *Crónica del Perú*, part 1, ed. Franklin Pease G. Y. (Lima, 1984), chap. 72.
20. [Miguel de Estete], "Relación de la conquista del Perú," in *Colección de libros y documentos referentes a la historia del Perú* (hereafter *CLD*), 2nd ser., vol. 8 (Lima, 1928), 38; Miguel de Estete, "Relación del viage . . . ," in Francisco de Xerez, *Verdadera relación de la conquista del Perú*, ed. Concepción Bravo (Madrid, 1985), 137; Hernando Pizarro to the Audiencia of Santo Domingo, in *CLD*, 2nd ser., vol. 3 (Lima, 1920), 176–77.

21. Estete, "Relación del viaje," 137; Pierre Duviols, *Cultura andina y represión: Procesos y visitas de idolatrías y hechicerías Cajatambo, siglo XVII* (Cuzco, Peru, 1986), 8; Maria Rostworowski, *Estructuras andinas del poder* (Lima, 1983), 42ff.

22. [Estete], "Relación de la conquista," 38–39; the translation is an abridged rendering of the text.

23. "Relación de la religion y ritos del Perú, hecha por los primeros religiosos Augustinos que allí passaron," in *Colección de documentos ineditos relativos al descubrimiento, conquista y organización de las posesiones españolas en America y Oceania* (hereafter *CDI*), vol. 3 (Madrid, 1865), 25–26.

24. Pedro Pizarro, *Relación del descubrimiento y conquista de los reinos del Perú* (Lima, 1978), 57ff.; Xerez, *Verdadera relación*, 127.

25. Cieza de León, *Crónica*, part 1, 44, Tumebamba; 89, Vilcas; 84, Xauxa. On Guaribilca, see also Cristóbal de Molina, *Relación de las fábulas y ritos de los Incas*, ed. Henrique Urbano and Pierre Duviols, in Cristóbal de Molina and Cristóbal de Albornoz, *Fábulas y mitos de los Incas* (Madrid, 1989), 53.

26. Cieza de León, *Crónica*, part 1, 62.

27. Ibid.; cf. 33, 51, 100–101.

28. Ciruelo, *Reprobación*, part 1, chap. 2; Cieza de León, *Crónica*, part 1, 43, 62; Pedro de Cieza de León, *Crónica del Perú*, part 2, ed. Francisca Cantú (Lima, 1985), 29.

29. Ciruelo, *Reprobación*, part 2, chap. 8; Cieza de León, *Crónica*, part 1, 48.

30. Cieza de León, *Crónica*, part 1, 62.   31. Ibid., 80.

32. Cieza de León, *Crónica*, part 2, 28.

33. See Sabine MacCormack, *Children of the Sun and Reason of State: Myths, Ceremonies, and Conflicts in Inca Peru*, 1992 Lecture Series, Working Papers no. 6, Department of Spanish and Portuguese, University of Maryland, College Park (1990).

34. See Cieza de León, *Crónica*, part 1, 43, Riobamba; cf. 41, Tacunga.

35. Cieza de León, *Crónica*, part 1, 62, Yungas.

36. Detailed documentation for such burial customs maintained in the seventeenth century in the central Andean highlands has been published by Duviols, *Cultura andina*; for continued ancestral cults a century later, see Frank Salomon, "Ancestor Cults and Resistance to the State in Arequipa, ca. 1748–1754," in Steve J. Stern, ed., *Resistance, Rebellion, and Consciousness in the Andean Peasant World, Eighteenth to Twentieth Centuries* (Madison, Wisc., 1987), 148–65.

37. Cieza de León, *Crónica*, part 1, 97.

38. Domingo de Santo Tomas, *Lexicon o vocabulario de la lengua general del Perú* (Valladolid, 1560; Lima, 1951), s.v. "pacari," fol. 158r.

39. See Frank Salomon, *Native Lords of Quito in the Age of the Incas* (Cambridge, 1987), 21ff.

40. Cieza de León, *Crónica*, part 1, 61.

41. "Religiosos Augustinos," in *CDI*, 3:25.

42. Ibid., 18, devil as eagle, and 39, as serpent; 26ff., sons of Catequil; 17ff., demonic vocation in a solitude; 19, demonic possession.

43. Ibid., 33–34.   44. Ibid.

45. Ibid., 30, *guaca* on campaign; 33, Inca irrigation cult; 41, cult of Sun.

46. Juan Polo de Ondegardo, *Los errores y supersticiones de los Indios*, in *CLD*, vol. 3 (Lima, 1916), 29; Brian P. Levack, *The Witch Hunt in Early Modern Europe* (New York, 1987), 40–45.

47. Juan Polo de Ondegardo, *Relación de los fundamentos acerca del notable daño que resulta de no guardar a los indios sus fueros*, in *CLD*, vol. 3 (Lima, 1916), 117.

48. At issue was the interpretation of the book of Genesis as history; see Don Cameron Allen, *The Legend of Noah: Renaissance Rationalism in Art, Science, and Letters* (Urbana, Ill., 1949). Since Polo and his contemporaries regarded the story of Noah as historical, they were committed to the opinion that Andean and Inca myths of origins, which they also interpreted historically, were false.

49. Juan Polo de Ondegardo, *Relación del linaje de los Incas*, in *CLD*, vol. 4 (Lima, 1917), 45, 48, 49.

50. "Informe del licenciado Juan Polo de Ondegardo al licenciado Briviesca de Muna-tones . . . ," *Revista histórica* (Lima) 13 (1940): 183–84.

51. For the date, see Edmundo O'Gorman, ed., Bartolomé de Las Casas, *Apologética historia* (Mexico City, 1987), xxi–xxxvi; in the vast literature on Las Casas and his intellectual world, note Anthony Pagden, *The Fall of Natural Man: The American Indian and the Origins of Comparative Ethnology* (Cambridge, 1982); Marcel Bataillon, *Estudios sobre Bartolomé de las Casas* (Madrid, 1976); Juan Friede and Benjamin Keen, *Bartolomé de Las Casas in History: Toward an Understanding of the Man and His Work* (DeKalb, Ill., 1971).

52. Las Casas, *Apologética historia*, chap. 126.

53. The story is in Exodus 17.11; quoted in Las Casas, *Apologética historia*, chap. 87, p. 450; also chap. 88.

54. This demonic influence on the weather stands at the core of the plot of Shakespeare's *Tempest*.

55. Aquinas *Summa theologica* 2.172.6; 2.174.5 ad 4.

56. Las Casas, *Apologética historia*, chap. 101; see also Augustine *Quaestiones ex Veteri Testamento* 27 (Migne *PL* 35.2232); *Quaestiones ad Simplicianum* 2.3 (Migne *PL* 40.1142); *Quaestiones ad Dulcitium* 6 (Migne *PL* 40.162); further, Heinrich Kraemer and Jakob Sprenger, *Malleus Maleficarum*, trans. Montague Summers (London, 1928; New York, 1971), 80; Martin de Castañega, *Tratado de las supersticiones y hechicerías* (Logroño, 1529; Madrid, 1946), 38.

57. Las Casas, *Apologética historia*, chap. 80, p. 417; note citation of Acts 16.16ff.

58. Las Casas, *Apologética historia*, chap. 245, Pedro de Córdoba; chap. 81, Adam and Eve.

59. Ibid., chap. 92.   60. Ibid., chaps. 87, 94.   61. Ibid., chap. 35.

62. Ibid., chap. 36.   63. Ibid., chap. 186.   64. Ibid., chap. 126.

65. Antonio Bautista de Salazar, *Relación sobre . . . Don Francisco de Toledo . . .* , in *CDI*, vol. 8 (Madrid, 1867), 280; letter by Don Francisco de Toledo, 20 October 1572, in Roberto Levillier, *Gobernantes del Perú: Cartas y papeles*, vol. 4 (Madrid, 1924), 345.

66. The *Apologética historia* remained unpublished until the nineteenth century, but it was liberally excerpted by Jerónimo Román in his *Repúblicas del mundo* (Medina del Campo, 1575; rev. ed., Salamanca, 1595). It was thus through Román's work, which circulated widely in Spain, that Las Casas's ideas on religion came before the reading public. For the European context of Las Casas's work, see the masterly essay by Arnaldo Momigliano, "Historiography of Religion: Western Views," in his *On Pagans, Jews, and Christians* (Middletown, Conn., 1987), 11–30.

67. See José de Acosta, *Historia natural y moral de las Indias*, ed. Edmundo O'Gorman (Mexico City, 1962), book 4, chap. 2, pp. 142ff., arguing that divine providence endowed the Americas with great mineral wealth so as to encourage missionary endeavors among the "less political" Indians; for the more noble and less noble parts of the world, see ibid., book 5, chap. 1, p. 218; Nicolas Antonio, *Censura de historias fabulosas . . . obra posthuma* (Valencia, 1742), 644, letter to Juan Lucas Cortés: people go to the Indies so as "to bury oneself in forgetfulness of everything that is virtuous

and precious about Europe." Note the revealing distinction in this work that Europe was favored by God not so that its denizens should go "to converse with Indians, but only in order to investigate the Indies."

68. Abraham de Mordechai Vaz Dias and Willem Gerard van der Tak, "Spinoza: Merchant and Autodidact," *Studia rosenthaliana* 16 (1982): 109–71.

69. A. J. Servaas van Rooijen, *Inventaire des livres formant la bibliothèque de Benedict Spinoza, publié d'après un document inédit* (The Hague, 1889), 143ff., Quevedo; 159, Góngora; 189, another copy of Góngora; 176, Cervantes; 183, Gracián. Gracián was neither named in the inventory nor identified by the editor, but the title *El criticón*, which is supplied by the inventory, makes the identification certain.

70. See Benedict Spinoza, Letters 55–60 (trans. R. H. M. Elwes, *On the Improvement of the Understanding; The Ethics; Correspondence* [New York, 1955]) to Hugo Boxel; for Spinoza's insistence that propositions, in order to be true, must be unequivocal see his *Treatise*, 50, 77ff. See also the newer translation, titled *Emendation of the Intellect*, by Edwin Curley in *The Collected Works of Spinoza* (Princeton, N.J., 1985).

71. Spinoza *Ethics* 1.36, appendix 1; see also Las Casas, *Apologética historia*, chap. 92, quoting Augustine on the just will of God.

72. See above, pp. 125–26, for Lope de Barrientos's description of Daniel; and Benedict Spinoza, *A Theologico-Political Treatise*, trans. R. H. M. Elwes (New York, 1951), 32.

73. Spinoza *Ethics* 2.17, scholium; in his *Opera posthuma* (n.p., 1677). I follow Curley's translation in *Collected Works*, 465, but have amended it slightly.

The Philosopher's Breviary:
Jean de Léry in the Enlightenment

IN THE SIXTEENTH CENTURY, France did not remain a stranger to the conquest of New Worlds. Several attempts at colonization were made, from 1555 to 1565, first in Brazil under the direction of the chevalier de Villegagnon, and then in Florida, under the administration of Jean Ribault and René de Laudonnière.[1] These ventures, which repeatedly ended in failure, nevertheless aroused great interest in Europe, much more than did the voyages of Jacques Cartier. Colonies located in tropical countries, unlike Canada with its harsh winters, exercised an undeniable power of fascination.

Moreover, the daring colonial enterprises in Brazil, and still more so that in Florida, had greater strategic importance than New France on the Saint Lawrence. By positioning himself near the Caribbean, Admiral de Coligny planned to strike the Spanish empire at its most vulnerable point, directly threatening the route of its galleons. But in both Brazil and Florida, the final catastrophe was proportionate to initial ambitions. The destruction of France Antarctique in Rio de Janeiro in 1560 and the worse disaster in Florida in the autumn of 1565, when a thousand colonists were methodically slaughtered by order of the *adelantado* Menendez de Avilés, figure among the most bloody episodes of the rivalry between European imperialisms at the dawn of the modern age.

These attempts at colonization were all carried out by Protestants. Under the protection of Coligny, they were led by privateers like Ribault and gentlemen like Laudonnière, all partisans of the Reformation. Both Normandy and Saintonge, areas where the new religion had followers even among the common people, sent colonizers and equipment. We know in this matter the role played by the city of Dieppe, the "Norman Geneva," in the Huguenot expansion across the seas.

Through the Protestant diaspora, news of these attempts soon reached cities such as London, Geneva, and Frankfurt, but it primarily stayed within the reformed milieu. We can see the formation of a mythology of the conquest of the New World in a series of texts that Marcel Bataillon has suggested we call the "Huguenot corpus on America."[2] These testimonies and commentaries form a continuous chain—from Jean de Léry's *Histoire du Brésil* and Urbain Chauveton's *Histoire nouvelle du Nouveau Monde* to Théodore de Bry's collec-

127

tion *Grands voyages*[3]—that lead directly to Montaigne's "Of Cannibals" and "Of Coaches."[4]

This Huguenot corpus, whose outlines become clear around 1580, is organized around two complementary themes: 1) a denunciation of the crimes of the Spanish Conquest, using for support the *Brevíssima relación* of Bartolomé de Las Casas, which was everywhere translated and accessible; 2) a defense of the free and happy savage, whom the bloody conquerors should have left to his native ignorance, even at the risk of his eternal damnation.

But this Protestant literature at the close of the Renaissance was not just anticolonialist. It appeared at the precise moment when the imperialist ambitions of England and later of Holland were awakening. Through a rewritten colonial history, it encouraged the current enterprises of Walter Ralegh in Virginia, of Martin Frobisher among the Eskimos, and of Francis Drake in his audacious circumnavigation of 1580–83. At the same time it reproduced conflicting points of view between principal figures at the heart of the Protestant cause: on the one hand, those who were anticolonialist for theological reasons, such as Jean Calvin or the Protestant minister Pierre Richer, or for ethical reasons, such as Jean de Léry; on the other, those with the geopolitical vision of Chauveton and of Philippe du Plessis-Mornay and, later, with colonial views as described at the turn of the seventeenth century by Marc Lescarbot and Antoine de Montchrestien.[5]

The Huguenot corpus described a scene and set a tone in which a satire of Catholic, conquering Europe was linked to an exaltation of the oppressed Indian. However, this polemic never amounted to a unified program or doctrine. A century and a half later, these interweavings of disparate texts acquired a coherence that they lacked at the beginning. Taken up again by the philosophy of the Enlightenment, reinvested in the service of a triumphant Reason that overthrew superstition and fanaticism, the Huguenot corpus was reduced and simplified, yielding the idealized figure of the Noble Savage, the pious image of an antiChristian religion.

The reworking of the iconography of the *Grands voyages* and *Petits voyages* of Théodore de Bry and his sons (1592–1634) in the *Ceremonies et coutumes religieuses* of Bernard Picart, a French engraver who took refuge in Holland after the Revocation of the Edict of Nantes (1685), provides an excellent example of this process. Through the adjusting and recentering of scenes, the already biased description of the Spanish conquest and its crimes was put to use in the philosophical combat against the Church of Rome.[6] The Mass was debased to the level of the primitive and sometimes repugnant rites of the Kaffirs and the Hottentots.

Repetitive uniformity and polemical schematization contributed to an impoverishment of the knowledge of distant lands and peoples. At the beginning of the Enlightenment all the symptoms of a veritable "anthropological recession" had developed, in part a consequence of the relative lack of exploration and discovery during the greater part of the Classical Age.

The Philosopher's Breviary

In order to illustrate these general points, I will take as example Jean de Léry's *Histoire d'un voyage faict en la terre du Bresil*, a work that both directly and indirectly influenced authors as diverse as John Locke and Pierre Bayle,[7] the Abbé Raynal, Denis Diderot, and Jean-Jacques Rousseau.[8] This travel narrative—the "philosopher's breviary" before it became, in Claude Lévi-Strauss's famous phrase, the "breviary of the ethnologist"[9]—was from its publication in Geneva in 1578 a European success. Five French editions appeared during the author's lifetime in addition to two Latin editions, among which was the "Digest" of Urbain Chauveton, included in the third volume of de Bry's *America* (1592). Conceived in the Calvinist milieu of French-speaking Switzerland, and relying for some of its material on existing Protestant sources, Léry's *Histoire* nonetheless exceeded in the import of its message the more narrow confines of its birth.

Léry's originality is not due to his presenting updated or new facts previously unavailable to his predecessors. The Tupinikin Indians of southern Brazil were already well known in France since the publication of the *Singularitez de la France Antarctique* by the Franciscan André Thevet in 1557. In 1575, the same author had provided in his *Cosmographie universelle* an expanded version of his ethnographic description, adding in particular several chapters on Tupi mythology. Aside from a "dialogue" or handbook of French-Tupi conversation and a musical transcription of Indian songs and dances, which remained available up through the *Encyclopédie* of d'Alembert and Diderot,[10] Léry's book added little to the previous documentary corpus.

The interest of Léry's work lies, rather, in the gaze and the conscience that emerge in the face of the other, in the course of an arduous ocean voyage that takes the narrator into the midst of naked and cannibalistic peoples. We could say that Léry's *Histoire* combines the *Bildungsroman* with the adventure novel, provided we do not forget that it is a testimony whose truth is affirmed at each point. Involuntary memories, whether olfactory, gustatory, or auditory, caused by the starchy odor of grated manioc, the intoxicating perfumes of the tropical forest, or the monotonous litany of dancers contribute to the mirage of an intact presence.

Léry's adventure is unique because, thanks to the acuity of his reported sensations and his dramatic account, he was able to create an illusion of reality without equal among Renaissance voyagers. But such a miracle of verisimilitude is fragile, and all the more threatened in that it is from the very start marked by mourning.

"I often regret that I am not among the savages," declares the narrator at the end of his account (342). This curious avowal, the first appearance in travel literature of nostalgia and remorse, two emotions that later become inseparable from the ethnological enterprise,[11] shows all the ambiguity of Léry's experience.

Exile creates the savages' beauty; their virtual death makes them desirable. When Léry evoked this perspective, in the chapter consecrated to "what we can call religion among the American savages" (230–61), he was not thinking of the physical disappearance of the Indians, menaced by the Portuguese and Spanish conquest; above all, he had in mind the "second death" that awaits them, the eternal damnation due to their remaining in error. The Indians are cannibals who go naked against the law of Nature and never pardon offenses, in spite of the exhortations of Christ. Every attempt by Léry and his followers to convert the Indians had failed.

Doubtless the song of Psalm 104 under the sunny foliage, filled with macaws and birds "which sung like nightingales," had made an ephemeral communion possible between Huguenot and savage through a common adoration of the Creator (257–58).[12] But once this instant of lyrical illusion had passed, the Indians forgot the Gospel's lesson of love and returned to their cannibal cuisine.

Léry, as a good Calvinist, sees in this failure the effect of predestination. The Indian, descended from Shem according to all evidence, is the object of a particular curse, and missionaries of whatever persuasion can do nothing for his salvation.

There would have been nothing unusual in this view if Léry had remained content, after Fernandez de Oviedo for example, with such a Manichean vision of the opposition between civilized and savage. He went beyond simple condemnation, however, in taking up a clearly anticolonialist position. The Indians were unconvertible; thus, the Spaniards had no right to occupy their land under the pretext of evangelization. At the same time that the American Indians were excluded from redemption, they were protected in their physical and cultural integrity.

Consequently, there is no contradiction between the sincere admiration that Léry felt for these well-proportioned people, not at all "monstrous or prodigious towards us" (95), whose moral virtues could be seen as superior to those of the Europeans, and a radical historical pessimism, which left these same people out of the divine plan of Redemption. The Indian, admirable in everything but for the notable exception of religion, was saved in this life but lost in the next. This distinction was of considerable significance for Léry; it should prevent us from simply seeing in his work a first example of the myth of the Noble Savage, even if it does first announce and form a point of departure for this myth.

Indeed, Léry's readers, during the next two centuries, only retained a partial, simplified view of this distinction. Some of them, like Locke and Bayle, were to emphasize its religious implications—but they represent the exception. The *Histoire*'s pessimistic conclusion in chapter 16, on the religion of the "Americans," contributed to the revolutionary hypothesis of the existence of atheist peoples. At a time—the dawn of the Enlightenment—when atheism was no longer feared, when its example could, on the contrary, be occasionally useful in the struggle against obscurantism and intolerance, the bitter conclusion of the Calvinist writer lost its dramatic character. On the contrary, it enabled a vehement attack on the dogma of universality claimed by Christian revelation.[13]

However, the majority of readers in the Classical Age were sympathetic to Léry's vivid portraiture; they felt complicitous with and at times friendly toward the free savages who lived in harmony with nature, ignorant of the evils that the accumulation of material goods and technical progress had brought. Most readers willingly ignored the sword brandished by the second horseman of the Apocalypse, mounted on a red steed, who, according to Léry, had prophesied to the Indians their destruction "by fire and by war" if they did not adhere to the truth (254–56).[14] For such readers, the seductive appeal of the savage life portrayed by the *Histoire* was brought about by a fundamental misunderstanding. They did not recognize the religious dimension of a spiritual autobiography; they ignored the fear of a terrible and jealous God that conferred an undefinable precariousness to the description of the customs and morals of Nature. Once the omnipresent curse springing from original sin is left out of Léry, what remains of the poignancy of condemned children? His remarks become insipid when deprived of their theological dimension. The ambiguous myth of exile on earth of Eden becomes reduced to a philosophical novelette.

However, this reading of Léry is not naive. The misunderstanding of the author's purpose occurs first because of a change in historical context but then arises from deliberate manipulations that, while secularizing the *Histoire d'un voyage*, transform it into a product perfectly adapted to the new exigencies of the intellectual marketplace.

In considering Léry as "son" of the Enlightenment, I will refer to his three "philosophical" avatars: the *Voyages de François Coréal*, published in Amsterdam in 1722; volume 16 of the *Histoire générale des voyages* by the Abbé Prévost (Paris, 1757); and the *Histoire des deux Indes* by the Abbé Raynal, first published in 1770. These three texts or series of texts seem at first to be very different.[15] The *Voyages de François Coréal*, the shortest of the three, claims to be an original account, while the other two are collections of diverse documents, letters, ambassadors' reports, and statistical surveys, with chapters on botany and zoology in Prévost, all linked by continuous commentary. However, the difference between the first and the following two is less than it appears. The alleged *Voyages de Coréal* is also part of a series of texts: accounts of Guiana by Ralegh and Captain Keymis, the journals of Captains Narborough's and Tasman's return from the South Seas, and so on. Even if we consider the *Voyages de Coréal*, properly speaking, which consists of scarcely half of the three-volume edition of 1722, we are struck by the heteroclite character of an account that juxtaposes a polemical reflection on the "causes of the decadence of the Spanish in the West Indies" (1:10) with a savage anticatholic satire in which the procession of the Holy Sacrament on the day of Corpus Christi is called a "buffoonery." We see the capers and somersaults of the assistants, we hear the mewing and grunting of cats and pigs swaddled like infants and creating with human voices "a most impertinent concert" (1:161). In another example of the heterogeneity of this text, a statistical table of colonial Brazil is followed by an account of the natives of the country. By all evidence, we may conclude that this poorly stitched patchwork is apocryphal.

Did François Coréal even exist? A loose plot frames the different sections of the account: as an eighteen-year-old adolescent impatient to get away from his parents, Coréal embarks in Cartagena "full of passion for traveling, and moved by that curiosity common to young men which, when not backed by good sense and means, degenerates easily into libertinage" (1:3–4). His voyages, not surprisingly, bring him to maturity. Upon returning, after a circumnavigation that takes him to all areas of Spanish America (we might think here of the *Tour de France par deux enfants*), he discovers that his parents are dead. He then leaves for new adventures after settling his inheritance. The second part of his *Voyages*, which opens with a journey to Bahia, depicts him in Brazil, in a geographical marathon as exhaustive as the first. The second part of this three-part adventure serves as a pretext for describing, in eight chapters plagiarized from Léry, the edenic condition of the savages of the country, whom one is astonished to encounter at that late date so close to the seacoast and even at the "Grande Ile" of the bay of Rio de Janeiro.[16]

There one sees how Nature, "completely simple and without ornament, is sometimes so agreeable" (1:183), one of the leitmotivs of the *Histoire d'un voyage*, which exalted the native beauty of the Indian women of Guanabara. The pseudo-Coréal lavishly expands on the hallowed theme of decent nudity as infinitely preferable to the gaudy ornamentation of worldly people in our hemisphere: "I believe that the attire of European women excites men's lust more quickly than the simple and plain nudity of the Indian women" (1:190–91).[17] The sentence is taken literally from Léry, but the man of the Enlightenment continues to deliberate at length on the erotic paradox: "It is indeed true that this nudity strikes newcomers at first, but they soon grow accustomed to it: lust becomes disgusting, and one recovers the cold sense of chastity sooner than expected. Whatever you may see in the future, your vision remains tranquil" (1:191). Léry's naturism is tainted with pruriency here. The spectacle of unclothed innocence did not have quite the same resonance in the century of Henry II, where its allegorical meaning was predominant, as in the France of the Regency, where a philosophical quest often became the pretext for complaisant exhibitionism.

At any event, both Coréal and the Abbé Prévost, who cited Coréal favorably while suspecting him of plagiarizing from Léry,[18] took from Léry all that agreed with the optimism and the hedonism of the Enlightenment. For both Coréal and Prévost, respect for simple nature is evident as much in an absence of clothing as in the treatment of children. Maternal nursing, already cited by the Huguenot as it later would be by Rousseau; education without constraint; the precocious apprenticeship of martial virtue; the lessons of natural theology under sun-dappled foliage filled with bird songs, all points of an educational program that the Philosophers would make their own.

We can observe, however, several significant differences from the Huguenot corpus and particularly from Léry's *oeuvre*. In the first place, the anthropology of the Enlightenment rationalized whatever escaped interpretation in the morals of the Indians. This caused a thorough incomprehension of customs, rites, and beliefs that Renaissance observers were content to record without always reducing them to a simple explanation. Such is the case with the weeping salutation, a ceremony in which a stranger was welcomed to a village by copious tears and moans. This paradoxical rite, in which hospitality appears as mourning, can be explained by the visitor's peculiar status for the Indians: arriving from elsewhere, even from the other world, the visitor was welcomed as a ghost, a relative returned to his family after metamorphoses and long wanderings.[19]

The pseudo-Coréal, a mask for some contentious philosopher, does not know how to penetrate such subtleties. He vulgarizes the strange ceremony of welcome into a rite of departure. Doubtless, when travelers arrived women squatted "on their hams and on their heels, while covering their faces with their hands," in conformity with Léry's account (1:237–38).[20] But it is not certain that they shed tears between their open fingers. On the contrary, they congratulated visitors on their "happy arrival." According to Coréal, the beautiful native women always remained in that uncomfortable position during the entire visit, and it was not until the moment of departure that, still squatting with their hands over their faces, they wept and sighed "because we were leaving" (ibid.).[21]

The odd fixity of this *tableau vivant* originates from an engraving by Léry doubtless under the eyes of the author at the moment he invented this episode of his imaginary voyages. But as he did not understand the meaning of the represented posture, he immobilized and extended it until the moment of separation, at which point it recovered its habitual logic and its apparent motivation. From that moment, the Indian custom was brought into agreement with the rules of Western politeness and seemed to be an expression of universal sentiments: savages, like Europeans, cried when they separated and not when they first made acquaintance.

The same observation can be made about the demonic apparitions, "sometimes in the guise of a beast or bird, or another strange form" (Léry, *Histoire*, 234), that tormented the unhappy Indians. Léry did not doubt for an instant in the reality of these persecutions of the devil, and he did not hesitate to represent in an engraving an infernal Brazil populated with sloths with sneering faces, with flying fish and winged demons, which whipped and pursued the frightened Indians in all directions (235).[22] Unlike atheists, who denied the existence of a devil as well as that of God, the author of *Histoire d'un voyage* declared with insistence "that the Americans are very visibly and actually tormented by evil spirits" (238). The author of the *Voyages de Coréal* did not share this belief. The claimed marvels of Satan were in fact a fraud perpetrated by "priests" whose essential business, in Brazil as in Europe, was to trick poor humanity. This use of the word *priests* to describe the Indian shamans is in itself revealing, for Léry used the words *false prophets* and *Caribs*.

The pseudo-Coréal aimed at the Catholic religion through the indigenous superstitions collected by Léry. These members of the Indian clergy "are skillful enough in their imposture to be able to play the role of Agnian and then to persuade the Savages that it is he who mistreats and torments them. They especially fear him at night. The night is more favorable for deception" (2:226). Henceforth, without the collaboration between the observer and the observed, the religion of others became devalued into trickery, the supernatural reduced to a gross fraud. To a great extent, this misinterpretation was deliberate, as it answered to a precise ideological end. But from the outset it came about through a blindness to the other, whose concrete individuality became effaced behind the general principle of a universal human nature.

The second feature of the more-or-less conscious deformation of the documentary heritage bequeathed by the Renaissance was the projection onto the other of phantasms and desires belonging to the European imaginary. I have referred to the prurient nature of certain commentaries added to the "naive" descriptions of travelers of the sixteenth century. Elaborating on Léry, Coréal goes on at length on the nudity, less "striking" than it might seem, of the native Brazilian women. In a similar fashion, we find in this author an eulogy of polygamy placed in the eloquent mouth of a savage who stigmatizes in consequence the hypocritical conduct of Christians, monogamous in principle but assiduous followers of public women (1:163). The apparent moralism of this tirade does not deceive: the real adversary is still devout Catholicism, which, under the appearance of sanctity, dissimulates indelible defects. In contrast to the free and innocent loves of a savage Eden, the syphilis contracted by the Creoles and the Spaniards of the Indies is attended by examples of the most ridiculous devotion: *grains benits*, signs of the cross, and *avés* were transported to the courtesan's bed but were powerless to ward off the fatal epidemic (1:164).

A dash of sentimentality is sometimes mixed into this literary libertinage, at the cost of the body of the savage, as can be seen later in Voltaire's *Candide*.[23] Thus the Abbé Prévost gives an involuntary comic turn to the description, taken from Léry, of a rudimentary medical technique in use among the Tupi-Guarani of Brazil: "In their maladies, the Brazilians mutually treat each other with such tender attentions, that if it is a matter of a wound, a Neighbor appears immediately to suck out that of another; and all the duties of friendship are performed with the same zeal" (284).[24] This "tenderness," so eighteenth century in tone, was foreign to the rough universe of Léry, an almost always fearless witness to cannibal feasts and the atrocities of the wars of religion. This illusory exotic tenderness refers again to a universal human nature posed a priori. The therapeutic suction of wounds dissipates into a kiss in order to definitively express the universality of human emotions, whose expressions would be similar across the division of oceans and cultures.

Prévost, who was also sensitive to the chaste nudity of Indian women, consistent in his eyes with "natural innocence" (281), is more respectful toward ethnographic reality than the pseudo-Coréal, who sacrifices it to the exclusive profit of antireligious combat. Prévost maintains a different attitude toward Léry's text: where the plagiarist suppresses his sources, Prévost cites them scrupulously. The liberties he takes with his model are more restrained; he has a perfect right to play with the difference between the original text and the continuous commentary surrounding it. The possibility of a dialogue can be found in the critical distance separating Prévost's commentary from Léry's account, which is respected even in "its naive style, of which one only wishes to change obsolete terms" (277) but which is quoted in rearranged fragments.[25]

This distance, however, becomes the occasion for another misunderstanding. The pseudo-Coréal claims to trace, not without duplicity or bad faith, the portrait of a nonperverted innocence. A stranger to every anti-Christian prejudice, the Abbé Prévost himself extends the myth of innocence to include the witness (Léry). The ascription of such a quality is not without ambiguity. If Léry can be compared to the Brazilians because of his innocence and his unstudied style, he, like them, belongs to the past. Praise of his simplicity does not occur without reservations by Prévost on the disorder of his narration, which combines "a mixture of examples, of reflections, of comparisons, and of strange citations" so that it represents "a muddy spring" where the compiler must draw with discernment (265). The savor of archaism that Prévost tastes when citing Léry adds one more illusion to the seduction of lost origins. Even so, this is no longer an absolute model that one must blindly follow. The charms of savage life are weakened by the insipidity of a language inherited from the good old days.

According to Abbé Raynal, who wrote some fifteen years after Prévost, the value of Léry's account stems to a great extent from that "naivety" of language which marvelously suited "the fine common sense of savages." He only took from the Huguenot's work a dialogue "written in this naive style which characterised the French language two centuries ago, and where one can still find attractions that are regrettably lost" (*Histoire des deux Indes*, 2:376). This dialogue, or more precisely this somewhat rhetorical personification of an "old man" among the savages, reproaching the European for his avarice and his instability, served as a prototype for Diderot for the celebrated oratorical piece within the *Supplément au Voyage de Bougainville*. The reproach of "madness" addressed to the vagrant and greedy French announced the "departure," how much more radical, of the Tahitian old man.[26] Thus the man of the Enlightenment only took from Léry what best suited his concerns: praise of natural liberty, with a trace of libidinous nostalgia, war against all institutional oppression, and a militant anticatholicism that soon became joined to the struggle against the Christian religion.

In this way the eighteenth century invented a sixteenth century in its own image, an anthropological prehistory that conformed to its desires. This refashioning, we have seen, did not occur without errors, the apparent simplicity of an antiquated language contributing to embellish the painting of the naked children of the New World.

The feature that completed the tableau, accomplishing the illusory adequation between a present ideology and its past premises, brings us back to our starting point: the censure of everything that concerns religion. This censure, which will be taken up on another level by Claude Lévi-Strauss,[27] affects Brazilian shamanism as much as the observer's belief. We have seen how in Coréal the incomprehensible rites and inexplicable apparitions were brutally reduced to mechanisms of trickery and imposture. In an analogous and symmetrical fashion, Léry's Calvinism was corrected most often through simple omission. In chapter 16 of the *Histoire*, "Of what one can call religion among the savages . . ." (230–61), Bayle and Locke saw a demonstration of the Indians' atheism; Coréal and Prévost only remarked on the anecdotal or the spectacular, the demonic apparitions and the dance of tobacco, during which sorcerers and "caraïbes" instilled "the spirit of courage" into warriors who were in a trance. Both groups forgot Léry's condemnation, in the name of Genesis, of the cursed race of Shem; his sad remarks on "that people forsaken by God," whose conversion was difficult and whose redemption by Grace was improbable; and finally, his prediction of an apocalyptic end for them (260).

Coréal was tempted to see an image of Hell, in which, indeed, he scarcely believed, in the "peppery" and poxed Creoles rather than in the Indians who were stubbornly resistant to evangelization. And Prévost, who skillfully combined Léry's text with the distorted imitation of Léry by the pseudo-Spaniard, emphasized the positive aspects of the natural religion of the Indians, who "are not at all in absolute ignorance of the Divinity and . . . even render him a kind of homage, by often lifting their hands toward the Sun."[28]

In this way the Noble Savage, created by anamorphosis and deletion, has just the thickness of a playing card. The ethnographic poverty of his description, in Coréal and Raynal, and to a lesser degree in Prévost, is obvious. Their accounts of the savage were no more objective than the Huguenot's or "political" pamphlets of the reign of Henri III.[29] The savage was a convenient and malleable mouthpiece for them, just as he was during the struggle against Spanish and Catholic hegemony. Now he became the herald of the imprescribable rights of Nature against the arbitrariness of established social and religious rules. From the Calvinist "breviary" of Léry, we have arrived at the breviary of the Philosopher. In this exchange, the Brazilian Indian, whose soul was already in doubt, lost his body as well.

—Translated by Katharine Streip

Notes

1. For an account of these attempts at colonization, see Charles-André Julien, *Les Voyages de découverte et les premiers établissements* (Paris, 1948), as well as Frank Lestringant, *Le Huguenot et le sauvage* (Paris, 1990), chap. 1.

2. Marcel Bataillon, "L'Amiral et les 'nouveaux horizons' français," *Actes du colloque "L'Amiral de Coligny et son temps," October 1972* (Paris, 1974), 41–52.

3. Jean de Léry, *Histoire d'un voyage faict en la terre du Bresil* (Geneva, 1578). I cite from the slightly expanded second edition (Geneva, 1580; facsimile ed., Geneva, 1975); further citations will be given in the text. Urbain Chauveton, *Histoire nouvelle du Nouveau Monde: Contenant en somme ce que les Hespagnols ont fait jusqu'à present aux Indes Occidentales, et le rude traitement qu'ils font à ces povres peuples-la . . .* (Geneva, 1579). On the *Grands voyages* of Théodore de Bry, whose fourteen volumes were published from 1590 to 1634, see Michèle Duchet et al., *L'Amérique de Théodore de Bry: Une Collection de voyages protestante du XVIe siècle* (Paris, 1987).

4. "Of Cannibals" and "Of Coaches," in *The Complete Essays of Montaigne*, trans. Donald M. Frame (Stanford, Calif., 1958), 150–58, 685–98. Gilbert Chinard has shown Montaigne's debt to Chauveton and Léry in *L'Exotisme américain dans la littérature française au XVIe siècle* (Paris, 1911; reprint ed., Geneva, 1978), 193–218.

5. Marc Lescarbot, *Histoire de la Nouvelle France* (Paris, 1609 and 1611; expanded ed., Paris, 1617). Antoine de Montchrestien, *Traicté de l'oeconomie politique* (Rouen, 1615). On these texts, see Paolo Carile, *Lo sguardo impedito: Studi sulle relazioni di viaggio in "Nouvelle-France" e sulla letteratura popolare* (Fasano, It., 1987).

6. *Cérémonies et coutumes religieuses de tous les peuples du monde représentées par des figures dessinées de la main de Bernard Picart*, vols. 1–4 (Amsterdam, 1723–37). On this editorial project and its ideological stakes, see Danièle Pregardien, "L'Iconographie des *Cérémonies et coutumes* de B. Picart," in D. Droixhe et P.-P. Gossiaux, eds., *L'Homme des Lumières et la découverte de l'autre* (Brussels, 1985), 183–90.

7. On Jean de Léry's influence, see S. Landucci, *I filosofi e i selvaggi, 1580–1780* (Bari, It., 1972), 218–20.

8. For a survey of readings of Léry and his influence in the eighteenth century, see Gilbert Chinard, *L'Amérique et le rêve exotique dans la littérature française au XVIIe et au XVIIIe siècles* (Paris, 1934), passim, as well as Afonso Arinos de Mello Franco, *O Indio brasileiro e a Revolução francesa* (Rio de Janeiro, 1937), 138–46, 249–51, and 304–6.

9. Claude Lévi-Strauss, *Tristes Tropiques* (Paris, 1954), 89.

10. These two "airs of savages in America" went from Léry to the article "Musique" in the *Encyclopédie*, plate 4, fig. 2, via Father Marin Mersenne, *Harmonie universelle* (1636), 148.

11. If we are to believe Jacques Derrida, "Nature, Culture, Writing: The Violence of the Letter from Lévi-Strauss to Rousseau," in *Of Grammatology*, trans. Gayatri Chakravorty Spivak (Baltimore, 1976), 101–40.

12. Cf. Léry, *Histoire*, 194.

13. See Giuliano Gliozzi, "Les Apôtres au Nouveau Monde: Monothéisme et idolâtrie entre révélation et fétichisme," in Francis Schmidt, ed., *L'Impensable polythéisme: Etudes d'historiographie religieuse* (Paris, 1988), 177–213 and particularly 184–85.

14. Léry interprets an Indian myth in terms of the Apocalypse.

15. François Coréal, *Voyages de François Coréal aux Indes Occidentales, contenant ce qu'il y a*

vû de plus remarquable pendant son séjour depuis 1666, jusqu'en 1697. Traduits de l'Espagnol. Avec une Relation de la Guiane de Walter Raleigh et le Voyage de Narborough à la Mer du Sud par le Detroit de Magellan. Traduits de l'Anglois, 3 vols. (Amsterdam, 1722). Abbé Antoine-François Prévost, *Histoire générale des voyages, ou Nouvelle collection de toutes les relations de voyages par mer et par terre*, 20 vols. (Paris, 1746). Abbé Guillaume-Thomas Raynal, *Histoire philosophique et politique des établissemens et du commerce des Européens dans les deux Indes*, 1st ed., 6 vols. (Amsterdam, 1770), 2nd ed., 4 vols. (Geneva, 1780). Further citations will be given in the text.

16. Coréal, *Voyages*, 1:180–81: "Two-and-a-half Spanish leagues from an isle that the French had formerly inhabited, and where one could still find ruins of a fort, there was another called the *grande Isle*, inhabited by the *Topinamboux*. It had a circumference of three leagues."

17. Cf. Léry, *Histoire*, 114.

18. Prévost, *Histoire générale*, 14:276: "Coréal, who appears to have taken much of his information from Léry, does not abstain from sometimes adding his own *Observations*." This temporary reservation did not keep Prévost from admiring elsewhere (13:431) Coréal's "unusual modesty" as well as "the extent of his journeys in the two parts of the Continent of America."

19. On the meaning of this rite, described by André Thevet and Jean de Léry, see Alfred Métraux, *La Religion des Tupinamba et ses rapports avec celle des autres tribus Tupi-Guarani* (Paris, 1928), 180–88.

20. Cf. Léry, *Histoire*, 283–86.

21. Cf. Léry, *Histoire*, 284: a wood engraving showing an Indian woman squatting and weeping before a French sailor seated in a hammock and bringing her hands to her face.

22. For a commentary on this plate, several of whose elements were taken from A. Thevet, see Lestringant, *Le Huguenot et le sauvage*, prologue.

23. One thinks especially of chapter 16 of *Candide*, and of the meeting of "two completely naked girls," pursued by two monkeys who bite their bottoms.

24. Cf. Léry, *Histoire*, 298.

25. A similar remark can be found in Prévost, *Histoire générale*, 14:201, concerning the story of the famine at sea during Léry's return to France: "We should doubtless regret that the end of this story is in another style than the Author's. How many touching details was it not necessary to sacrifice to elegance?"

26. Léry, *Histoire*, 176–77. See Denis Diderot, *Supplément au Voyage de Bougainville*, in *Le Neveu de Rameau et autres dialogues philosophiques*, ed. Jean Varloot and Nicole Evrard (Paris, 1972), 291–97.

27. On this point, see the introduction by Sophie Delpech to Jean de Léry, *Histoire d'un voyage fait en la terre de Brésil* (Paris, 1980), 24. "It is important to emphasize this double emptying out, that of the religious aspect in the Tupinambu world in Léry and that of the 'social' character of the societies which Lévi-Strauss studies."

28. Prévost, *Histoire générale*, 14:276, cites Coréal, *Voyages*, 2:228.

29. For a description of this polemical literature, in which there was frequent recourse to the savage victim of the Spaniards, see Frauke Gewecke, *Wie die neue Welt in die alte kam* (Stuttgart, 1986), 211–20, as well as Lestringant, *Le Huguenot et le sauvage*, chap. 8.

DAVID DAMROSCH

The Aesthetics of Conquest: Aztec Poetry Before and After Cortés

> *We lift our songs, our flowers,*
> *these songs of the Only Spirit.*
> *Then friends embrace,*
> *the companions in each other's arms.*
> *So it has been said by Tochihuitzin,*
> *so it has been said by Coyolchiuhqui:*
> *We come here only to sleep,*
> *we come here only to dream;*
> *it is not true, it is not true*
> *that we come to live on earth.*
> —*Cantares mexicanos*, 18.39

THE AZTEC NOBILITY of the fifteenth and sixteenth centuries created the most extensive, and in many ways the most exquisite, body of poetry ever known to have existed in Mesoamerica. The gentle melancholy and the delicate aestheticism found in so many of the older songs stands in sharp contrast to the violence that was endemic in Aztec political and religious life, during the entire period of imperial expansion that began under Itzcoatl in 1428 and ended only with the triumph of Cortés in 1521. Students of Mesoamerican culture have long recognized the importance of the several hundred surviving Aztec lyrics as providing insights into Aztec thought and culture.[1] And yet, the beauty and delicacy of these texts has almost always been used to provide a *respite* from the harsh realities of Aztec political life. For many Mesoamericanists, the poetry provides a way to salvage the culture from its own history:

It reveals a far fuller mentality than that which is generally known from the presentations in the history books. It contributes, in sum, to complete our image of the past in order to enable us to make a more just evaluation of ancient Mexico. . . . The traditional image of the Aztecs, often judged as cruel and bloody for their religious practices involving sacrifice, can be modified. We can see that this people . . . was at the same time capable of great delicacy and refinement, of an intense artistic creativity and a profound spirituality.[2]

My object here is to explore these haunting lyrics in such a way as to complicate this view. I wish to show that Aztec aestheticism was in fact deeply implicated in the carrying through of Aztec imperial policy, and indeed that it even contributed directly to the brutality with which that policy was pursued.

The political "impurity" of these poems is seconded by a further, historical complexity, for the lyrics, in the form we have them, are intimately bound to two very different periods: the decades before the Conquest, and the decades thereafter. We cannot simply wipe away a few Christian accretions and marginal glosses and recover a transparent window into "the ancient Nahuatl mind"; rather, we have to deal with a continual uncertainty as to whether a given poem responds to events of 1460 or events of 1560—if not to both at once.

Aztec poetry, then, is rarely pure and never simple, but I wish to argue that we should neither be embarrassed nor annoyed by its impurity and its complexity. The historical rootedness of the songs should be seen as part of their very fabric, and an important source of their compelling power as we read them today. By attending to the shifting historical contexts within which the poems functioned, we can both recover a fuller appreciation of the poems in themselves, and also use the study of these poems toward a more dynamic sense of Aztec culture as a whole, which even now is all too often treated in a static, essentializing fashion.[3] Finally, these poems give a striking instance of a very general problem: How do we read texts in an awareness of the ways in which their meaning can be altered by changes in the circumstances of their production and of their reception?

"I am a Quetzal Plume, I am a Song": Pre-Conquest Aestheticism

Something that can fairly be called aestheticism is widespread in the major bodies of surviving Aztec poetry, the codices known as the *Cantares mexicanos* and the *Romances de los señores de la Nueva España*, both collections dating from the mid to late 1500s, and both incorporating much earlier as well as much more recent material. Many of the evidently pre-Conquest poems discuss the nature and role of poetry itself. Often identified with the paired terms "flower" (*xochitl*) and "birdsong" (*cuicatl*), poetry encapsulates all that is both precious and transitory in earthly life, a combination found in the often mentioned quetzal plume—with which the poet may actually identify himself, as in my heading for this section (from *Cantares*, 50.8).[4] Often, the singer stresses the importance of beauty, and especially of beautiful works of art, in preserving some permanence in an ephemeral world:

> Painted are the Toltecs, completed are the pictures: all Your hearts are
> arriving. Here, through art, I'll live. . . .
> In song I cut great stones, paint massive beams, that this, in future
> time when I'm gone, shall be uttered, this my song-sign [or song-
> emblem, *nocuicamachio*] that I leave behind on earth. My hearts
> will be alive here: they'll have come, a remembrance of me. And
> my fame will live.
>
> (*Cantares*, 44.15–17)

Songs can preserve the individual's memory, and equally they can foster social bonds:

> Let there be friendship and mutual acquaintance through flowers. Songs shall be raised, then we're off to His home. . . .
>
> My heart hears songs, and I weep, I grieve, on account of these flowers. We're to go away and leave them here on earth. We merely borrow them, and we're off to His home.
>
> Let me take this multitude of flowers as my necklace. Let me have them in my hand. Let them be my flower crown. We're to go away and leave them here on earth. We merely borrow them, and we're off to His home.
>
> (82.17–19)

The individual shares primarily the flower's transience—"Listen, I say! On earth we're known only briefly, like the magnolia. We only wither, O friends" (18.29). The song, on the other hand, possesses the flower's fertility, and can bring the singer back to life through its powers of regeneration. The composition of songs is often compared to planting and harvest: "It seems that I myself am cultivating songs, keeping company with those who work the soil" (17.45). In particular, there are many references to mist and rain, the attributes of Tlaloc, the god of fertility: "My songs are ripening, my word-fruit sprouts; our flowers arise in this place of rain. Well! Cacao flowers, fragrant ones, come scattering down, spreading perfume: fragrant poyomatli drizzles down" (44.19–20).

In many poems, such evocations of delicate beauty and of social and natural harmony do indeed show a modesty, an awareness of mortality, a renunciation of ambition, and a friendship-oriented hedonism, which contrast sharply with the stark image of the rapacious imperialists sacrificing ever more captives to their equally rapacious gods.

> I'm to pass away like a ruined flower. My fame will be nothing, my renown here on earth will be nothing. . . .
>
> Friends, take pleasure! Let us put our arms around each other's shoulders here. We're living in a world of flowers here. No one when he's gone can enjoy the flowers, the songs, that lie outspread in this home of the Giver of Life.
>
> Earth is but a moment. Is the Place Unknown the same? Is there happiness and friendship? Is it not here on earth that acquaintances are made?
>
> (17.14–16)

There are dozens of stanzas, and even whole poems, that can support such claims as this: "Even at the moment of their ascendancy, no people were more conscious of the transient nature of life, of life as vibrant yet as frail as the flowers they so loved."[5]

There are, however, two problems with this view of the poetry. In general terms, it leaves us with an almost schizophrenic sense of a people of violent and unmediated dualities—vibrant and frail one day, ruthless and bloodthirsty the next. Indeed, unable to construct any clear relation between such opposed terms in Aztec culture, writers have often fallen into such, let us say, *paratactic* characterizations.[6] More particularly, a harmonious view of Aztec aestheticism can only be maintained by a highly selective reading of the poems themselves. Many poems very closely associate themes of ephemerality and the beauty of flowers with themes of warfare, bloodshed, and human sacrifice. Indeed, many of the most perfect expressions of the love of beauty and friendship serve to introduce the parallel beauties of battle. What are we to make of this linkage?

To begin with, I should say something about the cirumstances under which the poems were composed. The creation of poetry was closely tied to the religious and political needs of the empire. The great body of the surviving poetry stems from singers trained in the court (or court-and-temple) circles of the Aztec ruling class. The poems, some actually attributed to Aztec lords, were in general the work of professional poets employed by the Aztec rulers in the capital city, Tenochtitlan, and in some of the major centers of their allies, notably Tezcoco on the eastern shores of the Lake of Mexico. Many poems commemorate or otherwise reflect specific historical occasions from the mid 1400s through the early 1500s, as well as the empire's political geography and its trading patterns.

From the late 1420s onward, the Aztec emperors took great care in the ideological organization of society. Itzcoatl went so far as to burn the existing historical texts, and to have new ones painted, in order to give due prominence to the Aztecs and their favored deities, notably Huitzilopochtli, god of war. Religious festivals were increasingly used as political theater; their allies—and eventually even rulers of hostile territories—were invited to witness major festivals, with their pageants of song, dance, and human sacrifice. As Inga Clendinnen says, "The significance of the performances went well beyond a conventional politics of terror. . . . The problem was to persuade not only Aztecs but other tribes that Aztec domination was no mere freak of fortune, an incident in the affairs of men, but part of the design of the cosmos."[7]

Several kinds of professionals were involved in the creation, preservation, and performance of songs. "Houses of song" (*cuicacalli*) were attached to the palaces in Tenochtitlan, Tezcoco, and elsewhere, and employed a variety of specialists, according to Bernardino de Sahagún's sixteenth-century informants: the developer of themes (*cuicapiqui*), the composer of text and music (*cuicano*), and directors of music and of choreography.[8] Further, great care was taken to ensure both the appropriateness of the compositions and their careful memorization and exact transmission. According to the *Códice Matritense del Real Palacio*,

The conservator [*tlapizcatzitzin*] had charge of songs composed in honor of the gods, all the divine hymns. In order that no one should make a mistake, he took the greatest care in teaching the divine songs to people in all parts of the town. A public crier would announce a meeting of the people so they could learn the songs well. . . . The duty of the shaved priest of Epcohua Tepictoton was the following: he decided about the songs. When someone composed a song, he was informed so that the song could be presented; he gave orders to the singers, and they went to sing at his house. When anyone composed a song, he gave his opinion about it.[9]

While songs were disseminated generally among the people, they also formed an important part of the education of young warriors. Songs and dances were taught in the *calmecac*, houses where adolescent boys lived as they trained to become warriors, and the boys spent the evenings singing these with older warriors.[10]

With this new creation of an elaborate professional system of composition, instruction, and performance, and with Aztec society increasingly dependent on, and organized around, a state of ongoing warfare, it seems plausible to suppose that it was in this period (and in these circles) that Aztec poetry developed into the full and elaborate forms that are found in the surviving codices. It appears to have been in this period as well that Aztec aestheticism developed its close linkage to imperial expansionism. Certainly, the poems' elaborate diction, philosophical and aesthetic reflection, and pervasive militarism are all absent from the occasional surviving examples of folk poetry from outside court circles, as well as from such old hymns as may be said to stem from pre-imperial times.[11]

The songs' themes and verbal techniques directly reflect the militarization of culture in the imperial period. Next to the aestheticist *cuicaxochitl* or "song flower" we must place the militarist *chimallixochitl*—the "shield flower." The political dimensions of warfare are rarely alluded to in the poetry; instead, warfare is seen as an artistic act, and the warrior becomes a poet. There are, in fact, two ways to be reborn on earth: in poetry, and in warfare. It is in battle that nobles can achieve their true stature, and their greatest fame, by becoming "eagles and jaguars," the names for orders of seasoned warriors:

> Nobles and kings are sprouting as eagles, ripening as jaguars, in
>   Mexico: Lord Ahuitzotl is singing arrows, singing shields.
> Giver of Life, let your flowers not be gathered! . . .
> You've adorned them in blaze flowers, shield flowers.
>
> (31.3–4)

In these lines, as in many of the war poems, images of natural fertility and harmony are linked to the beauty of art, with shields adorning the warrior in the same way that poems adorn the poet. By this means, the battlefield itself, seemingly a place of death and destruction, is represented as a place of beauty, growth, and fertility. War becomes a kind of girls' picnic: "Get up sisters, and let's go! Let's go look for flowers. . . . Here they are! Here! Blaze flowers, shield flowers! Desirable, pleasurable war flowers!" (84.1). Singers in the imperial period seem to have vied with each other to create ever more striking images to link beauty and terror: "Jaguar flowers are opening, knife-death flowers are becoming delicious upon the field" (39.6).

The poets engage in virtuosic wordplay as they go about the project of aestheticizing war. In the two examples just quoted, we find several examples of the witty choice of flowers, and of neologisms that play on names of existing flowers. The "jaguar flower" (*oceloxochitl*) comes readily into use, as "jaguars" are an order of warrior. Similarly, the very often used "shield flower" (*chimallixochitl*, probably a sunflower), has obvious metaphoric value. Furthermore, actual shields were made of flowers for ritual use, and so the image of maidens gathering shield flowers links the battlefield both to the natural world and to the "flowered shields" used in the world of temple ritual.

At a further level of punning reference, the double compound "knife-death-flower" (*itzimiquilxochitl*) is a neologism (from *itztli*, "obsidian knife," + *miquiztli*, "death," + *xochitl*, "flower"), but one which plays on two different botanical terms. The underlying pun is between *miquiztli*, "death," and *quilitl*, "plant"—verbal roots that can resemble each other closely in different combinations. In this instance, the *itzimiquilxochitl* suggests an actual flower, the *itzmiquilitl*, a kind of portulaca. Further afield are mesquite bushes, suggested through the resemblance of *miquiztli*, "death," and *mizquitl*, "mesquite." The mesquite grows far from the field of battle envisioned in the poem, but it is found in the northern deserts, the home of the Aztecs before they settled in the Valley of Mexico; various poems refer to warriors as mesquite plants. The spiny flower of the mesquite, moreover, is called the *itzimizquixochitl*. Thus the "knife-death-flower" both plays upon the local image of a blossoming portulaca and envisions the warrior as embodying the hardy toughness of the plants of the distant ancestral homeland. Finally, the neologism involves a ritual reference as well, as the second and third terms of "knife-death-flower" invert the ritual term "flower death," *xochimiquiztli*, signifying the glorious death of a warrior upon the sacrificial stone (or, failing that, in battle itself).

Using such verbal techniques, the imperial poets adapt the "gentle" themes of fellowship and ephemerality to serve as an impetus for excelling in battle: "They that scatter are war flowers: many open, all wither. Yet as many eagles, jaguars as have gone away will come to life again near you and in your presence, O God. There beyond!" (21.7). The love of fellowship is directed away from life and toward death:

> And we? We won't be giving pleasure to the Giver of Life forever. Let us give ourselves pleasure with Your flowers, and with these songs! We merely borrow these flowers of His, merely borrow these yellow flowers.
>
> They're war flowers, spinning in the field, whirling in the dust. Princes make these blaze flowers, desiring them, seeking them. But is there pleasure? There's only death.
>
> They crave and seek these warm delicious ones. But is there pleasure? There's only death.
>
> (74.4–6)

In both of these passages, the identification of the warrior as a "war flower" (*yao-xochitl*) punningly inverts an existing term: the *xochiyaoyotl* or "flower war," a staged tournament, whose goal was not to kill the enemy but to take captives for sacrifice. As Clendinnen has acutely observed of the "flower war," "It was on that field of battle that the Aztec aesthetic of war could be most perfectly displayed and most profoundly experienced; and here 'aesthetic' must be understood to comprehend moral and emotional sensibilities."[12]

Aztec aestheticism, then, both could and often did directly serve the interests of Aztec imperialism. The expansion of the empire, and when necessary the brutal suppression of revolts within imperial territory, was clothed in all the delicate beauty, and all the moral urgency, that the poets could provide. The warrior, indeed, became the poet of empire par excellence, as in this song commemorating the emperor Axayacatl's Matlatzincan campaign in the 1470s:

> A song! Let it be carried from where He dwells in the Place Unknown.
>   It's here! And here are Your flowers. Let there be dancing.
> Your prize is a Matlatzincan! O Blade Companion, O Axayacatl! You've
>   come to tear apart the town of Tlacotepec! . . .
> These eagle shields he lays in Someone's hands are won in danger on
>   the blazing field.
> Just like our songs, just like our flowers, you, you Shaven Head, are
>   pleasing the Giver of Life.
> With eagle flowers lying in your hands, O Axayacatl—flood-and-blaze
>   flowers, sprouting—our comrades, all of them, are drunk.
>
>   (65.2–8)

Poetics Across History

The political cast of Aztec aestheticism, then, does not allow us to view it in isolation from history. At the same time, however, the poems must be seen in relation to several very different sets of historical circumstances, which can broadly be described as pre-imperial, imperial, and post-imperial. Pre-imperial poetry is almost entirely lost to us, and only general inferences can be made about it, such as my inference that war poetry, and especially the aestheticization of war, was greatly developed during the ninety years of the empire and its cult of war.

Matters are very different for *post*-imperial poetry, as the major collections of lyric poetry were made several decades after the Conquest, and reflect their situation in three ways: through new composition; through reworking of older material in light of new events; and through the shifting of old meanings under new circumstances, quite apart from any visible rewriting. In what follows, I wish to explore what became of Aztec aestheticism once it was no longer serving the greatest and most violent empire ever seen in the New World, and was instead confronted with the most crushing and inexorable *defeat* imaginable—Tzvetan

Todorov goes so far as to speak of genocide[13]—inflicted on the empire and, increasingly, on the entire culture as well.

In the first part of this article, I have used the historical and political context of the empire to give a grounding, a specificity, to Aztec aestheticism. In this way, I hope to point the way toward a better understanding of the poetry, as it appears to have functioned in the imperial era. But this quest for "the" meaning of the poetry works only up to a point, within the context of what is in fact a somewhat artificial locating of the poems within a single historical period. We can indeed learn much about the pre-Conquest Aztec world from these poems, but they do not speak of that period alone. For a full understanding of the poetry, it is necessary to take seriously its transmission, and its re-creation, during the first decades of the colonial period. We should attempt to read most of these poems *bivalently*, as if they were products both of 1450–1520 *and* of 1521–1570—as, given the nature of the oral tradition, many of them probably were.

To date, students of the poetry have almost invariably done their best to resolve this bivalence by wishing it away. The majority of scholars have used the poems to try to recover a sense of the "pure" Aztec culture of the time before the Conquest. Scholars from Daniel Brinton in the 1890s to Ángel María Garibay K. in the middle of this century and Miguel Léon-Portilla in the present have proceeded by bracketing such poems as are clearly post-Conquest compositions, and by supposing that most appearances of the names of God the Father, Jesus Christ, and Santa María are editorial emendations to otherwise "pure" pre-Conquest poetry. They have stressed the passages in early chronicles that describe memorization of old songs as indicating the faithful transmission of the poetry in post-Conquest times. Further, they have rightly noted that few poems in classical style are known to have been composed after 1570, and none after 1590, suggesting that the entire tradition died out along with the last generation trained in the imperial schools.

With these facts in mind, these scholars have taken historical references within the poems as evidence of the date (or at least the period) of composition, and have often identified figures named in the poems as the actual authors; Léon-Portilla has gone so far as to offer biographies and analyses of the oeuvres of a number of such figures.[14] Whole volumes have been devoted to the poetry attributed to Nezahualcoyotl (1402–72), a king of Tezcoco often mentioned in the poems, and credited as a great poet by the seventeenth-century historian Fernando de Alva Ixtlilxochitl.[15]

By contrast, John Bierhorst goes to the opposite extreme in his new edition of the *Cantares*. He argues that *all* of the poems in the codex are post-Conquest compositions, and indeed that all are representatives of a single genre, a "ghost song" used in rituals designed to bring about the return of deceased warriors to aid in the revitalization of Mexican culture and the military defeat of the Spaniards. He argues persuasively that figures like Nezahualcoyotl are only alluded to, and at times portrayed by, the singers of the poems, but in no case can pre-Conquest rulers be shown to have been the actual authors. Ixtlilxochitl in particular is essentially only glorifying an ancestor (he claimed Nezahualcoyotl as his great-great-great-great-grandfather), with no factual basis for his claims.

Further, in Bierhorst's view, the many references to figures like Dios, Jesucristo, Espíritu Santo, and Santa María are not editorial emendations, or ruses to escape monastic censorship, but valid reflections of the supplanting of the old deities in the early colonial period. Bierhorst admits that a number of poems appear to have pre-Conquest origins, but he insists that most historical references are vague, many are muddled, and all can be understood as part of the "revitalization movement" of the 1550s and 1560s that he sees the poems as reflecting.[16]

The problem with Bierhorst's revisionistic understanding of the poems is that the ambiguities of the poems can no better be resolved by disconnecting the poems from the decades before the Conquest than they can be by detaching them from the decades afterward. For his part, Bierhorst downplays the often quite detailed historical references in many poems, and ignores the evidence that Christian religious names often *have* been inserted in place of older names. Further, he homogenizes the interpretation of the codices, which most readers very reasonably see as rather heterogeneous collections of different sorts of songs, in his wish to see them as reflecting his putative revitalization movement—for which, as he admits, there is no direct evidence at all.

Both views of the dating of the poetry, then, achieve a desired univocality only at the cost of enormous extrapolations from slender evidence, or even from silence, together with the widespread suppression of contradictory evidence. I agree fully with Bierhorst that there are no good reasons for supposing that Nezahualcoyotl actually composed any more of the songs associated with his name than King David composed the Psalms credited to him; indeed, it seems ironically appropriate that Ixtlilxochitl openly regarded his ancestor as the Mexican King David.[17] The majority of the surviving poems reflect the post-Conquest period in various ways, implicit or explicit, and given their oral transmission there is no way to be confident that *any* poem has come down to us without any modification over the course of sixty or a hundred years.

At the same time, however, there is ample evidence that the basic image repertoire of the poetry was developed before the Conquest, together with the themes that I have been discussing so far. Apart from internal evidence (the presence of these themes in poems that even Bierhorst allows to be particularly closely tied to the pre-Conquest period), there is ample attestation in early chronicles from the years just after the Conquest of the traditional importance of the theme of ephemerality, for example, and there is confirming pictorial and archaeological evidence for the role of the "flower wars," "flowery death," "flower shields," and other cultural analogs for the aestheticist themes in the poetry.

The question I would like to pursue here is how this old image repertoire functioned in, and was affected by, the new circumstances of the Spanish presence in Mexico. I will take as an area for examination what may be the most striking, and the most readily visible, change in the poetry: the displacement of the old gods by the new. As noted above, most of the songs were composed by, or under the watchful guidance of, the Aztec priests, and they were performed on public occasions, ordinarily as part of religious celebrations and rituals. In the codices of the *Cantares* and the *Romances*, however, actual names of Aztec divinities are almost never found. What we do find are a variety of epithets that Sahagún and other chroniclers list as names for the gods, such as *Ipalnemoani*, "Giver of Life," a traditional appellation of Tezcatlipoca. It is impossible to say, in many instances, whether a poem addressed to Ipalnemoani represents a veiled appeal to Tezcatlipoca, or whether the term now refers to the Christian God—as seems more certainly to be the case with *Icelteotl*, "Sole God," a term occasionally used for major deities before the Conquest but now very explicitly associated with God the Father in post-Conquest poetry.

Very often, the names of God (*Dios*, or *Tios*, or *Tiox*) and other Christian figures appear in the manuscripts, and here too it is hard to say how often these names reflect the poet's own beliefs, or a deliberate ruse on the poet's part to escape censorship,[18] or a pious emendation by the native informants who collected the songs for Sahagún or other early Spanish ethnographers. The two poetic codices appear to take somewhat different formal approaches to the problem of emendation. In the *Romances*, the scribe often gives a marginal gloss to a traditional epithet. For example, next to the line *Acan huel ichan Moyocoyatzin*, "In no place is found the home of The One Who Creates Himself"—an epithet of Tezcatlipoca—the scribe notes in the margin: *yehuan ya dios glosa*, "this is to be read as 'God.'"[19] At other times, this marginal emendation appears where a divine name has simply been omitted, or else replaced with the generic term *teotl*, "god." By contrast, the *Cantares* manuscript pairs terms within the line itself, so that we often encounter lines such as this: *titeotl yehuan Dios an tinechmiquitlani*, which can be translated either as an "original" apostrophe—"O Spirit, O God, you want me dead"—or as an emendation: "O Spirit [i.e., God], you want me dead" (18.21).

As ambiguous as these namings often are, it is still more difficult to say how far, or in what ways, a cultural shift has taken place when Christian names *are* evidently being used by the poet. There are some poems in which we may feel that the old gods have simply disappeared, but there are others in which it seems more as though the old pantheon is simply being enlarged by the arrival of figures like Tiox, spilitu xanto (Espíritu Santo), and Santa Malia. The poems make no mention of Ometeotl, the "Dual God" or "God of Duality," simultaneously male and female, who had created all the other gods; but now, in some poems, Tiox and Santa Malia seem to rule together as king and queen of heaven, at times in quite un-Catholic settings:

> I scatter a multitude of flowers. Ho! I've come to offer songs. There's
> flower-drunkenness. And I'm a leering ribald. . . .
> You've come to give him pleasure, and it would seem that he is Tiox,
> that he is the Giver of Life, that she is Santa Malia, that she is our
> mother. The flowers are stirring, ah!
>
> (80.5–9)

The Christian deities now become the patrons of song: "Santa María the ever virgin comes loosening, comes unfolding, song marvels, flower paintings. Hear them! In Butterfly House, House of Pictures, God's home, in Roseate House she sings, she arrives, she, Santa María" (32.5–6). "To the white willows, where white rushes grow, to Mexico, you, Blue Egret Bird, come flying, you, O spirit, O Espíritu Santo! . . . You're here singing in Mexico" (35.3–4). In another poem, Espíritu Santo takes on a form suspiciously like that of a disguised Quetzalcoatl, the traditional patron of Aztec culture: "You come created, O Quetzal [*quetzalto-totl*, a term notably close to *Quetzalcoatl*], O spilitu xanto. You arrive! You come bringing your quechols, these angels [*ageloti*], these flower garlands, that loosen their songs and give you pleasure, O Giver of Life!" (71.5). It is no wonder that Sahagún complained that "they persist in singing their old songs . . . a practice that arouses much suspicion as to their Christian faith."[20]

The linkage of poetry and warfare continues in the late poems, and the same Tiox and Jesucristo who are the new patrons of song are also the new patrons of war, in those poems that do fit well with Bierhorst's stress on resistance to the Spaniards in the poetry.

> Gold is shining in your sapodilla house of trogons. Your home abounds
> in jade water whorls, O prince, O Jesucristo. You're singing in
> Anahuac. . . .
> You're hidden away at Seven Caves, where the mesquite grows. The
> eagle cries, the jaguar whines; you, in the midst of the field—a
> roseate quechol—fly onward, in the Place Unknown.
>
> (33.3–8)

Here the military reference is covert, encoded in the terms "mesquite," "eagle," and "jaguar," all suggesting warriors, as in several poems discussed above; the cry of the eagle, further, is a battle cry. Jesucristo is "hidden away at Seven Caves, where the mesquite grows," as though he is training warriors in the northern homeland in preparation for a return in force. In other poems, these references are more overt: "This jaguar earth is shaking, and the screaming skies begin to rip. Spilitu Xanto, Giver of Life, descends. Chalked shields are strewn away with love. And they that come to stand on earth are spines of His from Flower-Tassel Land" (71.1).

God himself, it seems, is spurring the Mexicans on to fight against the Spaniards who brought him:

> Montezuma, you creature of heaven, you sing in Mexico, in
>   Tenochtitlan.
> Here where eagle multitudes were ruined, your bracelet house stands
>   shining—there in the home of Tiox our father. . . .
> Onward, friends! We'll dare to go where fame, where glory's, gotten,
>   where nobility is gotten, where flower death is won.
> Your name and honor live, O princes. Prince Tlacahuepan!
>   Ixtlilcuechahuac! You've gone and won war death.
>
> (76.1–2, 5–6)

The old ideas are still here—but nothing is the same. In fact, the "old" ideas and images themselves are transformed. Not only is warfare a different proposition for a defeated people than for seemingly unconquerable armies, but the relations of beauty, the divine, and the ephemeral mortal life are all altered. Thus, in the lines just quoted, the bracelet house (a warrior's house) still stands shining, an enduring human artifact—but it survives amid the ruins of the warriors themselves who used to inhabit the house.

The flower death of heroic individuals used to take place against the backdrop of the ever-expanding empire, with its unshakable center, Tenochtitlan; now, the heroic death of the warrior achieves itself alone, with no certain result for the culture. The ephemerality of human culture, newly observed on an unprecedented scale, extends to the gods as well. Even as Dios is enlisted in the struggle, his foreignness, his unpredictability, remain apparent to the poets, and they seek to comprehend this fickleness. One poem begins with two ringing verses celebrating warriors in battle, but then comes up short:

> I grieve, I weep. What good is this? The shield flowers are carried
>   away, they're sent aloft. Ah, where can I find what my heart
>   desires?
> Incomparable war death! Incomparable flower death! The Giver of
>   Life has blessed it.
> I seek the good songs whence they come—and I am poor. Let me not
>   sing.
>
> (31.5–7)

The poet then confronts the possibility that the same Giver of Life who has blessed both warfare and poetry may not, after all, reward either:

> Perhaps these glorious jades and bracelets are your hearts and loved
>   ones, O father, O Dios, Giver of Life. So many do I utter near
>   you and in your presence—I, Totoquihuaztli. How could you run
>   weary? How could you run slack?
> Easily, in a moment might you slacken, O father, O Dios.
>
> (31.13–14)

The poem ends with the knowledge that the poet can become intoxicated not with any actual victories in battle but only with dreams of war, with his songs, while instead of celebrating great feats in battle and splendid flower deaths, the people must be content that anyone is still left alive:

> They make my heart drunk: they flower, they intoxicate me here on
> earth: I am drunk with war flowers.
> He shows mercy to everyone. Thus people are alive on earth. Heaven
> comes here! And I am drunk with war flowers.
>
> (31.15–16)

If songs cannot continue to reflect the enduring glory of the empire and the ageless fame of its victorious warriors, they still retain power, fortifying the singer through a newly deepened awareness of the possibilities for beauty in an existence far more ephemeral than anyone had imagined. "Only sad flowers, sad songs, lie here in Mexico, in Tlatelolco. Beyond is the Place Where Recognition Is Achieved. O Giver of Life, it's good to know that you will favor us, and we underlings will die" (13.1–2). In this poem, a raining mist comes down not from the beneficent Tlaloc but from the tears of the vanquished:

> Tears are pouring, teardrops are raining there in Tlatelolco. The
> Mexican women have gone into the lagoon. It's truly thus. So all
> are going. And where to, comrades?
> True it is. They forsake the city of Mexico. The smoke is rising, the
> haze is spreading. This is your doing, O Giver of Life.
> Mexicans, remember that he who sends down on us his agony, his fear,
> is none but Dios, alas, there in Coyonazco.
>
> (5–7)

The poem closes by affirming the power of song even in such devastating circumstances. The poet recalls the captivity of the Mexican leaders Motelchiuh and Tlacotzin, whom the Spaniards were said to have tortured with fire in hopes of learning the location of hidden gold:

> Weep and be guilty, friends. You've forsaken the Mexican nation, alas.
> The water is bitter, and the food is bitter as well. This is the
> doing of the Giver of Life in Tlatelolco.
> Yet peacefully were Motelchiuh and Tlacotzin taken away. They
> fortified themselves with song in Acachinanco when they went to
> be delivered to the fire in Coyohuacan.
>
> (9–10)

Strength and beauty can shine out even in defeat. The poet's song can persist too, perhaps no longer as the splendid embodiment of the ever-renewing flowers of empire, but rather as itself a newly ephemeral, even broken, artifact. To give one example of this idea, the long sixty-eighth song in the *Cantares* describes Cortés's arrival in Tenochtitlan and subsequent events, including a trip by several Aztecs to Rome, where they meet the Pope—"The pope [*i papa*] is on Tiox's mat and seat and speaks for him. Who is this reclining on a golden chair? Look! It's the pope. He has his turquoise blowgun and he's shooting in the world" (68.65). Cortés sends the Aztecs along with a shipment of gold for the Pope: "He's said: What do I need? Gold! Everybody bow down! Call out to Tiox in excelsis!" (68.100).

If the Europeans want all the gold, the Aztecs are left trying to preserve their water. The song is titled *Atequilizcuicatl*, "Water-Pouring Song," and in this poem "water" comes to stand for Mexico itself. One name for Tenochtitlan, reflecting its construction on islands in the Lake of Mexico, was *Atliyaitic*, "The Water's Midst." Water and fire were the great gifts of the two gods worshipped on the Templo Mayor in Tenochtitlan, the fertile Tlaloc and the war god Huitzilopochtli. Now, in this poem, God has taken control of both of these forces. Concerning fire: "Tiox and Only Spirit, you and you alone lay down the mirror and the flame that stands here in the world" (68.36), with the power over mirror and flame implicitly taken over from Tezcatlipoca, "Smoking Mirror." God's envoy Cortés enters the city with smoking guns: "Now woe! He gives off smoke! This is how he enters, this conquistador, this Captain" (68.9).

Those who control the fire, control the water as well. The Mexicans are forced to pour out their water for the invaders, and here water becomes a metaphor for the entire culture:

> We who've come to Water's Midst to marvel are Tlaxcalans: Mexican princes are pouring out their waters! Lord Montezuma's hauling vats of water. And the city passes on, ensconced in water-whorl flowers. Thus Mexico is handed over. Oh! The waters are His, and He drinks them, it's true.
>
> Iye! The lady María comes shouting. María comes saying, "O Mexicans, your water jars go here! Let all the lords come carrying." And Acolhuacan's Quetzalacxoyatl arrives. And Cuauhpopoca. Oh! The waters are His, and He drinks them, it's true.
>
> (68.10–11)

Once again, the poet finds an appropriate flower to symbolize his theme, as the city passes away "ensconced in water-whorl flowers." Perhaps there is also a play between "water-whorl flowers," *amalacoxochitl*, and "paper flowers," *amacaxochitl*, used in 60.55 to mean "poems"; the root, *amatl*, means "paper, book, songbook." The poet has also chosen his nobles deliberately, in order to contrast their humble duties as water carriers with the glorious possibilities suggested by their names. *Cuauhpopoca*, "Smoking Eagle," is a warrior's name par excellence, while *Quetzalacxoyatl*, "Plumed Needle," refers to the *acxoyatl*, an instrument used in ritual bloodletting and mock combats.

The poet sees only one refuge from the harsh labor being imposed on his people: to break the carved and painted jars that have been pressed into the lowly service of hauling water. In a shifting of the initial metaphor, the jars themselves become the Mexicans: "O Giver of Life, these urgently required ones have been broken, these, our water jars, and we are Mexicans. A cry goes up. They're picking them off at Eagle Gate, where recognition is achieved. Oh! The waters are His, and He drinks them, it's true" (12–13).

As his people dies, the poet sees his poem itself as a water jar, carrying his culture. And so his poem is to be broken along with the people:

> O nephews, hail! And hear a work assignment: we've come to do our
> water pouring. Now who will go and fetch the jadestone jars that
> we must carry? . . .
> Oh none of us shall work for tribute. We're to pass away. . . .
> I weep, I sorrow, and I sing: I've broken these, my turquoise gems, my
> pearls, these water jars.
> And let it be thus that I return them. Chirping for these flowers, let me
> head for home. At Flower Waters let me weep, composing them:
> I've broken these, my turquoise gems, my pearls, these water
> jars.
>
> (25–28, 31–33)

In these poems of the Conquest, the old imperial linkage of beauty and death in battle persists, but in new terms befitting such changed circumstances. Only a minority of the poems in the *Cantares* and the *Romances* reflect so openly upon the results of the Spaniards' arrival, and only a few poems in the entire corpus are so closely tied to pre-Conquest conditions that they have no visible relevance to the later time of their transmission. Most poems fall into an ambiguous grey area; they may be seen as coming from either period, or, in a very real sense, from both. Within their own lifetimes, the Aztec poets were compelled to sing their poems in light of the overturning of the world in which they were first composed. As the conquistador and historian Bernal Díaz del Castillo put it, writing during the period in which the *Cantares* were being collected, "Ahora todo está por el suelo, perdido, que no hay cosa" (Now all is in the dust, lost, there is nothing left).[21]

The poems are a testimony both to the truth of Díaz's observation and to its falsity. The conquistadors were too quick to congratulate themselves (and, more rarely, to reproach themselves) for the extirpation of the native cultures within a few short years; even now, Mesoamericanists too readily speak of "ancient" Nahuatl culture, considering the term as appropriate to, say, 1518 but opposed to the "colonial" culture of 1528. The Aztec poems are filled both with a sense of dramatic loss and with a sense of underlying continuity. It is, indeed, this double fact, the oxymoronic persistence of a disappeared culture, that enables and even requires us to read so many of the poems against both pre- and post-Conquest history.

In many cases stanzas, and even entire poems, change their valences dramatically across the great divide of 1519–21. The theme of ephemerality in the poems, for example, has often been read in modern times as expressing a detached, existential—even existential*ist*—philosophy. It is increasingly clear, however, that the poems were always closely tied to urgent religious and political concerns, and by this very engagement their meaning altered radically with the Conquest. The same images and verses that aided and even heightened the brutality of the imperial regime were turned to new purposes some years later: to strengthen the resolve of a conquered people to resist their total destruction.

Understanding this sort of shift helps us to read these poems more fully, and it has larger implications as well. The Aztec poems illustrate in exemplary fashion some of the ways in which any text alters and renews its meaning across time and across cultures. In their double historical grounding, these poems provide a real-life instance of the shifting of meaning over time explored fictively in Jorge Luis Borges's "Pierre Menard, Author of *Don Quixote*": "It is not in vain that three hundred years have passed, charged with the most complex happenings. . . . The text of Cervantes and that of Menard are verbally identical, but the second is almost infinitely richer."[22] In the case of Aztec poetry, though, the crucial passage of time was more like three years than three hundred, and in consequence the Aztec poets of the sixteenth century were perhaps among the first to be forced to confront this problem directly—in ways that bear comparison with poets' struggles with their cultural heritage on the *other* side of the Atlantic, though the vanishing past was not that of a remote antiquity but of the poets' own youth. In a variety of cases, indeed, the Aztec poets seem to have shaped their work to include this theme. The "water-pouring" poem discussed above is one such instance, as the theme of water, water carriers, and water jars develops—or implodes—during the course of the poem, with the poet finally evoking the breaking of his own poem in response to the very events that have given rise to it.

The theme may also be seen in other poems less directly concerned with the Conquest. To give one example, the forty-ninth poem in the *Romances* codex modulates the theme of the brevity of human life through a series of ironic changes.[23] It begins with a standard evocation of the joys of fellowship:

> Make your beginning, you who sing.
> May you beat again your flowered drum,
> may you give joy to my lords, the eagles, the jaguars.
> Briefly we are here together.

This last line is then given a suprising twist in the next stanza:

> The one heart's desire of the Giver of Life
> is jewels, is quetzal plumes: to tear them apart.
> This is his desire: to scatter apart the eagles, the jaguars.
> Briefly we are here together.

The brevity of existence has moved from a neutral fact of life to a direct consequence of a divine will to destruction. As the poem continues, the poet reverses the traditional image of the song as the bearer of immortality for mortal heroes:

And these our songs, these our flowers,
they are our shrouds. So be happy:
woven into them is the eagle, the jaguar;
we will go with them, there where it is all the same.

Like the broken water jar in the "Water-Pouring Song," the poem now takes its value by sharing in the destruction it is elsewhere represented as surviving. If the militarism of imperial songs becomes transvalued by the Conquest, so too does the aestheticist theme of ephemerality. This poem has no elements that mark it clearly either as a pre-Conquest or a post-Conquest composition; seen within one setting or the other, its message reads rather differently. In both contexts, though, the poem offers its audience a severe consolation, as in its closing lines, in which the problem of the brevity of life becomes its own ironic solution, the very source of strength:

So let us now rejoice within our hearts,
all who are on earth;
only briefly do we know one another,
only here are we together.
So do not be saddened, my lords:
no one, no one is left behind on earth.

The challenge these poems offer us is to read them in multiple senses, a multiplicity commonly taken on by texts over time, but in this case inscribed within the poems themselves, shaped as they have been by the poets' own multiple perspectives on their past triumphs and their present struggles. As they sang, and reworked, the old songs, perhaps some of the poets of the 1550s and 1560s recalled the archaic "Legend of the Suns," the central mythic description of the world's five ages, or suns, in which the Aztecs accounted themselves as living in the fifth age, named Four-Movement, the age of earthquakes. Perhaps, too, they thought that this final age of the world shared something of the violent second age as well:

It was called the Jaguar Sun.
Then it happened
that the sky was crushed,
the Sun did not follow its course.
When the Sun arrived at midday,
immediately it was night;
and when it became dark,
jaguars ate the people.
In this Sun giants lived.
The old ones said
the giants greeted each other thus:
"Do not fall down," for whoever falls,
he falls forever.[24]

Notes

1. Most notably, the lyrics are central texts in Miguel Léon-Portilla's pathbreaking study *La filosofía Náhuatl* (1956), revised and translated as *Aztec Thought and Culture: A Study of the Ancient Nahuatl Mind* (Norman, Okla., 1963).
2. Birgitta Leander, *In xochitl in cuicatl, flor y canto: La poesía de los Aztecas* (Mexico City, 1972), 3, 15.
3. This observation applies, for example, to recent studies by two literarily oriented scholars, René Girard and Tzvetan Todorov. Girard devotes a chapter of his *The Scapegoat*, trans. Yvonne Freccero (Baltimore, 1986), to a reading of an Aztec creation myth, and concludes that the religion as a whole was based on a centrality of brutal sacrifice; he closes by urging scholars to abandon their humanistic pretense to objectivity and admit that Aztec religion was morally repellent in its very essence. In *The Conquest of America: The Question of the Other*, trans. Richard Howard (New York, 1984), Todorov, with a far fuller and more sympathetic reading of sixteenth-century Spanish sources, largely accepts the Conquistadors' illusion that they were encountering an ancient and static society, rather than the very recent and unstable phenomenon that the empire in fact was.

   Among Mesoamericanists, while historical development is given full weight, we rarely find an equally dynamic sense of ideology. As Arthur Demarest has recently noted, "Unfortunately, when it comes to religious behavior or institutions, anthropologists and archaeologists interested in cultural evolution invariably slip into a kind of static functionalism which assigns ideology a passive role, or no role at all, in culture change"; "Overview: Mesoamerican Human Sacrifice in Evolutionary Perspective," in Elizabeth H. Boone, ed., *Ritual Human Sacrifice in Mesoamerica* (Washington, D.C., 1984), 227–43, 238.
4. Quotations from the *Cantares mexicanos* are taken, with some modifications, from John Bierhorst's splendid new edition, *Cantares Mexicanos: Songs of the Aztecs* (Stanford, Calif., 1985). Bierhorst's paleographic transcription of the Nahuatl manuscript far surpasses previous editions, as do his literal prose renderings. An accompanying volume, *A Nahuatl-English Dictionary and Concordance to the "Cantares Mexicanos"* (Stanford, Calif., 1985), is also a valuable supplement to the standard dictionaries of Rémi Siméon and Alonso de Molina. Citations are to song and stanza, in Bierhorst's numbering.
5. Andrew O. Wiget, "Aztec Lyrics: Poetry in a World of Continually Perishing Flowers," *Latin American Indian Literatures* 4 (1980): 1–11, 4.
6. To give one example, Jacques Soustelle reads the Aztec calendrical system as expressing a radically discontinuous sense of time and space:

   > In such a world, change is not conceived as a consequence of 'becoming' which gradually develops, but as something abrupt and total. Today the East is dominant, tomorrow the North; today we live in good times, and without a gradual transition, we shall pass into the unfavorable days (*nemontemi*). The law of the universe is the alternation of distinct qualities, radically separated, which dominate, vanish, and reappear eternally.

   La Pensée cosmologique des anciens mexicains (1940); quoted in Léon-Portilla, *Aztec Thought and Culture*, 57. Suffice it to say here that this characterization is very broadly overstated, and, further, passes silently over the many ways in which the Aztec priests would work to mitigate the effects associated with an unfavorable day or direction.

7. Inga Clendinnen, "The Cost of Courage in Aztec Society," *Past and Present* 107 (1985): 44–89, 53.

8. See Leander, *In xochitl in cuicatl*, 29.

9. Quoted in Miguel Léon-Portilla, *Pre-Columbian Literatures of Mexico*, trans. Grace Lobanov and the author (Norman, Okla., 1969), 78–79.

10. For a full description of warriors' training, see Ross Hassig, *Aztec Warfare: Imperial Expansion and Political Control* (Norman, Okla., 1988).

11. The most extensive and striking collection of traditional folk poetry (albeit recorded at a later date), is found in Hernando Ruiz de Alarcón's *Tratado de las supersticiones y costumbres gentilicas que oy viuen entre los Indios naturales desta Nueua España* (1629), recently translated by Michael Coe and Gordon Whittaker as *Aztec Sorcerers in Seventeenth-Century Mexico* (Albany, N.Y., 1982). On the hymns, see Ángel María Garibay K., *Veinte himnos sacros de los Nahuas* (Mexico City, 1958).

12. Clendinnen, "Cost of Courage," 62. It should be further noted that the important religious goals of the "flower war" did not preclude its use in quite specific practical circumstances. Ross Hassig has recently argued persuasively that the "flower wars" were undertaken as much for tactical as for religious purposes, to wear down opponents who were too strong to be taken by frontal attack without large losses; *Aztec Warfare*, 129ff.

13. Todorov, *Conquest of America*, 132–45.

14. See Miguel Léon-Portilla, *Trece poetas del mundo azteca* (Mexico City, 1967).

15. Fernando de Alva Ixtlilxochitl, *Historia chichimeca*, in his *Obras completas*, ed. Edmundo O'Gorman, 2 vols. (Mexico City, 1975–77); José Luis Martínez, *Nezahualcoyotl: Vida y obra* (Mexico City, 1972); Miguel Léon-Portilla, *Nezahualcoyotl: Poesía y pensamiento* (Mexico City, 1972).

16. Bierhorst argues his controversial thesis in his long introduction, *Cantares Mexicanos*, 3–109.

17. As Gordon Brotherton says, "Most of the time he did his best to make Nezahualcoyotl the Psalm King, the Mexican David complete with Uriah and Bathsheba and a good singing voice, whose very laments for the vanity of earthly things, whose predictions of Mexican catastrophe and whose invitations to the one (as yet) Unknown God, become a surreptitious invitation to the Spaniards to come to America and bring their bible with them"; "Nezahualcoyotl's 'Lamentaciones' and Their Nahuatl Origins: The Westernization of Ephemerality," *Estudios de cultura Náhuatl* 10 (1972): 393–408, 406.

18. This is the view taken by Leonhard Schultze Jena in his unfinished edition of the *Cantares*; *Alt-Aztekische Gesänge* (Stuttgart, 1957).

19. *Romances de los señores de la Nueva España*, fol. 4v, line 1; in Ángel María Garibay K., ed., *Poesía Náhuatl*, vol. 1 (Mexico City, 1964), 12. Something of the complexity of the circumstances in which these poems were recorded may be seen from the scribe's trilingual gloss, written as it is in a mixture of Nahuatl, Spanish, and Latin—in which native seminarians were already being trained soon after the Conquest.

20. From the prologue to Bernardino de Sahagún, *Psalmodia christiana* (1583), a collection of Nahuatl hymns he had composed, hoping to supplant the indigenous songs used in churches; quoted in Arthur J. O. Anderson, "Aztec Hymns of Life and Love," *New Scholar* 8 (1982): 1–74, 2.

21. Bernal Díaz del Castillo, *Historia verdadera de la conquista de la Nueva España*, ed. Joaquín Ramírez Cabañas (Mexico City, 1983), 159.

22. Jorge Luis Borges, *Ficciones*, trans. Anthony Kerrigan (New York, 1962), 51–52.

23. Text in Garibay, *Poesía Náhuatl*, 1:76–77.

24. *Anales de Cuauhtitlan*, fol. 2; quoted in Léon-Portilla, *Pre-Columbian Literatures*, 36. Wayne Elzey, in a study of twenty surviving variants of the "Legend of the Suns," has argued that the fifth age was in fact regarded as embodying the characteristics of the earlier ages; "The Nahua Myth of the Suns," *Numen* 23 (1976): 114–35. For an interesting discussion of the political uses of these and other myths, see David Carrasco, *Quetzalcoatl and the Irony of Empire: Myths and Prophecies in the Aztec Tradition* (Chicago, 1982).

SARA CASTRO-KLARÉN

Dancing and the Sacred in the Andes:
From the Taqui-Oncoy to Rasu-Ñiti

IF WE ASSUME THAT the Andean peoples interpreted the Spanish Conquest of the Inca empire as a Pachacuti—a cyclical destruction and restoration of the world[1]—we can view the Andean cosmos as a place of articulation, revision, and response to the challenge of Colonial rule. This assumption lets us step outside the European frame of reference for an understanding of cultural formations in the Andes.

There is no question that the arrival of the Spanish in 1532 meant disaster in the lives of the Andeans. But Andean society did not collapse and simply accept Spanish Colonial rule. Resistance and accommodation, even cooperation, marked the complex dynamics that ensued after 1532 in the Inca empire. Examining Andean responses, the French ethnohistorian Nathan Wachtel writes:

Defeat was experienced as a catastrophe of cosmic dimensions. . . . The clash coincided with the death of the son of the Sun, the Inca. He constituted the mediating point between the gods and men, and he was worshiped as a god. In some way he represented the bodily center of the universe. He was the guarantor of the harmony of the universe. Once that center was murdered, the living point of reference in the world disappeared. Universal order is thus brutally destroyed.[2]

Wachtel describes the Taqui-Oncoy, the cult and ritual of the sick dance that sprang up in 1565, as one of several Andean responses to the collapse of the Inca empire. He views the Taqui-Oncoy as a form of social resistance to the imposition of foreign rule and systematic dismantling of the Andean world. Wachtel calls this a period of "destructuration":

Spanish domination, while making use of Inca institutions, also caused their demise. This decomposition did not, however, mean the birth of a new universe radically different from the old one. On the contrary, it involved *destructuration*, which we understand as the survival of ancient structures or partial elements of these but displaced from the relatively coherent context in which they used to function.[3]

In this chapter I examine the discourse of the sacred implied in the practice and preaching of the Taqui-Oncoy and analyze the semiotic elements by which this cult addresses the experience of destructuration. My use of the term *discourse* is informed by Michel Foucault's *Archaeology of Knowledge*. Discourse is constituted by a group of statements, which in turn are not merely traces but modalities that

159

allow groups of signs to exist "in relation with a domain of objects and [prescribe] a definite position to any possible subject."[4] Foucault's principle of dispersion and redistribution of statements in discursive formations is pertinent here. Also, I indicate how the presence and cult of the *guacas*—exceptional features of the visible universe that represent the sacred and its connection to ancestry and descent[5]—continues, though transformed, to the present day as in the case of the scissor dancer (*danzak de tijeras*). Finally, I outline the links between the ritual of the Taqui-Oncoy and the ritual of the scissor dancer.

Before delving into the history of the religious cult and ritual dance of the Taqui-Oncoy, we need to examine the meaning of this name. In Quechua *taqui* refers to the ceremonial dances tied to the agricultural calendar. *Oncoy* means sick or sickness. It also refers to the Pleiades, who were among the major deities in the Andean pantheon. In one of his few references to the *taqui oncoy*, Guaman Poma de Ayala, a convert to Christianity, wrote that false shamans could make people sick by sucking their blood while the victims slept. They also sucked blood from the victims' bodies in order to cure them of "the sickness of the *taqui oncoy*."[6] He listed *taqui oncoy* along with seven other sicknesses that shamans treated by sucking blood in order to draw out the disease. These illnesses all seem to exceed the strict dimensions of the physiological in both cause and symptoms, for they involve the psychological phenomenon of utter fright, terror, hysteria, or hallucination. Their names alone reveal the psychosomatic conception of the illness and the cure. For example, *chirapa uncuy* is the sickness caused by the vision of rain with sunshine; *pucuy oncuy* is the sickness caused by a water spring; *capac uncuy* is the sickness caused by a major calamity; the *uaca macasca* refers to the state of being wounded by a guaca. It is important to note that these diagnoses rest on the notion of having been robbed of or hurt in one's vital force (*cama-quuen*)—an Andean concept incorrectly translated as "soul."

The so-called dancing sickness that Cristóbal de Albornoz, an almost totally unknown Spanish priest and visitor, discovered in 1564 was extirpated in less than three years after more than eight thousand Andeans had been accused and condemned for "idolatry" by the energy and zeal of the campaign led by Albornoz.[7] This extirpation of the Taqui-Oncoy preceded the better known and more thoroughly destructive campaigns of 1610 to 1620 by some fifty years.[8] Although the center of the Taqui-Oncoy was Huamanga, the cult had converts in Cuzco, Arequipa, Lima, and even La Paz. Some Spanish contemporaries of the Taqui-Oncoy accused the rebel Inca in Vilcabamba, Titu Cusi Yupanqui, of promoting this "apostasy."[9]

The cult's preachers announced the end of Spanish domination. The guacas, they said, were alive and were coming back to fight against Dios. The guacas were already expelling the Spaniards and their Dios. These local deities demanded the allegiance of their people, who must therefore not go into churches, listen to evangelizing priests, eat Spanish food, or dress in Spanish clothing, under threat of being turned into animals.

The sixteenth-century Spanish chronicler Cristóbal de Molina called the Taqui-Oncoy a "sect" and reported:

They thought that all the guacas of the kingdom, all such that the Christians had defeated and burned, had come back to life and had divided themselves into two groups. One group had gathered around the deity Pachacamac, and the other around Titicay. All of them were going about in the air giving orders to wage battle unto Dios in order to defeat him. [They said] that they were about to win, that when the marquess [Francisco Pizarro] entered this land, Dios had vanquished the guacas and the Spaniards [had defeated] the Indians; but that now the world was turning and thus Dios and the Spaniards would be defeated, and all the Spaniards would be dead and their cities would be flooded, because the sea was going to rise and drown them, and hence that there would be no memory of them.[10]

Although the Taqui-Oncoy was known to the students of the sixteenth century in the Andes, the study of this millenarian movement dates back a mere twenty-five years. Recent publication of chronicles and accounts by Albornoz and others charged with the extirpation of idolatries provide a good source for our interpretation of the dancing sickness.[11] Of particular relevance to discourse analysis are Franklin Pease's essays on the myth of Incarrí and on the Taqui-Oncoy. Pease shows how, after the defeat of the Sun in Cajamarca, older local gods gained a new preeminence.

Evangelistic indoctrination was simultaneous with the Conquest. The Andean peoples had to accept Christianity as the official religion that displaced the solar cult of Cuzco. At the same time they had to accept the rupture of *the sacred order* of their world. But this substitution of the Christians' Dios for the Sun did not include or affect all other Andean divinities, as the discovery of the Taqui-Oncoy, thirty years after the Spanish invasion, attests.[12]

The demise of the Sun and the subsequent profanation of Cuzco, the sacred center of the cosmos, disarticulated the Andean pantheon. Since the Andean deities were particularly tied to the system of kinship, social structure, and economic production, their demise meant not only the death of God, but the devastation of the visible and invisible worlds alike.[13] For this reason, we can also read the myth of Incarrí as a response to the end of the known social order. Most variants of the myth hold that Incarrí's head was hidden in the underground. There it grows, impervious to decay, so that one day the head and the body will be reunited. On that day, when the mutilated body becomes whole again, Incarrí will be restored to life on the surface of the Pachamama, and if Dios allows it, the son of the Sun will reign again. At the same time, the sacred order—that is, justice as harmony—will be restored to the Andeans.

Besides stating the kernel of a utopia, the Incarrí myth signals a clear affirmation of continuity of the Andean cosmos despite the rupture caused by the

Spanish Conquest, as Pease points out. But unlike the preaching by the Taqui-Oncoy or a utopian vision of return to the Andean administration by Guaman Poma, this myth of restoration no longer postulates immediate reestablishment of the sacred order of the time of the Incas. The myth of Incarrí, in all its versions—including those collected most recently by field anthropologists—defers restoration to a messianic time. This messianic moment is marked by a pair of ambivalent signs. On the one hand, its inauguration depends on the growth of the Inca's body, which in turn will leave the underground to reign on the Pacha-mama; on the other hand, this will happen only if Dios permits, a condition not at all predictable. Thus the myth speaks with forked tongue. While signaling the continuity of the Andean world, it paradoxically asserts its break with the Inca past, the defeat of the Cuzco solar divinity, and its new dependence on Dios.

The invasion of 1532 left Andean people with stark choices: either to accept or resist Spanish rule. They could give up their guacas and separate ethnic identities to become generic Indians, as viceroy Francisco de Toledo (1569–1581) planned, or they could struggle to resist or overthrow Spanish domination and the works of Dios.[14] If the choice was to fight back, the accompanying expectation included restoration, during their lifetime, of the autochthonous gods and reinstatement of themselves as masters of Andean material and social life. Even as late as 1621, when José de Arriaga published his work on the extirpation of idolatries, it was clear that the Andean people clung to the project of preserving their gods. Arriaga counseled future extirpators to beware of the Andeans' obstinate desire "to carry water on both shoulders, to have recourse to both religions at once . . . for they feel and even say that they can worship their huacas while believing in God the Father, the Son, and Holy Ghost. Thus what they offer for the worship of Jesus Christ, they generally offer their huacas."[15]

By 1564, when Cristóbal de Albornoz detected the Taqui-Oncoy, there had been several responses and forms of resistance to colonial rule. This is not the place to discuss how each mode of resistance came to be; Wachtel and Steve Stern deal extensively with them. The awareness that Spanish rule spelled out the brutal disappearance of the Andeans and their world had become a vivid and even obsessional preoccupation for the inhabitants of the former Inca empire.[16] Stern writes that the cult of the "Taqui-Oncoy expressed the painful truth dawning upon local societies—that conflict between the Andean and European elements of colonial society was at once inescapable, irreconcilable, and decisive."[17]

At least four serious types of resistance can be documented, all combining acts with discourse and all seeking the continuity of the Andean world. First, the survivors from the Inca ruling class took up arms and entrenched themselves in Vilcabamba. Their response was war, a war that they eventually lost. The rebel Inca Titu Cusi Yupanqui spoke for those who fought in Vilcabamba. Second,

Guaman Poma de Ayala embarked on an unparalleled adventure of writing a letter to the king of Spain. The thousand-page autobiography, utopia, ethnography, and deconstruction of European thought is known as *El primer nueva corónica y buen gobierno (1586–1615)*. Third, a large number of curacas, caciques, and other individuals took up resistance and sabotage through their use of the Spanish legal structure. They became the litigant corps of Andean society. In the attempt to save their lives, welfare, and rights to the land, these "native shyster lawyers"—as the Spaniards named them—ensured that Spanish colonial efforts to establish an extractive economy and a clearly Spanish-dominated society would be ensnared for the rest of the sixteenth century and well into the seventeenth century. Finally, the otherwise unknown Juan Chocne and his followers, as preachers and converts of the cult and its ritual known as the Taqui-Oncoy, struggled to empower the ancient local gods with the force and the discourse necessary to compete with and, eventually, to defeat the invading god, the Spaniards, and the pestilence that followed in their wake.

In the search for continuity of the Andean world, all four forms of resistance were like the myth of Incarrí. The corollary of their resistance was, of course, the expulsion or at least the separation—as Guaman Poma proposed—of the Spanish world from the Andean life and cosmos. It would appear, at first glance at least, that all four forms of struggle failed. The rebels attempting to revive an Inca state capitulated; Titu Cusi, along with what was left of the Inca nobility, converted to Christianity and even accepted Dios. Guaman Poma died (1616?) an old and poor man whose last hope was through suffering to attain sainthood, and whose ultimate consolation for relinquishing princely aspirations was authorship;[18] the utopia of his *Primer nueva corónica y buen gobierno* was deferred indefinitely but his keen-edged critique of a world upside down remains. The litigious Andeans did manage to curtail the immediate erosion of their civil and economic rights; yet because they needed money to pay the costs of fighting in the Spanish courts, they actually fell prey to the policies whose demise they sought. Finally, when the Taqui-Oncoy was uncovered by the Spanish bureaucracy, it was quickly extirpated by the inspections of the extirpators of idolatries.

By the last quarter of the sixteenth century the Andean world, with its posture of explicit resistance to and struggle against the new order of Spanish rulers, had come to terms with defeat. The once sacred order of the universe stood forever profaned, and the discourse of the local rebellious gods that once inspired Juan Chocne's preaching and Guaman Poma's writing had to seek refuge, as in the myth of Incarrí, in a sort of underground to avoid its absolute and complete obliteration.

We do not know exactly when the myth of Incarrí began. Some think it appeared after the rebellion of Tupac Amaru II in 1780–1782. However, as

Flores Galindo writes, the myth's presence coincided with the particular historical development of Peru's central highlands, the same area where the Taqui-Oncoy flourished:

There exists a clear link between the history of this utopia and the [life of the Indian] communities. If we were to draw a map of the principal manifestations of the utopia, it should include the places where both the myth of *Incarrí* and the story of the three ages of the world have been found in conjunction with communal theatrical representations of the capture of the Inca.[19]

It would seem, however, in light of the several versions of the myth to be found in the Andes today, that once the messianic myth was born, it remained almost unchanged in the oral tradition. The same cannot, of course, be said about the millenarian beliefs of the Taqui-Oncoy, which we understand were extirpated by Cristóbal de Albornoz and other envoys of Toledo. I suggest, however, given the Andean will for continuity and history's abundant evidence of surviving functions and structures in the Andes,[20] that we will not stray far off course if we view José María Arguedas's scissor dancer in the short story "La agonía de Rasu Ñiti" as rearticulating many elements that once constituted the discourse of the Taqui-Oncoy.

Dancing in the texts of Arguedas is not restricted to Rasu Ñiti. Dancers, music, and musicians appear on many critical occasions in Arguedas's fiction: Camac in *El sexto* (1961), Ernesto in *Los ríos profundos* (1958), Tankayllu in *Yawar fiesta* (1941), and Don Diego in *El zorro de arriba y el zorro de abajo* (1971) all engage in a delirious dance or *taqui* at key moments of dramatic intensity in the narrative.[21] It may be possible to trace the link between the Taqui-Oncoy and its surviving manifestations today in specific instances of ritual plays (*comparsas*) celebrated in Andean communities (the research remains to be carried out).[22] Manuel Burga's study of these plays as ritual reenactments of the people's sense of history (for example, the death of Atahualpa, the last Inca) shows how the symbols and ritual of the sacramental dance are still at work in the Andes.[23]

In the sixteenth-century preaching of the Taqui-Oncoy neither the Inca nor the Sun occupied any space or function. Juan Chocne's message about the fighting return of the guacas seemed to concede the defeat of the Sun as god of the Inca state. In fact, the Taqui-Oncoy departed from the notion that Dios, the state god of the Spaniards, had indeed triumphed over the Sun. It therefore became the function of the numerous guacas—deities or culture heroes—to fight and expel the invaders and their god.[24]

According to Arriaga, besides adoring the sun, the moon, the stars, and thunder, the Indians adored the land, the ocean, mountain springs, snowcapped peaks (razu), and their mythical places of origin (*pacarinas*); small things were also part of the sacred order. Arriaga noted that the Indians held their forebears within the category of guacas and that some of these heroes, such as Libiacancharco, were famous for their feasts and exploits. Thus not only did their heroic ancestors literally occupy the earth, but as Arriaga further observed fifty years after the Taqui-Oncoy had been extirpated, Andeans regarded the guacas as the guarantors of "life and health and food." The Christian examiner of the guacas seemed puzzled by the "fact" that the "Indians never ask for anything concerning the other life."[25]

Within this context of the sacred, Dios appeared rather remote, almost irrelevant, were it not that he was allied with the war-making machine of the Christians. The logic of the Taqui-Oncoy—rejecting Dios and with it Christianity as well as the universe that the discourse of the evangelizing priests sought to implant—radically distanced the Taqui-Oncoy from Guaman Poma's blueprint for future government. The author of *El primer nueva corónica* grows tiresome in his repeated embrace of Christianity and the new god. The author and self-styled prince not only willingly discarded the Sun and its cult as mere Inca superstition or error but even denied that Indians had worshiped the now satanized guacas: "They neither made devils their masters nor worshiped idols and guacas."[26] What is more, Guaman Poma's utopia—restoration of Andean administration with the king of Spain as the new Inca principle of order[27]—allowed room for two Spanish cultural tools: Christianity and writing. We can easily comprehend that the self-appointed lawyer of indigent "Indians" would have felt a logical aversion to the emotional contents of the actions and preachings of the frenzied dancing of the Taqui-Oncoy inasmuch as they derived from a cult that Guaman Poma, as a Christian convert, rejected.

Guaman Poma preferred a god even more abstract and distant than the Andean creator god(s). Above all Guaman Poma, the writer, opted for a god figured within and through a complex and ancient discourse. The teleology of the Christian discourse not only posited a single origin for the human species but also seemed flexible enough to permit the grafting of Andean time and peoples into its "universal" sacred and historical order. For Guaman Poma, Juan Chocne's advocacy of a return to the cult of the guacas suggested an intolerable answer to the burning question of the day: were the Indians the descendants of Adam and Eve and therefore human or had they a separate origin and were they thus beasts of some kind? What is more, Guaman Poma's indirect mention of the Taqui-Oncoy included it in his long section on sorcery. To distance himself from all the shamans and sorcerers whose practices he described, he said that he learned about them when he went along as an assistant to Cristóbal de Albornoz who "consumed all the guacas, idols, and sorcerers of the kingdom."[28]

Thus, contrary to Guaman Poma's political dreams, the Taqui-Oncoy rejected not only two state gods but all things belonging to Spain, from discourse to food and clothing. Besides vowing to drive the invaders into the sea, the Taqui-Oncoy promised the restoration of good health and an abundance of foodstuff for the Andean peoples. Such promises were eminently practical and took into account local conditions and feelings of despair before the daily agony of the everyday world. The Taqui-Oncoy thus addressed not only the psychological traumas of the Conquest and the defeat of the gods but also the very palpable needs of the body.

By 1565 it had become abundantly clear that the ecological disaster brought on by the European invasion threatened the physical end of the Andean population. Over and over, Guaman Poma begs God to grant him and his people biological continuity, if nothing else. "Let us not disappear" is one of his several refrains. Freedom from the killing epidemics caused by European diseases—from the common cold to smallpox—was one of the promises the return of the guacas signified to the followers of Juan Chocne.[29] The satisfaction of basic needs—healthy bodies and enough food to go on living—required in turn that people obey the injunction not to eat Spanish foods (which were poisons or carriers of disease) or wear Spanish clothes (which transformed the social and religious meaning of being), under threat of final extinction. The people who did not obey the injunctions would surely succumb: they would be turned into animals, losing all contact with culture and reverting to unconscious nature. The guacas threatened those who betrayed them with the very destiny that people feared most: the absolute and irretrievable end to self and to life as they knew it. A clear consciousness of facing the dreaded end, the holocaust, thus characterized the preaching of the sick dance.

Contemporaries of the Taqui-Oncoy failed to see its relation to the crisis of everyday life. As Cristóbal de Albornoz reported, the Taqui-Oncoy was dangerous but only inasmuch as it was an "apostasy," a return to the old beliefs. The visitor dedicated a great deal more ink and paper to enumerating the hundreds of hidden guacas or ritual objects that he discovered and whose immediate destruction he himself undertoook or supervised than to examining the subject matter of the cult. He reduced the Taqui-Oncoy to its bare essentials, elements that enabled him to speak about the destruction of guacas to his superiors in the Spanish ecclesiastical bureaucracy.[30]

Today, when we look at the bare semiotic elements that make up the discourse of the Taqui-Oncoy, a closer reading reveals a complex transformation of religious and political structures that formed the world of Juan Chocne, Guaman Poma, Cristóbal de Molina, and Cristóbal de Albornoz. The analysis of the discourse of the Taqui-Oncoy allows us to rearticulate its elements and to rediscover its presence in cultural forms that have survived until today. Somehow, nodal elements of the cult remain active in a secret and nonverbal inscription to be found in the ritual and choreography of scissor dancers in Andean towns of the central highlands, and reinscribed in José María Arguedas's story "La agonía de Rasu Ñiti."

The Taqui-Oncoy accepts the sky as the place of a superior divinity that originally the Sun occupied. The solar defeat at Cajamarca—the capture of the Inca by the Spaniards—leaves that space to Dios, another sky divinity. Although the Taqui-Oncoy reclaims the guacas as the active divinities at the center of its pantheon, it nevertheless assigns the celestial space—vacated by a (defeated) Dios—to a vaguely conceived aerial divinity. Albornoz says that they speak of "a being who went about in the air in a sort of basket."[31] Even though "the Inca figures as a large absence," as Franklin Pease notes,[32] the sky is still considered an appropriate place for the supreme divinity.

If the transformation in the sky divinity goes from Sun to Dios to one who gets about in a basket, a very different movement takes place on the land. Corresponding to the Sun in the sky, the old religion holds the guacas on the land. In a sacred (sacralized) universe, the guacas are the essence of the power of the divine on a tangible, material level. The guacas, inasmuch as they are believed to be or to have become rivers, monoliths, or snowcapped peaks, dot the sensorial world and, therefore, the psychological universe, with their presence. José de Arriaga comes to the conclusion that since even small and insignificant things or places can be held to be guacas, these cannot be destroyed in their material existence. Thus the only way he sees to remove idolatry is to wrench it from the hearts of the Indians. The Jesuit José de Acosta confirms the multiplicity and varied origins of the guacas. In his *Historia natural y moral de las Indias* (1590) he comments:

The devil was not satisfied when he made the Indians blind, so that they adore the sun and the moon and the stars and nature as a whole. He went on to give them small things as gods, many of them vile. . . . In Cajamalca de la Nazca they showed me a great mountain of sand. It was a principal worship site or guaca of the ancients. I asked what divinity they saw in it. They answered that it was indeed a marvelous thing, being such a high sand mountain among so many other peaks of rock.[33]

The guacas are literally everywhere and are numerous because the people hold them to be not only their place of origin but also their constant companions in life. They intervene daily in human affairs, especially matters of health. Drawing from José de Arriaga and the myths of Huarochirí, Karen Spalding notes that guacas are not only held to provide good fortune and prosperity but also considered to help conquer and protect new territories. Guacas wage war on one another: "The capture of *wak'as*—who continued to be honored and served by their new possessors—as well as the lands was part of the oral tradition of Huarochirí."[34]

Guacas are the object of public worship and their service is the responsibility of the larger lineages and clans. Worship of the guacas, numerous as they are, forms part of the preservation and transmission of communal histories. According to Spalding, a large number of priests preserve and interpret the guacas.

Christianity holds a parallel arrangement in sixteenth-century Peru. Corresponding to Dios in the sky, the new religion reserves a sacralized space on the land. In place of the ancient, sacred, but now silent or mistaken guacas stand the churches filled with the voices of praying converts and preachers who attempt to organize the whole of life under the dictates of God and the saints. In response to the Christian sacralization that envelops the land with its churches, "evangelizing priests," and sacraments, the Taqui-Oncoy proclaims the new powers of an alliance of great guacas ready to battle Dios for sovereignty of the Andean universe. From Chimborazo in Ecuador, through Pachacámac in Lurín, to Tiahuanaco in Bolivia, the guacas are making ready to fight Dios.

The Taqui-Oncoy's struggle with Christianity hinges on the question of the land. Because the Andean cosmos implies a sacralized nature, the struggle for control and meaning of the land signifies much more than the location and function of the churches or the guacas as places of private or public worship. Juan Chocne, his followers, and many others readily understand that the prohibition to worship the site of the guacas does not simply nullify the divine but also negates the link between the Andean peoples and their ancestors (the bodies of family members and even *mallquis*, the embalmed bodies of deceased Incas) and thus destroys their right to use and conceptualize the land—for every lineage derives its identity and claim to the land from a recognized ancestor, real or mythical. Not only do the Christians denounce the guacas as false gods who speak lies and mislead the people—the Spaniards destroy their sites and punish their priests— but deny the very connection of the people with their sacralized origin and extirpate their "idolatries." Moreover, the relationship between the myth of origin, the present life of the body, and the sense of an everlasting community, synthesized in the cultural formation of the guaca, is dashed to pieces in 1551 when the Inquisition's Council of Lima declares that the sacred ancestors of the Indians, the deceased Incas, are in fact burning in hell.[35] The paroxysms of fright and despair embodied in the Taqui-Oncoy's sick dance re-present the figures drawn in the churches for future converts. They hear that their deceased parents, children, and grandparents, condemned to suffer in hell, are being devoured by thirst and hunger and consumed by illness. Painfully aware of their kin in hell, they take the return of the guacas to the domain of the land to be a logical and utter necessity.

The discourse of the Taqui-Oncoy with its prohibition of Spanish food, dress, and systems of beliefs underscores the body as the point of articulation between a universe loaded with symbols and a desacralized and disarticulated—impossible—purely physical realm. In forbidding Indians contact with the new sacred spaces, the Taqui-Oncoy also forbids them the Catholic sacraments, which revolve around eating (Holy Communion), talking (confession), rites of corporeal cleanliness and renaming of people (baptism). Within Christian discourse, these sacraments preside over and institutionalize all the critical stages of life, giving way to the birth of a new sense of self.[36]

Nowhere is the power over terrestrial space more keenly disputed than at the level of names. "Indians" are especially forbidden to take Spanish names, so that they may not answer to a new function or identity. The guacas are reconnected with the power of speech and, above all, with a public discourse, so that they can once again transmit their sacred word (as Christian churches do). The guacas will protect their people, but only under certain conditions of loyalty to the old ways. No longer fixed to their place of wonder—a majestic peak, a breathless precipice, a clear spring—the guacas now live within the hearts of men and women (in their social and religious imagination). Cristóbal de Albornoz reports that the guacas "entered the bodies of the Indians and made them talk."[37] The gods are no longer restricted to their former function of oracles. They, like the Christian god, inhabit the individual's inner, invisible, nonmaterial space.

The return of the guacas is clearly identified with the return of a dominant Andean discourse, of health to the Andean people, and of plentiful Andean foodstuff. This signals a return to life as it was known before the rupture of the Conquest and the coming of a new god. All desires are oriented toward the wholeness and plenitude of the individual body, which in turn has become the site from which the divinity speaks. The Andean body, thus resacralized, must not be disguised under foreign clothing. Spanish clothing not only hides the Andean self but also distorts it. What the body wears must be in accordance with what the body, as a social and religious sign, signifies and contains.

In most religions, the underground is reserved for deities who oppose the being and works of the creators. A bottomless hole of darkness and heat is reserved for the devil in the Christian pantheon. The Andean imagination speaks of magic snakes—*amarus*—and other beings inhabiting holes, tunnels, and caves; but their sign is positive. We lack adequate knowledge to define the underground assigned to the body of Incarrí or explain the meaning of this underground as the place of regeneration for a celestial divinity. According to Luis E. Valcárcel, the cosmos of the ancient Andean peoples contains three elements: water, earth, and fire. The universe (*pacha*) is arranged in tiers: *hanaq pacha* or "above world," inhabited by gods such as the Sun, the moon, or thunder; *kay pacha* or "the world here," populated by living beings and spirits; and *ukhu pacha* or "inside world," inhabited by the dead and bacteria or germs. These three worlds maintain communication by means of channels and tunnels through volcanic craters, caverns, or springs at fixed points of entrance (*pacarinas*).[38]

In the case of the Taqui-Oncoy, preoccupied with a struggle for domination over the terrestrial plane and hopeful that "guacas would make another world" because "the guacas had already defeated the God of the Christians since their turn was already over," the underground has little place.[39] Understandably, the cult's discourse is silent in reference to the underground as a space to occupy or mobilize its imagination.

Both Millones and Pease show very convincingly how the Inca principle—the principle of order—generally goes underground after 1532. A similar, but more complex, trajectory transforms the discourse of the Taqui-Oncoy within the ritual dance of the scissor dancers.

"La agonía de Rasu Ñiti" (1962) is a short story Arguedas wrote in one of his best moments.[40] The old and sick scissor dancer Rasu Ñiti (he who steps on snow), prepares to dance his last or death dance. As he readies himself for the final rite of passage, a condor, visible only to the dancer and his wife, hovers over the dancer's head. The condor, the dancer tells his daughter, is the *Wamani*, the aerial divinity that protects him and listens to him as it does to the rest of the Andean peoples. The Wamani's hearing is such that it can even hear the growth of Incarrí.[41]

From the narrator's explanation we recognize that this divinity belongs to the sky. A silent presence overhead, it listens intently. Other deities live inside mountains or occupy sacred underground sites from which they inspire other scissor dancers in their rituals and celebrations.

In "La agonía de Rasu Ñiti," the body and performance of the dying dancer constitute fluid spaces inhabitable by either sky or underground divinities. The churches, formerly in dispute with the guacas, appear in the dancer's world as spaces particularly suited to the feats of his dance because their high towers are connected to the sacred inner sanctum of the churches by dark, snake-like or snail-like, inner stairways that the dancer climbs up and down with extraordinary skill, taken by the whirlwind of his abstracting and mesmerizing music.[42]

The former univocal quality of the sky, land, and underground as divine space delineated in the Taqui-Oncoy has, in the tale of Rasu Ñiti, been diffused or confused. The church has been integrated into the Andean articulation of space. It has lost the forbidden quality that the Taqui-Oncoy conferred on it during the struggles of the sixteenth century. The aerial god of the basket has disappeared, leaving perhaps Dios in its place or the condor as its visible sign. The scissor dancer of Arguedas has continuity with the ritual sick dancers of the Taqui-Oncoy because his body is an emblem of the Wamani's active presence in the world. His body mediates between the political sphere and the religious world; between the practical sphere and the mystical realm; between the churches' high towers to which no priest dares ascend and the space where God and his officiating priests secretly and darkly dwell.

Whereas the extirpations of Albornoz drove the Andean gods back into their natural sites and also drove the Inca principle underground, the scissor dancers, with their kinetic statement of splendor and song, survive right under the glaring light of Christianization and oppression. We recognize here the same ability to adapt and transform in order to continue the ancient beliefs that Arriaga saw as he cautioned his sixteenth-century fellow priests against the Andeans' ingenuity. "The dissimulation and boldness of the Indians has also reached such a point that during the feast of the Corpus Christi they have slyly hidden a small huaca on the very platform of the monstrance of the holy Sacrament."[43]

The dance of the Taqui-Oncoy was a space of transition that divided the voyage from sickness to health, from Pachacuti to restoration. A measure of such health was the preaching or discourse that the guacas granted to reward their adepts' dancing. In the face of the devastating epidemics and the thorough destructuration of the Andean social and economic system, the restoration of health to a sick and disintegrating world was more than an appropriate metaphor to express the significance of the cult to the gods. But the discourse of the guacas was also forced underground, leaving only the splendor of the dance as a sign of the desire for wholesome and harmonious integration.

In Arguedas's contemporary story, Rasu Ñiti gets up from his deathbed to dance for the last time because "my heart is letting me know."[44] In communication with the Wamani, the mountain divinity whose expression is the condor, the dancer tells his wife: "The Wamani speaks. You cannot hear." The gods have been driven underground or, rather, back into the land; they still communicate but only privately, secretly, with a few select and trusted individuals. The world and discourse that the guacas of the Taqui-Oncoy made public appear transformed in Arguedas's tale as a secret space, unattainable for the uninitiated. Its message resists all interpretation, all dissemination. The wife cannot hear the Wamani, but she can see and sense it. She must be satisfied by what her husband, the scissor dancer, tells her about the Wamani in their house. She perceives only that it is gray and hovers serenely over the dancer's head. Any act of verbal communication is forbidden to her.

Observing a precise and ancient ritual, Rasu Ñiti dresses in his glorious outfit. With religious fervor, he puts on each piece of clothing in a prescribed order. This dancer's costume is outstanding for its colors and its European slant; it does not observe the prohibitions of 1565. Its materials display the most precious Andean brocaded ribbons and the luxury of European silks and velvets. The tailoring of the pants and jackets is reminiscent of a bullfighter's; Arguedas calls it a "suit of light and color."

These elements of the dancer's clothing are his signs, his markings, in a semiotic sense. Satisfied with his dress and ritual, "already dressed by his decoration," Rasu Ñiti steps out into the sunlight before the people who have gathered to see him dance his farewell.[45]

Inverting the relationship of the people to the guacas in the Taqui-Oncoy, the Wamani does not speak publicly yet *hears* what all the Andean people know and think. One of Rasu Ñiti's daughters is told that she cannot "see" the Wamani because she is not yet *strong* enough to see him, but she can be sure that the

Wamani hears her. "'Yes, he hears,' answered the dancer. 'He also hears how our god is growing, how he is going to swallow the eyes of that horse of the master'" (148).

The Wamani listens and takes note, as St. Peter does, of any offenses perpetrated against the social order. And if it cannot or does not speak, it does communicate its loving presence through the dancer's performance. Discourse is not the privilege of this deity: through yet another transformation, the Wamani communicates with its people through music. In other words, of the fourfold combination of the Taqui-Oncoy (dance–preaching–music–ecstasy), three elements have survived and one, the preaching, has been lost. The music of the dancer's scissors (two unhinged steel blades "played" by one hand) is the range of sounds within which it signifies its presence, mood, and caring concern for the sorrows of its people. "Do you hear, my daughter? The scissors are not really played by your father's fingers. The Wamani plays them. Your father is only obeying" (148).

Once again we are in the presence of the possessed dancer of the Taqui-Oncoy. The narrator states:

They dance alone or in competition with each other. The feats they accomplish and the boiling of their blood during the figures of the dances depend on the [Wamani] who sits on their head and heart. While he dances or lifts and throws crowbars with his teeth, or pierces his flesh through with an awl, or walks in the air on a cord stretched between the very top of a tree and the tower of the town. (149)

In this regard, Martin Lienhard insists on the link between the competitive (dialogic) dancing of the foxes of the myths of Huarochirí, translated by Arguedas, and the "dancing delirium that takes possession of the characters and even of language" in *El zorro de arriba y el zorro de abajo*.[46]

As the anonymous participants in the Taqui-Oncoy did, Arguedas's narrator posits the Wamani not only as a divinity whose site is a place or a thing in nature, but also as a spirit residing within the dancer's body:

The genius of a scissor dancer depends on the spirit that inhabits him. It could be the spirit of a mountain [Wamani], or the spirit of a silent and transparent precipice. (149)

The "spirit" of the guacas thus survives in the dance of this possessed artist. However, mere survival is not their best achievement; for even as they cede the space of discourse, the guacas give back to the people, through the dancer and especially in his scissor's song, just for an ephemeral moment, the desired health or harmony of the sacred order so ruptured by the Conquest.

Arguedas's narrator remembers the feats of another scissor dancer, Unto:

The voice of the scissors exhausted all feeling. . . . It floated up to heaven only to return to the world as our eyes followed the dancer. . . . The music of the world will never again play so intensely on two blades of shining steel. (149)

In this music played by Rasu Ñiti, the world's sacred order is thus restored for all Andeans. The privileged relation of performer with Wamani is, through his dance and music, rendered communitarian.

As in a Pachacuti, Arguedas's story narrates the tale of death and rebirth. Rasu Ñiti gets up from his sickbed to perform his last dance, a dance in whose ritual and music he will pass his relation to the Wamani on to Atok Sayllu, his disciple. "He was born again, with the tendons of a young beast and the fire of the Wamani" (154).

In this transformed version of the Taqui-Oncoy, the divinity perpetuates itself in its people; they, in turn, find their continuity in the divinity. Arguedas's story thus ends with a double affirmation: the old dancer is to be buried and a new one is to be born. The young disciple is to marry, and thus the sorrow of death is mitigated by the promise of life. It is to the collectivity of Arguedas's story that we can attribute these last words: "Wamani is Wamani." Words that the adepts of the Taqui-Oncoy also enunciated in order to restore and assert the continuity of their world.

Notes

1. The cycle of Pachacuti was thought to occur roughly every five hundred years. For a discussion of the Pachacuti in Andean ideology see Franklin Pease, *El dios creador andino* (Lima, 1973); and Juan Ossio, ed., *Ideología mesiánica del mundo andino* (Lima, 1973). For the ways in which the idea of a Pachacuti intersects with the Christian idea of the Last Judgment, see Sabine MacCormack, "Pachacuti: Miracles, Punishment, and Last Judgment: Visionary Past and Prophetic Future in Early Colonial Peru," *The American Historical Review* 4, vol. 93 (October 1988): 960–1006.
2. Nathan Wachtel, *Los vencidos, los indios del Perú frente a la conquista española (1530–1570)* (Madrid, 1976), 58; this and all subsequent translations from Spanish are mine. The American historian Steve Stern has a similar focus on the Andean response; see his chapter in Nathan Wachtel, *Sociedad e ideología, ensayos de historia y antropología andina* (Lima, 1973), and Steve Stern, *Peru's Indian Peoples and the Challenge of the Spanish Conquest, Huamanga to 1640* (Madison, Wis., 1982).
3. Wachtel, *Los vencidos*, 135.
4. Michel Foucault, *The Archaeology of Knowledge* (New York, 1972), 107.
5. In 1621 the Spanish priest José de Arriaga (1564–1622), in trying to understand the objects and rites of worship in the Andes, listed the sun, the moon, and the Pleiades, then added guacas:

> They also worship and reverence the high hills and mountains and huge stones. They have names for them and numerous fables about their changes and metamorphoses. Saying that they were once men who have changed to stone . . . these are all huacas that they worship as gods . . . and every child who has learned to talk knows the name of the huaca of his clan. For every clan and faction has a principal huaca . . . and members of the clan take the

name of the community huaca. Some huacas are thought as the guardians and advocates of the town.

    The Extirpation of Idolatry in Perú, trans. and ed. Clark Keating (Lexington, Ky., 1968), 22–25. Among twentieth-century sources, María Rostworowski de Diez Canseco comments in her superb study of religious ideology and politics in pre-Hispanic Peru that Andean beliefs lacked both the abstract idea of God and a word to express it but had a strong sense of the sacred; "the word for this was *guaca*"; *Estructuras andinas del poder: Ideología religiosa y política* (Lima, 1983), 9. The glossary to Stern, *Peru's Indian Peoples* defines *Waká* as "a native Andean God; a sacred being or spirit, often thought of as an ancestor, and materialized in the form of hills, waters, stones or ancestors' mummies" (262).

6. Guaman Poma de Ayala, *El primer nueva corónica y buen gobierno* (1583–1615), eds. John Murra and Rolena Adorno (Mexico City, 1981), 1:253. For a penetrating study of shamanism in Peru, see Mario Chiappi, Moisés Lemlij, and Luis Millones, *Alucinógenos y shamanismo en el Perú contemporáneo* (Lima, 1985), and Rostworoski, *Estructuras andinas*, 10–11.

7. Stern, *Peru's Indian Peoples*, 51.

8. Alberto Flores Galindo (*Buscando un Inca: identidad y utopía en los Andes* [Lima, 1987]) writes, "Between 1610 and 1660, three campaigns to extirpate idolatries were unleashed on the peoples of the central highlands after a *criollo* [an indigenous person of Spanish descent] priest discovered that behind the pious celebrations of the Virgin of the Assumption there hid the worship of Pariacaca and Chaupiñamacc, two ancient pre-Hispanic deities." (90)

9. Wachtel, *Los vencidos*, 284.

10. Ibid., 285. Wachtel quotes this passage from the chronicle *El Cuzqueño* (1575) of Cristóbal de Molina.

11. See the account of Albornoz published by Luis Millones, "Un movimiento nativista del siglo XVI: el Taqui-Oncoy," in Ossio, ed., *Ideología mesiánica del mundo andino*. On Andean deities see Pease's work *El dios creador* and Rostworoski, *Estructuras andinas*; also Franklin Pease, ed., *El pensamiento mítico, antología* (Lima, 1982).

12. Pease, *El dios creador*, 70.

13. For detailed discussion of the origins, properties, and function of guacas see Karen Spalding, *Huarochirí: An Andean Society under Inca and Spanish Rule* (Stanford, 1984), 63–65.

14. A substantive account of the conversion of the many Andean ethnic societies into "Indians" is in Stern, *Peru's Indian Peoples*, 80–113.

15. Arriaga, *The Extirpation*, 72.

16. For an up-to-date examination of the demographic ruin caused by the European invasion of the Andes see D. N. Cook, *Demographic Collapse: Indian Peru, 1520–1620* (Cambridge, 1981).

17. Stern, *Peru's Indian Peoples*, 56.

18. For a discussion of Guaman Poma and the question of authorship in his work, see Sara Castro-Klarén, "Escritura y persona en el Nuevo Mundo," in *Escritura, transgresión y sujeto en la literatura latinoamericana* (Mexico City, 1989), 139–57.

19. Flores Galindo, *Buscando*, 88.

20. See for instance John V. Murra, *Formaciones económicas y políticas del mundo andino* (Lima, 1975), and Juan Ossio, "Cultural Continuity, Structure, and Context: Some Peculiarities of the Andean Compadrazgo," in *Kinship, Ideology, and Practice in Latin America*, ed. Raymond I. Smith (Chapel Hill, N.C., 1984), 118–46. See also Rodrigo

Montoya, Edwin Montoya, and Luis Montoya, *La sangre de los cerros, Urkukunapa Yawarnin* (Lima, 1987), and Francisco Carrillo, *Literatura Quechua Clásica. Enciclopedia histórica de la literatura peruana*, vol. 1 (Lima, 1986).

21. José María Arguedas, "La agonía de Rasu Ñiti," in *Amor, mundo y todos los cuentos* (Lima, 1967). José María Arguedas (1911–1969) was an anthropologist; he and Mario Vargas Llosa are considered to be the two major Peruvian novelists of the twentieth century. His narrative combines a highly original prose style with a realistic rhetoric that captures the world of the Andean people from their own vantage point and experience. Arguedas grew up in an Andean community of the central highlands. Translation of Arguedas's work into English has taken place only after his death; see Frances H. Barraclough's translation of Arguedas's major novel *Los ríos profundos* (1958) as *Deep Rivers* (Austin, Tex., 1978) and the short novel *Yawar fiesta* (1941; trans. Austin, Tex., 1985). *The Singing Mountaineers*, trans. Ruth Stephan, Kate Flores, and Angel Flores (Austin, Tex., 1957), contains *Canto kechua* and *Canciones y cuentos del pueblo quechua*.

22. Author's conversation with Luis Millones, 1989.

23. Manuel Burga, *Nacimiento de una utopía: Muerte y resurrección de los Incas* (Lima, 1988), especially chaps. 1 and 2.

24. In her study of the myths of Huarochirí, Spalding states, "Wak'as were regarded as hero-deities who had performed great exploits (constructing irrigation canals, for instance) and had turned themselves to stone to guard the resources they had created for their people"; *Huarochirí*, 63.

25. Arriaga, *The Extirpation*, 22–24, 50.

26. Guaman Poma, *El primer nueva corónica*, 1:45, 253.

27. "The king of Spain is assimilated to the notion of Pachacuti in the sense of 'renovator of the world,' which to our understanding was the principal attribute of the Inca in the pre-Hispanic past"; Gauman Poma, quoted in Ossio, *Ideología*, 200.

28. Guaman Poma, *El primer nueva corónica*, 1:253. Regarding the nature and efficacy of the (oracular) discourse of the Andean gods just before and after 1532, Manuel Burga writes, "Their gods, who spoke through professionals in Andean technology and knowledge, became fallible. They became liars. . . . The gods lost credibility and thus Andean peoples turned more often to an apocalyptic reading of normal events"; *Nacimiento*, 58.

29. The steep decline in the sixteenth-century population was so dramatic that the term "holocaust" no longer seems an exaggeration. The records show that between 1520 and 1600 there were twenty epidemics. People were dying at unprecedented rates not only because of diseases but also from forced labor, military conscription, dietary change, and psychological devastation. For a fuller appreciation of this picture of horror, see Max Hernández, Moisés Lemlij, Luis Millones, Alberto Péndola, and María Rostworoski, *Entre el mito y la historia: Psicoanálisis y el pasado andino* (Lima, 1987), especially "El Taqui-Oncoy, la enfermedad del canto," 111–35.

30. Millones, "Un movimiento," 86.

31. Albornoz, quoted in Millones, "Un movimiento," 1/22.

32. Pease, *El dios creador*, 80.

33. José de Acosta, *Historia natural y moral de las Indias* (1590), ed. Edmundo O'Gorman (Mexico City, 1979) 223–24.

34. Spalding, *Huarochirí*, 63–65.

35. Ibid., 245.

36. The struggle over the hearts and minds of the Andeans waged by the evangelizing priests recognized patronymics as a key element of self-identity. Whereas the Taqui-Oncoy forbade the taking of Spanish names, José de Arriaga in his section on prohi-

bitions explained that Andeans were not to keep their ancient names because these might have secret association with the guacas. The Jesuits even proscribed the name Santiago because the Indians appropriated it to make of the warrior saint of the Spaniards a new representation for their thunder god Illapa, associating the lighting of Santiago's harquebus with Illapa's own aerial manifestations; Arriaga, *The Extirpation*, 54.

37. Albornoz, quoted in Millones, "Un movimiento," 1/37.

38. See Luis E. Valcárcel, *Etnohistoria del antiguo Perú* (Lima, 1959) 137–62. A *pacarina* is also the place of origin for each ethnic group; its connection with the community's guacas is direct.

39. Albornoz, quoted in Millones, "Un movimiento," 1/17, 2/8.

40. The connection between the ritual character of the foxes and the dancing in Arguedas's *El zorro de arriba y el zorro de abajo* (1971) and the dancing foxes of Huarochirí myths seems inescapable. Neither Arguedas nor the critics who study his work have linked the scissor dancers to the foxes in the Huarochirí myths and the generally ritual sacred dances, of which the Taqui-Oncoy must be but one in a series.

41. In speaking of the famous hero-deity Libiacancharco, the Spanish priest José de Arriaga related that it was "in a shelter below a cave in a very steep mountain. It had its huama [*waman*, or falcon totem] or diadem of gold on its head and it was dressed in fine shirts of cumbi"; *The Extirpation*, 16.

42. In coming to terms with the Christian cosmos, Andean people not only occupied and subverted the new sacred space aboveground, the church, but also tried to change cemeteries into places for their expulsed *mallquis*; Flores Galindo quotes evidence from the account of an extirpation campaign: "In 1613, in a town located between Huancavelica and Ayacucho, upon the arrival of the preachers, a bolt of lightning destroyed a church. . . . The Jesuits who were evangelizing the Indians of the locality examined the ruins of the church only to discover behind the central altar a guaca, and under the floor a clandestine cemetery"; *Buscando*, 92.

43. Arriaga, *The Extirpation*, 70.

44. Arguedas, "La agonía de Rasu Ñiti," 146. Further references cited in the text.

45. This ritual dressing coupled to Arguedas's care in observing the order of the investiture points to the totemic nature of the dance. Luis E. Valcárcel writes of the surviving totemic dances of undoubted pre-Columbian origin. Like the performance of the scissor dancer, these totemic dances are executed by a single masked man whose clothing integrates either feline skin or feathers. See the prologue to Pierre Verges, *Fiestas y danzas en el Cuzco y en los Andes* (Buenos Aires, 1945), 12.

46. Martin Lienhard, *Cultura popular andina y forma novelesca, zorros y danzantes en la última novela de Arguedas* (Lima, 1981), 120.

LOUIS MONTROSE

The Work of Gender
in the Discourse of Discovery

> *Guiana is a countrey that hath yet her maydenhead.*
> —Sir Walter Ralegh, *The Discoverie . . . of Guiana*

I

IN A RECENT ESSAY on gender as a category of historical analysis, Joan Wallach Scott advances two integrally connected propositions: "Gender is a constitutive element of social relationships based upon perceived differences between the sexes, and gender is a primary way of signifying relationships of power."[1] The first proposition "involves four interrelated elements: first, culturally available symbols that evoke multiple (and often contradictory) representations"; "second, normative concepts that set forth interpretations of the meanings of the symbols, that attempt to limit and contain their metaphoric possibilities" (43); third, the realizations of those various alternative or contestatory possibilities that are marginalized or suppressed by the normative or dominant, and which must be recovered by subsequent critical-historical analysis; and fourth, the employment of such historically specific (though not necessarily stable or consistent) cultural representations in the making of gendered subjective identities. Scott's second proposition refers to gender as one of the fundamental modes in which ideological and material reality are organized:

Established as an objective set of references, concepts of gender structure perception and the concrete and symbolic organization of all social life. To the extent that these references establish distributions of power (differential control over or access to material and symbolic resources), gender becomes implicated in the conception and construction of power itself.

From this perspective, as "a persistent and recurrent way of enabling the signification of power in the West," the discourse of gender is not always or necessarily "literally about gender itself" (45). Among the flexible strengths of this analytical model are that it conceptualizes gender in terms of the reciprocally constituted and historically variable categories of Man and Woman; and that it also comprehends such gender systems as themselves reciprocally related, in multiple and shifting ways, to other modes of cultural, political, and economic organization and experience. Furthermore, to view gender representations historically—in terms of a multivalent ideological process that perpetually generates, constrains,

177

AMERICA.

Americen Americus retexit, & Semel vocauit inde semper excitam

FIGURE 1. *America*, ca. 1580. Engraving by Theodor Galle
after a drawing by Jan van der Straet (ca. 1575).
Photo: The Burndy Library, Norwalk, Conn.

and contests cultural meanings and values—is to reveal, beneath the apparent stability and consistency of collective structures, myriad local and individual sites of social reproduction, variation, and change.

This analytical model provides a theoretical groundplot for the particular historical and critical, local and individual, concerns of the present essay. At the center of these concerns is the gendering of the protocolonialist discourse of discovery prevalent in Western Europe in the sixteenth century; the projection into the New World of European representations of gender—and of sexual conduct, a distinct but equally *cultural* phenomenon; and the articulation of those representations with new projects of economic exploitation and geopolitical domination. I discuss some instances of the gendering of the New World as feminine, and the sexualizing of its exploration, conquest, and settlement. The frame of reference for this discussion is not a closed or autonomous discourse of gender or sexuality but rather an open field of historically specific ideological conjunctures and exchanges, in which issues of gender and sexual conduct participate.

Early modern Europe's construction of its collective Other in "the New World"—its construction of the "savage" or the "Indian"—was accomplished by the symbolic and material destruction of the indigenous peoples of the Western Hemisphere, in systematic attempts to destroy their bodies and their wills, to suppress their cultures and to efface their histories. This process of protocolonialist "othering" also engages, interacts with, and mediates between two distinctive Elizabethan discourses: one, articulating the relationship between Englishmen and Spaniards; the other, articulating the relationship between the woman monarch and her masculine subjects. The latter discourse is inflected by the anomalous status of Queen Elizabeth—who is at once a *ruler*, in whose name the discoveries of her masculine subjects are authorized and performed; and also a *woman*, whose political relationship to those subjects is itself frequently articulated in the discourses of gender and sexuality.[2] The paradoxes and contradictions implicit in each of these discourses are foregrounded when they are brought together in a conjuncture with the discourse of discovery. Within the intertwined and unstable terms of collective national and gender identity, I focus upon an individual Englishman and Elizabethan subject—Sir Walter Ralegh—whose production of these discourses in his writings and performances is marked by the idiosyncrasies of his personal history and circumstances.

The writings of critics, too, are necessarily subject to historical and idiosyncratic marking. I remain uncomfortably aware that the trajectory of this essay courts the danger of reproducing what it purports to analyze: namely, the appropriation and effacement of the experience of both native Americans and women by the dominant discourse of European patriarchy. It is necessary, I believe, not only to resist such a dominant discourse but also to resist too rigid an understanding of its dominance. In other words, it is necessary to anatomize these elements of heterogeneity and instability, permeability and contradiction, that perpetually forestall ideological closure.[3] Thus, while I have no illusion that I have wholly resisted complicity in the operations of that dominant discourse, my attempt has been to locate and discover a few of the places of stress where its operations may be critically observed.

II

By the 1570s, allegorical personifications of America as a female nude with feathered headdress had begun to appear in engravings and paintings, on maps and title pages, throughout Western Europe.[4] Perhaps the most resonant of such images is Jan van der Straet's drawing of Vespucci's discovery of America, widely disseminated in print in the late sixteenth century by means of Theodor Galle's engraving (fig. 1).[5] Here a naked woman, crowned with feathers, upraises herself from her hammock to meet the gaze of the armored and robed man who has just come ashore; she extends her right arm toward him, apparently in a gesture of wonder—or, perhaps, of apprehension. Standing with his feet firmly planted upon the ground, Vespucci observes the personified and feminized space that will bear his name. This recumbent figure, now discovered and roused from her torpor, is about to be hailed, claimed, and possessed as *America*. As the motto included in Galle's engraving puts it, "Americen Americus retexit, & Semel vocavit inde semper excitam"—"Americus rediscovers America; he called her once and thenceforth she was always awake." This theme is discreetly amplified by the presence of a sloth, which regards the scene of awakening from its own shaded spot upon the tree behind America. Vespucci carries with him the variously empowering ideological and technological instruments of civilization, exploration, and conquest: a cruciform staff with a banner bearing the Southern Cross, a navigational astrolabe, and a sword—the mutually reinforcing emblems of belief, empirical knowledge, and violence. At the left, behind Vespucci, the prows of the ships that facilitate the expansion of European hegemony enter the pictorial space of the New World; on the right, behind America, representatives of the indigenous fauna are displayed as if emerging from an American interior at once natural and strange.

Close to the picture's vanishing point—in the distance, yet at the center—a group of naked savages, potential subjects of the civilizing process, are preparing a cannibal feast. A severed human haunch is being cooked over the fire; another, already spitted, awaits its turn. America's body pose is partially mirrored by both the apparently female figure who turns the spit and the clearly female figure who cradles an infant as she awaits the feast. Most strikingly, the form of the severed human leg and haunch turning upon the spit precisely inverts and miniaturizes America's own. In terms of the pictorial space, this scene of cannibalism is perspectively distanced, pushed into the background; in terms of the pictorial surface, however, it is placed at the center of the visual field, between the mutual gazes of Americus and America, and directly above the latter's outstretched arm.

I think it possible that the represented scene alludes to an incident reported to have taken place during the third of Vespucci's alleged four voyages, and recounted in his famous letter of 1504. I quote from the mid-sixteenth-century English translation by Richard Eden:

At the length they broughte certayne women, which shewed them selves familier towarde the Spaniardes: Whereupon they sent forth a young man, beyng very strong and quicke, at whom as the women wondered, and stode gasinge on him and feling his apparell: there came sodeynly a woman downe from a mountayne, bringing with her secretly a great stake, with which she gave him such a stroke behynde, that he fell dead on the earth. The other wommene foorthwith toke him by the legges, and drewe him to the mountayne, whyle in the mean tyme the men of the countreye came foorth with bowes and arrowes, and shot at oure men. . . . The women also which had slayne the yong man, cut him in pieces even in the sight of the Spaniardes, shewinge them the pieces, and rosting them at a greate fyre.[6]

The elements of savagery, deceit, and cannibalism central to the emergent European discourse on the inhabitants of the New World are already in place in this very early example. Of particular significance here is the blending of these basic ingredients of protocolonialist ideology with a crude and anxious misogynistic fantasy, a powerful conjunction of the savage and the feminine.[7]

This conjunction is reinforced in another, equally striking Vespuccian anecdote. Vespucci presents a different account of his third voyage in his other extant letter, this one dated 1503 and addressed to Lorenzo Piero Francesco de Medici. Like the previous letter, this one was in wide European circulation in printed translations within a few years of its date. Here Vespucci's marvelous ethnography includes the following observation:

> Another custom among them is sufficiently shameful, and beyond all human credibility. Their women, being very libidinous, make the penis of their husbands swell to such a size as to appear deformed; and this is accomplished by a certain artifice, being the bite of some poisonous animal, and by reason of this many lose their virile organ and remain eunuchs. (*Letters*, 46)

The oral fantasy of female insatiability and male dismemberment realized in the other letter as a cannibalistic confrontation of alien cultures is here translated into a precise genital and domestic form. Because the husband's sexual organ is under the control of his wife and is wholly subject to her ambiguous desires, the very enhancement of his virility becomes the means of his emasculation.

In the light of Vespucci's anecdotes, the compositional centrality of van der Straet's apparently incidental background scene takes on new significance: it is at the center of the composition in more ways than one, for it may be construed as generating or necessitating the compensatory foreground scene that symbolically contains or displaces it. In van der Straet's visualization of discovery as the advance of civilization, what is closer to the horizon is also closer to the point of origin: it is where we have come from—a prior episode in the history of contacts between Europeans and native Americans, and an earlier episode in the history of human society; and it is now what we must control—a cultural moment that is to be put firmly, decisively, behind us. In the formal relationship of proportion and inversion existing between America's leg and what I suppose to be that of the dismembered Spanish youth, I find a figure for the dynamic of gender and power in which the collective imagination of early modern Europe articulates its confrontation with alien cultures. The supposed sexual guile and deceit that enable the native women to murder, dismember, and eat a European man are in a relationship of opposition and inversion to the vaunted masculine knowledge and power with which the erect and armored Vespucci will master the prone and naked America. Thus, the interplay between the foreground and background scenes of the van der Straet–Galle composition gives iconic form to the oscillation characterizing Europe's ideological encounter with the New World: an oscillation between fascination and repulsion, likeness and strangeness, desires to destroy and to assimilate the Other; an oscillation between the confirmation and the subversion of familiar values, beliefs, and perceptual norms.

Michel de Certeau reproduces the engraving of Vespucci's discovery of America as the frontispiece of his book *The Writing of History*. As he explains in his preface, to him this image is emblematic of the inception of a distinctively modern discursive practice of historical and cultural knowledge; this historiography subjects its ostensible subject to its own purportedly objective discipline; it ruptures the continuum "between a subject and an object of the operation, between a *will to write* and a *written body* (or a body to be written)." For de Certeau, the history of this modern writing of history begins in the sixteenth century with "the 'ethnographical' organization of writing in its relation with 'primitive,' 'savage,' 'traditional,' or 'popular' orality that it establishes as its other." Thus, for him, the tableau of Vespucci and America is

an inaugural scene. . . . The conqueror will write the body of the other and trace there his own history. From her he will make a historied body—a blazon—of his labors and phantasms. . . .

What is really initiated here is a colonization of the body by the discourse of power. This is *writing that conquers*. It will use the New World as if it were a blank, "savage" page on which Western desire will be written.[8]

"America" awakens to discover herself written into a story that is not of her own making, to find herself a figure in another's dream. When called by Vespucci, she is interpellated within a European history that identifies itself simply as History, single and inexorable; this history can only misrecognize America's history as sleep and mere oblivion. In 1974, when a speaker at the first Indian Congress of South America declared, "Today, at the hour of our awakening, we must be our own historians," he spoke as if in a long suppressed response to the ironic awakening of van der Straet's America, her awakening to the effacement of her own past and future.[9]

Although applied here to a graphic representation that is iconic rather than verbal, de Certeau's reflections suggestively raise and conjoin issues that I wish to pursue in relation to Sir Walter Ralegh's *The Discoverie of the large, rich, and beautifull Empire of Guiana* (1596) and some other Elizabethan examples of "writing that conquers."[10] These issues include consideration of the writing subject's textualization of the body of the Other, neither as mere description nor as genuine encounter but rather as an act of symbolic violence, mastery, and self-empowerment; and the tendency of such discursive representation to assume a narrative form, to manifest itself as "a historied body"—in particular, as a mode of symbolic action whose agent is gendered masculine and whose object is gendered feminine. Rather than reduce such issues to the abstract, closed, and static terms of a binary opposition—whether between European and Indian, Culture and Nature, Self and Other, or, indeed, Male and Female—I shall endeavor to discriminate among various sources, manifestations, and consequences of what de Certeau generalizes as the "Western desire" that is written upon the putatively "blank page" of the New World, and to do so by specifying the ideological configurations of gender and social estate, as well as national, religious, and/or ethnic identities, that are brought into play during any particular process of textualization.

III

An "inaugural scene" of Elizabethan New World colonialism is textualized in Arthur Barlowe's report to Ralegh. Fortuitously, it was on the fourth of July in 1584 that "the first voyage made to . . . America" at the "charge, and direction" of Ralegh "arrived upon the coast, which we supposed to be a continent, and firme lande."[11] Barlowe relates the Englishmen's discovery of America; having found the mouth of a river,

we entred, though not without some difficultie . . . and after thankes given to God for our safe arrivall thither, we manned our boates, and went to viewe the land . . . and to take possession of the same, in the right of the Queenes most excellent Majestie, as rightfull Queene, and Princesse of the same: and after delivered the same over to your use, according to her Majesties grant, and letters patents, under her Highnes great Seale. (94)

The letters patent issued to Ralegh on 25 March 1584 had granted

to our trusty and welbeloved servaunte Walter Raleighe Esquier and to his heyres and assignes for ever free liberty and licence from tyme to tyme and at all tymes for ever hereafter to discover search fynde out and viewe such remote heathen and barbarous landes Contries and territories not actually possessed of any Christian Prynce and inhabited by Christian people . . . and the same to have holde occupy and enjoye to him his heyres and assignes for ever. (82)

Barlowe does not perceive the natives to be barbarous but, on the contrary, "in their behaviour as mannerly, and civill, as any of Europe" (98–99). Nevertheless, unbeknownst to these heathens, not merely their alien religious practices but their very freedom from prior colonization, their unpossessed condition, has *in principle* sanctioned their dispossession even before Ralegh's expedition sets sail from England to discover them.

Barlowe writes that, having first taken legal and ritual possession in the queen's name, "Wee viewed the lande about us. . . . I thinke in all the world the like aboundance is not to be founde" (94–95). This abundant country is called, by the "very handsome, and goodly people" who already inhabit it, "Wingandacoa, (and nowe by her Majestie, Virginia)" (98–99). William Camden soon records that Virginia is "so named in honour of Queen Elizabeth, a virgin."[12] Significantly, the naming of "Virginia" was "the first such imperious act sanctioned by an English monarch."[13] Having authorized her subjects' acts of discovery and symbolic possession, the English monarch assumes the privilege of naming the land anew, and naming it for herself and for the gender-specific virtue she has so long and so successfully employed as a means of self-empowerment. Queen Elizabeth participates in an emergent colonialist discourse that works to justify and, symbolically, to effect the expropriation of what it discovers. Typically, this discourse denies the natural right of possession to indigenous peoples by confirming them to be heathens, savages, and/or foragers who neither cultivate the land nor conceptualize it as real property; or it may symbolically efface the very existence of those indigenous peoples from the places its speakers intend to exploit.[14] What was Wingandacoa is now rendered a blank page upon which to write Virginia. Thus, the Virgin Queen verbally reconstitutes the land as a feminine place unknown to man, and, by doing so, she also symbolically effaces the indigenous society that already physically and culturally inhabits and possesses that land. In this royal renaming, considerations of gender difference interact with those of ethnic difference; the discursive power of the inviolate female body serves an emergent imperialist project of exploration, conquest, and settlement.

Although England's first American colony was claimed in her name and named in her honor, Queen Elizabeth herself demonstrated little enthusiasm or material support for the various colonizing ventures that ignited the energy, imagination, and desire of many of her restive masculine subjects.[15] Preeminent among those subjects was Walter Ralegh. Ralegh's tireless promotion of exploration and colonization was driven not only by intellectual curiosity, and by a patriotic devotion to the creation of an overseas empire that would strengthen England against Spain both economically and strategically; it was driven also by his extraordinary personal ambition. In his social origins, Ralegh was the youngest son of a modest though well-connected West Country gentry family. Thus, he was wholly dependent upon the queen's personal favor not only for the rapid and spectacular rise of his fortunes but also for their perpetuation; in the most tangible and precarious way, Ralegh was Elizabeth's creature. The strategy by which he gained and attempted to maintain the royal favor was systematically to exploit the affective ambiguity of the royal cult; to fuse in his conduct and in his discourse the courtship of the queen's patronage and the courtship of her person.[16]

Observing Elizabeth's open display of intimacy with Ralegh during the Christmas festivities at court in 1584, a German traveler recorded that "it was said that she loved this gentleman now in preference to all others; and that may be well believed, for two years ago he was scarcely able to keep a single servant, and now she has bestowed so much upon him, that he is able to keep five hundred servants." In surveying the leading courtiers attending upon the queen at this event, Lupold von Wedel had already noted the earl of Leicester, "with whom, as they say, the queen for a long time has had illicit intercourse," and Sir Christopher Hatton, "the captain of the guard, whom the queen is said to have loved after Lester" (263).[17] Such opinions—which seem to have been offered readily to von Wedel by his native English informants, and which he duly noted in his diary— suggest that many at court did not regard the queen's perpetual virginity as a literal truth. This is not to suggest that they therefore necessarily regarded it as a mere fraud—although there is surviving testimony that at least a few of the queen's subjects thought precisely that. Many at court may have regarded the royal cult as a necessary and effective, collectively sustained political fiction, as a mystery of state quite distinct from the question of whether or not Elizabeth Tudor was a woman who had yet her maidenhead. Whatever the precise nature and degree of Ralegh's intimacy with Queen Elizabeth, in 1587 he succeeded Hatton as Captain of the Guard; in both physical and symbolic terms, he now officially protected, and controlled access to, the queen's body. However, whatever honors, offices, patents, and leases the queen might grant to her favorite, without clear title to great manorial lands he had no secure source of income and status, and no hope of founding and sustaining his own lineage. What the royal patent for Virginia and the subsequent commission for Guiana gave to Ralegh was the prospect of possessing vast riches and vast lands, a prospect that would never be available to him at home in England.[18]

Although, in the later 1580s, Ralegh was displaced as the queen's preeminent favorite by the earl of Essex, he nevertheless continued to enjoy considerable royal confidence and favor. In 1592, however, Queen Elizabeth learned of Ralegh's secret marriage to her namesake, Elizabeth Throgmorton, one of the young ladies attendant at court, and of the birth of their first child. Both offenders were imprisoned in the Tower for several months, and Ralegh continued in disgrace and away from the court for some time longer. In the extravagant and fragmentary complaint, *The Ocean to Cynthia*, Ralegh wrote of the queen as his royally cruel mistress: "No other poure [power] effectinge wo, or bliss, / Shee gave, shee tooke, shee wounded, shee apeased."[19] Perhaps it cannot be decided, finally, whether to attribute the queen's anger toward Ralegh (and toward other noblemen and courtiers in his circumstances) to the sexual jealousy of a mistress, betrayed by her lover; to the moral outrage of a virgin and the guardian of virgins, victimized by men's lasciviousness; or to the political perturbation of a militarily and fiscally weak ruler, whose attempts to maintain an absolute command over her courtiers' alliances and their attentions had been flagrantly flouted. Indeed, the various and conflicting recorded perceptions and attitudes of Elizabethan subjects strongly suggest that such undecidability is itself the historically relevant point; that it is, in fact, a structural feature of the Elizabethan political system. A strategic ambiguity that might be manifested as paradox, equivocation, or contradiction, it was of potential if limited utility both to the monarch and to her (masculine) subjects. For the latter, however—as Ralegh's case demonstrates—it also carried considerable potential liabilities.

The issuance in 1594 of a royal commission allowing Ralegh to maraud the Spanish Caribbean may be interpreted as a gesture of returning favor. Thus authorized, in 1595 he set sail for Guiana, about which he had been gathering reconnaissance and speculation for several years. By the beginning of the new decade, the focus of Ralegh's interest in the New World had begun to shift southward, to the Caribbean and the Orinoco basin. This was part of a larger strategy to confront England's mighty adversary directly at sea and on land, in both the old world and the new. In the public self-presentations of the *Discoverie*, Ralegh maintains that his aims are wholly patriotic and untainted by mercenary considerations. The goal is the destruction of Spain's economic and geopolitical hegemony in Europe and the Americas. England will be able to counter Spain's power if Englishmen can discover and conquer an indigenous American empire rivaling in riches those plundered by the Spanish in Mexico and Peru.[20] The imperial strategy presented to the queen and her councillors is that the extortion of gold from the (mythical) Empire of Guiana, either by tribute or by conquest, will load her shaky exchequer with more than enough resources to "defend all enemies abroad, and defray all expences at home" (430); it will make England prosperous and invincible. Despite his repeated representations of himself as un-self-interested, Ralegh's writings reveal him to be preoccupied with the prospect of enormous personal wealth and power, for which the unprecedented successes of Cortés and Pizarro now provided models. Ralegh's expedition traveled several hundred miles of the Orinoco basin, encountered numerous indigenous social groups, and conducted a few raids on Spanish outposts. They failed, however, to find the anticipated empire of El Dorado, the Inga of Manoa, or his fabled riches. Indeed, the tangible returns from the voyage were so negligible that some of Ralegh's more skeptical fellow countrymen raised doubts as to whether it had actually taken place. It was both to justify the recently concluded expedition and to promote further interest, support, and investment that in 1596 Ralegh published *The Discoverie of Guiana*.

We may regard with a certain skepticism the claim that Queen Elizabeth's virtues inspired virtuous conduct in her subjects; however, there is no doubting that the courtly politics of chastity bore acutely upon the commander of the Guiana voyage. An anonymous letter concerning the circumstances of Ralegh's disgrace in 1592 can provide us with a thematic link between that episode and the discourse of his *Discoverie* in 1596:

S. W. R., as it seemeth, have been too inward with one of Her Majesty's maids. . . . S. W. R. will lose, it is thought, all his places and preferments at Court, with the Queen's favour; such will be the end of his speedy rising. . . . All is alarm and confusion at this discovery of the discoverer, and not indeed of a new continent, but of a new incontinent.[21]

Although of uncertain provenance and authenticity, this wittily scurrilous text does help to foreground and contextualize the *Discoverie*'s recurrent references to Ralegh's restraint of himself and his subordinates, his repudiation of concupiscence and his strategic tempering/temporizing of his announced quest for wealth and power.

In his dedicatory epistle to Lord Howard and Sir Robert Cecil, Ralegh represents both the conduct of his discovery and the account in which he discovers it as intended to mollify the queen's displeasure and to regain her favor:

As my errors were great, so they have yeelded very grievous effects. . . . I did therefore even in the winter of my life, undertake these travels . . . that thereby, if it were possible, I might recover but the moderation of excesse, & the least tast of the greatest plenty formerly possessed. . . . To appease so powreful displeasure, I would not doubt but for one yeere more to hold fast my soule in my teeth, till it were performed. (339)

Indeed, Ralegh goes so far as to suggest that the narrative of his exploit should be read as a penitential journey, an act of fleshly purgation undertaken to expiate the incontinent lapse in his devotion to the queen:

I have bene accompanyed with many sorrowes, with labour, hunger, heat, sickenes, & perill. . . . [They] were much mistaken, who would have perswaded, that I was too easefull and sensuall to undertake a journey of so great travell. But, if what I have done, receive the gracious construction of a painefull pilgrimage, and purchase the least remission, I shall thinke all too litle. (339–40)

Read in the context of Ralegh's fall from grace, the *Discoverie* operates on the model of book 2 of Edmund Spenser's *Faerie Queene* (1590), as a compensatory "Legend of Sir Walter, or of Temperance." The hero of this exemplary autobiographical narrative of restrained desire and deferred gratification eschews both Avarice and Lust, both Mammon and Acrasia:

If it had not bin in respect of her highnes future honor & riches, [I] could have laid hands on & ransomed many of the kings & Casiqui of the country, & have had a reasonable proportion of gold for their redemption: but I have chosen rather to beare the burden of poverty, then reproach, & rather to endure a second travel and the chances therof, then to have defaced an enterprise of so great assurance, untill I knew whether it pleased God to put a disposition in her princely and royal heart either to folow or foreslow the same. (342–43)

I neither know nor beleeve, that any of our company one or other, by violence or otherwise, ever knew any of their women. . . . I suffered not any man . . . so much as to offer to touch any of their wives or daughters: which course so contrary to the Spaniards . . . drewe them to admire her Majestie, whose commaundement I tolde them it was. (391)

In short, Ralegh's discovery of a new continent discovers him to be newly continent. As if to redress his conduct with Elizabeth Throgmorton, in these and a number of other passages Ralegh pointedly defers the desired consummation with Guiana until a royal blessing has been secured. Nevertheless, it is the prospect of that consummation that drives the narrative.

Himself a man from a society in which women—with one extraordinary exception—are politically invisible, Ralegh is predisposed to characterize the indigenous societies of the New World as if they are exclusively masculine. The Tivitivas, for example, "are a very goodly people and very valiant, and have the most manly speech and most deliberate that ever I heard, of what nation soever" (382–83). Ralegh admires these alien nations for their collective virility. Nevertheless, at a higher level of abstraction and under stronger rhetorical pressure, these apparently masculine societies—societies from which women have already been verbally effaced—are themselves rendered invisible by a metonymic substitution of place for persons, a substitution of the land for its inhabitants. This land which is substituted for its manly inhabitants is itself gendered feminine and sexed as a virgin female body:

To conclude, Guiana is a countrey that hath yet her maydenhead, never sackt, turned, nor wrought, the face of the earth hath not bene torne, nor the vertue and salt of the soyle spent by manurance, the graves have not bene opened for golde, the mines not broken with sledges, nor their Images puld downe out of their temples. It hath never bene entred by any armie of strength, and never conquered or possessed by any christian Prince. (428)

In this concluding exhortation of his masculine readership, Ralegh's description of Guiana by means of negatives conveys a proleptically elegiac sympathy for this unspoiled world at the same time that it arouses excitement at the prospect of despoiling it. His metaphor of Guiana's maidenhead activates the bawdy Elizabethan pun on *countrey*, thus inflaming the similitude of the land and a woman's body, of colonization and sexual mastery.[22] By subsuming and effacing the admired societies of Amerindian men in the metaphorically feminine Other of the land, the English intent to subjugate the indigenous peoples of Guiana can be "naturalized" as the male's mastery of the female. The ideology of gender hierarchy sanctions the Englishmen's collective longing to prove and aggrandize themselves upon the feminine body of the New World, and, at the same time, the emergent hierarchical discourse of colonial exploitation and domination reciprocally confirms that ideology's hegemonic force.[23]

Queen Elizabeth names the eastern seaboard of North America, in her own honor, *Virginia*. When her "trusty and welbeloved servaunt Walter Raleighe" describes the northeast interior of South America as a virgin, the rhetorical motive is not an homage to the queen but rather a provocation to her masculine subjects: "Guiana is a countrey that hath *yet* her maydenhead" (428; italics mine). There exists an intimate relationship between the figurations of these two places, as there does between Elizabeth and Ralegh themselves: it is as if the queen's naming of Virginia elicits Ralegh's metaphor of Guiana's fragile maidenhead. Addressing Ralegh in a dedicatory epistle to his edition of Peter Martyr's *De orbe novo* (1587), Richard Hakluyt imagines "your Elizabeth's Virginia" as Ralegh's bride, her depths as yet unprobed for their hidden riches.[24] Hakluyt takes imaginative liberties in Latin; however, it is difficult to imagine that Ralegh himself, in a printed address to the queen's subjects, would be so impolitic as to represent the plantation of Virginia in the same terms that he uses to represent the conquest of Guiana. If he cannot write explicitly of Virginia's rape, this is because the queen and her courtier share a common discourse of discovery, grounded in a territorial conception of the female body.

As de Certeau suggests in his discussion of van der Straet's icon, the "historied" and gendered body of America calls attention to the affinity between the *discovery* and the *blazon*, two Renaissance rhetorical forms that organize and control their subjects—respectively, the body of the land and the body of the lady—by means of display, inventory, and anatomy. As Nancy Vickers has remarked, "The blazon's inventory of fragmented and reified parts [is] a strategy in some senses inherent to any descriptive project."[25] Typically, in both the blazon and the discovery, the dynamics of this descriptive situation are gendered in a triangulated relationship: a masculine writer shares with his readers the verbal construction/observation of a woman or a feminized object or matter; in doing so, he constructs a masculine subject position for his readers to occupy and share. In *The Arte of English Poesie*, George Puttenham exemplifies "your figure of *Icon*, or resemblance by imagerie and portrait," first by citing "Sir Philip Sidney in the description of his mistresse excellently well handled," and then by piecemeal quotation from one of his own *Partheniades*:

written of our sovereign Lady, wherein we resemble every part of her body to some naturall thing of excellent perfection in his kind, as of her forehead, browes and haire. . . . And of her lips. . . . And of her eyes. . . . And of her breasts. . . . And all the rest that followeth.[26]

Puttenham's *Partheniades* were conceived and presented as a New Year's gift, as a rhetorical instrument for ingratiating himself with the queen and eliciting some reciprocal benefit. Thus, subsequently, he can display in print an example of how he has, by figure, "excellently well handled" his sovereign. When an Elizabethan subject devises a blazon of his royal mistress, he gives an explicitly political charge to a poetic figure already marked by the politics of gender.

Queen Elizabeth might not only be figured in an erotic blazon but might also be troped in the similitude of land and body. In her special case, however, the representational strategies of the trope might well serve to aggrandize the sovereign rather than to subordinate the woman. Her own naming of Virginia for herself is a variation on such a strategy; another, from one of her speeches, will be discussed below. Here I want to consider the "Ditchley" portrait of Queen Elizabeth (ca. 1592), by Marcus Gheeraerts the Younger (fig. 2).[27] This striking painting, the largest known portrait of the queen, represents her standing, like some great goddess or glorified Virgin Mary, with her feet upon the globe and her head amidst the heavens. The cosmic background divides into sunlight and storm; according to the now fragmentary sonnet inscribed on the canvas, these signify, respectively, the heavenly glory and divine power of which the queen is the earthly mirror. She stands upon a cartographic image of Britain, deriving from Christopher Saxton's collection of printed maps. Like Saxton's 1583 map, the painting divides England into counties, each separately colored, and marks principal towns and rivers. Much of the monarch's island nation is enclosed by the hem of her gown, a compositional feature perhaps recalling the iconography of the *Madonna della misericordia*. This representation of Queen Elizabeth as standing upon her land and sheltering it under her skirts suggests a mystical identification of the inviolate female body of the monarch *with* the unbreached body of her land, at the same time that it affirms her distinctive role as the motherly protectress of her people. But the painting also asserts, in spectacular fashion, the other aspect of Elizabeth's androgynous personal symbolism—her kingly rule; it affirms her power *over* her land and *over* its inhabitants. The cartographic image transforms the *land* into a *state*; and by the division of the land into administrative units, its inhabitants are marked as the monarch's political and juridical subjects.[28] It is against such official figurations of the relationship between the woman ruler and her masculine subjects that Ralegh's figuration of his own and his fellows' relationship to Guiana resonates as a belligerent though displaced gesture of resistance.

IV

Ralegh's "discoverie" is both a text and an event; and the declaration in its title that this doubled discovery has been "performed in the yeere 1595 by Sir Walter Ralegh" compounds the difficulty in keeping them distinct: the text is also an event, and the event, a text. In his prefatory addresses to his powerful friends and patrons, Lord Howard and Sir Robert Cecil, and "To the Reader," Ralegh specifically cites and seeks to defend himself against charges that he had in fact "hidden in Cornewall" instead of sailing to Guiana; that he had planned to sell his services to none other than King Philip (339) instead of returning to England; that the few putative gold samples brought back from Guiana were actually worthless marcasite or, if genuine, had been bought in Barbary and then transported *to* Guiana (343–46). The only evidence Ralegh can adduce for his having physically performed his discovery is contained in the text itself, which purports to be a record of the event. The performance of Ralegh's discovery becomes socially accessible and meaningful only as a writing performance, as *ethnography*—only, that is, when it has been textualized as his *Discoverie*. However, the status of the *Discoverie* as an historical record is always vulnerable to subversion by its status as rhetorical invention. Thus, in his attempt to represent his *Discoverie* as the transparent record of his discovery, Ralegh must seek to deprecate its style: he humbly prays "that your honors will excuse such errors, as without the defense of art, overrun every part of the following discourse, in which I have neither studied phrase, forme nor fashion" (343). Ralegh's continuous attempts to document his experience in his narrative and his continuous attempts to ground his narrative in the objective reality of his experience can only prove mutually defeating.[29]

Ralegh can claim no more than to be the first *Englishman* to explore parts of the Orinoco basin, and to discover those parts to *English* readers. His text cannot and makes no attempt to erase the footprints of the Spaniards who have preceded him everywhere he goes, and who have either knowingly or unknowingly provided almost all of the practical information as well as the fantasies that have generated the motives and underwritten the execution of his project. Over the

FIGURE 2. Marcus Gheeraerts the Younger, the "Ditchley" portrait of Queen Elizabeth, ca. 1592. Photo: National Portrait Gallery, London.

course of more than three decades, more than two dozen groups of Spanish adventurers had explored the Amazon and Orinoco basins in search of El Dorado. Ralegh rehearses some of these undertakings in his *Discoverie*; he cites and quotes from Spanish books on the New World, both in Spanish and in English translation; he uses information gained from discussions with his captive, Don Antonio de Berreo, the governor of Trinidad; and he appends to his text relevant Spanish documents that had been intercepted at sea.[30] The notable lack of success of the prior Spanish undertakings in the region, despite their enormous scope, might well have discouraged further attempts. Ralegh, however, manages to construe the Spanish failures hopefully, as a sign of special providence: "It seemeth to mee that this empire is reserved for her Majesty and the English nation, by reason of the hard successe which all these and other Spanyards found in attempting the same" (362).

Spanish tales are the sources repeatedly invoked by Ralegh in his strained and circumstantial attempts to substantiate his own claims for the existence of "the great and golden citie of Manoa," which was said to have been founded somewhere in Guiana by the Incas after the fall of Peru. His descriptions of the wondrous riches of El Dorado are merely extrapolated from the Spanish narratives of Peru that he cites (see esp. 355–58). What is perhaps his most artfully circumspect and obfuscating position occurs near the end of the *Discoverie*:

Because I have not my selfe seene the cities of Inga, I cannot avow on my credit what I have heard, although it be very likely, that the Emperour Inga hath built and erected as magnificent palaces in Guiana, as his ancestors did in Peru, which were for their riches and rareness most marvellous and exceeding all in Europe, and I thinke of the world, China excepted, which also the Spaniards (which I had) assured me to be true. (424–25)

Ralegh's final position concerning the existence of Manoa ultimately relies upon assurances from the rivals and enemies who are temporarily within his power; furthermore, whatever their credibility, the precise subject of these Spanish assurances is rendered conspicuously obscure and ambiguous by Ralegh's syntax. In effect, the very Spaniards whom Ralegh's text repeatedly represents as the cruel and deceitful foes of Englishmen and Indians alike are also the authorities upon whose knowledge and experience Ralegh has pursued his own discovery.

The *Discoverie* is haunted by a subversive irony, one that it nowhere explicitly confronts but does frequently if obliquely register, such as when the writer anxiously strives to authenticate his narrative. This epistemological and ideological destabilization arises from Ralegh's repeated need to ground his own credibility upon the credibility of the very people whom he wishes to discredit. One of the central ways in which Ralegh attempts to obfuscate this predicament of dependency upon and identification with the enemy is through an absolute distinction of the Englishmen's sexual conduct in the New World from that of the Spaniards. The rhetorical operations of gender performed in the *Discoverie* are considerably more complicated than the familiar trope of the feminine land might at first suggest. This complication is in part related to the pervasive Spanish presence in Ralegh's text and in the country it purports to discover.

The priority of Iberian claims to much of the New World could be discredited by English and other Northern European and Protestant writers by an insistence upon the necessity for effective, material occupation rather than merely symbolic discovery and possession.[31] Regarding Guiana, in particular, English concerns about the validity of rival and prior Spanish claims were partially addressed by English arguments against both the moral and the strategic wisdom of conquest, and in favor of an alliance with the "Inga" or emperor of Manoa, or a persuasion of indigenous peoples to embrace English overlordship. By the persistent rehearsal of Spanish atrocities against the Indians, the English also tried to turn Spanish precedence to their own advantage. Ralegh could assure himself and his English readers that God had reserved Guiana for England's dominion; and at the same time, both to himself and to the Indians of Guiana, he could represent his own imperialistic venture as a holy and humanitarian war of liberation against Spanish oppression. For example, Ralegh relates that in his conversation with the chieftain Topiawari,

I made him knowe the cause of my comming thither, whose servant I was, and that the Queenes pleasure was, I should undertake the voyage for their defence, and to deliver them from the tyrannie of the Spaniards, dilating at large . . . her Majesties greatnesse, her justice, her charitie to all oppressed nations. (399)

The "oppressed nations" of the New World are to be liberated from the Spanish tyrant so that they may be more benignly and effectively subjected to the English savior.

Ralegh's ironic discovery of the Spaniards' prior discoveries drives home to his English readers the embarrassment of England's cultural and imperial *belatedness*. Many Elizabethan writers voice a nagging concern that—in military, commercial, and/or artistic terms—the English are a backward and peripheral nation. This concern is usually manifested as an anxious and impatient patriotism. For example, in *A Relation of the Second Voyage to Guiana*, Laurence Keymis writes that

it were a dull conceite of strange weaknes in our selves, to distrust our own power so much, or at least, our owne hearts and courages; as valewing the Spanish nation to be omnipotent; or yeelding that the poore Portugal hath that mastering spirit and conquering industrie, above us.[32]

Keymis was Ralegh's lieutenant, and performed this "second Discoverie" (441) in 1596, under Ralegh's instructions; his written account was printed in the same year. As this passage from Keymis clearly suggests, a belligerent and chauvinistic national consciousness is almost invariably expressed in the terms and values of a collective national character that is culturally encoded as masculine. Such encoding leads all too predictably to imagery such as Ralegh's, which figures

England and Spain as manly rivals in a contest to deflower the new found lands: at the beginning of his *Discoverie*, Ralegh invites his readers to "consider of the actions of . . . Charles the 5. who had the maidenhead of Peru, and . . . the affaires of the Spanish king now living" (346); at the end, he invites them to consider that "Guiana is a countrey that hath yet her maydenhead" (428). In order to represent Ralegh's discovery of Guiana iconically, we might triangulate the scenario of van der Straet's drawing: upon coming ashore, the Englishman discovers America in the arms of a Spaniard.

The ubiquitous figure of the Spaniard is an unstable signifier in the text of Ralegh's *Discoverie*: he is, at once, an authority to be followed, a villain to be punished, and a rival to be bested. For the Englishmen in the New World, the Spaniards are proximate figures of Otherness: in being Catholic, Latin, and Mediterranean they are spiritually, linguistically, ethnically, and ecologically alien. At the same time, however, England and Spain are intertwined with each other in an encompassing European system of economic, social, and political structures and forces; and they share an ambient Christian and classical cultural, moral, and intellectual tradition. The sign of the Spaniard in English discovery texts simultaneously mediates and complicates any simple antinomy of European Self and American Other.

We can begin to observe how gender and sexual conduct are figured into this complex textual play of otherness by juxtaposing two passages from Keymis's *Relation*. Near the end of his narrative, Keymis asks his English readers, rhetorically:

Is it not meere wretchednesse in us, to spend our time, breake our sleepe, and waste our braines, in contriving a cavilling false title to defraude a neighbour of halfe an acre of lande: whereas here whole shires of fruitfull rich grounds, lying now waste for want of people, do prostitute themselves unto us, like a faire and beautifull woman, in the pride and floure of desired yeeres. (487)

Here the already familiar similitude of the earth and the female body—"fruitfull rich grounds" and "a faire and beautifull woman"—is activated through a peculiarly dissonant and degraded fantasy of *self-prostitution*. It is as if the writer's imagination of the New World has taken corruption from his already disconcerting representation of the old one: we are exhorted to repudiate our homegrown and familiar greed and fraudulence, not because they are immoral but because they are paltry; they must be reconceived on a grander scale, in the large, rich, and beautiful empire of Guiana.

In an earlier passage, Keymis writes of the Indians' present predicament, that

for the plentie of golde that is in this countrey, beeing nowe knowen and discovered, there is no possibilitie for them to keepe it: on the one side they coulde feele not greater miserie, nor feare more extremitie, then they were sure to finde, if the Spaniardes prevayled, who perforce doe take all things from them, using them as their slaves, to runne, to rowe, to bee their guides, to cary their burthens, and that which is worst of all, to bee content, for safetie of their lives, to leave their women, if a Spaniard chance but to set his eye on any of them to fancie her: on the otherside they could hope for, nor desire no better state and usage, then her Majesties gracious government, and Princely vertues doe promise, and assure unto them. (472)

The Indians who are the collective subject of this passage are exclusively the Indian *men*; "their women" are the (male) Indians' most valued and most intimate possessions, serving to define and to make manifest their own freedom and masculinity. One of the most conspicuous ways in which the Spaniards assert their enslavement of native American men is precisely by their casual use of the bodies of native American women. In Keymis's representation of the Spaniards, the rape of the Indians' lands and the rape of "their women" go hand in hand. In the case of Englishmen, however, masculine sexual aggression against the bodies of native women has been wholly displaced into the exploitation of the feminized new found land. Indeed, the Englishmen's vaunted sexual self-restraint serves to legitimate their exploitation of the land. Furthermore, such masculine desires for possession have been subjected to a form of reversal, in that Keymis's discourse renders Englishmen not as territorial aggressors but rather as passive beneficiaries of the animated land's own desire to be possessed: "Fruitfull rich grounds, lying now waste for want of people, do prostitute themselves unto us, like a faire and beautifull woman." The sexual conduct of European men in the New World is sometimes explained away as the unbridled expression of an essential male lustfulness. It might be more useful to understand it as an ideologically meaningful (and overdetermined) act of violence. This violence is impelled by, enacts, and thus reciprocally confirms the imperatives of appropriation, possession, and domination that characterize the colonialist project in general, imperatives that are themselves discursively figured in gendered violence.

The topic of sexual conduct can become a point of convergence for a multiplicity of discourses—among them, gender, ethnicity, nationality, and social estate. I write of "ethnicity" and "social estate" rather than "race" and "class" because, in the Elizabethan context, some of the contemporary assumptions implicit in the terms "race" and "class" do not seem to be either adequate or appropriate.[33] For example, concerning "class": not only different categories of social rank but also different systems of social categorization and stratification sometimes overlapped, contradicted, or excluded one another. And concerning "race": prejudicial early English perceptions of native Americans—unlike contemporaneous perceptions of Africans—were not given a physical basis in their appearance and skin color but were based exclusively upon their supposed savagery. Furthermore, issues of "class" and "race" might be conflated. The statuses of "Indians" and "the meaner sort" of English people were sometimes analogized: Indians were said to be like English rogues and vagabonds, and unruly English forest dwellers like Indians.[34]

A particularly instructive convergence of Elizabethan discourses of sex, gender, ethnicity, nationality, and social rank is provided in the following extended passage from Ralegh's *Discoverie*, a part of which I have already quoted:

[The Arwacas] feared that wee would have eaten them, or otherwise have put them to some cruel death (for the Spaniards, to the end that none of the people in the passage towards Guiana or Guiana it selfe might come to speach with us, perswaded all the nations, that we were man-eaters, and Canibals) but when the poore men and women had seen us, and that wee gave them meate, and to every one something or other, which was rare and strange to them, they beganne to conceive the deceit and purpose of the Spaniards, who indeed (as they confessed) tooke from them both their wives and daughters dayly, and used them for the satisfying of their owne lusts, especially such as they tooke in this maner by strength. But I protest before the Majestie of the living God, that I neither know nor beleeve, that any of our company one or other, by violence or otherwise, ever knew any of their women, and yet we saw many hundreds, and had many in our power, and of those very yong, and excellently favoured, which came among us without deceite, starke naked.

Nothing got us more love amongst them then this usage: for I suffered not any man to take from any of the nations so much as a Pina, or a Potato roote, without giving them contentment, nor any man so much as to offer to touch any of their wives or daughters: which course so contrary to the Spaniards (who tyrannize over them in all things) drewe them to admire her Majestie, whose commaundement I tolde them it was, and also wonderfully to honour our nation.

But I confesse it was a very impatient worke to keepe the meaner sort from spoyle and stealing, when we came to their houses: which because in all I coulde not prevent, I caused my Indian interpreter at every place when wee departed, to know of the losse or wrong done, and if ought were stolen or taken by violence, either the same was restored, and the partie punished in their sight, or else was payed for to their uttermost demand. (390–91)

By a fine irony that Ralegh fails to appreciate, the spectral New World cannibals who so horrified and fascinated sixteenth-century European writers and readers appear to the equally horrified Arwacas to be Englishmen. The English unmask the Spanish deception by reversal: they offer to feed meat to the Indians rather than to eat them. (This is also a reversal in another sense, since perhaps the most commonly recorded initial gesture of friendship made toward Europeans by New World peoples was to offer food.)[35] Ralegh purports to have learned from the Indians that the Spaniards have misrepresented the English as anthropophagi: through this heavily mediated pattern of assertion and denial, Ralegh's text voices the Englishmen's own consuming desire to consume the Indians' land and goods; it registers a fleeting intimation that the "man-eaters, and Canibals" of the New World are actually a projection—and, by this means, a legitimation—of the Europeans' own predatory intentions toward their hosts.

Whereas the English bestow gifts upon the Indians, the Spaniards take from them, using Indian women "for the satisfying of their owne lusts." Although, for purposes of contrast to the Spaniards, it would have been necessary only to reaffirm the absence of sexual violence from English behavior, Ralegh insists that to the best of his knowledge none in his company, "by violence, *or otherwise*, ever knew any of their women" (italics mine). And he goes out of his way to suggest that this chaste conduct has been heroically maintained against the great temptations posed to the male concupiscible appetite by the young, well-favored, and naked women whom the Englishmen have held in their power. Ralegh is at pains to inhibit any culturally inscribed predisposition in his (masculine) readers that would identify the naked maidens in his text as conventional allegorical personifications of Lasciviousness and Indolence—such as those which populate the exotic pleasure gardens of Spenser's Legend of Temperance. Although he credits reports that the Amazons are both violent and lustful, the women whom he claims to have actually encountered in Guiana Ralegh represents as neither deceitful nor predatory—such attributes tend to be reserved for the Spanish men. However, in this passage and elsewhere, his contrary emphasis upon feminine innocence and vulnerability, upon the potential victimization of women, simultaneously disempowers them and legitimates their condition of dependency. It also reduces them to functioning as the collective instrument for making comparisons among *men*. It is crucial to Ralegh's text that what is at issue is not masculine sexual prowess but, on the contrary, the ability of European men to govern their concupiscible appetites. In *The Book named The Governor*, Sir Thomas Elyot writes that

continence . . . is specially in refraining or forbearing the act of carnal pleasure, whereunto a man is fervently moved, or is at liberty to have it. Which undoubtedly is a thing not only difficult, but also wonderful in a man noble or of great authority, but as in such one as it happeneth to be, needs must be reputed much virtue and wisdom, and to be supposed that his mind is invincible.[36]

Ralegh's concern with sexual conduct is not inscribed within an autonomous discourse about human, masculine, or personal sexuality; rather, it is the somatic focus of concerns that are fundamentally ethical, social, and political.[37] "We saw many hundreds, and had many in our power": it is precisely their refusal to abuse their own position of mastery over the Indians that is the measure of the Englishmen's collective self-mastery, that provides proof of the ascendancy of (what Sir Philip Sidney would call) their erected wits over their infected wills. And this self-mastery might not only help them to distinguish themselves as *Men* from Women, to whom unruliness and lasciviousness were traditionally ascribed; it might also help them to distinguish themselves as *Englishmen* from the lustful and un-self-governable Spaniards. Here misogynistic sentiments subserve anti-Spanish ones, in a project aimed at mastering native Americans.[38]

However, having made this moral distinction among men exclusively upon the ground of national difference, Ralegh goes on to say that he had to exercise vigilant control over the inherent tendency toward lawlessness among "the meaner sort" within his own company. He now shifts categories so as to mark hierarchical social differences among the Englishmen themselves. Now, within the restricted domain of Englishness, "the meaner sort" have become structurally equivalent to Spaniards—just as, in other Elizabethan and Jacobean ideological contexts, they are negatively represented as analogous to Indians.[39] If gentlemen have the capacity and the duty to govern themselves, they also have the prerogative and the obligation to govern their social inferiors, who are incapable of self-government. To quote Elyot once more,

To him that is a governor of a public weal belongeth a double governance, that is to say, an interior or inward governance, and an exterior or outward governance. The first is of his affects and passions, which do inhabit within his soul, and be subjects to reason. The second is of his children, his servants, and other subjects to his authority. (183)

Although it is "worke to keepe the meaner sort from spoyling and stealing," the perceived necessity that the gentleman undertake this burdensome duty defines and legitimates the hierarchical ordering of society; and by actually undertaking it, he reciprocally confirms the congruence of his status with his virtue.

The rhetorical shifting and swerving of Ralegh's text invite some scrutiny. In the first paragraph of the long passage quoted above, Ralegh represents the Englishmen as antithetical to the Spaniards, on the basis of their disinterested generosity toward the Indians: "Wee gave them meate, and to every one something or other, which was rare and strange to them"; in the second paragraph, we are circumstantially informed that although Ralegh forbade his men "so much as to offer to touch any of their wives or daughters," he did permit them to take other forms of Indian property, as long as reparation was made; in the third paragraph, we learn that Indian property was in fact being "stolen or taken by violence" by some of these same gift-giving Englishmen, though not without punishment by their commander. If English virtue becomes a little soiled in the working, an occasion is nevertheless provided to demonstrate containment of the poorer sort's petty thievery by the moral rectitude and judicial vigilance of their betters. Yet it is precisely by an emphatic insistence upon both triviality and scrupulosity—"I suffered not any man to take from any of the nations so much as a Pina, or a Potato roote"—that this discourse obfuscates the magnitude of the theft being contemplated and prepared by Ralegh himself, which encompasses nothing less than the entire land and everything in it.

The circuitous movement of Ralegh's discourse at once admires the Indians for their innocent trust and displaces onto the Spaniards the implicit betrayal of that trust which is at the heart of the English enterprise. However, the *Discoverie* also represents the Spaniards as brutally direct in their intentions toward the Indians. What Ralegh seems to be evading—and what his text nevertheless intermittently discovers—is a recognition that the most massive deception of the Indians is being perpetrated by Ralegh himself. And although evaded, this self-compromising perception may be surfacing obliquely in Ralegh's emphatic characterization of the Indian maidens who were held in his power as being "without deceit, starke naked": here the insidious erotic provocations of female nudity have been transformed into an emblematic, exemplary—and, perhaps, an obscurely self-admonitory—honesty. An appropriate gloss on Ralegh's naked maidens is provided by the emblem of the Graces in Spenser's Legend of Courtesy:

> Therefore they alwaies smoothly seeme to smile,
> That we likewise should mylde and gentle be,
> And also naked are, that without guile
> Or false dissemblaunce all them plaine may see,
> Simple and true, from covert malice free.
> (*Faerie Queene*, 6.10.24)

At several points in the text of the *Discoverie*, Ralegh discovers his systematic and strategic duplicity toward the Indians, thereby inviting his readers' admiration and complicity. For example, he explains to his readers that

I did not in any sort make my desire for gold knowen, because I had neither time, nor power to have a greater quantity. I gave among them manie more peeces of gold, then I received, of the new money of 20 shillings with her Majesties picture to wear, with promise that they would become her servants thencefoorth. (415)

To his readers, Ralegh once again represents himself as a masterful strategist, simultaneously covetous and generous, cynical and patriotic. The Indians' very acceptance of Ralegh's dissembled gifts betokens their uncomprehending entry into the circulations of England's nascent imperial economy—an economy to be fueled, in the future, by their own gold. This passage also allows us to observe something of the subtlety and guilefulness of Ralegh's rhetoric of address to his readers. He gains the confidence of his fellow countrymen by sharing with them what he claims to have withheld from the Indians; yet what he actually shares with them is another set of equivocations and excuses for his having returned empty-handed. As occurs repeatedly in the *Discoverie*, what Ralegh claims to be a deeply considered policy of restraint collapses into a series of circumstantial impediments and uncertainties. We may begin to wonder if Ralegh's representation of his duplicity toward the Indians is not a screen for his duplicity toward his readers, and perhaps toward himself.

Surely the most remarkable disruption of ideological consistency on the surface of Ralegh's text occurs just a paragraph earlier than this last example, in the course of yet another explanation/excuse for his failure to have plundered the (nonexistent) domain of the Inga of Manoa:

I thought it were evill counsell to have attempted it at that time, although the desire of gold will answere many objections: but it would have bin in mine opinion an utter overthrow to the enterprize, if the same should be hereafter by her Majesty attempted: for then (whereas now they have heard we were enemies to the Spaniards & were sent by her Majesty to relieve them) they would as good cheap have joyned with the Spaniards at our returne, as to have yeelded unto us, when they had proved that we came both for one errant, and that both sought but to sacke & spoile them, but as yet our desire of gold, or our purpose of invasion is not knowen unto them of the empire. (413–14)

At this point of ideological contradiction, the elaborate system of moral difference between the Englishman and the Spaniard is momentarily ruptured; the deep structural opposition that has in large part generated the narrative of the *Discoverie* threatens to collapse. This contradiction might be perceived from at least two perspectives. From one perspective, we apprehend the dissonance between two simultaneously held codes of value: on the one hand, the text's invocation of the normative moral beliefs and judgments nominally shared by its readers; and on the other, its solicitation of their complicity in and admiration for their fellow countryman's cunning and morally equivocal statecraft. From another perspective, we experience a brief eruption into discourse of the subliminal counter-awareness that English desires in the New World are fundamentally identical to Spanish ones, that *we* are really very much like *them*. This awareness is registered in the striking phrase, "We came both for one errant": Here the unusual form of the noun *errand* not only suggests a task, and a journey by which to accomplish it, but also intimates that the journey is wayward and the enterprise corrupt. That this passage may, even today, generate an intolerable ideological dissonance is perhaps indicated by its complete and unacknowledged effacement from the most readily available current edition of the *Discoverie*.[40]

Ralegh exhorts his English readers to liberate the Indians from Spanish exploitation and oppression; at the same time, he incites them to plunder Guiana for themselves. The ideological coherence of the *Discoverie* is destabilized by a fundamental contradiction in its hortatory aims, a moral contradiction between charity and avarice. In this intolerable situation, in which the Other is always threatening to collapse into the Same, feminine figures must be textually deployed in an attempt to keep Spaniards and Englishmen apart. Thus, distinctions between Man and Woman, and between European and Indian, may both qualify and be qualified by the pervasive textual operation of distinctions between Englishmen and Spaniards that are made on the basis of national identity, cultural and religious values, and social behavior. It is precisely by constructing and reiterating a moral opposition between Spanish lust and tyranny, on the one hand, and English continence and justice, on the other—an opposition epitomized in the contrasting conduct of Spanish and English men toward Indian women—that the discourses of Englishmen such as Ralegh and Keymis obscure the fundamental *identity* of English and Spanish interests in Guiana: "For the plentie of golde that is in this countrey, being nowe knowen and discovered, there is no possibilitie for [the Indians] to keepe it" (Keymis, 472); "We came both for one errant . . . both sought but to sacke & spoile them" (Ralegh, 414). Greed is here the common denominator of "Western desire."

V

Ralegh frequently writes respectfully and admiringly of the native Americans whom he purports to have encountered during his discovery. They are worthy to be the prospective allies and tributary peoples of the Empress Elizabeth. I think it important to acknowledge such sympathetic representations of various indigenous individuals and groups, while at the same time remaining aware that the very condition of sympathy may be enabled by prior processes of projection and appropriation that efface the differences and assimilate the virtues of the Indians to European norms. Furthermore, such instances of apparently enlightened familiarization cannot be considered in isolation from Ralegh's projection of radical and hostile Otherness elsewhere. This projection operates in two general directions, toward the foreground and toward the margins of the known world; and it also operates in two discourses, which might be called the discourses of morality and of wonder. In the discourse of morality, as I have already suggested, this Otherness is constituted in the proximate, ubiquitous, and tangible Spaniards. In the discourse of wonder, Otherness is figured in the spectacular myth of El Dorado, the Inga of Manoa (356–61), who is frequently represented as an imperial oppressor of Ralegh's tribal allies; and also in those residual Herodotean and Mandevillean curiosities such as anthropophagi, acephali, and Amazons, who haunt the margins of Ralegh's text and of whom he writes only circumspectly and at second hand. Unsurprisingly, from this latter catalogue of marvels it is the Amazons who most arouse Ralegh's interest.

Ralegh discovers the Amazons to his readers more than once during the meandering discourse of his journey. Although these occurrences may appear to be incidental to the *Discoverie*'s narrative, they have an integral place in its textual ideo-logic of gender and power. The matriarchal, gynocratic Amazons are the radical Other figured but not fully contained by the collective imagination of European patriarchy.[41] Sixteenth-century travel narratives often recreate the ancient Amazons of Scythia in South America or in Africa. Almost invariably, the Amazons are relocated just beyond the receding geographical boundary of *terra incognita*, in the enduring European mental space reserved for aliens. The notion of a separatist and intensely territorial nation of women warriors might be seen as a momentous transformation of the trope identifying the land with the female body. Implicit in the conceptual shift from *the land as woman* to *a land of women* is the possibility of representing women as collective social agents. Predictably, such a disturbing notion produces a complex and at best morally ambiguous masculine representation of feminine agency. In any event, such women as the Amazons are not merely assimilable to the landscape; nor are they assimilable to the goods and chattels possessed by the men of their group. Unlike the other indigenous societies described by Ralegh, in the case of the Amazons it is the women who are synonymous with the political nation; indeed, Amazon men are literally nonexistent. And as a particular (and particularly extreme) construction of the feminine gender, the Amazons enter into complex and multiple articulations, not only with the textual figurations of masculinity in the *Discoverie* but also with its other significant feminine representations: the women among the native American peoples encountered by Ralegh, who are victimized by the Spaniards, and the queen of England, to whom Ralegh himself is subject.

It is a discussion about the circulation of gold and other commodities among the peoples situated between the Orinoco and the Amazon that provides the immediate occasion for Ralegh's lengthy digression on the remarkable tribe for whom the latter river has been named:

> [I] was very desirous to understand the truth of those warlike women, because of some it is beleeved, of others not. And though I digresse from my purpose, yet I will set downe that which hath bene delivered me for trueth of those women. . . . The memories of the like women are very ancient aswell in Africa as in Asia. . . . In many histories they are verified to have bene, and in divers ages and provinces: but they which are not far from Guiana doe accompany with men but once in a yere, and for the time of one moneth, which I gather by their relation to be in April: and at that time all kings of the borders assemble, and queenes of the Amazones; and after the queenes have chosen, the rest cast lots for their Valentines. . . . If they conceive, and be delivered of a sonne, they returne him to the father; if of a daughter they nourish it, and reteine it: and as many as have daughters send unto the begetters a present; all being desirous to increase their owne sex and kind: but that they cut off the right dug of the brest, I doe not finde to be true. It was farther tolde me, that if in these warres they tooke any prisoners that they used to accompany with those also at what time soever, but in the end for certeine they put them to death: for they are sayd to be very cruell and bloodthirsty, especially to such as offer to invade their territories. (366–67)

This Amazonian anticulture precisely inverts European norms of political authority, sexual license, marriage and child-rearing practices, and inheritance rules. Such conceptual precision suggests that it was not merely the antiquity and wide diffusion of the idea of the Amazons that compelled Ralegh and his contemporaries to entertain seriously the possibility of their existence. Elizabethan perception and speculation were structured by the cognitive operations of hierarchy and inversion, analogy and antithesis. By the logic of these operations, a conceptual space for reversal and negation was constructed within the world picture of a patriarchal society. Among those figures which might occupy this space were the Amazons. Since they didn't exist, it proved necessary to invent them—or, in the case of the New World, to reinvent them.

Ralegh's ethnography of the Amazons divides into two antithetical parts, each largely defined by their collective conduct toward alien men: the first is focused upon the Amazons' orderly, periodic, and eminently civilized ritual cohabitation with men of neighboring tribes. Because it is performed for purposes of procreation—in order to ensure the perpetuation of "their owne sex and kind"—this apparently remote Amazonian practice is not without relevance to the always sensitive Elizabethan succession question. It may be that Ralegh was obliquely criticizing the queen's earlier refusal to marry and her ongoing refusal to designate a successor. In any case, the relevant point is that the centrality that had been given to such matters of state from the very inception of Elizabeth's reign predisposed Englishmen to take a keen interest in the ways in which other actual or imagined societies might structure the processes of political succession and social reproduction. Taking place at the margins of the Amazons' territory, on the boundary between matriarchal and patriarchal societies, this sexual rite serves to mark the feminine and masculine genders as mutually exclusive and, simultaneously, to mediate their radical difference through sexual intercourse. The second, strongly contrasted part of the digression is a brief but sensational account of the impulsive and random mixing of violence and lust in the Amazons' conduct toward their masculine captives. This latter mode of Amazonian behavior—an irascible and concupiscible distemper provoked by attempts "to invade their territories," to violate their body politic—inverts and doubles the violent and lustful conduct frequently associated with the masculine Spanish invaders. In Ralegh's narrative of the Amazons' response to invasion, sexual conduct takes the form of reciprocal aggression between the genders rather than a practice of either procreative or abstinent virtue. Construed as a struggle between women and men for the control and disposition of their own and of each other's bodies, the sexual is here synonymous with the political. Gender and rule, sex and power: these are the concerns that preoccupy Ralegh in his desire "to understand the truth of those warlike women"; we might expect such concerns to be of more than incidental interest to a gentleman who is subject to a woman monarch.

Although Amazonian figures might at first seem suited to strategies for praising a woman ruler, they are not conspicuous among the many encomiastic mirrors of Queen Elizabeth produced by her own subjects.[42] The one notable exception, the heroic Amazon Queen Penthesilea, may have been acceptable and appropriate precisely because she sacrificed herself not for the Amazonian cause but for the cause of patriarchal Troy, the mythical place of origin of the Britons. Otherwise, the sexual and parental practices habitually associated with the Amazons must have rendered them, at best, an equivocal means for representing the Virgin Queen. She herself seems to have been too politic, and too ladylike, to have pursued the Amazonian image very far. However, she could transform it to suit her purposes. If report speaks true of her, she did so most notably when she visited Tilbury in 1588, in order to review and to rally the troops that had been mustered in expectation of a Spanish invasion. According to the subsequent recollection of Thomas Heywood, among others, on that momentous occasion the Queen of England was "habited like an *Amazonian* Queene, Buskind and plumed, having a golden Truncheon, Gantlet, and Gorget, Arms sufficient to expresse her high and magnanimous spirit."[43] The theme of her speech was by then familiar to her audience:

Let Tyrants fear, I have always so behaved my self, that under God I have placed my chiefest strength, and safeguard in the loyal hearts and good will of my subjects. . . . I know I have the bodie, but of a weak and feeble woman, but I have the heart and Stomach of a King, and of a King of *England* too.[44]

Elizabeth's strategy of self-empowerment involves a delicate balance of contrary gestures. On the one hand, she dwells upon the feminine frailty of her body natural and the masculine strength of her body politic—a strength deriving from the love of her people, the virtue of her lineage, and the will of her God. In other words, she moderates the anomalous martial spectacle of feminine sovereignty by representing herself as the handmaiden of a greater, collective, and patriarchal will. On the other hand, she subsumes the gesture of womanly self-deprecation within an assertion of the unique power that inheres in her by virtue of her office and nation. Her feminine honor, the chastity invested in a body that is vulnerable to invasion and pollution, is made secure by the kingly honor invested in her body politic. She adds, defiantly:

I . . . think foul scorn that *Parma* or *Spain*, or any Prince of Europe should dare to invade the borders of my Realm, to which rather then any dishonour shall grow by me, I my self will take up arms, I my self will be your General, Judge, and Rewarder of everie one of your virtues in the field.

Queen Elizabeth's putative speech presents the threat of invasion in the most intimate and violent of metaphors, as the attempt by a foreign prince to rape her. Like the iconic effect of the Ditchley portrait, the rhetorical force of this speech is partly due to Elizabeth's identification of corporeal with geopolitical boundaries, to her subtle application of the land/body trope to herself: she identifies her virginal female body with the clearly bounded body of her island realm, threatened with violation by the masculine Spanish land and sea forces personified in King Philip and the duke of Parma. Such an illegitimate sexual union would contaminate the blood of the lineage and dishonor not only the royal house but the whole commonwealth. The Roman matron Lucretia submitted to and was ritually polluted by sexual violation, and her suicide was required in order to cleanse the social body. In contrast, the royal English virgin will defend and preserve both herself and her state. If Queen Elizabeth at Tilbury resembles the Amazons in her martial stance, she differs from them in leading an army of men. By insisting, however impractically, that she herself will be the leader of her army, the queen implies that she will not be merely the passive object of male power— even if the intended use of that power is to protect her against the aggression of others. Thus, Elizabeth's own gendered, metaphorical discourse anticipates Ralegh's: England is a country that has yet her maidenhead—and Ralegh's virgin queen, not wholly unlike his Amazons, will prove herself a virago toward those who offer to invade her territories.

In the wake of the Armada's failure, Ralegh can tell all the tribes he encounters in the New World that the queen will protect them as she has protected herself, her own people, and the Protestant cause in Europe:

> I made them understand that I was the servant of a Queene, who was the great Casique of the North, and a virgine . . . that shee was an enemie to the Castellani in respect of their tyrannie and oppression, and that she delivered all such nations about her, as were by them oppressed, and having freed all the coast of the Northren world from their servitude, had sent mee to free them also, and withall to defend the countrey of Guiana from their invasion and conquest. (353–54)

However, at the very end of his narrative, in a characteristically shameless display of his duplicity, Ralegh invites Elizabeth to betray the Indians' trust; in effect, he exhorts her to emulate "the Castellani in respect of their tyrannie and oppression" by undertaking her own conquest of Guiana:

> For whatsoever Prince shall possesse it, shall be greatest, and if the king of Spaine enjoy it, he will become unresistable. Her Majestie hereby shall confirme and strengthen the opinions of all nations, as touching her great and princely actions. And where the South border of Guiana reacheth to the Dominion and Empire of the Amazones, those women shall hereby heare the name of a virgin, which is not onely able to defend her owne territories and her neighbours, but also to invade and conquer so great Empires and so farre removed. (431)

Ralegh seems to insinuate that Elizabethan imperial designs upon the Empire of Guiana might be extended to the Empire of the Amazons. Ralegh's rhetorical tactic for convincing the queen to advance his colonial enterprise is apparently to associate her ambiguously with the Amazons, and then to offer her a means by which to distinguish herself from them. It is precisely by her pursuit of a policy of invasion and conquest that, in Ralegh's terms, "a virgin" may disassociate herself from "those women." He insinuates that a woman who has the prerogative of a sovereign, who is authorized to be out of place, can best justify her authority by putting other women in their places. He seeks to persuade the queen not merely to emulate the Amazons' vigilant territoriality but to overgo them by emulating the Spaniards' rampant invasiveness. In effect, by appropriating the royal tropes of feminine self-empowerment such as those employed in Elizabeth's Tilbury speech, Ralegh endorses a martial and heroic—a manly and kingly—image of feminine authority. But he does so precisely in order to bend the royal will to his own designs. Suffice to say that Her Majesty was unyielding.

VI

Ralegh's exhortation of Queen Elizabeth to overgo the Amazons by offensive warfare, and to outmaneuver King Philip of Spain by possessing Guiana, is immediately preceded by an exhortation of his masculine readership, who are potential volunteers and investment partners for the conquest and settlement of Guiana. Employing a gender-specific rhetorical strategy distinct from that addressed to the queen, Ralegh elaborates a geography of Elizabethan masculine desire, discovering that "there is a way found to answer every mans longing" (342). The object of this overdetermined desire encompasses identity and security, knowledge, wealth, and power. It seeks to know, master, and possess a feminized space—or, in the language of Ralegh's Virginia patent, "to discover search fynde out and view . . . to have holde occupy and enjoye"; it is a desire that is most vividly realized as the prospect of deflowering a virgin. In his prefatory address "To the Reader," he bids Englishmen to "consider of the actions of both Charles the 5. who had the maidenhead of Peru, and the abundant treasures of Atabalipa, together with the affaires of the Spanish king now living" (346); and, at the end, he exhorts them to emulate King Philip's father by taking Guiana's maidenhead just as he had taken Peru's. In urging these English gentlemen to emulate the rapacious and spectacularly successful Spanish imperialism that now threatens England's very existence, Ralegh holds out to them the prospect of rewards graded to their various statuses:

The common souldier shall here fight for golde, and pay himselfe in steede of pence, with plates of halfe a foote broad, whereas he breaketh his bones in other warres for provant and penury. Those commanders and chieftaines that shoot at honour and abundance shall finde there . . . rich and beautifull cities . . . temples adorned with golden images . . . sepulchres filled with treasure. (425)

As is common in the promotional literature for Elizabethan colonizing ventures, Ralegh envisions exploration, trade, and settlement abroad as an escape valve for the frustrations of disaffected or marginalized groups, and as a solution to endemic socioeconomic problems at home: "Her Majestie may in this enterprize employ all those souldiers and gentlemen that are younger brethren, and all captaines and chieftaines that want employment" (430). Thus, the potentially riotous malcontents among her majesty's masculine subjects may displace their thwarted ambitions into the conquest of virgin lands. Himself a younger brother, a soldier, and a gentleman in need of advancement, Ralegh might well be considered a special case of the general social problem that he here seeks to redress to his own inestimable advantage.

Together with his company, and his readers, Ralegh encounters in the New World the presence of England's implacable Spanish foe—the specular figure of desiring European Man. Thus recontextualized in the body of Guiana and in the body of Ralegh's book, the Englishman's relationship to the Spaniard manifests itself as a disturbing oscillation between identity and difference, between the acknowledgment and the obfuscation of their common longing. Ralegh can reassure his English gentleman readers that, although "Charles the 5 . . . had the maidenhead of Peru," there remain in the New World other countries that have yet their maidenheads. It is not the English monarch but rather her masculine subjects who are exhorted to emulate the king of Spain. Whether as the virgin protectress of the Indians or as their Amazonian conqueror, Queen Elizabeth cannot comfortably be analogized to Charles V; she cannot take maidenheads. As I have tried to show, the conjunctures, exchanges, and contradictions between the categories of gender and nation could be employed to produce moral distinctions between Englishmen and Spaniards. But they could also dispose English subjects to identify with Spaniards and with the king of Spain himself on the basis of their manly rivalry for possession of the feminized land. In the face of a tangible Spanish threat to what were perceived to be the mutual interests and shared identity of English men and women of all estates, Queen Elizabeth's Tilbury speech may have been relatively successful at producing an identification of the collective social body with the feminine body of the monarch. However, for its masculine Elizabethan readers, the violent rhetoric of Ralegh's *Discoverie* generates identifications with the agency of England's masculine enemies; and in this very process of identification and emulation, these Englishmen will necessarily be alienated from their own sovereign, who cannot occupy the position of the agent in such a gendered and sexed discourse.

The final sentence of the *Discoverie*, following immediately upon Ralegh's exhortation to the queen to overgo the Amazons, balances against its initial deferential gestures an ultimate assertion of the subject's resolve: "I trust . . . that he which is King of all Kings and Lord of Lords, will put it into her heart which is Ladie of Ladies to possess it, if not, I will judge those men worthy to be kings thereof, that by her grace and leave will undertake it of themselves" (431). Ralegh has good reason to doubt that the queen will be moved to action by his own imperial vision. The requisite phrase, "by her grace and leave," does little to qualify the assertion of a strong, collective, and defiant response by the queen's masculine subjects to her anticipated lack of enthusiasm. Invoking the aid of an emphatically masculine God, Ralegh employs the epithet "Lord of Lords" to figure superlative authority and potency; in contrast, his epithet for his monarch, "Ladie of Ladies," figures superlative feminine gentility. The *Discoverie*'s final clause—"I will judge those men worthy to be kings thereof, that by her grace and leave will undertake it of themselves"—envisions the queen's most manly subjects, like so many Tamburlaines, seizing the opportunity to repudiate their unworthy subjection and to make themselves kings by their deeds. Nor does Ralegh's perfunctory gesture of deference to the queen neutralize his bold, final symbolic act, in which he arrogates the authority to judge who is worthy to be a king. It seems to me that this closing period of Ralegh's *Discoverie* manifests a considerable strain between two Elizabethan subject positions and two different notions of the "subject": a strain between the subject's courtship of and deference to his queen, and his contrary impulse to assert his own masculine virtue and to put his sovereign in her place as a woman. Nevertheless—and the point cannot be made too strongly—however clever and rhetorically skillful the arguments and insinuations of Ralegh's text, they exerted no discernible power over the queen's policies. Whatever personal predispositions or pragmatic military, diplomatic, and fiscal considerations may have governed Elizabeth's refusal to endorse Ralegh's grandiose scheme, she was also, in effect, resisting his attempts discursively to construct and delimit her gender identity and her sovereignty, to influence her fantasy and to control her will.

Ralegh emphasizes that the Englishmen "had many" of the Indian women "in [their] power" (391); and he represents territorial conquest as the enforced defloration and possession of a female body. Such forms of discursive intimidation and violence may be identified as the compensatory tactics of a masculine Elizabethan subject who is engaged with his monarch in a gendered struggle for mastery and agency, authority and will. If we widen our perspective, however, Queen Elizabeth herself may be understood to be a feminine subject who had been engaged since the very beginning of her reign in compensatory tactics of her own. Elizabeth's political genius was to appropriate and maintain a space for feminine authority within the dominant masculine and patriarchal structures of Tudor society. However, to the extent that such tactics became a successful strategy of power, they also tapped the alternating current of misogyny in her ostensibly adoring and obedient masculine subjects.[45] Such attitudes of hostility, distrust, and contempt were expressed toward women and toward the category of Woman; and they were also expressed toward the sovereign, often indirectly or equivocally but also occasionally with remarkable bluntness. Thus, to formulate Ralegh's practices in terms of "compensatory tactics" may be merely to reobjectify Woman as the threatening Other of the masculine subject: his own gendered violence has now been rendered understandable—perhaps even sympathetic. In other words, unintentionally and unreflectively, such a formulation may be complicit in the very tactics that it describes.

Many who have not read Ralegh's *Discoverie* may, nevertheless, be familiar with the phrase, "Guiana is a countrey that hath yet her maydenhead." It has been cited and quoted frequently in studies of English Renaissance culture, and has been made the subject of discourses ranging from ideological analysis to prurient anecdote. Our contemporary discourses about rape emphasize its character as an act of rage, rather than an act of desire. Some would therefore deny it the status of a specifically sexual crime; others argue compellingly that, to the contrary, rape is always a socially sexed crime that must be contextualized within a larger system of gender politics. Whether the action is physical or metaphorical, whether its object is a woman, a man, or a "countrey," that object is always positioned as feminine.[46] These emphases are certainly relevant to Ralegh's notorious metaphor—and, equally, to the ways in which we critically re-present it. My immediate concern has been with the historically and textually specific work performed by this metaphor in Ralegh's *Discoverie*, and with its articulation among other rhetorical/ideological elements in the collective Elizabethan discourse of discovery. The female body maps an important sector of the Elizabethan cultural unconscious; it constitutes a veritable matrix for the forms of Elizabethan desire and fear. The feminized topographical and textual spaces of the new found land; the heroic, fecund, and rapacious Amazons; the young, well-favored, and naked maidens of Guiana; the pure and dangerous, politic and natural bodies of the Queen of England: it is through the symbolic display and manipulation of these feminine representations—in discursive acts of violence or adoration, or of violent adoration—that "every mans longing" is given a local habitation and a name.

The subject of Ralegh's *Discoverie* is a masculine subject, one who is textually defined not in terms of his subjective experience of sexuality but rather by means of a complex process of social positioning. The narrative and descriptive movements of Elizabethan texts construct multiple—and potentially contradictory—subject positions for writers and readers by means of continually shifting and recombined sets of oppositional or differential terms, terms that are culture-specific in their content and resonance. The project of Ralegh's prose tract, as of Spenser's heroic poem, is (in the words of Spenser's Letter to Ralegh, appended to *The Faerie Queene* in 1590), "to fashion a gentleman or noble person in vertuous and gentle discipline." In both texts, this fashioning is produced in a conjunction of identifications and distinctions that are made in terms of gender, nation, religion, social estate, and condition of civility or savagery (which we might call ethos). The system of Aristotelian ethics that provides a foreconceit for Spenser's Legend of Temperance also provides the conceptual framework within which Ralegh thinks his own daily actions and interactions. But whereas Spenser's polysemous allegorical fiction works explicitly toward a general system of moral virtue, Ralegh's ostensibly factual narrative inscribes elements of such ideological schemata into its intended representations of particular persons and events.

I have suggested some of the ways in which, through the construction/observation of his narrative and descriptive objects, the writing subject obtains coordinates for the constant if often subliminal process by which he locates his shifting position in moral and social space. Ralegh's observations of the Spaniards, of the warriors of Guiana and "their women," of the Amazons, and of "the meaner sort" of Englishmen all work interdependently so as to exemplify in Ralegh himself the ethical and political congruence of the temperate man and the governor, the national and social congruence of the Englishman and the gentleman. At the same time that the persona of the author is dialectically fashioned in relationship to the personae narrated and described in his text, he is also so fashioned in relationship to the readers whom he defines by addressing them in his text. In the case of Ralegh's *Discoverie*, as I have already suggested, these gender- and status-specific objects of address include Queen Elizabeth herself, who is obliquely addressed and directly discussed throughout the text; Lord Howard ("Knight of the Garter, Baron and Councellor, and of the Admirals of England the most renowmed"), and Sir Robert Cecil ("Councellor in her Highnesse Privie Councels")—two of the most powerful men in England, to whom the *Discoverie* is directly addressed; and a general readership of Elizabethan masculine subjects—gentlemen, soldiers, potential investors, and colonists—who are directly addressed in an initial epistle and at the close of the work.

However distinctive in detail, Ralegh's individual relationship to Queen Elizabeth was shaped by a cultural contradiction that he shared with all members of his nation, gender, and social estate: namely, the expectation that he manifest loyalty and obedience to his sovereign at the same time that he exercised masculine authority over women. His relationship to Howard and Cecil was also conditioned by a cultural contradiction, one specific to men of the social elite and the political nation: namely, that while mastery of oneself and one's social inferiors was central to the ideology of the gentleman, the extreme degree of stratification in Elizabethan society meant that most relationships between gentlemen were also hierarchical, and required elaborate if often subtle forms of deference toward social superiors. (At the very beginning of the *Discoverie*, Ralegh addresses Howard and Cecil as his patrons and protectors, giving them their full titles as quoted above, but he compensates for this requisite positioning of himself as a dependent by also addressing them intimately as his friends and, in Howard's case, as his kinsman.) In his strategies of address "To the Reader," Ralegh must make his appeal in terms of the interests, desires, and national identity he has in common with this general readership, but without compromising the position of distinction and superiority that is the basis of his claim to authority over them. A dissonance that is intermittently registered throughout the text of the *Discoverie* is powerfully foregrounded and heightened when, in the rhetorical violence that governs his final address to these readers, Ralegh abandons his previous claim and responsibility to govern their appetites. This dissonance between Ralegh's representation of his own conduct as temperate and judicious and his incitement of others to conduct that is passionate and rapacious has a multiple and contradictory ideological import that lies beyond the controlling intentions of the writing subject: it simultaneously affirms and subverts—and thus, ultimately, destabilizes—the identification of the *masculine* subject with the authority of his *feminine* sovereign; it destabilizes the moral distinction of the *virtuous* Englishman from the *degenerate* Spaniard, and of the *reasonable* gentleman from the *sensual* commoner; and it destabilizes the legitimacy of *civil* European attempts to possess *savage* America. Although Ralegh declares triumphantly that "there is a way found to answer every mans longing," the textual operations of the *Discoverie* discover the way to be errant and the answer equivocal.

Notes

For reading drafts of this essay, and for offering criticism and encouragement, I am grateful to Wai-chee Dimock, Stephanie Jed, Steven Mullaney, Frank Whigham, and, especially, to Roxanne Lin.

1. Joan Wallach Scott, *Gender and the Politics of History* (New York, 1988), 42.

2. I have discussed other aspects of this discourse in detail in earlier studies. Of particular relevance are Louis Montrose, "'Shaping Fantasies': Figurations of Gender and Power in Elizabethan Culture," *Representations* 2 (Spring 1983): 61–94; and "The Elizabethan Subject and the Spenserian Text," in *Literary Theory/Renaissance Texts*, ed. Patricia Parker and David Quint (Baltimore, 1986), 303–40. A few passages from those earlier studies reappear in the present essay in revised form.

3. I discuss some of these larger issues of theory and method more fully in Louis Montrose, "Texts and Histories," in *Redrawing the Boundaries: The Transformation of English and American Literary Study*, ed. Stephen Greenblatt and Giles Gunn (New York, 1992).

4. See Hugh Honour, *The New Golden Land: European Images of America from the Discoveries to the Present Time* (New York, 1975), chap. 4, esp. plates 76–84.

5. See the reproduction of van der Straet's drawing in Claire le Corbeiller, "Miss America and Her Sisters: Personifications of the Four Parts of the World," *Metropolitan Museum of Art Bulletin*, ser. 2, vol. 19 (1961): 209–23; fig. 1, p. 211 ("The Discovery of America, by Jan van der Straet [Stradanus]. Flemish, about 1575. Pen and bistre heightened with white"). Galle's engraving was originally issued in the early 1580s as the first in a set of twenty based on drawings of Stradanus, with the general title *Nova Reperta*; all the other engravings in this series illustrate inventions and technologies. The twenty engravings of *Nova Reperta* and the additional four engravings of *Americae Retectio* (celebrating Columbus, Vespucci, and Magellan) are reproduced in *"New Discoveries": The Sciences, Inventions, and Discoveries of the Middle Ages and the Renaissance as Represented in Twenty-four Engravings Issued in the Early 1580s by Stradanus* (Norwalk, Conn., 1953).

6. *A treatyse of the newe India, with other new founde landes and Ilandes . . .* , trans. Rycharde Eden (London, 1553); reprinted in *The First Three English Books on America*, ed. Edward Arber (1885; reprint ed., New York, 1971), 39. Latin, Italian, and French editions seem to have been in print within three or four years of the original date of Vespucci's letter. It was on the basis of this work that, in 1507, the cosmographer Martin Waldseemüller first used the name *America* on a map to mark the southern region of the New World. Although the authorship of Vespucci's letter appears to be genuine, its contents were proved to have been fabricated as early as the mid sixteenth century by none other than Bartolomé de Las Casas. There is a modern translation of the letter and of relevant passages from Las Casas in *The Letters of Amerigo Vespucci*, ed. Clements R. Markham, The Hakluyt Society, 1st ser., no. 90 (1894; reprint ed., New York, n.d.); see 37–38 for the passage I have quoted in my text in Eden's translation. (Throughout this study, I have silently modernized obsolete typographical conventions in quotations from Elizabethan texts.)

7. For a Lévi-Straussian analysis of the conjunction of savagery, anthropophagy, and gender in the sixteenth-century European imagination of the New World, see Bernadette Bucher, *Icon and Conquest: A Structural Analysis of the Illustrations of de Bry's "Great Voyages,"* trans. Basia Miller Gulati (Chicago, 1981). Also see the chapter on the Bra-

zilian travel narrative of Jean de Léry (1578) in Michel de Certeau, *The Writing of History*, trans. Tom Conley (New York, 1988), 209–43.

8. De Certeau, *Writing of History*, xxv–xxvi. The frontispiece of *The Writing of History* is labeled as an "Allegorical etching by Jan Van der Straet for *Americae decima pars* by Jean-Théodore de Bry (Oppenheim, 1619)." Part 10 of de Bry's *America* includes a text of Vespucci's voyages and several related engravings. However, the copies I have been able to examine do not contain an engraving of van der Straet's *America*.
    The engraving also serves as the frontispiece to Peter Hulme's stimulating study, *Colonial Encounters: Europe and the Native Caribbean, 1492–1797* (London, 1986), where it is also incorrectly attributed to van der Straet himself rather than to Galle ("'America' [c. 1600]; an engraving by Jan van der Straet [Stradanus]"). Hulme discusses the engraving briefly on pp. 1–2.

9. Address by Justino Quispe Balboa (Aymará, Bolivia) before the first Indian Congress of South America, 13 October 1974; quoted in Michel de Certeau, *Heterologies: Discourse on the Other*, trans. Brian Massumi (Minneapolis, 1986), 227.

10. Walter Ralegh's *The Discoverie of the large, rich and beautifull Empire of Guiana, with a relation of the great and golden citie of Manoa (which the Spaniards call El Dorado . . . Performed in the yeere 1595 by Sir Walter Ralegh* was first published separately in London in 1596 and went through three editions in that year; it was soon reprinted in the second edition of Richard Hakluyt's monumental collection, *The principal navigations, voyages traffiques & discoveries of the English nation*, 3 vols. (London, 1598–1600). Illustrated translations were printed in the Latin and German editions of Théodore de Bry's *Americae*, part 8 (Frankfurt, 1599). I quote the *Discoverie* from the modern edition of Hakluyt, *Principal Navigations*, 12 vols. (Glasgow, 1904; reprint ed., New York, 1969), 10:338–431. All parenthetical page references will be to vol. 10 of this edition.

11. Arthur Barlowe, "The first voyage made to the coastes of America, with two barkes, wherein were Captaines Master Philip Amadas, and Master Arthur Barlowe, who discovered part of the Countrey, now called Virginia, Anno 1584: Written by one of the said Captaines, and sent to sir Walter Raleigh, knight, at whose charge, and direction, the said voyage was set foorth," in *The Roanoke Voyages, 1584–1590: Documents to Illustrate the English Voyages to North America Under the Patent Granted to Walter Raleigh in 1584*, ed. David Beers Quinn, The Hakluyt Society, 2nd ser., nos. 104, 105 (London, 1955), 91–92. Barlowe's text was first printed in the 1589 edition of Richard Hakluyt's *Principall navigations, voiages and discoveries of the English nation*.

12. William Camden, *Annals* (1585), extract reprinted in *The Original Writings and Correspondence of the Two Richard Hakluyts*, ed. E. G. R. Taylor, 2 vols., The Hakluyt Society, 2nd ser., nos. 76–77 (1935; reprint ed., Nendeln, Liecht., 1967), 2:348.

13. John T. Juricek, "English Territorial Claims in North America Under Elizabeth and the Early Stuarts," *Terrae Incognitae* 7 (1976): 7–22; 11. Juricek presents an enlightening discussion of conflicting concepts of "discovery" and "possession" as employed by Iberian and Anglo-Dutch interests in the sixteenth and early seventeenth centuries, with particular reference to Virginia.

14. On theoretical justifications for the dispossession of New World peoples, see Wilcomb E. Washburn, "The Moral and Legal Justifications for Dispossessing the Indians," in *Seventeenth-Century America: Essays in Colonial History*, ed. James Morton Smith (Chapel Hill, N.C., 1959), 15–32; Juricek, "English Territorial Claims"; Anthony Pagden, *The Fall of Natural Man: The American Indian and the Origins of Comparative Ethnology*, rev. ed. (Cambridge, 1986); Pagden, *Spanish Imperialism and the Political Imagination: Studies in European and Spanish-American Social and Political Theory, 1513–1830* (New Haven,

1990), 13–36. On the effacement of indigenous peoples in later forms of colonialist discourse, see Mary Louise Pratt, "Scratches on the Face of the Country; or, What Mr. Barrow Saw in the Land of the Bushmen," *Critical Inquiry* 12 (1985): 119–43.

15. See the suggestive comments apropos of the Virginia patent in Joyce Youings, "Did Raleigh's England Need Colonies?" in *Raleigh in Exeter, 1985: Privateering and Colonisation in the Reign of Elizabeth I*, ed. Youings, Exeter Studies in History, no. 10 (Exeter, Eng., 1985):

> On the whole the colonial literature did not stress the advantages of extending the Queen's dominions, the authors knowing full well that the Queen had no territorial ambitions. . . . One of John Oxenham's companions had told his captors in 1579 that the Queen was the great obstacle to English colonial endeavours but that if she should die the floodgates would be open. Even in 1584, when England was virtually at war with Spain, Raleigh's patent confined him strictly to territory not yet occupied by any Christian prince. (52–53)

16. On Ralegh's self-fashioning in writing, speech, and conduct, see Stephen J. Greenblatt, *Sir Walter Ralegh: The Renaissance Man and His Roles* (New Haven, 1973). The standard documentary biography and edition of Ralegh's extant letters is still that of Edward Edwards, *The Life of Sir Walter Ralegh . . . Together with His Letters*, 2 vols. (London, 1868).

17. "Journey Through England and Scotland Made by Lupold von Wedel in the Years 1584 and 1585," trans. Gottfried von Bülow, *Transactions of the Royal Historical Society*, new ser., 9 (1895): 223–70; 265, 263.

18. Youings points out both the rapid elevation and the precariousness of Ralegh's social standing:

> Raleigh was knighted in January 1585, being then already member of parliament for Devon, both of these unusual achievements for a virtually landless gentleman. Later that year he was to succeed . . . as Lord Warden of the Stanneries, High Steward of the Duchy of Cornwall and Lord Lieutenant of Cornwall. As such he would enjoy power and patronage, but no landed inheritance, without which there was no future for his line. . . . Even if he invested what cash he had in English land rather than in colonial ventures, land suitable for gentlemen, that is manors and other revenue-producing property, was no longer readily available, even for purchase. ("Did Raleigh's England Need Colonies?" 54)

19. Walter Ralegh, *The 11th: and last booke of the Ocean to Scinthia*, printed from the undated holograph in *The Poems of Sir Walter Ralegh*, ed. Agnes M. C. Latham (1951; reprint ed., Cambridge, Mass., 1962), 27, lines 55–56. Conjectures as to the date of *The Ocean to Cynthia* range from 1589 to 1603, with the period immediately following the 1592 disgrace perhaps most often endorsed.

20. On Ralegh's early and continuing interest in Guiana, see Joyce Lorimer, "Ralegh's First Reconnaissance of Guiana? An English Survey of the Orinoco in 1587," *Terrae Incognitae* 9 (1977): 7–21. For an excellent geopolitical and economic contextualization of Ralegh's privateering and colonial projects, see Kenneth R. Andrews, *Trade, Plunder, and Settlement: Maritime Enterprise and the Genesis of the British Empire, 1480–1630* (Cambridge, 1984); Andrews discusses Ralegh's *Discoverie* on pp. 287–94.

21. Quoted in Edward Thompson, *Sir Walter Ralegh: The Last of the Elizabethans* (London, 1935), 83. The letter was first printed in J. Collier, "Continuation of New Materials for a Life of Sir Walter Raleigh," *Archaeologia* 34 (1852): 161.

22. See, for example, Eric Partridge, *Shakespeare's Bawdy* (1948; reprint ed., New York, 1960), s.v. "country" and "country matters."

23. Scott observes that "hierarchical structures rely on generalized understandings of the so-called natural relationships between male and female. . . . Power relationships among nations and the status of colonial subjects have been made comprehensible (and thus legitimate) in terms of relations between male and female"; *Gender and the Politics of History*, 48.

24. Hakluyt, *Writings and Correspondence*, 2:360–61, 367–68.

25. Nancy Vickers, "'The blazon of sweet beauty's best': Shakespeare's *Lucrece*," in *Shakespeare and the Question of Theory*, ed. Patricia Parker and Geoffrey Hartman (New York, 1985); 95–115; 95. For an introduction to the literary history of the woman/land trope, see Annette Kolodny, *The Lay of the Land: Metaphor as Experience and History in American Life and Letters* (Chapel Hill, N. C., 1975), esp. 10–25. Drawing upon the work of Kolodny, Vickers, and others, Patricia Parker discusses rhetorical and ideological aspects of the woman/land trope—the interplay of gender, commerce, and property—in *Literary Fat Ladies: Rhetoric, Gender, Property* (New York, 1987), 126–54.

26. George Puttenham, *The Arte of English Poesie* (1589), ed. Gladys Doidge Willcock and Alice Walker (Cambridge, 1936), 244.

27. For reproductions of details and analogues, and for a commentary different from but complementary to my own, see Roy Strong, *Gloriana: The Portraits of Queen Elizabeth I* (London, 1987), 134–41.

28. On Saxton's maps and the ideological implications of Elizabethan and Jacobean cartography, see Victor Morgan, "The Cartographic Image of 'The Country' in Early Modern England," *Transactions of the Royal Historical Society*, 5th ser., 29 (1979): 129–54; and Richard Helgerson, "The Land Speaks: Cartography, Chorography, and Subversion in Renaissance England," in *Representing the English Renaissance*, ed. Stephen Greenblatt (Berkeley, 1988), 326–61. Helgerson's thesis is that "the cartographic representation of England . . . strengthened the sense of both local and national identity at the expense of an identity based on dynastic loyalty. . . . Maps thus opened a conceptual gap between the land and its ruler" (332). His judgment that the Ditchley portrait, however, "enforces the royal cult" (331) accords with my own reading.

29. Most published discussions of Ralegh's *Discoverie* have been the work of historians and biographers, whose primary interest has been in the events narrated in the text and their extratextual reference. Such writings are frequently methodologically naive; they base their own accounts of Ralegh's activities in Guiana wholly upon his putatively factual account of them. The formal, stylistic, and rhetorical dimensions of Ralegh's text are given greater emphasis in Greenblatt, *Ralegh*, 99–112; and Mary B. Campbell, *The Witness and the Other World: Exotic European Travel Writing, 400–1600* (Ithaca, N. Y., 1988), 211–54. My understanding of the play of referentiality and textuality in Ralegh's *Discoverie* has benefited from a stimulating paper written for my graduate seminar by Lucia Folena.

30. In an exhaustive study introductory to his edition of the *Discoverie* (London, 1928), V. T. Harlow concludes that Ralegh's

> so-called 'Discovery' of Guiana merely consisted in traversing the Orinoco from its estuary to the cataract on the Caroni, a journey with which every Spanish soldier at Trinidad was perfectly familiar. . . . In fixing the site of Manoa near the source of the Caroni, Ralegh was simply adopting the theory which Berrio had laboriously constructed after ten years' arduous toil. Moreover, a large part of the accurate geographical knowledge of the upper Orinoco and its tributaries which Ralegh displayed . . . must again have been

derived from Berrio, who was then one of the few Europeans who had ever visited those regions. (xcvii)

It should be noted that, having debunked Ralegh's status as an explorer, Harlow goes on to praise him on distinctly chauvinistic grounds: "His Spanish predecessors in the quest had been valiant adventurers, but they had been solely intent upon plunder. Ralegh, on the other hand, undertook the search from the point of view of a statesman. If the monopoly of Spain was to be broken, she must be beaten on her own ground." In this passage, we may note the apparent suppression by Harlow of Ralegh's own clear indications that he indeed desired to plunder Manoa; Harlow's elevation of English—as distinct from Spanish—foreign policy and imperialism to the level of statesmanship; and the historical persistence, in Harlow's scholarly discourse, of a Western androcentric consciousness that genders the land as female and effaces the acts of expropriation that made Spain's colonies "her own ground."

31. See Juricek, "English Territorial Claims," 10: "Exactly what was required for such legitimate possession was never precisely defined, but the general idea was real domination. Evidence generally recognized as relevant to this matter included colonization, fortification, economic development, and tribute or other recognition from the natives."

32. Laurence Keymis, *A Relation of the Second Voyage to Guiana: Performed and written in the yeere 1596* (London, 1596), reprinted in Hakluyt, *Principal Navigations*. I quote Keymis's *Relation* from the 1904 edition of Hakluyt, *Principal Navigations*, 10:487. Parenthetical page references will be to vol. 10 of this edition.

33. Compare Eve Kosofsky Sedgwick, *Between Men: English Literature and Male Homosocial Desire* (New York, 1985), 11: "The subject of sex [is] an especially charged leverage-point or point for the exchange of meanings, *between* gender and class (and in many societies, race)." As Sedgwick herself notes, the constitution and interrelation of these categories—including "the subject of sex"—are societally and historically variable.

34. For varying interpretations of attitudes toward North American Indians in sixteenth-to-seventeenth-century English writings, see Karen Ordahl Kupperman, *Settling with the Indians: The Meeting of English and Indian Cultures in America, 1580–1640* (Totowa, N.J., 1980); and Bernard Sheehan, *Savagism and Civility: Indians and Englishmen in Colonial Virginia* (Cambridge, 1980). Kupperman emphasizes social rank as the fundamental category of difference and hierarchy, while Sheehan emphasizes savagery.

35. This is also the case elsewhere in the *Discovery*. On the significance of cannibalism and indigenous culinary practices in sixteenth-century colonial discourse, see Pagden, *Fall of Natural Man*, 80–90; Hulme, *Colonial Encounters*, 13–43; and Bucher, *Icon and Conquest*, passim.

36. Sir Thomas Elyot, *The Book named The Governor* (1531), ed. S. Lehmberg (London, 1962), 203–4.

37. On "sexuality" as a specifically modern, Western, and bourgeois mode of subjectification and subjectivity, see Michel Foucault, *The History of Sexuality*, vol. 1, *An Introduction*, trans. Robert Hurley (New York, 1978); Robert A. Padgug, "Sexual Matters: On Conceptualizing Sexuality in History," *Radical History Review* 20 (1979): 3–23; David M. Halperin, "Is There a History of Sexuality?" *History and Theory* 28 (1989): 257–74.

38. On the ideology of female unruliness in early modern Europe, see, for example: Natalie Zemon Davis, "Women on Top," in *Society and Culture in Early Modern France* (Stanford, Calif., 1975), 124–51; D. E. Underdown, "The Taming of the Scold: The Enforcement of Patriarchal Authority in Early Modern England," in *Order and Disorder in Early Modern England*, ed. Anthony Fletcher and John Stevenson (Cambridge,

1985), 116–36; and Linda Woodbridge, *Women and the English Renaissance: Literature and the Nature of Womankind, 1540–1620* (Urbana, Ill., 1984), passim.

39. Social status is so fundamental a marker of distinction in Elizabethan culture that, in the course of his narrative, Ralegh can praise the virtues of both a native American chieftain and his own Spanish rival because their social and political statuses are equivalent to his own. Thus, "This Topiawari is helde for the prowdest, and wisest of all the Orenoqueponi, and so hee behaved himselfe towardes mee . . . as I marveiled to finde a man of that gravitie and judgement, and of so good discourse, that had no helpe of learning nor breede" (401). Note that the political organization of this Amerindian society is assimilated to the European model of monarchy; that Topiawari's virtues— which include pride—are those appropriate to a great personage, like Ralegh himself; and that Ralegh's surprise at the existence of such virtues in such a person is not expressed in terms of assumptions about limited racial capacities but rather in terms of education and lineage—the same terms that Ralegh would have used had Topiawari been a sagacious English rustic.

Don Antonio de Berreo, governor of Trinidad and explorer of Guiana, was briefly Ralegh's captive during the voyage. Ralegh announces his desire to be revenged upon Berreo for his deception and betrayal of one of Ralegh's captains during a 1594 expeditionary voyage, which had resulted in the ambush and killing of eight Englishmen. Within three paragraphs, however, Ralegh is describing the Spaniard as "a gentleman wel descended . . . very valiant and liberall, and a gentleman of great assurednes, and of great heart: I used him according to his estate and worth in all things I could, according to the small meanes I had" (354). By his approval of Berreo's status-specific virtues, and by his own conduct toward his captive, Ralegh affirms a kind of transnational class solidarity with a fellow European gentleman, soldier, and colonial administrator. It should also be noted that in praising both Topiawari and Berreo, Ralegh is probably motivated in part by the necessity to enhance the credibility of two of his most crucial informants.

40. See the Penguin edition of Richard Hakluyt, *Voyages and Discoveries*, ed. Jack Beeching (Harmondsworth, Eng., 1972; reprint ed., 1982). The title page mentions this as an "abridged" edition, and the introduction refers to it as a "condensed version," but there is no explicit indication either in the introduction or in the text that the individual accounts which are actually included in this abridged edition have themselves been cut. This editorial silence concerning excisions is maintained despite the scrupulous notice that "on the very rare occasions when, for clarity, a word is here added to Hakluyt's text, it has been put in square brackets" (28). Among other unindicated cuts, the following passage is silently edited out of the text of Ralegh's *Discoverie* on p. 404 of this edition: "for then (whereas now they have heard we were enemies to the Spaniards & were sent by her Majesty to relieve them) they would as good cheap have joyned with the Spaniards at our returne, as to have yeelded unto us, when they had proved that we came both for one errant, and that both sought but to sacke & spoile them." I myself once assigned Ralegh's text to my graduate seminar in this easily available and affordable paperback edition, naively assuming it to be uncut. I owe the discovery of Beeching's elisions to Lucia Folena.

41. I use the term "patriarchy" to describe a system of social and domestic organization hegemonic in early modern England, in which authority resided in a masculine "head"—whether father, husband, elder, master, teacher, preacher, magistrate, or lord. On the political theory of patriarchy in early modern England, see Gordon J. Schochet, *Patriarchalism in Political Thought* (New York, 1975); on the interplay of

theory and practice at the level of household and village, see Susan Dwyer Amussen, *An Ordered Society: Gender and Class in Early Modern England* (Oxford, 1988).

42. For a sense of the ubiquity of Amazonian representations in Elizabethan culture, see the valuable survey by Celeste Turner Wright, "The Amazons in Elizabethan Literature," *Studies in Philology* 37 (1940): 433–56; and, for Amazons and viragos in Elizabethan and Jacobean dramatic and nondramatic writings, see Simon Shepherd, *Amazons and Warrior Women: Varieties of Feminism in Seventeenth-Century Drama* (Brighton, Eng., 1981). For analyses and speculations regarding Amazonian representations of Queen Elizabeth, see Winfried Schleiner, *"Divina virago*: Queen Elizabeth as an Amazon" *Studies in Philology* 75 (1978): 163–80; and Gabriele Bernhard Jackson, "Topical Ideology: Witches, Amazons, and Shakespeare's Joan of Arc," *English Literary Renaissance* 18 (1988): 40–65.

43. Thomas Heywood, *The exemplary lives and memorable acts of nine the most worthy women of the world* (London, 1640), 211. Among Heywood's three "Heathen" female worthies is the Amazon "Penthisilaea" (96–109); the ninth and culminating female worthy is, of course, England's late queen (182–212).

44. The speech is recorded in an undated letter: "Dr. [Leonel] Sharp to the Duke of Buckingham," printed in *Cabala, Mysteries of State, in Letters of the great Ministers of K. James and K. Charles* (London, 1654), 259. Sharp had been present in the queen's retinue at Tilbury.

45. Here I am using *strategies* to connote practices by which a dominant ideology seeks to maintain or extend its hegemony, and *tactics* to connote improvised appropriations of dominant practices by marginalized subjects. This distinction is indebted to Michel de Certeau, *The Practice of Everyday Life*, trans. Steven Rendell (Berkeley, 1984).

46. I am indebted to the discussion of this controversy in Teresa de Lauretis, "The Violence of Rhetoric: Considerations on Representation and Gender," in *The Violence of Representation: Literature and the History of Violence*, ed. Nancy Armstrong and Leonard Tennenhouse (London, 1989), 239–58, esp. 244–45.

MARY C. FULLER

Ralegh's Fugitive Gold:
Reference and Deferral
in *The Discoverie of Guiana*

> *If from time to time I envy*
> *the pure annunciations to the eye*
>
> *the* visio beatifica
> *if from time to time I long to turn*
>
> *like the Eleusinian hierophant*
> *holding up a single ear of grain*
>
> *for return to the concrete and everlasting world*
> —Adrienne Rich,
> "Cartographies of Silence"[1]

I

WITH THE 1596 PUBLICATION OF *The Discoverie of the Large, Rich and Bewtifvl Empire of Gviana*, Walter Ralegh promised Elizabeth I a gold-rich empire more lucrative than Peru—whose inhabitants, moreover, were eager to swear allegiance to "*Ezrabeta Cassipuna Aquerewana*, which is as much as *Elizabeth, the great princesse or greatest commaunder.*"[2] In 1616, Ralegh staked his life on his ability to find, claim, and work the Guianan gold mines of which he had written so confidently twenty years earlier—and lost. The *Declaration of the Demeanor and Cariage of Sir Walter Raleigh*, appearing after Ralegh's execution to relate at James's behest "the true motiues and inducements which occasioned His Maiestie to Proceed in doing Iustice upone him, as hath bene done," accused Ralegh of twofold duplicity; given a commission only "to discouer and finde out some commodities and merchandizes in those Countries [the Americas] . . . whereof the Inhabitants there make little or no use or estimation,"[3] his intentions, as revealed in action, were

first, to procure his libertie, and then to make new fortunes for himselfe, casting abroad onely this tale of the Mine as a lure to get aduenturers and followers; hauing in his eye the *Mexico* Fleete, the sacking and spoyle of Townes planted with Spaniards, the depredation of Ships, and such other purchase. (4)

The *Declaration* had some distance to go in convicting Ralegh of intentions to turn pirate, to sack Spanish towns, to ally himself with the French. True, Ralegh's company sacked the inland settlement of San Thomé, but Ralegh himself was not present, detained at the coast by serious illness. Ralegh's lieutenant Lawrence Keymis (or Kemys), returning with news of the proscribed engagement with the Spaniards in which Ralegh's son died, offered the explanation that the fort at San Thomé had moved since the last English visit: the Spanish settlement formerly at a safe distance "was newly sett up within three miles of the mine," where the English happened on it and became involved with the Spaniards by mischance.[4] Keymis's suicide followed his less than appreciative reception.

The *Declaration* then tries, since it cannot attack Ralegh's own actions, to build a case on his intentions as reflected by members of his company. Perhaps the climax of invective—as well as irony—is reached with the attribution of these words to Ralegh's son as he led the ill-omened attack on San Thomé: "Come on my hearts, here is the Mine that ye must expect, they that looke for any other Mine, are fooles."[5] (Ralegh would say at his trial: "The voyage had no success but what was fatal to me, the loss of my son and wasting of my estate").[6] The anonymous author goes on to comment that

with this did well concurre that which followed . . . For this Mine was not onely imaginary, but moueable, for that which was directed to bee 3. miles short of Saint *Thomé*, was after sought 30. miles beyond S. *Thomé*. (35)

For "30," one should probably read "300";[7] this was, according to Spanish sources, the distance Keymis traveled beyond San Thomé in his purported search for the mine.

Where Ralegh himself was concerned, the text focused on the way in which he talked—or failed to talk—about that "golden baite," the mine or mines reportedly indicated to himself and to Keymis by Indian informants during their expeditions in 1595 and 1596.

After, when hee was once at Sea, hee did not much labor to nourish and maintaine the beliefe, that he meant to make his voyage vpon the profite of the Mine, but fell a degree, as if it were sufficient to bring home certainty and visible proofe, that such a Mine there was, though hee brought not the riches of it. (29)

Ralegh seems to be *charged* with neglecting a "labor" of "nourishing" and "maintaining" belief—belief that "he meant to make his voyage upon the profite of the Mine"—as if this labor of belief were an essential part of working the mine. He is charged with having an interest not in profit but in proof—intending to "save his credit" with one basket of ore, rather than restore the king's credit with "the riches of it."

Hee confessed the speech, with this argument and inference, that if there had beene a handfull of the Mine, it followed there was a Mine to be confessed; as if so many Ships, so many liues of men, such charge of prouisions, and such an honourable Commission, had beene but for an experiment. (29)

The *Declaration* here accuses Ralegh *not* of lying about his knowledge of a mine, as I have tried to show it does; rather, he is charged with "falling a degree," with a culpable shrinking of intention from *working* the mine to merely bringing back "certainty and visible proofe, that such a Mine there was." Ralegh "confessed" this intention. It seems that he conceived of his project, not as one of justifying the expenditure of ships, men, and provisions by a commensurate profit, but of enabling him to substantiate his own language with material proof—a token of reliability to generate further credit. As the *Declaration* reasonably points out, the voyage was not commissioned and funded solely for this purpose; James expected payment in full.

In a sense, the question of Ralegh's intentions here is moot. Whatever they were, the expedition went badly awry, and failed to bring back either profit *or* proof.[8] The *Declaration's* dramatic language—"charged," "confessed"—seems oddly excessive: the point driven home is not that Ralegh's talk of working a mine was a cover for piracy, sacking towns, and tobacco (all culpable intentions for a king both pro-Spanish and antismoking); revealed instead is a preoccupation on Ralegh's part with bringing back tangible evidence and thus reestablishing his credit as a truthful speaker.[9] This intention appears to be less criminal than inappropriate—not only from James's point of view, but from the standpoint of self-interest, self-preservation. Ralegh did not have to return to England at all; as he wrote to James, "When I had gotten my liberty . . . I voluntarily lost it. . . . When I was master of my life I rendered it again . . . though I might elsewhere have sold my ships and goods, and put five or six thousand pounds in my purse, I have brought her into England."[10] What caused the matter of proof to assume such curious primacy?

James's accusations amount to an intensely skeptical critique of Ralegh's language. He claims that Ralegh's writing is a screen not for *things* but for culpable intentions; that the *things* of which he writes are imaginary, and that their objective properties—such as physical location—are constructs responsive to the wish and will of the writer; that these *things* lack even the substance lent to imaginative constructs by the sustained labor of an author. We ought to recall here Spenser's version of such an accusation in the proem to book 2 of *The Faerie Queene*: "that all this famous . . . history / Of some th' aboundance of an idle braine / Will iudged be, and painted forgery, / Rather than matter of just memory."[11] How does one validate memory? Ralegh, it seems, intended to do so by bringing back matter, "a handfull of the Mine."

If matter, the material, can validate language as just memory, it would seem that the writer of discovery texts disposes of resources not available to the mere poet: speaking of gold, he puts a piece of ore in the refiner's hand. The resources of the material appear to be limited only by material conditions: Ralegh can neither bring a Guianan mine to James, nor bring James to the mine; he thinks to produce a "handfull of the Mine" as testimony to the mine itself. Things, then, would stand in the place of mute and incorruptible witnesses, already and always defended from the kinds of skepticism to which Ralegh's texts were subject.

Two problems present themselves with this claim. First, the *things* produced by Ralegh and others as underpinnings for representations of the New World were always and everywhere fully implicated with rhetorical procedures: substitutions of part for whole, transportations, translations, ellipses. Second, in the particular case of Ralegh, the part-for-whole synecdoche of *handfull* for mine masks a previous figure of metonymy—in fact, a congerie of previous figures. For in fact, Ralegh has never been to Guiana, but only to the country on the borders of the borderers of Guiana, and the furthest penetration into these borders was made not by him but by his "right hand," Lawrence Keymis; he has not been to a mine, but he has spoken to Indians who have. Ralegh's second expedition is underwritten by an original voyage, but that voyage itself failed to substantiate Ralegh's claims, and indeed gave rise to the same accusations of fabrication and misrepresentation that met the second.

Ralegh's problem was symptomatic of a more widespread attitude toward the material, and also of a writing situation with peculiar constraints: one in which the issue of *truth*, veracity, was particularly at stake and also particularly difficult to check. The problems of writing America, of producing "true reports," tested the limits of the material as a resource for verifying the nonfictional text.

In English writing about the New World, *discovery* frequently carried the sense of revealing, laying open something previously hidden, bringing to light something previously dark. William Strachey writes, for instance, that

Yt now pleased the eternal wisdome . . . that those misteryes and secrettes of this goodly workemanshippe of his, should to his utmost boundes be extended, reveyled, and layd open, and those goodly Nations and regions discovered.[12]

Discovery, then, makes what exists at a distance—troped as inwardness, secrecy, darkness—visible, accessible, understood. Discovery is the project of moving what is "in there," the inwardness of the New World, to "out here"—the public space of England—in a simple motion of unveiling. That motion of unveiling tropes the multiple operations and transmissions intervening between the eye which sees and the *I* printed on the page as a single act, as if these movements were ones of mechanical replication. As if the movement between two contiguous stages—e.g., senses and memory, memory and writing, and all the other possibilities of mediation—would present no challenge to the integrity of the transmission but be simply the transportation of a faithful image; or as if "the meaning aimed at by these figures [were] an essence rigorously independent of that which carries it over."[13] And yet the thesis so stated by Jacques Derrida is a thesis about metaphor, "the figure of transporte";[14] in other words, models that tend toward describing memory or discovery as modes of transportation applied to images or even objects, and that attempt to secure discovery and memory in a milieu of voiceless physical procedures, arrive immediately in the midst of figurative language, the poet's lie.

Such a model invites us to separate into two parts the issues given play by the distance between English audiences and the New World, that distance the book seems provisionally to bridge: first, the modes of transportation, of communicating the New World; second, those things—objects, words, pieces of information, bodies—that are communicated *as* the New World. Irma Staza Majer describes the first issue as one of translation: "from one language to another, from one place to the other, and . . . from a lived experience, a *voyage*, to a written experience, a *récit*."[15] Along similar lines, Tzvetan Todorov characterizes the discovery of America in terms of its radical difference both from any prior history and from any other "discovery." For Todorov, America implies an encounter with that which is prior to knowledge, prior to a language capable of adequately describing it. "Nothing is known" about the Indians of America, though knowledge of other populations was projected onto them.[16] The "otherness" or difference of the New World in both these discussions, that which must be translated, is the otherness of being *outside language*—as if America were, finally, the referent *par excellence*, a purely empirical domain unmapped, unmarked, unsullied by a history of writing and speaking. We find ourselves beginning to assume (again) that there is some*thing* self-evident, unambiguous, unified on the other side of language, which that language ideally serves merely as Christopher served Christ, "to carry across."[17]

Edmundo O'Gorman writes that the idea that Columbus "discovered" America "springs from a previous assumption . . . that things are something in themselves, *per se* . . . that all things are endowed for all time, for anyone and anywhere, with a set being, predetermined and unalterable."[18] O'Gorman's analysis opens the way for an interrogation of what underwrites our understanding of discovery and of the New World. When Majer or Todorov construct the New World through a series of oppositions (between languages, places, cultures; between "lived experience" and "written experience"; between self and other), this construction seems to posit a domain of things outside the order of language, located beneath it as a guarantee; above it as a privileged locus of authenticity and authority; beside it, at the end of a process of translation or transportation that allows it to be glimpsed at a distance. How does the text relate itself to a proposed domain of things, to what it constitutes as "outside itself"—and how does it constitute or imply that "outside"?[19]

Early writings about America such as Ralegh's *Discoverie* offer a peculiarly attractive entrance to the question of the material, and this for several reasons. The colonialism they herald will form a relationship between the imperial power and its colony in which the latter will have the role of supplying raw materials, will *become* the place of the material. Second, they document a situation of enunciation in which the matter of speech, the topic, the referent, physically existed but was always going to be physically absent from the place of speaking and listening. Finally, these texts record the transmission from America to Europe of substantial bodies: artifacts, animals, plants, ore—Indians. It is as if, in despair of making the New World present in words, language were materialized in some naive way, as a movable container faultlessly conveying meaning or an attempt at the wordless communication fantasized by Adrienne Rich's poem when "language cannot do everything": "holding up a single ear of grain / for return to the concrete and everlasting world." If the records of discovery show anything, however, they show that those bodies which are to speak for or manifest the other do so no less ambiguously than the compromised or inadequate language which they supplement. The move into silence, into the material world, fails to produce the kind of transparency fantasy promises, because finally there is no such move being made: what appears to be a turn away from language into "the concrete and everlasting world" dissolves into multiple references back into the order of language.

II

Michel de Montaigne, in the essay "Des caniballes," offers experience and presence as the path to producing a true report of travel. He derides those who

if . . . they have seene *Palestine*, will challenge a privilege, to tell us newes of all the world besides. I would have everie man write what he knowes, and no more: not only in that [topography] but in all other subjects. For one may have particular knowledge of the nature of one river, and experience of the qualitie of one fountaine, that in other things knowes no more than another man.[20]

What is privileged here is physically seeing, being in the presence of the thing: the memory of that experience becomes authoritative writing. The writing Montaigne enjoins needs only memory to guarantee it: not skill, learning, authorities, other travels, but just that memory of presence, being with the thing. Even experience, however, may be vitiated by the speaker's desires, his use of language as a means of effecting social and rhetorical transactions.

Subtile people . . . never represent things truly, but fashion and maske them according to the visage they saw them in; and to purchase credit to their judgement, and draw you on to beleeve them, they commonly adorne, enlarge, yea, and Hyperbolize the matter. Wherein is required either a most sincere Reporter, or a man so simple, that he may have no invention to build upon, and to give a true likelihood unto false devices, and be not wedded to his owne will. (162)

Michel de Certeau describes the first part of Montaigne's essay as a "critical journey through the languages which compel belief":[21] common opinion, tradition, observation. Each of these languages in turn finds itself discredited as an adequate means for knowing other places, and this critique "constitutes language in its relation to that which it is unable to appropriate," to the New World that exists outside language. It is the inhabitant of that other world, the cannibal, who offers an alternative to the languages Montaigne explodes.

The cannibal appears "precisely as a (t)exterior [*hors-texte*], as an image" in the second part of "Des caniballes": "After the critical journey through the languages which compel belief, now we get to 'see' savage society." This part of Montaigne's essay offers an "experience" more amazing than imagination, recounted by (for de Certeau) a reliable reporter, "the simple man." De Certeau privileges the words of the simple man and of the cannibals, in the name of which the narration proceeds. The discourses of the simple man and the cannibals "are both reliable, sustained by bodies that have been put to the test—of travel . . . or combat . . . and that . . . have not been altered by the ability of discourse to conceal particulars beneath the fiction of generality (the simple man 'has not the stuff to build,' and the Cannibals have 'no knowledge of letters')" (73). If these tested bodies—of the simple man, of the cannibal—guarantee an unaltered language that does not conceal what it claims to represent, de Certeau omits to say what guarantees these bodies *for us*—how we can tell that they have in fact undergone those experiences which allow them to guarantee language, how we can distinguish them from other bodies. By the legible signs those experiences leave on a body "touched, carved, tested by experience"?[22] This argument has to rely on a prior commitment to give to one level of reading—reading the body—a privileged simplicity and force. Even given this assumption, nothing allows us to pass with certainty between the level of accurately reading the body—"this body has traveled"—to the level of the guarantee—"because this man has traveled, he speaks the truth concerning a distant place."

De Certeau's discussion places a kind of transcendant value on the body, in particular the "savage" body, that the mechanics of Montaigne's text belie. It is well known, as de Certeau points out, that the essay "hides the literary sources at its basis beneath the authority of 'simple' speech: these sources include Gomara, Thevet, probably Léry, and not Las Casas, and so on." It would appear that the savage body guaranteeing language is, in fact, a body of writing, a *corps-texte* (to turn the pun). De Certeau goes on to declare that "an appeal to the senses . . . and a link to the body . . . seem capable of bringing closer and guaranteeing . . . the real that was lost by language. Proximity is thus necessary; for Montaigne, it takes the double form of the traveller and the private collection, both of which are his and in his home" (74). Proximity—this term glides surreptitiously into the place vacated by experience, by presence. And as proximity (to Indian artifacts, the simple traveler) replaces experience of the "real" in de Certeau's argument, it seems we are once again talking about interpretation, building upon objects—body, artifacts, cassava—grasped as signs or metonymic figures (73).[23] To be in proximity is not to be or to be with: nothing tells us that these material signs mean what we take them to mean, that the route from the "real" to that fragment we possess can be retraced—or that there was a recoverable beginning to that route at all, a "beautiful body 'without divisions'" (73). We have to speak of metonymy rather than synecdoche: How do we know of what whole the object forms a part? De Certeau himself leaves ambiguous the relationship of filiation between Montaigne's narrative and the materials he has collected—servant, museum, library. And these, in order for Montaigne to own them as "his and in his home," must themselves be movable, detachable from other proximate bodies, sources, filiations.

Let me recall for a moment Montaigne's critique, alluded to earlier, of subtle speakers who "Hyperbolize the matter" of their testimony "to purchase credit to their judgement, and draw you on to beleeve them" (162). The economic terminology introduced here is suggestive (the original French has "pour donner crédit à leur jugement et vous y attirer"); these speakers detach their narrative from its referent ("experience of a particular fountain," for example) in order to increase their "credit," the social or rhetorical value of their speech. This inflation *depends* for its possibility on severing an initial reliance of words on things: "They never represent things truly, but fashion and maske them according to the visage they saw them in." This severance, and the consequent drift of representation away from the referent (from "things" to "visage" to "maske"), defines the impropriety of their language for Montaigne. However, a similar drifting or voyaging stands as the necessary precondition for Montaigne's proximity to the New World in "the double form of the traveler and the private collection, both of which are his and in his home." What becomes Montaigne's property, actually and rhetorically (under the sign of "je voy"), must already have been "carried from a place in which it is proper to one in which it is not proper."[24] The objects of the private collection have undergone the process that makes words figurative or metaphorical; what Derrida says concerning the potential separation of metaphors from their origins surely applies here also: "There being no longer any properly named reference in such a metaphor, the figure of speech sets out on a voyage into a long and hidden sentence, a hidden recitative, with no assurance that we shall be led back to the proper name."[25]

Montaigne claims that the reliable report emerges at the end of an unbroken line from writing, to the memory of experience, to the experience of a particular thing, to the thing itself. It is the presence of that *thing* at the beginning which authorizes such writing—for de Certeau, the presence of a savage or simple body that authorizes speech. The conditions for Montaigne's proximity to American objects and to the body of the simple reporter are, first, that these be detachable from their places of origin, movable, and capable of participating in symbolic and economic systems of exchange; then, that they can be owned or hired, that is, subjected to an order and to a name that are not their own. What underlies Montaigne's text, however, is not the presence of bodies or things but a chain of metonymies, of signs whose filiation is indeterminate. What Montaigne proposes as the proper goal and end of language, and as what rescues language from figurative drift—Spenser's "matter of just memory"—exists in his text only as constructed by several orders of artifice: ownership, plagiarism, and the rhetorical figures of metaphor (carrying across) and metonymy (transfer). If the solidity of these bodies and things can be dissolved as it was constructed, by an analysis of rhetorical procedures, we may wish to give a different account of the discovery text, as well as of things and bodies.

Ralegh's *Discoverie* identifies itself as a defensive gesture against the potential ambiguity of the material in its broadest reference: the content of narrative, marks of experience on the body, objects.

Because there haue been diuers opinions conceiued of the golde oare brought from *Guiana*, and for that an Alderman of London and an officer of her maiesties minte, hath giuen out that the same is of no price, I haue thought good by the addition of these lines to giue aunswere as well to the said malicious slaunder, as to other obiections. . . . Others haue deuised that the same oare was had from Barbery, and that we caried it with vs into *Guiana*: surely the singularitie of that deuice, I do not well comprehend, for mine owne parte, I am not so much in loue with these long voiages, as to deuise, thereby to cozen my selfe . . . to sustaine the care and labour of such an enterprize, excepte the same had more comfort, then the fetching of *Marcasite* in *Guiana*, or bying of gold oare in Barbery. (xi–xiii)

In the introductory material to the *Discoverie*, Ralegh announces that text as his response to three allegations, two of which appear above: that the gold ore he brought back from Guiana contains no gold; that Ralegh acquired the ore not in Guiana but in East Africa; that Ralegh never left England at all, but concealed himself in Cornwall for the duration of the supposed voyage. Language—the discovery narrative—must step in to verify the object and the "parched and withered" body; but those *things* were themselves supposed to testify, to prop up or substantiate Ralegh's claims.

Edmund Spenser's "Dedicatory Sonnet" to Ralegh accompanying *The Faerie Queene* excuses his "unseasoning" of Ralegh's ear by claiming that his own unworthy poem occupies a place left vacant by the deferral or withholding of Ralegh's "golden showre" of words:

> Yet till that thou thy Poeme wilt make knowne,
> Let thy faire Cinthias praises be thus rudely showne.

Ralegh's career as a discoverer, as well, associates itself with places whose location does not appear to remain fixed, and with arrivals or consummations continually deferred—over hours, years, decades, centuries.

III

When wee landed we found few people, for the Lord of that place was gone with diuers Canoas *aboue 400 miles of, vpon a iourney towards the head of* Orenoque *to trade for gold . . . who afterward vnfortunatly passed by vs as we rode at an ancor in the port of* Morequito *in the dark of night, and yet came so neer vs, as his* Canoas *grated against our barges: he left one of his companie at the port of* Morequito, *by whom we vnderstood that he had brought . . . diuers plates of gold, and had great store of fine peeces of cotton cloth, and cotton beds. (56–57)*

Ralegh's text is a tissue of distances: distance from home, the distance and time one traverses in the narrative, the distance between oneself and the thing one is attempting to "discover"—gold mines, a golden city, at least the canoe of a chief who has traded for gold. The distance from discovery persists, reiterated time and time again in the *Discoverie*, so much so that one begins to wonder if this distance is not as much a product of human wish as are the fantastic objects it conceals.

Ralegh's expedition is literally a search for the referent, a place to which can be attached the proper names *Manoa* and *El Dorado*. At the same time, there seems to be some considerable force in the text working against trying to close the distance between words, or fantasies, and things. Ralegh's pursuit of gold swerves and halts as if that desire mingled with a willful misprision or holding back. It isn't that Ralegh does not find El Dorado—there was nothing there to find, at least nothing like what El Dorado appeared to mean to him. Rather, at the moments when, on his own account, he comes close to a place where words might be tried against things, invariably both narrator and narrative turn away. Again and again, divergences and distractions mark the moments where we might expect to find "real" discoveries, if not the kinds of discoveries Ralegh set out to make at least discovery of what was *there* in the places the Indians pointed to, golden city or wilderness.

For many of Ralegh's missing referents we can at least describe the trajectory of their passage, or rather a genealogy, a trace that might have been the history of a thing.[26] This is the case with *Manoa* and *El Dorado*. As Richard Schomburgk, Ralegh's nineteenth-century editor, tells it, "The name El Dorado was not originally used to designate any particular region, but a custom, which, as related by the Indians, was in itself sufficiently remarkable."[27] The accounts fell into two schools: according to one, the religious custom of a certain sect was for the chief priest, before the sacrifice, to smear his hands and face with grease and have "powder of gold" sprinkled on them; the other rumor was of "a sovereign prince . . . who on public occasions appeared with his body sprinkled over with gold-dust; hence the name El Dorado was given to him, meaning in Spanish 'the gilded' or 'golden,' which was afterward applied to the whole region." By 1539, Schomburgk continues, Gonzalo Pizarro was looking for "a great prince, of whom report related that he was covered with powdered gold, so that from head to foot he resembled a golden figure worked by the hands of a skilful artist" (xlix). The presumed locale of the king passed from place to place, accumulating details: a "gold-covered" city, surrounding mountains "so impregnated with gold, they shone with a dazzling splendor," a vast lake, even a genealogy and promotion for the prince—"The Emperour now raigning is discended from those magnificent Princes of Peru of whose large territories, of whose pollicies, conquests, edifices, and riches *Pedro de Cieza, Francisco Lopez*, and others haue written large discourses" (*Discoverie*, 11).

Ralegh relates a terminal version of the story, which runs as follows:

Those *Guianians* and also the borderers, and all others in that tract which I haue seen are marueylous great drunkardes . . . and at the times of their solemne feasts when the Emperor carowseth . . . the manner is thus. All those that pledge him are first stripped naked, and their bodies annoynted al ouer with a kinde of white *Balsamum* (by them called *Curcai*) of which there is great plenty and yet very deare amongst them, and it is of all other the most pretious, wherof we haue had good experience: when they are annointed all ouer, certaine seruants of the Emperor hauing prepared gold made into fine powder blow it thorow hollow canes vpon their naked bodies, vntill they be al shining from the foote to the head, and in this sort they sit drinking. . . . The same is also confirmed by a letter written into *Spaine* which was intercepted, which master *Robert Dudley* told me he had seen. (20)

We might be excused for understanding this passage as a narrative of firsthand observation. The lead in to the El Dorado material certainly does claim a source in experience: "in that tract which I haue seen" (Jonathan Goldberg has pointed out the submerged pun on *tract*, a piece of writing). In what follows, similar traces of the first person punctuate the body of the narrative, laying claim to details that in turn seem to substantiate the whole: the vice "in which I think no nation can compare with them"; the ointment "wherof we haue had good experience"; the letter "master *Robert Dudley* told me he had seene." Imperceptibly, Ralegh moves from the drunken festivities he did witness to another narrative altogether, the relation of "the first that euer sawe *Manoa* . . . *Iohannes Martines* master of the munition to *Ordace*" (17)—it is this "relation" from which Ralegh derives the material he lays out in such proprietary fashion. Nor does he derive his information directly: "The relation of this *Martynes* . . . is to be seene in the Chauncery of *Saint Iuan de puerto rico*, whereof *Berreo* had a coppie."[28]

Martines—so the story goes—spent seven months in Manoa, the fabled El Dorado, and on his departure was escorted by "diuers *Guianians* . . . all loden with as much gold as they could carrie." Unfortunately, the company was robbed by the Orenoqueponi before reaching civilization, leaving only two gourds filled with gold beads; at his death, Martines delivered both the relation and the remnant gold to his confessor. Schomburgk cites Alexander von Humboldt's opinion that the "relation of this Martynes" was itself a compendium of other travelers' tales.[29] Ralegh goes on to describe subsequent attempts at invading Guiana (which sometimes, as here, apparently means Manoa—although not always) by a succession of Spaniards, all unsuccessful. Their failure, he argues, shows the discovery is "reserued for her Maiestie and the *English* nation" (22).

Ralegh deploys Spanish "relations of the countrie" in two quite opposite ways. On the one hand, we hear of many Spaniards who have been to Manoa—not only Martines, and the "Frier, and those nine Spaniards" killed by Morequito (80), but that indeterminate group, never named or enumerated, who have seen the city and "assure" Ralegh that its riches exceed that of any city in the known world. At the same time, he gives repeated examples of Spanish failure not just to conquer Manoa but to *find* Guiana, from "Diego Ordace" (18), "Agiri" (22), up to Berreo in the present, who "neuer could enter so far into the land as my selfe with that poore troupe or rather a handfull of men" (25). Guiana remains elusive—difficult to find, without "passage or entrance." Only on Lawrence Keymis's second voyage, the following year (1596), did he succeed in obtaining the seemingly preliminary information that "*Muchikeri* is the name of the countrie where *Macureguerai* the first towne of the Empire of *Guiana* is seated."[30] Macureguerai is referred to in Ralegh's text as "the first ciuill towne of *Guiana*" and "the frontier towne of the Empire" (80, 81). Ralegh's men, in their furthest penetration inland, do not reach it.

The moment of Ralegh's furthest movement inland gives quite spectacular form to the divergence I want to delineate. Topiawari, the 110-year-old king of Arromaia, comes fourteen miles on foot to bring pineapples and other victuals to the English, and discourses to them of the recent history and geography of the area, specifically "as touching Guiana" (74). Directed by him, Ralegh and his company sail westward up the Orinoco River toward the Caroli River, "as well bicause it was maruellous of it selfe, as also for that I vnderstood it led to the strongest nations of all the frontires, that were enimies to the *Epuremei* [inhabitants of Macureguerai], which are subiects to *Inga*, Emperor of *Guiana*, and *Manoa*" (78). When they arrive, the rivers have risen so high it is impossible to row up the Caroli against the stream, but Ralegh sends a company of men overland toward a town some twenty miles away, where they are to seek a guide for the next town, which "adioyned to *Macureguarai*, which was the frontier towne of the Empire" (81). (The "Empire" appears as the last term in a series of adjoining towns, related as "next . . . next.")

At this point, Ralegh himself with "some halfe a dosen shot" marches overland in a different direction, to see the Caroli's marvelous waterfalls. As they approach the falls, Ralegh's prose becomes increasingly lyrical, culminating in what a penciled note in the margin of my edition calls "the great prose set piece of this work" and which Stephen Greenblatt compares both to the Red Crosse Knight's vision of the New Jerusalem and to Calidore's vision of Mount Acidale.[31]

I neuer saw a more beawtifull country, nor more liuely prospectes, hils so raised heere and there ouer the vallies, the riuer winding into diuers braunches, the plaines adioyning without bush or stubble, all faire greene grasse, the ground of hard sand easy to march on, eyther for horse or foote, the deare crossing in euery path, the birdes towardes the euening singing on euery tree with a thousand seuerall tunes, cranes and herons of white, crimson, and carnation pearching on the riuers side, the ayre fresh with a gentle easterlie wind, and euery stone that we stooped to take vp, promised eyther gold or siluer by his complexion. (82)

The casual stooping to take up stones, and the promise of their complexion, develop into a scene of frustration, confusion, and growing anxiety. The promising stones taken up by the company "were for the most part but culored . . . yet such as had no iudgement or experience kept all that glistered" (83). These stones, along with pyrite from Trinidad, will be returned to London to be assayed, and there "[breed] an opinion that all the rest is of the same." Ralegh quotes a Spaniard's opinion that the stones were "*El Madre deloro*, and that the mine was farther in the grounde"—and quickly moves to distance himself from such fantasy: "It shall bee founde a weake policie in mee, eyther to betray my selfe, or my Countrey with imaginations." Some stones of another kind they scratch out of the rock itself, which is "like a flint, and altogether as hard or harder, and besides the veynes lie a fathome or two deepe" (82).

This is the ultimate scene of Ralegh's discovery, its furthest reach. What was promised: a land where nature shimmered with gold, and art produced golden replicas of the ordinary world—a land where the inhabitants are eager to surrender themselves, a land "reserved" for the English, which "hath yet her Maydenhead" (115). Instead, they find themselves off the track, left behind, scrabbling with fingers and daggers against a hard rock, wanting "all thinges requisite saue onlie our desires" and those desires effective only to collect pieces of pyrite, fool's gold. From this point in the text to the point at which "we left the mouth of *Caroli*, and arriued againe at the port of *Morequito* where we were before" (90)—indeed, in the remainder of his narrative—Ralegh makes no mention of the expedition sent out toward the borders of Guiana. That moment—if not of discovery, of the nearest approach to one—disappears under the marvels of the waterfall, the rush of Ralegh's description.

Ralegh makes the same move that he was to "confess" in the *Declaration* twenty years later—he turns away from discovery to a discussion of credibility and credit, or belief: the credit wrongly accorded the crew's "fool's gold"; the credulity Ralegh disavows concerning the Spaniard's assertion; the credibility of a body willingly submitted to "that lodging, watching, care, perill, diseases, ill sauoures, bad fare, and many other mischiefes that accompany these voyages" (83). (Soon after we arrive at a circumstantial account of headless men, one of the scandals—for historians—of Ralegh's narrative.) Keymis's expedition party never returns and reports; at a certain point they silently rejoin the company—perhaps while

Topiawari is telling Ralegh that Macureguarai is "fower daies iourney from his towne" (92)—and when Keymis is next named, he is being dispatched again toward a rumored mine (99).

Ralegh wrote *The Discoverie of Guiana* about not discovering Guiana; twenty years later, he is still eager to prove that there was something there "to be confessed"—that is, "made known" or discovered. This hidden residue is registered in the primary meaning of *to confess*: "to declare or disclose (something which one has kept or allowed to remain secret as being prejudicial or inconvenient to oneself)" (*OED*).[32] (We might recall, at this point, Spenser's chiding of Ralegh for his reluctance to "make knowne" his promised or projected poem to Elizabeth/Cinthia.) What could be "prejudicial or inconvenient" to Ralegh in discovering Guiana? To put it differently, what would be the interest in falling short of a complete disclosure?

The *Discoverie* suggests a succession of terms for the place of the hidden deposit. Ralegh composes lengthy apologetics for not having investigated Spanish gold mines of which an Indian pilot informed him. The rivers were rising; the company lacked men and equipment; the best mines were "defended with rocks of hard stone." These were the physical obstacles to reaching and working the mine—but *finding* it would have been strategically unwise.

I thought it best not to houer thereabouts, least if the same had been perceiued by the company, there would haue bin by this time many barks and ships set out, and perchance other nations would also haue gotten of ours for Pilots, so as both our selues might haue been preuented, and all our care taken for good vsage of the people been vtterly lost, by those that onely respect present profit. . . . Such a quantitie as would haue serued our turnes we could not haue had, but a discouery of the mines *to our infinite disaduantage* we had made. (59–60; italics mine)

Ralegh makes explicit in this passage his dissociation from "those that onely respect present profit." It would be misleading, however, to leave this statement undiscussed; Ralegh was far from uninterested in profit. It is the nature of the profit that must be understood.

Ralegh writes, in the "Epistle Dedicatorie" to Charles Howard and Robert Cecil, "I haue chosen rather to beare the burthen of pouerty, then reproch, & rather to endure a second trauel & the chaunces therof, then to haue defaced an enterprise of so great assurance" (x). We can particularize, I believe, the kind of reproachful acts and the kind of defacement that were chiefly at issue. Todorov writes of Cortés in a similar situation that

he will severely punish pillagers in his own army because the latter *take* what must not be taken and *give* an unfavorable impression of themselves. . . . The reason for these actions is precisely Cortés' desire to control the information the Indians receive: "In order to avoid the appearance of avarice on their part, and to dispel the notion that their single motive for coming was to acquire gold, all should pretend ignorance of it." . . . We note the role incipiently taken by the vocabulary of pretense: "appearance." (111)[33]

Ralegh also makes clear that his company was not permitted to "take what must not be taken": "I suffred not anie man to take . . . so much as a *Pina*, or a *Potato* roote, without giuing them contentment" (61). As Todorov points out, such actions aim primarily at creating a certain impression; Ralegh will present himself to the inhabitants of Trinidad and Guiana not as an invader but as offering a relationship of tutelage and protection.

I made them vnderstand that I was the seruant of a Queene, who was the great *Casique* of the north, and a virgin . . . that she was an enemy to the *Castellani* in respect of their tyrannie and oppression, and that she deliuered all such nations about her, as were by them oppressed, and . . . had sent me to free them also, and withal to defend the countrey of *Guiana* from their inuasion and conquest. (8)

Ralegh engages a kind of fantasy here, of a conquest by love rather than violence. In one lyrical moment of the narrative, he will write of seeing on his voyage "the most beautifull countrie that euer mine eies beheld," but the particular beauty of the country is its appearance of being *already* conquered, *already* domesticated.

Heere we beheld . . . in diuers parts groues of trees by themselues, as if they had been by all the art and labour in the world so made of purpose: and stil as we rowed, the Deere came downe feeding by the waters side, as if they had beene vsed to a keepers call. (57)

The absence of an actual keeper figures as an internalization of order, figuring not wildness, lack of "discipline," but only an unoccupied place of enjoyment or exploitation.

This colonial romance seems to extend itself to "taking" in general; while Berreo acquires by trade quite a cargo of gold, Ralegh sends to his patrons two examples "recovered by chance," explaining that "I did not in any sort make my desire of golde knowen. . . . I gaue among them manye more peeces of Golde then I receaued of the new money . . . with her Maiesties picture" (96). Elsewhere, Ralegh's desire assumes a franker tone, at least in the text.

I was enformed of one of the *Cassiqui* of the valley of *Amariocapana* which had buried with him a little before our arriuall, a chaire of Golde most curiously wrought. . . . But if wee shoulde haue grieued them in their religion at the first, before they had beene taught better, and haue digged vppe their graues, wee had lost them all. (110)

Here alone in the *Discoverie* is mention made of converting the Indians. This passage, following as it does a detailed and not unsympathetic account of American religious, marital, and funeral customs, seems not so much to exist in tension with that account as to gloss it. The *Discoverie* operates on two levels, and that second level of the gloss underlies the level of romance, so well understood or so fully withheld it surfaces only at rare moments. When these do occur, the effect is to cast the remainder of the text as blandly ironic: "(Whereas now they haue heard we were enemies to the Spaniards and were sent by her Maiestie to relieue them) they would as good cheape haue ioyned with the Spanyardes at our returne, as to haue yeelded vnto vs" (95). A few pages later, Ralegh will describe the willingness of certain chieftains to ally themselves with the English, after they "perceiued our purpose, and sawe that we came as enemies to the Spanyardes onely" (103).

Ralegh's discovery seems to require a kind of strategic balancing: between opening up what is hidden—discovering the other—and discovering or revealing one's own unacceptable violence. Ralegh conceives of "discovering" Guiana precisely as a violent act—yet he withholds that violence in action and, at least partially, in his language. After all, it is not from the Indians that Ralegh fears reproach but from the queen, and it is to her that he repeatedly defers: "Although the desire of gold will aunswere many obiections . . . it woulde haue been . . . an vtter ouerthrowe to the enterprize, if the same should be hereafter by her Maiestie attempted" (95); "And therefore I held my first resolution, that her maiesty should eyther accept or refuse the enterprise, ere any thing shoulde be done that might in any sort hinder the same" (110).

The *Discoverie* is thus a text, like Ralegh's famous letter to Cecil from prison, addressed to the queen under guise of addressing others.[34] The "Epistle Dedicatorie" identifies Ralegh's aim in making the voyage and producing the report as "euen to appease so powrefull a displeasure" (iv). The voyage to Guiana, then, occurs between potential reproach and past displeasure, concerning a prior fault that William Camden famously names as sexual transgression: "Walter Ralegh, captain of the Queen's Guard, having violated the queen's maid of honor, later married her."[35] Willard Wallace quotes an anonymous letter writer on Ralegh's fault: "All is alarm and confusion at this discovery of the discoverer, and not indeed of a new continent, but of a new incontinent."[36] The fault was not merely "incontinence"; Arthur Marotti has noted the politicization of sexual activity at the court, and the displacement of male sexual advances onto the maids of honor who surrounded the queen.[37] Jonathan Goldberg identifies Ralegh with the figure of Timias in *The Faerie Queene*, book 4, whom Belphoebe punishes for what she misunderstands as lust for another woman: "Elizabeth's court was a place of endless courting . . . and woe to the courtier who, like Ralegh (like Timias), sought favor elsewhere. Other marriages were betrayals in Elizabeth's eyes."[38]

It seems clear that Elizabeth punishes Ralegh for a sexual fault; we might ask whether her anger results from betrayal—his displacement of desire onto Elizabeth Throckmorton as a surrogate for the queen—or his incontinence, the symbolic impropriety of deflowering a woman who was precisely a surrogate for the queen. In either case, Ralegh's transgression amounted to a crude or naive disruption of the economy of symbols and desires in and by which Elizabeth ruled. The *Discoverie of Guiana* reenacts and rewrites the scene of Ralegh's transgression, enacting fidelity and continence over and over.

Both Ralegh and Keymis will image Guiana as a woman, and a woman specifically presented as a sexual object.[39] Ralegh sums up his discovery in the famous passage: "To conclude, *Guiana* is a Countrey that hath yet her Maydenhead. . . . It hath neuer been entred by any armie of strength, and neuer conquered or possessed by any Christian Prince" (115). This maidenhead, for Ralegh, is "what must not be taken"; Guiana's virginity is preserved at the symbolic level as well as the literal:

> I protest before the maiestie of the liuing God, that I neither know nor beleeue, that any of our companie one or other, by violence or otherwise, euer knew any of their women, and yet we saw many hundreds, and had many in our power, and of those very yoong, and excellently fauored which came among vs without deceit, starke naked. Nothing got vs more loue among them then this vsage . . . which course . . . drew them to admire hir Maiestie, whose commandement I told them it was. (61)

Ralegh's feminization of Guiana, which construes discovery and conquest as forms of sexual violence, allows him also to represent at the symbolic as well as the literal level the absence of rape, the withholding of male desire. In that space of absence, the power of the queen can be celebrated in a new and flattering way, as a power between women that relegates men to an instrumental status: "Where the south border of *Guiana* reacheth to the Dominion and Empire of the *Amazones*, those women shall heereby heare the name of a virgin, which is not onely able to defend her owne territories and her neighbors, but also to inuade and conquere so great Empyres and so farre remoued" (120).[40]

George Chapman's "De Guiana, carmen Epicum," prefixed to Keymis's narrative of his own voyage, gives the most explicit expression to this version of the royal romance:

> *Guiana*, whose rich feet are mines of golde,
> Whose forehead knockes against the roofe of Starres,
> Stands on her tiptoes at faire *England* looking,
> Kissing her hand, bowing her mightie breast,
> And euery signe of all submission making,
> To be her sister, and the daughter both
> Of our most sacred Maide: Whose barrenness
> Is the true fruite of vertue, that may get,
> Beare and bring foorth anew in all perfection,
> What heretofore sauage corruption held
> In barbarous *Chaos*; and in this affaire
> Become her father, mother, and her heire.[41]

Here, masculine sexuality, indeed male bodies altogether, are not merely discreet but altogether absent. In their place is Elizabeth's ability to reproduce herself symbolically, in contrast to the "corruption" and "chaos" of biological reproduction. Chapman's poem substitutes metaphorical for biological relations, bringing together terms that properly speaking are separate: father and mother, sister and daughter. The elision or elimination of biology in this parthenogenetic scene allows for the representation of improper combinations without impropriety: although Guiana is both sister and daughter, her symbolic filiation to Elizabeth as mother and father cancels the incestuous mingling that "sister and . . . daughter both" would otherwise entail. Elizabeth and Guiana approach each other by a system of (family) relations whose engendering term, or whose engenderment, must not appear; the appearance of a bodily father would manifest, in Sophocles' words, "an incestuous kinship of fathers and brothers and sons, of brides and wives and mothers, yes, all the foulest shame that is wrought among men!"[42] With Oedipus, we find ourselves at the classic place of the thing that must not be disclosed. As Aristotle says, "The deed is outside the play."[43] Held in reserve, then, is that unthinkably present body which connects and engenders all relations in the play. From a mine, to the desire for profit; from that desire to an intention to take profit; from the intention to the violence of carrying it out; from the violence of conquest to the violence of sex; from sexual violence to the male body, from the male body to the father, and from the father to Oedipus: Ralegh's strategy of representing potential actions held in reserve resembles the exclusion of Oedipus' deed from that which can be represented in a play. But the appearance of something in reserve is in a way simply that, an appearance generated by the series of contiguous terms I describe. As James discovered, what Ralegh had in reserve was precisely *no*thing.

Chapman's scene of a parthenogenetic relation drawn between Elizabeth and Guiana draws its terms—virgin queen, virgin land—from Ralegh's personification of Guiana as a virgin whose defloration the queen forbids. Behind that image are multiple scenes and multiple figures both at home and abroad: not only the virgin body of Elizabeth Throckmorton and Ralegh's fault of incontinence, but a continent of virgins and a continence or deferral that could be called failure. Ralegh represents his command to his men not to rape Guianan women as obedience to the queen's prior command, a command that had never actually been given. Deferral or withholding of sexual violence then becomes a figure for Ralegh's general relation to Guiana, his repeated turning away from the aims of his "discovery": Guiana itself, Manoa, gold mines, tombs rich with gold—gold in general, whether mined, traded for, conquered or stolen.[44] This turning away could be otherwise construed, however: as a failure to reach or achieve what was sought, to find the place known as "El Dorado," the gold of the referent.

But didn't Ralegh "fail" just because what he was looking for did not exist? And if that is all that happened, is there really any more to say? At least here, the question can be answered in particular: El Dorado *existed* as the latest—if not necessarily the last—link in a chain of metonymies that Schomburgk traces or retraces. At the beginning, the "strange custom" of a priest gilding his face and hands; from the priest to a king who gilds his entire body; from that king to an emperor whose gilded courtiers sit feasting "by twenties and hundreds"; from that court to a city in which every animal, artifact, and natural object has "the counterfeat in gold."

All the vessels of his home, table, and kitchin were of gold and siluer. . . . He had in his wardroppe hollow statues of golde which seemed giants, and figures in proportion and bignes of all the beastes, birdes, trees and hearbes, that the earth bringeth forth: and of all the fishes that the sea or waters of his kingdome breedeth. Hee had also ropes, budgets, chestes and troughs of golde and siluer, heapes of billets of golde that seemed woode, marked out to burne. (14)

Priest/hands and face; king/body; emperor/courtiers; city/men, animals, nature, art: movement along the links of this chain, however, seems to violate the decorum of figurative language. For Derrida, "Metaphor is able to display properties, to relate to each other properties which have been abstracted from the essence of different things, to make them known on the basis of their resemblance, without ever directly, fully, or properly stating the essence, without itself making visible the truth of the thing itself" (50). On this Aristotelian model, we begin with "the essence" or the "thing itself"; we detach from that thing itself what participates in it but is at the same time detachable: a property. That property may then be exchanged with a second property, which itself may stand next to a second thing to which it is "proper"—or next to a third property to which it is related "on the basis of . . . resemblance," and so on.

Even when that chain of exchanges departs on such an indefinite voyage, the presumption remains that somewhere, somehow, we began with the "properly named reference," that initial inversion between property and essence, and departed from that thing in successive exchanges. We might recall, for instance, the chain of substitutions Montaigne sees in subtle speech: things → visage → mask, where the use of ornamented language leads to a progressive attenuation of substance. In the case of El Dorado, however, we move back toward the first link by synecdoches: the court is only part of the city, the king only a member of the court, the priest only a function of the king. Each reconstitution, rather than bringing us closer to a full instantiation, entails a loss. We begin with golden mountains; we arrive at a pair of hands powdered with gold that perform a ritual.

If, looking for the material body or the properly named referent on which depends the genealogy of figures terminating in the city "El Dorado," we find at our furthest reach a moment of artifice, in which the pervasive gold has faded to a dusting, we must say not that we have arrived but that we have reached some point of exhaustion. Exhaustion of gold, which glimmered as the link between El Dorado, the emperor's manifold "counterfeats" and some natural place, some mine concealing raw ore in limitless abundance; exhaustion, also, of the narrative "proper." Behind the golden hands (if they are "real hands"—and what does it mean to ask that?) must be, somewhere, a not necessarily limitless mine; but a mine producing only dustings of gold belongs to another narrative, certainly not the narrative of El Dorado. Ralegh's turning back permits that narrative to continue, permits the body or the thing to glimmer still at the limit of exhaustion—albeit the way back is only the way to that word still lacking substance, to further voyages, and further tropes.[45]

Ralegh writes to Howard and Cecil, "Your loues sought me out in the darkest shadow of aduersitie . . . which though I cannot requite, yet I shal euer acknowledge: and the great debt which I haue no power to pay, I can doe no more for a time but confesse to be due" (iii–iv). From the exhausted and belated language of the "Epistle Dedicatorie" emerges the emblem of that gesture which deposits its "material" at the border of the text: "the great debt . . . I . . . confesse to be due."

Notes

1. Adrienne Rich, *The Dream of a Common Language: Poems 1974–1977* (New York, 1978).
2. Walter Ralegh, *The Discoverie of the Large, Rich and Bewtiful Empire of Gviana, with a Relation of the Great and Golden City of Manoa (which the Spaniards call El Dorado) and the prouinces of Emeria, Arromaia, Amapaia and other Countries, with their riuers, adioyning* (1596), ed. Robert Schomburgk (London, 1848), 9. Further references cited in the text.
3. *A Declaration of the Demeanor and Carriage of Sir W. Ralegh* (1618; New York, 1971), 9. Further references cited in the text.
4. V. T. Harlow, *Ralegh's Last Voyage* (London, 1932), 277; Willard M. Wallace, *Sir Walter Ralegh* (Princeton, N.J., 1959), 279.
5. *Declaration*, 35.
6. Harlow, *Last Voyage*, 303.
7. See Wallace, *Ralegh*, 280. Documentary evidence concerning Ralegh's final expedition is extensive and too complex to be discussed in any detail here. Harlow prints many of the relevant letters and other documents, including Spanish and French sources; he also offers a detailed interpretation of the evidence.
8. Wallace notes that "subsequent explorers have confirmed . . . that gold is to be found in Guiana (now Venezuela)"; *Ralegh*, 120.
9. "To most of [Ralegh's contemporaries], his *Discovery* was simply a fantastic potpourri of well-told fabrications, a verdict agreed to as late as the eighteenth century by the historian David Hume"; ibid. Ralegh's namesake defends him: "The disappointing results of the expedition are accurately recorded, but so strong is the author's belief in his preconceived idea, that, from the title onward, his narrative conveys the impression of great things on the verge of achievement and untold wealth ready at the touch to fall into England's lap"; Walter A. Raleigh, "The English Voyages of the Sixteenth Century," in Richard Hakluyt, *The Principall Navigations*, vol. 12 (Glasgow, 1904), 73.
10. Wallace, *Ralegh*, 298.
11. Edmund Spenser, *The Faerie Queene*, ed. A. C. Hamilton (New York, 1977), book 2, proem.
12. William Strachey, *Historie of Travell into Virginia Brittania*, ed. Louis B. Wright and Virginia Freund (London, 1953), 138.
13. Jacques Derrida, "White Mythology," *New Literary History* 6 (1974): 29. Further references cited in the text.

14. George Puttenham, *The Arte of English Poesie* (Kent, Ohio, 1970), 189.

15. Irma Staza Majer, *The Notion of Singularity: The Travel Journals of Michel de Montaigne and Jean de Léry* (Ph.D. diss., The Johns Hopkins University, 1982), 4.

16. Tzvetan Todorov, *The Conquest of America: The Question of the Other*, trans. Richard Howard (New York, 1984), 5.

17. Here, as will appear later in my discussion of Montaigne and de Certeau, we see not only an ontological but also an ethnological presumption: that the New World's inhabitants could not write, that their relationship to language was at once simpler and less skilled than that of Europeans. Recent work on Mesoamerican culture has challenged the historical basis of this theory, which I will critique on primarily rhetorical grounds. Stephen Greenblatt traces the genesis of the idea in "Learning to Curse: Aspects of Linguistic Colonialism in the Sixteenth Century," in *First Images of America*, ed. Fredi Chiapelli, 2 vols. (Berkeley, 1976), 2:561–80. Gordon Brotherston, in "Towards a Grammatology of America: Lévi-Strauss, Derrida, and the Native New World Text," notes Lévi-Strauss's "failure to mention the fact of . . . literacy" in his native American subjects, and goes on to describe the persistent cultural uses of script and paper in Mesoamerica (a region whose archaeological definition depends, Brotherston notes, "in part on the manufacture and use there of screenfold books of paper and parchment"); in *Literature, Politics, and Theory*, ed. Francis Barker et al. (London, 1984), 205. José Piedra, in a paper entitled "Gnawing at the New World Edge of the Renaissance" delivered at the 1988 convention of the Modern Language Association, details the production and consumption of Mesoamerican paper both by native Americans and by the colonial Spanish; a fuller version of this argument, "The Value of Paper," appears in *Res* 16 (Autumn 1988): 85–104.

18. Edmundo O'Gorman, *The Invention of America* (Bloomington, Ind., 1961), 40–41.

19. J. Hillis Miller makes the point that "'materiality,' or 'the material,' or 'the material base' is a catachrestic trope, side by side with others, for what can never be approached, named, perceived, felt, thought, or in any way encountered as such, though it is the hidden agent of all those phenomenal experiences"; "The Triumph of Theory, the Resistance to Reading, and the Question of the Material Base," *PMLA* 102 (May 1987): 289. While I find Miller's argument about agency somewhat problematic, I agree with him on the notion of "the material" as trope.

20. Michel de Montaigne, *The Essayes of Michael Lord of Montaigne*, trans. John Florio (1603; London, 1928), 163. Further references cited in the text.

21. Michel de Certeau, *Heterologies: Discourse on the Other* (Minneapolis, 1986), 73. Further references cited in the text.

22. Philip Sidney tells, in the *Apology for Poetry*, an exemplary story on the perils of taking marks on the body as a guarantee of authentic or truthful speech; *An Apology for Poetry*, ed. Forrest G. Robinson (Indianapolis, 1970). The story of the faithful servant appears an an instance of historical fidelity in the *Apology*:

    > Herodotus and Justin do both testify that Zopyrus, King Darius' faithful servant, seeing his master long resisted by the rebellious Babylonians, feigned himself in extreme disgrace of his king, for verifying of which he caused his own nose and ears to be cut off: and so flying to the Babylonians, was received, and for his known valor so far credited that he did find means to deliver them over to Darius. (33)

    Sidney notes that Xenophon's "poetic" version ameliorates the example by allowing the servant to keep his face intact; in either case, the servant's fidelity consists in betraying his auditors.

238   Mary C. Fuller

23. For a similar argument, see Eugenio Donato, "The Museum's Furnace: Notes Towards a Contextual Reading of *Bouvard and Pécuchet*," in Josué V. Harari, ed., *Textual Strategies* (Ithaca, N.Y., 1979), 213–38:

> The set of objects the Museum displays is sustained only by the fiction that they somehow constitute a coherent representational universe. . . . Should the fiction disappear, there is nothing left of the *Museum* but "bric-a-brac," a heap of meaningless and valueless fragments of objects which are incapable of substituting themselves either metonymically for the original objects or metaphorically for their representations. (223)

24. The author cited is Quintilian, defining a "figure of thought"; my source is Eugene Vance, "Chaucer, Spenser, and the Ideology of Translation," *Canadian Review of Comparative Literature* 8, no. 2 (Spring 1981): 217–38, 220n.

25. Derrida, "White Mythology," 44.

26. See the map facing p. 99 in Harlow, *Ralegh's Last Voyage*, showing the successive locations of San Thomé—a town that did in fact move, although not until after Ralegh's time.

27. Schomburgk, introduction to Ralegh, *Discoverie*, 1.

28. Don Antonio de Berreo was at the time of Ralegh's voyage governor of Trinidad, and Ralegh claims to have taken him prisoner.

29. Schomburgk, in Ralegh, *Discoverie*, 18.

30. Lawrence Keymis, *A Relation of the Second Voyage to Guiana* (1596; New York, 1968), sig. C3r.

31. Stephen Greenblatt, *Sir Walter Ralegh: The Renaissance Man and His Roles* (New Haven, 1973), 110.

32. See also sense 5 in the *OED*: "To make known or reveal by circumstance; to be evidence of; to manifest, prove, attest."

33. Todorov refers here to F. Lopez de Gomara, *Historia de la conquista de Mexico* (Mexico City, 1943).

34. The letter is quoted by Greenblatt, *Ralegh*, 23–24, and Wallace, *Ralegh*, 95; Greenblatt gives the source as Edward Edwards, *The Life of Sir Walter Ralegh . . . Together with His Letters*, 2 vols. (London, 1868), 2:51–52.

35. Schomburgk, in Ralegh, *Discoverie*, xliii, n. 1.

36. Wallace's source is J. Collier, "Continuation of New Materials for a Life of Sir Walter Raleigh," *Archaeologia* 34 (1852): 161.

37. I refer here to my notes of Arthur Marotti's seminar "Literary Text and Social Text" at The Johns Hopkins University, fall 1983.

38. Jonathan Goldberg, *Endlesse Worke* (Baltimore, 1981), 49, 132.

39. Taken in context of their audience, it is hard to decide which version is the most uneasy. Keymis portrays Guiana as a prostitute in search of custom: "Whole shyeres of fruitfull rich groundes lying now waste for want of people, doe prostitute themselues vnto us, like a faire and beautifull woman in the pride and flower of desired yeares"; *Relation*, sig. F2v.

40. Of five illustrations to the Latin edition of the *Discoverie* (Nuremberg, 1599), two are of the Amazons—the description of whom occupies slightly more than a page in the 1596 edition; 23–24, 27–29.

41. Keymis, *Relation*, sig. A1v.

42. Moses Hadas, ed., *The Complete Plays of Sophocles* (New York, 1971), 111.

43. Aristotle *Poetics* 1453b29–32, cited by Derrida, "White Mythology," 29.

44. John Donne also famously conjoins penetration of American mines and of the female

body: "O my America! my new-found land,/My kingdom, safeliest when with one man manned,/My mine of precious stones, my empery,/How blest am I in this discovering thee!"; "Elegy XIX. To His Mistress Going to Bed," lines 27–30.

45. Here my argument runs parallel to Derrida's, in substance and in trope; see "White Mythology," 45.

DAVID QUINT

Voices of Resistance:
The Epic Curse
and Camões's Adamastor

I

I N 1 6 1 0 G A S P A R P E R E Z D E V I L L A G R Á published a minor epic poem in unrhymed heroic verse, the *Historia de la Nueva Mexico*. It chronicles the Spanish exploration and conquest of what is now the American Southwest. Villagrá was an eyewitness and participant at the events he recounts, and while his poem is of small literary value, it is our chief, often exclusive historical source for the exploits of the New Mexican conquistadors. It is with the 1599 siege and destruction of the Acoma pueblo that Villagrá finds his true epic subject—events that inevitably evoke Troy, the model of all doomed epic cities.[1] The rebellious Acomans had ambushed and massacred eleven members of a Spanish patrol; the four-hundred-foot heights of their pueblo could not save them from a frightful retribution.

A punitive expeditionary force was sent out under the command of Vicente de Zaldívar, whose own brother lay among the Acomans' victims. It took only two days for the Spaniards to storm the seemingly impregnable pueblo, which they burned to the ground. Hundreds of its Indian defenders died, many committing suicide by throwing themselves into the flames of their houses or over the pueblo's sheer cliffs. It was later alleged that Zaldívar butchered others who had surrendered, avenging his brother's death. The remaining inhabitants of the pueblo were subsequently put on trial and condemned for their revolt. All over the age of twelve were sentenced to twenty years of servitude; males over twenty-five were to have one foot cut off as well.

Villagrá's poem does not describe the trial or the fate of the survivors. It ends instead with a highly dramatic incident during the mopping-up campaign that followed Acoma's downfall. Two fugitives from Acoma, Tempal and Cotumbo, had been taken prisoner and held in a kiva in the pueblo of San Juan. The prisoners now barricaded themselves in the kiva and kept their captors at bay, hurling stones at anyone who approached them. After three days they asked the Spanish general, Don Juan de Oñate, for two daggers with which to kill themselves. After vain attempts to persuade them to surrender and convert to Christianity, Oñate instead sent them two ropes. The captives made two nooses, placed them around their necks, came out into the open, and climbed into the branches of a nearby tree. Fastening the ropes to its boughs, they turned and spoke defiantly to their conquerors.

> Soldados advertid que aqui colgados,
> Destos rollizos troncos os dexamos,
> Los miserabiles cuerpos por despojos,
> De la victoria illustre que alcancastes,
> De aquellos desdichados que podridos,
> Estan sobre su sangre rebolcados,
> Sepulcros que tomaron, porque quiso,
> Assi fortuna infame perseguirnos,
> Con mano poderosa y acabarnos.
> Gustosos quedareis, que ya cerramos,
> Las puertas al vivir, y nos partimos,
> Y libres nuetras tierras os dexamos,
> Dormid á sueno suelto, pues ninguno,
> Bolvio jamas con nueva del cammino
> Incierto y trabajoso que llevamos,
> Mas de una cosa ciertos os hazemos,
> Que si bolver podemos a vengarnos,
> Que non parieron madres Castellanas,
> Ni barvaras tampoco en todo el mundo,
> Mas desdichados hijos que â vosotros.

[Soldiers, take note that here we give you our miserable bodies, hanging from these sturdy boughs, as spoils of the famous victory that you have obtained, the reward for those wretched companions of yours we have killed who lie rotting drenched in their blood, the only burial that they found. Because infamous Fortune has thus wished to hound and destroy us with her powerful hand, you will remain here content, for now we close our gates on this life and take leave, and we freely give you our lands. Sleep with untroubled dreams, since no one ever returned with tidings from the uncertain and toilsome road upon which we set out; but we make you certain of one thing: that if we can return to avenge ourselves, no sons born to Castilian or Indian mothers in the whole wide world will be as wretched as you.][2]

With this ringing curse, the two Indians drop from the branches and hang themselves. Villagrá immediately brings his poem to an end with a brief address to his king.

This powerful closing scene transcends the doggerel verse in which it is told. The doomed but valiant Indians, cursing to the end, become their own executioners rather than surrender to the Spaniards. It makes a good story, and popular historians have included it in their narratives of Southwestern history.[3] But did the incident take place as Villagrá recounts it? One reason for doubt is that it repeats an episode in an earlier Spanish epic of New World conquest, the *Araucana* of Alonso de Ercilla, an account—here, too, by an eyewitness—of the wars in Chile against the Araucanian Indians.[4] Villagrá knew and modeled his own poem on Ercilla's epic, which was printed in three installments in 1569, 1578, and 1589 and remains a classic of Spanish literature. He was a relation of Don Francisco de Villagrá, the conquistador of Chile, who is one of the heroes of Ercilla's poem. At the beginning of his twenty-seventh canto, he compares the punitive campaign against Acoma to the wars against "those valiant savages of Arauco" (233r).

Ercilla's episode takes place in canto 26 of the *Araucana*. After the battle of Millarapue (1557), the Spaniards chose twelve chieftains from among the captured prisoners and sentenced them to be hanged. Ercilla writes that he himself was moved to pity, and he tried to save one of the condemned Indians from execution. This prisoner turns out to be Galbarino, a major Indian character of the poem, whom the Spanish had captured once before; at that time they had cut off both of his hands as punishment for his rebellion (22.45–54). Galbarino had then proceeded to the council of the Araucanian chiefs, where the testimony of his bloody stumps overcame the pleadings of the peace party and resolved the Indians to continue their struggle (23.6–17). Recaptured, he now preferred to die, turning his sword upon himself, rather than to grant his conquerors the power to show him mercy (26.26).

> Muertos podremos ser, mas no vencidos
> ni los animos libres oprimidos.
> (26.25)

[We can be killed, but not vanquished, nor can our free souls be enslaved.][5]

This defiance causes Galbarino to be condemned along with his counterparts. His death, however, is self-inflicted, just as he wanted it to be. For, Ercilla reports, there were no executioners available, and the sentence was carried out in an unheard-of way: each of the Indians took a rope, climbed into the trees, and hanged himself. One chieftain hesitated and begged the Spaniards for mercy but, rebuked by the indomitable Galbarino, he, too, placed the noose around his neck and dropped from the treetop to his death. Last of all, Galbarino died in the same manner (26.31–37).

While Villagrá's poem is virtually the only firsthand report of what happened at Acoma, Ercilla's epic can be compared to other historical sources. The story of the Indians hanging themselves is confirmed in the 1558 chronicles of Gerónimo de Bibar,[6] but a somewhat different version of the aftermath of Millarapue is presented by Alonso de Góngora Marmolejo, another veteran and eyewitness of the wars whose history of the Araucanian wars, composed in the 1570s, was first published in 1850.

Ten caciques were taken prisoner, their chief lords who served the office of captain: Quepulican, the commander-in-chief, fled and escaped. Don Garcia ordered that all these chieftains be hanged. There was seen one cacique, a warlike man and a chief lord, who had served well in the time of Valdivia, an Indian of good understanding; he had endeavored that they grant him his life, but was unable to obtain it, although many tried to intercede for him because he was so well known. Seeing that they had hanged the others, he greatly implored the constable that they hang him above the others on the highest branch of the tree, so that the Indians who passed by there should see that he died in the defense of his country.[7]

In Marmolejo's narrative the central character is the Indian who first pleads for his life through Spanish intercessors and subsequently, when he realizes that he has no alternative, dies with patriotic dignity. Ercilla divides this character in two: the figure who implores mercy is relatively minor, the unnamed Araucanian whom Galbarino rebukes. Galbarino, probably a fictional composite of several historical figures, takes over center stage, rejecting efforts to intercede for him, choosing to die along with his like-minded companions. What Marmolejo recounts as a single noble gesture performed by an otherwise pathetic and even craven victim becomes for Ercilla a collective act of courage and firmness. Ercilla depicts the Indians' acting as their own hangmen—a feature that does not appear in Marmolejo's history—as an expression of their stoic valor. Their deaths become a mass suicide, like the one recounted in Lucan's *Pharsalia*, Ercilla's favorite epic model, where a surrounded band of Caesarian soldiers turn their swords upon each other (4.474–581). The Araucanians seem to have learned Lucan's stoic moral (576–77): "Non ardua virtus/Servitium fugisse manu" (It is no arduous feat of virtue to escape slavery by one's own hand).

When the two Indians hang themselves at the end of Villagrá's *Historia*, the scene is already an epic *topos*. The other component of the episode, the dying curse of the Acomans, can similarly be broken down into a series of traditional rhetorical attitudes assumed by the vanquished in epic poetry, but here their literary provenance cannot be so clearly determined. It is Fortune who has led them to defeat, the Acomans say: so complains Turnus as he heads toward his fatal duel with Aeneas at the end of the *Aeneid* (12.676–77, 693–95); so the anti-imperial Lucan makes Fortune the god of the conquering Caesar in the *Pharsalia* (1.225; 5.570; 7.796); so Galbarino attributes the Araucanian downfall to "los fieros hados variables" (26.25), to fates that are harsh but also variable. The epic loser ascribes the victor's success to Fortune—to chance rather than to the victor's superiority or to some kind of historical necessity—thus leaving the possibility open that Fortune may change in the future. The Indians tell the Spaniards to sleep with untroubled dreams; after the great victory of Caesar's troops at Pharsalia, Lucan's poem recounts that they were afflicted by nightmares as the ghosts of the dead rose to haunt their sleep (7.764–68). It is the possibility, however remote or unlikely, of such a return of the dead that the Acomans raise in their curse. Similarly, the furious, suicidal Dido threatens to become a fury hounding Aeneas after her death in the *Aeneid* (4.384–86), and the defeated Solimano in Tasso's *Gerusalemme liberata* takes up her words:

> Risorgerò nemico ognor più crudo
> cenere anco sepolto e spirito ignudo.
> (9.99)

[I shall rise again, a still fiercer enemy, even as buried ashes and naked spirit.][8]

Solimano is modeled not only on Dido, who also prophesies the avenging Hannibal rising from her buried bones (*Aeneid* 4.625–29), but on that Hannibal himself, as he is depicted in the *Punica* of Silius Italicus. Defeated at Zama at the end of the epic, Hannibal pledges to fight on so that Roman mothers will know no peace (17.614–15); at the poem's beginning, in a scene where Hannibal swears vengeance on Rome in the temple of Dido, it is said that his victories will cause the mothers of Latium to refuse to bear children (1.111–12). The Acomans suggest that Villagrá's Spaniards may come to regret the day their mothers gave them birth.

The historical factuality of Villagrá's final scene becomes more and more difficult to pin down. We can probably assume that the Spaniards hanged two rebellious Indians in the San Juan pueblo in 1599. The rest—their self-execution and curse—blends into an inherited poetic tradition. By isolating the traditional epic fictions and tropes that are interpolated into Villagrá's chronicle, we can observe their ideological function in a particular historical occasion. This function typically does not so much present a single official viewpoint; it seeks to contain, rather than resolve, conflicting ideological messages. Moreover, it cannot be separated from the episode's *formal* function, its placement at the very end of the *Historia*: the form both determines and constitutes part of the ideological content itself.

For the power of this epic ending is that it calls the idea of ending into question. Acoma has been destroyed, the war is over, the last rebels die at the hangman's tree—and yet the words of their curse echo on, a threat that all is not over. To be sure, the doomed Indians acknowledge their defeat and the loss of their lands; they admit that no one has ever returned from the realm of death. But they proceed to promise just such a ghostly revenge, an uncanny afterlife that reveals its affinity to other psychic forms by the Indians' reference to the dreams of their conquerors. Their curse raises the specter of a real future retribution, one that will take the shape of periodic insurrections, renegade raids, and acts of sabotage by a people who can never be reconciled to colonial rule. However gnomic its form, the curse amounts to an alternative history of resistance that competes with Villagrá's narrative of conquest, the narrative of the *Historia* that presents itself as a complete and finished epic action but that, at the very moment of formal closure, suggests a bloody and unending sequel.

The two Indians are thus lent a voice of their own—a momentary glimpse of what history looks like from the perspective of the losers—a voice that cannot simply be suppressed by Spanish force. They earn this voice by their invincible valor and self-execution. And even if this scene is lifted from the epic of Ercilla, who had himself embellished his historical narrative by portraying the Araucanians as stoic suicides, Villagrá's Indians are nonetheless linked to the other Acomans who jumped to their deaths from the heights of their citadel rather than surrender to their conquerors. There is a symbolic analogy between their mastery of their own deaths and their possession of an autonomous voice and history. Both the Acomans' self-execution and their curse are removed from the control of the victorious Spaniards, who can make complete and unconditional neither their conquest nor their version of the conquest: a stubborn core of native resistance remains and cannot be eradicated.

But this resistance can, perhaps, be contained within limits. The pose of stoic autonomy that the cornered Indians adapt as they hang themselves cannot disguise the fact that they are doing the Spaniards' work for them. The space in which they assert themselves as independent agents has been drastically reduced and circumscribed by their conquerors. The fate of Acoma itself recalls other cases of mass suicide by the defenders of besieged cities, Masada or Numantia— the latter, explicitly mentioned by Villagrá, held a special place in the sixteenth-century Spanish imagination.[9] These desperate measures are open to more than one interpretation. If the losers stake their claim to freedom and invincible heroism upon suicide, the victors can complacently view the same act as the inevitable outcome of their victory, an act of which they, the victors, are the true authors. Shakespeare's Octavius, soon to be Augustus, expresses this idea clearly when he appropriates the suicides of Antony and Cleopatra: "High events as these / Strike those that make them" (*Antony and Cleopatra*, 5.2.359–60). And Scipio Aemilianus, the conqueror of Numantia, adapted the title *Numantinus* as a trophy of its inhabitants' destruction.[10]

The Indians' curse may similarly be appropriated by their Spanish masters. This is obviously true in the sense that the curse is contained within Villagrá's poem, expressed in his language and mediated, as we have seen, through the terms of his literary tradition. But it is true in a more sinister sense as well, for the curse can be used against the Indians. The undying hatred and resistance to which they give voice warrants the harshness of the Spaniards' countermeasures, such as the sentences meted out on the survivors of Acoma. De Oñate and Zaldívar were, in fact, charged in 1609 and brought to trial in 1614 to answer for the brutal conduct of the Acoma campaign. Villagrá's *Historia* of 1610 is involved in a case of special pleading: the poet seeks to exonerate his commanders who, he suggests, had no other recourse against an enemy who admitted no quarter.[11] The Acomans' curse may thus be fitted into the conquistadors' own self-understanding. If it is a projection of their dread of future Indian revolts and retribution—and, hence, in some sense a veiled expression of their feelings of guilt—it also justifies, with the logic of a vicious circle, the severity of their present policy.

In this sense, too, the Indians' resistance is suicidal, for it only brings on further reprisals. And the same may be said for the future history that is projected by their curse, the narrative that would go beyond and compete with Villagrá's official history. The fact that this narrative is paired with and mirrored by the Indians' hanging themselves may suggest that it is, in fact, a narrative with no place to go, a chronicle merely of further, self-destructive defeats. If the curse challenges the formal closure of the *Historia*, it may not so much foretell an overthrow of Spanish rule, which has indeed been won once and for all in the completed action of the poem, as a series of abortive rebellions that can disturb, but not alter, the new political status quo. The Indians are condemned to a future of scattered suicidal gestures, ultimately without aim or direction. Thus if the Acomans' curse may represent the attempt of the victors' poet to identify imaginatively with the losers and to portray their fiercely independent version of history, it simultaneously suggests that they have no real history—their own story is rather a sequence of incomplete and unconnected events that cannot be linked together into a coherent narrative: they have a voice and role only within the history made by their Spanish masters. The ending of Villagrá's poem allows for diametrically opposed readings as it confronts the victims of the Spanish conquest, both endowing them with and denying them a separate identity and perspective. One cannot say whether this uncertainty and conflict of meaning is the effect or the cause of the epic tropes to which Villagrá has recourse in order to end his poem, but it is at such moments that these tropes seem most ideologically charged.

Because the epic forms at the end of the *Historia* are inserted into what presents itself as a factual history, they call attention to themselves and to their ideological function. By a reverse process, the particular historical occasion of the *Historia* may disclose ideological meanings in these forms that were latent or not fully articulated. A poem of small literary merit like the *Historia* can thus have something to say about the canonical epic tradition with which it claims affiliation. As a chronicle that reports, in however distorted a version, real historical events, it suggests that behind the fictions of epic poetry lie other similar events: episodes of political struggle and colonialist violence. Above all, it reminds us of the presence of real victims: the two Indians whom the Spaniards executed in the San Juan pueblo in 1599 and whom Villagrá's poem does not easily lay to rest.

The Indians' defiant curse invites us to reconsider other imprecations of epic losers against their conquerors, losers who may initially appear to have mythological or purely fictional, rather than historical, identities. The epic curse, in fact, constitutes its own distinctive *topos*, whose morphology and history can be traced from the *Odyssey* and the *Aeneid* to a celebrated central episode in the *Lusíadas*. Camões's poem provides another, similar instance of a traditional epic type scene imported into a historical narrative of Renaissance imperialism and native victims. But, unlike Villagrá's *Historia*, it does so with the self-consciousness of "high" literature. Its representation of native resistance takes *both* historical and mythopoetic forms, and it plays these off against one another. It thus lays bare the process by which real events become transformed into epic fictions, fictions that depend—and Camões explicitly declares their dependence—upon earlier epic fictions; at the same time it interrogates the historical basis of those earlier epics. Yet even as Camões demonstrates how suppressed populations may find a voice— if only one that curses—in the epic fictions of their conquerors, his poem works to appropriate that voice, to contain and neutralize the unsettling implications that the inherited *topos* of the curse might have for its own triumphalist narrative of empire. The resources of the epic tradition are drawn upon here simultaneously to represent and disfigure the defeated and their version of history.

II

The tradition of the epic curse properly begins when the blinded Polyphemus cries out to his father Poseidon for vengeance upon Odysseus at the end of book 9 of the *Odyssey*. His curse concludes an episode that has been recognized and well interpreted by modern critics, most notably Max Horkheimer and Theodor Adorno, as a colonialist encounter between a "superior," civilized Greek and an underdeveloped barbarian.[12] Homeric scholars have associated aspects of Odysseus' wanderings with Greek colonizing ventures in the Mediterranean that began in the eighth century B.C., and Odysseus' glowing appraisal (9.131–41) of the island that lies off the cyclopes' coast—fit for all crops, rich in meadows, a suitable site for vineyards, a good harbor, a fresh water spring—reveals a colonist's mentality.[13] The land is there for the taking, especially since the neighboring cyclopes lack the ships to get there themselves; they also lack the agricultural skills to exploit it properly. But when Odysseus goes "to find out about these people, and learn what they are" (9.174), the cyclopes turn out to be a pesky lot indeed. By means of verbal guile and technological improvisation, Odysseus is able to outwit and blind the backward cannibal Polyphemus, and he and the surviving remnant of his companions make good their escape. But they cannot escape the cyclops's ensuing curse, which predicts and determines the subsequent plot of the *Odyssey*.

> Hear me, Poseidon who circle the earth, dark-haired. If truly
> I am your son, and you acknowledge yourself as my father,
> grant that Odysseus, sacker of cities, son of Laertes,
> who makes his home in Ithaka, may never reach that home;
> but if it is decided that he shall see his own people,
> and come home to his strong-founded house and to his country,
> let him come late, in bad case, with the loss of all his companions,
> in someone else's ship, and find troubles in his household.
>
> (1528–35)[14]

The curse shifts its focus midway through from ends to means. Polyphemus seems to concede Odysseus' homecoming, the narrative goal of the *Odyssey*, as predetermined and inevitable, and instead specifies the conditions that will defer the hero's return and make it a hollow achievement: the destruction of his ships and companions, the struggle with Penelope's suitors that awaits him before his homecoming can be complete. But the result of the curse will be to qualify the poem's completion as well: Teiresias later instructs Odysseus that to appease Poseidon for the blinding of his son he will have to depart from Ithaka again on a new voyage to the ends of the earth (11.10–138), instructions that Odysseus repeats to Penelope (23.264–284) just before their much delayed sexual reunion in their marital bed. Penelope takes heart in Teiresias' final words that promise Odysseus a prosperous old age after his sea of troubles, but the strength of the curse, greater than Polyphemus himself seems to imagine, is to prevent the *Odyssey* from ending happily ever after. Thus here, as in Villagrá's *Historia*, the victim's curse works against closure as the epic poem creates and defines it. The wrath of Poseidon affects the poem's ending both before and after: the god obstructs and delays Odysseus's homecoming through the storms that twice attack him at sea; the expiation required by the god demands that Odysseus leave home again.

The kinship of Polyphemus to Poseidon, the god of sea and storms, extends a process of dehumanization that has already begun by portraying the barbarian native as a cyclopean giant, one-eyed and slow-witted because of his primitive culture, monstrously big because of his willingness to use force against the colonizing stranger.[15] Through his divine father the native is further identified with the hostile elements that Odysseus must battle along his voyage. The conquest of native peoples becomes assimilated with efforts to dominate nature, but this familiar ideological equation merely suggests here how difficult and inconclusive conquest may prove to be. The *Odyssey* presents a failed colonialist scenario in book 9, even if it leaves a native victim behind. Odysseus loses six men, devoured by Polyphemus, in the course of the episode, and the curse of the cyclops will eventually cost him the rest of his crew and literally untold hardships beyond the ending of the epic itself. The price of colonialist violence seems prohibitively high.

Virgil uses the curse of Polyphemus, cast at the fleeing ship of Odysseus, as a literary model for the great curse that the abandoned Dido utters as she sees the ships of Aeneas leaving Carthage and just before she mounts the funerary pyre she has constructed and commits suicide. This is well known, but critical commentary on the *Aeneid* has not discussed how the curse fits into larger patterns of Homeric allusion in the Dido episode, nor has it tended to recognize the full extent of Virgil's identification of Dido with the Homeric cyclops. Dido does not at first look like such a monster. The Carthage episode in books 1 and 4 of the *Aeneid* performs *through allusion* the same literary itinerary as Aeneas' narrative of his wanderings across the Mediterranean in book 3: both retrace backward the wanderings of Odysseus in books 5–13 of the *Odyssey* and both conclude with imitations of the Polyphemus episode, with Aeneas' own encounter with the cyclops at the end of book 3, with Dido's curse at the end of book 4.[16] But before her curse and death Dido and her Carthage suggest other Odyssean locales with their presiding female figures. When Aeneas shoots the deer in book 1 to feed and comfort his companions, the African setting recalls the island of Circe (*Odyssey* 10.156–84); when Mercury summons Aeneas to leave Dido (4.219–78), Carthage becomes a version of Calypso's isle (*Odyssey* 5.43–147); most obvious, Aeneas' enjoyment of Carthaginian hospitality and his inset narrative of his past wanderings at the banquet of books 2 and 3 make the Punic city another Phaiakia (*Odyssey* 6–13) in which Dido alternately plays the role of the wise woman ruler Arete and the enamored princess Nausikaa. But the first sighting of the Carthaginian coast in book 1 casts Dido as still another Odyssean heroine, for the harbor into which the storm-tossed Trojan fleet sails (1.159–67) is a close imitation of Homer's description of the harbor of Ithaka with its Cave of the Nymphs (*Odyssey* 13.96–112). This momentary, shadowy resemblance to Ithaka makes Carthage look like the longed-for homeland, and it casts Dido as the chaste and circumspect Penelope: she tells us in book 4 that she has rejected the proposals of her local Numidian suitors (534–36). This opening view of Carthage is particularly illusory and tragic, as if Aeneas and the Trojans could reach their destination in the first book of the *Aeneid* without the travails and sufferings of the rest of the poem, as if they could accept Dido's invitation to them to stay and settle in her newly founded city (1.572–74), as if she and Aeneas could be united in marriage. It is set in deliberate contrast to the final Odyssean characterization of Dido as Polyphemus in book 4, and measures the extent of her erotic downfall. Once aroused through the combined agency of Venus and Juno, her passion for Aeneas will transform the Carthaginian queen from chaste consort and ruler into a monster.

But perhaps she has been a monster all along.[17] The encounter with the cyclopes that Aeneas recounts retrospectively in book 3 is the last extended episode of the Trojans' wanderings before they reach Carthage, hurled there by the storm of book 1; this proximity in the chronological sequence of the wanderings is reinforced by the narrative sequence that reverts from Aeneas' story back to Dido's court in book 4. This proximity has a Homeric basis, for we learn in the *Odyssey* (6.3–6) that the cyclopes and the men of Phaiakia were once neighbors. Homer seems to suggest that the wealthy and hypercivilized Phaiakians are as alien to the Greek world as the primitive Polyphemus. Virgil takes this idea a step further, for opulent Carthage, closely modeled upon Phaiakia, is not only narratively adjacent to his Polyphemus episode but also offers a second version of that episode: in both book 3 (666–67) and book 4 (571–80), the Trojans cut the anchor cables of their ships in their haste to escape Cyclopean shores.[18] The two sides of the barbarian in the *Odyssey* have become one in a Carthage viewed in the anti-Eastern terms of Roman propaganda: the outward refinement of the city merely covers up a monstrous irrationality that, according to the same propaganda, associates the East with womankind and that here is embodied in Dido herself.[19] Thus, alongside his dramatic version of Dido's progressive disintegration as she loves and is abandoned—a version that puts a share of the blame and guilt on Roman Aeneas—Virgil also presents a less sympathetic, ideologically colored view of Dido: her transformation into a raging Polyphemus merely allows her true nature to appear.

The *Aeneid* thus wavers between a human understanding and a demonization of Dido—and of the historical enemies of Rome whom she represents: the Carthage of the three Punic Wars and Cleopatra, the African queen of Virgil's own time. The history of this emnity is foretold in Dido's curse. The first part of her curse is much like the curse of Polyphemus: just as the cyclops conceded that Odysseus might return home but called down the troubles in store for him there, Dido, acknowledging that Aeneas may be fated to reach Italy, invokes the hardships he will face in the second half of the *Aeneid*.

> si tangere portus
> infandum caput ac terris adnare necesse est,
> et sic fata Iovis poscunt, hic terminus haeret:
> at bello audacis populi vexatus et armis,
> finibus extorris, complexu avolsus Iuli,
> auxilium imploret videatque indigna suorum
> funera; nec, cum se sub leges pacis iniquae
> tradiderit, regno aut optata luce fruatur,
> sed cadat ante diem mediaque inhumatus harena.
> haec precor, hanc vocem extremam cum sanguine fundo.
>   (4.612–21)

[If this detested creature must touch harbor and sail to the shore—if thus the fates of love demand, and if this end is fixed and determined:

nonetheless harried by war and the swords of a daring people, exiled from his home and torn from the embrace of Iulus, let him beg for aid and watch the shameful deaths of his own people; nor, when he has yielded to the terms of an unjust peace, may he enjoy his kingdom or the light of day, but let him fall before his time unburied amid the sand. This is my prayer; I pour out these last words with my blood.][20]

The war with Turnus, Aeneas' alliance with Evander and the Etruscans, the death of Pallas: these are all contained in Dido's words. They are the immediate consequences of her curse for the rest of the poem. Moreover, whereas the effect of Polyphemus' curse was to send Odysseus off onto another protracted voyage and thus to unsettle the ending of the *Odyssey*, Dido predicts Aeneas' premature death after the Trojans' victory in Italy closes the *Aeneid*: here, too, the hero has little chance to live happily ever after. But Dido's curse does not stop here. She calls upon her compatriots to continue her hatred of the Trojans; her curse extends beyond the ending of the poem and enters into history.

> tum vos, o Tyrii, stirpem et genus omne futurum
> exercete odiis, cinerique haec mittite nostro
> munera. nullus amor populis nec foedera sunto.
> exoriare, aliquis nostris ex ossibus ultor,
> qui face Dardanios ferroque sequare colonos,
> nunc, olim, quocumque dabunt se tempore vires.
> litora litoribus contraria, fluctibus undas,
> imprecor, arma armis; pugnent ipsique nepotesque.
> (4.622–29)

[Then you O Tyrians, practice your hatred against all his race and future stock, and send these offerings to my ashes. Let there be no love or treaty between our peoples. Rise up, you, unknown avenger, from my bones, to pursue the Dardan settlers with fire and sword, today, hereafter, whenever you have the power to do so. Let shore oppose shore in battle, I pray, sea against sea, sword against sword; let them and their children's children have war.]

It is now not simply the narrative ending of the *Aeneid* that is in question, but the closure that the *Aeneid* projects upon Roman history: their empire without end foretold by Jupiter. The curse operates as a rival prophecy, set alongside the prophecies in the *Aeneid* of future Roman greatness. Dido foretells the other side of the story, the saga of the conquered who refuse to stay conquered and of the repeated wars that the African foes of Rome will wage against her supremacy. Rome's unbroken rule will be periodically challenged, Dido predicts, every time that the defeated Africans regain sufficient strength. The defeated find consolation in the occasions that future history will offer them for retaliation and revenge.

Dido's call for an avenger rising from her bones, the avenger who will be Hannibal, is the most celebrated moment of her curse. It chilled Roman readers with historical memories and would continue to exert its fascination upon subsequent readers, including Freud, a Jew in a Catholic culture who identified with victimized Semites seeking revenge upon Rome.[21] Virgil's scene darkly evokes a mythic parallel: the Phoenix, the fabulous bird who, in one version of the myth, constructs the fragrant pyre upon which it will burn itself in order to be reborn from its ashes.[22] So Phoenician Dido—"Phoenissa" as Virgil repeatedly calls her (1.670, 714; 4.348, 531)—prepares the pyre for her own immolation. When Dido earlier unfastens her sandal and girdle (4.581), the ancient commentator Servius notes that she is summoning the presence of Juno in her aspect of Lucina, the patroness of childbirth.[23] Juno will send down Iris at the end of book 4 to put an end to Dido's death agony and to release her struggling spirit from her confining, fastened limbs (*nexosque resolveret artus*; 695); the action and language parody labor and delivery. Something terrible has been born—in place of the child whom Dido longed to have had by Aeneas (327–30). It is Hannibal whom her curse raises up, Phoenix-like, from the remains of her pyre.

The Phoenix myth applies to Carthage itself, the city several times vanquished and destroyed that rises again and again from its defeat. Within Roman epic tradition, the cyclical repetition of Carthage's rise and fall is mirrored in a second myth, that of the Libyan giant Antaeus who falls to the earth, his mother, in order to rise even mightier from her sustenance. It is the myth of the autochthonous native par excellence, the native who must be literally uprooted from his elemental relationship to the land by his foreign conqueror. The story of Hercules' defeat of Antaeus is recounted in the *Pharsalia* (4.593–660), where Lucan treats it as a mythical analogue to Scipio's victory at Zama over Hannibal, Dido's avenger himself.[24] Ariosto will later couple Antaeus and Hannibal when he cites them as native predecessors to his own African warrior Rodomonte (*Orlando furioso*, 18.24.4), and Tasso continues this epic typology, no longer African but more generally Eastern, with the figure of the Sultan Solimano, the Turkish adversary of the first crusaders in the *Gerusalemme liberata*. Tasso both models Solimano upon the Hannibal of the *Punica* of Silius Italicus and compares him to Antaeus when, after a career of defeats and comebacks, he is killed in the final decisive battle of the poem.[25]

> 'l Soldan, che spesso in lunga guerra,
> quasi novello Anteo, cadde e risorse
> più fero ognora, al fin calcò la terra
> per giacer sempre.
> (20.108.1–4)

[The Sultan, who often in long warfare, almost a new Antaeus, fell and rose again still fiercer, at last fell to earth to lie there forever.]

This is the same Solimano who promised, echoing Dido's words, to return from the grave as a naked, avenging spirit. Tasso depicts Solimano as an ancestor of the Saladin who would historically avenge the deaths of the defenders of Jerusalem. So, in some sense, the warrior Sultan *does* return. And again and again: in Tasso's lifetime the invading army of a Turkish Sultan Suleiman had reached the gates of Vienna.

There is something demonic in this historical repetition—and Milton will compare his Satan to Antaeus at the end of *Paradise Regained* (4.563–568)—in a foe who refuses to die a natural death and whose hatred is transmitted to successive generations. Dido as Phoenix, Carthage as Antaeus embody a life force that paradoxically both assimilates them to the regenerative cycles of nature and marks them as unnatural and monstrous. As her curse begets Hannibal, the otherwise barren, sexually frustrated Dido takes on the uncontrolled, diseased fertility of an Africa that is always producing monsters, a nature gone wild. This monstrosity reinforces Dido's similarity to Polyphemus, the controlling literary model behind her curse, and completes her dehumanization as a figure of Rome's foreign enemy, of a Carthage that must be destroyed. This figure must be read alongside the all-too-human Dido, wronged by the Roman she has loved and befriended, whose story has invited the Carthaginian St. Augustine and other readers to weep for her and to identify with her loser's perspective, even with her curse and its projected history of resistance. Even if that history is not read—through the Roman victors' ideology—as a kind of demonic repetition, it is nonetheless marked by failure from the beginning, for, as was the case at the end of Villagrá's *Historia*, the loser's curse is accompanied by suicide—though, as opposed to the stoical autonomy and self-mastery displayed by Villagrá's Indians, Dido's death marks an irrational loss of self-control.[26] It suggests that the harm her successors will inflict upon the Roman conquerors will always involve self-inflicted harm as well. The last of these, Cleopatra, took her own life, probably at the order, certainly with the connivance, of Augustus.[27] When Dido, *after* uttering her curse, declares that she will die unavenged (*moriemur inultae*; 4.659), this reversal may mean more than that she cannot have immediate revenge, that history must wait for the Punic wars and Hannibal. In the long run, Rome's rule will be shaken but not overturned, and the continuing resistance of her subject peoples breaks down into a series of periodic, suicidal measures. Theirs is a repeated history of failures, a failed history.

III

In the fifth canto of the *Lusíadas*, Vasco da Gama is the guest of the African king of Melinde on the east coast of Africa. He narrates the story up to this point of his voyage from Portugal: Camões's obvious models are Odysseus telling his adventures to Alcinous in Phaiakia and Aeneas recounting his wanderings to Dido in Carthage. Da Gama describes the moment when his fleet is about to approach the Cape of Good Hope. Suddenly, there appears a black cloud out of which, in turn, an enormous giant emerges, looming over them in the air. This menacing figure announces to the Portuguese the punishments that await them for their daring and presumption (*atrevimento*; 5.42.6) in opening up the new maritime route to the Indian Ocean. He briefly mentions (5.42.7–8) the arduous wars they will have to fight to subjugate the seas and lands of their empire. Then he foretells at length (5.43–48) the storms and mishaps that the cape itself has in store for future Portuguese fleets, culminating in the terrible Sepulveda shipwreck of 1552. The monster would continue this dire prophecy, but da Gama interrupts him to ask his identity. He replies that he is Adamastor, one of the earthborn Titans who, during their rebellion against the gods, led an assault against Neptune to gain control of the sea. He was stirred by his love for the sea nymph Thetis, who lured him out of battle only to deceive and spurn him. In his shame and disdain he fled to the Southern Hemisphere, where the gods punished him for his presumption (*atrevimento*; 5.58.8) by turning him into the land mass of the cape itself. There he is still erotically tantalized and frustrated, for Thetis still swims around him in the encircling sea (50–59). Having told his story, the giant disappears as the black cloud dissolves, and the Portuguese sail by the cape (61) without further incident and continue their voyage.

It is a much admired scene: the giant rising up at the midpoint of Camões's ten-canto epic, at the geographical midpoint and boundary of da Gama's journey. More than any other episode of the *Lusíadas*, it has given the poem its place in world literature, a place to which Camões and even his hero da Gama self-consciously lay claim. At the end of his narrative, da Gama favorably compares it to the maritime adventures recounted in the *Odyssey* and the *Aeneid*.

> Cantem, louvem e escrevam sempre extremos
> Dêsses seus semideuses e encareçam,
> Fingindo magas Circes, Polifemos,
> Sirenas que co'o canto os adormeçam;
> Dem-lhe mais navegar a vela e remos
> Os Cicones e a terra onde se esquecem
> Os companheiros, em gostando o loto;
> Dem-lhe perder nas águas o pilôto;
>
> Ventos soltos lhe finjam e imaginem
> Dos odres e Calipsos namoradas;
> Harpias que o manjar lhe contaminem;
> Descer às sombras nuas já passadas:
> Que, por muito e por muito que se afinem

Nestas fábulas vãs, tão bem sonhadas,
A verdade que eu conto, nua e pura
Vence tôda grandiloca escritura!

(5.88–89)

[Let them sing, praise, and write, always in the highest terms, of those
demigods of theirs and let them exaggerate, feigning sorceress Circes,
Polyphemuses, Sirens that put men asleep with their song; let them still
voyage with sails and oars among the Ciconians and to the land where
their companions, having tasted the lotus, become forgetful, let them
lose their helmsman in the sea. Let them feign and imagine winds
released from wineskins and enamored Calypsos, Harpies that foul their
food; let them descend to the naked souls of the dead: for as much, as
greatly as they refine these empty fables, so well dreamed up, the truth
that I tell, naked and pure, outdoes all their grandiloquent writings.][28]

The claim to historical truth certainly appears odd after da Gama has narrated
the apparition of a prophesying cloud-born giant. The mention of Polyphemuses, moreover, is a tip-off that discloses the literary descent of Adamastor from
the fantastic inventions of Homer and Virgil. But the burden of Camões's episode—and the basis of its alleged superiority to classical epic—is to show how such
poetic inventions can be historical.

The commentators of the *Lusíadas* have noted that Adamastor is modeled
upon Homer's and Virgil's depictions of the cyclops Polyphemus.[29] His prophecy
of future Portuguese hardships and disasters at the cape recalls the curse of the
cyclops in the *Odyssey*, while his monstrous body, "horrendo e grosso" (5.40.5),
echoes Virgil's description of Polyphemus: "monstrum horrendum, informe,
ingens" (3.658). Adamastor's name also seems to allude to Virgil's cyclops episode,
for Achaemenides, the companion of Odysseus whom Aeneas rescues from the
cyclopes' coast, tells us that he is the son of Adamastus (3.614).[30] But Adamastor's
story of his passion for Thetis recalls still another Polyphemus, the one whose
unrequited love for another sea nymph, Galatea, is recounted in *Idyls* 6 and 10 of
Theocritus, in Virgil's *Eclogue* 9, and in the thirteenth book of Ovid's *Metamorphoses*. Following a typical Renaissance literary practice of imitative *contaminatio*,
Camões has combined all the classical representations of Polyphemus into his
mythical figure. In doing so he has also managed to capture something of Dido's
spurned love and irrationality in Adamastor, for Virgil's queen is depicted as a
kind of cyclops in love. Ovid, in fact, remembering how the frenzied Dido became
another Polyphemus, makes *his* enamored Polyphemus, as he turns upon Galatea's lover Acis (13.865–6), echo Dido's vindictive speech (4.600–601) seven lines
before it turns into her great curse. Thus Dido and Polyphemus had achieved a
kind of reciprocity—between monstrous passion and a passionate monster—in
the classical literary tradition that informs Camões's fiction. Dido's presence can
also be felt in the future orientation and historical concreteness of Adamastor's

prophecy. Polyphemus cursed Odysseus alone, but, like Dido, Adamastor directs his words not so much against the epic hero as against his imperialist successors.

Da Gama's insistence upon the truth of his narrative is balanced by an earlier passage in canto 5 where he addresses those purely theoretical armchair scholars who deride the marvelous phenomena reported in sailors' tales, and insist that either the sailors have made them up or misunderstood what they have seen (*falsos ou mal entendidos*; 17). Da Gama goes on to describe a waterspout, a prodigy of nature undreamt of by such scholars or by the ancient philosophers on whose works they rest their authority.[31] It is one of the many marvels he has himself encountered at sea: all can be narrated, without lying, as pure truth (*E tudo, sem mentir, puras verdades*; 23). There is a polemic of moderns against ancients here, one that prefigures the experimental attitudes of the New Science. But the passage has a curious relationship to the later Adamastor episode, for if the land-lubber scholars are wrong to doubt the factual existence of waterspouts, they may still be skeptical about a sailor's story of a giant hovering in the air above his ship— all the more since the waterspout itself offers a naturalistic explanation for the giant. Both are described as a black cloud (*a nuvem negra*; 21.8, 60.3), and the poem suggests that the encounter with Adamastor is a second version of da Gama's sighting of the waterspout. The episode is true in the sense that he did really see a waterspout, and that waterspouts really do exist.

But the episode that immediately follows the description of the waterspout offers a second, historical explanation for Adamastor. The Portuguese make a landfall on the southern tip of Africa and, at stanza 27, they encounter a Hottentot who is out gathering wild honey. He shows no interest in the gold and silver they show him, but is delighted by their trade goods: beads, bells, and a red cap. The next day he returns with his fellow tribesmen, who are eager to see the same trinkets. They appear so tame (*domesticos*; 5.30.5) and friendly that one member of the crew, Fernão Veloso, dares (*atreva*; 30.7) to go off with them to see the manner of their land and customs. The next thing that da Gama sees is Veloso running at full speed down the hill toward the ships with the Africans in hot pursuit. Da Gama leads a rescue party to pick him up from the shore, where the natives have prepared a further ambush. The Portuguese drive them off, though da Gama receives a wound in the leg in the process. The tone of the episode is nonetheless lighthearted, for the narrator da Gama makes a joke about giving red caps indeed to the bloodied Hottentots, and it ends when all hands have safely returned on board ship with a humorous bantering between the crew and Veloso, who is teased about his hasty retreat. But this mood quickly changes, for the apparition of Adamastor immediately follows.

The episode historically took place. It is recorded in the log of da Gama's ship and in Camões's sources, the histories of João de Barros and Damião de Gois.[32] It seems to be a trivial vignette of colonialist violence, but Camões evidently saw in it another version of the encounter between Odysseus and Polyphemus in the

Odyssey. Veloso has an Odyssean curiosity to learn about the natives and their customs; as de Gois puts it, he wished "to go to see their dwellings, and the manner of life they kept in their homes."[33] But, like Odysseus, the Portuguese explorer is forced to make a run for his ship. Camões invites us to note the analogy at the very beginning of the episode when he describes the honey-gathering Hottentot as "more savage than the brutish Polyphemus" (*Selvagem mais que o bruto Polifemo*; 5.28.4), and then directly follows the episode with the horrific spectral appearance of the Polyphemus-like Adamastor. The skirmish with the natives is paltry and one-sided enough; yet even so da Gama is wounded in the fray, and the giant Adamastor is a blown-up figure of the African natives and of the price that will be exacted by their resistance to Portuguese mastery and conquest. Adamastor's name means "the untamed one," and he suggests the nature of the Africans who turned out to be less domesticated than they first appeared. In this light it is significant that the first foreign lands that da Gama passes as he sets out on his voyage at the beginning of canto 5 are those of Moslem Mauretania, "the land over which Antaeus once reigned" (*Terra que Anteu num tempo possuiu*; 5.4) where the sixteenth-century Portuguese were involved in crusading and colonizing projects that would lead up to their disastrous defeat at Alcazarkebir in 1578, six years after the publication of Camões's poem. Like Antaeus, Adamastor is an autochthonous son of the Earth (5.51) and a figure for an Africa that cannot be definitively subdued by European arms.[34]

Canto 5 thus moves in sequence from da Gama's description of the waterspout to Veloso's encounter with the Hottentots, then to the apparition of Adamastor, who is a demonic composite of the natural and human foes faced by the Portuguese imperial enterprise. The canto self-consciously discloses the historical basis of its own act of mythmaking, both on the part of the narrator da Gama and of the poet Camões. For the explorer a native chasing, and hitting, you with a spear can turn into a giant, a waterspout can appear to be a supernatural power; for the poet an episode in the chronicles can suggest the story of Odysseus and Polyphemus and bring a whole literary tradition—Homer, Virgil, Theocritus, Ovid—into play. This self-consciousness allows the poet to assert a historicity and human truth for his fabulous classicizing invention. At the same time it can restore the original Polyphemus episode of the *Odyssey* to human dimensions: it suggests that Homer's story is itself a mythic retelling of a similar encounter of colonialist and native. The *Lusíadas* can indulge in a process of myth-making by simultaneously exposing the mechanism of that process: the poem brings classical myth forward into the modern world by simultaneously subjecting it to a rationalizing, euhemerist critique. Camões's episode is thus able both to enter into and exploit the imaginative power of a classical epic tradition, a power that in no small part accounts for the hold that the figure of Adamastor has had upon readers, what has made the episode a part of "world literature."[35]

If Camões can both demystify his mythic fiction and have it too, the same may be said for its ideological content. The self-consciously constructed nature of the Adamastor episode does not diminish its capacity for ideologial manipulation: it may, on the contrary, augment it. The Africans' resistance to Portuguese rule, the retribution due for the violence done to them—not only da Gama's skirmish with the Hottentots but the later destruction of Kilwa and Mombasa mentioned in the monster's prophecy (45)—are summoned up in the apparition of Adamastor. But Adamastor also embodies the storms that gave the cape its first name. If the kinship of Homer's Polyphemus to Poseidon suggested a relationship between the barbarian native and the natural elements, here the two become inextricably conflated in a third figure: the cloud-born giant that is Camões's mythopoetic creation. This conflation is already suggested when da Gama describes the black band of Hottentots showering missiles at him as a thick cloud (*espessem nuvem*; 33.1), and it is nicely maintained in the series of historical disasters that Adamastor prophesies will befall the Portuguese: Diaz, the discoverer of the cape, will be lost in a hurricane at sea in 1500 (44); the first viceroy Almeida will land to provision there in 1509 and be massacred along with fifty of his men by Hottentots more successful than those who attacked da Gama (45); and the Sepulvedas will suffer both from the stormy elements and at the hands of the natives when they are shipwrecked in 1552 (46–48). In this curse the natives remain nameless, and the specificity of the events it foretells is determined by their notable Portuguese victims; there is no prediction here of any avenging Hannibal. The Africans fade into the workings of an anonymous nature. Such nature does not have a history, and if Adamastor might seem to project a loser's narrative that would rival the Portuguese victors' own version of history, the events he predicts are no more connected than recurrent storms.

Moreover, this assimilation of the native African resistance with the hostility of nature overlooks and suppresses the Portuguese aggression that kindled the resistance in the first place. Adamastor suggests that the storms of the cape rise out of some motive of retribution for the actions of the Portuguese, but, in fact, storms are impersonal and aimless—they are not even hostile, however much they may seem to be to those humans who happen to enter into their path. The natives' violence appears unmotivated: we do not know quite why the Hottentots should have turned on Veloso, whose sole crime is his explorer's curiosity and desire to penetrate into their territory—though their refusal to let him go any further (36) may be a miniature version of Adamastor's rage against the Portuguese for crossing the boundary of the cape and invading the seas that he has long guarded and controlled (41). Da Gama concludes that the Hottentots are simply bestial, brutal, and evil by nature (*gente bestial, brutal, e malvada*; 34.4).[36] And according to his own mythic story, Adamastor was already an angry, literally tempestuous monster *before* the Portuguese ever arrived.

The resistance that the Portuguese face is thus reduced to a kind of blind fury of nature, a resistance that is not particularly directed at them or the result of their own acts of violence: they have simply wandered into a region of storms. And because such storms are not consciously out to harm the Portuguese, they may even help them. This is the case of the great storm that strikes da Gama's fleet in the following canto (6.70–91), and that actually drives his ships *toward* their Indian destination of Calicut. This tempest is carefully balanced against the apparition of Adamastor, and together the two episodes constitute the center of the ten-canto *Lusíadas*. Camões signals the relationship between the two episodes by having each follow a scene involving Fernão Veloso; in canto 6 Veloso has been telling the story of the Twelve of England when the storm suddenly strikes (70) with a telltale black cloud (*nuvem negra*; 70.8) that recalls Adamastor himself. The poem's mythological machinery at first makes the storm seem to be an enactment of the monster's curse, for it has been sent by Neptune (35), and thus recalls the storms that Poseidon unleashes in the *Odyssey* to avenge Polyphemus. But the storm is subsequently ended by Venus, who sends a band of sea nymphs to woo and calm the winds. The episode pointedly inverts the opening scene of the *Aeneid*, where it is Neptune (1.124ff.) who must calm the storm that has risen from the sexual bribe, in the form of the nymph Deiopea (72) that Juno offered to Aeolus, god of the winds. In Camões's fiction, moreover, the nymph sent to tame the south wind, Notus, is none other than Galatea (90), the Galatea loved unsuccessfully by Polyphemus and the model for Adamastor's stormy romance with Thetis. As opposed to Adamastor's failure and continuing frustration, his desire for the tantalizingly close but unattainable Thetis, canto 6 features a second mythic story of storm demon and nymph that concludes with a promise of sexual consummation. As the storm at sea subsides, da Gama's lookouts catch sight of the coast of Calicut, the desired end and consummation of his voyage. The storm that has seemed to run backwards the beginning of *Aeneid* 1 thus also reverses the digressive movement of the Virgilian model: whereas Aeneas was blown away from the Italy he sought into the potential dead end of Carthage, da Gama is driven across the Indian Ocean from the hospitable, Carthage-like Melinde to his goal in southern India. In fact, the storm probably represents the violent August monsoons of the Indian Ocean region. The historical da Gama took advantage of these winds, and their seasonal repetition was a vital part of the Portuguese trade route.

Furthermore the marriage of winds and sea nymphs looks forward to the final two cantos of the *Lusíadas* where da Gama's crew are sexually rewarded for their successful labors. Venus sends an enchanted island floating into their path and populates it with enamored Nereids—willing native girls in a thin mythological disguise (9.18). Da Gama himself receives Tethys (85) as his consort. Her name (*Tétis*) closely resembles that of Thetis (*Tetis*), so much so that Renaissance mythographers were at pains to keep them apart.[37] So, in the symbolic economy of the poem, Adamastor's loss looks very much like da Gama's gain. This final consummation, a reward to the Portuguese for their mission accomplished, becomes in the last canto of the epic an eschatological allegory of the pleasures of immortal fame and a prophecy of Portuguese empire without end.

It is this sense of ending—both of the completed narrative action of the poem and of the finality of an imperial conquest that claims to remain permanent through history—that we have seen unsettled by the *topos* of the epic curse, by the promise of the defeated to return, in some form, to disturb the victor's achievement and rule. Adamastor and his dire prophecy are indeed symbolically connected to the ending of the *Lusíadas* and the celebration on Venus' island of love. But the relationship between these two most famous episodes of the epic is one of inversion: the Portuguese get the girls—and consummate fame and power— while the enemy monster is consumed with frustration. The diametrical contrast suggests how completely the epic, by its end, has overcome the resistance— including the resistance to its own closure—that Adamastor represents. But, in fact, this resistance has already been overcome and left behind well before the celebratory ending of the poem. The first of the two middle cantos of the *Lusíadas* raises the specter of storms and disasters that might stop or sidetrack the Portuguese progress to India—that might halt Portuguese history as it is in the making. But the second immediately dispels this specter: one such storm rises, merely to turn to the advantage of the Portuguese, propelling them toward their destination and imperial destiny. The prophecy of Camões's Jupiter in book 2 (44–55) describes Portuguese history as an undeviating line of conquest across world geography: the center of his epic narrative turns potential deviation into linearity. By confining Adamastor to its narrative center, the poem turns his prophecy into a question of means—the costs that empire will incur along its way—rather than final ends. And because those imperial ends are assured and untouched by his prophecy, the costs, while they may be more considerable than a mere scar on da Gama's leg, are no less incidental.

What is particularly remarkable is the way in which the monsoon of book 6— a seasonally recurring storm that crosses the Indian Ocean from west to east— manages to combine the aimless repetition of Adamastor's squalls with the narrative direction and teleology of da Gama's voyage, how it manages to transform the former into the latter. In terms of narrative structure, the middle of Camões's poem enacts the twofold dynamics of the typical *narrative middle*, that indeterminate space where the repetition that constitutes narrative either may become purely, compulsively repetitive and hence collapse back upon itself or may move forward, repeating with difference, toward a predetermined goal.[38] In epic this moment of narrative suspension is characteristically dramatized in the suspense of battle, where the power of the emergent victor ensures the possibility of narrative, what epic identifies with its own teleological plot; the losers come to embody a principle of non-narratable repetition. In the uncertainty whether the monsoon of book 6 will carry out Adamastor's curse and drive da Gama off course to destruction or will blow his ships to their epic goal, the alternative forms of repetition are as clearly politicized as they are in the undecided epic battle. And here, in addition, they are sexualized. The monsoon winds move in a fixed direction and therefore arrive at a destination that Camões's poem characterizes as a union with the nymphs of the sea: similarly the Portuguese conquest of the waves and lands of the East will turn into a sexual conquest. By contrast, the aimless storms of Adamastor, rising only to subside just as the risen giant himself dissolves along with his cloud, mirror his unconsummated passion for Thetis, and his sexual frustration itself perpetuates the original failure of his rebellion against the gods. The storms and disasters that Adamastor foretells are the product of an impotent fury, the rage of those powerless to stop, hardly able even to slow, an inevitable Portuguese triumph.

In Adamastor the human identity of the Africans has begun to disappear as they are merged with the storms of the cape. We have already seen how epic can dehumanize foreign and subject peoples in order to characterize imperial conquest as the triumph of culture over nature. The continuing resistance of these peoples turns into a cyclical repetition that seems to be a version of nature's repeated regenerative cycles, but one that has been unnaturally thwarted and become demonic: like Dido's barrenness, Adamastor's frustration begets a monstrous future. But quite beyond this familiar ideological trick, the *Lusíadas* make available a further reading of the figure of Adamastor that would displace the natives altogether. Or perhaps, it suggests, they were never quite present in the figure to begin with.

The readings of Adamastor advanced so far have depended on an implicit relationship between the apparition of the giant and the two episodes that precede it—the description of the waterspout and the encounter with the Hottentots. The poem offers clues to this relationship and invites the reader to draw it out of its text, especially by its self-conscious assertion of its historical truth. But in a literal reading of the poem that simply follows its narrative sequence, Adamastor's apparition and prophecy constitute a discrete episode, unconnected to what has gone before. Adamastor makes no mention of Veloso and the natives. Rather he tells the Portuguese that they will be punished for their daring, their "atrevimento"—the word suggests pride and presumption—in going into seas where no (European) men have gone before. In fact, this also glosses the curiosity of Veloso, who dares (*atreva*) to go off to visit the Hottentots, as a kind of overweening pride.

But it so happens that it was for Adamastor's own "atrevimento," the proverbial pride of the rebellious giants, that the gods transformed him into the cape. In this context, Adamastor's love for Thetis is another version of his presumptuous rebellion, for, according to myth, the nymph was prophesied to give birth to a son destined to be greater than his father, one who might therefore pose a threat to the rule of Zeus. Thus Adamastor becomes an image of the transgressive pride and daring of the Portuguese themselves.[39] By venturing into uncharted seas, the Portuguese had been earlier compared to the proud, aspiring giants

(2.112), and the monsoon that assails de Gama's ships in book 6 is likened to the destruction wrought by heaven upon the warring giants (78) and upon their biblical counterparts, the builders of the Tower of Babel (74).[40] The Portuguese transgress not only geographical limits but a whole vision of the world that had endured since antiquity and that the voyages of discovery were to change forever. Adamastor's presumption mirrors the pride of the modern, no longer content to be a dwarf standing on the shoulders of giants but claiming to be a giant himself— the modern who claims to be mightier than the classical fathers he dislodges. We are brought back to da Gama's reference to the "antigos filosofos" (5.23) who had no knowledge of the lands and marvels he has seen at first hand, and to the end of his narrative and his assertion that his story surpasses the poems of Homer and Virgil: Camões's own presumptuous claim to overgo his ancient models.

The Portuguese and their poet may see themselves in the *hybris* of Adamastor and stand back in awe of their own achievements. This specular gaze seems to involve as much self-satisfaction as dread at having gone too far. For when the gigantomachy is read as an allegory of the moderns' attempt to outdo the ancients and overthrow their authority, the Portuguese may claim victory where the mythical giants met defeat. The continuing contrast in the poem between Adamastor's failure and da Gama's success can be reinterpreted to suggest just how successful the revolutionary accomplishments of the Portuguese have been.

But what is most striking in this potential moment of self-knowledge, as the Portuguese find their daring mirrored in Adamastor, is that the African natives have vanished from sight. The "other" in which the Portuguese are reflected is the monstrous mythopoetic figure, not the natives whose historical encounter with da Gama's fleet might seem to have generated the black giant in the first place; indeed, if that historical episode still stands behind Adamastor's apparition, the giant now seems to have grown out of Veloso's overconfident daring rather than from the wrath of the natives. The poem avoids a mutual recognition between colonialist and native, and in this reading of Adamastor as the projection of a (justifiable) Portuguese pride the Africans are virtually canceled out. The production of self-knowledge that might be held to be laudable in itself is here involved with a twofold suppression of the other, one by which the figure of Adamastor is both substituted for the Africans and simultaneously emptied of their presence and made to point instead to their Portuguese masters. This suppression repeats the original act of violence against the Hottentots, a violence that was doubled in Camões's text by da Gama's joke about the wounded natives and the comic dismissal of the whole episode.

This self-reflection that takes place at the expense of the natives can be linked to the remarkable self-consciousness of the Adamastor episode as a whole: the way in which the epic announces and points to its own act of creating a new myth out of the stuff of history. We are accustomed, I think, to see such self-consciousness as an undoing of ideology. Insofar as it insists upon the historicity of Adamastor, Camões's poem may indeed allow us to glimpse the violence and victims that lie behind its own and other epic fictions. But its calling attention to the constructed nature of the giant figure does not necessarily question the ideological operation that the figure effects: an assimilation of the African natives with the storms of nature that deprives them once again of an historical identity and of an identity as victims. Moreover, in his very self-consciousness, the poet seems to become complicit with a reading that still further erases the historical natives by turning Adamastor into an image of Portuguese pride and achievement. For Camões stakes his own claim to excel Homer and Virgil upon the figure of the giant, who not only lends a proper heroic awe and epic magnitude to da Gama's relatively uneventful journey but also presents the poet with an occasion to demonstrate his powers in a kind of epideictic display. The figure of Adamastor can be read to be what, at a literal level, it declares itself to be: the poet's daring and aggrandizing figure of his Portuguese heroes', and his own, daring and greatness. When the figures of poetic language are read as self-reflexive figures, history and human beings begin to disappear.

The African natives have indeed disappeared for readers of the poem, whose textual strategies may work only too well: the relationship between Adamastor and da Gama's encounter with the Hottentots has virtually escaped previous commentary on the episode. And equally submerged into the implicit symbolic relations of the text and in its web of poetic and historical sources is the *topos* of the epic curse, the classical model that informs the fiction of the giant, but that the ideology of the *Lusíadas* deforms in turn. We have seen that the curse typically lends the epic loser something of an autonomous voice and identity. But here it issues from a giant cloud rather than a human agent. Its characteristic prophecy of a future history of resistance that may unsettle the political dominance and closed histories of the victors turns into a weather forecast. And even the storms it predicts as obstacles to the Portuguese have the capacity to turn into their opposites and facilitate the building of a Lusitanian empire without end. This deformation of the *topos* suggests even more forcefully than our earlier examples that epic's representation of its losers, its attempt to adopt their perspective, may not be able to escape appropriation by the victors' ideology. And such appropriation would become complete when the representation, the giant Adamastor, is read no longer as a figure of the native loser but as a mirror image of the Portuguese victor himself.

And yet subsequent readers have not failed to experience an uncanny frisson produced by the episode of Adamastor. This may be due precisely to the way in which the not-so-hidden presence of the natives—and with it the *topos* of the curse and the earlier literary voices of Polyphemus and Dido—are displaced and swallowed up in Camões's giant, the way they are covered over, as it were, by alternative readings: a textual suppression that creates the effect of a return of the repressed. In *Billy Budd*, Herman Melville writes of the "wars which like a flight of harpies rose shrieking from the din and dust of the fallen Bastille," and then shifts epic figures to remark of the Napoleonic period: "The genius of it presented an aspect like that of Camoens' 'Spirit of the Cape,' an eclipsing menace mysterious and prodigious."[41] Melville suggests a genealogical posterity for Adamastor and his curse, of oppressed voices and insurgent ghosts heard at last, that is no less distinguished than their Homeric and Virgilian ancestry. Camões's monster, born of the initial encounter of Portuguese imperialism and its native subjects, is the first in a line of specters haunting Europe.

Afterword: Fracastoro's *Syphilis*

In *Syphilis* (1530), his celebrated Neolatin poem that gave the new epidemic its name, Girolamo Fracastoro provides one further example of the *topos* of the epic curse functioning in the context of Renaissance exploration: in this case in an account of the very first contact between Europeans and the New World. Book 3 of the poem narrates a highly fictionalized version of the first landing of Columbus and his men on Hispaniola. They have hardly come ashore when they see and begin to hunt with their guns the myriad bird life of the island (3.151ff.). This episode recalls the violence that Aeneas and his men commit against the harpies in *Aeneid* 3 (234ff.), and it ends with one of the birds, like Virgil's harpy Celaeno, launching a prophetic curse against the attackers.[42]

> "Qui Solis violatis aves, sacrasque volantes,
> Hesperii, nunc vos, quae magnus cantat Apollo,
> Accipite, et nostro vobis quae nunciat ore.
> Vos quanquam ignari, longum quaesita, secundis
> Tandem parta Ophyrae tetigistis littora ventis.
> Sed non ante novas dabitur summittere terras,
> Et longa populos in libertate quietos,
> Molirique urbes, ritusque ac sacra novare,
> Quam vos infandos pelagi terraeque labores
> Perpessi, diversa hominum post praelia, multi
> Mortua in externa tumuletis corpora terra.
> Navibus amissis pauci patria arva petitis,
> Frustra alii socios quaeretis magna remensi
> Aequora: nec nostro deerunt Cyclopes in orbe.
> Ipsa inter sese vestras discordia puppes
> In rabiem ferrumque trahet: nec sera manet vos
> Illa dies, foedi ignoto quum corpora morbo
> Auxilium sylva miseri poscetis ab ista,
> Donec poeniteat scelerum."
>
> (3.174–92)

["You who have done violence to the birds of the Sun, his sacred flying creatures, you men of Hesperia hear now what almighty Apollo prophesies, what he declares to you by our mouth. Although you do not know it, you have with favoring winds at last touched and gained the shores of the Ophyre you sought so long. But it will not be granted you to place in subjection new lands and a people that have enjoyed long liberty and peace, to construct cities and change rites and customs, until, having suffered to the bitter end unspeakable trials by land and sea, and after battling against men on all sides, many of you bury dead bodies in a foreign land. Ships will be lost so that few of you will make for your home lands; others retraversing the mighty seas will search for comrades in vain. Nor will cyclopes be wanting in this hemisphere. Discord herself will drag your crews into mad and murderous disputes; and a day lies in wait for you, close at hand when, your bodies filthy with an unknown disease, you will in your wretchedness demand help of this forest until you repent of your crimes."][43]

This curse, apparently uttered on behalf of the soon-to-be-subjected natives of the New World but not by them, may well have been a model for Camões, and it enacts a series of displacements that are similar to those performed by the curse of Adamastor. Unlike Adamastor's curse, which followed an encounter with the human natives, this curse immediately precedes an encounter, which here is entirely amiable: the people of Hispaniola feast and trade with Columbus, and there are no unfriendly incidents. The shooting of the birds and the ensuing curse thus acknowledges, if only in a symbolic version, the historical violence inflicted by the gun-toting Spaniards upon the natives of America. The mention of cyclopes joins the curse of Fracastoro's Hispaniola bird (probably a parrot) back to Homer's Polyphemus and the origin of the *topos*. At the same time it refers to the cannibalism that was the most notorious trait of the Amerindian peoples. It reduces the Americans on the one hand to a part of the wildlife and, on the other, hints at a monstrous savagery that equally dehumanizes them. The Spanish violence, for its part, while having something of the mythical resonance of Odysseus' men eating the cattle of the Sun—a violation of nature—is comparatively innocent and trivial: a hunting scene.

Yet the impression of dread remains, not least because of the association that the curse makes in this poem about syphilis between the threat of the disease and the retribution that awaited the Europeans for their treatment of the American natives. For syphilis was widely, probably correctly, thought to have been brought back to Europe by Columbus's crew, the true curse and revenge of the New World upon the Old. But here, too, the power of the curse is displaced and contained. At the opening of his poem (1.33ff.), Fracastoro explicitly rejects the idea of an American origin for syphilis. If we can see the curse bringing this idea back once again, we should also note that it ends *not* simply with the disease—which the poem will shortly depict the Spaniards bringing with them to the New World *from*

Europe (3.381ff.)—but rather with the prospect of its cure: by means of the Guaiacum tree growing in the American forests. In this instance, the curse—and the discovery and conquest of America—turn into a blessing.

Notes

1. So Villagrá's Zaldivar proclaims at the end of canto 33: "A qui fue Troia" (Here was Troy); Gaspar Perez de Villagrá, *Historia de la Nueva Mexico* (Alcalà, 1610), 276v. The poem has been translated by Gilbert Espinosa and annotated by F. W. Hodge as *History of New Mexico* (Los Angeles, 1933).

2. Villagrá, *Historia de la Nueva Mexico*, 285r; my translations.

3. See, for example, Paul Horgan, *Great River: The Rio Grande in North American History*, 2 vols. (New York, 1954), 1:209.

4. The indebtedness of Villagrá's episode to Alonso de Ercilla's *Araucana* (1569–89) has been noted by Daníel Wogan in "Ercilla y la poesía mexicana," *Revista iberoamericana*, 3, no. 6 (1941): 371–79, esp. 374–75.

5. Citations from de Ercilla's *Araucana* are taken from the edition introduced by Ofelia Garza de del Castillo (Mexico City, 1972).

6. Gerónimo de Bibar, *Crónica y relación copiosa y verdadera de los regnos de Chile hecha por Gerónimo de Bibar natural de Burgos MDLVIII*, ed. Irving A. Leonard, 2 vols. (Santiago, 1966), 2:203.

7. Alonso de Góngora Marmolejo, *Historia de Chile*, chap. 26, in *Colleción de historiadores de Chile y documentos relativos a la historia nacional*, vol. 2 (Santiago, 1862), 76; my translation. Marmolejo may have written to counter Ercilla's poem, and he shows little of the latter's sympathy for their Araucanian foes. See his remarks on Ercilla in his dedicatory letter (xii). But his description of the aftermath of Millarapue cannot be a response or rival version to Ercilla's account, which he presumably would not have known: it appeared in the second part of the *Araucana* in 1578, two years after Marmolejo's death. Since Ercilla, Bibar, and Marmolejo all claim to be eyewitness reports, there is little way to determine the actual historical facts over which they disagree.

8. Citations from the *Gerusalemme liberata* are taken from the edition of Torquato Tasso's *Opere*, ed. Bruno Maier, 5 vols. (Milan, 1964); my translations.

9. Villagrá, *Historia de la Nueva Mexico*, 280r. See also Bibar, *Crónica*, 2:203, who compares the Araucanians who hang themselves to "those ancient Numantines." For the sixteenth-century sources that lie behind Cervantes's *Cerco de Numancia* (and also of Francisco de Rojas-Zorillas's two Numantia plays), see Cervantes, *Comedias y entremeses*, ed. Rodolfo Schevill and Adolfo Bonilla, 6 vols. (Madrid, 1922), 6:38–60. For an anti-imperialist reading of the Cervantes play that links it to the *Araucana*, see Willard F. King, "Cervantes' *Numancia* and Imperial Spain," *Modern Language Notes* 94 (1979): 200–221.

10. See the chillingly cynical comments of Appian in the *Roman Histories* 6.15.98.

11. Along with the *Historia*, Villagrá two years later published a pamphlet exonerating de Oñate: *El Capitan Gaspar de Villagrá, para justificcación de las muertes, justicias, y castigas que el Adelantado don Iuan de Onate dizen que hizo en la Nueva Mexico . . .* (Madrid, 1612). I am indebted for this reference to Michael Murrin, who is preparing a full discussion of Villagrá and Acoma. The documents surrounding de Oñate's career and trial are

collected and translated by George P. Hammond and Agapito Rey in *Don Juan de Oñate: Colonizer of New Mexico, 1595–1628*, 2 vols. (Albuquerque, 1953). Villagrá was himself tried and ultimately condemned, but for unrelated charges: he had executed two deserters without trial and had written a letter to the Mexican viceroy falsely extolling the richness of fertility of New Mexico. See *Don Juan de Oñate*, 2:1116.

12. Max Horkheimer and Theodor W. Adorno, *Dialectic of Enlightenment*, trans. John Cumming (New York, 1972), 43–69. See also Norman Austin, *Archery at the Dark of the Moon* (Berkeley, 1975), 143–49.

13. See John H. Finley, *Homer's Odyssey* (Cambridge, Mass., 1978), 61–63; and, for a negative argument, M. I. Finley, *The World of Odysseus*, 2nd ed. (New York, 1980), 156.

14. I cite the translation of Richmond Lattimore, *The Odyssey of Homer* (New York, 1965).

15. One can compare the famous passage in chapter 3 of Jean-Jacques Rousseau's *Essay on the Origin of Languages*: "Upon meeting others, a savage man will initially be frightened. Because of his fear he sees the others as bigger and stronger than himself. He calls them *giants*"; *On the Origin of Language: Two Essays by Jean-Jacques Rousseau and Johann Gottfried Herder*, trans. John H. Moran and Alexander Gode (New York, 1966), 13. Rousseau is anticipated—perhaps inspired—by a narrative of a Renaissance European explorer in the New World. In his celebrated account of his wanderings, Cabeza de Vaca remarks of the Indians that he and his companions first encountered after being shipwrecked off the coast of Texas in 1528: "Whatever their stature, they looked like giants to us in our fright." See chapter 18 of de Vaca, *Adventures in the Unknown Interior of America*, trans. and ed. Cyclone Covey (New York, 1961), 56.

16. For this backward pattern, to which Virgil tips off the reader at *Aeneid* 3.690–91— "Achaemenides, the unhappy companion of Ulysses, showed these things to us as he retraced backward the coast along which he had wandered" (*talia monstrabat relegens errata retrorsus/litora Achaemenides, comes infelicis Ulixi*)—see David Quint, "Painful Memories: *Aeneid* 3 and the Problem of the Past," *Classical Journal* 78 (1982): 31–38, esp. 32–33. The visit to the cyclopes' coast and to Carthage belong to the *end* of Aeneas' Odyssean wanderings, while the episode of Polyphemus in *Odyssey* 9 takes place toward the beginning of the wanderings of Odysseus; similarly the eating of the cattle on the island of the harpies that occurs earlier in Aeneas' journey (3.209–67) corresponds to the eating of the cattle of Helios in *Odyssey* 12, the final episode of Odysseus' narrated wanderings. But this pattern of reversal is also countered by the storm of *Aeneid* 1 that, in the chronological order of Aeneas' voyage, follows the episode of the cyclopes at the end of book 3 and partly corresponds to the storm at the end of *Odyssey* 12 that drives Odysseus to Calypso's island—here the *Aeneid* seems to follow the order of its Homeric model. And, similarly, Virgil places a prophetic curse in the mouth of the harpy Celaeno that recalls the curse of Polyphemus and suggests a correspondence between the harpy episode and the Homeric episode of the cyclopes—again conforming to the narrative order of the *Odyssey*.

Celaeno's curse—that the Trojans will be so consumed with hunger that they will eat their tables (3.255–7)—turns out to have a happy resolution in book 7 when Ascanius jokes that the Trojans' bread cakes are edible tables (7.116ff.). The monster's curse is thus comically appropriated by her enemies—and Aeneas, in fact, attributes her prophecy to Anchises (123), completely removing Celaeno from memory. Celaeno is related to Dido through her curse and her gender (both are female versions of Polyphemus), and the impotence of her prophecy may reflect in miniature upon Dido's own curse, which, however effective it may be in summoning up Hannibal and the Punic Wars, and perhaps Cleopatra after them, cannot stop the eventual victory of Roman power.

17. The view of the Carthaginian coast in book 1 is, in fact, a *conflation* of the description of Ithaca in *Odyssey* 13 with the description of the harbor of the Laestrygonians in *Odyssey* 10.87–94. Thus from the very beginning Carthage is seen in its double aspect: as a potential homeland and site of a high civilization rivaling Rome *and* as a place of monstrous cannibalism. Moreover, the allusion to the Laestrygonians frames the entire Carthage episode. For while Aeneas' cutting of the anchor cables of his ships to escape in haste from Carthage echoes within the *Aeneid* his flight from the coast of the cyclopes, it also imitates *Odyssey* 10.126–27, where Odysseus similarly cuts the ship ropes in order to save his crew from the Laestrygonians. The cyclopes and Laestrygonians are coupled in the *Odyssey* (10.199–200) by their monstrous size and cannibalism.

18. See the preceding note for the Odyssean parallel.

19. I have described the misogynist, anti-Eastern propaganda of the *Aeneid* and its afterlife in later Western epic poetry in "Epic and Empire," *Comparative Literature* 44 (1989): 1–32. See the classic article of M. P. Charlesworth, "The Fear of the Orient in the Roman Empire," *Cambridge Historical Journal* 2 (1926): 1–16.

20. All citations from the *Aeneid* are taken from *P. Vergili Maronis opera*, ed. R. A. B. Mynors (Oxford, 1969).

21. In the case recorded in chap. 2 of *The Psychopathology of Everyday Life*, Freud describes a young Jewish man "of academic background" obsessed with the (misquoted) words of Dido's curse. See *The Standard Edition of the Complete Psychological Works of Sigmund Freud*, ed. James Strachey et al., 24 vols. (London, 1953–1973), 6:8–14. It seems likely that Freud was referring to himself, for in *The Interpretation of Dreams*, chap. 5b, he describes his own identification with Hannibal and the Carthaginians and his inability to reach Christian Rome; *Standard Edition*, 4:195–98. In *Fin-de-Siècle Vienna* (New York, 1980), 181–207, Carl E. Schorske discusses this latter passage in a stimulating reading that shows how Freud's feelings of political resentment and resistance could be internalized in his psychoanalytic theory.

22. There are two versions of the myth of the Phoenix. The one in which the bird immolates itself and is reborn from its ashes can only be unambiguously attested after Virgil, in poems of Statius (*Sylvae* 2.4.37) and Martial (5.7). An earlier attested version describes the young Phoenix generated out of the decomposing body of its parent and then burning the parent's body in an act of piety: see the version attributed to Manilius in Pliny's *Natural History* 10.4 and, for a parallel account, Pomponius Mela *De chorographia* 3.84. But see the persuasive arguments of R. van den Broek for the equal antiquity of the myth of generation from self-immolation in *The Myth of the Phoenix* (Leiden, 1972), 409–11.

23. Servius on *Aeneid* 4.581, in *Servianorum in Vergilii carmina commentariorum*, ed. A. F. Stocker and A. H. Travis (Oxford, 1965), 420.

24. See the excellent discussion by Frederick M. Ahl in *Lucan: An Introduction* (Ithaca, N.Y., 1976), 88–107.

25. Tasso's imitations of Silius are particularly numerous in canto 9, where Solimano's attack on the Crusader army is modeled on the battle of Cannae in books 9–10 of the *Punica*. Solimano's promise of booty to his Arab troops repeats Hannibal's exhortation on the eve of Cannae (9.195ff.); the episode of Latino and his sons (9.27–39) imitates Silius's Crista (10.92–169); and the simile of the lioness at octave 29 repeats

10.124–27. Further, the death of Lesbino, the object of Solimano's pederastic affection (9.81–88), is modeled upon the death of Cinyps, the favorite of Hannibal, in *Punica* 12.226–52.

26. I risk oversimplification here, for, as usual, Virgil has it at least two ways. Dido seems to regain her composure and dignity following her curse and at the moment of her suicide (4.651ff.); her words at verse 653—"vixi et quem dederat cursum Fortuna peregi" (I have lived and completed the course that Fortune set for me)—earned the admiration of Seneca (*De beneficiis* 5.17.5). Thus her death combines stoic autonomy and fatalism with an erotic loss of self-mastery. See the commentary of R. G. Austin to *P. Vergili Maronis Aeneidos liber quartus* (Oxford, 1955), 188–90.

27. See W. W. Tarn and M. P. Charlesworth, *Octavian, Antony, and Cleopatra* (Cambridge, 1965), 137–39.

28. Citations from the *Os lusíadas* are taken from the edition of Francisco da Silveira Bueno (São Paulo, 1960).

29. The classical models of the Adamastor episode have been excellently traced by Américo da Costa Ramalho in his *Estudios camonianos* (Coimbra, 1975), 33–53.

30. Ibid., 35.

31. Frank Pierce notes parenthetically that the waterspout is "a kind of natural Adamastor" in his essay "Camões' Adamastor," in *Hispanic Studies in Honour of Joseph Manson* (Oxford, 1972), 207–15, esp. 209. See also the helpful remarks on the Adamastor episode by C. M. Bowra in *From Virgil to Milton* (London, 1945), 123–25.

32. Cf. decade 1, book 3, chaps. 3–4 of the *Asia de Joam de Barros*, ed. António Baiao (Coimbra, 1932), 127–29; part 1, chap. 35 of Damião de Gois, *Cronica do Felicissimo Rei D. Manuel*, ed. David Lopes Gagean, 4 vols. (Coimbra, 1949), 1:74–75. For the log of da Gama's voyage, see *Portuguese Voyages, 1498–1663*, ed. Charles David Ley (London, 1947), 3–38. The episode of Veloso and the Hottentots is found on pp. 5–6.

33. De Gois, *Cronica*, 1:75.

34. Ramalho, *Estudios*, 44–45, notes a connection between the allusion to Antaeus and the figure of Adamastor.

35. For a description of the "dialectical" literary imitation at work here in Camões's rewriting of Homer, see the heuristic model proposed by Thomas M. Greene in *The Light in Troy* (New Haven, 1982), 45–47.

36. This was a not untypical expression of Portuguese attitudes toward the natives of black Africa, although these attitudes could vary considerably with respect to different African peoples and in different regions. See C. R. Boxer, *Race Relations in the Portuguese Colonial Empire, 1415–1825* (Oxford, 1963).

37. See, for example, Boccaccio in book 3 of the *Genealogie deorum gentilium libri*, ed. Vincenzo Romano, 2 vols. (Bari, 1951), 1:122–23; and Natalis Comes in book 8, chap. 2 of *Natalis Comitis mythologiae* (Padua, 1616), 428–30.

38. The best description of this double structure of narrative repetition is found in Peter Brook's chapter, "Freud's Masterplot: A Model for Narrative," in his *Reading for the Plot* (New York, 1984), 90–112. Brooks examines the description of the repetition compulsion in *Beyond the Pleasure Principle* and sees in narrative teleology an attempt to master repetition that the double nature of repetition always calls into question. It is possible that Freud's model of psychic empowerment may be informed by the political master narratives of his literary tradition, particularly epic. It is not perhaps coincidental that his example of traumatic repetition in *Beyond the Pleasure Principle* is drawn from Tasso's *Gerusalemme liberata*. On this and related points, see Margaret Ferguson, *Trials of Desire* (New Haven, 1983), 126–33, 189–93; see also note 22 above.

39. This conclusion is briefly considered by Cleonice Berardinelli in her *Estudios camoni-anos* (Rio de Janeiro, 1973), 40.

40. The comparison of daring seafarers to the rebellious giants has a classical precedent in the *Silvae* of Statius (3.2):

> Quis rude et abscissum miseris animantibus aequor
> fecit iter solidaeque pios telluris alumnos
> expulit in fluctus pelagoque immisit hianti
> audax ingenii? nec enim temeraria virtus
> illa magis, summae gelidum quae Pelion Ossae
> iunxit anhelantemque iugis bis pressit Olympum.
>
> (61–66)

[Who made the rough and sundered sea a path for miserable mortals, and, daring of character, cast the devoted children of the firm earth out onto the waves and threw them into the yawning ocean? For not more presumptuous was the valor that joined frozen Pelion to the top of Ossa and pressed upon panting Olympus with the double mountains.]

See *Statius*, trans. J. H. Mozley, 2 vols. (London, 1961), 1:160. For Rabelais's treatment of this *topos*, see the *Tiers Livre*, chap. 51.

41. Herman Melville, *Billy Budd*, chap. 7, in *Shorter Novels of Herman Melville*, ed. Raymond Weaver (New York, 1928), 255.

42. For Celaeno, see note 16 above.

43. Both text and translation are cited from *Fracastoro's Syphilis*, ed. and trans. Geoffrey Eatough (Liverpool, 1984).

FIGURE 1. From Theodore de Bry's *Americae Tertia Pars* (Frankfurt-
am-Main, 1593). Cf. *Nashes Lenten Stuffe* (1599): "A pipe of
Tobacco to raise my spirits and warm my brain . . ."
Photo: The Bancroft Library, University of California,
Berkeley.

Elizabethan Tobacco

TOBACCO'S FIRST ENTRY INTO English poetry doesn't strike the modern reader as a particularly auspicious one. In book 3 of *The Faerie Queene* (1590), during a hunt, the fairy Belphoebe discovers the unconscious body of Prince Arthur's seriously wounded squire Timias:

> Into the woods thenceforth in hast she went,
>   To seeke for hearbes, that mote him remedy . . .
>   There, whether it divine *Tobacco* were,
>   Or *Panachaea*, or *Polygony*,
>   She found, and brought it to her patient deare
> Who al this while lay bleeding out his hart-bloud neare.
>
>   (3.5.32)[1]

What could be more fleeting a reference? A plant growing in not only distant but fairy woods, and then only one of three alternatives for the herb Belphoebe actually does fetch, applied in the most unusual way, as a wound wart, not in a pipe—and Spenser's poetry never mentions the word, the novelty, again. Yet this seemingly offhand reference, and the newly introduced plant itself, had a surprising impact on later writers: no epithet for tobacco comes close to being as standard in later Elizabethan literature as Spenser's "divine,"[2] a fact almost as remarkable as the meteoric rise of tobacco smoking during the same period. In 1603, the first year for which official records of tobacco importation survive, 16,000 pounds of tobacco passed through official channels, perhaps that much again unofficially.[3] And a year after that, marking the new power at once of tobacco and king, James issued his *A Counter-Blaste to Tobacco*, which denounced the "toy" as England's ruination.[4] In fact, "As the literature of the day indicates," says tobacco historian Jerome Brooks, "[tobacco] was nowhere more heartily taken up, after about 1590, than in England."[5] The paradoxical combination of triviality and power in both tobacco and Spenser's reference to it seems perfectly foreshadowed by Spenser's oxymoronic-sounding epithet itself—the weed's divine.

What makes tobacco's rise to power even more impressive, and helps in part to account for James's disgust, is the fact that the sole owner of the New World from which tobacco came was the enemy, Spain. One would have guessed the knowing Englishman to have shied away from tobacco as a constant reminder of the belatedness Richard Hakluyt in *Divers Voyages Touching the Discovery of America*

273

(1582) begins his dedication to Sidney by deploring: "I marvel not a little (right honorable) that since the discovery of America (which is now full fourscore and ten years), after so great conquests and plantings of the Spaniards and Portingales there, that we of England could never have the grace to set fast footing in such fertile and temperate places as are left as yet unpossessed of them."[6] Not only did Spain monopolize America's land, souls, and especially gold while England settled for a New World weed, but Spain further increased her fortune, and decreased England's, by selling that same weed to England. And yet tobacco in Spenser's passage represents not an exacerbation of a bad case but its cure.

A brief consideration of Spenser's allegory in the Timias and Belphoebe passage helps begin explaining how the English could accommodate tobacco's representation of their own triviality. For tobacco is only one of many grand trifles that figure in Spenser's passage. Neither Timias nor Belphoebe could be considered the most significant character in this or any other book of *The Faerie Queene*, and yet they represent what were in 1590 the two most powerful people in England—Spenser's patrons, Raleigh and the queen. Oddly, the rise to power of these figures—Raleigh the fourth son of a country gentleman; Elizabeth excommunicated, "illegitimate," and female—is itself as miraculous as tobacco's, almost a pledge of England's own potentiality.[7] As a celebration of his small country's enormous spiritual and imperial claims, Spenser's poem matches the paradoxicality of its subject, here in the Timias and Belphoebe passage by the lowly pastoral meant "to insinuate and glance at greater matters,"[8] and everywhere by the epic representation of "our sovereign the Queen, and her kingdom in" the nothing of "Faery land."[9] But then "divine" Spenser himself,[10] the poor scholar turned poet laureate, testifies to the latent power of English trifles, producing with his contemporaries what generally has been considered "the greatest literature our language has known" at a time when it would seem that imperial-minded Englishmen had little reason to exult.

Insofar as literary historians have highlighted the paradoxical nature of Elizabethan England's ebullience, they have tended to consider that expansiveness merely compensatory or wish-fulfilling, arising from the need to hide the truth about Elizabethan banality and impotence. For example, G. K. Hunter, whose evaluation of Elizabethan literature I've just quoted, assumes that what drove writers like Spenser to the heights of literary sublimity was precisely their "frustration"—with their own political careers, most directly, but also implicitly with England's as a whole.[11] Similarly, in a classic analysis of the extravagant praise these writers lavished on the queen, Frances Yates calls Elizabeth's own "divinity" a sublimated expression of repressed anxiety about England's fate: "The lengths to which the cult of Elizabeth went are a measure of the sense of isolation which had at all costs to find a symbol strong enough to provide a feeling of spiritual security in face of the break with the rest of Christendom."[12] Yet tobacco's own cult demonstrates that it is at least as accurate to say that the Elizabethans actively celebrated what they themselves considered overtly trivial.

Indeed, some Elizabethans expected tobacco not merely to exemplify by analogy the divine potential of other English trifles, but actually to help *produce* those divinities, even so far as to transform little England into a heaven on earth. Spenser's association of tobacco with Raleigh and Elizabeth suggests the real basis of England's hopes for an overseas empire, the American colony that Raleigh had already founded in Elizabeth's name—Virginia. This English foothold in the New World would be different from Spain's empire not only in location, as Hakluyt recommended, but in theory and practice. Thomas Cain has convincingly demonstrated that the Mammon episode in *The Faerie Queene*'s second book represents in part Spenser's warning about New World gold;[13] according to Spenser, the Spanish, in their typically idolatrous fashion, have blinded themselves by worshipping an earthly god. Cain oddly assumes, however, that Spenser is in particular warning Raleigh to "manage the gold of Guiana" temperately. The conclusion is anachronistic—Raleigh did not sail for Guiana till 1595—but more important misses Spenser's contrast between the gold-feverish Spanish colonies and "*fruitfullest* Virginia" (2.proem.2.9; my emphasis). The point of this essay is to show what Spenser and his contemporaries take this contrast to mean, and why it gets elaborated by talk about a smokeable American "fruit." The first section of the essay will briefly review the medical benefits tobacco was supposed to offer, and suggest why neither these supposed benefits nor tobacco's inherent pleasures can alone account for tobacco's popularity in the 1590s, again precisely the period when England owned no New World empire from which to import tobacco and so was forced to buy it from the enemy who did; the second section will outline Raleigh's and Elizabeth's crucial roles in tobacco's popularization; and the third and fourth sections will examine English claims about tobacco's divinity in relation to the literary tradition for tobacco inaugurated by Spenser and most fully worked out by John Beaumont's mock panegyric, *The Metamorphosis of Tabacco* (1602).[14] In general, tobacco's advocates and critics agree that the materially poor English are nevertheless Spain's ideological superiors, but disagree about whether tobacco will help or hurt this "fairy" superiority. The tobacco critic considers the imported weed pagan and earthly, qualities that infect England and lower its sights profoundly. A tobacco advocate like Beaumont counters that, with less persuasive claims to inherent value than gold, tobacco bespeaks the mind's power to create value, and so continually alerts the English mind (even physiologically, as I'll show) to its own abilities. Later, in Stuart England, this idealism centering on tobacco would help foster a new economics of imperialism, one that began to displace gold as an imperialist preoccupation in favor of commodities previously understood as trivial.[15] But Elizabethan propagandists of tobacco— drawn to medical and economic rationales for smoking yet pursuing such rationales only confusedly or ironically—were finally less concerned with tobacco's material than with its ideal import. Indeed, these writers believed that the immediate reward of gold had tricked the Spanish into equating imperial with economic success; tobacco was supposed to dramatize that, on the contrary, something like what we would now call ideology was true power. While the Spanish enslaved themselves to gold, tobacco taught the English to limit their ambitions to nothing—or, at least, to nothing but smoke.

I

Though Columbus sighted tobacco on his very first voyage, "the first original notice in English of the use of tobacco by the Indians" does not appear till 1565, in John Sparke's account of Sir John Hawkins's second slaving voyage:[16] "The Floridans when they travel," observes Sparke,

> have a kind of herb dried, who with a cane and an earthen cup in the end, with fire, and the dried herbs put together, do suck through the cane the smoke thereof, which smoke satisfieth their hunger, and therewith they live four or five days without meat or drink, and this all the Frenchmen [Jean Ribault's men, about to be massacred by the Spanish] used for this purpose: yet they do hold opinion withal, that it causeth water & phlegm to void from their stomachs.[17]

Such a report of tobacco's double and, as Sparke's "yet" signifies, slightly paradoxical power—at once to nourish and to purge—gets reiterated by English writers too many times to bother citing, though when William Harrison (1573) and the elder Hakluyt (1582) acknowledge that tobacco is now being planted in England, they naturally single out not its nutritional but its medicinal virtue as the benefit required by certainly well-to-do buyers: tobacco, they say, eases the rheum.[18]

Now the rheum—what we call an allergic reaction or the common cold—was enough of a worry in Tudor England to make a remedy for it seem marvelous indeed. Sir Thomas Elyot's *The Castel of Helth* (1541), for instance, claims that "at this present time in the realm of England, there is not any one more annoyance to the health of man's body, than distillations from the head called rheums."[19] Ever since the Tudor peace, Elyot believes, the disease has become more frequent, the English head more watery, as the English have increasingly devoted themselves to excess, like "banqueting after supper & drinking much, specially wine a little afore sleep" (80a). Indeed, in Elyot's account the rheum's symptoms—"Wit dull. Much superfluities. Sleep much and deep" (3b)—look just like its causes; one might conclude that the rheum not only mirrors but helps perpetuate the complacence and corruption of manners producing it.

Given this sociological understanding of the disease, however, tobacco seems an unusual choice for a remedy. If it is relatively easy to imagine a physical opposition between tobacco and the rheum, the rheum as cold and moist being driven out by tobacco as hot and dry, it is much less easy to see how an expensive novelty could help do anything but augment the intemperance Elyot decries.[20] "A Satyricall Epigram" in Henry Buttes's *Dyets Dry Dinner* (1599) mocks tobacco—though only its "wanton, and excessive use," a qualification to which I'll return—as simply the latest foreign luxury helping to drown the English character: "On English fool: wanton Italianly;/Go Frenchly: Dutchly drink: breath Indianly."[21] Later, "Philaretes" in his *Work for Chimny-Sweepers* (1602) denounces tobacco not only as a foolish toy but as the devil's invention, a fact amply demonstrated, he believes, by the herbalist Nicolas Monardes' observations on tobacco's American heritage:

The Indian Priests (who no doubt were instruments of the devil whom they serve) do ever before they answer to questions propounded to them by their Princes, drink of this *Tobacco* fume, with the vigor and strength whereof, they fall suddenly to the ground, as dead men, remaining so, according to the quantity of the smoke that they had taken. And when the herb had done his work, they revive and wake, giving answers according to the visions and illusions which they saw whilst they were wrapt in that order.[22]

(The devil aside, tobacco here even exaggerates the physical symptoms, the dullness and sleepiness, associated with the rheum: the priests fall down "as dead men.") The odd truth about this kind of argument, however, is that Philaretes' is the first full-scale attack on tobacco to be launched in English, some thirty years at the very least after its use in England begins.[23] Even Monardes himself, in the herbal that proved to be "the most frequently issued book of overseas interest in the Elizabethan period,"[24] concludes that tobacco's superstitious application shows only how "the Devil is a deceiver, and hath the knowledge of the virtue of Herbs";[25] by Philaretes' own account "Monardus" is one of the "many excellent & learned men" who "do commend this plant as a thing most excellent and divine" (A3r). What was there about tobacco that enabled it for so long not only to escape the censure one would expect but to receive such lavish praise instead?

One answer is provided by Philaretes' anxiety about his pamphlet's reception. So strong are the voices for tobacco, and so rare the voices against it—"many excellent Physicians and men of singular learning and practice, together with many gentlemen and some of great accompt, do by their daily use and custom in drinking of *Tobacco*, give great credit and authority to the same" (A3r)—that Philaretes feels he must embark on a disputation against Authority (citing Plato and Aristotle in his defense) before his tobacco argument can proceed (A4v). But to claim that tobacco prospered because the mighty took it under their wing is only to rephrase the question: what enabled tobacco to win such powerful favor?[26] The two most obvious explanations, that tobacco is inherently likeable, not to say addictive, and that tobacco's novelty added luster to its intrinsic charm, fail fully to account for the particular circumstances of tobacco's reception in late sixteenth-century England. First, with the help of herbalists like Monardes, tobacco came to be regarded as not just a rheum distiller but an all-round wonder drug; since tobacco was not the only American herb celebrated this way, its own virtues, whatever they may be, would seem to say less about its identification as a cure-all than about its eventual ascendancy over other New World candidates for Panacea like sassafras. Second, the English craze for smoking, like its taste for America in general, developed much later than on the Continent, later even than its introduction to England as a novelty.[27] Here the demonstrably false legend about Raleigh introducing tobacco to England gains a certain kind of credence: just as Raleigh hardly invented the idea of English colonies in America and yet was the first to start one, so we might imagine the most powerful Englishman in 1590 not as tobacco's original but its most persuasive proponent.[28] The legend about Raleigh in fact derives from the 1590s—Buttes says, "Our English *Ulysses*, renowned Sir *Walter Raleigh* . . . hath both far fetcht it [tobacco], and dear bought it" (P5v–P6r)—though James himself lends greater authority to the claim:

With the report of a great discovery for a Conquest, some two or three Savage men, were brought in, together with this Savage custom. But the pity is, the poor wild barbarous men died, but that vile barbarous custom is yet alive, yea in fresh vigor: so as it seems a miracle to me, how a custom springing from so vile a ground, and brought in by a father so generally hated, should be welcomed on so slender a warrant.[29]

The denunciation makes sure that James's subjects understand tobacco's political significance: for tobacco to be attacked means for Raleigh to have fallen, and at the same time, though only implicitly here, for pathetic, unprofitable Virginia to have been confiscated by the Crown. I'd like to turn now to the surviving evidence about Raleigh and tobacco in order to determine the attractions tobacco held for the man who focused England's attention upon it.

II

The first description and commendation of tobacco one can safely associate with Raleigh is the work not of Raleigh himself—indeed, Raleigh is for the most part above speaking on the subject—but of his servant Thomas Harriot, in Harriot's *A Briefe and True Report of the New Found Land of Virginia* (1588).[30] The purpose of Harriot's tract, to advertise and justify Raleigh's American efforts, helps in an obvious way to account for both Harriot's praise of tobacco there and the many other claims about tobacco's medicinal wonders in general: if one wants to convince potential investors that Virginia "may return you profit and gain" (5), then a miraculous Virginian herb will come in very handy. What is less obvious is the close relation between the specific properties Harriot claims for tobacco and the kinds of economic returns he and writers like him expected America would bring to little England. The historian D. B. Quinn has called what he considers the most important of these expectations the supplementary economy, the complementary economy, and the emigration thesis.[31] The first, the supplementary economy, meant "that America could produce many of the products which England herself produced but in greater quantities," and so could bolster, expand the limited homeland; Harriot is thinking this way when he lists potential Virginian commodities like woad, "A thing of so great vent and use among English Dyers, which cannot be yielded sufficiently in our own country for spare of ground," but which "may be planted in Virginia, there being ground enough" (11). The second model, though "of primary importance," imagined the New World supplying the English, as Harriot says, "with most things which heretofore they have been fain to provide, either of strangers or of our enemies" (6). Since the Renaissance believed that the same latitude meant the same climate, and the same climate was all one country needed to produce the same commodities as another country, Virginia, as "answerable" in climate "to the Island of *Japan*, the land of *China*, *Persia*, *Jury* [Jewry], the Islands of *Cyprus* and *Candy* [Crete], the South parts of *Greece*, *Italy*, and *Spain*, and of many other notable and famous countries" (31),[32] held out to England the hope that, in Quinn's words, "the English economy would . . . become virtually independent of imports from all but tropical lands." The final model, the emigration thesis, Quinn explains this way: "The tendency for population to increase after the mid-century, together with endemic unemployment associated with the decline of certain branches of the cloth trade, impressed—over-impressed—almost all those who thought about it with the idea that there was a surplus population which ought to be exported." John Hawkins, in a prefatory poem to Sir George Peckham's *True Reporte* (1583), describes the "impression" more vividly:

> But Rome nor Athens nor the rest, were never pestered so,
> As England where no room remains, her dwellers to bestow,
> But shuffled in such pinching bonds, that very breath doth lack:
> And for the want of place they crawl one o'er another's back.[33]

It is with such hysteria in mind that Harriot extols "the dealing of *Sir Walter Raleigh* so liberal in large giving and granting of land" in Virginia; "The least that he hath granted hath been five hundred acres to a man only for the adventure of his person" (32). In the light of these hypotheses about increased "home" production, freedom from the threat of foreign embargoes, and room in which to "vent" England's surplus, part of Harriot's description of tobacco's powers looks like a synecdoche for America's expected impact on the English body politic as a whole: tobacco, says Harriot, "openeth all the pores & passages of the body" (16) or, in Hawkins's terms, lets England breathe.

The easiest way to grasp the economic constraints that tobacco as America might be imagined resolving is to think of them all as effects of one master problem—England's limitation to an island, in particular a northern island hemmed in by enemies. In his *A Defence of Tabacco: With a Friendly Answer to Worke for Chimny-Sweepers* (1602), Roger Marbecke traces to this cause even England's peculiar susceptibility to the rheum: "But for that we are Islanders . . . we are by nature subject, to overmuch moisture, and rheumatic matter";[34] Harriot's captain Ralph Lane, on the other hand, writes to Sir Francis Walsingham from Virginia that "the climate is so wholesome, yet somewhat tending to heat, As that we have not had one sick since we entered into the country; but sundry that came sick, are recovered of long diseases especially of Rheums."[35] While Marbecke immediately goes on to agree with Elyot that excessive eating and drinking produce rheum also, these factors too signal the anxieties of a country unable to produce for itself, taking too much in—as it were, drowning for want of land.[36] With a whole world to themselves, the Indians, remarks Harriot, are moderate eaters, "whereby they avoid sickness. I would to god we would follow their example. For we should be free from many kinds of diseases which we fall into by sumptuous and unseasonable banquets, continually devising new sauces, and provocations of gluttony to satisfy our unsatiable appetite" (60). It is important to remember that in this dietetic case, as in the case of the rheum, tobacco's cure is not merely figurative, representing the extra world little England hopes to acquire; tobacco smoke, said Sparke, "satisfieth their hunger," and Harriot classifies tobacco with other "such commodities as Virginia is known to yield for victual and sustenance of man's life, usually fed upon by the natural inhabitants, as also by us during the time of our abode" (13).

But no matter how convenient for understanding tobacco in relation to England's economic ills, this classification by Harriot actually forces consideration of some problems about Virginian tobacco I've so far overlooked. If America is to help England by freeing it from the twin dangers of excessive importation and unexportable surplus, one might have expected to find tobacco listed not only with the native foods that would support a displaced English population but with the "merchantable commodities" (7) that would feed and enrich home also—which is in fact where Harriot places that other panacea "of most rare virtues," sassafras (9).[37] Presumably Harriot knows something about the marketability of Virginian tobacco that he doesn't want to say directly, something like the "biting taste" that prevented Englishmen from becoming interested in colonial tobacco until John Rolfe imported Trinidadian seeds to Virginia in 1610–11;[38] most of the tobacco Englishmen "drank" before that time was indeed the enemy's—Spain's—so rather than alleviate England's trade woes, tobacco actually only exacerbated them.[39] Good reason for sticking to tobacco's nutritional value, but the classification as food is problematic in its own way: Harriot never explicitly mentions the hunger-depressant power he could have found out about not only from the Indians but from such written sources as Monardes—to whom, oddly enough, Harriot refers the reader in sassafras's case, not in tobacco's.[40] Whatever the real reason for Harriot's enigmatic silence here, he himself wants the reader to know both that his praise of Virginian tobacco has been cut short and that his reticence about it corresponds to his especially high regard for it: "We our selves during the time we were there used to suck it after their manner, as also since our return, & have found many rare and wonderful experiments of the virtues thereof; of which the relation would require a volume by it self." It is a regard the Indians share. "This *Uppowoc*"—Harriot's preference for the native instead of the well-known Spanish name is itself significant—

is of so precious estimation amongst them, that they think their gods are marvelously delighted therewith: Whereupon sometime they make hallowed fires & cast some of the powder therein for a sacrifice: being in a storm upon the waters, to pacify their gods, they cast some up into the air and into the water: so a weir for fish being newly set up, they cast some therein and into the air: also after an escape of danger, they cast some into the air likewise. (16)

If I'm right to say that Harriot has some difficulty *placing* tobacco in his colonial argument, this description of native or "natural" superstition, intended after all as a weak form of argument from authority, allows Harriot the liberty to speak of tobacco as a panacea without having to rationalize the claim in terms either of physiology or of England's peculiar needs.[41] Harriot doesn't show the Indians believing, in other words, that tobacco has some chemical or synecdochical relation to storms, weirs, or danger; simply, the gods like it, one casts it on an action and it works.

Yet a more common colonial logic, more common even in Harriot's own tract, makes citing Indians as any kind of authority on value look strange. For the most salient fact about savages is that they always hold the wrong thing in "precious estimation"—not gold, for instance, but trifles. One could find Harriot's version of the first confrontation between Americans and Europeans in innumerable travel books:

As soon as they saw us [they] began to make a great and horrible cry, as people which never beforehand had seen men appareled like us, and came a way making out cries like wild beasts or men out of their wits. But being gently called back, we offered them of our wares, as glasses, knives, babies [i.e., dolls], and other trifles, which we thought they delighted in. So they stood still, and perceiving our Good will and courtesy came fawning upon us, and bade us welcome. (45)

When Harriot speaks elsewhere of the Indians' powers of estimation, it is only copper "which they much esteem" (46), "which they esteem more than gold or silver" (71);[42] in other words, they "do esteem our trifles before things of greater value" (25). While such proofs of Indian misprision are meant no doubt to tickle Harriot's readers, and to demonstrate how cheaply Indian favor can be bought,[43] the savage love of trifles speaks directly to England's fears, once again, about its own trading habits. Worried as Elyot is with extravagances at home, Clement

Urmeston, for example, deplores the taste of his fellow countrymen for foreign "trifles, whereby all strangers in other realms hath work, and English men hath none"; what is worse, the stranger will not "take cloth nor English commodities" for his useless ware, but that which, for the sixteenth-century economist, constituted value itself, "rials, angels and other fine gold."[44] If English economists could regard their European trade, then, as a delusion—the foolish English venting the solid good of bullion in exchange for mere pestering trifles—the still more foolish American savage represented the hope of turning passive victimization into active victimizing. England would be able not only to import gold for next to nothing but to export all its own weaknesses onto America: Sir Humphrey Gilbert trusts that by western voyages Englishmen will "have occasion, to set poor men's children, to learn handy crafts, and thereby to make trifles and such like, which the Indians and those people [the Chinese] do much esteem: By reason whereof, there should be none occasion, to have our country cumbered with loiterers, vagabonds, and such like idle persons."[45]

The only catch in Harriot's case is that his credulous Indians don't *have* any gold; his prefatory letter warns the understanding reader to discount "as trifles that are not worthy of wise men to be thought upon" the ill reports of such former colonists who "after gold and silver was not so soon found, as it was by them looked for, had little or no care of any other thing but to pamper their bellies" (6). In light of these disaffected gold hunters, with whom Harriot might reasonably expect a very large proportion of his audience to sympathize, Harriot's praise of Indian moderation takes on a colonial significance: if only Englishmen could regard America as the Indians do, and learn to live as colonists like them, "free from all care of heaping up Riches for their posterity, content with their state, and living friendly together of those things which god of his bounty hath given them" (56). Once again, in the displacement of gold as a measure of value, Indian tastes assume a kind of authority; looking back on Harriot's interest in their "precious estimation" of tobacco, one might say, then, that tobacco supplies the lack of the precious metal—or that by declaring a relation of tobacco's virtues "would require a volume by itself," as if tobacco were a New World all its own, Harriot builds both gold's missing value, and the fact that gold is missing, into tobacco.[46]

It is a substitution that tobacco's critics later found the English people all too willing to make themselves. That is, not only a lack of Indian gold seemed to these critics to defeat expectations of happy returns from America: somehow even savages had managed to palm off a trifle on the ever eager English consumer. John Aubrey's life of Raleigh (c. 1669–96) records how near the turn of the century the exchange of a trifle for a precious metal was quite literal: tobacco "was sold then for its weight in silver. I have heard some of our old yeoman neighbors say, that when they went to Malmesbury or Chippenham Market, they culled out their best shillings to lay in the scales against the tobacco."[47] Thomas Campion complains that such skewed powers of estimation yield the Spaniards profit:

Aurum nauta suis Hispanus vectat ab Indis,
  Et longas queritur se subijsse vias.
Maius iter portus ad eosdem suscipit Anglus,
  Ut referat fumos, nuda Tobacco, tuos:
Copia detonsis quos vendit Ibera Britannis,
  Per fumos ad se vellera cal'da trahens.

[The Spanish raider carries gold from his Indies and laments that he has
gone on long journeys. The Englishman undertakes a longer way to the
same parts so that he can bring back your smoke, unadorned Tobacco,
which Spanish wealth sells, by this smoke stripping and drawing to itself
the hides from the Britons.][48]

Tobacco even clarified the old fears about England trading its solid commodities
for nothing by dramatizing the exchange in a way never before possible: whenever an Englishman lit his pipe,[49] he could be seen to demonstrate unequivocally
how "the Treasure of this land is vented for smoke."[50]

Yet a well-known anecdote about Raleigh, first reported by James Howell
(1650), shows how, when Raleigh makes a bet with Elizabeth about the amount of
smoke tobacco actually does hold, the substitution of gold for smoke could work
in an Englishman's favor:

But if one would try a pretty conclusion how much smoke there is in a pound of Tobacco,
the ashes will tell him, for let a pound be exactly weighed, and the ashes kept charily and
weigh'd afterwards, what wants of a pound weight in the ashes cannot be denied to have
been smoke, which evaporated into air; I have been told that Sir *Walter Raleigh* won a wager
of Queen *Elizabeth* upon this nicety.

In another version of the anecdote the queen adds in paying, "Many laborers in
the fire she had heard of who turned their gold into smoke, but *Raleigh* was the
first who had turned smoke into gold."[51] The story compactly illustrates so much
of Raleigh's relation to the queen, even down to the carefully staged destruction
of his property, like his muddied cloak or his melodramatically desperate postur-
ings, bringing him greater wealth. But this manner of enriching oneself via the
New World and its products is crucially different from the colonial models and
tobacco uses I've specified: unlike a chemical or alchemical transformation of the
English body or body politic, Raleigh's tobacco simply wins him a bet; the gold
comes neither from the New World nor its inhaled representative but from Elizabeth. There seems nothing about tobacco's place in the story, in other words,
that some other inflammable object might not fill—the operative term is, after
all, smoke.

But perhaps tobacco's replaceability here is what helps make its appearance
in the story, and in the story of Raleigh's life, so inevitable: for the story must be
about Raleigh, not tobacco, and it must show that what Raleigh does to tobacco,
turning smoke to gold, is only what he has done to himself—as Stephen Green-

blatt reminds us about Raleigh in his prime, he was "perhaps the supreme example in England of a gentleman not born but fashioned."[52] Contemporaries did not miss the correspondence, famously dramatized by Raleigh before his execution, between Raleigh's smoking and his pride, his aloofness; whether or not Raleigh smoked at the execution of his rival Essex also, the story sounded so plausible and epitomizing that, at his own execution, Raleigh was forced publicly to deny it.[53] Others quickly adopted the flourish a pipe could bring them. In his mock travelogue *Mundus Alter et Idem* (1605), Joseph Hall "discovers" Raleigh and tobacco in Moronia Felix or, in Hall's own gloss, the "Land of braggarts, or of conceited folly."[54] Everyone in Moronia Felix, like Raleigh, pretends to noble birth, though their claims, like their sumptuous buildings, "are exceedingly flimsy, and whatever their external splendor promises, on the interior they are sordid beyond measure" (94). Lacking funds and good sense, "most of the inhabitants feed neither on bread nor on food but on the fume" of their own vanity and of tobacco:[55] "And while their nostrils exhale smoke high in the air, their kitchens have passed completely out of use" (96). The wager anecdote captures very well both the insubstantiality of Raleigh's position as Hall sees it—"Without a power-base of any kind . . . Raleigh was totally dependent on the queen"[56]—and Raleigh's irritating or enviable ability to capitalize on that insubstantiality, to give it weight, to turn the smoke of his own bravura, and of Elizabeth's favor, to account.

If tobacco figures in the anecdote, then, as little more than the personal trademark of the Queen's Alchemist, Raleigh's America similarly distances itself from the national hypotheses about New World benefits that I've outlined. Even the primary advocate of such hypotheses, Richard Hakluyt, succumbs to the pressure of Raleigh's self-allegorizing vision of America; in dedicating to Raleigh the newly edited *De Orbe Novo* (1587) of Peter Martyr, Hakluyt praises Raleigh's

letters from Court in which you freely swore that no terrors, no personal losses or misfortunes could or would ever tear you from the sweet embraces of your own Virginia, that fairest of nymphs—though to many insufficiently well known,—whom our most generous sovereign has given you to be your bride[.] If you persevere only a little longer in your constancy, your bride will shortly bring forth new and most abundant offspring, such as will delight you and yours, and cover with disgrace and shame those who have so often dared rashly and impudently to charge her with barrenness. For who has the just title to attach such a stigma to your Elizabeth's Virginia, when no one has yet probed the depths of her hidden resources and wealth, or her beauty hitherto concealed from our sight? Let them go where they deserve, foolish drones, mindful only of their bellies and gullets, who fresh from that place, like those whom Moses sent to spy out the promised land flowing with milk and honey, have treacherously published ill reports about it.[57]

The jolting reference to Virginia's imputed barrenness not only demands that the possibly vague or nominal comparison between Elizabeth and Virginia be taken seriously, but that the analogy be extended into what one might consider the most dangerous territory. Yet in similarly dwelling on the possible throwaway about Raleigh's "sweet embraces" with his "bride," the lavish sexual imagery that follows, the hidden beauty and the probeable depths, shows that taking liberties is precisely Hakluyt's point: the racy language is itself part of the dalliance between Elizabeth and Raleigh that Virginia enables.[58] Like tobacco smoke, Virginia's whole beauty here in relation to Raleigh lies in its essential malleability, the ease with which it stands for a marriage, and the fruits of a marriage, otherwise impossible. But it is crucial to see that in allegorizing Virginia as a substitute Elizabeth, the passage drives toward claiming what Virginia's critics claim also, that Virginia has no attractions per se. And indeed Elizabeth will allow Raleigh to probe her Virginia only if he stays "at Court"—near Elizabeth, certainly, but far from the vicarious deflowering.[59]

I don't mean to argue, however, that Raleigh's self-aggrandizing vision of America is entirely at odds with other more nationally oriented New World views, that Hakluyt himself, the writer here, does not desire and enjoy this vision, as others would desire and enjoy Raleigh's smoking, also. After all, Elizabeth's virginity, or more negatively her barrenness, betokened national concerns not merely by way of analogy: since Elizabeth's foreign suitors represented the possibility of international alliances, her favor meant money and power, and her offspring would hopefully ensure a peaceful succession, the queen's maidenhead would seem more than merely symbolic of both national isolation and the "want of place" at Court.

But the continuation of Hakluyt's allegory beyond the bridal motif demonstrates how the particular reduction of Virginia to a metaphor for an available queen only isolates a hidden tendency common to other more strictly economic colonial theorizing, a tendency to understand Virginia as only a *substitution*, not a different place and, possibly, a different home. Hakluyt's comparison of the English people to the Jews highlights the problem of Englishmen's finally exclusive attachment to England itself by ineptly running counter to that attachment: the switch from Raleigh and Elizabeth to Moses seems to leave Elizabeth behind, and Raleigh too even if he gets to be Moses, for Moses, of course, never entered "the promised land"; but then Virginia as the promised land neither complements, supplements, nor relieves England but leaves the island, like the Wilderness, behind altogether. In brief, the difference between Elizabeth and Moses in Hakluyt's allegory is the difference between regarding England or Virginia as home. Yet this puts the matter too crudely. Hakluyt can hardly be intending to suggest that England be abandoned; in calling Virginia "the promised land" he clearly overcompensates for *Virginia's* felt lack of intrinsic merit, a lack he at other times even helps, oddly enough, to publicize: the 1589 *Navigations* record the verdict on Virginia of one more Raleigh underling, Ralph Lane again, who affirms "that the discovery of a gold mine, by the goodness of God, or a passage to the Southsea, or someway to it, and nothing else can bring this country in request to be inhabited by our nation."[60] On the other hand, Hakluyt can, of course, hardly mean that Englishmen should never settle Virginia; when in his address to Raleigh Hakluyt deplores as Harriot will those excolonists "mindful only of their bellies and gullets," it is the profiteering English view—that gold in hand is the only thing worth leaving home and probing Virginia's depths for—which he means, again like Harriot, to condemn. Hakluyt wants to say that Virginia supplies a "milk and honey" that satisfies something more than bellies, something like Raleigh's impossible desire for Elizabeth, which hopes to "occupy" at once both Elizabeth and Virginia, though in a far from literal way. A manna made "of conceited folly," of air—yet an air the Elizabethans thought substantial enough to "drink"—tobacco helps represent both the expansionist desire and its chimerical satisfaction. Harriot's ambiguous position about tobacco/*uppowoc*, classifying it as nourishment to be exploited "there" while describing its use "here," begins to make more sense: requiring a volume all its own, tobacco helps suspend the question of Englishmen's true home, as if the metaphorical identification between England and Virginia were as good as, indeed better than, a solider settlement.

III

Tobacco enters *The Faerie Queene* carrying with it this question of mediation, posed once again in terms of Raleigh's desire for Elizabeth. The "Letter to Raleigh" and the proem to *The Faerie Queene*'s third book identify Belphoebe in two ways, first as representing one aspect or "person" of Elizabeth—"a most vertuous and beautiful Lady" as distinguished from "a most royal Queen or Empress" ("Letter," 737), or Elizabeth's "rare chastitee" as distinguished from "her rule" (3.proem.5)—and second as fashioned after Raleigh's "own excellent conceit of Cynthia" ("Letter," 737); by removing the impediment of Elizabeth's high station and presenting an Elizabeth after Raleigh's own conceit, Spenser's Belphoebe moves Elizabeth closer to Raleigh's desires in much the way Hakluyt's Virginian bride does also. Tobacco enforces the analogy to Hakluyt. With it, Belphoebe heals Timias' spear wound (received in a battle reminiscent of Raleigh's well-publicized Irish skirmishes),[61] but inflicts a love wound she cannot bring herself to cure: "But that sweet Cordiall, which can restore / A love-sick hart, she did to him envy" (50.6–7). The cordial happens to be "that dainty Rose" (51.1), "her fresh flowring Maidenhead" (54.6) in both a literal and figurative sense (i.e., the rose is literal enough to be "dispred" in mild weather [51.9], and figurative enough to be lodged "in gentle Ladies brest" [52.7]). Though Spenser's pathos here hardly figures in Hakluyt's passage (nor, for that matter, in Spenser's source),[62] the general allegorical point is basically the same: Raleigh is dying for Elizabeth's Rose, yet she grants him another flower, "divine Tobacco," as at once a compensation and demurral. At the same time, the pastoral landscape that supports two classical herbs and an American one, and that presents the choice between them as almost indifferent, ignores practical distances and distinctions (as far as Spenser might safely do so) in favor of one commanding distance, between not classes but states of mind, Timias' "mean estate" (44.7) and Belphoebe's "high *desert*" (45.7, my emphasis).[63]

But Spenser's characterization of tobacco as "divine" seems, in some vague or esoteric way, to take the allegory further; if not to the second, theological part of Hakluyt's own passage, his comparison of Virginia to "the promised land," at least to some argument that would help explain, again, the surprising notoriety of this briefest of references to tobacco. In part that notoriety would seem due simply to Belphoebe's, and therefore Elizabeth's, association with this view of tobacco, especially since tobacco requires divinity in the episode so as to render it more commensurable to "the heavenly Mayd" (43.4), but this reinvokes the comparison to Hakluyt, and to tobacco as miraculous food and healer, as manna:[64] what heavenly aspect of Elizabeth exactly do tobacco and Virginia complement? In part subsequent writers may echo Spenser's term because they accept a Continental tradition Spenser himself seems to echo,[65] but then what made Continental writers adopt the term? The influence of Indian "estimation" seems once again difficult to deny, as James demanded his subjects to consider:

Shall we . . . abase our selves so far, as to imitate these beastly *Indians*, slaves to the *Spaniards*, refuse to the world, and as yet aliens from the holy Covenant of God? Why do we not as well imitate them in walking naked as they do? in preferring glasses, feathers, and such toys, to gold and precious stones, as they do? yea why do we not deny God and adore the Devil, as they do? (B2r)[66]

If the charges against Marlowe and Raleigh and his followers may be believed, the king's hysteria was not entirely unwarranted: the infamous snitcher Richard Baines reported Marlowe's assertion "that if Christ would have instituted the sacrament with more ceremonial Reverence it would have been had in more admiration, that it would have been much better administered in a Tobacco pipe," and a lieutenant of Raleigh's was allegedly seen to "tear two Leaves out of a Bible to dry Tobacco on."[67] Philaretes comments, "Our wit-worn gallants, with the scent of thee, / Sent for the Devil and his company." To the tobacco hater, tobacco doesn't complement English values, it inverts them, hell for heaven; Philaretes too believes the comparison with Elizabeth explains tobacco, though not as her surrogate, a bride, but as her travesty, a whore: "O I would whip the quean with rods of steel, / That ever after she my jerks should feel" (Br).[68]

The problem is the same one posed by Elyot's analysis of the rheum—how can a far-fetched luxury associated with the depths of superstition come to any good?—and yet some of tobacco's advocates not only excused tobacco but exalted it as England's "divine" savior from just that decadence and superstition it would seem to exacerbate. A poem attributed in the earl of Essex's lifetime to Essex offers the pathos Spenser associates with tobacco as its justification. The poem, "The Poor Laboring Bee" (1598),[69] laments Essex's singular and undeserved bad luck: "Of all the swarm, I only could not thrive, / yet brought I wax and Honey to the hive." Even before any mention of tobacco Essex invokes the terms of Timias' unhappiness—the other bees "suck" Elizabeth's flowers, the "Rose" and "eglantynes"—but the poem's conclusion makes Essex's debt to Spenser unmistakeable: "If this I cannot have; as helpless bee, / Wished Tobacco, I will fly to thee" (the Egerton MS of the poem reads "*Witching* Tobacco," which moves the poem closer to Philaretes' pessimism about the exchange). Yet tobacco's cure works not by compensating for but by dramatizing and generalizing Essex's disappointment as the fate of all worldly desires:

> What though thou dye'st my lungs in deepest black.
> A Mourning habit, suits a sable heart.
> What though thy fumes sound memory do crack,
> forgetfulness is fittest for my smart.
>> O sacred fume, let it be Carv'd in oak,
>> that words, Hopes, wit, and all the world are smoke.

Calvin says that "not only the learned do know, but the common people have no Proverb more common than this, that man's life is like a smoke."[70] And so Essex transforms Philaretes' attack on tobacco as "smoking vanity" (Br) into the very basis of tobacco's claim to sacredness: that is, tobacco's insubstantiality leads Essex to a sublime view of the world as itself insubstantial, to *contemptus mundi*,[71] while in the same way the otherwise humiliating exchange of solid good for smoke—as a character in Thomas Dekker has it, "Tobacco, which mounts into th'air, and proves nothing but one thing . . . that he is an ass that melts so much money in smoke"[72]—here proves tobacco a less delusory taste than love of precious metals, "sweet dreams of gold."

Henry Buttes similarly turns tobacco's deficits to spiritual advantage, though more optimistically than Essex. The title page of *Dyets Dry Dinner* oddly takes for granted that a meal should be "served in after the order of Time universal," or to put it another way, that the ontogeny of one's banquet should recapitulate the phylogeny of human culture; so the meal begins with the food "Adam robbed [from] God's Orchard" (A7v)—fruit—then proceeds through dishes consequent on new developments in "humane invention," until our itch for "voluptuous delight" (A8r) leads us to that most odious of luxuries, sauces. It is at this point, as in Elyot, that the rheum arrives, the bodily counterpart to a superfluity, a running over, on two oddly correspondent scales of time, of a meal and of a human history that have both lasted too long:

Thus proceeded we by degrees, from simplicity and necessity, to variety and plenty, ending in luxury and superfluity. So that at last our bodies by surfeeding, being overflown and drowned (as it were) in a surpleurisy or deluge of a superfluous raw humor (commonly called Rheum) we were to be annealed (like new dampish Ovens, or old dwelling houses that have stood long desolate). Hence it is that we perfume and air our bodies with *Tobacco* smoke (by drying) preserving them from putrefaction. (A8v)

Yet of course, as the phylogenic scheme of the meal demands that we see, tobacco is the ultimate superfluity, and Buttes himself later spells out the rheumlike "hurt" tobacco can do: it "mortifieth and benumbeth: causeth drowsiness: troubleth & dulleth the senses: makes (as it were) drunk: dangerous in meal time" (P5r). Presumably his pharmacology is, then, homeopathic: a little more excess somehow eradicates excess altogether. But the moral is quite different from Essex's, who prizes tobacco for dramatizing the true nature of all "voluptuous delight." Buttes's homeopathy cuts two ways. Fire to rheum's water, tobacco as after-dinner mint replaces the grand conclusion to our history, the Conflagration that follows our punishment by Deluge;[73] in other words, as at once the latest luxury and earliest apocalypse, tobacco homeopathically cures, in Buttes's mind, both decadence and God's judgment upon that decadence.

Though one is tempted to dismiss this conclusion, like so many other Elizabethan arguments about tobacco, as a particularly eccentric joke, Philaretes' theological view of England seems basically the same as Buttes's, a belief that Englishmen are somehow in a peculiarly good position to mediate between worldly delights and a divine contempt for them. Philaretes' problem with tobacco is that it is too grossly of the world—its priestly user "dead sleeping falls, / Flat on the ground"—and so threatens to undo England's compromise between *contemptus* and carnality, heaven and earth: "But hence thou Pagan Idol: tawny weed, / Come not with-in"—not our Christian but—"our *Fairie* Coasts to feed" (Br; my emphasis).[74]

Buttes defends tobacco's role in preserving this compromise by sidestepping overt theology and invoking instead what he considers commonsense physiology. According to *The Breviary of Helthe*, for instance, rheum causes sleepiness by producing "great gravidity in the head," by weighing the head down; John Trevisa elaborates this analysis in terms of a clogged spirit:

For sometime rheumatic humors cometh to the spiritual parties & stop the ways of the spirit and be in point to stuff the body. Then cometh dryness or dry medicines. & worketh & destroyeth such humors. & openeth the ways of the spirit / & so the body that is as it were dead hath living.[75]

By this account hot and dry tobacco would seem, in other words, to oppose grossness, and so Marbecke argues even against Philaretes' interpretation of Monardes' report on tobacco's superstitious usage:

For take but *Monardus* his own tale: and by him it should seem; that in the taking of *Tobacco*: they [the priests] were drawn up: and separated from all gross, and earthly cogitations, and as it were carried up to a more pure and clear region, of fine conceits & actions of the mind, in so much, as they were able thereby to see visions, as you say: & able likewise to make wise & sharp answers, much like as those men are wont to do, who being cast into trances, and ecstasies, as we are wont to call it, have the power and gift thereby, to see more wonders, and high mystical matters, then all they can do, whose brains, & cogitations, are oppressed with the thick and foggy vapors, of gross, and earthly substances. Marry, if in their trances, & sudden fallings, they had become nasty, & beastly fellows: or had in most loathsome manner, fallen a-spewing, and vomiting, as drunkards are wont to do: then indeed it might well have been counted a devilish matter: and been worthy reprehension. But being used to clear the brains, and thereby making the mind more able, to come to herself, and the better to exercise her heavenly gifts, and virtues; me think, as I have said, I see more cause why we should think it to be a rare gift imparted unto man, by the goodness of God, than to be any invention of the devil. (58–59)

Now smoke for substance is a godly exchange: the mind comes to herself, though still clogged and hamstrung by the body; carried up in ecstasies to a more pure and clear region, though still on earth.[76]

Freeing Englishmen from the body's limitations as well as from their small, embattled, rheumatic island, tobacco removes a secondary curb on the English mind—particularly, on English poetry. In light of the Renaissance theory that warmer climates are more conducive to mind than colder ones,[77] Harriot's list of the warm countries, like Greece and Italy, to which Virginia's climate is answerable takes on a new significance: Virginia can be understood as opening for England not merely economic but intellectual and poetic vistas, vistas to which tobacco's own heat contributes. But to see Virginia's and tobacco's advantages in this light is to render finally untenable the reduction of tobacco's powers merely to synecdoches for Virginia's: in order to warm up Englishmen the Virginian way, one must ship them many miles and latitudes hence; yet tobacco brings to Englishmen Virginian heat—what Beaumont will call the "Indian sun"—without their having to leave the comforts of home. But then all of tobacco's benefits, like its after-dinner annealing in Buttes, are immediate, and Virginia's only anticipated; insofar as those benefits are taken seriously, tobacco does not merely stand for the New World but stand *in* for it, by transforming England into a New World all its own.[78]

Of course that is just the point tobacco's critics make also: Hall's name for Raleigh in *Mundus*'s tobacco passage, *Topia-Warallador*, buries *Raleigh* in the name of the Indian cacique Raleigh met in Guiana, *Topi-Wari*, and the Spanish word for discoverer, *hallador*, so as to suggest how an Englishman's interest in America can un-English him. The physiological side to this argument is that tobacco smoke makes an Englishman as black on the inside (inside the body, inside England's bounds) as the Indian is on the outside (on his body's outside, outside England).[79] But to the tobacco advocate smoke is precisely the key for proving that tobacco converts the New World into a disposable remedy—and now even Raleigh's self-aggrandizing bet, in which tobacco's smoke becomes his substance, seems to have its national correlative: tobacco purges the pent-up body, opens its pores, warms its brain, helps it breathe, by itself going up in smoke. Opposing Philaretes' fear that tobacco will instead turn the English body into a torrid zone, Marbecke even denies that smoke has the power seriously to alter anything:

The taking thereof, especially in fume, (which as your self granteth, *hath very small force to work any great matter upon our bodies*) can cause no such fiery, and extreme heat in the body, as is by you supposed, but rather, if it do give any heat, yet that heat is rather a familiar, and a pleasing heat, than an immoderate, extraordinary, and an aguish distemperature (19)[80]

The heat is familiar, so that England can become capable of New World powers without having to stop being England—*alter et idem*: tobacco only helps the rheumatic English mind "come to herself."

IV

A commendatory epigram to Beaumont's *The Metamorphosis of Tabacco* compares tobacco's self-consuming influence to Beaumont's poetry:

TO THE WHITE READER

Take up these lines Tobacco-like unto thy brain,
And that divinely toucht, puff out the smoke again.
(272)

Beaumont himself quickly implies that the primary metamorphosis of his title is tobacco's transformation into his poetry, a transformation unabashedly evoking the savage practice Monardes describes and Philaretes abhors:

But thou great god of Indian melody . . .
By whom the Indian priests inspired be,
When they presage in barbarous poetry:
Infume my brain, make my soul's powers subtle,
Give nimble cadence to my harsher style;
Inspire me with thy flame, which doth excel
The purest streams of the Castalian well.
(276–77)

Where Marbecke tries to reconcile savage to Christian value, Beaumont characteristically insists on celebrating those features of Indian smoking, the superstition and barbarity, that most stand in the way of such a reconciliation. Beaumont's dedicatory poem to Michael Drayton had warned readers that Beaumont would prove irreverent, since it emphasizes that the dedication is meant to be as much an affront to the powerful as a compliment to a friend: Beaumont claims he "loathes to adorn the triumphs of those men, / Which hold the reins of fortunes, and the times." The Latin tag ending the dedication, from Catullus' dedication of his own work, embraces the poet's professed marginality less militantly, joking now about Beaumont's intellectual poverty: who better should I dedicate my poem to, asks Beaumont, "namquam tu solebas / Meas esse aliquid putare nugas," than you who used to think my trifles (*nugas*) something.[81] Yet with the rigor of a puritanical antagonist Beaumont in his invocation completes the traditional assault on "trifling" poetry by allying his poem not only with poverty and nugacity but with superstition. For Beaumont subscribes to an alternative—in his view Spenserian—system of "estimation," whose genius is "the sweet and sole delight of mortal men, / The cornu-copia of all earthly pleasure" (275).[82] If poetry's influential critic Henry Cornelius Agrippa declares that poets "super fumo machinari omnia," or, in the Elizabethan version, "devise all things upon a matter of nothing [*fumo*, smoke]" (33), then Beaumont will celebrate the "Castalian well" of *fumo*—tobacco.[83]

Indeed, after its invocation, Beaumont's poem embarks on two myths of tobacco's creation that celebrate tobacco's worth as against the religious and temporal orthodoxy separately scorned in dedication and invocation but now combined in the figures of the Olympian gods. In the first myth, Earth and her subjects frustrate their oppressor, Jove, by enlivening Prometheus' subversive creation, man, with the flame of tobacco (277–86); in the second, less contentious tale, Jove courts a beautiful but standoffish American nymph who outshines Apollo: Juno angrily transforms her into a plant—tobacco—but Jove retaliates by further metamorphosing his former love into "a micro-cosm of good" (286–304). While both myths associate tobacco's value with the victimized and profane, one last hypothesis about tobacco moves value closer to conformity, though only in order to attack still another kind of tyranny. This hypothesis takes the premise of the second myth further, and decides that the gods must always have been ignorant of tobacco, or else, "had they known this smoke's delicious smack, / The vault of heav'n ere this time had been black." The more the Olympians are imagined as prone to love "the pure distillation of the earth" (304), the more their powers and authority are blotted out, blackened; for their love of tobacco assimilates them to Harriot's Indian gods, and by implication the pagan Greeks and Romans to the pagan Indians.[84] In other words, Beaumont involves tobacco in a rebellion now against not only religious or temporal authority but "the purest stream of the Castalian well," the authority of the classics. Even the gods' ignorance of tobacco damns the classical world, by reminding Beaumont's readers of one of the first and most powerful intellectual reactions to America's discovery, the realization that the ancients had, for all their intimidating genius, proven profoundly benighted—"Had but the old heroic spirits known" (305)![85]

Yet Beaumont does not want the subversion of one orthodoxy to become a triumph for another: he now explicitly asserts that those "blinder ages" (306) were indeed wrong to worship Ceres, for instance, but only because they ought to have worshiped tobacco instead. Modern times, he claims, have not abandoned superstition but discovered improvements on it:

Blest age, wherein the Indian sun had shin'd,
Whereby all Arts, all tongues have been refin'd:
Learning, long buried in the dark abysm—
Of dunstical and monkish barbarism,
When once the herb by careful pains was found,
Sprung up like Cadmus' followers from the ground,
Which Muses visitation bindeth us
More to great Cortez, and Vespucius,
Than to our witty More's immortal name,
To Valla, or the learned Rott'rodame.

                                    (314–15)

To keep his distance from both orthodoxy and superstition, Beaumont now orthodoxly eschews *papist* superstition, "dunstical and monkish barbarism," yet in the name not of Humanism nor of the True Church but of Tobacco.

This last profanity derives a special bite from the fact that, to many of Beaumont's readers, the distinction between Indian and papist paganism would have seemed a nice one indeed. We've already seen how Marlowe conflates the two kinds of "ceremonial reverence" (and apparently some Catholic priests overseas felt the same temptation: in 1588 the Roman College of Cardinals was forced to declare "forbidden under penalty of eternal damnation for priests, about to administer the sacraments, either to take the smoke of *sayri*, or tobacco, into the mouth, or the powder of tobacco into the nose, even under the guise of medicine, before the service of the Mass").[86] George Chapman's Monsieur D'Olive mocks the similar views of Marlowe's enemies—here, a Puritan weaver reviling tobacco:

Said 'twas a pagan plant, a profane weed
And a most sinful smoke, that had no warrant
Out of the word; invented sure by Satan
In these our latter days, to cast a mist
Before men's eyes, that they might not behold
The grossness of old superstition
Which is as 'twere deriv'd into the church
From the foul sink of Romish popery.

                                    (2.2.199–206)

The difference for Beaumont seems to be one of proximity: England has just escaped papistry's "dark abysm," while Indian superstition is at once too distant and too primitive a threat to be taken seriously. The superior status of a blest age freed from papist barbarism now leads Beaumont to affirm that

Had the Castalian Muses known the place
Which this Ambrosia did with honor grace,
They would have left Parnassus long ago,
And chang'd their Phocis for Wingandekoe.

                                    (315)

The wit of the final line depends on perceiving the two place names, one Greek, one Indian, as equally outlandish and barbaric, on the suggestion, again, that the ancients were no better than the Indians, or still more wishfully, that the authority of the classics, as of the Indian "people void of sense" (315), depends on the playful attribution of that authority by the enlightened English reader.

One might say that the comical mixture of classical with Indian subject matter focuses power on England as the excluded middle,[87] whose perfect representative would seem now to be "our more glorious Nymph" (315), the virgin more successful than tobacco in withstanding the encroachments of the powers that be, of superstition East and West—that "heretical" authority, Elizabeth. Earlier in the poem Elizabeth had enabled Beaumont to make a provisional act of obeisance to the status quo by his claim that, as tobacco has replaced Ceres in the heaven of the superstitious, so Elizabeth has replaced tobacco. Wingandekoe, the American home of the tobaccoan nymph, "now a far more glorious name doth bear / Since a more beauteous nymph was worshipt there": as Beaumont's note explains, "Wingandekoe is a country in the North part of America, called by the Queen, Virginia" (286–87). The moral would seem to be that Elizabeth outshines the dreams of the superstitious pagan, and indeed the Cult of Elizabeth as E. C. Wilson, Yates, Roy Strong, and Greenblatt, among others, have characterized it worked by substituting itself for the cast-off "superstitions" primarily of Catholic ritual so as to absorb Catholicism's displaced authority.[88] Yet here Elizabeth does not stand apart, virginal, from the superstition whose authority she absorbs. The terms of praise for Elizabeth that follow—the queen is, for example, "our modern Muse, / Which light and life doth to the North infuse," "In whose respect the Muses barb'rous are, / The Graces rude, nor is the phoenix rare"—sound if anything indistinguishable from the ones Beaumont previously applied to tobacco; in his poem at least, Elizabeth's authority, like the poem's itself, depends on highlighting its *inseparability* from overt superstition.[89] The comparison of queen to poet helps clarify the distinction: just as Beaumont refuses to name his own religion outright and instead presents his sophistication only negatively, masquerading as Indian or ancient barbarism, so Elizabeth's accomplishments are defined only negatively, by the degree to which she does tobacco or ancient Muse one better, and so, as Beaumont says, "exceeds her predecessors' facts." Beaumont nicely captures the paradox of Elizabeth's alliance to and difference from superstition when he asserts, "Nor are her wondrous acts, now wondrous acts."

The obscure advantages of such definition by negation seem a little more explicable in an overseas context, as "the improvisation of power,"[90] when the English want the natives both to love them and yet still look foolish; Raleigh's lieutenant Lawrence Keymis (1596) reports how on his return to Guiana the year after Raleigh's visit, he found the natives constant in the devotion Raleigh taught them:

Thus they sit talking, and taking *Tobacco* some two hours, and until their pipes be all spent. . . . No man must interrupt . . . for this is their religion, and prayers, which they now celebrated, keeping a precise fast one whole day in honor of the great Princess of the North their Patroness & Defender.[91]

Of course, Catholic polemicists like Nicholas Sanders could ignore the distinction between the savage and civilized "estimation" of Elizabeth as easily as antitobaccoans ignored the distinction between savage and civilized smoking;[92] but this problem aside, and the problem aside also of the actual depth of Indian commitment to the queen, what practical benefits did this Indian chapter of the Cult of Elizabeth actually yield England? The purpose behind Beaumont's own version of the Cult seems obscurer still when the one "fact" of Elizabeth upon which Beaumont decides to elaborate is perhaps the most dubious one he could have chosen: he extols the queen for having

> uncontroll'd stretcht out her mighty hand
> Over Virginia and the New-found-land,
> And spread the colors of our English Rose
> In the far countries where Tobacco grows,
> And tam'd the savage nations of the West,
> Which of this jewel were in vain possest.
>
> (316)

The last anyone had seen of England's single New World tamer at the time, the 1587 Roanoke colony, was more than fourteen years before, and the law presumed missing persons dead after seven; John Gerard's *Herball* (1597) musters as bright an optimism about the Lost Colony as could be expected when he mentions "Virginia . . . where are dwelling at this present Englishmen, if neither untimely death by murdering, or pestilence, corrupt air, bloody fluxes, or some other mortal sickness hath not destroyed them."[93] As the poem now turns to more strictly imperialist talk, Beaumont himself contradictorily emphasizes the hardships that still await English New World enterprise: Jove hates tobacco "as the gainsayer of eternal fate," and so "this precious gem / Is thus beset with beasts, and kept by them." Besides, "a thousand dangers circle round / Whatever good within this world is found," and not the least of the dangers England continues to face are the Spanish, "far more savage than the Savages," who indeed "have the royalty / Where glorious gold, and rich Tobacco be" (317). Beside the possibly apocryphal exportation of Elizabeth-idolatry to a small tribe in Guiana, the "facts" to which Beaumont must be pointing when he claims that Elizabeth has already tamed America, then, are presumably speech acts like Elizabeth renaming Wingandekoe Virginia, Hakluyt calling Virginia Raleigh's Elizabeth-like bride, Spenser placing Belphoebe in a tobacco field, and Beaumont himself writing this poem: in other words, the importation of barbarism, and especially of its representative "jewel" tobacco, into civilized discourse.

Again symbolic returns from the New World seem almost preferable to something more substantial, and again this preference gets elaborated, in the poem's climax, as esteeming tobacco more than gold:

> For this our praised plant on high doth soar,
> Above the baser dross of earthly ore,
> Like the brave spirit and ambitious mind,
> Whose eaglet's eyes the sunbeams cannot blind;
> Nor can the clog of poverty depress
> Such souls in base and native lowliness,
> But proudly scorning to behold the Earth,
> They leap at crowns, and reach above their birth.
>
> (317–18)

The sentiment, the contemning of mere fortune, is the same one introduced in the dedication to Drayton, but now oddly transformed from an antipolitical and individualistic pose to a national, imperialist argument: tobacco is the key to England's late and unlikely imperial hopes, "the gainsayer of eternal fate," precisely because it signals that the Spanish "have the royalty" of both it and gold, while the English have no empire at all. Both Beaumont's surprising metamorphosis and his peculiar theory here follow logically, however, from his disdain for those worldlings who, like Samuel Daniel's Philocosmus (1599), declare of "trifling" poetry: "Other delights than these, other desires, / This profit-seeking age requires."[94] Indeed, what in a contemporary work, the last of the *Parnassus* plays (1601), represents a poet's lament about contemptuous patrons, would in Beaumont's poem constitute a patriotic brag: "We have the words, they the possession have." (At one point in the plays another poet even imagines this envied "possession" to be "the gold of India"; as Dekker [1603] says, "Alack that the West Indies stand so far from Universities!")[95] Like the Virginia of Harriot and Hakluyt, poetry for Beaumont cannot please the material-minded, and by the same token Virginia requires "the brave spirit and ambitious mind" of the man professionally equipped to see the substance in what appears substanceless—the poet: "For verses are unto them food, / Lies are to these both gold and good."[96]

But what inspiration is to be had from one's total outflanking by the enemy? A standard Christian explanation of the value of such trouble—here Calvin's explanation, in the chapter where he notes that "man's life is like a smoke"— seems at first miles apart from Beaumont's probable response: "For, because God knoweth well how much we be by nature inclined to the beastly love of this world, he useth a most fit mean to draw us back, and to shake off our sluggishness, that we should not stick too fast in that love."[97] But in justifying the imperial difficulties for which tobacco stands, Beaumont simply lowers the sights Calvin sets. Gold has tricked the Spanish into making the literalizing, bestializing mistake of filling their bellies, while tobacco teaches the English a limited form of *contemptus* instead: "the clog of poverty" that tobacco represents—in short, England's limitation to its island home—does not "depress" Englishmen in their "base and native lowliness" because that clog is made of smoke (and imported smoke at that). Poor Englishmen harness the rarefying power of Apollo, the sun, create a new Golden Age, not by embracing as the Spanish do the "terrestrial sun" of gold but by attaching themselves to something as nearly nothing as possible.

It's crucial to remember here, however, that in rejecting any binding, material correlative to its powers, the ambitious mind does not on the other hand appeal to a heavenly correlative either; though the idea of leaping at crowns and reaching above one's birth certainly suggests an aspiration, in spite of original sin, for a heavenly crown, tobacco smoke does not ascend that high: true, "our sweet herb all earthly dross doth hate, / Though in the Earth both nourisht and create," but when it "leaves this low orb, and labors to aspire," it ends up only "mixing her vapors with the airy clouds" (318), which then drop "celestial show'rs" on English heads. Beaumont wants a crown somewhere between earth and heaven, both off the ground and of it, distinguished only from the frivolous low superstition that negatively defines its purview. Tobacco's limited, homeopathic dose of *contemptus*, its minor and embraceable Conflagration, cures the pangs both of worldly trouble and of *contemptus* itself; it helps the ambitious mind, aware now of its own unfading substance, come to itself.

An alternative explanation of Beaumont's resistance to articulating his theology more clearly would note his multiple convictions for recusancy a few years later,[98] which raises the question whether any other tobacco advocate actually holds Beaumont's possibly anomalous position. It has not been my intention to demonstrate, however, that the writers I've discussed hold any one position about tobacco at all. Rather, they share certain assumptions about tobacco that are based on prior physiological, economic, poetic, and theological claims, claims that are themselves analogous and cohere around the central premises concerning England the island, limited, rheumatic, and late: either the analogies may or may not be pursued, or the writer may or may not recognize the consequences of those analogies he does pursue. Indeed, the primary value of tobacco for these writers is its negativity, its ability to mediate between normally opposed terms—between purging and feeding, high and low, superstition and religion, home and away, heaven and earth—by displacing both terms and substituting its own neither material nor spiritual "essence" instead. The negativity of Beaumont's theological argument, for instance, substituting tobacco worship for either Protestant or Catholic polemic, may suit both his rebelliousness and his fears about recusancy convictions, but its efficacy, or danger, does not stop there. How does the imperialist reconcile his earthly ambitions to his heavenly ones? Recent scholarship, most notably Richard Bauckham's *Tudor Apocalypse*, has rejected the notion advanced by William Haller that Elizabethans perceived the millennium of Revelations 20 as a prophecy that England would establish a godly kingdom on earth; rather, "the vast majority of Tudor Protestant writers . . . interpreted the millennium of that chapter as a period in the past history of the church."[99] Yet Bauckham notes that, especially after the Armada, an historical and even imperialist optimism began to exceed orthodox bounds. Beaumont's tobacco argument both makes and unmakes a *contemptus* superiority to the "carnal" millennium that worried the Elizabethans, by characterizing both a worldly and an otherworldly estimation with the same figure, smoke.

Tobacco's critics perceive this negativity simply as negation, a problem to which even Beaumont draws attention when at the end of his poem (in lines reminiscent of the end of *The Shepheardes Calender*) he asks his Muse, now ambiguously "clok'd with vapors of a dusky hue," to "bid both the world and thy sweet herb, Adieu"—the poem too goes up (or down?) in smoke. But then the poem's motto, from Virgil's *Culex*[100]—"Lusimus, Octave, &c."; in Spenser's version, "We now have played (Augustus) wantonly"—has already cast this apparently wanton and excessive use of tobacco as itself dispensable, a mere fledgling poetic attempt soon to be transcended by a more properly imperial invention; the tobacco pipe simply tunes the modern pastoral. Later, when England and the newly created Virginia Company begin to pursue their imperial goal more directly, colonists like John Pory try to make the same argument about Virginia's own tobacco craze: while deploring the idea of a settlement based on a commodity that "in fumu . . . evanitio," Pory asserts that "the extreme Care, diligence, and labor spent about it [i.e., tobacco], doth prepare our people for some more excellent subject."[101] Yet the conveniently replacing and replaceable tobacco, the baseless fabric of this vision, refuses to fade away.[102] The Company's repeated assurances that some more substantial commodity will soon arise sound less and less convincing;[103] in fact, the more essential to Jamestown tobacco becomes, the more ambiguous becomes even James's distaste. In 1619 the College of Physicians declared home-grown tobacco unhealthy, and James banned its production, ostensibly to protect both the English smoker and the Virginian grower, but James had a personal, highly lucrative stake in the ban: in exchange for it, the Virginia Company allowed the Crown much higher duties on their tobacco imports.[104] The colony that was supposed to expand the English economy by providing material "otherwise obtainable only 'at the courtesy of other Princes, under the burthen of great Customs, and heavy impositions,'"[105] had been transformed by James, then, into simply one more foreign power, with James its extortionist lord—a king not of Fairyland but of thin air.[106]

Notes

I'd like to thank the Graduate Division of the University of California, Berkeley, for a grant that enabled me to research this topic; and Paul Alpers, Stephen Greenblatt, Dorothy Hale, Steven Knapp, Walter Michaels, James Schamus, and Lynn Wardley for reading earlier drafts of this essay and providing indispensable advice.

1. I cite A. C. Hamilton's edition of Edmund Spenser, *The Faerie Queene* (London, 1977) throughout. I have modernized all spelling excluding Spenser's poetry and the titles of Renaissance texts—which I have nevertheless capitalized.

2. See, e.g., Jerome E. Brooks, ed., *Tobacco: Its History Illustrated by the Books, Manuscripts, and Engravings in the Library of George Arents, Jr.*, 5 vols. (New York, 1937–52), 1:327, 334, 368, 378, 392, 448–49, 455, 464; 2:21–22, 77, 166; the list is by no means exhaustive. Brooks's work, an extraordinary sourcebook for the study of tobacco, cites almost all the tobacco references I'll examine; see also the supplement to Brooks, *Tobacco: A Catalogue of the Books, Manuscripts, and Engravings Acquired Since 1942*, parts 1–7, ed. Sarah Dickson (New York, 1958–62); parts 8–10, ed. Perry Hugh O'Neil (New York, 1967–69); hereafter cited as *Supplement*. Dickson's *Panacea or Precious Bane: Tobacco in Sixteenth-Century Literature* (New York, 1954) is a fine one-volume history.

   John Lyly parodied Spenser's episode in his *The Woman in the Moon* (c. 1591–93); see *The Complete Works of John Lyly*, ed. R. W. Bond, 3 vols. (Oxford, 1902), 3:1.65–70; and Dickson, *Panacea*, 177–78.

3. *Calendar of State Papers, Domestic, 1603–1610*, 140; the figures actually cover Michaelmas 1603 to Michaelmas 1604.

4. James I, *A Counter-Blaste to Tobacco* (London, 1604).

5. Brooks, *Tobacco*, 1:381.

6. Richard Hakluyt, *Divers Voyages Touching the Discovery of America*, ed. John W. Jones, Hakluyt Society no. 7 (London, 1850), 8.

7. Cf., e.g., George North in *The Stage of Popish Toyes* (London, 1581): "The whole course of her Majesty's life is miraculous" (95).

8. [George Puttenham], *The Arte of English Poesie* (London, 1589), 31.

9. "Letter to Raleigh," in Spenser, *Faerie Queene*, 737.

10. Cf., e.g., Thomas Nashe: "divine Master *Spenser*, the miracle of wit" (1589); "heavenly *Spenser*" (1592); in *Works of Thomas Nashe*, 5 vols., ed. R. B. McKerrow (London, 1904–10); ed. F. P. Wilson, revised ed. (Oxford, 1958), 3:323 and 1:243.

11. These quotations derive from the first chapter of G. K. Hunter's *John Lyly: The Humanist as Courtier* (Cambridge, Mass., 1962), 34, where Hunter attacks the "Whig" notion that "the 'spaciousness' of Elizabeth's reign is a setting for a new-found freedom of the human spirit" (3).

12. Frances Yates, "Queen Elizabeth as Astraea" (1947); reprinted in *Astraea: The Imperial Theme in the Sixteenth Century* (London, 1975), 59.

13. Thomas Cain, *Praise in "The Faerie Queene,"* (Lincoln, Neb., 1978), 91–101.

14. John Beaumont, *The Metamorphosis of Tabacco* (1602), reprinted in *The Poems of Sir John Beaumont*, ed. Alexander B. Grosart (Blackburn, Lancs., 1869), 263–321; all references to the poem will be to page numbers of this edition.

15. Carol Shammas, in "English Commercial Development and American Colonization,

1560–1620," in Kenneth R. Andrews et al., eds., *The Westward Enterprise: English Activities in Ireland, the Atlantic, and America, 1480–1650* (Liverpool, 1979), 151–74, argues that Elizabethan imperialism was gold-centered, while its Jacobean counterpart moved toward commodities-centered schemes. Joan Thirsk's *Economic Policy and Prospects: The Development of a Consumer Society in Early Modern England* (Oxford, 1978) sees more Elizabethan interest in commodification than Shammas allows. This essay, on the other hand, tries to highlight a strand of Elizabethan expansionism at once uneasy about gold and, finally, indifferent to commodification.

16. For Columbus, see Brooks, *Tobacco*, 1:17–18; for Sparke, see ibid., 1:45.

17. Sparke's account first appeared in Richard Hakluyt, *The Principall Navigations, Voyages, and Discoveries of the English Nation* (London, 1589); reprinted in 2 vols. by the Hakluyt Society, ed. D. B. Quinn, R. A. Skelton, and Alison Quinn (Cambridge, 1965); 2nd ed., *The Principal Navigations, Voyages, Traffiques & Discoveries of the English Nation*, 3 vols. (London, 1598–1600); reprint ed., 12 vols. (Glasgow, 1903–5), 10:57. Further references will be to the second edition in the Glasgow printing.

18. William Harrison, "Great Chronologie [of England]," MS entry for 1573, quoted in Brooks, *Tobacco*, 1:298; Richard Hakluyt the elder, "Remembrances . . . for a principall English Factor at Constantinople 1582," in *Principal Navigations*, 5:242.

19. Thomas Elyot, *The Castel of Helth* (London, 1541), 77.

20. James's *Counter-Blaste* asserts that some of the gentry have been "bestowing three, some four hundred pounds a year upon this precious stink" (C4v).

21. Henry Buttes, *Dyets Dry Dinner* (London, 1599), P4r.

22. "Philaretes," *Work for Chimny-Sweepers* (London, 1602), F4v.

23. Brooks, *Tobacco*, 1:381. The title character in George Chapman's *Monsieur D'Olive* (1605; published 1606) seems to allude to this unusual time lapse when he describes tobacco as "an ancient subject, and yet newly / Call'd into question"; *Monsieur D'Olive*, 2.2.151–53, in *The Comedies of George Chapman*, ed. Thomas Marc Parrott, 2 vols. (1913; reprint ed., New York, 1961), 1:329.

24. John Parker, *Books to Build an Empire: A Bibliographical History of English Overseas Interests to 1620* (Amsterdam, 1965), 76, on Nicolas Monardes, *Segunda parte . . . de las . . . Indias Occidentales* (Seville, 1571), translated by John Frampton as *Joyfull Newes out of the Newe Worlde* (London, 1577). (For the complicated publishing history of Monardes' work, see Brooks, *Tobacco*, 1:245–46, 263–64.) Parker, whose *Books* is a valuable starting point for research into Renaissance English travel literature, adds that "two issues in 1577, another in 1580, and still another in 1596 were not in keeping with the tendency of most English travel books of this period to appear in only one edition, even when they were vigorously imperialistic." His explanation of Monardes' exceptional popularity, "its utilitarian value to medical practitioners," sounds plausible enough but skirts two problems. First, the timing of the various editions matches two small waves of Elizabethan propaganda about America, the earlier stimulated by Martin Frobisher's Northern voyages (1576–78), the later by Raleigh's Guianan expedition (1595). Second, the translator Frampton was, as Parker notes, a former victim of the Spanish Inquisition and an ardent imperialist: he translated five other exploration tracts, including Marco Polo, in hopes to spur his countrymen into action. Parker maintains that this first translation is "the only one . . . in which the political motive is not evident," which is to say, perhaps, only that Frampton became increasingly explicit about his motives. Parker's bibliography of travel literature (243–65) makes clear that his own definition of politics, like the definitions of so many other researchers into travel literature, does not include plants—no tobacco books, not

even James's, appear there. My own explanation of Monardes' popularity, which I hope this essay will make more convincing, is that his herbal provided the sort of information about America that most interested Elizabethans in general.

25. Monardes, *Joyfull Newes*, 86.

26. Even James, in his proclamation of 17 October 1604 that levied a heavy custom on the weed, distinguished between "the better sort," who "have and will use the same with Moderation to preserve their Health," and "a number of riotous and disordered Persons of mean and base Condition, who, contrary to the use which Persons of good Calling and Quality make thereof, do spend most of their time in that idle vanity . . . and also do consume that Wages which many of them get by their Labor"; quoted in Brooks, *Tobacco*, 1:406–7. Cf. Doctor Clement in Ben Jonson's *Every Man in His Humour* (1598; published 1601) pretending to hold a similar position and scaring Cob the tobacco hater:

> What? A tankard-bearer, a thread-bare rascal, a beggar, a slave that never drunk out of better than pisspot mettle in his life, and he to deprave, and abuse the virtue of an herb, so generally receiv'd in the courts of princes, the chambers of nobles, the bowers of sweet Ladies, the cabins of soldiers—Peto, away with him, by god's passion, I say, go to. (3.3.108–14)

In C. H. Herford and Percy and Evelyn Simpson, eds., *Ben Jonson*, 11 vols. (Oxford, 1925–52), 3:246. Whether or not Jonson and Chapman are mocking James in particular, as Brooks assumes (1:424), Chapman's D'Olive too claims to believe that tobacco's "lawful use" should be "limited thus: / That none should dare to take it but a gentleman, / Or he that had some gentlemanly humor, / The murr, the headache, the catarrh, the bone-ache, / Or other branches of the sharp salt rheum / Fitting a gentleman" (*Monsieur D'Olive*, 2.2.290–95)—so the rheum itself has come to seem a high-class affectation, like spleen.

27. "On the Continent tobacco had been generally accepted as a panacea since 1560, and as such had been woven into daily life there. But in England, about three decades later (after its fairly limited reception as a wonder-working simple) smoking suddenly and triumphantly became a social force, developing into an almost national recreation"; Brooks, *Tobacco*, 1:43.

28. Ibid., 1:47–49; Dickson, *Panacea*, 170–74. It is Raleigh's authority that Philaretes seems to have particularly in mind when in a prefatory poem he anxiously tries to distinguish his special attack on tobacco from his general endorsement of Raleigh's American projects: "Let none deny but *Indies* soil can yield, / The sov'reign simples, of *Apollos* field. / Let England Spain and the French *Fleur de Lis* / Let Irish Kern and the Cold seated *Freese* / Confess themselves in bounden duty stand / To wholesome simples of *Guiana* land"; *Chimny-Sweepers*, A4v.

29. James, *Counter-blaste*, B2v; William Camden too, in his *Annales* (London, 1615), trans. Robert Norton as *The Historie of . . . Elizabeth* (London, 1630), says that Raleigh's colonists "were the first that I know of, which brought into *England* that *Indian* plant. . . . Certainly from that time, it began to be in great request, and sold at an high rate"; quoted in Brooks, *Tobacco*, 2:156.

30. For Raleigh, see Brooks, *Tobacco*, 1:68; Thomas Harriot, *A Briefe and True Report of the New Found Land of Virginia* (London, 1588), reprinted by Theodore De Bry in four languages as the first volume of his *America* (Frankfurt, 1590); De Bry added to the original text some engravings from the watercolors of Harriot's fellow colonist John White, along with Harriot's commentary on them. I cite Paul Hulton's edition of the De Bry text (New York, 1972) throughout.

31. D. B. Quinn, "Renaissance Influences in English Colonization," *Transactions of the Royal Historical Society*, ser. 5, no. 26 (1976): 82–83. Quinn is following George Louis Beer, *The Origins of the British Colonial System, 1578–1660* (1908; reprint ed., Gloucester, Mass., 1959), 32–77.

32. Cf. Harriot, *Briefe and True Report*, 7, 12.

33. George Peckham, *A True Reporte, of the Late Discoveries, of the Newfound Landes* (London, 1583), reprinted in D. B. Quinn, ed., *The Voyages and Colonising Enterprises of Sir Humphrey Gilbert*, 2 vols., Hakluyt Society ser. 2, nos. 83–84 (London, 1940), 2:439.

34. [Roger Marbecke], *A Defence of Tabacco: With a Friendly Answer to Worke for Chimny-Sweepers* (London, 1602); on the identification of Marbecke as the author of the *Defence*, see Brooks, *Tobacco*, 1:389. Cf. William Barclay's "To my Lord the Bishop of Murray," from his *Nepenthes, or The Vertues of Tabacco* (Edinburgh, 1614), unpaginated: "A stranger plant, shipwrecked in our coast,/ Is come to help this poor phlegmatic soil."

35. D. B. Quinn, ed., *The Roanoke Voyages, 1584–1590*, 2 vols., Hakluyt Society ser. 2, nos. 104–5 (London, 1955), 1:202.

36. Marbecke cites idleness also in his etiology, which brings the following simile about English humidity even closer to descriptions of economic and social surpluses:

> For as Conduits, if they had not vents for to spend their waste water, would in time, either break, or else become unprofitable: so in our bodies, this unnatural, and over great increase of unnecessary humidities and moistures, being made by those means which I mentioned before, would breed great annoyances, if they were not lessened and wasted, by some device, or other.

> *Defence*, 34.

37. As "good Merchandize" Ralph Lane mentions only "Sassafras, and many other roots & gums"; Quinn, *Roanoke Voyages*, 1:273. For sassafras as the primary New World commodity garnered by Raleigh's man Samuel Mace in 1602, and by Bartholomew Gosnold in a voyage unlicensed by Raleigh the same year, see D. B. Quinn, *England and the Discovery of America, 1481–1620* (New York, 1974), 408, 414–16; tobacco is not mentioned.

38. See William Strachey, *The Historie of Travaile into Virginia Britannia* (MS 1612), ed. R. H. Major, Hakluyt Society no. 6 (London, 1849), 121, 31; quoted in Brooks, *Tobacco*, 1:525–26; and see ibid., 1:86. Ralph Hamor says Rolfe "first took the pains to make trial thereof" in 1612; *A True Discourse of the Present Estate of Virginia* (London, 1615; facsimile ed., Richmond, Va., 1957), D4b; quoted in Brooks, *Tobacco*, 1:524.

39. Of course, England must have acquired a good deal of tobacco in a happily indirect way also, via privateering; see Kenneth R. Andrews, *Elizabethan Privateering: English Privateering During the Spanish War 1585–1603* (Cambridge, 1964).

   For the interesting history of homegrown tobacco in the English Renaissance, see Joan Thirsk, "New Crops and Their Diffusion: Tobacco-Growing in Seventeenth-Century England," in C. W. Chalklin and M. A. Havinden, eds., *Rural Change and Urban Growth, 1500–1800: Essays in Honour of W. G. Hoskins* (London, 1974), 76–103.

40. See Monardes, *Joyfull Newes*, 90–91; Harriot, *Briefe and True Report*, 9. Cf. Hakluyt's "Discourse of Western Planting" (1584), in *The Original Writings and Correspondence of the Two Richard Hakluyts*, ed. E. G. R. Taylor, 2 vols., Hakluyt Society ser. 2, nos. 76–77 (London, 1935), 2:223–24.

41. The continuation of Harriot's sentence seems to mark a separation from Indian barbarity, as if the superstitious use of tobacco hadn't been felt as entirely barbarous

before: "but all done with strange gestures, stamping, sometime dancing, clapping of hands, holding up of hands, & staring up into the heavens, uttering therewithal and chattering strange words & noises."

42. These two quotations, from Harriot's captions to John White's drawings, are Hakluyt's translations of Harriot's Latin.

43. For example, "*Deer Skins . . .* are to be had of the natural inhabitants thousands yearly by way of traffic for trifles"; Harriot, *Briefe and True Report*, 10. Apparently Harriot came to be regarded as England's resident authority on the subject of Indians misvaluing things. When Christopher Newport returned to England in January 1609 with one of Powhatan's sons,

> Harriot advised that no expensive gift be made to him but that he would be satisfied with copper decorations only, so that there duly appeared in the [Northumberland house] accounts a payment of three shillings 'for 2 Rings and other pieces of Copper given to the Indian prince.' Similarly, we can identify as probably chosen by Harriot, amongst the goods sent to George Percy in July 1608, 'for blue beads' six shillings and 'for Red copper' nineteen shillings and sixpence, objects Harriot had long ago found the Indians anxious to have."

D. B. Quinn, "Thomas Harriot and the New World," in John Shirley, ed., *Thomas Harriot: Renaissance Scientist* (Oxford, 1974), 50. Cf. Harriot's memoranda for Mace's 1602 voyage, in which we witness the odd spectacle of England's premier scientist carefully directing the production of copper trifles for the Indians; Quinn, *England and the Discovery of America*, 410–13.

44. Clement Urmeston, "A Treatise Concerning the Staple and the Commodities of this Realm" (c. 1519–35), in R. H. Tawney and Eileen Power, eds., *Tudor Economic Documents*, 3 vols. (1924; reprint ed., New York, 1962), 3:109–10. Cf. ibid., 2:45 and 3:346–59; Thomas Smith, *A Discourse of the Commonweal of This Realm of England* (1549), published in 1581 under the title *A Compendious or Brief Examination*, ed. Mary Dewar (Charlottesville, Va., 1969), 62–65; and R[obert] W[ilson], *The Three Ladies of London* (London, 1584).

45. Humphrey Gilbert, *A Discourse of a Discoverie for a New Passage to Cataia* (1578), in Quinn, *Gilbert*, 1:161. Cf. Peckham, *True Reporte*, in Quinn, *Gilbert*, 2:462; and Hakluyt, "Discourse," 2:235, 270.

46. Shortly before his disastrous second voyage in search of El Dorado, Raleigh reportedly boasted "that he knew a Town in those parts, upon which he could make a saving Voyage in *Tobacco*, though there were no other spoil"; quoted in Brooks, *Tobacco*, 1:68, n. 8, from *A Declaration of the Demeanour and Cariage of Sir Walter Raleigh* (London, 1618).

47. Quoted in Brooks, *Tobacco*, 1:50.

48. Thomas Campion, "In tabaccam," in *Epigrammatum libri II* (1619); *Campion's Works*, ed. Percival Vivian (Oxford, 1909), 238; translated by Dickson in *Supplement*, 4:191.

49. Though Englishmen had smoked tobacco before Lane's men returned home (see, e.g., Brooks, *Tobacco*, 1:240, 298), Charles de L'Ecluse's Latin abridgment of Monardes, *Segunda parte*, notes that "the English returning from thence [i.e., Virginia] brought the like [Indian] Pipes with them, to drink the smoke of Tobacco; and since that time, the use of drinking Tobacco hath so much prevailed all *England* over, especially amongst the Courtiers, that they have caused many such like Pipes to be made to drink Tobacco with"; *Exoticum Libri Decem* (Leyden, 1605), trans. J. R. in his edition of Gilles Everard, *Panacea; or, the Universal Medicine* (London, 1659); quoted in

Brooks, *Tobacco*, 1.417–18. Quinn explains that "what the colonists apparently introduced was the smoking pipe used in Roanoke Island as a model for English pipe-makers"; *Roanoke Voyages*, 345–46, n. 3.

50. C. T., *An Advice How to Plant Tobacco in England* (London, 1615), A3v. This most common of tobacco jibes could appear in the mouths of foreigners—"Both *Spaniards* & all other Nations say tauntingly to us, when they see all our goods landed (to use their own words) *Que todo esso sepagtaa con humo*; that all will be paid in smoke"; Edward Bennett, *A Treatise . . . Touching the Inconveniences that the Importation of Tobacco Out of Spaine, Hath Brought Unto This Land* (London, c. 1620), unpaginated—and of kings: a proclamation of Charles I (January 1631) prohibited the importation of foreign tobacco so that "our Subjects may not unthriftily vent the solid Commodities of our own Kingdom, and return the proceed thereof in Smoke"; cited in Beer, *Origins*, 82.

51. Quoted in Dickson, *Panacea*, 172. While it has long been recognized that Lucian presents a similar anecdote (*Lucian*, trans. A. M. Harmon et al., Loeb Classical Library, vol. 1 [New York, 1915], 163), Dickson sensibly observes that this coincidence alone doesn't prove the story apocryphal: "It is even possible that Raleigh, having read the story in a Greek or Latin edition of Lucian, carefully arranged the matter of the wager to amuse his royal mistress." As it is, I am less concerned with the anecdote's authenticity than with the testimony it offers about contemporary opinions of Raleigh and tobacco.

52. Stephen Greenblatt, *Renaissance Self-Fashioning: From More to Shakespeare* (Chicago, 1980), 285–86, n. 29.

53. See Dickson, *Panacea*, 174; cf. T. W. on the Gunpowder Plotters: "In the time of their imprisonment, they rather feasted with their sins, than fasted with sorrow for them; were richly appareled, fared deliciously, and took Tobacco out of measure, with a seeming carelessness of their crime"; *The Araignment and Execution of the Late Traytors* (London, 1606); quoted in *Supplement*, 3:133.

54. Joseph Hall, *Mundus Alter et Idem* (Frankfurt, n.d. [London, 1605]), trans. John Healey as *The Discovery of a New World* (London, 1609); ed. Huntington Brown (Cambridge, Mass., 1937); new translation by John Millar Wands (New Haven, 1981), whose edition I cite (93).

55. Cf. the braggadocio Bobadillo in Jonson's *Every Man in His Humor*: "I have been in the Indies (where this herb grows) where neither my self, nor a dozen Gentlemen more (of my knowledge) have received the taste of any other nutriment, in the world, for the space of one and twenty weeks, but Tobacco only. Therefore it cannot be but 'tis most divine"; 3.2.70–75.

56. Stephen Greenblatt, *Sir Walter Raleigh: The Renaissance Man and His Roles* (New Haven, 1973), 56.

57. Taylor, *Original Writings of the Hakluyts*, 1:367–68; quoted by John Seelye, *Prophetic Waters: The River in Early American Life and Literature* (New York, 1977), who comments: "So Raleigh's constancy to Elizabeth, his loyalty to his colony, the Queen's barrenness, and Virginia's ill repute are all spun into an ambiguous fabric of allusion, ending by associating the New World with the paradisiac promised land of the Mosaic epic" (43). Seelye also observes that "Hakluyt lifts himself to a level of expression which he seldom attained" (42); the quality may in fact be Raleigh's: Hakluyt writes to him that "if there be anything else that you would have mentioned in the epistle dedicatory, you shall do well to let me understand of it betimes"; Taylor, *Original Writings of the Hakluyts*, 1:355.

58. The Latin in the original compensates to some degree for this raciness, as Hakluyt's characterization of Martyr's Latin suggests: "He depicts with a distinguished and skillful pen and with lively colors in a most gifted manner the head, neck, breast, arms, in brief the whole body of that tremendous entity America, and clothes it decently in the Latin dress familiar to scholars"; Taylor, *Original Writings of the Hakluyts*, 363.

59. Indeed, Raleigh is free to enter America only when he has been barred Elizabeth's presence. He pursued his *Discoverie of the Large Rich, and Bewtiful Empyre of Guiana* (London, 1596), Raleigh explains in his dedication, "that thereby if it were possible I might recover but the moderation of excess, and the least taste of the greatest plenty formerly possessed" (4)—as if, that is, he took Hakluyt's metaphor literally, and accepted in place of the lost Elizabeth her occupiable American body. But it was such a "vicarious" intercourse with Elizabeth Throckmorton that lost Elizabeth the queen originally; Raleigh's point in the now famous assertion "Guiana still hath her maidenhead" is that, as restitution, he has foregone the more substantial surrogate bride. Nor is his propitiatory restraint (which, incidentally, had been standard English policy before Raleigh's fall) simply economic or political: none of his men, he repeatedly emphasizes, "ever knew any of their women, and yet we saw many hundreds, and had many in our power, and of those very young, and excellently favored which came among us without deceit, stark naked" (44).

60. Quinn, *Roanoke Voyages*, 273.

61. For the most recent compilation of evidence that Timias represents Raleigh, see James P. Bednarz, "Ralegh in Spenser's Historical Allegory," *Spenser Studies* 4 (1984): 52–54.

62. Unfortunately I don't have the space to consider the question of Spenser's precise intentions here, but in a longer work on which I'm currently engaged I argue that Spenser writes this scene in part to try to correct misreadings, deliberate and otherwise, of Spenser's "Aprill" eclogue. Readers of that eclogue like Thomas Blenerhasset and George Peele either ignore or eschew the fact that Colin has forsaken pastoral celebrations of Elizabeth of the sort that Hobbinol rehearses. Spenser is anxious about complacence regarding Elizabeth's virginity and the anti-imperial stasis that complacence represents; in the *Faerie Queene* episode he wants to single out Raleigh's pathos in relation to the queen's virginity as a step beyond Colin's old views, but nevertheless pastoral and static in its own way.

63. Raleigh at least understood "Belphoebe" as the queen made approachable; he laments of the angry Elizabeth after his disgrace, "A Queen she was to me, no more Belphoebe, / A Lion then, no more a milk-white dove"; *XIth Book of Ocean to Cinthia* (MS 1592), 327–28; ed. Walter Oakeshott in his *The Queen and the Poet* (New York, 1961), 193.

64. For James tobacco is the food of the belly fillers who *reject* manna; he sees the English "lusting after it as the children of Israel did in the wilderness after Quails"; *Counterblaste*, C4r:

> And a number of people that was among them, fell a lusting, and turned themselves and wept (as did also the children of Israel) and said, who shall give us flesh to eat? We remember the fish which we did eat in Egypt freely, and the cucumbers, and melons, leeks, onions, and garlic. But now our soul is dried away: for we can see nothing else but Manna.

Num. 11.4–6; Bishops' Bible (London, 1568; revised ed., 1572). God answers this intemperance by sending "quails from the sea" (31), which bring plague with them;

what makes the story particularly apt for James is not only this projected punishment for smokers but the chance for himself to identify with Moses, who warns the Jews that "the Lord will give you flesh, and ye shall eat. Yet ye shall not eat one day, nor two, nor five days, neither ten, nor twenty days: But a whole month, until it come out at the nostrils of you" (18–20).

65. "It was before 1560, in or about Lisbon, that the gospel of tobacco as panacea was evolved"; Brooks, *Tobacco*, 1:236; see Dickson, *Panacea*, 57–80. The most influential publicists of tobacco's divinity were Jean Liebault, in his edition of Charles Estienne's *L'Agriculture et maison rustique* (Paris, 1570), and Pierre Pena and Matthias de L'Obel, *Stirpium Adversaria Nova* (London, 1570–71); see Brooks, *Tobacco*, 1:232–42. Frampton's English edition of Monardes (1577) includes a translation of Liebault on tobacco's "divine effects"; *Joyfull Newes*, 93; see Brooks, *Tobacco*, 1:232.

66. James I, *His Majesties Gracious Letter* (London, 1622) to the earl of Southampton, treasurer of the Virginia Colony, includes this similar appraisal by the master of the king's silk works, John Bonoeil: "Sure there is some such sorcery in this weed; it was first sown (it seems) by some Indian Enchanter's hand, with spells and Magic verses, or otherwise you could never so much dote on it"; *Supplement*, 5:206.

67. Quoted in John Shirley, *Thomas Harriot: A Biography* (Oxford, 1983), 182–83, 192.

68. The most common way to represent fears about tobacco's ill effect on the English character is to personify tobacco as a witch or whore: e.g., "that Witch *Tobacco*" (James I, *The Peace-maker* [1618]; quoted in Dickson, *Panacea*, 156); "that Indian whore" (William Fennor [1617]; quoted in *Supplement*, 4:158); "a swarty *Indian* [who]/ Hath played the painted English *Courtesan*" (Philaretes, *Chimny-Sweepers*, A4v); "The *Indian Devil*, our bawd, witch, whore, man-queller" (Thomas Scot [1615–16]; quoted in Brooks, *Tobacco*, 2:8). This particular stigmatization of tobacco is due in part to tobacco's associations with fast living—"It is a thing his soul doth most adore," says John Taylor (1614) of the tobacco taker, "To live and love Tobacco, and a whore"; Brooks, *Tobacco*, 1:522—but more generally to worries that tobacco will block the production of legitimate Englishmen; William Vaughan (1612) wanted smokers to memorize this rhyme: "Tobacco, that outlandish weed,/ It spends the brain, and spoils the seed:/ It dulls the sprite, it dims the sight,/ It robs a woman of her right"; quoted in Brooks, *Tobacco*, 2:131. This physiological argument aside, writers often depict wives complaining about the greater *affection* their husbands feel for tobacco; the most elaborate diatribe occurs in John Deacon, *Tobacco Tortured* (London, 1616): e.g., "Why dost thou so vainly prefer a vanishing filthy *fume* before my permanent virtues"; quoted in Brooks, *Tobacco*, 2:12; for more references see ibid., 5:280 under "Smokers, wives of." Uncannily enough, the first Englishman to begin growing commercially successful tobacco in Virginia was also the first Englishman to marry an Indian: in the same breath Ralph Hamor praises John Rolfe's importation of tobacco seeds and his marriage to Pocahontas, both done "merely for the good and honor of the Plantation"; *True Discourse*, D4v; quoted in Brooks, *Tobacco*, 1:524. (Marlowe associates tobacco with a third un-English choice: he reportedly declared "That all they that love not Tobacco & Boys were fools"; quoted in Shirley, *Harriot*, 182.)

69. See Brooks, *Tobacco*, 1:352–58, and Dickson, *Panacea*, 198–99. I cite Brooks's edition of the poem, one of thirteen extant MS versions. Ray Heffner, "Essex, the Ideal Courtier," *English Literary History* 1 (1934): 23, notes that William Browne alludes to the poem in the course of his meditation on Essex's career in *Britannias Pastorals*, 1.4.685–760, in *Works*, ed. Gordon Goodwin (London, 1894); Heffner gives 1625 as the date, though book 1 was first published in 1613. What Heffner fails to note,

however, is Browne's allusion in the same passage to Timias and Belphoebe also: returning from war, Essex searches for Elizabeth in the hope that "her skill in herbs might help remove" a wound Envy gave him, but she mistakes him for a beast and kills him. To Browne's mind, Spenser's Timias and Essex's poem describe the same man.

70. Jean Calvin, *The Institution of the Christian Religion*, trans. T[homas] N[orton] (London, 1561). Cf. Ps. 102.3, Isa. 51.6, Hos. 13.3.

71. Thomas Jenner turned this allegorical potential of tobacco-smoking into a very popular poem (1626):

> The Indian weed withered quite
> Green at noon, cut down at night
> Shows thy decay, all flesh is hay,
> Thus think then drink *Tobacco*.
>
> The Pipe that is so lily white
> Shows thee to be a mortal wight,
> And even such, gone with a touch,
> Thus think, then drink *Tobacco*.
>
> And when the smoke ascends on high,
> Think, thou behold'st the vanity
> Of worldly stuff gone with a puff:
> Thus think, then drink *Tobacco*.
>
> And when the Pipe grows foul within,
> Think on thy soul defil'd with sin,
> And then the fire it doth require
> Thus think, then drink *Tobacco*.
>
> The ashes that are left behind,
> May serve to put thee still in mind,
> That unto dust, return thou must,
> Thus think, then drink *Tobacco*.

Quoted in Brooks, *Tobacco*, 2:128; see ibid., n. 2, for a bibliography of the poem's popularity. As if to emphasize the ambiguity of Jenner's position here—does he approve or disapprove of smoking?—the poem was published "Answered by *G. W.* [George Wither?] thus,/Thus think, drink no *Tobacco*." Incidentally, Wither came full circle on tobacco, and published a similar *contemptus* "Meditation Whilst He Was Taking a Pipe of Tobacco" (1661) lauding tobacco's educative powers, which he composed during his third incarceration at Newgate; see Brooks, *Tobacco*, 4:421–23.

72. Thomas Dekker, *Old Fortunatus* (1600), in *Dramatic Works of Thomas Dekker*, ed. Fredson Bowers, vol. 1 (Cambridge, 1953), 1.1.336–37; quoted in *Supplement*, 3:116. Fortunatus himself refers to "that lean tawny face Tobaccionist death, that turns all into smoke."

73. Cf. 2 Pet. 3. Buttes's awkward comparisons of the gluttonous eater to an empty oven and desolate house depend on this apocalyptic resonance for their coherence. Both occur in the Psalms as figures for God's judgment upon David's enemies (21.9, 69.25); Christ also warns the Jerusalem that will not recognize him as its Messiah, "Behold, your habitation shall be left unto you desolate" (Mat. 23.38; Geneva Bible [Geneva, 1560]). The most revealing allusion, one by which tobacco is made to seem a cure both for itself as luxury and for the punishment of luxury, may be to Revelations and the fall of Babylon: the sea-traders "cry, when they see the smoke of her

burning, . . . Alas, alas, the great city, wherein were made rich all that had ships in the sea by her costliness: for in one hour she is made desolate" (19.18–19).

74. Once again I must defer to another study the question of Spenser's connection to this interpretation of Fairyland.

75. "The Extravagants," not by Borde, in Andrew Borde, *The Breviary of Helthe* (London, 1547; revised ed., 1598), 18v; Anglicus Bartholomaeus, *Bartholomus De Proprietatibus Rerum*, trans. [John Trevisa] (MS 1398; 1495), 4.3.evi.b/2. Cf. Stephen Bateman's version of *Bartholomus*, *Batman Uppon Bartholome* (London, 1582), 4.3.fiii.a/1.

76. For a different account of this process of sublimation, see William Vaughan, *The Spirit of Detraction, Conivred and Convicted* (London, 1611), whose prefatory epistle has certain "Cavaliers and Gentles" simply aping Monardes' Indian priest: after smoking,

> they fain themselves so long ravished as it were in an ecstasy: until after a thorough perambulation of their barren wits . . . they have coined some strange accident worthy the rehearsal among their boon companions. Then as though they started out of an heavenly trance . . . they recount tales of ROBIN-HOOD, of RHODOMONTING rovers, of DONZEL DEL PHOEBO, of a new ANTI-CHRIST born in BABYLON, of lying wonders, blazing out most blasphemous news, how that the DEVIL appeared at such a time with lightning and THUNDRING majesty . . . and if they had not suddenly blessed themselves better, he had carried away with him men, women, houses, and all right into hell.

Quoted in *Supplement*, 4:158.

77. The standard reference on this subject is Z. S. Fink, "Milton and the Theory of Climatic Influence," *Modern Language Quarterly* 2 (1941): 67–80, supplemented by Thomas B. Stroup, "Climatic Influence in Milton," *Modern Language Quarterly* 4 (1943): 185–89; the theory derives from Aristotle's *Politics* 7.7. For other English speculations on New World climate, see Karen Ordahl Kupperman, "The Puzzle of the American Climate," *American Historical Review* 87 (1982): 1262–89.

78. A satiric epigram from *Humors Antique Faces* (1605) by Samuel Rowlands nicely illustrates, by way of mockery, the idea that tobacco as miraculous fare might alone cure the economic wants Virginia was supposed to supply:

> A Poor Slave once with penury afflicted,
> Yet to Tobacco mightily addicted
> Says, they that take Tobacco keeps their health,
> Are worthy fellows in a common wealth.
> For if (sayth he) Tobacco were our cheer,
> Then other victuals never would be dear.
> Fie on excess it makes men faint and meek,
> A penny loaf might serve a man a week.
> Were we conform'd to the Chamelion's fare,
> To live by smoke as they do live by air.
> O how our men oppress and spoil their sense,
>   in making havoc of the elements.
> He can give reason for what he hath spoke,
> My Salamander lives by fire and smoke.
> Necessity doth cause him to repeat,
> Tobacco's praise for want of other meat.

Quoted in *Supplement*, 3:131–32. An imp in William Warner's *A Continuance of Albions England* (London, 1611) takes the opposite view, and celebrates the "*Indian* weed /

That fum'd away more wealth than would a many thousands feed"; quoted in Brooks, *Tobacco*, 1:436.

79. Hall's account of the invention of smoking concerns "certain Indian chiefs of the Torrid Zone, so renowned for smoking that they had blackened their insides. It is clear that this color pleased them, for it did not seem right that the inner part of their bodies should differ from their outer"; *Mundus Alter et Idem*, 96. Marbecke believes on the other hand that tobacco compensates for any residue it may leave in the body by purging rheum: "It bringeth no more thither, than it carrieth away from thence"; *Defence*, B3r. James counters that what tobacco smokers take for rheum is really only smoke condensed, "and so are you made free and purged of nothing, but that wherewith you willfully burdened your selves"; *Counter-blaste*, B4v.

80. Marbecke's emphasis; cf. *Defence*, 16, 20, and 63–65.

81. Catullus, *Poems*; trans. Francis Warre Cornish, in *Catullus, Tibullus, and Pervigilium Veneris*, Loeb Classical Library (New York, 1912), 2. Noted by Grosart; see Beaumont, *Metamorphosis*, 266.

82. Beaumont and his friends subscribe to the Spenserian tobacco tradition with a vengeance: five times in the commendatory verses and poem is tobacco called "divine," five times "sacred," three times "celestial," five times its effects are "blest"; and then it is also "ethereal," "heavenly," "metaphysical," "immortal"—in short, a "god"; *Metamorphosis of Tobacco*, passim.

For Spenser's peculiar insistence on highlighting the ostensible triviality of his own poetry, see my "Error as a Means of Empire in *The Faerie Queene* 1," *English Literary History* 54 (Winter 1987). The idea of Spenser as an impoverished poet arose almost immediately after his death—for instance, in *The Return to Parnassus Part 2* (1601): "And yet for all, this unregarding soil / Unlac't the line of his desired life, / Denying maintenance for his dear relief: / Careless ere to prevent his exequy, / Scarce deigning to shut up his dying eye"; J. B. Leishman, ed., *The Three Parnassus Plays, 1598–1601 (The Pilgrimage to Parnassus, The Return to Parnassus Part 1, The Return to Parnassus Part 2*; London, 1949), 220–24. See Ray Heffner, "Did Spenser Die in Poverty?" *Modern Language Notes* 48 (1933): 221–26; and Alexander Judson, *The Life of Edmund Spenser* (Baltimore, 1945), 202–3.

83. Henry Cornelius Agrippa, *De Incertitudine & Vanitate Scientiarum & Artum* (Antwerp, 1530); trans. James Sandford as *Of the Vanitie and Uncertaintie of Artes and Sciences* (London, 1569), ed. Catherine M. Dunn (Northridge, Calif., 1974).

84. In his *De Orbo Novo*, Peter Martyr includes an epitome of a treatise on Indian rites by Ramon Pane, a friar who accompanied Columbus on his second voyage. Pane describes the superstitious use of the herb *cohoba*; the ceremony is very similar to the tobaccoan one Monardes reports, and in fact by the end of the sixteenth century commentators accepted *cohoba* as tobacco; Brooks, *Tobacco*, 1:196. Martyr adds to the future Charles V: "Now (most noble Prince) what need you hereafter to marvel of the spirit of *Apollo* so shaking his Sibyls with extreme fury? You had thought that superstitious antiquity had perished"; trans. Richard Eden (1555), in Edward Arber, ed., *The First Three English Books on America* (Birmingham, 1885), 101–2.

85. Cf. Samuel Walsall's praise of tobacco in his commendatory poem to Buttes: "Sovereign Nepenthes, which Tobacco hight, / Tobacco not to Antique Sages known, / Sage wizards that Tobacco knewen not?"; Buttes, *Dyets Dry Dinner*, Aa3v. For Beaumont on tobacco replacing moly, see *Metamorphosis of Tobacco*, 313.

86. Jose de Acosta, ed., *Concilium limense* (Madrid, 1591); translated in *Supplement*, 2:102.

Acosta "appears to have formulated the decrees and defended them against opponents" (ibid.).

87. Cf. W. B.'s commendatory poem: "There didst thou gather on Parnassus clift,/This precious herb, Tobacco most divine,/Than which ne'er Greece, ne'er Italy did lift/A flower more fragrant to the Muses' shrine:/A purer sacrifice did ne'er adorn/Apollo's altar, than this Indian fire"; Beaumont, *Metamorphosis of Tobacco*, 268–69. Nothing English figures in this account of the poem except Beaumont's head, which W.B. compares to a tobacco pipe.

88. For the Virgin Queen appropriating the Cult of the Virgin, for instance, see E. C. Wilson, *England's Eliza* (Cambridge, Mass., 1939), 200–23; Yates, *Astraea*, 78–79; and Roy Strong, *The Cult of Elizabeth: Elizabethan Portraiture and Pageantry* (London, 1977), 126.

The clearest explanation of this process, and the terms I've used, are Greenblatt's, in his discussion of an Accession Day celebration that seems to combine both classical allusion and Catholic ceremony: "The Roman mythology, deftly keyed to England's Virgin Queen, helps to fictionalize Catholic ritual sufficiently for it to be displaced and absorbed"; *Renaissance Self-Fashioning*, 230.

89. Cf. *The Masque of Flowers* (London, 1614; E. A. J. Honigmann, ed., in *A Book of Masques: In Honour of Allardyce Nicoll*, ed. T. J. B. Spencer et al. [Cambridge, 1967]), produced by Francis Bacon for Somerset's marriage in 1614, which stages a kind of mock Great Instauration celebration of modern times. The masque begins with a debate about the relative merits of wine, represented by Silenus, and tobacco, represented by an Indian god described by Harriot, "Kiwasa" or "Kawasha." Part of Kawasha's argument is that "Nothing but fumigation/Doth chase away ill sprites,/Kawasha and his nation/Found out these holy rites" (166). The joke on tobacco is first that Kawasha is himself an ill sprite, and second that no one wants to chase him away, not entirely: the scene of the masque is a walled city, before which sit "on either side a temple, the one dedicated to Silenus and the other to Kawasha" (161). The debate soon gives way to a more explicit account of Britain's superiority to either classical or Indian barbarism, when James transforms some painted flowers—metamorphosed gentlemen, we discover—back into men; a song helps explain the allegory:

> Give place you ancient powers,
> That turned men to Flowers,
> For never Writers pen
> Yet told of Flowers return'd to Men:
> *Chorus*: But miracles of new event
> Follow the great Sun of our firmament.
>
> (168)

The apparent euhemerism of the allegory, in which the enlightening sun of James reverses the classical transformation of men into myths or "flowers"—poesies—does not demand that superstition be discarded; rather, the enlightened song is itself sung by twelve "Garden-gods," also referred to as "Priests." The masque wants Britain to retain superstition so that potentially heretical claims for Britain's superiority, indeed for its millennialness, may be maintained, but negatively: Britain is here simply "fit to be" the millennial "fifth monarchy" of Dan. 7.27.

90. I refer to the title of the last chapter of Greenblatt's *Renaissance Self-Fashioning*.

91. Lawrence Keymis, *A Relation of the Second Voyage to Guiana*, C3r; quoted in Dickson,

Panacea, 138. When Beaumont referred earlier to Elizabeth being "worshipt" in America, he may have been either misremembering this Guianan anecdote or alluding to the much less dramatic submission of the Virginian *weroance* or chief Menatonon, who ordered his vassal king Okisko "to yield himself servant, and homager, to the great Weroanza of England"; Menatonon seems to have been impressed less by Elizabeth's virtues than by the fact that at the time Lane held his "best beloved son prisoner with me"; Quinn, *Roanoke Voyages*, 279, 262.

92. See, e.g., Yates, *Astraea*, 80–81.

93. John Gerard, *The Herball or Generall Historie of Plantes* (London, 1597); quoted in Quinn, *England and the Discovery of America*, 445, 444.

94. Samuel Daniel, *Musophilus* (London, 1599), 12–13; reprinted in *Poems and a Defense of Rhyme*, ed. Arthur C. Sprague (Chicago, 1930), 69.

95. Leishman, *Return Part 2*, 403; *Return Part 1*, 368; Thomas Dekker, *The Wonderfull Year* (London, 1603); quoted in Robert Ralston Cawley, *The Voyagers and Elizabethan Literature* (Boston, 1938), 298, n. 152. The *Parnassus* plays, when optimistic, also transform the scholar's material poverty into his spiritual purity: on his way to Parnassus, Philomusus declares, "Though I foreknow that dolts possess the gold,/Yet my intended pilgrimage I'll hold"; while Studioso adds the moral, "Within Parnassus dwells all sweet content,/Nor care I for those excrements of earth"; *Pilgrimage*, 5.594–97. In the later plays of the trilogy, however, after the scholars return to the quotidian world, this otherworldliness becomes more difficult to maintain, and tobacco soon surfaces as a correlative to ambivalence about poetical "spirit," sometimes like ale inspiring mere vapors (*Return Part 2*, 160–62), other times representing a more positive but still jocular alternative to the gold scholars lack: Philomusus, pleased with Luxurio's wit, prays that "long for a reward may your wits be warm'd with the Indian herb" (*Return Part 1*, 432–34).

96. Agrippa, *Vanitie*, 33.

97. Calvin, *Institution*, 167v.

98. Sell, *Shorter Poems*, 8–10.

99. Richard Bauckham, *Tudor Apocalypse: Sixteenth-Century Apocalypticism, Millennarianism, and the English Reformation* (Oxford, 1978), 209; William Haller, *Foxe's "Book of Martyrs" and the Elect Nation* (London, 1963). See also Viggo Norskov Olsen, *John Foxe and the Elizabethan Church* (Berkeley, 1973); Paul Christianson, *Reformers and Babylon: English Apocalyptic Visions from the Reformation to the Eve of the Civil War* (Toronto, 1978); and Katherine R. Firth, *The Apocalyptic Tradition in Reformation Britain, 1530–1645* (Oxford, 1979).

100. Noted by Grosart, in Beaumont, *Metamorphosis of Tobacco*, 265.

101. John Pory to Edwin Sandys, 16 January 1620, in William S. Powell, ed., *John Pory, 1572–1636: The Life and Letters of a Man of Many Parts* (Chapel Hill, N.C., 1977), microfiche suppl. p. 81.

102. For tobacco's fortunes in the seventeenth century, see Edmund S. Morgan's superb *American Slavery, American Freedom: The Ordeal of Colonial Virginia* (New York, 1975).

103. James's silk master Bonoeil had warned the colony, "Do not then still *Ixion*-like, embrace a cloud, for *Juno*, and smoke for substance"; *Letter*, quoted in *Supplement*, 4:206; but even James soon had to admit that tobacco had truly become a miraculous nourishment: in 1624 he noted how "the planters of Virginia have implored consideration for their languishing colony, which can only subsist at present by its tobacco"; *Calendar of State Papers, Domestic, 1623–25*, 290.

104. On the tobacco deals between Company and Crown, see, e.g., Charles M. Andrews, *The Colonial Period of American History*, 4 vols. (New Haven, 1934), 1:55–57. Thirsk notes that "in no other country did merchants and planters manage to secure a total prohibition on domestic cultivation for the sake of the colonial trade"; "New Crops," 87.

105. Beer, *Origins*, 67, quoting *A True and Sincere Declaration of . . . Virginia* (London, 1610).

106. Such imposts eventually helped reduce Charles to smoke: "Almost to a man prominent Virginia traders supported the Parliamentarian cause"; John R. Pagan, "Growth of the Tobacco Trade Between London and Virginia, 1610–40," *Guildhall Studies in London History* 3 (1979): 262. Pagan is following the work of Robert Brenner, of which he provides a bibliography on p. 262, n. 93.

LUCE GIARD

Epilogue:
Michel de Certeau's Heterology
and the New World

> *Our world has just found an other.*
> —Montaigne, *Essays*, 3.6

MICHEL DE CERTEAU would have been honored by this collection of articles dedicated to his memory by *Representations*, and even more touched by the gesture of friendship, for he was a man who never separated intellectual activity from a warm and enthusiastic regard for others. He had been associated with *Representations* from its very beginning, and its combination of disciplines and viewpoints could only delight him, as it agreed almost too well with his own practice of transversality.[1]

The Space of the Voyage

After finishing *La Fable mystique*, Michel de Certeau had wished to dedicate all of his time to the question of the New World. As we reread his writing up to the point at which it was interrupted by his death, we can see more clearly how and why accounts of voyages to the Americas interested him. He had begun to formulate this question as a decisive moment in his attempt to constitute a "science of the Other," a *heterology* as he liked to call it.[2] Indeed, this heterology was the chief object of his thought in its various modes of inquiry, the final (and thus unattainable) goal of his voyages of exploration across the ocean of knowledges and methods.

To exemplify this heterology, I will first consider de Certeau's essay on Jean de Léry's *Histoire d'un voyage faict en la terre de Brésil* (1578), which appears in part 3 of *The Writing of History* and which is an essential piece in the structure of that book.[3] The book opens onto a threshold of critical epistemology that describes, with fierce irony, the prejudices and conventions regulating the historian's practice within his or her professional institution. Beyond that, three equally important questions are addressed in innovative ways; these concern respectively the complete transformation of religious practices in the seventeenth century, which reversed their meanings as they became politicized; the status of the "voice" and of the "savage," when in the sixteenth century Scripture lost the power to speak the truth and Christian Europe began to propagate beyond its boundaries the Revelation it had already ceased to believe; and finally the relevance of Freud and psychoanalysis for history, which help show the discourse of history in its true status as a strange mix of science and fiction in which the imaginary returns within rationality. The three areas under investigation, in other words, lead toward the Other—whether God, other men in other societies, or that alterity in oneself against whom the most painful battles are played out.

It is altogether evident that the search for God is a journey toward the Other; de Certeau had pointed out, without dwelling on the matter, that all types of voyages are the same. Thus he remarked that, "unfortunately, travel literature has not yet been studied systematically as a great complement to and displacement of demonology. Yet the same structures are common to both."[4] In another essay, de Certeau discusses the seventeenth-century autobiography of Jean-Joseph Surin, who had been confined as mad for close to twenty years, as a travel narrative in which madness and reason exchange roles, an account that "illuminates the questions that every voyage tries to articulate within the double modality, both geographical and textual, of the opening of another space."[5] This inquiry, as de Certeau adds in a note, would have developed into a book on travel narratives.[6]

De Certeau was only able to complete the preliminary work for this project: a noteworthy rereading of Montaigne's essay "On Cannibals,"[7] which should be seen as a complement to the chapter on Léry; a study of Joseph-François Lafitau, the eighteenth-century Jesuit whose *Moeurs des sauvages amériquains comparées aux moeurs des premiers temps* (1724) in a way founded anthropology as an autonomous science;[8] and several additional pieces along with, in his archives, many files of notes and fragments. But a first outline of the general project exists, presented to the Centre national de la recherche scientifique in the spring of 1978, when de Certeau was still hesitating whether to leave Europe for a teaching position in the United States. The center did not accept his proposal, and he left for the University of California at San Diego,[9] where he made this project the subject of several courses he taught between 1978 and 1984. The description of the project is appended here in translation; it illuminates the perspective that would have guided de Certeau in his study of narratives of journeys between France and Brazil from the sixteenth to the eighteenth centuries. The proposal revives regret for the book that we will never read, as well as leaves unexplained the origins of de Certeau's interest in a marginalized literary genre rarely studied by historians.

I can only offer conjectures as to the reasons for his interest in such accounts. Some of these reasons stem from external influences, others from subjective factors of his intellectual trajectory. In the foreground, there is the influence of Alphonse Dupront (1905–90), who is not well known outside France due to his unusual habits of publication. The student and intellectual heir of Paul Alphandéry, a medievalist, Dupront began his studies with the Crusades but then enlarged his field of inquiry to include all occasions of the sacred, both in itself and in its social manifestations. He was captivated by rites, sacred places, images, and pilgrimages, and combined a historian's erudition with metaphysical and theological preoccupations as well as with a sustained interest in depth psychology. This combination was unique, and its originality was increased by being expressed in a language equally inimitable, sometimes lyrical, archaic, and precious, but always precise.

Dupront was for a long time a professor at the Sorbonne and the Ecole des hautes études. He was thus at the center of a network of historians, without observing the usual customs of publication but influencing numerous historians in and outside the medieval sphere such as Mona Ozouf, Dominique Julia, and de Certeau. One of Dupront's habits was to disperse the fragments of his work, always presented as provisional and partial, in a hundred improbable places (collections of limited circulation, obscure local reviews, and so on), as if he wished to make the fruit of his studies invisible. Perhaps he wished to impose on his reader an initiation like that of the holy grail; only if one knew how to discover its trace could one accede to the sacred texts.[10]

De Certeau, who never had a taste for rites of initiation or for Jungian pan-symbolism, admired Dupront and for a time participated in his seminar. He sometimes alluded to it as a completed moment of the past, but always with respect and a kind of regret for what it might have accomplished.[11] In reading Dupront's book (published in 1987 and not seen by de Certeau), one begins to understand what in the old master could have interested, irritated, and disappointed his junior. Three notable themes in Dupront would have attracted de Certeau: the question of the Other, the problem of space, and the privilege granted to vision. These themes, which can be recognized in all levels of de Certeau's work, were profoundly imbricated in de Certeau's thought and stem from experiences that date from before his being acquainted with Dupront.[12] But Dupront certainly influenced de Certeau's reflections, if only by obliging him to clarify his position on essential points on which he differed from Dupront, particularly on the religious phenomenon and its possible psychoanalytic interpretation. This negative influence can be found especially in de Certeau's opposite approach to the history of mysticism. However, it also played a positive role in his recognition of the importance of the historical encounter with the Other and of the experience of space.

This becomes clear if one returns to Dupront's definition of the pilgrimage as a "physical act of mastery over space," a "march to elsewhere" that is "an instance of the Other."[13] De Certeau often mentioned a long article in which Dupront meditates on the emergence of Christian Europe from the Middle Ages and from its geographical frontiers: "The occidental discoverer indeed is the conqueror of the earth: this conquest saw itself as a crusade or a mission even before the passions of imperialism had found the courage to declare themselves."[14] In rereading Dupront's article, one notices two similarities with de Certeau's work. On the one hand, Montaigne is given an important place, and his essay on cannibals is the object of a commentary;[15] a comparison of the two readings by Dupront and de Certeau is instructive on their different styles, methods, and intentions. On the other hand, there is a strong insistence on vision and the visual appropriation of space. Dupront cites as well Marc Lescarbot's *Histoire de la Nouvelle France* (1609), in which the discoverer is "desirous not so much of traveling as of ocularly recognizing the earth," and then Montaigne, again in connection with the cannibals, to conclude: "[Possessing the thing through vision] provides the definition of modern knowledge, whose progress is made in the reading of space. . . . [Modern knowledge] is expressed in the act of description as a figure for the thing, in other words a shifting from space traversed to space that is read."[16] Such a theme of seeing, in almost the same terms and with similar consequences, runs through all of de Certeau's work and, in particular, permeates his most secret and autobiographical text on the question of mysticism.[17]

However, it would be wrong to attribute de Certeau's interest in space itself and accounts of it to his contact with Dupront. De Certeau's membership in the Jesuits and the contribution of their determinate and very rich tradition was chronologically anterior and intellectually more significant. From its foundation, the Society had turned its efforts toward missionary work, especially in the Americas and in Asia. Little by little a complete network of houses and colleges was established, and an abundant correspondence was regularly maintained between Rome and the diverse Jesuit provinces both within and outside Europe. From 1547 Ignatius of Loyola expressly asked Jesuits scattered across the world to provide information to the Roman center on apostolic activity, its objective conditions and specific problems due to the circumstances and traditions, the customs and the conceptions of the host country, as well as to submit to the collective judgment of the Society all decisions taken. There is thus an abundance of precise and detailed documentation on distant countries. This provided material for three series of texts: an interior correspondence, limited to governance within the order (of which a large part is preserved today in various archives); the *Lettres édifiantes et curieuses*, which represent the public part of this correspondence, circulated in print for the information of the students of the colleges, the families of benefactors, devout circles, and social elites; and finally a scholarly literature embodied in the *relations de voyage* and other *descriptions*, which offer remarkable scientific treatises on the geography, language, and customs of distant countries and their inhabitants.[18]

As a young historian, de Certeau had been asked by the Society to devote himself for a time to the history of its early development. He naturally read closely these sources, printed and in manuscript, for the history of the order. This coincided with his own interest in missionary work: he had entered the Society with the desire to leave for China, although the political situation made this impossible; later there was a possibility that he might be sent to Cameroon; in the end, he remained in France, where his voyage was first intellectual and mystical although he made numerous sojourns in European countries and especially in North and South America after 1966. It is possible, as well, that an encounter that occurred in the Society had an influence on his later reflections on space; this was with François de Dainville (1909–71), a specialist in the history of education and cartography.[19] For several years Dainville and de Certeau lived in the same Jesuit community in Paris, and while it does not seem that their proximity led to very close ties, there certainly existed an intellectual exchange and a reciprocal esteem. De Certeau knew Dainville's work well and spoke on occasion of sessions spent together over ancient maps, objects that fascinated him and to which he dedicated his last public lecture in Paris in December 1985.

These encounters, readings, the tradition of the Society, his desire to leave as a missionary did not, however, create in de Certeau his passionate interest in voyages, space, and the act of seeing, even if they nourished it. He had had from childhood an intense desire, in his own words, to "not belong," to free himself, to overcome the limits of family, of milieu, of a province and a culture, and to encounter the Other in order to be, at the same time, again in his own words, "transformed" and "wounded." At the basis of this vocation for the Other, which determined his way of being in the world, there was a fundamental intensity of seeing, a feature to be found everywhere in his work. This essential experience inspired a striking commentary on Maurice Merleau-Ponty, who was also driven by the same passion for seeing:

Vision "captivates" us not only because it is a journey toward external things, but also because it is a *return* to a reality of origin, which is represented in these objects perceived at a distance. In this respect, moreover, it already functions like all true journeys (the traveler inventories and discovers little by little the place he comes from), and bears a special relationship to travel: to travel is to see, but seeing is already traveling.[20]

Speaking the Other

In the studies gathered in this special issue, one immediately notices the diversity of voices that intersect and respond to each other, voices of the past and of the present, the whole composing a single narrative of the same *destructive violence* that Europe inflicted on the American Indian societies. Underneath the sound and fury of this violence, de Certeau heard the rumor of another one, more secret but equally important, the *transformative violence* of the meeting with the Other whose shock waves had finally reached Europe to undermine its old certainties. He often remarked that "no one returns unchanged" from an encounter with the Other. In a sense, it was the meditation of this encounter in all its forms, past and present, external to each or internal to the soul, that preoccupied his mind throughout his life. His collection of essays, *Heterologies*, is indicative of nothing else. It shows how the unity of this interrogation ("What about the Other?") produced a unity of investigation that ranges over such diverse terrains as history, mysticism, literature, and psychoanalysis. In the final analysis, the stakes of this work are to constitute a "science of the Other," for which each inquiry localized by its object provided elements but which de Certeau knew had not yet resulted in a final edifice.

It is not certain that de Certeau thought such a "science of the Other" to be constructible; rather, it constituted a horizon of intelligibility toward which his work addressed itself in its entirety. This could not be otherwise, for his thought resisted all systematization and equally rejected the pious consolation of global hypotheses. His lasting frequentation of Hegel, whom he studied closely as a graduate student in the Society of Jesus, made him definitively skeptical about "absolute knowledge." His studies of religious history from the Renaissance to the Enlightenment had familiarized him with theological-political quarrels and the way in which they justify the fragile equilibrium of antagonistic forces in society. From this lucid exigency stemmed his rejection of unified explanations and global theories, but it resulted as well in an acute and almost painful awareness of the limits of each historical figure that rationality displayed. Thus he could never be satisfied with one method, one period, one discipline, and hence his habit of subjecting each model he employed to a rigorous epistemological critique. In this way he established his distance from certainties and voluntarily remained on the margins of the institution—an itinerant on the frontier, impossible to make sedentary even after he became successful.

For de Certeau, to interrogate each figure of rationality without privileging a stable center of perspective from which to contemplate their succession was to forbid the establishment of an exempted position from which their totalization could be produced. It would thus be impossible to give a definitive form to the science of the Other, and it would be necessary as well to replace this first enterprise with one, more modest, of illuminating the formality of practices without delineating an ordering principle. This necessity explains de Certeau's reticence toward Aristotle and his interest in Wittgenstein; all desire to systematize would engender a possible totalization that de Certeau suspected of missing the point. The price he paid was indeed the necessity of giving up ever producing a complete theory or a finished science, but the advantage of this limitation was the marvelous freedom it allowed him in his choice of objects, modes of interrogation, and criteria for examination.[21]

The science of the Other was thus condemned to remain an unattainable but always beloved object of desire for de Certeau, always escaping any appropriation. In order to emphasize this impossibility, he repeatedly used the same troubling formulas—"*That's not it*; one cannot rest *here* nor be satisfied with *that*"—whether it was a question of mysticism[22] or of Montaigne's objection to received images of the "savage."[23] Constructible neither by nature nor in principle, the science of the Other, both desired and rejected, was thus the motive force of a thought never in repose. Of this itinerancy, however, de Certeau did not provide any travel narrative: differing from the voyager at his return, he did not feel he was endowed with "the authority to speak in the name of the Other and command belief";[24] he was too lucid to consent to follow the law of genre and, by a rhetoric of the Other, end in a reduction to the Same.[25]

De Certeau did not want to play such a role, for he had no intention of speaking the truth. To claim to do so would have meant that he believed himself "authorized" to do so, but by what authority? The logic of the position he adopted denies all identification with a determined place chosen as the center of power from which the law is announced and from which the ownership of property is organized. De Certeau accounts for this refusal very clearly in *The Practice of Everyday Life*, distinguishing between a strategy always inscribed in the logic of the proprietor and the ephemeral tactics of an anonymous crowd with neither wealth nor a place of their own. He made no mystery of his preferences; it suffices to return to that work where several lines, dedicated to others, trace without his knowing it a marvelous self-portrait:

I know of investigators experienced in this art of diversion, which is a return of the ethical, of pleasure and of invention within the scientific institution. Realizing no profit (profit is produced by work done for the factory), and often at a loss, they take something from the order of knowledge in order to inscribe "artistic achievements" on it and to carve on it the graffiti of their debts of honor.[26]

In this sense de Certeau's intellectual itinerancy was not a random activity but was centered and unified by the untiring activity of reading and writing. These were so inextricably linked for him that they came to constitute an entirely unusual reading/writing (*lirécrire*) that referred, on the theoretical level, to the status he gave to the appearance of a "scriptural society" from the time of the Renaissance. While the object of this reading/writing changed ceaselessly, its procedures were maintained without their resulting in a code, a definitive grid of reading transportable from one text to another, and even less in a statement of method.[27] Never psychologizing, this interpretative practice was in a sense completely Freudian, not in that it submitted the text to the dictates of Freudian orthodoxy but for what it caused to surge up. There is in his mode of interpretation something mysterious and consummate, surprising and captivating, a delicate and precise perfection by which one can follow the subtlest articulations of the text being analyzed in order to discover the internal necessity that, in its turn, reveals its finality.

De Certeau read all kinds of texts in this manner, from mystical works to literature, from philosophy to travel narratives. Thus he presented the autobiography of Surin as a remarkable voyage through madness and suffering up to the point that Surin recovered the possibility of writing and through this his access to reason. In this agonized text, whose narrator loses himself, divided between an "I" and a "he," de Certeau sought neither to give a precise diagnosis of Surin's temporary madness, nor to distinguish between the true and the false in his account, but to "hear what the discourse says of his body," following as if by a musical score the fundamental musical line.[28] Full of tact and showing an extreme sensitivity in listening, this manner of proceeding was analytic in its composition and thus foreign to all synthetic ambition. This does not mean that it was without force or coherence; it is because it had both qualities that it has gained the respect of readers in different languages and contexts, as its many translations show.

Michel de Certeau was fond of quoting a verse from the *Aeneid*: "Her walk reveals the goddess." This image had for him a secret and profound resonance that he also found in *Flowers of Evil* in the sonnet dedicated "To a Woman Passing By." In similar terms he invoked the image of Christ as a man lost in the crowd, happy to disappear there, "that illustrious passerby."[29] I had often thought, in the happy time when he was among us, that this verse of Virgil, transferred to the intellectual sphere, described perfectly what was at the heart of his untiring work of reading/writing. It was an "art of doing," as he liked to say, that consisted "*of passing* more than of founding" in the "gesture of clearing a path, without cease."[30] François Hartog has drawn up a just portrait of his admirable and inimitable art:

He discovered, but without measuring, he traveled through, but without inhabiting, this heterological space of which he was, in a certain way, the inventor and the historian, but a historian without territory, the instigator of a proceeding rather than the founder of a new discipline.[31]

Michel de Certeau would have liked this way of inscribing his work within the space of the Other, as he would have liked to engage in dialogue the voices from the sixteenth century in this collection of essays, brought back by voices from our own century, and then to disappear into the oceanic rumor of the crowd.

—Translated by Katharine Streip

Notes

1. On the development of Michel de Certeau's thought, see Luce Giard, ed., *Michel de Certeau* (Paris, 1987); Giard et al., *Le Voyage mystique: Michel de Certeau* (Paris, 1988), which contains a complete bibliography; and the dossier "Michel de Certeau, historien," *Le Débat* 49 (March–April 1988): 83–121.
2. Michel de Certeau, *Heterologies: Discourse on the Other*, trans. Brian Massumi (Minneapolis, 1986). This collection has no equivalent in French; I have reprinted half of its texts in de Certeau, *Histoire et psychanalyse entre science et fiction* (Paris, 1987).

3. Michel de Certeau, *The Writing of History*, trans. Tom Conley (New York, 1988), 209–43.

4. Ibid., 242, n. 52.

5. Michel de Certeau, "Voyage et prison: La Folie de J.-J. Surin," in Bernard Beugnot, ed., *Voyages, récits, et imaginaire* (Paris, 1984), 439–67, esp. 443.

6. Ibid., 463, n. 13.

7. Michel de Certeau, "Montaigne's 'Of Cannibals': The Savage 'I,'" in *Heterologies*, 67–79.

8. This article first appeared in English; Michel de Certeau, "Writing vs. Time: History and Anthropology in the Works of Lafitau," *Yale French Studies* 59, *Rethinking History* (Summer 1980): 37–64.

9. Michel de Certeau, "Californie, un théâtre de passants," *Autrement* 31, *Californie, rêve et cauchemar* (1981): 10–18.

10. Alphonse Dupront, *Du sacré: Croisades et pèlerinages, images et langages* (Paris, 1987). The work begins with a very long "itinerary," pp. 11–235, which ends on an unusual juxtaposition of two citations, one from Alain, the other from Pascal, as if Dupront had wanted, once more, to cover his tracks.

11. See, for example, de Certeau, *The Writing of History*, 38–39, on the "relation with the Other" for the historian.

12. Cf. what I have called, in one of his accounts, "the primal scene": Luce Giard, "La Passion de l'altérité," in *Michel de Certeau*, 19–20.

13. Dupront, *Du sacré*, 53, 55.

14. Alphonse Dupront, "Espace et humanisme," *Bibliothèque d'Humanisme et Renaissance* 8 (1946): 7–104, esp. 54. De Certeau mentioned this article several times, particularly in *The Writing of History*, 241, n. 25.

15. Dupront, "Espace et humanisme," 61–65.

16. Ibid., 95–96.

17. See Michel de Certeau, *La Fable mystique, XVIe–XVIIe siècle*, vol. 1 (Paris, 1987), chap. 2 on Hieronymus Bosch; de Certeau, "The Gaze: Nicholas of Cusa," *Diacritics* 17, no. 3 (Fall 1987): 2–38. See as well de Certeau, "The Madness of Vision," *Enclitic* 7, no. 1 (Spring 1983): 24–31. On the city, seeing, and narratives of space (which are also, he says, "travel narratives"), see de Certeau, *The Practice of Everyday Life*, trans. Stephen Rendall (Berkeley, 1984), chaps. 7 and 9. On mysticism, as for his most personal text, see de Certeau, *La Faiblesse de croire* (Paris, 1987), 315–18.

18. For a brief presentation of this immense literature, see the article "Jésuites" in *Dictionnaire de spiritualité*, vol. 8 (Paris, 1973), cols. 1033–35.

19. François de Dainville, *La Géographie des humanistes* (Paris, 1940); Dainville, *L'Education des jésuites, XVIe–XVIIIe siècles* (Paris, 1978), a collection edited by Marie-Madeleine Compère, who has established Dainville's bibliography, pp. 537–49.

20. De Certeau, "Madness of Vision," 26.

21. De Certeau, *Heterologies*, chap. 15, "History: Science and Fiction"; see also the text of the project for the Centre national de la recherche scientifique, following this essay.

22. De Certeau, *La Fable mystique*, 411.

23. De Certeau, *Heterologies*, 69.   24. Ibid.

25. De Certeau, "Voyage et prison," 444.

26. De Certeau, *Practice of Everyday Life*, particularly chap. 3; my citation is at the end of chap. 2, p. 28.

27. Ibid., chap. 12. See also Anne-Marie Chartier and Jean Hébrard, "*L'Invention du quotidien*: Une Lecture, des usages," and Jacques Le Brun, "De la critique textuelle à la lecture du texte," in *Le Débat* 49 (March–April 1988): 97–108, 109–16.

28. De Certeau, "Voyage et prison," 453. The musical metaphor is my own.

29. De Certeau, *La Faiblesse de croire*, 292, 302, 304.

30. De Certeau, "Ecritures," in *Michel de Certeau*, 13–14.

31. François Hartog, "L'Ecriture du voyage," in *Michel de Certeau*, 127.

MICHEL DE CERTEAU

Travel Narratives of the French to Brazil: Sixteenth to Eighteenth Centuries

Subject

THIS RESEARCH PROJECT is situated at the intersection of history and anthropology. It proposes to analyze a corpus that could be considered as a series over the long term. This research continues work undertaken in history (*mentalités* and spirituality in the sixteenth and seventeenth centuries; possession in the seventeenth century; religious thought and practices in the seventeenth century; Leibniz; linguistic policies and theories at the end of the eighteenth century) and in anthropology (possession; sorcery and mysticism; the concept of "popular culture"; investigations conducted in Brazil, Chile, and Argentina since 1966; the regular teaching of historical and cultural anthropology at the University of Paris VII since 1972; the foundation of DIAL, a center for information on Latin America).

The project presented here originates from several questions that could receive answers through an analysis of the dossier:

1) The information provided by the French on Indian ethnic groups living in Brazil and on Brazil itself during these three centuries of relations with Latin America puts into question the relation between systems of interpretation (conceptual apparatuses, mythologies, grids of analysis, dominant ideas, and questions) and their historical contexts (institutional, economic, political, social, professional, and religious). In defining the corpus under study by a geographical bipolarity, I hope to locate more easily the modifications that were introduced in the production of texts by changes relative to the forms of contact (for example between the French and the Tupis), to the international situation, to the recruitment of "voyagers," and so on, and thus to study which elements affect the reproduction of a scientific and literary genre that goes back to the medieval *itinerarium* (stages in the knowledge of another world) as well as to the ancient odysseys of pilgrims, heroes, and merchants, and how they bring about these changes. In this

way we can appreciate the impact of history on a symbolic structure of knowledge: the voyage.

2) Travel narratives also constitute interdisciplinary laboratories in which categories of analysis, scientific concepts, and taxonomic systems demarcating and classifying observations on social organization, linguistic and juridical formations, technologies, myths and legends, geography, a new experience of the body, as well as biological, zoological, and medical factors, can come into play and interact. These areas of exchange and of scientific confrontation (within the science of that time) are collections set in the form of narratives (in a period when collections of objects and curiosities, like the written collection of information and knowledge theorized, notably, by Francis Bacon, came into being). For this reason these narratives are of interest to a history of science: in them, mobile configurations of evolving disciplines intersect, grow distinct, and become ordered; in them, as in the archives, units become determinate which will exercise their constraints on the sciences destined to express them within systems.

3) As scientific narrativity, this literature refers to modes in which an account "represents" technical operations (observations, controls, rules, procedures) and their results. At once a staging (fiction, in the English sense of the term) and an ordering (discourse), travel narratives offer to analysis various combinations between the practices of scientific investigation (that *ars inveniendi*, another form of the quest for *methodus*, which haunts writers from Rodolphus Agricola to Leibniz and Jean-Henri Lambert) and their figurations in a literary space-time. In order precisely to establish the status of this scientific writing, I will particularly investigate: a) the narrative description of the series of operations that characterize a study (in comparing these accounts with other "histories" of scholarly, medical, chemical discoveries, and so on);[1] b) the imaginary, the beliefs and the ideologies that a rationality postulates, produces, or critiques; c) the relation of these representations of itineraries (where the "works" of the researchers/voyagers are expressed through "portraits" of visited societies) to the systems of figuration of the period (thus the literary accounts, the cartographic projections, and the engraved scenes or figures obedient to the rules of perspective, to the hierarchical types of "painting," together form interlacings of complementary writings).[2] How, under the name of travel narratives, were these *fictions*, at once models and representations of scientific operations, produced? This will be the main issue.

4) Through a specific investigation (of the series France/Brazil), it seems to me possible to grasp the slow formation of what will receive in 1836 the name of "ethnology"—in other words, to delineate an archeology of ethnology and to show how a science of man is detached, modified, and specified between the rupture of the Renaissance and the end of the Enlightenment. The successive definitions of ethnic difference or of "superstition," the progressive elaboration of concepts of "fable" or of "myth," the distinctions between writing and orality will

require special attention.[3] These points either involve strategic elements of Western culture or enact classifications that refer back to the social divisions that organize knowledge, or conversely, are divisions that have structured the social agency of science.

5) Finally, since these accounts enter into the more general category of a science of the Other or "heterology," it is important to ask, starting from Brazilian sources in particular or from the confrontation of different documents: a) how the specificity of another society, for example, that of the Tupi, resisted occidental codifications; b) how the fragments of a historicity proper to other societies (with, notably, differing relations to time, to space, and so on), elements capable of inscribing these societies within a duration, a memory, and a space of their own, were first brought into use; c) how, in the text of the ethnographic project, oriented initially toward reduction and preservation, are irreducible details (sounds, "words," singularities) insinuated as faults in the discourse of comprehension, so that the travel narrative presented the kind of organization that Freud posited in ordinary language: a system in which indices of an unconscious, that Other of the conscience, emerge in *lapsus* or witticisms.[4] The history of voyages would especially lend itself to this analysis by tolerating or privileging as an "event" that which makes an exception to interpretative codes. In so doing, it would constitute only one variant of more contemporary forms of heterological voyages.

Constitution of the Corpus

Fundamentally, the material of the corpus will be provided by various reference works.[5] My research bears only on the narratives of travelers, and not— except for texts unavailable elsewhere—on the innumerable *recueils* or *histoires générales des voyages* that attempt, as compilations or anthologies, to repeat the ancient cosmographic model or to constitute a totalization of the encyclopedic type.[6] The proposed research will extend thus from the voyage of Paulmier de Gonneville (1504) to the voyages of Alexander von Humboldt (1799–1804): although the latter author was not French, his texts will be explored because they mark a rupture in the conception of ethnologic exploration. In France, this same division is traced by the works of Démeunier (1776), Volney (1795), Dégérando (1800), and Jauffret (1803) on ethnology,[7] and also by the new definition then given to "anthropology" (for example, in A.-C. Chavannes's *Anthropologie ou science générale de l'homme*, 1788).

Since this research analyzes the relationship between the actual encounter of a different society (what will become a "terrain" at the end of the eighteenth century) and a type of discourse (the narrative), I will privilege texts that treat Indian ethnic groups, even if their progressive effacement and overlapping with the colonizers, half-breeds, and mulattos in the *observations* of the voyagers (and how could this have been otherwise, given the racial mixtures characteristic of Portuguese colonization and the demographic hecatomb brought about by the Europeans) prevent me from limiting the corpus to texts that speak only of Indians. I will add that, during my different periods of work in Latin America since 1966, I have paid particular attention to the vestiges of Indian cultures and to the present situation of these groups.[8]

Likewise, it will be necessary to investigate the relations between travel narratives and contemporary "philosophers" (for example Jean de Léry and Montaigne, Bougainville and Diderot), mathematicians (see the exemplary case of Cook), biologists (Léry and Wotton, for example). On this aspect of the problem, substantial studies already provide a foundation.[9] I will rely on manuscripts in the National Archives (colonial series), the Archives of the French Overseas Territories (deposits on fortifications of the colonies), and the Archives of Foreign Affairs (memoirs and documents) only to illuminate particular dossiers. The same will be true for the archives preserved at Lisbon (Biblioteca nacional), at Porto (Museu de etnografia e história), at Rio de Janeiro (Instituto histórico e geogràfico brasileiro), and at Recife (Instituto Joaquim Nabuco de pesquisas sociais), where I have made preliminary inquiries, relying on important information from Brazilian historians.[10]

Methodology

There is an abundant scientific literature on this subject.[11] The richness of these studies and of this accumulated material enables and calls for a different way of reading and discussing these travel narratives. In addition to the research, which aims to construct the corpus defined above (a corpus that has not been the object of any of the studies cited), I wish to indicate three concerns that will help clarify my methodology.

1) The first involves the treatment of the texts. The studies that I have published and the teaching that I have regularly engaged in at the Centre international de sémiotique in Urbino and in Paris since 1969 lead me to think that it is possible to associate a semiotic analysis of documents with a historical problematic. As narratives, these texts particularly lend themselves to studies concerning narrativity, enunciation, the modalities and the functioning of the text. In this way, I hope to define a literary structure of scientific work, a narrative instrumentality of investigation, in sum a kind of writing relating to the process of research more than to its results. The work of Alain Girard on nineteenth-century diaries, of Tzvetan Todorov on the fantastic novel during the same period, or of Philippe Lejeune on autobiography already demonstrate the historical interest of this kind of analysis.

2) The identification and the historical variants of this scientific "genre"

authorize comparison with other kinds of narratives of travel and discovery: scholarly, chemical, astronomical, mystical, and so on. In this way, a kind of research and discourse that crosses distinct fields, and opens the objective possibility of interdisciplinary work, becomes available. Between differentiated sciences, a historical cohesion appears that concerns not only postulates, ideologies, and objects of knowledge common to these sciences but a manner of proceeding linked to a manner of writing, that is to say, to a method. Doubtless, referring results to the manner of "producing" them (that is to say, to the discovery and the manifestation of these results) corresponds to an essential aspect of modernity, to an historicization of knowledge (which precedes theories of history).[12]

3) Finally, research already undertaken to elaborate a concept of "science/fiction," that is to say not a reduction of science to fiction but a mixture of narration and scientific practices, leads me to try to locate in travel narratives the forms that this combination of the rules of literary production and those controlling scientific production takes. The travel narrative oscillates between these two poles and permits the elaboration of a theory of this association: the travel narrative is a text of observation haunted by its Other, the imaginary. In this way it corresponds to its object, a "culture" haunted by its "savage" exteriority. It appears to offer a particularly interesting field for the construction of an epistemological model that "legitimates" the actual functioning of the human sciences. Current research (for example at the Department of Philosophy at Cambridge University) on the relation between scientific discourse and metaphor, belief and the imaginary (such as the work of Gerald Holton on the central role of theme in scientific creativity) suggest a promising simultaneity of work in this direction.[13]

Through the travel narrative, an ideal of science becomes available for analysis, and with it a configuration of the ensemble of knowledge. But only a local study, partial and precise, can permit the detailed disassembling of the subtle mechanisms that articulate between themselves narrativity, scientificity, and the efficacy of each.

—Translated by Katharine Streip

Notes

1. See, for example, the *Ortus medicinae* of Jean Baptiste van Helmont; *Le Labyrinthe du monde et le paradis du coeur* of Comenius, the heuristic notations of Girard Desargues on his "projective" geometry, and so on.
1. I will rely here on the work of Erwin Panofsky, François de Dainville, and Jacques Guillerme.
3. I have already studied this theme in the case of Jean de Léry. See Michel de Certeau, *The Writing of History*, trans. Tom Conley (New York, 1988), 209–43.
4. I have already dedicated two studies to the way in which Freud's contribution interrogates and illuminates the work of the historian; see *The Writing of History*, 287–354.
5. See Georges Raeders and Edson Nery da Fonseca, *Bibliographie franco-brésilienne* (Rio

de Janeiro, 1960); Anatole Louis Garraux, *Bibliographie brésilienne: Catalogue des ouvrages français et latins relatifs au Brésil, 1500–1898*, 2nd ed. (Rio de Janeiro, 1962). It is of course necessary to add Edward Godfrey Cox, *A Reference Guide to the Literature of Travel*, 4 vols. (Seattle, 1935–38); and catalogue O of the Bibliothèque nationale, *Historia exotica, peregrina, sive rerum africanarum, asiaticarum, americanarum, et novi orbis . . . scriptores, itinera, seu peregrinationes et navigationes variae, 1500–1864*. These two collections complete the two preceding and permit me to establish an initial list of French voyages to Brazil.

6. See Franco Simone, "La Notion d'Encyclopédie: Elément caractéristique de la Renaissance française," in Peter Sharratt, ed., *French Renaissance Studies, 1540–1570* (Edinburgh, 1976), 234–62.

7. See Sergio Moravia, *La scienzia dell'uomo nel settecento* (Bari, It., 1970).

8. See Michel de Certeau, "The Politics of Silence: The Long March of the Indians," in *Heterologies: Discourse on the Other*, trans. Brian Massumi (Minneapolis, 1986), 225–33.

9. Urs Bitterli, *Die Wilder und die Zivilisierten* (Munich, 1976); Sergio Landucci, *I filosofi e i selvaggi, 1580–1780* (Bari, It., 1972); Moravia, *La scienzia dell'uomo*; Michèle Duchet, *Anthropologie et histoire au siècle des Lumières* (Paris, 1971).

10. See especially Jose Honorio Rodrigues, *As fontes da historia do Brasil na Europa* (Rio de Janeiro, 1950); Rodrigues, *Historiografia del Brasil, siglo XVII* (Mexico City, 1963); Florestan Fernandes, *Organização social dos Tupinambà* (São Paulo, 1963); Fernandes, *A função social da guerra na sociedade Tupinambà* (São Paulo, 1952).

11. Since the pioneering work of Atkinson, in particular, see the work of Baudet, Boxer, Bucher, Gandia, Gerbi, Gove, Hanke, Buarque de Holanda, Manuel, Morison, Penrose, Skelton, not forgetting the catalogue *L'Amérique vue par l'Europe* (Paris, 1976).

12. Here we can extend to scientific writing the perspectives opened by Lucien Braun, *Histoire de l'histoire de la philosophie* (Paris, 1973); Claude-Gilbert Dubois, *La Conception de l'histoire en France au XVIe siècle* (Paris, 1977); or by Donald R. Kelley, *Foundations of Modern Historical Scholarship* (New York, 1970).

13. The same is true for historical works such as Charles Webster, *The Great Instauration: Science, Medicine, and Reform, 1626–1660* (London, 1975); and Betty J. T. Dobbs, *The Foundations of Newton's Alchemy* (Cambridge, 1975).

CONTRIBUTORS

STEPHEN GREENBLATT is the Class of 1932 Professor of English Literature at the University of California, Berkeley. His books include *Shakespearean Negotiations* (Berkeley, 1988) and *Marvelous Possessions: The Wonder of the New World* (Chicago, 1991).

MARGARITA ZAMORA is Associate Professor of Spanish and Latin American and Iberian Studies at the University of Wisconsin, Madison. Her research and teaching focus on the discourses of discovery, conquest, and colonization of America. She is the author of *Language, Authority, and Indigenous History in the Comentarios reales de los incas* (Cambridge, 1988) and a forthcoming book on the Discovery, *Reading Columbus* (Berkeley).

INGA CLENDINNEN was awarded the Conference on Latin American History Bolton Prize in 1987 for her *Ambivalent Conquests: Maya and Spaniard in Yucatan, 1517–1571* (Cambridge, 1987); her latest book is *Aztecs: An Interpretation* (Cambridge, 1991). She is Reader in History at La Trobe University, Australia.

ROLENA ADORNO is Professor of Romance Languages and Literatures at Princeton University, where she teaches Hispanic literature of the sixteenth and seventeenth centuries. She is the author of *Guaman Poma: Writing and Resistance in Colonial Peru* and has just completed a monograph on the odyssey of Alvar Núñez Cabeza de Vaca.

ANTHONY PAGDEN is a fellow at King's College, Cambridge, and the author of *The Fall of Natural Man: The American Indian and the Origins of Comparative Ethnology* (Cambridge, 1982) and *Spanish Imperialism and the Political Imagination* (New Haven, 1990). His current project is a history of the human sciences in the Enlightenment.

SABINE MacCORMACK writes about the religious and cultural history of late antique Rome, imperial Spain, and early colonial Peru. Her books include *Art and*

329

Ceremony in Late Antiquity (Berkeley, 1982) and *Religion in the Andes: Vision and Imagination in Early Colonial Peru* (Princeton, 1991). She is Alice Freeman Palmer Professor of History at the University of Michigan, Ann Arbor.

FRANK LESTRINGANT is Professor of French Literature of the Sixteenth Century at the University of Lille. He recently published *Le Huguenot et le sauvage: L'Amérique et la controverse coloniale, en France, au temps des Guerres de Religion* (Paris, 1990), and he is now completing a book on cosmography in the Renaissance, *L'Atelier du cosmographe*.

DAVID DAMROSCH has written *The Narrative Covenant: Transformations of Genre in the Growth of Biblical Literature* (New York, 1987) and is working on a book on alienation and community in the contemporary university. He is Associate Professor of English and Comparative Literature at Columbia University.

SARA CASTRO-KLARÉN is Professor of Latin American literature at Johns Hopkins University. She writes on the contemporary novel and on the formation of Latin American culture. She recently published *Escritura, sujeto y transgresión en la literatura hispano-americana* (Puebla, 1989) and, with Sylvia Molloy and Beatriz Sarlo, the anthology *Women's Writing in Latin America* (Boulder, 1991).

LOUIS MONTROSE is Professor of English Literature at the University of California, San Diego. He has published on theory and method in the historical analysis of literature. The present essay is excerpted from a longer study of the Elizabethan discourse of discovery, which will form part of a book to be called *The Subject of Elizabeth*.

MARY C. FULLER is Assistant Professor of Literature at the Massachusetts Institute of Technology. She is currently completing a book titled *Genealogies of the Real: English Writing on the New World*.

DAVID QUINT is Professor of Comparative Literature and English at Yale University. He is the author of *Origin and Originality in Renaissance Literature* (New Haven, 1983) and of the forthcoming *Epic and Empire: Politics and Generic Form from Virgil to Milton* (Princeton).

JEFFREY KNAPP is Assistant Professor of English at the University of California, Berkeley, and the author of *An Empire Nowhere: England, America, and Lit-*

erature from Utopia *to* The Tempest (Berkeley, 1992), from which this essay is excerpted. He is currently working on a book concerning the relation between national and personal identity in Shakespeare's history plays.

LUCE GIARD is Research Fellow at the Centre national de la recherche scientifique, Paris, and Visiting Associate Professor at University of California at San Diego. She is executor of Michel de Certeau's estate and author, with Hervé Martin and Jacques Revel, of *Histoire, mystique, et politique: Michel de Certeau* (Grenoble, 1991).

MICHEL DE CERTEAU (1925–1986), Directeur d'études at the Ecole des hautes études en sciences sociales (Paris), was Professor at University of California, San Diego, from 1978 to 1984. He published approximately twenty books on Renaissance history, mysticism, historiography, and contemporary cultural anthropology, three of which were translated into English, most recently *The Mystic Fable* (Chicago, 1992).

Acoma, 241, 243, 245, 247

Acosta, José de, 167

Adamastor, 257, 262, 260; on Portuguese, 259

Adorno, Theodor, 248

Aeneid: Carthage episode in, 250; Dido in, 245, 251; epic curse and, 248; fatal duel in, 244; as model, 255; prophecies of, 252; storm in, 260; violence in, 265

Aestheticism: of Aztecs, 139; as delicate beauty, 141; and origin of Aztec poetry, 142; political, 145; pre-Conquest, 140–45. *See also* Poetry

Africans, 262, 263

"Agonía de Rasu Ñiti, La" (Arguedas), 170

Agricola, Rodolphus, 324

Agrippa, Henry Cornelius, 292

Alcaraz, Diego de, 71, 72

Allies, 38, 39

Alvarado massacre, 21, 22, 47n

Amadis of Gaul, 94

Amazon, 192, 201–3, 207

America: alternative history of, xviii; discovery of, 222; Europeans and, 86; as female nude, 179–80; gendered body of, 189; as savage, 210; Vespucci and, 179, 181, 182. *See also* New World

America (Bry), 129

Amerindians. *See* Indians

Anales de Tlatelolco, 35

Ancestors, 114

Andeans: and Christianity, 176n; deities of, 161; demons among, 112, 118; devil among, 115; on land, 113; litigious, 163; physical end of, 166; pilgrimage of, 108; religion of, xi–xii, 110; resistance of, 163. *See also* Incas

Antaeus, 253

Anthony the hermit, 104, 120

Antonio de Berreo, Don, 192

Apologetic History of the Indies (Las Casas), 89, 95, 117, 120

Apurimac, 111

Aquinas, Thomas: cognitive problems for, 101; on demons, 118; Eucharistic visions for, 105; on reason and senses, 102–3; on visions, 103

Araucana (Ercilla), xv

Arawak, 85

Arbadaos, 61

Archaeology of Knowledge (Foucault), 159

Arguedas, José María, xiii, 164, 167, 175n

Aristotle, 235; and civility, 97n; de Certeau's resistance to, 318; on property, 236; on reason and senses, 102–3, 119; and sensory perception, 87; and Spenser, 209

Arriaga, José de, 162, 167

Arte of English Poesie, The (Puttenham), 189

Arwacas, 196

Atawallpa, 108, 110, 115

Atshualpa, 95

Avavares: healing among, 57; overland trek from, 51; Oviedo y Valdés on, 57; Spanish leave, 61; terrorizing, 59

Aztecs: aestheticism of, 139; Christianity and, xiii; culture and, xiii; divinities of, 148; monolithic view of, 25; poetry among, 139–40; political aestheticism and, 145; songs of, 142; after Spanish conquest, xiii

Bacon, Francis, 310n, 324

Barchilon, 87, 88

Barlowe, Arthur, 183

Barrientos, Lope de, 105, 106

Barros, João de, 257

Bataillon, Marcel, 127

Battle, 26

"Battle of Otumba," 32, 33
Bauckham, Richard, 297
Bayle, Pierre, 129, 130
Beaumont, John: alternative explanation of, 297; and Calvin, 296; *Metamorphosis of Tabacco*, 275, 291; and Queen Elizabeth, 294; tobacco and poetry of, 291; on tobacco's divinity, 275
Belphoebe, 274, 286
Bible, 118, 121–22
Bierhorst, John, 146, 147
Bilbar, Geronimo de, 243
Blenerhasset, Thomas, 305n
Book named The Governor, The (Elyot), 197
Book of Kings, 118
Borde, Andrew, 289
Borges, Jorge Luis, 154
Borinque, 8
Bosch, Hieronymus, 104
Braudel, Fernand, x
Brazil, 129, 323
Breviary of Helthe, The (Borde), 289
Brevísima relación de la destrucción de las Indias (Las Casas), 76, 89, 91, 95, 128
Briefe and True Report, A (Harriot), 278
Brinton, Daniel, 146
Brooks, Jerome, 273
Bry, Théodore de, 127, 128
"Bundle of Years" (*Xiumolpilli*), 31
Burga, Manuel, 164
Buttes, Henry, 277, 288, 289

Cabeza de Vaca, Alvar Núñez: on colonization, 73; conquest history of, 71; on epidemic, 66; and European-American interaction, 52; on healing, 73; on idolatry, 84; and Indians, x; on journal of survival, 50, 51; on Mala Cosa, 59, 60; and nonshaman, 65; in Nueva Galicia, 69; on peaceful conquest, 74; and people of the cows, 67; return to Spain of, 48; on rules of sacking, 66; on shamanism, 58; among Susolas, 56; on terror, 53; trading of, 54; on warriors, 61
Cain, Thomas, 275
Calvin, Jean, 128, 288, 296
Camden, William, 183, 184, 233
Camões, 261, 264, 266. See also *Lusíadas*

Candide (Voltaire), 134
"Caniballes, Des" (Montaigne), 128, 223–26, 314
Cannibalism, 27; in Carthage, 269n; Europeans on, 196; Montaigne on, 223, 314; and sexuality, 181; Spanish, 80n; warriors and, 45n
Cannon, 39
Cantares, 148, 153
Capac, Guayna, 111, 116
Capac uncuy, 160
Carthage, 250, 254, 269n
Cartier, Jacques, 127
Cassirer, Ernst, 86
Castel of Helth, The (Elyot), 276
Castile, 5, 6
Catalan, Juan, 19
Catequil, 110, 115
Catholic Church: cardinalate in Indies, 7; Coréal on, 134; and demonic power, 107; sacraments of, 168–69; versus tobacco, 293. See also Christianity
Cecil, Sir Robert, 209–10, 231, 233
Celaeno, 265, 268n
Cempoalla, 20
Cérémonies et coutumes religieuses (Picart), 128
Cervantes, 154
Chapman, George, 234, 293
Charles V (emperor of Spain): Cabeza de Vaca and, 74; chronicles of, 12; minister of, 92; Moctezoma and, 16; and Queen Elizabeth, 207
Chauveton, Urbain, 127, 129
Chichimecatecle, 46n
"Children of the sun" (*hijos del sol*), 58, 76–77
Chocne, Juan, 163, 164, 165, 166
Cholula massacre, 21
Christianity: Andeans and, 176n; in Aztec poetry, 148–49; and Aztecs, xiii; and colonization, 73; of Columbus, xiv, 7, 85–86; conversion to, 77; and food, 65; healing in, 63, 64; Indians and, 72; and Jews, 106, 107; medieval, 101; natives and, 67; and peaceful conquest, 74; Renaissance, 101; ritual blessing of, 66; Spanish, 19–20, 165; suffering and martyrdom in, 53; and

Taqui-Oncoy, 165, 168. *See also* Catholic Church

Church of God. *See* Catholic Church

Cieza de León, Pedro: on Andean politics and economy, 114; devil of, 111; on funerary observance, 112; on land, 113

Ciruelo, Pedro, 106

Civility, 97n

Cleopatra, 254

Climate, 290

Clothing, 166, 168, 169, 171

Códice Matritense del Real Palacio, 142

Colonization: Christianity and, 77; of Greeks, 248; of Nueva Galicia, 73; Protestant, 127; Queen Elizabeth and, 205, 206; Walter Ralegh and, 184, 206, 222

Columbus, Christopher: on alien world, xi; announces Discovery, 1; on cardinalate for son, 7; and Catholic Church, 7; Christianity of, xiv, 7, 85–86; *Diario*, 1; on Europe and America, 86; on Europeans as strangers, 68; first letter of, xiv; on gold, 6, 85–86; on Indian religion, 5; on Indian women, 5, 8; on Indies, 3–5, 6, 7; on language, 6; on letter in barrel, 9n; *Libro Copiador*, 1; names islands, 3; Oviedo on, 85–86; on religion, vii; on tobacco, 276. *See also* "Letter to the Sovereigns"

Combat, 24

Communication, 222

Conquest, Spanish, 13

Conquest of America, The (Todorov), 13

Conquistadores, 93–94, 96

Conversion: Cabeza de Vaca on, 74; Indians and, 232; of Las Casas, 90, 92, 96; of natives, 64; "peaceful," 71

Córdoba, Pedro de, 71, 119

Coréal, François, 132, 136; *Voyages*, 131, 133

Cortés, Hernando, 12; and allies, 38; and Alvarado, 47n; blockade of, 37; Cempoallan assault of, 20; as conservationist, 36; in control, 22; destroys Moctezoma, 23; on Díaz, 44n; on disciples of war, 43n; as god, 16; and horses, 30; *Letters of Relation*, 88; lit-

eracy of, 13; as manipulator, 39; massacre and, 38; Mexican religion and, 21; on Moctezoma, 15, 17–18, 19, 41; mystification of, 28–29; narratives of, 15; profile of, 19; on Spanish advantage, ix; as Spanish ruler, 13; speech of, 23; tactics of, 27, 28; on Tacuba, 24; and Tenochtitlan, 14, 18, 37, 38, 151; and terror, 37; Todorov on, 231

Counter-Blaste to Tobacco, A (James I), 273

Cristóbal, Don, 111

Cristóbal de Albornoz, 162, 164, 166, 169

Cristóbal de Molina, 161

Cuba, 8, 22

Cuchendados, 61, 62

Cuitlahuac, 34

Culiacán, 71, 72, 75

Culture: combat and, 24; Elizabethan, 216n; Europeans on, x; Indian and European, 95; militarization of, 143; natives on, x

Cusi, Titu, 163

Cutalchuches, 58

Cuzco, 117

Da Gama, Vasco, 254, 259

Dainville, François de, 317

D'Alembert, 129

Dance: last, of Rasu Ñiti, 173; scissor, 160, 170, 172; sick, 159; songs and, 143; of Taqui-Oncoy, 171; in texts of Arguedas, 164; totemic, 176n

Daniel (prophet), 122

Daniel, Samuel, 296

David, King, 147

Dead, 112, 114

De Certeau, Michel: and Dupront, 315; on first-person utterance, 88; as Jesuit, 316; on language, 238n; on Montaigne, 223–24; and Other, 317–18; and *Representations*, 313; and Vespucci, 182; *Writing of History*, 182

Declaration of the Demeanor and Cariage of Sir Walter Raleigh, The, 218–20

Defence of Tobacco, A (Marbecke), 279–80

Deiopea, 260

Deity, 81n, 120, 148, 161. *See also* Dios

Dekker, Thomas, 288

Demons, 107; in Andes, 112, 118; in Bible, 118; Ciruelo on, 106; as dead, 118; in Europe, 119, 121; of Mediterranean, 119

Derrida, Jacques, 221, 236

De Soto, Hernando, 48

Destiny, 45n

Destructuration, 159

Devil, 111, 115

Diario (Columbus), 1

Díaz del Castillo, Bernal, 153; Cortés on, 44n; and Cortés speech, 23; on Spanish bravery, 24; and Spanish horses, 29; on success story, 15

Díaz, Melchior, 71, 72, 73

Diderot, 129, 135

Dido: abandoned, 250; avenger of, 253; curse of, 252; demonization of, 251; literary voice of, 264; and Solimano, 254; vindictive speech of, 256

Dionysius the Areopagite, 120

Dios: and *guacas*, 168; rejected by Taqui-Oncoy, 165; as sky divinity, 167; and Sun, 164, 167

Discourse, definition of, 159

Discoverie of Guiana (Ralegh): and destabilization, xiv, 192; intentions toward Indians in, 198; moral contradictions of, 200; patriotism of, 186; promises gold, 218; and violence, 233; as "writing that conquers," 182

Discovery: Santángel-Sánchez version of, 1–2; as unveiling, 221; van der Straet on, 181

Dismemberment, 181

Divers Voyages Touching the Discovery of America (Hakluyt), 273–74

Divine Names (Dionysius the Areopagite), 120

D'Olive, Monsieur, 293

Dorantes de Carránza, Andres, 50, 53

Drake, Francis, 128

Dreams, 105. *See also* Visions

Dupront, Alphonse, 314–15

Duran, Diego, 17

Dyets Dry Dinner (Buttes), 277, 288

Eden, Richard, 180

El Cid, 93

El Dorado: failure to find, 186; and Manoa, 228; and Otherness, 201; Ralegh on, 235; searching for, 192, 227

Elizabeth (queen of England): Amazon and, 205, 207; as androgynous, 190; Chapman on, 235; and Charles V, 207; colonization and, 205, 206; and Guiana, 235; Ralegh and, 185, 285; reproduction of, 234; as ruler and woman, 179; self-empowerment of, 204; tobacco and, 275, 283, 284, 287, 294; Virginia and, 183–84, 285, 286

Elizabethan culture, 216n

Elliott, J. H., 16

Elyot, Sir Thomas, 197, 276–77, 280, 287

Encyclopédie (d'Alembert and Diderot), 129

Enemies, Mexicans on, 40

England, 274–75

Englishman: in New World, 194; Ralegh as, 179; Spanish and, 206; and tobacco, 276; view of Spanish, 198

Enlightenment: anthropology of, 133; and nature, 132; on Noble Savage, xii, 130, 131

Epidemic, 66

Ercilla, Alonso de, xv, 243, 244

Española, 4, 5, 6

Esquivel, 56

Essex, Earl of, 288

Estevanico, 50, 53

Estimation, Indian powers of, 281, 287, 295, 303n

Ethnicity, 195

European Discovery of America, The (Morison), vii

Europeans: alternative history of, viii; and America, 86, 181; and Amerindian interaction, 52; came "from heaven," 68; civil, 210; cultural understanding of, x; demons among, 119, 121; diseases of, 166; and gourds, 65; as historical subject, viii; native fear of, 68; and native state, 12; as thinkers, 13

Fable mystique, La (de Certeau), 313

Fact, 96

Faerie Queene (Spenser): "Dedicatory

Sonnet" of, 226; Legend of Courtesy in, 199; Legend of Temperance in, 197, 209; Mammon episode in, 275; on memory, 220; on Ralegh, 187; Timias in, 233; tobacco in, 273–74, 286. *See also* Spenser, Edmund

Fate, 31

Ferdinand (king of Spain), 1

Fernandina, 3

Florentine Codex (Sahagún), 16, 28, 35

Florida, 78

Flowers, 143–45, 147

Flowers of Evil (de Certeau), 320

Food, 65, 166, 168

Foucault, Michel, 159

Fracastoro, Girolamo, 265

Francesco de Medici, Lorenzo Piero, 181

Frobisher, Martin, 128

Fuentes, Carlos, 88

Fuller, Mary, xiv

Funerary observances, 112, 114

Galbarino, 243, 244

Galindo, Flores, 164

Galle, 180

Galveston Bay, 52

Garibay K., Ángel María, 60, 146

Geertz, Clifford, 92, 96

Gender, 177, 195

Gentleman of Elvas, 48

Gerard, John, 295

Gerusalemme liberata (Tasso), 245, 253

Gheeraerts, Marcus, 189

Gilbert, Sir Humphrey, 282

Girard, Alain, 326

God, 148. *See also* Deity; Dios

Gois, Damião de, 257

Gold: Columbus on, 6, 85–86; Indians and, 282; in islands, 6; New World, 275; Ralegh on, 218, 226; Spanish and, 276

Goldberg, Jonathan, 228, 233

Gonneville, Paulmier de, 325

Gourds: Europeans and, 65; healing virtues of, 82n; Natives and, 62; Spanish and, 64, 67

Government, 4

Granada, 55

Grands voyages (Bry), 128

Great Speaker, 34

Greenblatt, Stephen, 229

Gregory (pope), 101

Guacas: as companions, 167; cult of, 160, 165; dance of, 172; Dios and, 168; discourse of, 171

Guamachuco, 110, 115, 116

Guascar, 110, 115

Guatemala, 71

Guiana, 208; discovering, 233; feminization of, 234; Keymis on, 194; plunder of, 200; Queen Elizabeth and, 235; Ralegh and, 221, 229, 231, 235; Ralegh describes, 188, 305n; Todorov on, 232; and Virginia, 189

Gulf of Mexico, 52

Gulliver's Travels (Swift), vii

Hakluyt, Richard: *Divers Voyages Touching the Discovery*, 273–74; on ex-colonists, 286; metaphor of, 305n; and tobacco, 273–74, 276, 284; on Virginia, 189

Hall, Joseph, 284

Haller, William, 298

"Hamburg Box," 43n

Hannibal, 245, 253, 254

Harriot, Thomas, 278, 280, 282, 286, 290

Harrison, William, 276

Hatton, Sir Christopher, 185

Healing, 51; among Avavares, 57; Christianity and, 63, 64; Karankawa, 53; Malhado, 54, 57; in Nueva Galicia, 69

Hegel, 318

Herball (Gerard), 295

Heroes, 36

Herrera, Antonio de, 73

Heterologies (de Certeau), 318

Heywood, Thomas, 203

Hidalgo, 48, 52. *See* Nobleman

Hijos del sol, 58, 76–77

Histoire de la Nouvelle France (Lescarbot), 316

Histoire des deux Indes (Raynal), 131

Histoire du Brésil (Léry), xii, 127, 129, 131, 313

Histoire générale des voyages (Prévost), 131

Histoire nouvelle du Nouveau Monde (Chauveton), 127

Historia de la Nueva Mexico (Villagrá), xv, 241, 247
Historia general de las Indias (Gómara), 76
Historia general y natural de las Indias (Oviedo), 85, 88
Historia natural y moral de las Indias (Acosta), 167
Historians, 92–93
History of the Conquest of Mexico (Prescott), 12
History of the Indies (Las Casas), 89–91, 93, 94, 95
Holton, Gerald, 327
Homer, 256, 259
Horkheimer, Max, 248
Horses, 29
Hottentots, 257, 258, 259
Howard, Lord Charles, 209–10, 231
Howell, James, 283
Huarochiri, 167, 176n
Huguenot, 132, 133, 135
Humors Antique Faces (Rowlands), 308n
Hunter, G. K., 274

Idolatry, 84, 111, 160
Ignatius of Loyola, 316
Imagination, xii, 102, 103
Imperialism, xvii
Incarrí, myth of, 161, 162, 163, 169
Incas: cults of, 116, 120; divine sun of, 120; funerary observances of, 112; order in, 170; Pachacamac among, 109; religion of, xi, 110, 120; and state, 114; at war, 162. *See also* Andeans
Indians: accounts of victory by, 14; on animals, 29; in Brazil, 323; and Christianity, 72; conversion of, 232; description of, 4; destruction of, 178; duplicity toward, 199; English and female, 208; and European interaction, 52; on fate and time, 31; fear of, 268n; and gold, 86, 282; government and, 4; as historical subject, viii; and killing, 27; language and, 222–23; Las Casas on, 90, 95; names of, 169; and natural reason, 119; nudity of, 135; origins of, 165; Polo on, 117; and powers of estimation, 281, 287, 295,

303n; Ralegh on, 199; rape of, 195; religion of, 5; rights of, 89; on San Salvador, 3; as smokers, 291, 295, 309n; society of, 120; Spaniards and female, 195, 196; Spanish compared to, 198; Spanish maltreatment of, 36; suicide of, 246–47; as thinkers, 13; Tupinikin, 129; valiant, 242; versus Spanish warriors, 31; Villagrá on, 246. *See also* Andeans; Incas; Natives; Noble Savage; Savage
Indies, 8; Columbus on, 3–5, 6, 7
Inga of Manoa, 186
Isabela, 1, 3
Isla de Malhado: death and epidemics on, 76; healing on, 53–54; Spanish named, 52
Islam, 52, 55, 107
Islands, 3, 5. *See also* Indies
Isle of Ill Fate, 52
Italicus, Silius, 245
"I" witness, 92
Ixtlilxochitl, Ferdinand de Alva, 146, 147

"Jaguar flower," 144
Jamaica, 8
James I (king of England): *Counter-Blaste to Tobacco*, 273; critiques Ralegh, 220; on tobacco, 278, 298
Jerome, Saint, 120
Jesuits, 318
Jews, 106, 107
John of the Cross, 101
Josephus, 93
Juana, 4, 5, 8
Juan II (king of Castile), 105
Judaism, 106, 107
Juno, 253, 260, 292

Karankawa, 53, 54, 56
Keegan, John, 33, 38
Keymis, Laurence: in Guiana, 221, 229; patriotism of, 193; on sexual conduct, 194, 195; on voyage, 234
Kilwa, 259
"Knife-death-flower," 144
Krieger, Alex D., 50

Lafaye, Jacques, 51, 77
Lafitau, Joseph-François, 314
Lambert, Jean-Henry, 324
La Navidad, 4, 5, 6
Land, 113, 168, 201, 230
Lane, Ralph, 280
Language: of cannibals, 224, 225;
    Columbus on, 6; de Certeau on, 238n;
    and Indians, 222–23; Montaigne on,
    223–24, 238n; and savage, 225
Las Casas, Bartolomé de: on American
    religion, 120; *Apologetic History of the
    Indies*, 89, 95, 117, 120; *Brevísima rela-
    ción de la destrucción*, 76, 89, 91, 95,
    128; compared to Oviedo, 92; conver-
    sion of, 90, 92, 96; on demons, 119;
    History of the Indies, 89–91, 93, 94, 95;
    on Indians, xi; "peaceful conversions"
    of, 71; on perceptions of God, 119; on
    reign of terror, 76; on rights of
    Indians, 89
La Spañola, 5
Laudonnière, René de, 127
Law, 91, 96, 163
"Legend of the Suns," 155
Leibniz, 324
Lejeune, Philippe, 326
León, Alonso de, 81n
Léon-Portilla, Miguel, 146
Léry, Jean de, xii; on America, 87; Cal-
    vinism of, 136; on civilized and savage,
    130–31; on culture, 95; *Histoire du
    Brésil*, xii, 127, 129, 131, 313; naturism
    of, 132; as "son" of Enlightenment,
    131
Lescarbot, Marc, 128, 316
"Letter to the Sovereigns" (Columbus), 2;
    Church of God in, 7; on Indians, 4–5;
    Indian women in, 8; on islands, 3–4;
    and language, 6
Lévi-Strauss, Claude, 58, 65, 129, 136
Libro Copiador (Columbus), 1
Lienhard, Martin, 172
Lienzo de Tlaxcala, 69
Literacy, 13
Locke, John, 129, 130
Lope de Oviedo, 55
Lucan, 244

Lusíadas (Camões), 248; and Adamastor,
    256, 260; ideology of, 264; storms and
    disasters in, 261; Vasco da Gama in,
    254–55

Machuca, Vargas, 96
Macureguerai, 229
Majer, Irma Staza, 222
Mala Cosa, 59, 60
Maldonado, Alonso Castillo, 50
Maliacones, 61
Manoa, 192, 193, 227, 228
Marauders, 64
Marbecke, Roger, 280
Mariames, 50, 51, 56, 59
Marina, Doña, 17
Marlowe, 287, 293
Marmolejo, Alonso de Góngora, 243,
    244
Marotti, Arthur, 233
Martyr, Peter, 284
Martyrdom, 53
Mediterranean, demons of, 119
Menendez de Avilés, 127
Merleau-Ponty, Maurice, 317
Metamorphosis of Tabacco, The (Beaumont),
    275, 291
Methodology, 326–27
Mexicans: capture enemies, 40; conquest
    of, 12; on horses, 29; Moctezoma as
    ruler of, 13; religion of, 21; and siege,
    30; on Tlaxcalans, 40, 43n; view of
    empire, 35; as warriors, 31
Mexico, 25, 36
Millarapue, battle of, 243
Millenarian movement, 161, 164
Millones, Luis, 170
Milton, John, 254
Miracle cures. *See* Healing
Missionaries, 36
Moctezoma: authority of, 18; Cortés on,
    15, 17–18, 19, 41; Cortés destroys, 23;
    death of, 14; downfall of, 23; Durán
    on, 17; as Mexican ruler, 13; prestige
    of, 22; Sahagún on, 16, 44n; shackled,
    22; and Tlaxcalans, 40
Moeurs des sauvages amériquains (Lafitau),
    314

Mombasa, 259
Monardes, Nicolas, 277, 289, 300n
Montaigne, Michel de, 128, 223–26,
    238n, 314
Montchrestien, Antoine de, 128
Moral collapse, 33
Morison, Samuel Eliot, vii
Mundus Alter et Idem (Hall), 284
Muslims, 52, 55, 107

Names, 169
Narváez, 50
Nationality, 195
Natives: and Christianity, 67; conversion
    of, 64; cultural understanding of, x;
    fear Europeans, 76; and fear of
    strangers, 64; Nuño de Guzmán and,
    69. *See also* Indians
Nature, 132
Naufragios (Cabeza de Vaca), 48
New World: communication, 222;
    Englishman in, 194; European on,
    181; gold, 275; Ralegh on, 188;
    Spanish in, 194; symbolic returns
    from, 296; transportation, 222; writing
    about, 221
Nezahualcoyotl, 146
Ñiti, Rasu, 164, 170, 172
Niza, Marco de, 95
Nobleman, 48, 52
Noble Savage: of anti-Christian religion,
    128; Coréal on, 136; Enlightenment
    on, xii; first example of, 130; Prévost
    on, 136; Raynal on, 136. *See also*
    Indians; Savage
Nudity, Indian, 135, 180
Nueva Galicia, 69, 73, 75
Nuño de Guzmán, 69, 76
Nursing, 132

Ocean to Cynthia, The (Ralegh), 185
Odyssey: colonization in, 248; curse of
    cyclops in, 256; epic curse and, 248; as
    model, 255; Poseidon in, 260
Oedipus, 235
O'Gorman, Edmundo, 222
Oñate, Don Juan de, 241
*Only Way to Attract the People to the True
    Religion, The* (Las Casas), 71

Orbe Novo, De (Martyr), 284
Origins, 113–14, 117, 164
Orinoco, 191, 202
Otherness, 201, 317–18, 325
Oviedo y Valdés, Gonzalo Fernández de:
    on Avavares healing, 57; on Columbus,
    85–86; compared to Las Casas, 92;
    and European-American interaction,
    52; on healing, 73; *Historia general y
    natural*, 85, 88; on journey of survival,
    50; on natives and Christianity, 67; on
    terror, 52

Pachacamac, 109, 110, 118
Pachacuti, 159
Pachamama, 161, 162
Pacification, 74
Pagden, Anthony, 16
Pané, Ramon, 85
Pánuco, 53
Paradise Regained (Milton), 254
Partheniade (Puttenham), 189
Patinir, Joachim, 104
Pearl Coast, 71
Pease, Franklin, 161, 167, 170
Peckham, Sir George, 279
Peele, George, 305n
Penelope, 249
Penthesilea (queen of Amazon), 203
"People from the sky," 68
"People of the cows," 67
Peru, 108, 164, 206
Phantasia, 87, 88
Pharsalia (Lucan), 244, 253
Philaretes, 277, 287, 288
Philip II (king of Spain), 104, 190, 205
Philocosmus, 296
Phoenix myth, 253, 269n
Picart, Bernard, 128
"Pierre Menard, Author of *Don Quixote*"
    (Borges), 154
Pilgrimage, 108
Pillages, 63
Pizarro, Gonzalo, 228
Pizarro, Hernando, 44n, 109, 110, 118
Plessis-Mornay, Philippe du, 128
"Plumed Needle" (*Quetzalacxoyatl*), 149,
    152
Poetry, 139–40; Aztec origin of, 142;

Christianity and, 148–49; dating of, 147; post-imperial, 145; and warfare, 149–50, 153

Politics (Aristotle), 120

Polo de Ondegardo, 116

Polyphemus: Dido's similarity to, 254; epic curse and, 248, 250; Hottentot compared to, 258; literary voice of, 264; and Odysseus, 252; and Poseidon, 249; Virgil on, 256

Poma de Ayala, Guaman, 160, 163, 165, 166

Portuguese, 259, 261, 263

Poseidon, 248, 249, 259, 260

Practice of Everyday Life, The (de Certeau), 319

Preaching, 163, 172

Prescott, W. H., ix, 12

Prévost, Abbé, 131, 136

Primer nueva coronica, El (Poma de Ayala), 163, 165

Prohibitions, 166, 168

Prophecies, 110

Protestants, 127

Psalms, 147

Pucuy oncuy, 160

Punica (Italicus), 245

Puttenham, George, 189

Pyramid of Huitzilopochtli, 32

Quauhtemoc, 34, 38, 46n

Quetzalacxoyatl ("Plumed Needle"), 152

Quetzalcoatl, 35, 149

Quevenes, 55

Quinn, D. B., 278, 279

Quiroga, Pedro de, 87

Ralegh (also Raleigh), Sir Walter: on Amazons, 201–3, 205, 207; charges against, 287; and colonization, 184, 206, 222; courtly conduct of, 186; de Certeau on, 182; "demeanor and carriage" of, 218–20; on discovery, 187, 233; on El Dorado, 192, 227, 228, 235; as Englishman, 179; and exploration, 184; as explorer, 214n; and feminization of Guiana, 234; on gold, 218, 226; and Guiana, 214n, 221, 229, 231, 235; Hakluyt's address to, 286; and ideology, viii; on Indians, 199; and Indian women, 208; James I critiques, 220; on land, 230; letter to Cecil from, 233; Louis Montrose on, xiv; on Manoa, 227, 228; *Ocean to Cynthia*, 185; and Protestant literature, 128; and Queen Elizabeth, 185, 285; in San Thomé, 219; on sexual conduct, 197; social standing of, 213n; text of, 190; tobacco and, 275, 278, 283, 284, 287; and "virgin" land, 188. See also *Discoverie of Guiana*

Raynal, Abbé, 131, 135, 136

Relation of the Second Voyage to Guiana, A (Keymis), 193, 194

Religion: Andean, xi–xii, 110; censure of, 136; Cortés and Mexican, 21; and dead, 114; Inca, xi, 110; of Indians, 5; Mexican, 21; of Spanish, 19–20; underground in, 169

Renaissance, 134

Requerimiento, 72, 73

Resettlement, 75, 76

Resistance, 163

Rheum, 289

Ribault, Jean, 127

Richer, Pierre, 128

Rituals, 66, 164

Rolfe, John, 280

Romances, 148, 153

Rousseau, 132

Rowlands, Samuel, 308n

Rumeu de Armas, Antonio, 1

Sacraments, 168–69

Sahagún, Bernardino de: on Conquest, 12; *Florentine Codex*, 16, 28, 35; on Indian life, 16; on magicians and mountebanks, 60; on Moctezoma, 44n; on Spanish in battle, 24, 33

Sahlins, Marshall, x

Samuel (prophet), 118

Sánchez, Rafael, on Discovery, 1–2

Sanders, Nicholas, 295

San Martín, 33

San Salvador, 3

Santa María, 149

Santa María de la Concepción, 3

Santángel, Luis de, on Discovery, 1–2

San Thomé, 219
Satan, xii, 254
Savage: America, 210; body of, 224, 225; destruction of, 178; and feminine, 181; society, 224; speech, 225. *See also* Noble Savage
Schomburgk, Richard, 227, 235
Science, 324, 327
Scott, Joan Wallach, 177
Senses, 102–3, 119
Sepúlveda, Juan Ginés, 12
Seven Caves, 149
Sexuality: abstinence from, 85; in Amazons, 203; cannibalism and, 181; as cultural phenomenon, 178; masculine, 234; race and class in, 195; Vespucci on, 181
Shaman, 53, 54, 58
"Shield flower," 143, 144, 147
Shipwreck, 48
Short Account (Las Casas), 89, 91, 95
Shrines, 110
Sick dance, 159, 168
Sickness, psychosomatic, 160
Siculus, Diodorus, 95
Siege, 30
Signs, 33, 34, 45n
Simon, Alvar, 101
Slavery, abolition of, 76
Smallpox, 24
"Smoking Eagle" (*Cuauhpopoca*), 152
Social class, 195
Social status, 216n
Society, 120, 224
Society of Jesus, 318
Solimano, 245, 253, 254
Songs, 142, 143
Sophocles, 235
Soto, Domingo de, 91
Spain, 274
Spalding, Karen, 167
Spanish: accounts of victory, 14; and Atawallpa, 110; captivity, 52; clothing, 169; colonizing, 73; Conquest, 13; conquest of Aztecs, xiii; and Englishman, 206; English view of, 198; epidemics on Malhado, 76; faith of, 19–20; fear of, 76; and gold, 276; and gourds, 64, 67; healing practices of, 51; and

horses, 29–30; imperialism, xvii; Indians versus, 31; and Indian women, 195, 196; and Karankawa, 56; and killing, 27; on land, 113; legal structure, 163; maltreatment of Indians, 36; and native state, 12; in New World, 194; party as divine, 81n; prohibition of food and clothing among, 166, 168; in Ralegh's text, 194; religion of, 19–20; and siege, 30; story-making, 15; Taqui-Oncoy rejected, 165; weapons of, 27, 45n
Spenser, Edmund, 187, 197; and Aristotle, 209; "Dedicatory Sonnet" to, 226; frustration of, 274; on gold, 275; on memory, 220; on tobacco, 273–74, 287, 309n. See also *Faerie Queene*
Spinoza, Baruch, xii, 121–22
Starvation, 53
Stern, Steve, 162
Stevenson, M. C., 58
Strachey, William, 221
Suffering, 53
Suicide, 246–47
Sun: in Cajamarca, 161; children of the, 58, 76–77; cult of the divine, 116, 120; as deity, 81n, 120, 164; Dios and, 167; Poma's rejection of, 165
Surin, Joseph, 314
Susolas, 56
Swift, Jonathan, vii–viii
Syphilis, xv
Syphilis (Fracastoro), 265

Tacuba, 24
Tainos, 82n
Taqui-Oncoy: Christianity and, 168; Cristóbal de Albornoz on, 166; dance of, 159–60, 171; Dios rejected by, 165; discourse of, 166; and divine space, 170; and land, 168; as millenarian movement, xiii, 161, 164; rejected Spanish, 165; as sect, 161; and sick dance, 168; sky of, 167
Tasso, 245, 253
Tenochtitlan-Tlatelolco: battle for, 26; and Cabeza de Vaca, 50; closed politics of, 16; Cortés and, 18, 37, 38, 151; criminals in, 31; cruelties in, 41; as

imperial city, 14, 35, 37; songs of, 151; Spanish ejection from, 24; warriors of, 44n

Terror, 37

Testera, Jacobo de, 71

Texas, 50, 51

Texcoco, 19, 20

Text, xvi–xvii, 89, 97n, 190

Tezcatlipoca, 44n, 148

Thevet, Andre, 129

Throckmorton, Elizabeth, 233, 235

Time, 31–32

Timias, 274

Tivitivas, 188

Tlaxcala, 21, 29; as allies, 39; hatred of, 34; and Mexicans, 40, 43n; warriors of, 39

Tobacco, xv–xvi; attack on, 277; Catholic Church versus, 293; Columbus on, 276; creation of, 292; critics and advocates of, 275; and Elizabethan England, 274, 283, 284, 287, 294; English and, 276; in English poetry, 273; Hakluyt on, 276, 284; Indians and, 291, 295, 309n; James I on, 278, 298; as metaphor, 286; Ralegh and, 275, 278, 283, 284, 287; as remedy, 276–77; sacredness of, 288; for savage and civilized, 295; Spenser on, 309n; in Virginia, 275, 278–79, 280, 285; as whore, 306n

Todorov, Tzvetan, ix, 13, 222, 231, 326; *Conquest of America*, 13

Toledo, Francisco de, 162

Topiawari, 229

Topos, 248, 266

Transportation, 222

Trevisa, John, 289

Trinidad, 232

True Reporte (Peckham), 279

Tudor Apocalypse (Bauckham), 297

Tumebamba, 111

Tupac Amaru, 163

Tupinamba, 87

Tupinikin Indians, 129

Uaca macasca, 160

Urcos, 114

Van der Straet, Jan, 179, 181, 189

Vassals, 43n

Veloso, Fernão, 257, 259, 260, 262

Venus, 260

Vera Paz, 71

Vespucci, 179, 180, 181, 182

Veyne, Paul, 14

Vickers, Nancy, 189

Vilcabamba, 162

Villagrá, Gaspar Perez de: on Acoma campaign, 247; curses of vanquished in, xv; epic poem of, 241, 243; final scene of, 245; *Historia de la Nueva Mexico*, xv, 241; on Indians, 246

Viracocha, 120

Virgen del Camino (Virgin of the Road), 101

Virgil, 256, 268n

Virginia: climate of, 290; named for queen, 183–84, 188; and Queen Elizabeth, 285, 286; Ralegh on, 189; tobacco in, 275, 278–79, 280, 285

Virgin Mary, 20, 190

Virgin of the Road (Virgen del Camino), 101

Visions, 101, 103, 105

Vital force, 160

Voltaire, 134

Von Humboldt, Alexander, 325

Von Wedel, Lupold, 185

Voyages de François Coréal, 131, 133

Wachtel, Nathan, viii, 159, 162

Wallace, Willard, 233

Walsingham, Sir Francis, 280

Wamani, 170, 172, 173

War, 25, 26, 162

Warfare, 150, 153

"War flower," 145, 147

Warriors: Cabeza de Vaca describes, 61; cannibalism of, 27, 45n; Eagle, 34; heroic deeds of, 34; Indians as, 28; Mexicans as, 31; Ocelot, 34; regalia of, 26; Spanish, 27; Spanish attack on, 28; Tlatelolcan, 44n; Tlaxcalan, 39

"Water-Pouring Song" (*Atequilizcuicatl*), 152, 154–55

Weapons, 27, 45n

Wingandacoa (Wingandekoe), 183, 184, 294
Wittgenstein, 318
Women: Cuchendado, 62; English and Indian, 208; in Indies, 8; land of, 201; nudity of Indian, 135; Spanish and Indian, 195, 196
Work for Chimny-Sweepers (Philaretes), 277
Writing, 163, 165, 221; Spanish and, 165
Writing of History, The (de Certeau), 182

Xauxa, 111
Xiumolpilli ("Bundle of Years"), 31

Yates, Frances, 274
Yucatán, 71
Yupanqui, Titu Cusi, 162

Zaldívar, Vicente de, 241
Zuni, 58

REPRESENTATIONS BOOKS

1. *The Making of the Modern Body: Sexuality and Society in the Nineteenth Century*, edited by Catherine Gallagher and Thomas Laqueur

2. *Representing the English Renaissance*, edited by Stephen Greenblatt

3. *Misogyny, Misandry, and Misanthropy*, edited by R. Howard Bloch and Frances Ferguson

4. *Law and the Order of Culture*, edited by Robert Post

5. *The New American Studies: Essays from REPRESENTATIONS*, edited by Philip Fisher

6. *New World Encounters*, edited by Stephen Greenblatt

Library of Congress Cataloging-in-Publication Data

New world encounters / edited by Stephen Greenblatt.
     p. cm. — (Representations books ; 6)
    Includes bibliographical references and index.
    ISBN 0-520-08020-3 (alk. paper). — ISBN 0-520-08021-1 (pbk. :
alk. paper)
    1. America—Early works to 1600—History and criticism.
2. America—Discovery and exploration—Sources. I. Greenblatt,
Stephen Jay. II. Series.
E141.N48   1993
970.01—dc20   92-19328
                                                 CIP